LEGENDS OF PRO WRESTLING

LEGENDS OF PRO WRESTLING

150 YEARS OF HEADLOCKS, BODY SLAMS, AND PILEDRIVERS

Tim Hornbaker

SPORTS
PUBLISHING

Sports Publishing books may be purchased in bulk at special discounts for sales promotion, corporate gifts, fund-raising, or educational purposes. Special editions can also be created to specifications. For details, contact the Special Sales Department, Sports Publishing, 307 West 36th Street, 11th Floor, New York, NY 10018 or sportspubbooks@skyhorsepublishing.com.

Sports Publishing® is a registered trademark of Skyhorse Publishing, Inc.®, a Delaware corporation.

Visit our website at www.sportspubbooks.com

10 9 8 7 6 5 4 3 2 1

Library of Congress Cataloging-in-Publication Data
Hornbaker, Tim. Legends of pro wrestling : 150 years of headlocks, bodyslams, and piledrivers / Tim Hornbaker ; foreword by Jimmy "Superfly" Snuka.
p. cm. Includes bibliographical references.
Previous edition ISBN: 978-1-61321-075-8 (pbk. : alk. paper)
1. Wrestling--Juvenile literature. I. Title. GV1195.3H67 2012 796.812--dc23

2012015014

ISBN: 978-1-61321-808-2

Printed in China

Cover photos courtesy of:
Top Row:
Andre the Giant by Pete Lederberg
Randy Savage by Dr. Mike Lano
Hulk Hogan by Pete Lederberg
The Rock by Dr. Mike Lano
John Cena by Mike Mastrandrea

Middle Row:
Mick Foley by Pete Lederberg
Ric Flair by Pete Lederberg
Ricky Steamboat by Pete Lederberg
Jerry Lawler by Pete Lederberg
Billy Graham by Pete Lederberg

Bottom Row
The Sheik by Pete Lederberg
Sgt. Slaughter by Pete Lederberg
Sting by Pete Lederberg
Stan Hansen by Pete Lederberg
Wahoo McDaniel by Pete Lederberg

To my grandmother Virginia and my mother Barbara, who are both an inspiration in strength, courage, and unyielding love.

TABLE OF CONTENTS

III. Heroes and Villains Wage War in the Sacred Territories

IV. New Legends Are Born: From Hulking Up to the G.T.S. — 354

I. The Pioneers Blaze a Trail
Pro Debut Between 1850 and 1920

At the heart of the professional wrestling business, more important than the weekly television ratings, pay-per-view buy-rates, and even attendance numbers, are the wrestlers themselves, who, in many cases, have devoted their entire lives to the industry. At great personal risk, these men and women have stepped through the ropes to entertain audiences, and their profound love for the sport cannot be equaled by any other form of athletics. While grappling is a time-honored tradition of combat with roots in Ancient Greece and India, modern professional wrestling has rapidly evolved over the last 150 years, and the wrestlers themselves have transformed in many imaginative ways.

With courage and sensibility akin to bare knuckle fighters, wrestlers going back to the American Civil War were tough to the bone and adept at battling opponents in a raw, brutal fashion that ended with the toughest competitor winning. There was very little flashiness, no grand match entrances, and the wrestlers didn't achieve success because of their "look" or by the push of a promoter. At some juncture, and historians don't exactly know when, the sport went through an important metamorphosis, and wrestlers heightened their performance in matches with predetermined finishes. Audiences responded positively to the adjustment, although the modification of its genuineness was kept from fans. For those inside the business, the overhaul of the fundamental blueprint for wrestling was almost necessary to keep it relevant to the public. In fact, the implementation of creativity into what used to be exhaustively contested matches that could last hours turned wrestling into a multi-million dollar business.

Colonel McLaughlin, William Muldoon, Tom Jenkins, and Farmer Burns were key athletes during the latter part of the 1800s. They were world-class wrestlers in both the Greco-Roman and catch-as-catch-can styles and had a heavy influence on the next generation of wrestlers—which included Frank Gotch—the greatest American wrestling champion in history. Through shear invincibility and magnetism, Gotch garnered mainstream attention in the 1900s and 1910s, and made professional wrestling respectable for middle- to upper-class followers. He was an indomitable spirit, and his legitimate wrestling knowledge, quickness, and aggressiveness made him unbeatable. Gotch was also able to work matches and create tension-filled situations that kept fans on the edge of their seats. Gambling was prevalent during this time-frame, and Gotch was as informed as anyone when it came to making money.

The business turned toward three men during the mid-to-late 1910s: Ed "Strangler" Lewis, Earl Caddock, and Joe Stecher. Each brought a unique personality and talent to the ring, and continued to build upon the strengths forged by their predecessors. Forward-thinking promoters were trying to stay ahead of the game by implementing intriguing concepts and introducing new wrestlers who'd keep the sport popular. Gimmicks and vociferous hype were on wrestling's doorstep, and fans embraced both the perceived competitive nature of the sport and the theatrical atmosphere of vaudeville. It all combined to create a world-wide phenomenon that is still being appreciated today.

Make no bones about it, anyone who undertakes the painstaking journey as a pro wrestler should be lauded for their commitment. *Legends of Pro Wrestling* honors the men and women who have awed and inspired fans everywhere through their actions on the wrestling mat, and these heroes will forever be cherished.

Born:	December 25, 1883
Height:	5'10"
Weight:	210
Real Name:	August John Schoenlein
Career Span:	1902–21
Died:	July 17, 1958, Bowleys Quarters, MD 74 years old

Titles Won:	At least 3
Days as World Champion:	55
Age at first World Title Win:	30
Best Opponents:	Frank Gotch, Stanislaus Zbyszko, Fred Beell

AMERICUS - GUS SCHOENLEIN

Americus

A natural athlete from an early age, Gus Schoenlein grew up in Baltimore, Maryland, the son of German parents. When he began wrestling professionally, after a successful stint as an amateur, he adopted the name "Americus" to hide his occupation from his father, who wanted him to follow in his footsteps and become a building contractor. But Americus enjoyed the challenge of wrestling, and although he was but 145 pounds when he started, he was fearless against larger opponents. He was quick, aggressive, and possessed astonishing conditioning, able to wrestle matches lasting several hours in length. Through the years—and as he gained weight—he advanced through the various divisions, finally winning the World Light Heavyweight Title twice, the first time over Fred Beell in 1908 and then over Charles Olson in 1910. On March 13, 1914, he beat Beell again, this time for the World Heavyweight crown in a match supported by the retired champion, Frank Gotch. His reign was brief, losing to Stanislaus Zbyszko less than two months later. Upon retirement, he finally joined his father's contractor business while also coaching both the Maryland State Police in hand-to-hand combat and Princeton's wrestling squad.

Born:	January 17, 1876
Height:	5'6"
Weight:	170
Real Name:	Friedrich A. Beell
Parents:	Wilhelm and Augusta Beell
Wife:	Anna Beell
Military:	Company A, Second Wisconsin Regiment
Trained by:	Lee Tepfer, Louis Cannon, Evan Lewis, Farmer Burns
Nickname:	Wisconsin Wizard, Wisconsin Whirlwind
Career Span:	1896–1919
Died:	August 5, 1933, Marshfield, WI 57 years old

Beell, Fred

Titles Won:	At least 4
Days as American Champion:	16
Age at first American Title Win:	30
Best Opponents:	Frank Gotch, Tom Jenkins, Ed Adamson
Halls of Fame:	1

There have been scores of acknowledged upsets in professional wrestling history, but none were more spectacular than the December 1, 1906, match between the unconquerable American champion Frank Gotch and Fred Beell, the pride of Marshfield, Wisconsin. The championship bout saw Beell, outweighed by 35 pounds, defeat Gotch and win the title in dramatic fashion. Born in Saxony, West Prussia, in 1876, Beell developed his athletic prowess by engaging all comers across Wisconsin while displaying an extraordinary cleverness. He beat a laundry list of renowned foes including Harvey Parker and Americus, and his stunning win over Gotch was undoubtedly a landmark moment in his illustrious career. Sixteen days after his remarkable victory, Beell traded the title back to Gotch in Kansas City, but what the general public didn't know was that the two matches were part of a coordinated effort by the Gotch–Beell–Farmer Burns syndicate to cash in on the gambling opportunities surrounding the matches. It was all a rouse that worked perfectly, and Beell reportedly made $4,000 alone on their first match. At other times, Fred claimed the middleweight and light heavyweight championships, and was always known for his extraordinary strength. After retirement, he became a police officer and was killed in the line of duty when he confronted robbers at the Marshfield Brewing Company in 1933. His 1906 win over Gotch still ranks amongst the greatest shockers in grappling history.

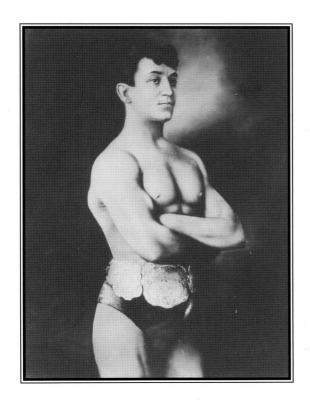

Photo Courtesy of the Pfefer Collection, Department of Special Collections, University of Notre Dame

Born:	June 5, 1867
Height:	5'6"
Weight:	125
Trained by:	William Brown
Finisher:	Scissors hold
Career Span:	1897–1918
Died:	November 20, 1954, Bronx, NY 87 years old

Titles Won:	At least 2
Best Opponents:	Tom Jenkins, Harvey Parker, Eugene Tremblay

Bothner, George

An icon in New York sporting circles for decades, George Bothner was regarded as one of the best lightweight professional wrestlers in the sport's history. The son of a piano maker, he grew up in borough gymnasiums and trained in a number of different combat styles, including jiu-jitsu, catch-as-catch-can, and Greco-Roman wrestling. A legitimate shooter, he took on all challengers while touring with bare-knuckle legend John L. Sullivan, and had a long-running feud with Harvey Parker. In 1901, he claimed the World Lightweight Title and, two years later, won the Richard K. Fox belt with a victory over Tom Riley of England. Although he was without a formal education, Bothner was incredibly wise and loved to impart his wisdom as an athletic coach, initially at the Pastime and Knickerbocker Athletic Clubs and later at his own private institution on West 42nd Street in Manhattan. Upon his retirement from active wrestling, Bothner became a leading referee and was the third man in the ring for most of New York City's most important matches during the 1920s and '30s. In 1949, just five years before his death, the eighty-two-year-old Bothner engaged in a gymnasium wrestling workout session with "The Russian Lion" George Hackenschmidt, a former champion himself, then in his early seventies. The two, never having lost their original competitiveness, put on a clinic of old school wrestling science that left their spectators in awe.

Caddock, Earl

Born:	February 27, 1888
Height:	5'10 ½"
Weight:	190
Real Name:	Earl Charles Caddock I
Parents:	John and Jane Caddock
Wife:	Grace May Caddock
Military:	United States Army (WWI)
Amateur Titles:	National AAU Heavyweight Title (1915), National AAU Light Heavyweight Title (1915), AAU Light Heavyweight Title (1914)
Trained by:	Martin Delaney, Ernest Kartje, Ben Reuben
Nickname:	The Berea Tiger, Man of a 1000 Holds
Career Span:	1915–22
Died:	August 25, 1950, Walnut, IA 62 years old

Titles Won:	3
Days as World Champion:	1,026
Age at first World Title Win:	29
Best Opponents:	Joe Stecher, Ed Lewis, John Pesek
Halls of Fame:	4

Born in Huron, South Dakota—the third of four children to English settlers—Earl Caddock was, pound for pound, one of the greatest wrestlers in history. Shy and unusually reserved, he pursued amateur wrestling as a boy in Iowa, and later more formally while a member of the Chicago Athletic Association in the 1910s. In 1915, he won National AAU championships in two different weight divisions and turned professional a short time later. Known as the "Man of 1,000 Holds," he was an exceptional genuine grappler, ingenious in the ring, and was credited with inventing dozens of new maneuvers. When on top of his game, Caddock was unbeatable. Ironically, though, he was only in his finest form as a pro wrestler for three years, between 1915 and '18, prior to being shipped off for Army duty in France during World War I. But in that time, he proved invincible, and on April 9, 1917, he beat Joe Stecher for the World Heavyweight Title. Caddock went overseas to fight while still reigning as champion, and was gassed in the trenches. Despite his courageous efforts to resume his career, he was never the same. He lost his title to Stecher in New York on January 30, 1920, wrestled until 1922, and then retired. He maintained a garage back in Iowa until the early 1930s, and lived a quiet life away from the spotlight until succumbing to cancer in 1950.

Born:	September 2, 1884
Height:	6'0"
Weight:	225
Real Name:	Charles Leroy Cutler
Parents:	Wallace and Christine Cutler
Wife:	Marie Cutler
Trained by:	Frank Gotch, Jack Coleman
Identities:	Kid Cutler
Career Span:	1905–30
Died:	December 25, 1952, Paw Paw, MI 69 years old

Titles Won or Claimed:	At least 6
Days as World Champion:	135 (plus unknown time for other claims)
Days as American Champion:	Around 726
Age at first World Title Claim:	28
Best Opponents:	Frank Gotch, George Hackenschmidt, Joe Stecher

Cutler, Charles

The third of five siblings born to a Coopersville, Michigan, blacksmith, Charles Cutler built his strength as a logger as a young man and began training in regional gyms as a boxer in the early 1900s. By 1906–07, he began traveling with the legendary John L. Sullivan as a sparring partner in theatrical exhibitions. Wrestling was a natural progression, and like his younger brother Marty, Charles worked as a "combination man," appearing before crowds in dual roles as both a boxer and wrestler. Physically powerful, Cutler was picked by Frank Gotch as his replacement to the heavyweight championship throne around 1912–13, and Charley also held the American title at least four times. Before captivated sportswriters in the offices of the *Chicago Tribune* on February 20, 1915, he boldly asserted that he was the rightful World champion over and above anyone else, and initiated a new lineage separate from that of Gotch. He ended up losing the title a few months later to Joe Stecher in Omaha. Notably, Cutler was an early manager and trainer for the "Great White Hope" Jess Willard, and his brother Marty was a sparring partner for boxer Jack Johnson. Cutler retired in 1930 and passed away in the small village of Paw Paw, Michigan, near Kalamazoo, in 1952.

Born:	October 22, 1886
Height:	6'0"
Weight:	205
Real Name:	William Diaman Demetral
Nickname:	Greek Demon
Career Span:	1904–39
Died:	August 13, 1968, Oak Forest, IL 81 years old

Titles Won:	At least 2, claimed to be champion of Greece
Best Opponents:	Frank Gotch, Stanislaus Zbyszko, Adolph Ernst

Demetral, William

In 1904, eighteen-year-old Vassilios Demetralis disembarked a passenger ship from his native Greece and stepped on American soil for the first time. Within months, he had changed his name to "William Demetral" and began what would ultimately be a 35-year career as a pro wrestler. Along with Jim Londos, he was an idol for his countrymen and gained a prominent role as a headliner all over the United States. Demetral held versions of the World Light Heavyweight and American Heavyweight championships while battling all of the greats, including Londos and Ed "Strangler" Lewis. During the 1920s, he became known as an independent grappler or a "trustbuster" for his status outside the established syndicates. He was denied top-tier bouts for that reason and quickly became disgruntled by the business. As a result, he publicly exposed insider secrets in 1927 and effectively broke kayfabe, confirming the crookedness of wrestling to many people who already suspected its dishonesty. His outsider role ended later in the 1920s and he returned to the national circuit, ending his career as a journeyman in 1939. Demetral was a longtime resident of Chicago and he died in suburban Oak Forest, in 1968.

Born:	June 3, 1887
Height:	5'9 ½"
Weight:	180
Real Name:	Clarence Gust Eklund
Parents:	August and Julia Eklund
Wife:	Florence Eklund
Trained by:	Farmer Burns
Career Span:	1908–34
Died:	January 4, 1981, Buffalo, WY 93 years old

Titles Won:	14
Best Opponents:	Earl Caddock, Mike Yokel, Ad Santel
Published Books:	1

Eklund, Clarence

Clarence Eklund was a nine-time World Light Heavyweight champion and retired as the undisputed titleholder in 1930. Born outside Miltonvale, Kansas, he left home and got a job as a teacher when he was just eighteen years old. However, Eklund had the spirit of a nomad and went on the road, ending up at a Canadian lumber camp. It was there that he learned how to wrestle, and debuted as a pro a few years later. He won titles in two weight divisions in Canada, and settled in Johnson County, Wyoming, around 1916. With victories over A. A. Britt, Sam Clapham, and others, Eklund claimed the World Light Heavyweight crown in early 1917, and affirmed his claim by defeating Pet Brown later that year. Over the next ten years, he lost and regained the title four more times, and then won a major tournament in Australia to determine the undisputed champion on November 20, 1928. In 1934, as his career was winding down, he told a reporter: "I haven't exactly quit wrestling on my own account, but it isn't often I can get matches with fellows of my class." He wasn't being conceded—it was true. Eklund, among light heavyweights across the globe, was simply in a class by himself. He settled in Buffalo, Wyoming and, in 1947, released a book entitled *Forty Years of Wrestling*. Eklund passed away at the age of ninety-three in 1981.

Born:	February 15, 1861
Height:	5'10"
Weight:	165
Real Name:	Martin Burns
Parents:	Michael and Mary Burns
Wife:	Amelia Burns
Career Span:	1869–1913
Died:	January 8, 1937, Council Bluffs, IA 76 years old

Titles Won:	At least 2
Days as World Champion:	920
Age at first World Title Win:	34
Best Opponents:	Evan Lewis, Dan McLeod, Tom Jenkins
Number of Wrestlers Trained:	Estimated at 1,600 over a forty-five-year period
Halls of Fame:	4

Farmer Burns

During the early twentieth century, a vast number of people ordered the Farmer Burns School of Wrestling correspondence course, and paid one dollar a month to be provided with the same instruction the legendary Frank Gotch had received, albeit in the written form. Of course, the hands-on training Burns gave to hundreds of athletes was far more effective, and his lessons produced many superior grapplers. His name was synonymous with wrestling greatness and his reputation is still pristine today, over a hundred years later. The third of seven children to Irish immigrants, Burns grew up in Springfield in Cedar County, Iowa. Legend has it that he wrestled his first pro match as early as eight, competing with a schoolyard friend and winning fifteen cents. Quick and strong with a 20-inch neck, Burns dedicated himself to building his body into a machine, and refrained from alcohol and tobacco. By the latter part of the 1880s, he had substantive backing for his claim to be the Iowa champion.

Helping popularize the catch-as-catch-can style in America, Burns won the world championship of that form when he beat the original "Strangler," Evan Lewis on April 20, 1895; although he would lose his title to Dan McLeod on October 26, 1897, in Indianapolis. Two years later, he met a youngster named Frank Gotch in Fort Dodge, Iowa, and was impressed by his natural strength and skill. He took Gotch under his wing and coached him to the American and World Heavyweight Titles, including two historic victories over George Hackenschmidt. Burns and Gotch traveled the country as part of an organized combine, working with a number of other top wrestlers of the era, making bundles of money in the process. Reportedly, Burns himself wrestled thousands of matches and crossed the continent twenty-seven times during his career. He was also known for his unusual hangman stunt that saw him survive a six-foot drop with a noose around his neck, which exhibited his extraordinary neck muscles and defied the laws of both gravity and rationality.

Born:	March 10, 1889
Height:	5'10"
Weight:	200
Olympics:	Greco-Roman Wrestling (1912) (Representing Italy) (DNP)
Career Span:	1914-40
Died:	September 29, 1940, San Paulo, Brazil 51 years old

Titles Won:	None known, claimed Italian Title
Best Opponents:	Jim Londos, Joe Stecher, Ed Lewis

Gardini, Renato

Among the international contingent migrating to the US in the 1910s to wrestle professionally was former Olympic star, Renato Gardini. Gardini was a highly-recognized Greco-Roman grappler from Bologna, Italy, and was the winner of several major tournaments in his home country. In December 1914, he arrived at Ellis Island just in time for the big tournaments in New York City, and quickly made a name for himself. A hero for Italians across the nation, Gardini claimed the championship of his native country, and was a significant challenger for world titleholders Ed "Strangler" Lewis and Joe Stecher, as well as holding wins over Jim Londos and Wladek Zbyszko. Acknowledged as a "pal of Mussolini" by a reporter in 1933, Gardini spent a lot of time in South America, where he helped popularize the sport. He promoted and mentored innumerable young wrestlers and, while in Brazil in 1940, suffered a fatal heart attack. Notably, *NWA Official Wrestling* called Gardini the "first millionaire wrestler" in its October 1952 issue.

FRANK GOTCH

Born:	April 27, 1877
Height:	5'11"
Weight:	215
Real Name:	Frank Alvin Gotch
Parents:	Frederick and Amelia Gotch
Wife:	Gladys Gotch
Finisher:	Toehold
Career Span:	1899–1917
Died:	December 16, 1917, Des Moines, IA 40 years old

Titles Won:	5 (Claimed other titles while barnstorming)
Days as World Champion:	3,544 (until death)
Age at first World Title Win:	30
Best Opponents:	George Hackenschmidt, Tom Jenkins, S. Zbyszko
Halls of Fame:	5

Gotch, Frank

Frank Gotch was an American wrestling icon. He was the first man to garner widespread celebrity status, and his popularity rivaled the top athletes from any other professional sport of his time. He was the face of wrestling as it evolved into a more socially acceptable form of entertainment, and was an invincible force of nature who dominated the profession. His unrelenting style of catch-as-catch-can wrestling inspired audiences from coast to coast, and there was no one, either home-grown or from an international location, who could beat him. Gotch's presence became so much that he demanded five figures per appearance later in his career, and his two defeats of strongman George Hackenschmidt will forever be part of wrestling lore. In terms of talent, he had it all, and reigned as the unconquered heavyweight champion of the world from 1908 until his death in 1917. Arguably, he is the most important American wrestler in history.

The ninth child born to German parents, Frank Gotch grew up in Springvale (later renamed Humboldt), Iowa, and was a child of the farm, building his muscles and stamina doing hard labor on the family homestead. In 1899, he matched up against the renown ex-champion Farmer Burns at Fort Dodge, and held his own, impressing the veteran so much that he took him as his apprentice. Gotch was rough around the edges and needed to zero in on the fundamentals, while retaining his natural instincts. Burns helped bring out the best in him and the two devised well-crafted plans to not only boost Gotch's reputation, but to make money. Gotch later admitted that he was only in the business to make a living, and understood from an early stage of his wrestling campaign that there were many different ways to earn cash. Some were in straight matches, while others were in bouts against members of his own touring troupe. There is no better example of this than Gotch's 1901 trip to the Yukon Territory during the gold rush.

Under the guise "Frank Kennedy," Gotch wrestled two of his partners, Joe Carroll Marsh and Colonel James McLaughlin in a series of matches, winning some and losing others, and there was a remarkable amount of gambling going on. When it was all said and done, Gotch earned as much as $30,000 during the tour. The lessons he learned on how to work the emotions of crowds, mixing athleticism and showmanship, and the substance of gambling in matches, were invaluable. On January 28, 1904, he beat Tom Jenkins for the first of three American Heavyweight Titles, defeating his opponent in two straight falls. Jenkins regained the championship at Madison Square Garden in New York on March 15, 1905, but lost it back to Gotch on May 23, 1906 in Kansas City.

Another example of Gotch's unparalleled mastery when it came to making money came on December 1, 1906 when one of pro wrestling's greatest upsets occurred. That evening in New Orleans, he was beaten by an opponent he outweighed by 30 pounds, and needless to say, was the heavy favorite going into the affair. An estimated $10,000 changed hands when Fred Beell, the "Wisconsin Wonder," won two of three falls and captured the title. Gotch and his cronies made a bundle of money and sixteen days later, he regained the American championship in Kansas City, winning with two straight falls.

The next major obstacle for Gotch was George Hackenschmidt, the World Heavyweight champion and a man he'd been after since 1905. Their supremely anticipated match occurred on April 3, 1908 in Chicago, and Gotch won the undisputed championship when the "Russian Lion" gave up after more than two hours of action. There was no denying that he was the best wrestler in the world and his fame increased to a level not seen by any professional wrestler to date.Over the next few years, Gotch toured when he wanted to make money, and spent time on his farm when he yearned for life away from the public eye. A rematch against Hackenschmidt was the most logical moneymaker and Gotch agreed to it once he was guaranteed upwards of $21,000 for the September 4, 1911 bout. More than 25,000 people turned out to see the Chicago match, and once again, Gotch proved victorious, winning in two straight falls. The gate of $87,953 was the largest ever for a wrestling match.

Gotch announced his retirement from the mat numerous times, and after every instance, he returned for one last match . . . but he was smart, waiting for the right payday, and unfortunately for him, the wrestling landscape lacked another foe like Hackenschmidt. Rather than rushing into another match, Gotch bided his time, proclaiming other grapplers champion, and enjoyed farm life with his wife and young son. Just as Joe Stecher was rising to fame and a potential match of the century was on the horizon, Gotch suffered a broken leg in an exhibition, and then became deathly ill. He passed away in 1917.

Gotch was inducted into the WWE Hall of Fame as part of its inaugural "Legacy" class in 2016.

Born:	Around 1878
Height:	5'7 ½"
Weight:	250
Real Name:	Ghulam Mohammad Baksh
Family:	Brother of Imam Baksh
Identities:	Gama Pahalwan
Nickname:	Lion of the Punjab
Career Span:	Debut unknown, retired around 1955
Died:	May 21, 1960, Lahore, Pakistan 82 years old

Titles Won:	2 (Indian and world championships)
Days as World Champion:	Claimed title for around four decades
Best Opponents:	Raheem Baksh Sultani Wala, Stanislaus Zbyszko
Halls of Fame:	1

Great Gama, The

Modern stories of The Great Gama are almost folklore and it is difficult to separate fact from fiction when researching this cultural icon from India. The tales of his otherworldly commitment to training, the remarkable five-figure crowds that always attended his matches, and the way he beat his foes with such ease make him a figure of such unique importance to pro wrestling history. Even if only a quarter of the stories are true about Gama, he is still a no-brainer for any Hall of Fame. He was undefeated during his entire career, beating Dr. Roller and Stanislaus Zbyszko without any trouble, and wrestled into his early 70s, still claiming to be the undefeated World Heavyweight Champion. Although Gama never toured the US or faced Frank Gotch when both were in their prime, his status as a wrestling legend is very secure.

Born:	February 19, 1896
Height:	6'3"
Weight:	200
Real Name:	Fred Joseph Grobmeier
Parents:	Joseph and Eva Grobmeier
Trained by:	Farmer Burns
Nickname:	Legs, Grubby
Finisher:	Figure four hook scissors
Career Span:	1918–44
Died:	March 24, 1970, Harrison, AR 74 years old

Titles Won:	None known, claimed regional honors in Iowa
Best Opponents:	Joe Stecher, Jim Browning, Jim Londos

Grobmier, Fred

Fred Grobmier of Harlan, Iowa, looked more like a string bean than a wrestler and, throughout his career, sportswriters would comment on his tall and lanky appearance. His modest look and country boy attitude worked perfectly at carnivals and AT shows, where he wrestled and usually beat touring champions who assumed he didn't have an athletic bone in his body. As "Toots" Mondt later explained, "[Grobmier] would go into towns, hang around the pool halls, and drink soda water out of a bottle so you'd think he was drunk. When some fellows would try and help him home, he'd say, 'I'm not drunk, I can lick anybody.' And they'd say, 'Oh, yeah, well we got a wrestler here in town…' And that's how he'd get most of his matches." He'd take the local champion out, twist his long legs around them like a vine, and squeeze the courage out of them, winning money from gambling bets in the process. The truth was that Fred was an extraordinary shooter, and few wrestlers had a chance with him in legitimate matches. During the 1920s, he was known primarily as an independent grappler, meaning that he wasn't tied to the syndicates and was sometimes referred to as a "trustbuster." He worked his way east and joined the major circuits, performing in a journeyman capacity while making others look good in the ring. Grobmier mentored many wrestlers, including a young Buddy Rogers, and worked as a guard for the New York Shipbuilding Corporation during World War II.

Born:	July 20, 1877
Height:	5'9"
Weight:	230
Real Name:	George Karl Julius Hackenschmidt
Parents:	George and Ida Hackenschmidt
Wife:	Rachel Marie Hackenschmidt
Military:	Russian Army (WWI)
Trained by:	Vladislav von Krajewski
Nicknames:	The World's Strongest Man, Hack
Career Span:	1900–11
Died:	February 19, 1968, London, England 90 years old

Hackenschmidt, George

Titles Won:	2, won several tournaments and claimed various other championships
Days as World Champion:	1,065 (catch title only)
Age at first World Title Win:	27
Best Opponents:	Frank Gotch, George Lurich, Stanislaus Zbyszko
Halls of Fame:	4

The "Russian Lion" George Hackenschmidt was a wrestling phenomenon at the beginning of the 20th century. He was also a noted strongman and weightlifting pioneer, often compared to the legendary Sandow. Between 1905 and 1911, he crossed the Atlantic from England to the United States four times and cemented his role in grappling history by meeting Frank Gotch in two of the most momentous matches ever staged. Of German and Swedish parents, Hackenschmidt was born in Dorpat, Estonia and possessed above average intelligence. In fact, he extensively studied psychology and philosophy and learned to speak six languages fluently. As an amateur wrestler at the Reval Athletic and Cycling Club in Estonia, he was a quick learner in the Greco-Roman style, and proceeded to win tournaments all over Europe. His extraordinary strength set him apart and he consistently improved in his weight training, developing his body into one of the most impressive physiques in the world.

By the time Hackenschmidt made his professional debut in June 1900, he was already a feared matman, able to overcome his lack of experience with his remarkable power. That applied to matches in the catch-as-catch-can style as well since he'd primarily trained in the Greco-Roman form. Tom Jenkins, the Cleveland catch great, ventured to London to face Hackenschmidt in July 1904 and agreed to Greco rules, where Hackenschmidt won in two straight falls. They faced off a second time during "Hack's" first tour of the US on

May 4, 1905 in a bout for the catch-as-catch-can World Title. The match, at Madison Square Garden in New York, was again won by Hackenschmidt in two straight falls. There wasn't a more acclaimed wrestler in the world, and it would be nearly three years before he returned to the United States to meet a credible opponent. Gotch, the American king, was a national hero to wrestling fans, and his prime challenger. The match was being promoted as the biggest in history—and it truly was.

Chicago's Dexter Park Pavilion hosted the April 3, 1908 contest and Hackenschmidt was extended two hours and one minute before he gave in, surrendering the title to Gotch. In October 1910, he returned to the US to rebuild his reputation, and beat many top stars in the hopes he'd land a big money rematch with Gotch. Some of the victories he logged were against Henry Ordemann, Americus, and Charles Cutler. Once the financial terms were established, the contest was staged on September 4, 1911, again, in Chicago. Little did the fans know that Hackenschmidt had suffered a severe right leg injury during training that should have postponed the bout. With so much money on the line, he decided to go forward despite his handicap, and lost in two quick falls, the first in 14:18 and the second in 5:32. It was an embarrassing performance and the audience of 25,000-plus, paying a record $87,953, was wholeheartedly disappointed. Hackenschmidt retired from the business and became a scholar.

In 2016, he was inducted into the WWE Hall of Fame as part of its inaugural "Legacy" class.

Photo Courtesy of Tom Ellis

Born:	August 3, 1872
Height:	5'9 ½"
Weight:	195
Parents:	Thomas and Mary Jenkins
Wife:	Lavinia Jenkins
Nickname:	Ham, Pop
Career Span:	1891–1914
Died:	June 19, 1957, Norwalk, CT 84 years old

Titles Won:	At least 3
Days as American Champion:	1,146
Age at first World Title Win:	29
Best Opponents:	Frank Gotch, Dan McLeod, Farmer Burns
Halls of Fame:	3

Jenkins, Tom

An outstanding catch-as-catch-can grappling phenomenon, Tom Jenkins bridged the gap between the era of "Strangler" Evans and Frank Gotch. Training under Mark Lamb at the latter's Ontario Street gym in his hometown of Cleveland, Ohio, Jenkins made his debut at twenty years of age, and obtained his first real taste of fame when he downed the great Farmer Burns on November 17, 1897 in two straight falls. On

November 7, 1901, Jenkins met champion Dan McLeod in Cleveland and won in two straight falls, capturing the American Title. McLeod won a rematch on Christmas in 1902, but Jenkins regained the championship on April 3, 1903. He also traded the crown with Gotch in 1904 and 1905, and then lost a match for the vacant World Title against George Hackenschmidt in May 1905. Gotch beat him for the American claim for the final time on May 23, 1906. Two months later, Jenkins became the wrestling instructor at West Point and taught over 13,000 cadets over his thirty-seven years at the military academy.

Photo Courtesy of John Ketonen

Born:	May 16, 1891
Height:	5'7"
Weight:	155
Real Name:	August Kallio
Career Span:	1916–42
Died:	March 2, 1962, Monroe, LA 70 years old

Titles Won:	8
Best Opponents:	Clarence Eklund, Charles Fischer, Jack Reynolds

Kallio, Gus

The quickness and technical abilities displayed by Gus Kallio turned the welterweight division upside down during the latter part of the 1910s, and his ability to counteract any maneuver was extraordinary. A devoted student of Farmer Burns, Kallio beat Jack Reynolds for the World Welterweight Championship on October 3, 1921, and he held the title for several years. By 1927, the Finnish superstar was a full-fledged middleweight, and with a decision over Charles Fischer in Chicago, he was recognized as the disputed champion of the middleweight division. Kallio later won a tournament in 1930 for NWA backing, and reigned as a claimant through the late 1930s, losing and regaining the title several times. He also promoted wrestling in Monroe, Louisiana for twenty years.

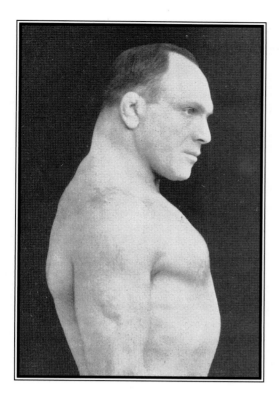

Born:	June 24, 1890
Height:	5'7"
Weight:	170
Real Name:	Alexander Karasick
Trained at:	Olympic Club in San Francisco
Nickname:	Russian Lion, Gentleman Al
Career Span:	1920–36
Died:	May 24, 1965, Honolulu, HI 74 years old

Titles Won:	At least 1, claimed others
Best Opponents:	Ted Thye, Walter Miller, Mike Yokel

Karasick, Al

A colorful wrestler in the ring and a leading authority behind the curtain, Al Karasick was involved in professional wrestling for over forty years. He was born in Babruysk, Russia, and was a member of Anna Pavlova's Ballet Company before settling in Oakland, California, in the 1910s. After becoming a member of the famed Olympic Club in San Francisco, he took to wrestling, claiming local honors in the welterweight, middleweight, and light heavyweight division thereafter. On December 30, 1925, he beat Ted Thye in Portland for the World Light Heavyweight championship, but lost it two weeks later to Mike Yokel. Karasick was often unorthodox in his style, utilizing methods often associated with heel wrestlers. It was part of his ring repertoire, and he was quite successful. But his fame didn't end when he hung up his boots. He continued as a promoter, opening up the Civic Auditorium in Honolulu to weekly wrestling, and brought all of the big names to the Islands, including Lou Thesz, the Sharpe Brothers, and Rikidozan. Beginning in 1949, he was a member of the National Wresting Alliance and was instrumental in the spread of the American style of wrestling to Japan. He sold his promotion to Ed Francis in 1961 for $10,000, and passed away four years later at the age of seventy-four.

Photo Courtesy of the Pfefer Collection, Department of Special Collections, University of Notre Dame

Born:	July 5, 1888
Height:	5'6 ¾"
Weight:	155
Real Name:	Waino Alexander Ketonen
Wife:	Selma Ketonen
Career Span:	1910–34
Died:	December 1, 1974, Boylston, MA 86 years old

Titles Won:	At least 4, claimed others
Best Opponents:	Mike Yokel, Joe Carr, Billy Riley

Ketonen, Waino

Recognized as "one of the most scientific wrestlers in the world" by a sportswriter in 1916, Waino Ketonen was a dominant natural wrestler with expert proficiency. He began grappling in the Greco-Roman style in his home country of Finland, where he won a number of medals. In 1910, he sailed from Tampere to the United States and began his pro career, adjusting to the more popular catch-as-catch-can style. His transition was flawless, and by 1915 he was claiming the world middleweight championship. With fierce, cat-like speed, Ketonen was respected throughout the sports community for his outstanding grappling knowledge, and when he wasn't performing in arenas he often worked carnivals, taking on all comers in genuine matches. If Ketonen had been larger in size, his level of skill would have put him in the exclusive Joe Stecher-Earl Caddock class of heavyweights, but as it was, he performed memorable matches against Mike Yokel, Ira Dern, and Joe Turner. In Europe during the early 1920s, he beat the invincible Billy Riley, and spent many years as a coach. Once praised by the legendary Farmer Burns, Ketonen retired to his Rutland, Massachusetts, farm in 1934.

Lewis, Ed "Strangler"

Born:	June 30, 1890
Height:	6'1"
Weight:	210-290
Real Name:	Robert Herman Julius Friedrich
Parents:	Jacob and Molla Friedrich
College:	University of Kentucky
Military:	United States Army (WWI) (Physical instructor at Camp Grant)
Trained by:	Fred Beell, Billy Schober, Charlie Olson
Finisher:	Headlock
Managed by:	Billy Potts (1910), Jerry Walls (1912–15), Billy Sandow (1915–32)
Career Span:	1906–48 (approximate debut year)
Died:	August 7, 1966, Muskogee, OK 76 years old

Titles Won:	At least 12, claimed others
Days as World Champion:	Over 1,927
Age at first World Title Win:	26
Best Opponents:	Joe Stecher, Stanislaus Zbyszko, Earl Caddock
Halls of Fame:	5
Movies:	5

The illustrious Ed "Strangler" Lewis was a physically gifted man who was known for being full of life. He tackled pro wrestling with an enthusiasm the sport lacked and leapt over all of his peers to become an icon, adored by fans and press alike. His outgoing personality got him places his wrestling ability couldn't, and was able to make connections throughout the sporting world so high that he was considered a peer of celebrities from other sports. It was recognition that mostly eluded professional wrestlers. Although Lewis wasn't the only superstar of his era, he received the best press, and his story has been told and retold so many times, some of it has become myth. Lewis was, without question, the truest of wrestling legends—a one-of-a-kind force that shaped the industry for decades. He also remained relevant even after stepping away from the ring himself. His story was atypical, but indicative of a sporting idol with far-reaching influence.

Born in Wood County, Wisconsin, Lewis was the third of five children, and a natural athlete. As a teenager, he played baseball with the Nekoosa city team and labored at Johanna Gutheil's general store in Nekoosa, handling stock and making deliveries. In early matches with locals, he displayed great strength and coordination, and with that, his confidence rose. He journeyed to neighboring states for contests with wrestlers of greater skill, and ultimately went to Lexington, Kentucky, where he adopted his trademark name, "Strangler Lewis." Sports writers in Chicago were soon calling him one of the great young stars in the sport, and Lewis' manager, Billy Sandow, a gregarious veteran, added that he was already better than world champion Joe Stecher. Lewis versus Stecher soon became the match everyone wanted to see. However, the two matches between them in 1915 and 1916 were horrible failures. The second, in Omaha on July 4, 1916, ended up going five hours to a draw and was an abysmal exhibition.

On May 2, 1917, Lewis beat John Olin for his first claim to the heavyweight title, albeit a secondary championship to the main line titleholder, Earl Caddock. Even after he lost to Wladek Zbyszko, Lewis and Sandow continued to claim he was champion, furthering their media manipulations. Over the next two years, he beat both Stecher and Zbyszko and held the strongest claim to the title outside Caddock, but then was defeated by Stecher in July 1919. It wasn't until March 3, 1922 that Lewis regained the world championship, beating Stanislaus Zbyszko, and was finally universally accepted as the king of the heavyweights. For nearly three years, Lewis was champion, demonstrating time after time that his headlock could hospitalize opponents. He went out of his way to draw the ire of crowds, laying the foundation for heel wrestlers, and adding to the passion of frenzied audiences. This component was revolutionary, as was the way they used dramatic angles to prepare challengers in cities on their circuit.

In 1925, Lewis and Sandow propped up a former football player named Wayne Munn and temporarily passed the title to him in an attempt to resurrect declining houses. The idea went south when Munn was double-crossed out of the championship by Stanislaus Zbyszko, and in an instant, the momentum of the wrestling war shifted to an opposing faction. Lewis, in 1928, regained the World Title with a defeat of Stecher, and then sold the crown to Gus Sonnenberg. The loss to Sonnenberg was contingent on the basis that when he was ready to lose the title, he'd do so back to Lewis. That didn't happen, and Lewis had to shoot on Sonnenberg's successor, Ed Don George, to physically take the title back in April 1931. Ironically, Lewis himself was the victim of a shady deal in Montreal the following month, and lost the title to Henri DeGlane. Although he was suffering from an eye disease, trachoma, and had fallen far out of shape, he was still a box office attraction, and returned to the World Title again in New York in 1932.

Lewis was so important to the business that promoters utilized him whenever they could, either as a wrestler, referee, or ambassador to help with publicity and spike attendance . . . and this went on well into the 1950s. Of course, by that point, he was no longer lacing up his boots, but he still was on the road, teaching guys like Lou Thesz and Bob Ellis, and promoting whatever needed to be promoted. Financially crippled, Lewis relied on a special salary from members of the National Wrestling Alliance from 1949 to 1956, and eventually needed donations from old friends to help him survive. When he stepped away from the limelight, he was completely blind and often spoke about religion from the heart. His love of life was apparent, and what he brought to pro wrestling was unlike anyone else in history. Ed "Strangler" Lewis was a game changer, a man who added new levels of ingenuity to the sport, and defied the odds by leaving his small Wisconsin town and rising up to the utmost pinnacles of professional wrestling.

In 2016, he was inducted into the WWE Hall of Fame as part of its inaugural "Legacy" class.

Photo Courtesy of the Pfefer Collection, Department of Special Collections, University of Notre Dame

Londos, Jim

Born:	January 2, 1894
Height:	5'8"
Weight:	210
Real Name:	Christopher Theophelus (many spelling variations)
Wife:	Arva Londos
Trained by:	George Miehling, Al Lavene, Pete Loch
Identities:	Chris Londos
Finishers:	Japanese sleeper, Airplane Spin
Career Span:	1914-59
Died:	August 19, 1975, Escondido, CA 81 years old

Titles Won:	5, claimed various other titles
Days as World Champion:	Over 9,600
Age at first World Title Win:	36
Best Opponents:	Ed Lewis, Joe Stecher, Dick Shikat
Halls of Fame:	3

During the Great Depression, while people surged toward arenas to be absorbed by the colorful wrestling business and distract themselves from the harsh realities of life, Jim Londos was king of the mountain. He was the heart of the business as World Heavyweight Champion between 1930 and 1935, and was the catalyst for the largest period of growth wrestling had ever seen. His ability as a showman to draw around the country was extraordinary—everyone knew his name and even non-fans were stricken by the urge to see him in person. For Londos, a man who didn't know the proper way to spell his birth name or what year he was truly born, all the success was coming naturally after years of dedication to the sport he loved. Initially an amateur for the San Francisco YMCA and then the Olympic Club, Londos had the spirit to be a champion from day one. He captured the Pacific Athletic Association Light Heavyweight Championship in March 1912 and made his debut as a professional two years later in Oakland.

Londos engaged in years of straight competition and picked up many tricks of the trade, effectively making him a dangerous shooter . . . the only drawback being his size. However, Londos was bigger than life, and overcame that obstacle time and time again. He began touring, picking up wins from many established wrestlers, even earning a two-hour-and-thirty-minute draw with the mighty Ed "Strangler" Lewis in 1918. Londos was mainly wrestling in secondary cities, and even though he was gaining respect, he didn't rise over the hump until he impressed the New York market with his January 5, 1920 victory over William Demetral.

However, promoters kept him out of the upper echelon, and throughout the 1920s, he bowed against the principal class of heavyweights, losing matches to "Strangler" Lewis, John Pesek, Joe Stecher, Earl Caddock, and others. He bided his time and gained key promotional allies in St. Louis, Philadelphia, and New York, which would catapult him to the top of the ranks.

On June 6, 1930, he beat Dick Shikat for the World Heavyweight Title, and was later recognized by the National Wrestling Association. Unlike his early years, Londos was now unbeatable, toppling opponent after opponent, and winning matches with a flamboyance that sealed his legendary status. His fame at this juncture was comparable to any superstar athlete in any other pro sport, and Londos drew thousands and thousands of fans regularly. He was a true icon during a terrible economic period. Jealousy reared its ugly head, and Londos was faced with a severe backlash after breaking from New York promoter Jack Curley to form his own syndicate in 1932. In retaliation, he was double-crossed in Chicago by a Curley wrestler, Joe Savoldi, on April 7, 1933—and Londos lost a match by pinfall in an unsatisfactory manner. The defeat did little to hurt his reputation.

Following the unification of rival promoters into the "Trust," matches that were previously off limits were being held across the nation, and on June 25, 1934, he beat the New York champion Jim Browning for local recognition. On September 20, he wrestled a dream match against Ed Lewis in Chicago. The affair set a new national gate record when 35,265 fans paid $96,302 to see Londos win. A substantial amount of money was needed for Londos to drop the title, and he was handsomely paid to lose to the "Trust's" next big thing, Danno O'Mahoney, on June 27, 1935 at Fenway Park, ending his reign at 1,847 days. Initially threatening to retire, he quickly changed his tune, and toured Europe and South Africa before returning during the summer of 1937. Within three months, he won a claim to the World Title and was once again doing his part to lure fans to arenas, especially those who'd turned their backs on the sport following the double-cross of O'Mahoney. Huge crowds turned out in Detroit, Philadelphia, and Los Angeles.

Because of his outstanding success, promoters had no other choice but to elevate Londos to the heavyweight throne once again. On November 18, 1938, he beat Bronko Nagurski to win the championship, and would never give up this claim to the world title—maintaining it until his retirement in 1959. Times had changed, and because of the down-slope of the marketplace, he was unable to recapture the same sort of glory he attained in the early part of the 1930s, although he continued to be successful. His athleticism and conditioning were always tip-top, which was surprising for his age, and he had a number of solid showings at the box office, particularly against Primo Carnera and Maurice Tillet. He initially retired in 1954, but had one final run five years later in Australia, of course, going undefeated. Londos' clean cut image and immortal legacy as the undefeated champion are as important to wrestling history as any other single figure to ever grace the ring.

Born:	March 17, 1897
Height:	5'11"
Weight:	210
Real Name:	Joseph Malcewicz
Parents:	Anthony and Helen Malcewicz
Family:	Brother of Frank Malcewicz
High School:	Utica Free Academy (NY)
Identities:	The Black Terror
Nicknames:	Utica Panther
Finisher:	Flying Scissors
Promoted:	San Francisco, California (1935–62)
Career Span:	1913–38
Died:	April 20, 1962, San Francisco, CA 65 years old

Malcewicz, Joe

Titles Won:	At least 3, claimed several others
Days as World Champion:	Claimed World Title three times for unknown period of time
Age at first World Title Claim:	Around 24
Best Opponents:	Ed Lewis, Joe Stecher, Earl Caddock
Halls of Fame:	1

Born and reared in Utica, New York, Joe Malcewicz was the son of local grocers and began wrestling and playing football at a young age. Joined by his brother Frank, he starred on the gridiron for the Utica Knights of Columbus, and took up training under Herbert Hartley to enter the pro wrestling ranks in 1913. He was a standout light heavyweight competitor and, after honorable service in the US Army during World War I—achieving the rank of sergeant—he rejoined the wrestling field in and around New York. In 1926, he was a last-minute substitute against World Heavyweight champion Joe Stecher in an attempted double-cross in Boston, and after the latter left the ring in protest, Malcewicz was named a title claimant. Press accounts attributed two other claims to the title as well, but none held any real weight. He was also the California champion on two occasions. From 1935 to '62 he promoted San Francisco and booked the Northern California territory with great success, and was known for his honest payoffs and leadership. Malcewicz was compassionate as well—a rarity in wrestling circles—and helped Bill Longson with his medical expenses after "Wild Bill" suffered a broken back in 1937. Malcewicz died a short time after his retirement in 1962.

Born:	June 30, 1891
Height:	5'11"
Weight:	310
Real Name:	Frank Simmons Leavitt
Identities:	Soldier Leavitt
Nickname:	Hell's Kitchen Hillbilly
Career Span:	1916–40
Died:	May 29, 1953, Norcross, GA 61 years old

Titles Won:	None known
Best Opponents:	Jim Londos, Ed Lewis, Vincent Lopez
Movies:	8

Man Mountain Dean

Truly a "Man Mountain," Frank Leavitt was a giant man with a giant personality. Originally from New York City, he was first known as "Soldier Leavitt" based on his military background, but was repackaged as "Man Mountain Dean" in 1932. The hillbilly gimmick worked perfectly, and his lengthy beard made his appearance even more imposing. Weighing upwards of 310 pounds, he tossed opponents around the ring with ease and the wrestling drama played out in exciting fashion as wrestlers worked to knock him off his feet. He was surprisingly agile and, during a run in Southern California in 1934, was a massive box office attraction. On October 10, 1934, for a match against World Champion Jim Londos, Dean helped draw a record house of more than 38,000 people to Wrigley Field in Los Angeles. He was defeated in two-straight falls, however. Three years later, he suffered a broken leg in a bout and quietly retired. A veteran of both World Wars, Dean was an actor in seven films while doing stunt work in another. One of his appearances came in the 1949 movie *Mighty Joe Young*, in which Dean fittingly portrayed a strongman.

Born:	June 8, 1842
Height:	6'1"
Weight:	240
Real Name:	James Hiram McLaughlin
Parents:	Martin and Elizabeth McLaughlin
Military:	24th New York Cavalry (1864)
Career Span:	1859–1902
Died:	September 11, 1905, Fairbanks, AK 63 years old

Titles Won:	Won several, claimed others
Days as World Champion:	Held collar and elbow title for years
Age at first World Title Win:	27
Best Opponents:	James Owens, William Miller, Homer Lane

McLaughlin, Colonel James

James McLaughlin lived a full life; he was a railroad conductor, gold prospector, military leader, and, last but not least, a champion wrestler. After service in the Civil War, he wrestled all the greats over the next few decades, and in 1901, while in the Klondike, he faced Frank Gotch during their infamous gold-rush tour. McLaughlin scored impressive victories over Louis Ainsworth and Homer Lane early in his career en route to claiming the collar and elbow title of America. On March 10, 1870, he won a tournament in Detroit, capturing a diamond belt, one of the first ever produced. Along with his championships, he also had memorable matches against John McMahon, Henry Dufur, and James Owens. In February 1874, McLaughlin had a notable bout in San Francisco versus a local hero named "Corduroy" Michael Whalen. Gamblers wagered an astonishing $15,000, but McLaughlin likely disappointed many of them when he won with two straight falls. He was on business in Alaska when he died, and was survived by his widow and daughter.

Born:	June 14, 1861
Height:	5′6 ¾″
Weight:	170
Real Name:	Daniel Stewart McLeod
Identities:	George Little, Dan Stewart
Career Span:	1890–1913
Died:	June 19, 1958, Los Angeles, CA 97 years old

Titles Won:	At least 3
Days as American Champion:	1,571
Age at first American Title Win:	36
Best Opponents:	Tom Jenkins, Farmer Burns, Frank Gotch

McLeod, Dan

Sturdy Dan McLeod was an authority of catch-as-catch-can wrestling at the turn of the twentieth century. Born in Illinois to Scottish parents, McLeod enjoyed a whirlwind journey that took him across the US and Canada, and ended up in San Francisco, California, around 1890. He joined the famous Olympic Club and awed contemporaries in a number of track and field events, including the hammer throw and pole vault, as well as on the mat. He worked out regularly with boxing champion James J. Corbett and, between 1897 and 1903, held the American Heavyweight Wrestling Championship twice—engaging in a spectacular feud with Tom Jenkins. His sheer gracefulness in competition was inspiring, and many pros idolized him. As a trainer, he was just as influential, and trained scores of athletes while instructor at the Los Angeles Athletic Club between 1913 and '20. Among his students were Pet Brown and future women's champion Cora Livingston. He was nearly killed in an auto accident later in life, and his unbelievable fitness contributed to his recovery. In October 1957, he appeared as a special gathering of athletic figures in Southern California, and the ninety-seven-year-old reflected on his long athletic career. A friend at the event summed it up when he said: "[McLeod] was as great a wrestler as there ever was." Everyone wholeheartedly agreed.

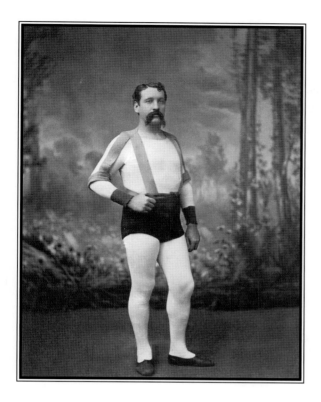

Born:	July 7, 1841
Height:	5'11"
Weight:	180-197
Parents:	Hugh and Bridget Owens McMahon
Military:	Company G, 13th Regiment, Vermont Volunteer Inf. (1862-1863)
Career Span:	1861–92
Died:	April 3, 1911, Bakersfield, VT 69 years old

Titles Won:	At least 2, claimed several others
Days as World Champion:	Claimed collar and elbow title for over 2,900 days
Age at first World Title Win:	Around 38
Best Opponents:	Henry Dufur, James Owens, James McLaughlin

McMahon, John

Civil War veteran John McMahon of Vermont was an early American wrestling legend. He was a master at the collar-and-elbow style, and demonstrated his profound athletic prowess by throwing seventeen of his fellow soldiers one evening at Brattleboro. As a member of the Vermont Volunteer Infantry, McMahon served in combat for two years and gained his earliest fame as a grappler in 1873 when he won matches against Homer Lane and Perry Higley. In November 1878, McMahon won an exciting contest from Colonel McLaughlin and then topped his cousin James Owens on August 6, 1879. McMahon claimed the World Title, and carried a belt to signify his status. He ran into perhaps his greatest opponent, Henry Dufur, in 1880. Dufur also claimed to be champion and their first match was a competitive six-hour draw. Their second bout in December 1883 ended when McMahon forfeited, and then Dufur won the title from him on September 3, 1887. McMahon retired in 1892 and suffered from rheumatism before passing away on his brother's farm. At the time of his death, McMahon still held his prized collar and elbow belt.

Born:	January 18, 1894
Height:	5'11"
Weight:	225
Real Name:	James Ervin Mondt
Parents:	Frank and Lula Mondt
Wife:	Alda Mondt
Trained by:	Farmer Burns
Identities:	The Masked Marvel, Tudor Mondt
Career Span:	1910–32
Died:	June 11, 1976, St. Louis, MO
	82 years old

Titles Won:	Claimed a variety of regional titles
Best Opponents:	Ed Lewis, John Pesek, Joe Stecher
Halls of Fame:	2

Mondt, Joe "Toots"

The history of Joe "Toots" Mondt is a complicated one, full of impressive achievements and dramatic catastrophes. Born in Iowa, Mondt grew up in Weld County, Colorado, and was one of eight children. Along with his brother Art, he appeared in vaudeville shows throughout the region, and featured exhibitions of strength and colorful wrestling demonstrations, which mixed light drama and comedy. Mondt gained a sense for entertaining audiences and fulfilling the desires of paying customers, playing to their emotions in the athletic realm. Soon, he was also wrestling in carnivals and testing his physical abilities in straight contests. These contests carved out the "shooter" he'd become, a dangerous wrestler in possession of genuine abilities. Mondt mixed his legitimate skills with fanciful showmanship, becoming a uniquely powerful figure in the business, particularly as it related to his position in the Ed Lewis combine between 1922 and 1927.

In addition to being a sturdy challenger to Lewis, Mondt was an intelligent force outside of the ring. His knack for drama helped conceive what are commonly known as "angles," devised to stir up interest through in-ring disputes or other means. This built up a system of challengers for Lewis throughout their circuit, creating a buzz and spiking attendance. His innovative ideas were embraced by top managers and promoters, and by the late 1920s, he was working behind the scenes in New York City. "Toots" spent time in Los Angeles before returning to New York in 1940, and managed a sizeable booking office, including lucrative operations at Madison Square Garden. By 1954, however, Mondt had driven his company into bankruptcy, and his infatuation with the race track was at the heart of his issues. Still looked to for wisdom, he acted in an advisoral role in Vincent J. McMahon's WWWF (forefather to the WWF, then WWE). He retired to St. Louis in the early 1970s.

Born:	May 25, 1845
Height:	5'9"
Weight:	210
Real Name:	William H. Muldoon
Parents:	Patrick and Marie Muldoon
Family:	Brother of Martin Muldoon
Trained by:	Professor William Miller
Nicknames:	Solid Man
Career Span:	Early 1870s–94
Died:	June 3, 1933, Purchase, NY 88 years old

Titles Won:	At least 3
Days as World Champion:	Over 2,700 days (not counting 1886–90 claim)
Age at first World Title Win:	34
Best Opponents:	William Miller, Evan Lewis, Duncan Ross
Halls of Fame:	2

Muldoon, William

Perhaps no man has had more of an impact on both professional wrestling and boxing than William Muldoon. His influence was far reaching, inside the ring and out, and lasted more than fifty years. These statements are not embellishments of the facts, but revealing of a man, known as the "Iron Duke," who was known as the best Greco-Roman wrestler of his day and the czar of boxing. He didn't hold both distinctions concurrently, but did so over the span of his career. Beginning as a young man, Muldoon wrestled initially for the athletic challenge, later on for financial gain, and continued after becoming a police officer in New York City around 1876. He was versed in a number of different styles, but none more than the Greco-Roman, and began to make a real name for himself at the annual Police Athletic Games in 1877-1878. Taking a win from James Quigley, a patrolman on the force, he annexed the club's heavyweight "challenge" medal, only to vacate the title of champion to challenge the known professionals of America.

Muldoon won a gold medal with his January 19, 1880 victory over Thiebaud Bauer and claimed the World Heavyweight Title. He accepted the challenge of Professor William Miller two months later and the two men wrestled to a seven-hour draw at Madison Square Garden. His quickness and clever abilities fended off Miller's size advantage, and neither was able to secure a fall. Muldoon's conditioning was tested again in a six-hour match against Clarence Whistler the following January. He often wrestled in mixed-style matches and was occasionally defeated, but Muldoon remained the closest to undisputed Greco-Roman champion until June 28, 1886, when he was defeated by Evan "Strangler" Lewis in Chicago in a controversial bout. Upon losing the first fall and then winning the second, Muldoon gave Lewis the match, claiming to be sick.

However, it was also reported that Muldoon quit because the crowd was small, and that his title wasn't on the line. Lewis believed otherwise, but Muldoon continued to claim his title.

In 1889, Muldoon was the primary trainer for legendary bare-knuckle boxing champion John L. Sullivan, preparing the latter for his famous bout against Jake Kilrain. Their camp was at Muldoon's childhood home in Allegany County, New York. On May 28, 1889 in Cincinnati, the two men even wrestled an exhibition, and went ten rounds to a draw. Muldoon shaped Sullivan into a warrior, giving him the tools he'd need to withstand seventy-five rounds against Kilrain in Richburg, Mississippi. In 1891, Muldoon announced his intention to retire, specifically telling his longtime foe, "Strangler" Lewis that he wasn't going to defend the Greco-Roman title anymore. He touted his star pupil Ernest Roeber, his successor as claimant, and backed him financially. Muldoon ran an athletic combination for some time, appeared as an actor, and, in 1921, became an original member of the newly-established New York Athletic Commission. He remained a pivotal voice in athletics until his death in 1933.

Photo Courtesy of the Pfefer Collection, Department of Special Collections, University of Notre Dame

Born:	December 6, 1898
Height:	5'10"
Weight:	175
Real Name:	Clifford Hugh Nichols
Parents:	George and Lucile Nichols
Wife:	Elizabeth Nichols
Finisher:	Double Japanese toehold
Career Span:	1919–38
Died:	December 15, 1956, Hollywood, CA 58 years old

Titles Won:	8, claimed others
Best Opponents:	Clarence Eklund, Ted Thye, Billy Edwards

Nichols, Hugh

Speedy Hugh Nichols was a rare breed of wrestler, capable of holding world championships in two separate weight divisions simultaneously. Born in Cedar Rapids, Iowa, he was discovered by Jack Reynolds, and further trained by the legendary Farmer Burns. Destined for greatness, Nichols ventured to Dallas and built a strong following of fans, and then beat Billy Edwards for his first World Light Heavyweight Title on March 7, 1927. The following September, he defeated Joe Parelli for a claim to the World Middleweight belt, becoming a double champion. Over the next decade, he'd win the light heavyweight championship at least five more times. In 1939, he became the matchmaker at Hollywood Legion Stadium and also promoted shows in San Diego until his suicide in 1956. During his career, he was an important and influential advocate for non-heavyweight wrestlers. His clever, scientific approach to wrestling was lauded, and yet he was willing to get down and dirty and fight with the best of them.

Born:	June 26, 1882
Height:	5'11"
Weight:	210
Real Name:	Henry Gyntner Ordemann
Wife:	Margaret Ordemann
Finisher:	Toehold
Career Span:	1907–24
Died:	June 8, 1947, Minneapolis, MN 64 years old

Titles Won:	At least 3, claimed others
Days as World Champion:	Unknown
Age at first World Title Win:	32
Best Opponents:	Frank Gotch, Jess Westergaard, Stanislaus Zbyszko

Ordemann, Henry

Decades before Verne Gagne ruled Minneapolis wrestling rings, Henry Ordemann was the local hero and a heavyweight sensation. Originally from Bergen, Norway, where he was an accomplished bicyclist and oarsman, Ordemann came to the United States in 1903. He built upon his strength as a blacksmith and joined a Minneapolis gym, training with well-known police wrestler John Gordon. In 1908, he met Frank Gotch and went on the road with the champion, learning many aspects of the business, including how to be successful with the toehold. Ordemann beat Dr. Roller, Fred Beell, and Charles Olson, and then won the American Title on October 25, 1910, when Gotch gave up the championship to the winner of Ordemann's bout with Charles Cutler. The latter defeated him for the crown he following February, but Ordemann reentered the championship picture in December 1911, when he toppled Jess Reimer (Westergaard) for the title in Minneapolis. Cutler again beat Ordemann for the championship—this time at the Globe Theater in Chicago—on March 25, 1912. Over his career, he wrestled every great wrestler of the era, from Frank Gotch to Ed "Strangler" Lewis, and stood among the finest legends of the sport. Following retirement in 1924, he entered the insurance business in Minneapolis and passed away in 1947.

Photo Courtesy of the Pfefer Collection, Department of Special Collections, University of Notre Dame

Born:	August 9, 1895
Height:	6'0"
Weight:	210
Real Name:	Nathaniel Greene Pendleton
College Ach.:	Two-Time Eastern Conference Champion (1914–15)
Amateur Titles:	Two-Time AAU Champion
Trained by:	George Bothner
Finisher:	Japanese armlock
Career Span:	1920–32
Died:	October 12, 1967, San Diego, CA 72 years old

Titles Won:	None
Best Opponents:	John Pesek, Wladek Zbyszko, Ivan Poddubny

Pendleton, Nat

Wrestler-turned-actor Nat Pendleton performed in more than 100 television and film projects, while wrestling professionally for a dozen years. Originally from Davenport, Iowa, he was educated at Columbia University and was an amateur grappler at the New York Athletic Club. He won a number of titles, and then took the silver medal at the 1920 Olympics in Antwerp. Later that same year, he turned pro, and began an impressive winning streak. In 1923, he confidently went to Boston to face an unknown wrestler promoted by a rival troupe, and was thrashed by "Tigerman" John Pesek, suffering torn ligaments in his leg during the brutal contest. The loss, his first on the pro mat, shattered the mystique of invincibility surrounding Pendleton, and Nat ultimately became more interested in what Hollywood had to offer. He acted alongside many legends of the screen to include Lionel Barrymore, James Stewart, Humphrey Bogart, and the Marx Brothers between 1924 and 1956.

Photo Courtesy of the Pfefer Collection, Department of Special Collections, University of Notre Dame

Born:	February 3, 1893
Height:	5'11"
Weight:	185
Parents:	Martin and Anna Pesek
Wife:	Myrl Pesek
Family:	Older brother of Charles Pesek, father of Jack Pesek Jr.
Trained by:	Clarence Eklund
Finisher:	Toehold, bar-arm wrist lock, double-wristlock
Career Span:	1913–59
Died:	March 12, 1978, Ravenna, NE 84 years old

Pesek, John

Titles Won:	4, awarded and claimed others
Days as World Champion:	Over 3,816
Age at first World Title Win:	38
Best Opponents:	Ed Lewis, Joe Stecher, Earl Caddock
Halls of Fame:	4

In wrestling history, very few have had comparable talents to the "Tigerman," John Pesek of Buffalo County, Nebraska. Sporting cat-like reflexes and speed, and a mastery of holds, he was nearly unbeatable. Pesek's aggressive style had widespread box office appeal, and had wrestling been completely on the level, he would've been a hard man to topple from the mountain. At a time in which reputations were everything, Pesek was thoroughly respected by his peers for what he was capable of on the mat. One of seven children born to a Bohemian farmer, Pesek was naturally gifted and relied heavily on his instincts. His extraordinary ability shone through during his first couple years in the profession, and he was already far more advanced than the veterans in the region. Pesek showed no fear going into matches against opponents of greater repute or weight, and beat one after another. The vanquished reads like a who's who of pro wrestling: Clarence Eklund, Charles Cutler, and Wladek Zbyszko were among them.

Pesek joined the Ed "Strangler" Lewis combine in 1921 and became one of the top challengers to Lewis' world heavyweight championship. Lewis utilized Pesek's otherworldly talents as his protector against independent wrestlers, meaning that if an outsider wanted a crack at the title, they'd have to earn it by beating Pesek first—and that wasn't happening. Having Pesek around was a major deterrent. In 1931, after years of being dubbed the uncrowned champion, he was recognized as the MWA World Titleholder in Ohio, and he'd hold MWA recognition three separate times, and in September 1937, he was also supported by the National Wrestling Association as World Champion. Away from the squared circle, Pesek was a champion greyhound racing owner, leading hall of fame dogs "Gangster," "Just Andrew," and "Tell You Why." During the last twenty years on the mat, Pesek was never defeated clean in the ring, and he's since been enshrined in four halls of fame, recognizing his remarkable achievements.

Photo Courtesy of the Pfefer Collection, Department of Special Collections, University of Notre Dame

Born:	July 20, 1887
Height:	6'2"
Weight:	240
Wife:	Lucritza Plestina
Trained by:	Charles Cutler, Farmer Burns, Frank Gotch, Pete Loch
Nickname:	Tarzan of the Mat, Marin the Mauler
Career Span:	1910–39
Died:	December 26, 1945, Chicago, IL 58 years old

Titles Won:	None, claimed world title in 1920
Days as World Champion:	Unknown
Age at first World Title Claim:	Around 32
Best Opponents:	Ed Lewis, John Pesek, Joe Stecher

Plestina, Marin

Out of middle of the chaotic Frank Gotch era came Marin Plestina, a Yugoslavian transplant to Chicago who was a common headliner, but played second fiddle to many of the more well-known heavyweights. Powerfully built, he worked out of the Gotch camp early in his career, gaining victories over Fred Beell and Ed "Strangler" Lewis, but losing to Joe Stecher, Charles Cutler, Earl Caddock, and Stanislaus Zbyszko. By 1918, Plestina had gained boisterous J.C. Marsh as his manager and announced that everyone of importance was dodging him. After failing to overcome the syndicate policeman, John Pesek, in two controversial matches, Plestina eventually decided to end the charade of being a trustbuster and went to work for the major troupes, but he never again made headlines like he did when he was besmirching every champion and declaring them unworthy.

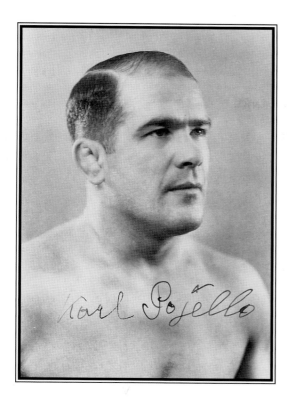

Born:	Around 1883
Height:	5'8"
Weight:	205
Real Name:	Karl Antonovich Pojello
Wife:	Olga Pojello
Career Span:	Unknown debut year–1945
Died:	August 3, 1954, Chicago, IL 71 years old

Titles Won:	Claimed at least two
Best Opponents:	Jim Londos, Jim Browning, Yvon Robert

Pojello, Karl

Commonly described as being unsuspecting in appearance, Karl Pojello was a dangerous wrestler with all the tools to break an opponent's bones with ease. Originally from Steigvilai, Lithuania, he wrestled the Greco-Roman style exclusively before venturing westward across Siberia and into China and Japan, where he practiced jiu-jitsu and other combat forms. Pojello toured the United States beginning in 1923, and was acknowledged as the Lithuanian Light Heavyweight champion. During World War II, he gained national notoriety after battling a Japanese jiu-jitsu expert to a bloody draw before military officers in attempt to show that old-fashioned wrestling was a more effective hand-to-hand fighting style. Pojello was sixty-years-old at the time and was facing a man half his age. His greatest accomplishment was the discovery of the extraordinary "French Angel" Maurice Tillet in Singapore. Tillet possessed unusual strength and had such a unique appearance that he became a worldwide sensation. Pojello managed Tillet for the remainder of his life and the two were inseparable friends. During the last year of their lives, both were bedridden and cared for by Karl's wife, Olga, in their adjoining rooms in Chicago. And after Karl died of lung cancer on August 3, 1954, Tillet, heartbroken, died only hours later.

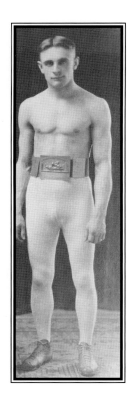

Photo Courtesy of the Pfefer Collection, Department of Special Collections, University of Notre Dame

Born:	February 7, 1894
Height:	5'6 ½"
Weight:	145
Real Name:	Charles Voris Reynolds
Parents:	William and Nancy Reynolds
Wife:	Alice Dale Reynolds
Family:	Brother of Art Reynolds
High School:	Center Point High School (IA)
Career Span:	1910–38
Died:	January 9, 1945, Covington, KY 51 years old

Titles Won:	15
Best Opponents:	Matty Matsuda, Bobby Chick, Robin Reed

Reynolds, Jack

In 1936, Bruce Dudley of the *Louisville Courier Journal* revealed that multi-time World Welterweight champion Jack Reynolds smoked cigarettes, drank alcohol, and shunned regular training practices. His behavior was completely abnormal for a pro wrestler, let alone a man considered one of the best at his weight (145 pounds) in history. Clever, fast, and scientific, the Cedar Point, Iowa, product was the youngest of seven sons, and trained with Farmer Burns and Frank Gotch early in his career. On January 8, 1914, he beat Cyclone Parker in Idaho Falls to capture his first welterweight title, and would hold the championship a total of fourteen times. Nicknamed the "Fox," Reynolds was also a capable showman and a successful draw all over the country. In 1934, he was charged with second-degree murder after a man died in a bar fight he was involved in, but was later acquitted. Later in the 1930s, he ran a wrestling outfit of non-heavyweights on the West Coast, sometimes staging athletic (AT) shows at carnivals, and retired from the ring in 1938. Following his death in 1945, a Louisville promoter said that "[Reynolds] was to wrestling what Jack Dempsey was to boxing."

Born:	June 22, 1896
Height:	5'10 ½"
Weight:	175
Real Name:	William Harold Riley
Parents:	Patrick and Jane Riley
Wife:	Sarah Riley
Family:	Father of Ernie Riley
Trained by:	Billy Charnock
Trained:	Bert Assirati, Karl Gotch, Billy Joyce, Billy Robinson, Jack Dempsey, Roy Wood, and scores of others
Career Span:	1909–68
Died:	September 15, 1977, Wigan, England 81 years old

Titles Won:	At least 2
Days as World MW Champion:	Reportedly claimed title for 18 years
Best Opponents:	Jack Robinson, Bobby Myers, Billy Moores

Riley, Billy

The "Old Master" Billy Riley taught the legitimate art of professional catch-as-catch-can wrestling at the renowned "Snake Pit" training center in England. He kept it up well after the need for real wrestlers had disappeared from the marketplace, as promoters sought hulking and colorful performers. It didn't matter to Riley. Some of his graduates were among the best catch grapplers in the world. From Wigan, Lancashire, Riley turned pro at fourteen and made a tour of the US in 1923. A year later, he claimed the World Middleweight Title, and his *Wigan Observer* obituary stated that he remained champion for eighteen years. In 1933-1934, he toured South Africa, furthering his international exposure. Back at his gym, more and more youngsters learned his famous teachings, and his influence was felt in all corners of the wrestling world— and still is to this day.

Born:	September 18, 1862
Height:	5'7"
Weight:	195
Real Name:	Ernst Roeber
Managed by:	William Muldoon
Managed:	Ernest Siegfried, Egeberg, Charlie Cutler
Career Span:	1885–1903
Died:	December 14, 1944, Auburndale, NY 82 years old

Titles Won:	At least 2, claimed others
Days as World Champion:	Around eight years
Age at first World Title Win:	29
Best Opponents:	Terrible Turk, Bech-Olsen, Tom Jenkins

Roeber, Ernest

The powerful Ernest Roeber was born in Wulsdorf, Germany, and settled in New York as a boy in 1870. He found employment in a tobacco factory, but his real calling was as a Greco-Roman wrestler; studying the sport endlessly in local Manhattan gymnasiums. Fearless, he battled the likes of Young Bibby prior to turning pro, and the legendary William Muldoon became his mentor in the late 1880s. For upwards of a dozen years, Roeber traveled and trained with Muldoon, and on July 25, 1892, he beat Apollon for the Greco-Roman World Title. Five years later, in 1897, he trained Bob Fitzsimmons to a victory over world boxing heavyweight champion James J. Corbett in Carson City, Nevada. Danish superstar Bech-Olsen took his World Title in March 1900 at Madison Square Garden, and Roeber retired from the sport in 1903. Roeber retired and operated a pub until Prohibition, while also working as a referee for the New York Athletic Commission during the early 1930s. Robert Edgren of the *New York Evening World* once described Roeber as a "short, thick set, stocky fellow with no neck and a head like a bullet, perfectly built for his own game." And as a Greco-Roman grappler, very few were better.

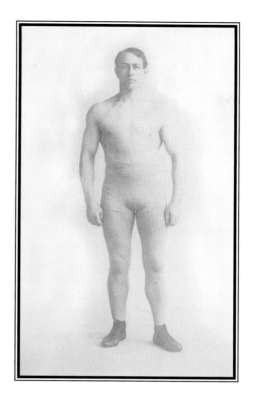

Born:	July 1, 1876
Height:	6'0"
Weight:	210
Real Name:	Dr. Benjamin Franklin Roller
Parents:	Phillip and Emily Roller
Colleges:	De Pauw University, University of Pennsylvania
Trained by:	Frank Gotch, Joe Carroll Marsh
Identities:	Frank Roller
Career Span:	1906–19
Died:	April 20, 1933, New York, NY 57 years old

Titles Won:	At least 3, claimed others
Best Opponents:	Frank Gotch, Great Gama, Stanislaus Zbyszko

Roller, Dr. B.F.

An unsung warrior of the early twentieth century, Dr. Roller's success as a professional wrestler is often obscured by the legend of Frank Gotch, as is the case for most heavyweights during that period. For Roller of Newman, Illinois, he was a highly distinctive individual and earned his own place in pro wrestling history. Although from a poor family, he earned his way into DePauw University and later the University of Pennsylvania, where he earned a medical degree. He was a standout football player and participated in games throughout college, as well as at the professional level in the early 1900s. Discovered in Seattle in 1906, he became a pro wrestler and entered the industry to make money, pure and simple. He had a natural gift for playing to audiences, working gimmicks, and feeding into the athletic drama. His most famous act was faking injuries during matches, and he sold the storyline all over the country. Roller traveled across North America and Europe, wrestling all the greats—including the Great Gama—and was, notably, one of George Hackenschmidt's trainers for his 1911 bout with Gotch. He claimed the American Heavyweight Title on several occasions, and intersected with every superstar wrestler from Farmer Burns to Earl Caddock.

Born:	April 7, 1887
Height:	5'9"
Weight:	185
Real Name:	Adolph Ernst Santel
Trained by:	Dick Sorensen, Joe Rogers, Charles Olsen
Identities:	Mysterious Carpenter, Otto Carpenter
Career Span:	1908–33
Died:	November 10, 1966, Oakland, CA 79 years old

Titles Won:	At least 3, claimed others
Best Opponents:	John Pesek, Ed Lewis, Joe Stecher

Santel, Ad

Although he stood only 5'9", Ad Santel was a giant in the world of catch-as-catch-can wrestling. He began his career in Chicago under the name "Adolph Ernst" after emigrating from Germany in 1907, and was an astute student of various wrestling and martial arts fundamentals. He was the only man to train with both Frank Gotch and George Hackenschmidt before their two legendary matches. By 1913, he claimed the World Light Heavyweight Title and affirmed his status as the rightful champion into the late 1920s. He successfully toured Japan in 1921, defeating jiu-jitsu expert Tokugoro Ito, and spread interest in American-style wrestling abroad. For over fifteen years he made San Francisco his headquarters and battled all the big names that toured through the city. In 1931, he partnered with his brother-in-law, Ernest Feddersen, to promote Oakland, and he would continue until the region was monopolized by Roy Shire thirty years later. As a trainer and mentor, Santel was a phenomenal influence on a number of wrestlers, including the legendary Lou Thesz. Dory Detton, a well-known grappler and promoter, told a reporter in 1957: "Santel was not only a great wrestler, he was the finest teacher I have ever met. He taught me more about wrestling than all others in my life."

Born:	October 18, 1894
Height:	6'0"
Weight:	225
Real Name:	Ivan Seric
Trained by:	Farmer Burns
Nickname:	Blackjack
Finisher:	Half-Nelson and scissors
Career Span:	1917–50
Died:	October 11, 1969, Los Angeles, CA 74 years old

Sherry, Jack

Titles Won:	None known, claimed at least 3
Days as World Champion:	Unknown
Age at first World Title Win:	Around 26 when he claimed title in 1920
Best Opponents:	John Pesek, Ed Lewis, Henri DeGlane

In the mixed realm of wrestling showmen and shooters, Jack Sherry was as legitimate as they came; a genuine grappler with the skill to hold his own with any of the best heavyweights of his era. Born in Yugoslavia and billed by promoters as an Alaskan Indian, Sherry was trained by the legendary Farmer Burns and began his career in 1917. It didn't take long for him to develop a reputation of a "trustbuster," and he found it exceedingly difficult to find matches with the protected grapplers of the major syndicates. For years Sherry chased the acknowledged titleholders without much success, and finally declared himself the "uncrowned champion of the world." In 1927, he battled syndicate policeman John Pesek in Columbus and scored a rare pinfall on the famed "Tigerman." Pesek, however, responded by throwing Sherry from the ring in anger and the latter won the match by disqualification. Six years later, he again proclaimed himself champion, stating that "Strangler" Lewis ran out on a bout with him at Philadelphia. Sherry wrestled all over the world and was recognized as titleholder during his tours of England. As late as 1948, Sherry was still confidently issuing challenges, and nearly came to grips with Lewis for a shoot in Hawaii in January of that year, but it was canceled at the last minute. Sherry retired in 1950 and died in Los Angeles in 1969 at the age of seventy-four.

Born:	January 11, 1897
Height:	6'1"
Weight:	225
Real Name:	Richard Scheckat
Family:	Brother of Joe and Paul Scheckat
Wife:	Ereka Schikat
Career Span:	1918–53
Died:	December 3, 1968, New York, NY
	71 years old

Titles Won:	3
Days as World Champion:	351
Age at first World Title Win:	32
Best Opponents:	Jim Londos, Ed Lewis, Stanislaus Zbyszko
Halls of Fame:	1

Shikat, Dick

From Ragnit, East Prussia, Dick Shikat excelled in the Greco-Roman style of wrestling following his naval service in World War I. Along with Hans Steinke, he came to the US on October 9, 1923, and quickly adapted to the American catch-as-catch-can ring method, proving to be a valuable asset to promoters. His quickness and aptitude earned him the respect of fans, and adding his size and strength, made him a top newcomer. In 1928, he received a significant push in Philadelphia, and, after taking "Toots" Mondt as his manager, was directly in line for a shot at the vacant World Heavyweight Title, supported by the Pennsylvania and New York Athletic Commissions. Before an estimated 30,000 fans at the Municipal Stadium in Philadelphia, Shikat took a popular victory from Jim Londos for the championship on August 23, 1929, and was presented with a belt valued at $5,000. Ironically, a few days later, Shikat left his new belt in the back of a New York City taxi and never saw it again.

The meteoric rise of Londos as a superstar in the industry was not ignored by promoters, and the Greek wrestler succeeded Shikat as the titleholder. Shikat's reign, lasting until June 6, 1930, was successful, and he reportedly made $250,000 while he was champion. For most of the next five years, he toiled around the wrestling circuit, drawing good houses in big matches, and performing as promoters expected. That would change on March 2, 1936, when he decided to lash out at the wrestling "trust" by double-crossing world champion Danno O'Mahoney at Madison Square Garden, and winning the title by submission. He remained champion until April 24, 1936, losing the championship to Ali Baba in Detroit. After his wife's unexpected death in early May 1936, Shikat scaled back his commitment to wrestling. He owned a bar in Buenos Aires for a time and became a Merchant Marine. On several ocean liners in the 1950s, he worked as a physical instructor and pool attendant.

Born:	April 5, 1893
Height:	6'0"
Weight:	225
Real Name:	Joseph James Stecher
Parents:	Frank and Anna Stecher
Wife:	Frances Ehlers Stecher
Military:	United States Navy (WWI)
Finisher:	Scissors leghold
Career Span:	1912–34
Died:	March 26, 1974, St. Cloud, MN 80 years old

Titles Won:	6
Days as World Champion:	2,224
Age at first World Title Win:	22
Best Opponents:	Ed Lewis, Earl Caddock, John Pesek
Halls of Fame:	4

Stecher, Joe

On a very short list of greatest natural professional wrestlers in history, "Scissors" Joe Stecher, who held the World Heavyweight Title five times, including the undisputed championship in 1920, is most certainly one of them. He was a low-key athlete, very much unlike his number one ring adversary, Ed "Strangler" Lewis, who commanded attention. They were different in so many ways, from personality to body type, but when they faced off, there was a distinct struggle for superiority that neither wanted to give in to. Stecher, from Dodge, Nebraska, was one of ten children born to Bohemian parents, and worked on their farm in his youth. At the age of nineteen, he ventured to Iowa to labor on the farm of Frank Petit, and in April 1912, he opposed a local in a wrestling match at a hall in Berea. His opponent was none other than Earl Caddock, a future world champion himself—and one of Stecher's greatest all-time opponents. Before thirty-one people, Stecher won the first and third falls, garnered a few bucks, and became a pro wrestler.

Stecher trained exceptionally hard, focusing on his leg muscles, and developed his famous scissors hold that would finish off many of his rivals. He went on a tear following his debut, defeating opponent after opponent, and went undefeated for over four years. In the midst of his run, he toppled Charles Cutler for a claim to the World Heavyweight Title on July 5, 1915. Although he beat Cutler fair and square and was given a $3,000 gold belt emblematic of the championship, Stecher's rightful claim to the title was still somewhat disputed. That was because American hero Frank Gotch had never lost his title in the ring. Promoters tried every conceivable way to match the two, but Gotch suffered a broken leg in an exhibition, and died a year later, with Stecher versus Gotch being the best match in wrestling history that never happened. As the defending champion, and against all types of opponents, Stecher demonstrated his ring mastery, and lived up to expectations wherever he traveled.

However, there were exceptions, especially when it came to his first two pro losses. While on tour of the east, Stecher inexplicably walked out during a lengthy match against John Olin in Springfield, Massachusetts on December 11, 1916, and the defeat soured his reputation as a title claimant. On April 9, 1917, he was officially stripped of his World Title by Caddock, again, under somewhat dubious circumstances. Apparently, it was claimed that he told officials he was unable to continue, which was later denied. Nevertheless, Caddock was declared the champion. With victories over Wladek Zbyszko and Ed Lewis, Stecher regained a claim to the World Title in 1919, and waited for his return match against Caddock, who'd been injured during the war.

Things came together for a huge spectacular at Madison Square Garden in New York on January 30, 1920, pitting the rival championships of Stecher against Caddock. That night, Stecher became the undisputed titleholder after more than two hours of competition.

Lewis beat Stecher in December 1920, and instead of continuing to chase the title, he went into semi-retirement, focusing more on baseball and other interests. He returned to beat Stanislaus Zbyszko for his fifth and final reign as World Titleholder on May 30, 1925, and held the championship until February 20, 1928, when Lewis won a three-fall encounter in St. Louis. Following his loss, Stecher took a backseat to the next generation of superstars and embraced a role as perpetual challenger. An injury in 1934 sidelined him, and Joe soon announced his retirement. In the years that followed, he was haunted by considerable financial problems. The *Associated Press*, on July 14, 1937, reported that the forty-four year-old Stecher was near death at a VA hospital in St. Cloud, Minnesota after suffering a nervous breakdown. Once an unbeatable force, Stecher was faltering mentally and physically, and never regained his health. He remained hospitalized until his passing in 1974.

Born:	February 8, 1900
Height:	5'11"
Weight:	215
Real Name:	Peter Sauer
Parents:	Conrad and Catharina Sauer
Family:	Uncle of George Sauer
Wife:	Annie Sauer
Trained by:	George (Barnes) Sauer, Lloyd Carter
Identities:	Roy Steele, The Masked Marvel
Career Span:	1918–49
Died:	September 11, 1949, Warm Lake, ID 49 years old

Titles Won:	7
Days as World Champion:	Around 580
Age at first World Title Win:	36
Best Opponents:	Jim Londos, Ed Lewis, Clarence Eklund
Halls of Fame:	3

Steele, Ray

Feared shooter Ray Steele was also a well-liked practical jokester, who was known for keeping things lively behind the scenes. However, his wrestling was anything but funny. Over the course of his thirty-one year career, he was highly successful and influential, winning championships in the ring and teaching others what he knew about the business. Born in Nokra, Russia, Steele was raised by an uncle and aunt in Lincoln, Nebraska, and took an interest in grappling after his older brother George began competing as a middleweight. Steele trained under Farmer Burns, and then wrestled as an amateur before making his pro debut as a teenager. Within a year, he'd travel to Wyoming and had several grueling matches against one of the best in the industry, Clarence Eklund. Despite his age, Steele was very impressive in his bout. Steele was already considered a future champion, and honed his skills in further training with John Pesek, the famed "Tigerman."

Victories over the British and Canadian claimants set up a rematch with Eklund in October 1922 in Santa Paula, California, which Steele won and claimed the World Light Heavyweight Title. Around 1927, he adopted the name "Ray Steele," using it in certain cities and his real name in others. Heavyweight champion Jim Londos would become his greatest in-ring rival, and the two met numerous times before huge throngs of people. Little did people know that Steele, in fact, worked as Londos's "policeman," meaning that he protected the champion from rogue opponents. Steele was briefly World Champion in Ohio in 1937, and then won the National Wrestling Association championship from Bronko Nagurski on March 7, 1940—holding it for a little more than year. He also held the National Wrestling Alliance Title in Iowa in 1943-1944. The always competitive Steele was planning a comeback when he died unexpectedly in 1949.

Photo Courtesy of the Pfefer Collection, Department of Special Collections, University of Notre Dame

Born:	February 22, 1893
Height:	6'3"
Weight:	250
Real Name:	Johannes Steinke
Nickname:	The German Oak
Hollywood:	Appeared in the films, *Deception* (1932), *Island of Lost Souls* (1933) with Constantine Romanoff and Ali Baba, *Sweet Cookie* (1933), *Reckless* (1935—scenes deleted), *Once in a Blue Moon* (1935), *People Will Talk* (1935), *Nothing Sacred* (1937), and *The Buccaneer* (1938)
Career Span:	1919–49
Died:	June 26, 1971, Chicago, IL 78 years old

Steinke, Hans

Titles Won:	Claimed several titles
Days as World Champion:	Unknown time as claimant
Age at first World Title Win:	35
Best Opponents:	Jim Londos, Dick Shikat, Ed Lewis

Incredibly powerful and sometimes unpredictable and unruly, Hans Steinke of Stettin, Germany, was an amateur Greco-Roman wrestling sensation in Europe around the time of World War I. In 1923, he ventured to the US and adjusted to the American catch-as-catch-can form under the tutelage of Johnny Meyers and Wladek Zbyszko. Steinke was embraced by promoter Jack Curley of New York City and especially by the German population in Ridgewood, Queens, where a special "Hans Steinke Social Club" was organized with approximately 3,000 members. After Ed "Strangler" Lewis won the World Heavyweight Title in 1928 and refused to wrestle Steinke, Hans supporters began billing him as the "uncrowned champion." For several years he toiled as Jim Londos's policeman and worked the national circuit until retiring to Chicago in the 1940s. Sam Cordovano, a journeyman grappler in the 1930s, told a reporter in 1943: "The toughest man of all was Hans Steinke, the German giant. He hurt me every time he touched me."

Photo Courtesy of the Pfefer Collection, Department of Special Collections, University of Notre Dame

Born:	January 6, 1887
Height:	6'1"
Weight:	220
Real Name:	John Taylor
Parents:	James and Euphemia Taylor
Military:	United States Army (WWI)
Career Span:	1911–39
Died:	May 19, 1956, Edmonton, Alberta 69 years old

Titles Won:	At least 3, claimed variety of state titles
Days as World Champion:	90
Age at first World Title Win:	27
Best Opponents:	Joe Stecher, Ad Santel, John Pesek
Halls of Fame:	1

Taylor, Jack

Legendary Canadian heavyweight Jack Taylor was born in Greenock, Ontario, the second of six children. He made history when he beat Charlie Cutler in a controversial match in Winnipeg on November 25, 1914, defeating the latter by disqualification and taking a claim to the World Title. In February 1915, he lost the championship to Joe Stecher. Taylor bought some land in Buffalo, Wyoming near the homestead of friend and mentor Clarence Eklund in 1917, and served in the Army during the war. He also faced and defeated many top names in the sport, including the Zbyszko Brothers, Ad Santel, and Bob Managoff. In the 1920s and early 1930s, he held the Canadian and British Empire Titles. A difficult man to beat, Taylor was instrumental in the careers of Earl McCready and Stu Hart.

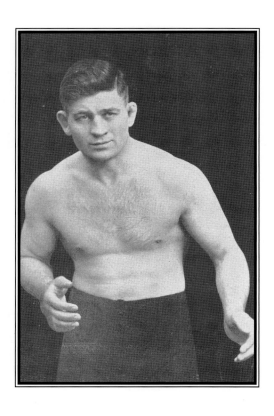

Born:	August 26, 1890
Height:	5'8"
Weight:	175
Real Name:	Theodore Thye
Parents:	Andrew and Bertha Thye
Trained by:	Dave Burns, Dr. John Berg
Career Span:	1915–35
Died:	March 21, 1966, Portland, OR 75 years old

Titles Won:	7, claimed at least one other
Best Opponents:	Clarence Eklund, Mike Yokel, Walter Miller

Thye, Ted

Globetrotting Ted Thye was a celebrated wrestler, and in the 1920s, helped popularize the American style of grappling in Australia. Originally from Frederick, South Dakota, he migrated to the Pacific Northwest and took up wrestling at an amateur club in Spokane, Washington. By 1915, he was claiming the middleweight championship of the Pacific Coast. He beat Walter Miller, a career-long ring nemesis, in June 1919 for a claim to the disputed World Middleweight Title. Rarely did a sportswriter remark that a Thye match was anything but "thrilling," and he was overwhelmingly popular in his hometown of Portland. A master of leverage and proponent of the wristlock submission hold, Thye moved up to the light heavyweight division, and held the world title six times between 1920 and 1927. He first went to Australia in 1924, and in each of the next three years, returned to that country to headline, drawing huge crowds at shows. Later, he worked as a booking agent in the Pacific Northwest territory, Australia, and throughout the South Pacific.

Born:	February 28, 1882
Height:	6'2"
Weight:	220
Real Name:	Nels Jesse Reimer
Wife:	Anna Reimer
Managers:	Oscar Thorson, Emil Klank
Career Span:	1905–25
Died:	September 4, 1956, Houston, TX 74 years old

Titles Won:	3
Best Opponents:	Frank Gotch, George Hackenschmidt, and Stanislaus Zbyszko

Westergaard, Jess

The heartland of the United States was bursting with wrestling talent during the first quarter of the twentieth century. Among them was Jess Westergaard of Des Moines, Iowa, a Swedish transplant and star heavyweight grappler. Having immigrated to the US from Kristianstad in 1901, and with a fine athletic background, Westergaard used his striking size and an education taught by Farmer Burns to tie up opponents. Also known in certain cities as "Jess Reimer," he ascended up the heavyweight ladder until he beat Chares Cutler for the American championship in 1911, and regained it in January 1913 with a victory over Henry Ordemann. He built a strong Midwest following and trained regularly with world champion Frank Gotch. Westergaard stepped off the mat to serve as a Des Moines deputy sheriff, and later settled in Houston, where he entered the oil business. In 1939, he returned to Des Moines after a fourteen-year absence and the local newspaper remembered him as an "outstanding drawing attraction." Westergaard retained his interest in pro wrestling until his death in 1956.

Zbyszko, Stanislaus

Born:	April 1, 1879
Height:	5'9"
Weight:	240
Real Name:	Stanislaus Cyganiewicz
Parents:	Martin and Caroline Cyganiewicz
Family:	Older brother of Wladek Zbyszko
Nickname:	The Mighty Pole
Finisher:	Bearhug
Career Span:	1901–32
Died:	September 23, 1967, St. Joseph, MO 88 years old

Titles Won:	3, claimed others
Days as World Champion:	Over 346 (unknown time for 1914 claim)
Age at first World Title Win:	35
Best Opponents:	Frank Gotch, Joe Stecher, Great Gama
Halls of Fame:	2
Movies:	2

When Stanislaus Zbyszko arrived in America in September 1909, the wrestling landscape changed forever. Although he wasn't adept to the tricky American style of catch-as-catch-can grappling, he was a pure athlete and a proven champion. Born near Krakow, Poland, he began wrestling in 1897 as an amateur and took to the pro sport three years later in Charlottenburg, Germany. He became a world-class Greco-Roman wrestler and engaged in tournaments in Germany and France, and had wins over Ivan Podubny, Alex Aberg, Nouroulah, and George Lurich. He adapted quickly to the rules of catch grappling, using his intellect to outwit opponents, and when he displayed signs of inexperience, he could rely on his extraordinary strength. A prime-time superstar, Zbyszko wanted nothing more than a match with the unconquerable World Champion Frank Gotch. However, when he finally met Gotch on June 1, 1910, things went much different than he hoped—he was beaten in two straight falls and the first was scored in only six seconds.

Educated at the University of Vienna and able to speak eleven languages, Zbyszko was a signature wrestler in the era of Gotch and George Hackenschmidt, and following World War I, he returned to the US to make a further impression on wrestling audiences. On May 6, 1921, he beat Ed "Strangler" Lewis for the World Title and held the championship until March 3, 1922, when he lost it back to Lewis. In a defining moment in the sport's history, he double-crossed Wayne Munn for the heavyweight title on April 15, 1925, and single-handedly seized power from one syndicate and gave it to another, of course for the right price. Zbyszko was briefly the matchmaker at Madison Square Garden in 1930 and made big news in 1932 when he issued a challenge to any college football team for a handicap wrestling match. He boasted that he could beat the entire team within an hour, claiming that he'd defeat the Princeton, Yale, and Harvard squads all in the same night. Zbyszko also appeared in several films, most notably portraying "Gregorius the Great" in the 1950 flick, *Night and the City*.

Photo Courtesy of John Pantozzi

Born:	November 30, 1891
Height:	6'0"
Weight:	230
Real Name:	Wladek Cyganiewicz
Parents:	Martin and Caroline Cyganiewicz
Family:	Younger brother of Stanislaus Zbyszko
Identities:	The Great Apollo (masked)
Nickname:	Polish Hercules
Military:	United States Army (WWI)
Career Span:	1911–50
Died:	June 10, 1968, Savannah, MO 75 years old

Titles Won:	5
Days as World Champion:	126
Age at first World Title Win:	25
Best Opponents:	Ed Lewis, Joe Stecher, Earl Caddock
Halls of Fame:	2

Zbyszko, Wladek

Wladek Zbyszko is often overshadowed by his older brother, Stanislaus, but he too had a hall of fame career. Zbyszko was a claimant to the heavyweight championship at least four different times, and between 1916 and 1921, he was one of the best wrestlers in the world. Born in Krakow, he wrestled the Greco-Roman style in Europe before venturing to the US in December 1912. Like his brother, he adjusted to the catch-as-catch-can system of wrestling, and was a sensation on both coasts. In 1917, he beat Ed "Strangler" Lewis two separate times for the World Title, and did it again in March 1919. Owning a part of the Buenos Aires promotion, Zbyszko held his fourth title in Argentina in 1935. He settled in Northwestern Missouri and remained passionate about wrestling, even sending letters to regional promoters about the monopolistic actions he felt were threatening the sport.

II. Gimmicks and Ingenuity Rekindle Wrestling's Popularity
Pro Debut Between 1921 and 1950

A drop-off in attendance in the 1920s pushed innovators Joe "Toots" Mondt, Jack Curley, and Paul Bowser to enhance the sport with creative mechanisms that transformed things once again. The melding of wrestling and football was the most critical concept that was introduced, and former All-American Gus Sonnenberg was the man who revolutionized the business on the mat. His array of ring moves and likeable personality recharged the sport, and it became almost mandatory, regardless of the level of talent, for wrestlers to adopt his famous flying tackle as a finisher. It was so popular that fans demanded it, and the unpredictability of the move was very entertaining for audiences coast-to-coast.

With that said, no single wrestler was more popular than Jim Londos, and his success between 1930 and 1935 was unparalleled at that time. It wasn't until Hulk Hogan came along in the 1980s that Londos' remarkable run was similarly achieved. Londos was the hero that carried wrestling on his back through the Depression years, and even after stepping away from the limelight, promoters beckoned for his star power to reignite lagging arena sales. The late 1930s saw the rise of Lou Thesz to prominence and his legitimate wrestling aptitude was a throwback to the legends of yore. Thesz had all the qualities to dominate the heavyweight division and outside a few years of service during World War II, he did, and his supremacy continued well into the 1960s.

This time period saw the development of the first real wrestling villains, grapplers who purposefully antagonized audiences. Ed "Strangler" Lewis, during his reign as heavyweight champion between 1922 and 1925, drew the ire of crowds with his famed headlock stranglehold, and not only hospitalized opponents with the borderline illegal maneuver, but displayed arrogance in press interviews. Lewis's actions paled in comparison to the rowdy rule-breakers that emerged in the 1930s and 1940s, among them "The Golden Terror" Bobby Stewart and box office sensation "Wild" Bill Longson. The wrestling villain became a fundamental aspect of pro wrestling, and its relevance is as important today as it was seventy years ago.

For a number of reasons, the popularity of grappling went into a tailspin in the late 1930s and remained lackluster throughout North America during World War II with the exception of a few local divisions. The television boom did wonders for wrestling beginning around 1947 and sensational performers like Gorgeous George and Antonino Rocca were overnight phenomenons. Once again, wrestling was at the forefront of American entertainment, and this time around, there were many more intriguing characters on the circuit than at any time in history. Buddy Rogers, Killer Kowalski, and Verne Gagne were among the young stars ready to make a real dent in the industry, and with that kind of talent, wrestling's future looked immensely bright.

Born:	July 9, 1908
Height:	5'7"
Weight:	280
Real Name:	Bartolomeo Assirati
Wife:	Marjorie Assirati
Trained by:	Atholl Oakley, Henry Irslinger, Billy Riley at his famous Wigan Gym
Career Span:	1928–60
Died:	August 31, 1990, Brighton, England 82 years old

Titles Won:	6
Days as World Champion:	237
Age at first World Title Win:	38
Best Opponents:	Dara Singh, King Kong Czaja, Henri DeGlane
Halls of Fame:	1

Assirati, Bert

An acrobat, strongman, and wrestler with an unprecedented reputation, Bert Assirati was a terrifically dangerous grappler. His offensive weapons of submission were occasionally hazards to rivals expecting to meet in worked affairs, as he was known to be uncooperative in some instances during bouts. With all that, Assirati was still one of the truest of pro wrestlers in the sense that he appreciated the legitimate art of the sport. Originally from London and of Italian parents, Assirati journeyed to the US early in his career to garner experience and competed at around 210 pounds. By the time he was in his prime, he weighed as much as 280. Standing only 5'7", he was a block of muscle, with coordination and quickness to spare. In search of further conquests, Assirati toured the world, from Germany to Singapore, and beat King Kong Czaja, Felix Miquet, and Maurice Tillet. He claimed the British Heavyweight throne for well over a decade, and held the World Title following a tournament in 1947. In 1957, he sought a match with Lou Thesz, but the highly-anticipated bout never materialized. Years later, well-known writer Gerald Kersh described Assirati's "odd" proportional size, and stated: "In the ring he was like nothing so much as a grand piano broken loose and rushing about the deck of a rolling ship." Assirati passed away in 1990 at the age of eighty-two.

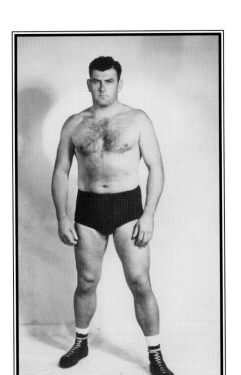

Born:	July 19, 1910
Height:	6'1"
Weight:	250
Real Name:	Robert Frederick Atkinson
Nickname:	Hard Rock from Down Under
Finishers:	Airplane Spin, Piledriver
Career Span:	1934–71
Died:	May 15, 1988, Crystal Beach, Ontario 77 years old

Titles Won:	9
Best Opponents:	Billy Watson, Pat O'Connor, Don Leo Jonathan

Atkins, Fred

During his thirty-year career, Fred Atkins was a champion in Australia, Canada, and the United States. Originally from New Zealand, Atkins was a rugged individual in the ring, using his strength to overpower opponents, and relied on heel tactics, although he had the ability to really wrestle. He began his lifelong journey in grappling as an amateur and became a breakout star in Australia after turning professional in 1934. He held the Australian national heavyweight championship for a number of years, and faced off with the biggest names touring the "Land Down Under," many of whom were from the US and Canada. It wasn't long before an opportunity arose for Atkins to travel to North America, and Fred was ready. Upon arriving in San Francisco in 1947, he told a reporter: "I was good enough in Australia and will be good enough here." And he was. He beat "Whipper" Billy Watson for the British Empire crown in 1949, and formed a successful tag team with Ray Eckert in San Francisco, winning the Pacific Coast Tag Title on two occasions. Known for his immense discipline and training style, he imparted his wisdom as a coach, teaching many up-and-comers the fundamentals of grappling. Among his protégés were Giant Baba, Tiger Jeet Singh, and Adrian Adonis.

Born:	September 14, 1901
Height:	5'6"
Weight:	205
Real Name:	Arteen "Harry" K. Ekizian
High School:	Pasadena High School (CA)
College:	Pasadena Junior College
Trained by:	Farmer Burns
Identities:	Harry Ekiz, Ali Yumid
Nickname:	The Terrible Turk
Career Span:	1924–50
Died:	November 16, 1981, San Luis Obispo, CA 80 years old

Titles Won:	2
Days as World Champion:	63
Age at first World Title Win:	34
Best Opponents:	Ed Lewis, Ray Steele, Dick Shikat

Baba, Ali

On April 24, 1936, the "Terrible Turk" Ali Baba dethroned Dick Shikat for the World Heavyweight Title in Detroit, and then beat him again in New York on May 5. His two victories propelled him from virtual obscurity to national prominence, and in press accounts his handlers billed him as a relative newcomer to the United States who didn't speak English and answered questions with mostly hand gestures. However, Baba's true history was soon revealed to the public. He was born in Armenia, but raised and schooled in California. Not only did he speak English well, he served two enlistments in the US Navy and performed as an extra in several Hollywood flicks. But Baba was a unique-looking character, complete with a bald head and handlebar mustache. His reign as titleholder was sabotaged through a calculated double-cross by Dave Levin and Jack Pfefer in Newark, and Levin captured the championship on June 13, 1936. Baba continued to claim the title until losing again to Everette Marshall later that month. Baba wrestled into the TV era, retiring in 1950, and settled in California. During his career, he scored wins over Ed "Strangler" Lewis, Lou Thesz, Gus Sonnenberg, and Ray Steele, and, to this day, is remembered as one of the earliest world champions to also use a colorful gimmick.

Born:	March 27, 1929
Height:	6'0"
Weight:	225
Parents:	John and Grace Barend
Wife:	Annie Barend
High School:	Jefferson High School (NY)
Finisher:	Airplane Spin
Career Span:	1948–72
Died:	September 20, 2011, Avon, NY 82 years old

Titles Won:	23
Best Opponents:	Buddy Rogers, Johnny Valentine, Bobo Brazil

Barend, Johnny

Johnny Barend began wresting at eight years of age in his hometown of Rochester, New York, and served in the US Navy during World War II. After his discharge, he studied pro wrestling under former Olympian Ed Don George and made his debut in 1948. Technically inclined, because of his lengthy amateur background, Johnny was a natural babyface. He was a guy who could deliver an entertaining, personality-driven interview and then wrestle an exciting match. He was completely versatile, a headliner in singles and tag team bouts, and a proven commodity to promoters in need of a steady worker. Barend won US championships in the WWWF and in Hawaii, and held the World Tag Title with Enrique Torres and Ronnie Etchison. During the 1950s, he morphed into a heel known as "Handsome" Johnny, and formed a tag team with Magnificent Maurice, managed by Mr. Kleen. Barend and Maurice were the ultimate vain "bad guys," carrying mirrors and wearing top hats and capes to illustrate their utter arrogance. But they were a brilliant combination. Barend found another successful tag team partner in "Nature Boy" Buddy Rogers, and the two captured the United States Tag Title in the Capitol Wrestling region in 1962. He retired in the early 1970s and passed away in 2011.

Born:	February 19, 1931
Height:	5'9"
Weight:	220
Real Name:	Rolland Garland Bastien
Parents:	Oliver and Helen Bastien
Military:	United States Navy
Trained by:	Einar Olsen, Henry Kolln
Identities:	Texas Red
Nickname:	The Flying Redhead
Finisher:	Sleeperhold
Tag Teams:	The Fabulous Redheads w/ Red Lyons
Career Span:	1949–80
Died:	August 11, 2012, Minnetonka, MN 81 years old

Bastien, Red

Titles Won:	22
Best Opponents:	Johnny Valentine, Verne Gagne, Maurice Vachon
Movies:	1

Born in Bottineau, North Dakota, Red Bastien began his pro wrestling career as a middleweight, and was a fine showman from an early age. He was athletic to the bone, competently performing rapid maneuvers and clever in the way he handled heavier opponents. He could chain wrestle and brawl, and his flying head-scissors leveled many foes with ease. Bastien grew up in Minneapolis, and was trained and learned the ropes from Verne Gagne and Joe Pazandak. Along with his faux brother, Lou Bastien, he won the US Tag Title from the Graham Brothers twice in 1960, and then traded the belts with the Fabulous Kangaroos. He also teamed with powerful Hercules Cortez to win the AWA Tag Title in May 1971. Cortez was killed in a car accident in July of that year, and Crusher joined Red as his championship partner. As a singles grappler, Bastien held the Florida and Texas State Titles.

From 2001 to '07, he served as the President of the Cauliflower Alley Club, and passed away at the age of eighty-one in 2012. Bastien was classy in and out of the ring and admired by fans and peers across the world.

Born:	January 12, 1914
Height:	5'10"
Weight:	225
Real Name:	George Peter Becker
Finisher:	Alligator Clutch
Career Span:	1935–72
Died:	October 25, 1999, Fort Walton Beach, Florida 85 years old

Titles Won:	25
Days as World Champion:	91
Age at first World Title Win:	32
Best Opponents:	Enrique Torres, Dave Levin, Ernie Dusek

Becker, George

The son of Russian parents, George Becker entered the wrestling business in 1935 under the management of Jack Pfefer in New York, and appeared across North America for thirty-seven years. His crowning achievement as a singles performer was his September 11, 1946, victory over Babe Sharkey in Portland for a claim to the World Heavyweight championship. He held the title until the following December, losing it to Enrique Torres in Los Angeles. In other parts of the country, including parts of Connecticut, Alabama, and Florida, he was recognized as the junior and light heavyweight champion, and was a tag titleholder with his "brother" Bobby Becker. In the 1950s, George began appearing in the Mid-Atlantic region for Jim Crockett Sr., and soon found a permanent base of operations. He became one of the most popular wrestlers in the area and formed several successful tag teams. Becker also booked the territory for a time. He retired from active wrestling in 1972 and later moved to Florida. His wife, Joyce, was also a grappler for a short time.

Born:	November 20, 1906
Height:	5'8"
Weight:	200
Real Name:	Ralph Berry
Parents:	James and Ella Berry
Trained by:	Dutch Klem
Finisher:	Gilligan Twist, Stepover toehold
Managed:	The Fabulous Kangaroos (1957–63), Hans Mortier (1963–68), Max Mortier (1964), Gorilla Monsoon (1964–68), Smasher Sloan (1964–65), Tank Morgan (1966–67), Bull Ortega (1966–67), Professor Toru Tanaka (1967–68)
Career Span:	1927–65
Died:	July 28, 1973, Pittsburg, KS 66 years old

Berry, Red

Titles Won:	20
Best Opponents:	Danny McShain, Verne Gagne, Leroy McGuirk
Halls of Fame:	2

From a rabid grappler to a smooth talking manager, "Wild" Red Berry experienced just about everything there was to experience in more than a four-decade involvement in pro wrestling. He was from Pittsburg, Kansas, a small town in the southeastern part of the state, and gave up schooling as a teenager to help support his family. Initially a boxer, he shifted to grappling after earning but $30 for a brutal six-round fight, and was a pioneer in wrestling's light heavyweight division. Berry was unrestrained around the ring, utilizing his speed and devious tricks to win matches. Fans, in turn, loved to hate him, and he feuded violently with the likes of Danny McShain and Paavo Katonen. Between 1937 and '47, he won the light heavyweight title thirteen times and was a big star in light heavyweight centers in both Hollywood, California, and Tulsa, Oklahoma. Extremely verbose, he lashed out at his enemies with a flair more associated with promos seen in modern wrestling. Berry was ahead of his time, and his animated personality earned him both popularity and ire. In 1969, he told a reporter: "I've had forty-two years of it, and more than 10,000 matches. And I've never lost my enthusiasm for wrestling." To the spectators who watched him, that much was obvious every time he stepped from behind the curtain.

Blassie, Fred

Born:	February 8, 1918
Height:	5'11"
Weight:	235
Real Name:	Fred Kenneth Blassie
Parents:	Jacob and Anna Blassie
Family:	Gimmicked brother of Billy McDaniels, Jack Blassie and Mickey Blassie
High School:	McKinley High School (MO) (attended briefly)
Trained by:	Billy Hansen, George Tragos
Identities:	Bill Blassie, Freddie Beal, Fred McDaniels
Nicknames:	Sailor, Butcher Boy, Ayatollah, Fashion Plate of Wrestling
Finisher:	Neckbreaker, Atomic Drop
Tag Team:	The McDaniels Brothers w/ Billy McDaniels
Managed:	Waldo Von Erich (1975), Stan Hansen (1976), Muhammad Ali (1976), Tor Kamata (1976-1977), Baron Von Raschke (1976), Mr. Fuji (1977), Professor Tanaka (1977), Spiros Arion (1977–78), Peter Maivia (1978), Victor Rivera (1978–79), Nikolai Volkoff (1979), Swede Hanson (1979), Hussein Arab (1979), The Hangman (1980), Hulk Hogan (1980–81), Stan Hansen (1980–81), Tor Kamata (1980), Killer Khan (1981), George Steele (1981), Adrian Adonis (1981–82), Jesse Ventura (1981–82), John Studd (1983), Iron Sheik (1983–84), Nikolai Volkoff (1983–84), Kamala (1984), George Steele (1985), Cpl. Kirschner (1986)
Career Span:	1942–85
Died:	June 2, 2003, Hartsdale, NY 85 years old

Titles Won:	41
Days as World Champion:	479
Age at first World Title Win:	43
Best Opponents:	The Destroyer, John Tolos, Mr. Moto
Halls of Fame:	3
Movies:	4

"Classy" Freddie Blassie was a Hall of Fame heel, a shrewd master of the squared circle who outsmarted his opponents and then talked trash about them in promos. He was a treasured wrestler to promoters around the world, literally for decades, and his act was as good in 1957 as it was in 1972. Blassie could draw immense heat from crowds and sold the intensity of feuds as well as anyone in the business. From St. Louis, he was a devoted athlete in his youth, training extensively at local gyms and athletic clubs. He initially majored in boxing, and rounded out his ring experience by learning holds and counters on the mat. In 1942, he not only joined the Navy, but turned pro, wrestling when he could break away from his duty station at Lambert Field in St. Louis. From 1944-1945, he served in the Philippines and weeks after his discharge in October 1945, he resumed his grappling career.

Blassie was known primarily as a fan favorite for the first half of the 1950s, respected for his scientific and clean style . . . but that changed as fans throughout the Southeastern US were exposed to his rulebreaking antics. He feuded for years with Don McIntyre and Ray Gunkel and held the Southern Heavyweight championship more than ten times between 1954 and 1960. At points, he was part owner and booker of the Atlanta office. In 1961, he settled in Los Angeles and challenged Edouard Carpentier for the WWA World Title on June 12, drawing 13,200 fans and a gate of $40,000. Blassie won the championship in three falls and retained it in defenses against Ricki Starr, Primo Carnera, Antonino Rocca, and Dick Hutton. He'd trade the title with Rikidozan and The Destroyer over the next two years, and then win his fourth championship from Carpentier in January 1964. On April 22, 1964, Blassie lost the title to Dick the Bruiser. In addition to his collective body of work in Southern California, Blassie was a legend in Japan.

Blassie sold out Madison Square Garden in New York in matches against Bruno Sammartino and ended up passing the proverbial torch to John Tolos in their dynamic Los Angeles feud that culminated in a $140,000+ gate in August 1971. Blassie stepped away from the ring to become a manager in the WWWF during the 1970s and 1980s, and was a key ingredient in the promotion's success. His arrogance and verbal aptitude was still charging up fans and his color helped get comparatively colorless workers over with audiences. Outside the ring, he made a number of well-received TV and film appearances and wrote a telling autobiography in 2003 that revealed much about his life. He was honored by induction into the WWE Halls of Fame in 1994.

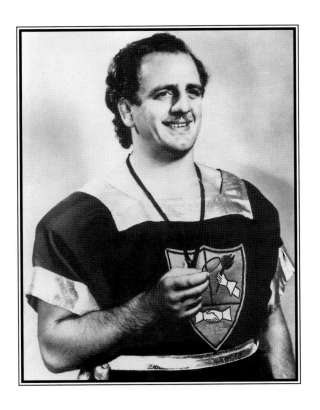

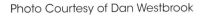

Born:	August 13, 1923
Height:	6'0"
Weight	225
Real Name:	James Ranicar Blears
Wife:	Leonora Blears
Identities:	Jan Blears, Mr. X
Nickname:	Tally Ho
Career Span:	1945-1973
Died:	March 3, 2016, Honolulu, HI 92 years old

Titles Won:	13
Best Opponents:	Lou Thesz, Sandor Szabo, Wilbur Snyder
TV Appearances:	4
Movies:	3

Blears, Lord James

Twenty-two-year-old James Blears arrived in New York City on June 17, 1946, and hooked up with Al Mayer, the booking agent who'd arrange his first series of matches around the northeast. Blears, born in Tyldesley, England, served as a radio operator on a merchant ship during the war, and barely survived a Japanese submarine attack that sank his vessel. In the ring he was a skilled performer and won a claim to the World Light Heavyweight Title from "Wild" Red Berry in 1947. He soon adopted a royal heritage, took Captain Leslie Holmes as his manager, and was a major television star on programs emanating from Los Angeles and Chicago. Along with Lord Athol Layton, he won a string of tag team championships and was also an influential grappler and personality in Hawaii, where he made his home. Away from active wrestling, he appeared in three films and four TV shows, including two episodes of *Magnum P.I.* in 1982 and '83. Additionally, he provided commentary for the AWA's national programs on ESPN during the 1980s. The legendary "Lord" Blears died in March 2016 at the age of ninety-two.

Born:	October 12, 1922
Height:	5'7"
Weight:	150
Real Name:	Alejandro Munoz Moreno
Wife:	Gregoria Moreno
Career Span:	1948–88
Died:	December 16, 2000, Mexico City, Mexico 78 years old

Titles Won:	6
Best Opponents:	El Santo, Karloff Lagarde, Rayo de Jalisco
Halls of Fame:	1
Movies:	27

Blue Demon, The

An iconic wrestler with superhero status, The Blue Demon was a legend in his native Mexico. Originally from Rodriguez in Coahuila, he developed into a premier athlete under Rolando Vera, and first donned his famed blue mask in 1948. Extremely popular and inspiring, the Blue Demon won the NWA World Welterweight belt from Mexico's other lucha libre hero, El Santo, on July 25, 1953, and held it for over four years. He was also the Mexican National Welterweight Champion three times over. Dedicated to health and training, he was a real role model, and his protégé and namesake, Blue Demon Jr., upholds the same honorable traits he made famous—and is very successful all over the world, even winning the NWA World Heavyweight Title in 2008.

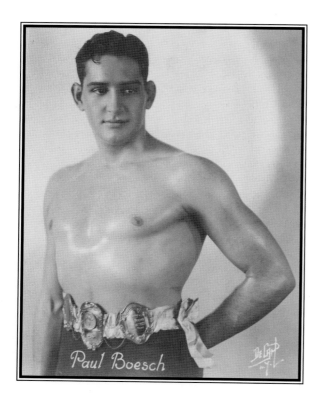

Photo Courtesy of the Pfefer Collection, Department of Special Collections, University of Notre Dame

Born:	October 2, 1912
Height:	6'1"
Weight:	215
Real Name:	Paul Max Boesch
Parents:	Max and Delia Boesch
Wife:	Valerie Boesch
High School:	Long Beach High School (NY)
Military:	United States Army (WWII)
Military Unit:	G Company, 121st Infantry Regiment, 8th Division
Military Honors:	Earned two Silver Stars, two Bronze Stars, two Purple Hearts and the Croix de Guerre Award
Promoted:	Houston (1967–87, 1988–89)
Career Span:	1932–65
Died:	March 7, 1989, Sugarland, TX 76 years old

Boesch, Paul

Titles Won:	Claimed at least 1
Best Opponents:	Bill Longson, Ray Steele, Buddy Rogers
Halls of Fame:	2

Popular Paul Boesch of Brooklyn, New York was a war hero, an author, lifeguard, wrestler, TV announcer, promoter, and genuinely nice guy. Discovered on the shores of Long Beach by promoter Harry Bloomfield, he was ushered into the business by Jack Pfefer in 1932. Pfefer sent him out onto the main New York circuit, and Boesch's speed and flawless execution were a big hit with fans. He ventured into Canada and landed in the Pacific Northwest, where he bought into the territory and acted as a promoter in Seattle throughout 1938. After service in World War II, where he distinguished himself on the battlefield and earned medals of valor, Boesch returned to the business, and was a valuable aide to Houston promoter Morris Sigel. Beginning in 1949, he was the voice behind the local TV program and took over the promotion when Sigel died. The always charitable Boesch ran Houston for two decades, and it was consistently a top-tier town because of his hard work.

Born:	September 19, 1923
Height:	5'10"
Weight:	325
Parents:	Alex and Angeline Bollas
High School:	Harding High School (OH)
College:	Ohio State University (1945–46)
Trained at:	Al Haft's Gym in Columbus
Identities:	The Intercollegiate Dark Secret
Career Span:	1947–68
Died:	January 28, 1977, Akron, OH 53 years old

Titles Won:	4
Days as World Champion:	42
Age at first World Title Win:	25
Best Opponents:	Lou Thesz, Verne Gagne, Buddy Rogers
Halls of Fame:	1

Bollas, George

Amateur wrestling great George Bollas was the son of Greek parents and the last of four children born in Warren, Ohio. Weighing in excess of 300 pounds, he was a dominant collegiate grappler, winning two Big Ten championships and the NCAA crown in 1946 while attending Ohio State University. He became a pro wrestler and, in the summer of 1948, adopted the famous gimmick of the "Zebra Kid," a masked, black-and-white striped mastodon. Booked by the famed Jack Pfefer, Bollas terrorized arenas all over the country and won the troupe's version of the World Heavyweight Title from Buddy Rogers in July 1949. At the Wilmington Bowl in the Los Angeles area, he beat Sandor Szabo for the KECA-TV Wrestling Jackpot on December 23, 1952, and held onto honors until February, when Szabo won a rematch. The Zebra Kid also won the Hawaii Heavyweight crown and battled all the top heroes from Rikidozan to Lou Thesz. He was unmasked at least nine times in the ring and toured the world until an eye injury ended his career. Bollas died in 1977 at the age of fifty-three.

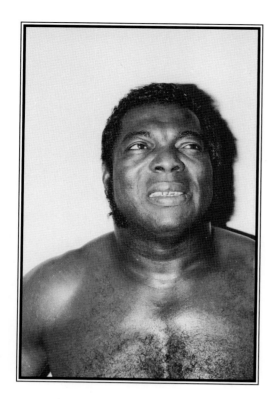

Born:	July 10, 1924
Height:	6'6"
Weight:	275
Real Name:	Houston Harris Sr.
Family:	Father of Bobo Brazil Jr.
Trained by:	Joe Savoldi, Rex Sheeley, Jimmy Mitchell
Finisher:	Coco Butt, Cobra Twist, Abdominal Stretch
Tag Team:	The Young Lions w/ Wilbur Snyder
Career Span:	1949–93
Died:	January 20, 1998, St. Joseph, MI 73 years old

Brazil, Bobo

Titles Won:	52
Days as World Champion:	Around 520
Age at first World Title Win:	42
Best Opponents:	The Sheik, Dick the Bruiser, Buddy Rogers
Halls of Fame:	3

In interviews, Bobo Brazil affirmed that he drew great strength from cheering crowds, and that fans across the world were the catalyst for his courage against the biggest heels in the industry. When Brazil was fired up, he was aggressive in his approach and willing to utilize all parts of the ring to batter his opponents. Of all his maneuvers, the one he relied upon the most was his famed "Coco Butt," which was his version of the headbutt, and it was applied with such immense force that it usually floored his foe right then and there. Throughout his forty-four year career, he also displayed a wide assortment of technical moves, which counterbalanced his brawling attack. It didn't matter to the fans which style he used, as they were on his side regardless. Originally from the northeastern part of Arkansas, Brazil and his family relocated to Benton Harbor, Michigan after the death of his father, and he played some municipal baseball before taking to the pro wrestling mat.

Brazil was a quick learner and his lack of formal education didn't hinder him in the slightest. Initially wrestling as "Huston Harris," he adopted the signature name "Bobo Brazil" in 1950. A powerful African American, he was met with resistance by racist promoters unwilling to exploit his tremendous drawing ability. However, he made plenty of waves across North America from Toronto to Los Angeles and received national TV coverage. Brazil meant big money at the box office, and he chased NWA champion Buddy Rogers for a lengthy period of time, coming close to winning the belt many times. He captured the WWA World Title in both Los Angeles and Indianapolis and was an eleven-time United States Champion between 1961 and 1976, with violent feuds with Dick the Bruiser, The Sheik, and Abdullah the Butcher. Brazil was arguably the most influential African American wrestler in history and his legacy will forever be honored for all the positivity he brought to the business.

Born:	March 10, 1908
Height:	6'3"
Weight	235
Real Name:	Orville E. Brown
Parents:	Clarence and Ellen Brown
Wife:	Grace Brown
Family:	Father of Richard Brown
Trained by:	Ernest Brown
Finisher:	Indian Deathlock, Piledriver, Stepover Toehold
Career Span:	1932–50
Died:	January 24, 1981, Lees Summit, MO 72 years old

Titles Won:	17
Days as World Champion:	Around 5,734, including overlapping claims
Age at first World Title Win:	32
Best Opponents:	Lee Wykoff, Bobby Bruns, Jim Londos
Halls of Fame:	1

Brown, Orville

The most influential wrestler when the National Wrestling Alliance expanded in 1948 was Orville Brown of Kansas. As the group's initial heavyweight champion, he was expected to proudly represent the budding organization across a growing list of territories . . . and that's exactly what he did. His first taste of regional success came as a rookie when he dethroned Alan Eustace for the Kansas State crown in 1932. Within a few years, he was challenging Jim Londos for the World Title and doing shows all over the eastern part of the country. Around 1940, he returned to Kansas and established himself as the preeminent hero throughout the central states, gaining widespread popularity. In eight years at the top of the Kansas City promotion, Brown captured eleven Midwest Wrestling Association World Championships, and had sensational matches with Lee Wykoff, Bobby Bruns, Sonny Myers, and many others.

After years of being acknowledged as the "National Wrestling Alliance" champion in Iowa, Brown collaborated in an effort to expand the organization nationally, and his credibility as heavyweight champion was imperative as the new NWA tried to gain footing. Brown's group went head-to-head against National Wrestling Association champion Lou Thesz until the two entities made peace and it was agreed that both NWA titles would be unified in November 1949. But weeks before his match against Thesz, Brown was nearly killed in a car accident, and his career as a wrestler was essentially over. He remained a booking agent, controlling a wide region in the central states until his power came into question during a real world feud with Gust Karras of St. Joseph, and, in 1963, he decided to walk away from the business. Brown's influence as a founder of the NWA and as its original ambassador has not, and will never, be forgotten.

Born:	March 31, 1903
Height:	6'2"
Weight:	240
Real Name:	James Orville Browning
Parents:	James and Anna Browning
Wife:	Mary Browning
High School:	Verona High School (MO)
Trained by:	Oscar Kimmons, Leo Dysart
Identities:	Young Stecher
Finisher:	Turnover Scissors
Career Span:	1924–36
Died:	June 19, 1936, Rochester, MN 33 years old

Titles Won:	1
Days as World Champion:	490
Age at first World Title Win:	29
Best Opponents:	Ed Lewis, Jim Londos, Ray Steele

Browning, Jim

Jim Browning was a low-key champion during the Great Depression; the kind of man who was extraordinary in the ring, but not outgoing in terms of personality. According to many of his peers, he was one of the greatest genuine wrestlers of all-time. His size and strength were overwhelming, and considering the years he spent as a carnival shooter early in life, was tough as nails. A product of Southwestern Missouri, Browning went to work to help his family following the death of his father in 1917. He wrestled his way out of Missouri and Kansas onto the national circuit, and made a big impression on promoters. By the early 1930s, he was easily one of the top five legitimate heavyweights in the sport. Winning New York recognition as world champion from Ed "Strangler" Lewis on February 20, 1933, was undoubtedly the greatest achievement of his career. He was titleholder when the new promotional alliance known as the "Trust" erased syndicate boundaries and he took on all his top challengers until losing the title to Londos on June 25, 1934, at the Madison Square Garden Bowl. An eye disease, trachoma, forced him into retirement before succumbing to a pulmonary embolism at thirty-three years of age.

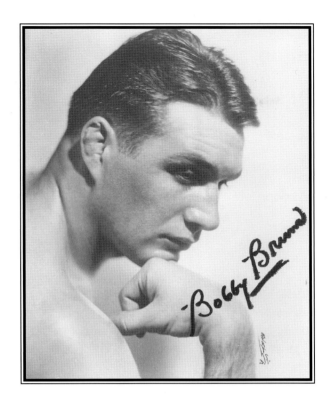

Photo Courtesy of the Pfefer Collection, Department of Special Collections, University of Notre Dame

Born:	July 12, 1914
Height:	6'1"
Weight:	225
Real Name:	Robert Harry Bruns
Parents:	George and Charlotte Bruns
Military:	United States Navy (WWII)
Nickname:	Bruiser, The German Apollo
Career Span:	1935–67
Died:	January 23, 1983, St. Joseph, MO 68 years old

Titles Won:	13
Days as World Champion:	270
Age at first World Title Win:	25
Best Opponents:	Jim Londos, Lee Wykoff, Dick Shikat

Bruns, Bobby

Influential globetrotter Bobby Bruns sported a brilliant mind for the business and was a key booker in many cities during the 1950s and '60s. Born in Chicago, he was the son of a railroad engineer and was an expert swimmer during his youth He competed in amateur meets as a member of the Beilfuss Natatorium, and was a lifeguard at Lincoln Park when he was called upon to train with Jim Londos prior to the latter's bout with Ed Lewis in 1934. Within a short period of time, Bruns made his wrestling debut, and soon ventured to New York, where his career took off. On November 10, 1939, he beat Maurice Boyer for the World Light Heavyweight Title, which morphed into a "heavyweight" title claim for Jack Pfefer's enterprises. He lost the crown to Orville Brown, on June 13, 1940. Most fans were unaware that Bruns and Brown were actually good friends outside the ring. Nine years after the title switch, the two were riding between towns when the car they were riding in collided with a stalled truck on a dark country road. Bruns was seriously injured in the wreck, while Brown was forced to retire due to injuries. In 1951, Bruns trained future legend Rikidozan and wrestled him in his pro debut in Japan. He was a booker all over the world, and was Sam Muchnick's main matchmaker in St. Louis for most of the 1960s.

Born:	May 2, 1913
Height:	5'10"
Weight:	245
Real Name:	Fred Thomas Koury Sr.
Parents:	Nelson and Mary Koury
Family:	Father of Fred Curry
Career Span:	1932–79
Died:	March 6, 1985, Columbus, OH 71 years old

Titles Won:	27
Best Opponents:	Bruno Sammartino, Johnny Valentine, The Sheik

Bull Curry

"Wild" Bull Curry was hardcore before the term was even coined. He was a gifted showman, known for his gigantic eyebrows, and gave fans their money's worth through a mixture of terror and excitement. Curry attended Hartford, Connecticut, schools through the eighth grade, and joined a local carnival as a wrestler who'd take on all comers. Supporting his family after the death of his father, Curry joined a pro wrestling circuit in 1932, and for the next forty-seven years he brawled, gouged, and bludgeoned opponents with a distinctive zeal. He served as a police officer in Hartford, and gained national attention for boxing Jack Dempsey in a Detroit exhibition, which he lost in the second round. Between 1953 and 1967, he held the

Texas Brass Knuckles Title, a championship representing the "extreme" style, twenty times. In Boston, he engaged in a lengthy feud with popular hero Frank Scarpa and beat the latter twice for the United States championship in 1962 and '63. Curry hung up his boots in 1979, and passed away six years later in March 1985, at the age of seventy-one.

Born:	August 5, 1915
Height:	5'2"
Weight:	135
Real Name:	Mildred Bliss
Parents:	Bruce and Bertha Bliss
Family:	Adopted mother of Janet Boyer Wolfe
High School:	Manual High School (MO)
Nicknames:	Millie the Mauler, Wrestling Queen
Finisher:	Alligator Clutch
Managed by:	Billy Wolfe (1935–52)
Career Span:	1935–55
Died:	February 18, 1989, Northridge, CA 73 years old

Burke, Mildred

Titles Won:	4
Days as World Champion:	Around 7,000
Age at first World Title Win:	21
Best Opponents:	June Byers, Clara Mortensen, Nell Stewart
Halls of Fame:	3
Movies:	1

Long before the Divas and Knockouts took the spotlight, women wrestlers were generally considered a sideshow, there more for eye candy than presenting a sound athletic performance. By the 1930s, there were a handful of coordinated outfits featuring women grapplers on the pro circuit, usually centering around one particular superstar attraction who claimed to be the champion. It remained loosely organized until Billy Wolfe, a Missouri middleweight grappler, discovered a short teenage waitress named Mildred Bliss from Coffeyville, Kansas in 1934, and ultimately built an entire syndicate around her. Although he didn't know it at first, Bliss was his ticket to fame and fortune, and Wolfe put her through the wringer before realizing her potential. She went out on the carnival circuit and demonstrated her perseverance against men of all sizes, defeating virtually everyone she was matched against. She literally wrestled her way out from under circus tents and into arenas all across Missouri and into the surrounding states.

Wolfe changed her name to "Burke," and on January 28, 1937, gained her first big slice of national attention when she defeated Clara Mortensen in Chattanooga and claimed the women's title. She lost a rematch two weeks later, but returned to avenge the defeat on April 19, 1937 in Charleston. From that moment on, Burke positioned herself at the top of the women's pyramid, and helped build now husband,

Wolfe's stable of female workers into the best the sport had ever seen. She dominated her competition as a fighting champion and drew the largest crowds for any woman grappler in history. Her success continued into the early 1950s, and, in 1951, a web of personal issues between Mildred, Wolfe, and Wolfe's son, G. Bill, threatened the sustainability of their working arrangement. In September of that year, Burke was badly injured in a car accident while driving through the Mojave Desert, and things were further complicated when Wolfe demanded that Burke lose the World Championship to June Byers or Nell Stewart.

The personal war between Burke and Wolfe descended into chaos and Mildred was steadfast in her plight, protecting her championship and the value it meant to her. The situation was seemingly resolved when Burke paid Wolfe $30,000 for all of the latter's booking interests, but after the transaction, Wolfe refused to walk away from the business, reneging on his pledge to do so. He pushed Byers to the World Title in 1953 and conspired to taint Burke's good name every chance he got; but Burke was still the most widely recognized champion and her fiery demeanor was well appreciated by wrestling's faithful. She agreed to meet Byers in Atlanta to straighten out their rival title claims, and on August 20, 1954, they met in what was a deeply hostile shoot. Both of their reputations were on the line, and after Byers won the first fall, and the match was stopped before a result could be established in the second, the confusion in the feminine grappling ranks continued, especially as both walked away still claiming the title.

Burke was instrumental in spreading interest in women's grappling to Japan when she toured the country in late 1954. She never lost her championship in the ring and retired as titleholder. For sixteen years, between 1937 and 1953, she was the most well-regarded female wrestler in the business, and proved that women were not only sideshow attractions, but the main event. In many cities, she drew better than her male counterparts, and certainly was able to outperform men, giving audiences a more impressive wrestling display. Burke was a key figure in the evolution of women's wrestling and the dignity she brought to the ring and the championship paved the way for Moolah and every female grappler who followed. After leaving the ring, she operated a wrestling school in Southern California and also promoted on a small-time scale. The complete story of Burke's rise to superstardom and her trials and tribulations with Billy Wolfe is told in Jeff Leen's 2009 book, *The Queen of the Ring*.

In 2016, she was inducted into the WWE Hall of Fame as part of the inaugural "Legacy" class.

Born:	May 25, 1922
Height:	5'7"
Weight:	150
Real Name:	DeAlva Eyvonnie Sibley
Parents:	Arthur and Ruby Sibley
Husbands:	G. Bill Wolfe, Sam Menacker
Trained by:	Shorty Roberts, Mae Young, Bobby Managoff, Karl Davis
Finisher:	Flying Dropkick
Career Span:	1944–64
Died:	July 20, 1998, Houston, TX 76 years old

Titles Won:	5
Days as World Champion:	Around 3,400
Age at first World Title Win:	32
Best Opponents:	Mildred Burke, Nell Stewart, Lillian Ellison
Halls of Fame:	1

Byers, June

A pin-up star for two decades, June Byers mixed glamour with legitimate wrestling knowledge and athletic ability. Originally from Houston, she became acquainted with amateur grappling as a teenager, learning the rudiments from her uncle. She worked as a lab technician, and only after her first husband passed away unexpectedly, leaving her with a young baby, did she consider wrestling professionally. Not before long she was traveling upwards of 100,000 miles a year on the national circuit, wrestling the likes of Nell Stewart, Elviry Snodgrass, and the Women's World champion Mildred Burke. Women's wrestling, which had been managed by promoter Billy Wolfe, was destabilized in 1953 after Wolfe had a falling out with his wife, Burke, and Byers was soon elevated to the number one spot. On April 14, 1953, she won a tournament in Baltimore to become World Champion of the powerful Wolfe office. Since there was still controversy over who was the rightful queen, Byers faced Burke in Atlanta on August 20, 1954. Their infamous bout contained elements of a "shoot," because neither trusted the other. Byers ended up with a stained victory, and remained a claimant until retiring in 1964. She was inducted into the Professional Wrestling Hall of Fame in 2006.

Born:	October 26, 1906
Height:	6'6"
Weight:	265
Parents:	Sante and Giovanna Carnera
Wife:	Pina Carnera
Pro Sports:	Boxing (1928–37, 1945–46)
Trained by:	Hardy Kruskamp
Nickname:	Da Preem, Alpine Atlas, Ambling Alp
Managed by:	Louis Soresi, Leon See, Bill Duffy, Walter Friedman, Harold Harris, Joe "Toots" Mondt, Babe McCoy, Hardy Kruskamp, and others
Career Span:	1945–62
Died:	June 29, 1967, Sequals, Italy 60 years old

Carnera, Primo

Titles Won:	2 (claimed several others)
Best Opponents:	Jim Londos, Killer Kowalski, Verne Gagne
Boxing Record:	88-14 (72 by knockout)
Days as Boxing World Champion:	350
Age at first World Title Win:	26
Halls of Fame:	2
Movies:	15

Primo Carnera was a longtime member of the athletic community, first as a champion boxer and later as a wrestling sensation. Throughout it all, he was the pawn of a long list of managers, all of whom sliced up his pay and manipulated him to the utmost of extremes. Carnera took orders from parties with underworld ties and even from Fascist leaders of his native Italy. His push in boxing was incredible despite his less-than-stellar fighting skills, and on June 29, 1933, he beat Jack Sharkey in the sixth round for the World Heavyweight boxing championship. Carnera was titleholder until June 14, 1934, when he lost a landslide fight to Max Baer, getting knocked down eleven times. Barely surviving World War II, he returned to the US in July 1946, and launched his mat campaign. He garnered a lot of attention based on name recognition and was even billed as a title claimant on occasion. Carnera was a successful international draw and remained a fixture on the circuit into the early 1960s.

Born:	December 4, 1908
Height:	6'0"
Weight:	225
Real Name:	Stephen Casey
Parents:	Mike and Bridget Casey
Family:	Seven brothers including Jim, Paddy, Mick, and Tom Casey
Wife:	Mary Casey
Military:	United States Army (WWII)
Trained by:	Mike "Big Mick" Casey, Jack Albright
Finisher:	Kerry Crush, Killarney Flip
Career Span:	1933–51
Died:	January 10, 1987, Brockton, MA 78 years old

Casey, Steve

Titles Won:	6
Days as World Champion:	1,680
Age at first World Title Win:	29
Best Opponents:	Maurice Tillet, Frank Sexton, Lou Thesz
Halls of Fame:	1

Based on the quality of advertising out of Boston promoter Paul Bowser's office, there were remarkably high expectations for the Irish newcomer, Steve Casey, in 1936. Casey was touted as better than his fellow countryman, former undisputed champion Danno O'Mahoney, and was reportedly undefeated in more than 200 matches. Fans responded positively to him from the start, and, unlike O'Mahoney's crash and burn, "Crusher" Casey could protect himself from a double-cross through sheer toughness. That attribute would benefit him through six AWA World Heavyweight Title reigns, the first beginning on February 11, 1938 when he beat Lou Thesz. He'd also win the championship from the likes of Gus Sonnenberg, Maurice Tillet, and his final victory in 1945 over Frank Sexton. In addition to his outstanding mat career, Casey was a champion rower with his brothers, and later ran a popular bar in Boston, appropriately named, "Crusher Casey's."

Born:	September 9, 1924
Height:	5'10"
Weight:	210
Real Name:	Christopher J. Clancy
Parents:	John and Mary Clancy
Nickname:	Irish
Career Span:	1945–67
Died:	June 15, 1988, Tulsa, OK
	63 years old

Titles Won:	12
Best Opponents:	Lou Thesz, Verne Gagne, Fred Blassie

Clancy, Mike

"Irish" Mike Clancy was a clever grappler who reigned supreme as NWA World Junior Heavyweight champion for the better part of two years. Born in Woburn, north of Boston, Massachusetts, he attended the Warren Academy and began wrestling as an amateur at a local YMCA during his youth. In 1945, following service in the Coast Guard during World War II, he turned professiona, and was a reliable performer regardless of his place on the bill. He wrestled across the country and built an ever-growing popularity. On April 10, 1956, he dethroned Ed Francis for the NWA World Junior Title in Tulsa, and finally released his grip on the belt on February 28, 1958, when Angelo Savoldi defeated him in Oklahoma City. Clancy beat Jackie Fargo for the Southern Junior Title in December 1959, and held that championship for nearly a full year. He also won the World Tag Team championship with Oni Wiki Wiki and the US Tag Title with Al Lovelock. Following his retirement in 1967, he retired to Tulsa, Oklahoma, where he was a prominent businessman and county sheriff.

Born:	March 8, 1910
Height:	5'11"
Weight:	225
Real Name:	Elmer Claybourne
Parents:	James and Ella Claybourne
Identities:	The Black Panther, The Black Secret
Finisher:	Dropkick
Career Span:	1932–58
Died:	January 7, 1960, Los Angeles, CA 49 years old

Titles Won:	3 (claimed several others)
Days as World Champion:	Unknown
Age at first World Title Win:	Around 33
Best Opponents:	Yvon Robert, Bobby Managoff, Billy Watson

Claybourne, Jack

Blazing a trail as a pioneering African American wrestler, Jack Claybourne was born in Mexico, Missouri, one of four children, and labored on local farms with his father and older brothers. He took to athletics, playing baseball and later becoming a wrestler on a small Missouri circuit. Not before long he was competing in Kansas City, and moved on to major metropolises across North America. Facing prejudices in many states, including Texas, where African Americans were prohibited from wrestling Caucasian grapplers, he gained a terrific popularity with fans of all cultures, and it was hard not to recognize his excellent wrestling abilities. An Ohio sportswriter in 1938 wrote: "Claybourne is the athlete who has set fans of the middlewest talking, with speedy action such as has seldom been witnessed [and] has been an instant hit wherever he has shown his wares." And Claybourne was a sensation in the US, Canada, Mexico, Australia, and New Zealand. He claimed the Negro Light Heavyweight and Heavyweight Titles, and reigned as titleholder in Hawaii from 1948 to '49. Claybourne retired from wrestling in 1958 and, sadly, committed suicide two years later.

Born:	September 20, 1905
Height:	5'3"
Weight:	220
Real Name:	Abe Kelmer
Parents:	Shaya and Chevet Kelmer
Married to:	June Coleman
Career Span:	1927–57
Died:	March 28, 2007, Fresh Meadows, NY 101 years old

Coleman, Abe

Titles Won:	Claimed at least 1
Best Opponents:	John Pesek, Jim Londos, Ray Steele
Halls of Fame:	1

Standing 5'3", Abe Coleman was an underdog through and through, and fans always wanted to see him score an upset against his usually larger foes. But Coleman's incredible strength and agility were a great equalizer, and he earned plenty of cheers for his competitive style. A Jewish grappler from Zychlin, Poland, he followed his brother to Nova Scotia, Canada, in December 1923, and later settled in the New York City area. Discovered by promoter Rudy Miller around 1927, he appeared across the North American wrestling circuit for the next three decades and was often billed as the Jewish Heavyweight champion. He also toured Australia and was an early proponent of the dropkick. Coleman's brother Alex joined the wrestling business in the 1930s as a promoter in Asbury Park, New Jersey. At 101 years of age, in 2006, Coleman became one of the oldest living pro wrestlers in history, and passed six months later. He was honored by induction into the Professional Wrestling Hall of Fame in 2012, and fans worldwide celebrated his outstanding career.

Costello, Al

Born:	December 14, 1919
Height:	5'10"
Weight:	225
Real Name:	Giacomo "Jack" Costa
High School:	Christian Brothers High School (Sydney, Australia)
Military:	Australian Army (WWII)
Trained by:	Jim Bonos
Managed:	Tony Charles, Les Thornton, Don Kent, John Heffernan
Career Span:	1939–87
Died:	January 22, 2000, Clearwater, FL 80 years old

Titles Won:	33
Age at first World Tag Title Win:	38
Best Opponents:	Lou Thesz, Bruno Sammartino, Edouard Carpentier
Wrestlers Managed:	11
Halls of Fame:	2

Many years before he became one half of the famous Fabulous Kangaroos tag team, Al Costello was being ushered by his parents toward a career as a singer, and had the tenor voice to do it. Instead, he graduated from his father's Australian fruit business and focused on the squared circle, where he fought and wrestled as an amateur, then as a professional grappler beginning in the late 1930s. Dedicated to weight-lifting and learning the scientific aspects of the business, Costello formed more of an identity as a showman after working with Dr. Len Hall, an established American grappler. He traveled around the globe, and in May 1957, formed the Kangaroos with Roy Heffernan in Canada. Together, they were an unstoppable force of nature, winning World and US Tag Team Titles from coast to coast, and their success as a duo was unrivaled to that point in history. Costello also teamed with Don Kent in a new version of the Kangaroos, and worked as a manager into the 1980s.

Born:	July 11, 1926
Height:	6'0"
Weight:	245
Real Name:	Reginald J. Lisowski
Parents:	John and Angeline Lisowski
Wife:	Faye Lisowski
High School:	South Milwaukee High School (WI)
College:	Marquette University
Identities:	Crusher Machine
Finisher:	Clawhold, The Neck Crusher, The Crusher Bolo
Career Span:	1949–89
Died:	October 22, 2005, Milwaukee, WI 79 years old

Crusher, The

Titles Won:	29
Days as World Champion:	265
Age at first World Title Win:	36
Best Opponents:	Verne Gagne, Buddy Rogers, Nick Bockwinkel
Halls of Fame:	3

A former high school football letterman, Reginald Lisowski was stationed at Heidelberg Army Base in Germany and learned his first wrestling holds from a military athletic instructor. He added to his knowledge at the Milwaukee Eagles Club, training under two part-time pros: Ivan Racey and Bud Tassie. Early on, he appeared on a circuit based out of Chicago and was featured nationally on the ABC and DuMont networks. Lisowski formed one of the most formidable teams of the 1950s with Stan Holek, who used the moniker "Stanley Lisowski." Adopting the name "The Crusher," he captured both the Nebraska and AWA World championships in 1963. He'd win the AWA crown three times total. Partnered with the rowdy Dick the Bruiser, Lisowski took his fame to another level, and the Bruiser and Crusher were unstoppable. They won the AWA Tag Team Title five times and the WWA Title six times. The duo also went overseas to Japan and won the JWA International Tag Team Title in 1969.

Born:	August 1, 1917
Height:	5'10"
Weight:	220
Real Name:	Jose Jesus Becerra Valencia
Identities:	Apollo Anaya
Finisher:	Cobra Twist
Career Span:	1941–60
Died:	January 4, 1999, Del Rio, TX
	81 years old

Titles Won:	11
Days as World Champion:	Around 140
Age at first World Title Win:	31
Best Opponents:	Walter Palmer, Lou Thesz, Dory Funk Sr.

Cyclone Anaya

A sensational grappler from Quitupan, Jalisco, Mexico, Cyclone Anaya was initially a boxer and was discovered by an old pro wrestler named Joe Parelli. Parelli supervised his transition to grappling and Anaya was an instant hit. By 1944, he was wrestling in and around Chicago for promoter Fred Kohler, and became a local mainstay. On July 13, 1949, he beat Walter Palmer for Chicago's localized World Heavyweight Title and retained the championship through mid-November, when he was defeated by Don Eagle. A short time later, in the Ohio territory, he beat Frankie Talaber for the MWA World Junior belt. Since Anaya was proving a valuable draw, the National Wrestling Alliance Board of Directors was seriously considering him for a reign with the World Junior Title, but the idea was scrapped. Even so, his success continued unabated. He won regional championships in Alabama and Texas, and traveled the nation based on his TV appearances out of Chicago. In 1950, a writer in Pennsylvania wrote: "Cyclone is an imposing figure as he climbs into the ring, and once in action, is a smooth and deadly as a panther." Anaya wrestled out of Houston until he was forced into retirement by a serious injury in 1960. From there, he opened a chain of successful restaurants.

Born:	February 25, 1926
Height:	5'10"
Weight:	220
Real Name:	William Darnell
Trained by:	Buddy Rogers
Identities:	Billy Rogers
Nickname:	Leopard Boy
Finisher:	Airplane Spin
Career Span:	1943–62
Died:	September 7, 2007, Maple Shade, NJ 81 years old

Titles Won:	8
Days as World Champion:	41
Age at first World Title Win:	22
Best Opponents:	Buddy Rogers, Ruffy Silverstein, Don Eagle

Darnell, Billy

Boyhood friends with Buddy Rogers from Camden, New Jersey, Billy Darnell attended Temple University, where he played football under Ray Morrison. During the early 1940s, he gave up his job as a lifeguard to become a professional wrestler, learning the ropes from Rogers, and made his debut in 1943. Under the management of the quirky Jack Pfefer, Darnell began touring and spent time in New York, Philadelphia, Ohio, and Southern California. On October 26, 1948, he beat Rogers in San Diego for the Pfefer claim to the World Heavyweight Title. He would lose it to The Demon in Hollywood on December 6, 1948. In the early 1950s, he joined the Chicago syndicate and became a national TV star. A wrestling reporter in New York, in 1953, wrote: "The twenty-seven-year-old Darnell provides action wherever he appears. There's never a dull moment when he's around." The writer also shared the belief of "experts," who felt Darnell would win the main line of the World Title "in a year or two," explaining that he had "all the equipment" to do so. However, Darnell never rose to that level of success. He held the World Tag Title with Bill Melby and his career-long "feud" with Rogers were among his most noteworthy career moments. Darnell retired from wrestling in 1962 and worked as a chiropractor.

Born:	June 22, 1902
Height:	5'10"
Weight:	220
Real Name:	Henri Francois DeGlane
Wife:	Suzanne DeGlane
Amateur Wrestling:	French National Champion (1923)
Trained by:	Celestin Moret, Dan Koloff
Career Span:	1925–48
Died:	July 7, 1975, Paris, France 73 years old

Titles Won:	At least 3 (claimed several others)
Days as World Champion:	647 (not counting European claims)
Age at first World Title Win:	28
Best Opponents:	Gus Sonnenberg, Ed Don George, Yvon Robert
Halls of Fame:	1

DeGlane, Henri

French wrestling legend Henri DeGlane was popular in the United States and Canada, as well as all across Europe. He was born in Limoges, France, and trained extensively as an amateur. DeGlane won gold at the 1924 Olympics in Greco-Roman grappling, and turned pro the following year. With high expectations, he arrived in New York in late 1927, and adjusted to the flashier American catch-as-catch-can style. He won a controversial match against Ed Lewis on May 4, 1931, and captured the AWA World Heavyweight Title. The finish saw Lewis DQ'd after the "Strangler" reportedly bit DeGlane, but it was also claimed that DeGlane really bit himself to double-cross his opponent. Two months later, on July 30, he drew one of the largest houses in North American wrestling history (to date), when an estimated 30,000 saw him defeat Gus Sonnenberg at Boston's Braves Field in two-of-three-falls. He would end up losing the crown to another Olympian Ed Don George on February 9, 1933. Later in the 1930s, he was recognized as the world champion in Europe and spent many years working as a firefighter in Paris after his career, and he aided Allied soldiers as part of the French Resistance during World War II.

Born:	June 27, 1908
Height:	6'1"
Weight:	210
Real Name:	Dean Henry Detton
Parents:	Joseph and Hilva Detton
Family:	Brother of Dory, Reed, Gene, and Glen Detton
Trained by:	John Anderson, Ira Dern
Nickname:	Salt Lake City Flash
Finisher:	Airplane Spin
Career Span:	1931–51
Died:	February 23, 1958, Hayward, CA 49 years old

Titles Won:	14
Days as World Champion:	274
Age at first World Title Win:	28
Best Opponents:	Ed Lewis, Jim Browning, Ray Steele

Detton, Dean

Originally from Idaho, Dean Detton was the second of eleven children, and was an above average wrestler and football player at the University of Utah. He also grappled for the famed Deseret Gym in Salt Lake City and, in 1930, won the AAU Intermountain Titles in two different weight divisions. He turned pro in February 1931, utilizing football tactics and technical skills in his matches, and earned the respect of many people in the business within a very short amount of time. By 1935, he was considered a top young prospect for the national "Toots" Mondt syndicate, and became the number one contender to the world title when he won a tournament in February 1936, defeating the legendary Ed "Strangler" Lewis in the finals. In touting him, the *Philadelphia Inquirer* compared his toehold to that of Frank Gotch, and it seemed apparent that he was in line for a championship run. On September 28, 1936, Detton beat Dave Levin for the heavyweight title and was recognized in more than twenty states. He held the belt until being defeated by ex-footballer Bronko Nagurski on June 29, 1937. In San Francisco, Detton also held the Pacific Coast Title ten times between 1939 and 1946. Following his retirement in 1951, he operated a tavern in Northern California.

Mike Di Biase
UNIVERSITY OF NEBRASKA

Born:	December 24, 1923
Height:	6'1"
Weight:	225
Real Name:	Michael DiBiase
Parents:	John and Christine DiBiase
Family:	Husband of Helen Hilde, stepfather of Ted DiBiase
High School:	Omaha Tech High School (NE)
College:	University of Nebraska
College Ach.:	Three-Time Big Seven Heavyweight Champion (1947–49)
Career Span:	1950–69
Died:	July 2, 1969, Lubbock, TX 45 years old

DiBiase, Mike

Amateur Titles:	7
Titles Won:	30
Days as World Champion:	28
Age at first World Title Win:	43
Best Opponents:	Dory Funk Sr., Verne Gagne, Lou Thesz
Halls of Fame:	2

Out of the tremendous class of amateur wrestlers to turn pro in the early 1950s, one of the most spectacular was "Iron" Mike DiBiase. The son of Italian immigrants, DiBiase grew up in Omaha, Nebraska and was a standout tackle on his high school football team. In addition, he picked up two high school wrestling championships in 1941 and 1942. While serving in the Navy, he won the National AAU Title in 1946, and dominated the Big Seven Conference heavyweight division between 1947 and 1949 He was trained by famous welterweight Adam Krieger, and made his debut in April 1950. Over the next nineteen years, he won the Rocky Mountain, Southern, and North American Titles, the WWA World Title in Los Angeles, and tag team titles in the United States and Japan. He was also holder of the NWA World Junior Title in 1959. DiBiase, a hard-hitting and talented shooter, died of a heart attack during a match with Man Mountain Mike. He was married to women's wrestler Helen Hilde, and his son Ted DiBiase also grappled professionally, along with his grandsons, Mike, Ted Jr., and Brett.

Born:	November 8, 1914
Height:	5'9"
Weight:	215
Real Name:	Sterling Blake Davis
College:	Texas A&M University
Identities:	The Satin Kid
Nickname:	Dandy, Orchid, Gardenia
Career Span:	1935–60
Died:	December 19, 1983, Rockwall County, TX 69 years old

Titles Won:	10
Best Opponents:	Ray Gunkel, Duke Keomuka, Red Berry

Dizzy Davis

Crafty and colorful, Dizzy Davis was a graduate of the same Houston minor league circuit that Gorgeous George sprouted from. In fact, Davis was developing his own "dandy" gimmick when George made it famous and became a cultural sensation. A product of a broken home, Davis had a difficult childhood and learned to fight from a young age on the streets of Houston. He attended Allen Academy in Bryan, Texas, and entered a semi-pro wrestling circuit in the 1930s, where he honed his grappling skills. Davis learned to wrestle scientifically, but also knew how to brawl in the violent Texas style. In 1949–50, he joined a group of prominent businessmen in an attempt to buck the Houston wrestling syndicate, only to be rebuffed at every turn. He eventually fell back into the good graces of the dominant combine, including members of the NWA, and found great success in the West Texas territory. There, he won the World Tag Title twice with partners Sonny Myers and The Great Bolo, the North American championship, and the Southwest States Junior Heavyweight crown. In 1959, he fought professional boxer Archie Moore in a losing effort in Odessa. Davis was a psychologist outside the ring and gained national news when he hired a commando to break his son out of a Mexican jail in 1976.

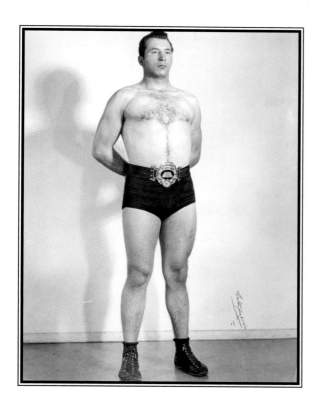

Born:	August 4, 1910
Height:	6'3"
Weight:	230
Real Name:	Roy Harvey Dunn
Parents:	Laurence and Estella Dunn
High School:	Gate High School (OK)
Colleges:	Northwestern Oklahoma, Oklahoma A&M
Olympics:	Freestyle Wrestling (1936) (HWT) (Representing the US) (DNP)
Amateur Title:	National AAU Title (1936) (HWT)
Career Span:	1937–55
Died:	June 10, 2000, Holly, CO 89 years old

Titles Won:	3
Days as World Champion:	Around 3,700
Age at first World Title Win:	30
Best Opponents:	Ede Virag, John Pesek, Lou Thesz

Dunn, Roy

Roy Dunn was a magnificent wrestler, amateur and professional, and was one of the toughest independent grapplers in the business. Fresh out from the Olympics at Berlin, Dunn was confronted with the opportunity of turning pro after his teammate at Oklahoma A&M, Tom Hanley, made the jump. Dunn followed suit in 1937, and both men were coached by another ex-Aggie, Charles Strack. Dunn wrestled throughout the northeast early in his career before settling for a circuit closer to home, based out of Wichita. In January 1941, he was named the inaugural National Wrestling Alliance Champion and remained titleholder until April 1942, when he was defeated by Ede Virag. Dunn would regain the belt in April 1946, and eventually retired as a champion. After the NWA expanded and a controversial promotional war broke out in Dallas in 1953, he reemerged with his manager, Billy Sandow, and sought a showdown with rival World Champion Lou Thesz. It was asserted that Dunn could beat both the NWA World Heavyweight and Texas Heavyweight champions in the same night, and that Roy would donate his share of the gate to charity. But, despite the verbal jousting, the matches were never made. In 1955, Dunn retired from the ring and later settled in Southeastern Colorado.

Born:	January 26, 1909
Height:	5'10"
Weight:	235
Real Name:	Ernest Hason
Parents:	Anton and Maria Hason
Family:	Brother of Rudy, Emil, and Joe Dusek
Wife:	Lillian Hason
Trained by:	Rudy Dusek
Career Span:	1929–63
Died:	April 11, 1994, Omaha, NE 85 years old

Titles Won:	At least 14
Days as World Champion:	54
Age at first World Title Win:	30
Best Opponents:	Jim Londos, Ruffy Silverstein, Killer Kowalski
Halls of Fame:	2

Dusek, Ernie

Of the four members of the famous "Riot Squad" Dusek Brothers, Ernie was seen as the most marketable. He was the complete package; combining athleticism and showmanship, and was often identified with being excessively rough during his matches. He had the tendency to play outside the rules, which rubbed fans the wrong way, and earned him a reputation that sold tickets at arenas all over North America. He was such a big star that he was being considered as a replacement for undisputed World Heavyweight Champion Danno O'Mahoney in 1936. On August 8, 1939, he beat O'Mahoney in a tournament final to become the top challenger to the local Montreal crown, but after champion Cy Williams was stripped, Dusek was named titleholder. He was a multiple-time tag team champion with his siblings and held numerous regional titles, including the California and Nebraska State championships. In 1950, he beat Primo Carnera for the Omaha city title. After his retirement from active competition, Dusek became a referee on the Nebraska circuit.

Born:	January 25, 1901
Height:	5'10"
Weight:	220
Real Name:	Rudolph Hason
Parents:	Anton and Maria Hason
Family:	Brother of Emil, Ernie, and Joe Dusek
Trained by:	Tommy Ray, Farmer Burns
Promoted:	Was involved in booking of New York City area (1932–57)
Career Span:	1922–53
Died:	October 27, 1971, Passaic, NJ 70 years old

Dusek, Rudy

Titles Won:	At least 2
Days as World Champion:	73
Age at first World Title Win:	35
Best Opponents:	Jim Londos, Dick Shikat, Ed Lewis
Halls of Fame:	2

Although he didn't have an extensive formal education, Rudy Dusek was a bright man, and was able to successfully wield power over the rich New York City region for twenty-five years as a booking agent. Originally from Omaha, Nebraska, Dusek grew up along the banks of the Missouri River and was an avid outdoorsman. He wrestled as a member of the Omaha YMCA squad, and acquired the name "Dusek" during an early tour of Wyoming. In 1929, he landed in New York, and was a key figure in the various wrestling wars of the early 1930s as a wrestler and booker. Eventually, he became the lead matchmaker for more than fifty towns, extending up and down the east coast. In 1936, he took a victory from Danno O'Mahoney in Philadelphia by reverse decision and claimed the highly-disputed World Title. He was part of the group that brought wrestling back to Madison Square Garden in 1949 and remained a booker into 1957, when he was pushed out by rival promoters. Aside from promoting, Dusek also trained three of his eight brothers for the ring.

Born:	August 25, 1925
Height:	6'1"
Weight:	225
Real Name:	Carl Donald Bell
Parents:	John Joseph and Emma Bell
Family:	Son of Chief Joseph War Eagle (John Joseph Bell)
Indian Heritage:	Mohawk
Pro Sports:	Boxing (1947–48)
Trained by:	Chief War Eagle
Finisher:	Indian Death Lock
Career Span:	1945–64
Died:	March 17, 1966, Caughnawaga, Quebec 40 years old

Eagle, Don

Titles Won:	3
Days as World Champion:	Around 980
Age at first World Title Win:	24
Best Opponents:	Frank Sexton, Bill Miller, Buddy Rogers
Boxing Record:	15-4

Enormously popular, "Chief" Don Eagle was a fixture on television sets across the United States during the late 1940s and into the 1950s. A Native American from the Caughnawaga Reservation outside Montreal, Eagle performed a ceremonial war dance in the ring prior to matches and always wore his tribal headdress. The outward celebration of his heritage, along with his profound wrestling abilities, earned him sizable crowd support wherever he appeared. Eagle was adept in numerous sports as a teenager, including lacrosse and fencing. He followed his father to Cleveland to work as a structural iron worker and joined the Papke Athletic Club. In 1945, he participated in the local Golden Gloves tournament and proved victorious in the heavyweight division. A few short weeks later, he debuted as a pro wrestler. Jack Kearns, Jack Dempsey's former manager took notice of Eagle's potential, and signed him to a boxing contract in 1946. Over the next two years, he fought professionally, often appearing at the Marigold Arena in Chicago.

By September 1948, he was back in the wrestling ring, and because of his exposure as a boxer, Eagle was a major draw in the "Windy City." Also proving valuable in Columbus, Ohio and Boston, Massachusetts, he received a consistent push into 1950, when he was booked against the AWA World Champion of five years, Frank Sexton. Their match occurred on May 23, 1950 in Cleveland at the Public Hall, and Eagle prevailed, winning the AWA crown. However, three nights later in Chicago, Eagle was caught in a politically-motivated double-cross staged by Kohler and perpetrated in the ring by Gorgeous George. Eagle seemingly lost the championship that night, but because it was an unscripted event, Haft and Bowser continued to recognize him as titleholder—and he even won a rematch over George on August 31. Around the middle of 1952, he suffered a serious back injury and forfeited the title in November. He continued his career, off and on, through the early part of the 1960s.

Photo Courtesy of Scott Teal/Crowbar Press

Born:	January 4, 1917
Height:	6′3″
Weight:	250
Real Name:	Floyd William Eckert
High School:	Soldan-Blewett High School (MO)
Identities:	Sandy O'Donnell
Career Span:	1935–55
Died:	July 7, 1996, California, MO 79 years old

Titles Won:	17
Best Opponents:	Lou Thesz, Enrique Torres, Sandor Szabo

Eckert, Ray

Born into a large family in St. Louis, Missouri, Ray Eckert began wrestling at a local boys' club and was competitive as a middleweight in high school and in AAU events. Ray grew into his size, developing into a 250-pound bruiser, and learned much from ex-champ Ed Lewis who, at one point, bestowed upon him the famous "Strangler" moniker. The redheaded Eckert wrestled both as a fan favorite and heel, and had his greatest success in Northern California. In San Francisco, he was an eight-time Pacific Coast Champion between 1948 and '53, and had memorable feuds with Enrique Torres and Sandor Szabo. He was also a three-time World Tag Team Champion with Hard Boiled Haggerty, Frederick Von Schacht, and Fred Atkins, and briefly held the Hawaii Heavyweight championship during the summer of 1950.

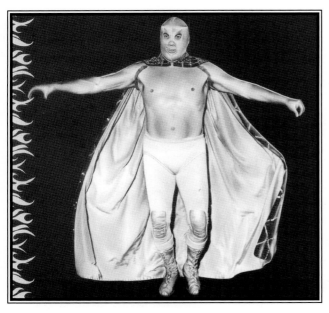

Born:	September 23, 1917
Height:	5'8"
Weight:	215
Real Name:	Rodolfo Guzman Huerta
Parents:	Jesus and Josefina Guzman Huerta
Identities:	Rudy Guzman
Career Span:	1934–82
Died:	February 5, 1984, Mexico City, Mexico 66 years old

Titles Won:	12
Best Opponents:	Blue Demon, Perro Aguayo, Bobby Bonales
Halls of Fame:	2
Movies:	54

El Santo

In all of history, few wrestlers have been able to transcend the business and become a national hero known casually by both fans and non-fans of the sport. El Santo did this in his native Mexico. He was embraced as a legitimate superhero, a bestowment that was fostered by his appearances in film, comic books, and other areas of popular culture. Becoming the masked El Santo in 1942, he proceeded to win the NWA World Welterweight and Middleweight Titles, and was a multiple time Mexican National Champion in three different weight classes. His last reign as National Middleweight Champion lasted just shy of four years. Between 1961 and 1982, he appeared in over fifty films and occasionally toured US rings. His older brother, Black Guzman, was also a wrestler of note, and his son, El Hijo del Santo, is a top star known worldwide.

Born:	May 6, 1920
Height:	6'1"
Weight:	230
Real Name:	Ronald Louis Etchison
Parents:	Everett and Lucille Etchison
Wife:	Almedia Etchison
High School:	Central High School (MO)
Trained by:	Warren Bockwinkel, Lou Thesz, Ray Villmer
Finisher:	Giant Swing
Promoted:	St. Joseph, MO (1976–79)
Career Span:	1938–80
Died:	March 4, 1994, St. Joseph, MO 73 years old

Titles Won:	31
Days as World Champion:	Around 70
Age at first World Title Win:	26
Best Opponents:	Orville Brown, Killer Kowalski, Gene Kiniski

Etchison, Ronnie

Popular ring veteran Ronnie Etchison wrestled in six different decades and won honors all over the wrestling spectrum. He began as a light heavyweight Golden Gloves boxer in his hometown of St. Joseph, Missouri, and then turned pro under Gust Karras in 1938. Within a few months of his debut, he annexed the St. Joseph City trophy and would later be given permanent possession of the title. During World War II, he served with the 6th Armored Division and received four Bronze Stars and a Purple Heart. In October 1946, he claimed to be "NWA" World Champion in Montana, and gave the real titleholder, Orville Brown, many tough matches. On June 20, 1962, Etchison dethroned Killer Kowalski for another claim to the World Title in Saskatoon. He also held the US and Missouri State Championships on a number of occasions. Following the death of Karras, Etchison took over as the promoter in St. Joseph in 1976, and operated for three years. He had his last wrestling match in 1980 and quietly retired. Etchison passed away in 1994 at the age of seventy-three.

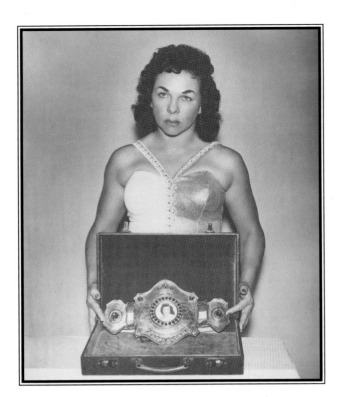

Photo Courtesy of the Pfefer Collection, Department of Special Collections, University of Notre Dame

Born:	July 22, 1923
Height:	5'5"
Weight:	138
Real Name:	Mary Lillian Ellisor (changed to Ellison)
Parents:	Henry and Mary Ellisor
Family:	Married to Buddy Lee
High School:	Columbia High School (SC)
Trained by:	Billy Wolfe, Mae Young
Identities:	Slave Girl Moolah, The Spider Lady
Nicknames:	Little Wildcat
Managed (Valet):	Buddy Rogers, The Elephant Boy
Trained:	She ran a women's wrestling school in Columbia, South Carolina and trained hundreds of aspiring athletes including Leilani Kai, Joyce Grable, Donna Christanello, and Vickie Williams.
Career Span:	1948–2005
Died:	November 2, 2007, Columbia, SC 84 years old

Fabulous Moolah, The

Titles Won:	At least 13
Days as World Champion:	10,708
Age at first World Title Win:	33
Best Opponents:	Daisy Mae, June Byers, Judy Grable
Halls of Fame:	3

The internationally recognized Fabulous Moolah was the primary women's wrestling attraction for several decades, and held a claim to the world championship for nearly all of twenty-eight years between 1956 and 1984. Born in Kershaw County, South Carolina, she was the last of five children, and the only daughter of a hard working farmer, Henry Ellisor. This story is very different from the tale claiming that she had thirteen brothers and was originally from Johannesburg, South Africa, "facts" which were made up to spice up her wrestling persona. She attended high school in Columbia and became a pro wrestler in 1948 under the leadership of Billy Wolfe. Wolfe was the dominant force in women's wrestling, and booked several troupes of ladies throughout the country at any single time. Instead of putting up with Wolfe's controversial behavior, Moolah affiliated herself with another powerful booking agent, Jack Pfefer, and was just as successful. She had lengthy feuds with Darling Dagmar and Daisy Mae and reigned as junior champion.

On September 18, 1956 in Baltimore, Moolah won an 8-woman tournament and captured the World Title, and was presented with a belt by the chairman of the Maryland commission after the match. When the Wolfe circuit collapsed, she controlled the strongest troupe of women grapplers in the nation, and was able to travel from territory to territory with a stable of credible challengers to her title. Over the next twenty-eight years, she had three short breaks as titleholder, losing the championship temporarily before regaining it. In 1983, she made a financial deal to sell her title to the WWF, and lost her crown to the Cyndi Lauper-managed Wendi Richter on July 23, 1984. She won the title three additional times, the last in October 1999 over Ivory. All through the 1990s and up until several months before her death in 2007, she made many appearances on WWE television, mostly with her close friend, Mae Young. She was featured in the documentary *Lipstick and Dynamite* and inducted into the WWF Hall of Fame in 1995.

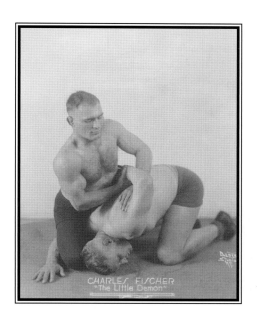

Photo Courtesy of the Pfefer Collection, Department of Special Collections, University of Notre Dame

Born:	January 2, 1898
Height:	5'3"
Weight:	165
Real Name:	Charles Berthold Fischer
Parents:	Berthold and Frances Fischer
Nickname:	Midget
Career Span:	1925–54
Died:	November 16, 1982, Butternut, WI 84 years old

Titles Won:	5
Best Opponents:	John Pesek, Johnny Meyers, Joe Banaski

Fischer, Charlie

A remarkable athlete, Charles Fischer proved time after time that his stature (standing 5'3") was not a handicap, and had a compelling career as a wrestler. He began as an amateur in Chicago in 1924 and won several regional AAU honors. He then turned pro, and his quickness and deceiving strength took opponents of all weight classes by surprise. When he had his rivals worn down, he applied his famed piledriver, a move that he invented. In 1929, he won claims to both the World Middleweight and World Light Heavyweight Championships, and held them both simultaneously for years. He retired as champion in both divisions to his hometown of Butternut, Wisconsin.

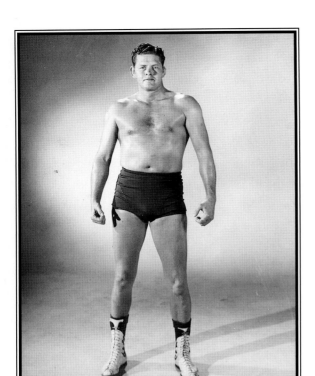

Born:	March 24, 1925
Height:	6'1"
Weight:	230
Real Name:	Edward Andy Welch
Parents:	Roy and Alma Welch
Family:	Father of Robert and Ron Fuller
Trained by:	Roy, Lester, and Herb Welch
Career Span:	1947–81
Died:	January 15, 1996, Pensacola, FL 70 years old

Titles Won:	20
Days as World Champion:	42 (excluding second Pfefer reign)
Age at first World Title Win:	38
Best Opponents:	Gene Kiniski, Lou Thesz, Eddie Graham

Fuller, Buddy

The eldest son of wrestler and promoter Roy Welch, Buddy Fuller spent his early years in Carter County, Oklahoma, and served as a Merchant Marine during World War II. He became a wrestler as a young man, often teaming with his uncles, Lester and Herb Welch. Not unusual, considering the success of his father, Buddy was also an enterprising promoter and restructured the Gulf Coast territory into a thriving region. He also bought booking rights to Louisiana and later entered into a partnership in Georgia as well. In Chicago, after Johnny Valentine walked out on Jack Pfefer, Buddy worked as "George Valentine" and won the vacant IWA World Heavyweight Title on October 4, 1963. He held the championship until losing to Jackie Fargo on November 15, 1963. Fuller held the Georgia and Gulf Coast Heavyweight Titles and, in 1966, held the Southern Heavyweight championship on two occasions. Fuller engaged in his last pro match in 1981.

Born:	May 4, 1919
Height:	6'1"
Weight:	235
Real Name:	Dorrance Wilhelm Funk
Parents:	Adam and Emma Funk
Wife:	Betty Funk
High School:	Hammond High School (IN)
HS Ach.:	Two-Time Indiana State Wrestling Champion (1936–37)
College:	Indiana University
Trained by:	Lou Thesz, Balk Estes
Finisher:	Spinning Toehold
Owned:	A percentage of the Amarillo promotion (1955–73)
Career Span:	1942–73
Died:	June 3, 1973, Amarillo, TX 54 years old

Funk, Dory Sr.

Titles Won:	52
Best Opponents:	Mike DiBiase, Fritz Von Erich, Lou Thesz
Halls of Fame:	4

An accomplished amateur and patriarch of the legendary Funk Family, Dory Funk Sr. grew up in Hammond, Indiana and was the son of a policeman. He initially wrestled on a Chicago-based circuit prior to joining the Navy in 1943, and resumed his career upon his discharge three years later. In January 1948, he debuted in Amarillo, which would become his home base, and remained so until his death. Funk was an accomplished junior heavyweight, and won the NWA World Junior Title on June 5, 1958 from Angelo Savoldi. He was just as potent as a heavyweight, winning the North American crown two dozen times, and always giving any of the touring NWA heavyweight champions a tough match. The Amarillo circuit was known for its innovative matches and grueling contests, and blood was a normal sight on Thursday nights at the Arena. Funk trained his two sons, Dory Jr. and Terry to become top-flight champions themselves, and when he wasn't brawling around the ring, he was devoting time to the Boys Ranch, where he worked as a superintendent.

Gagne, Verne

Born:	February 26, 1926
Height:	6'0"
Weight:	225
Real Name:	Laverne Clarence Gagne
Parents:	Clarence and Elsie Gagne
Family:	Father of Greg Gagne
Wife:	Mary Gagne
High School:	Robbinsdale High School (MN)
HS Ach.:	High School State Championship (1943)
College Ach.:	Four-Time Big Ten Champion (1944, 1947–49)
NFL Draft:	Chicago Bears (1947) (16th Round)
Trained by:	Joe Pazandak and Paul Boesch
Finisher:	Sleeperhold
Promoted:	American Wrestling Association (1960–91)
Career Span:	1949–86
Died:	April 27, 2015, Bloomington, MN 89 years old

Amateur Titles:	8
Titles Won:	34
Days as World Champion:	5,277 (including overlapping reigns)
Age at first World Title Win:	32
Best Opponents:	Nick Bockwinkel, Lou Thesz, Dick the Bruiser
Halls of Fame:	6

Few individuals in the annals of history have contributed to the legacy of professional wrestling like Verne Gagne. From the moment he first stepped into the ring, he was destined for greatness, and at a time in which many amateurs were breaking into the business, Gagne was at the head of the class. He became the foremost television superstar outside of Gorgeous George and Antonino Rocca, and one of the biggest draws of the 1950s. His accomplishments only grew from there, and between 1960 and 1981, he reigned as the American Wrestling Association World Heavyweight Champion ten times. His Minneapolis-based promotion sprouted roots throughout the Upper Midwest and westward to California, and was considered one of the "Big Three" organizations along with the NWA and WWWF. Gagne, at his training camp, coached a number of future champions to include Ric Flair, Sgt. Slaughter, Iron Sheik, and Ricky Steamboat.

Throughout his school years, Gagne was a proven winner, and his natural competitiveness was on display every time he stepped onto the mat or football field. His collegiate career at the University of Minnesota was broken up by service in the Marines during the war, and the few added years of life experience bolstered his confidence in route to three consecutive Big Ten championships from 1947 to 1949, and two NCAA titles in 1948 and 1949. Additionally, he was a member of the 1948 Olympic squad, but did not compete. A short time after winning the National AAU championship in 1949, he made his pro debut in Minneapolis, and was thrust into matches against NWA champion Lou Thesz and other heavyweights of impressive stature, like Killer Kowalski. Although Gagne only weighed around 200 pounds, his speed and science made it appear possible for him to beat any foe on any given night . . . he was just that good.

From 1950 to 1951, he brought much credibility to the NWA World Junior championship, and was fast becoming one of the biggest draws in the industry. Chicago was the site of Gagne's early success and the Saturday night TV show emanating from the Marigold Arena across the DuMont Network made him a national celebrity. He was a top challenger to Thesz's crown, and the two drew over 10,000 fans to the Amphitheater on January 25, 1952. Gagne held the champion to an hour draw and many fans anticipated him being Thesz's successor. He was booked in cities that carried the DuMont program and had enormous success from Milwaukee to Boston. At the 1953 annual convention of the NWA, members approved recognition of Gagne as United States champion, and he was presented with a belt emblematic of the title on September 12. Despite his status as one of the biggest box office attractions, he never succeeded Thesz as expected. In fact, Gagne never wore the NWA World Heavyweight Title.

Gagne's initial reign as US Champion lasted thirty-one months, and he captured the title several other times. On August 9, 1958, in Omaha, he won his first claim to the World Title with a defeat of Edouard Carpentier for local recognition. He soon bought interest in the Minneapolis territory, and formed the AWA, which was integrated as the sanctioning body in 1960. An initial heavyweight champion of the AWA was declared, and it was Gagne, after it was claimed that the NWA titleholder Pat O'Connor failed to defend against him. Gene Kiniski was the first man to conquer him for the belt on July 11, 1961, but Gagne regained the title on August 8. Over the next two years, he won the championship four additional times, defeating Mr. M, Fritz Von Erich, and Crusher Lisowski twice. Another former Olympian, Maurice Vachon, beat him for the title in Minneapolis on October 20, 1964, and it took Gagne a few years, until February 26, 1967, to return to the top of the mountain.

His ninth reign started in 1968 after trading the belt with Dr. X and lasted an astounding 2,625 days until November 8, 1975, when Nick Bockwinkel beat him in St. Paul. On June 6, 1979, he teamed with his longtime rival, Vachon, to win the AWA Tag Team Title from Pat Patterson and Ray Stevens. Before a large crowd at Chicago's Comiskey Park on July 18, 1980, he won his final AWA World Championship, defeating Bockwinkel with his famous sleeperhold. Following his May 19, 1981 victory over Bockwinkel, Gagne retired as World Champion, something only a few others have ever done. He made a few appearances after that showing, his final on April 20, 1986 when he beat Sheik Adnan el Kaissey. A world champion in four different decades, Gagne was an impressive wrestler in every area. He was fundamentally gifted, intelligent, had quick reflexes, and was entertaining. He ranks, in terms of wrestling legends, as one of the very few legitimate icons of the sport.

Born:	March 19, 1907
Height:	5'11"
Weight:	220
Real Name:	Sam Curcuru
Parents:	Joseph and Lucy Curcuru
Family:	Brother of Chick, Ralph, Tony, and Joe Garibaldi
Career Span:	1928–61
Died:	December 10, 1984, Los Angeles, CA 77 years old

Titles Won:	12
Days as World Champion:	29
Age at first World Title Win:	36
Best Opponents:	Jim Londos, Joe Stecher, Lou Thesz

Garibaldi, Gino

Gino Garibaldi grew up in DuQuoin, Illinois, the son of a coal miner, with four brothers and two sisters. He enjoyed training at the Rock Springs Athletic Club in St. Louis while in his early twenties, and worked out with wrestlers including Ray Steele, Billy Scharbert, and Joe Sanderson. Lloyd Carter trained him to be a pro wrestler and Gino debuted in 1928, under the name "Vito Rinaldi." By 1929, however, he adopted the name "Gino Garibaldi," which had been recommended by a St. Louis sportswriter. During the 1930s wrestling boom, he was a strong challenger to champion Jim Londos, and the two drew more than 15,000 to the inaugural show at Maple Leaf Gardens in Toronto, on November 19, 1931. Gino also had an ongoing feud with the Dusek Brothers, especially in the northeast. On May 12, 1943, he beat Yvon Robert for the Montreal World Title and held it a second time in 1944. His son, Leo, followed him into the business and they teamed up on many occasions, winning the World Tag Title in Southern California in 1951. Garibaldi was a father figure to many wrestlers, including a young Buddy Rogers and Nick Bockwinkel.

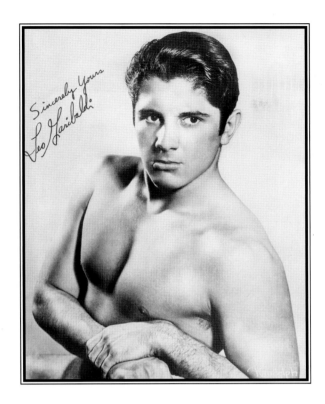

Born:	July 19, 1929
Height:	6'1"
Weight	210
Real Name:	Leo Gino Garibaldi
Family:	Nephew of Chick, Ralph, Tony, and Joe Garibaldi
Wife:	June Garibaldi
High School:	New York Military Academy
Trained by:	Gino Garibaldi
Identities:	Frank Garza
Career Span:	1947-61
Died:	May 12, 2008, Las Vegas, NV 78 years old

Titles Won:	10
Best Opponents:	Buddy Rogers, Johnny Valentine, Danny McShain

Garibaldi, Leo

A popular wrestling idol, Leo Garibaldi was a talented grappler and matchmaker. He was the son of veteran grappler Gino Garibaldi, and broke into the sport as a teenager in 1947. Born in St. Louis, he attended military school before joining the wrestling circuit, teaming often with his father during his rookie year. He was a star by 1950 and, on March 3 of that year, he beat Billy Varga for the first of three World Junior Heavyweight Titles. He would regain the belt from Varga during the summer of 1950, and then also trade the title with Baron Michele Leone. In late 1951, he entered the Air Force and served four years, wrestling when he had the opportunity. During a stint in Texas, he won the regional junior championship and captured the World Tag Team crown with partner Sonny Myers in 1957. A serious injury ended his active career and he went behind the curtain to promote in upstate New York and Austin, Texas. In addition, he was a booker in Georgia and Florida. Garibaldi was well respected for his wrestling knowledge and brought many creative ideas to the business.

Born:	October 1, 1924
Height:	6'1"
Weight:	245
Real Name:	Robert Frederick Geigel
Parents:	Fred and Leota Geigel
Wife:	Vera Geigel
High School:	Algona High School (IA)
College Ach.:	Four-Time letterwinner in football (1946–49), Three-Time letterwinner in wrestling (1947–49)
Military:	United States Navy (WWII)
Promoted:	Kansas City (1963–88), World Wrestling Alliance (1988–89)
Career Span:	1950–77
Died:	October 30, 2014, Kansas City, MO 90 years old

Geigel, Bob

Titles Won:	33
Best Opponents:	Sonny Myers, Bob Ellis, Mike DiBiase
Halls of Fame:	1

An All-American wrestler from the University of Iowa, Bob Geigel placed third in the 1948 NCAA tournament and was runner-up the following year in the National AAU tourney after losing a decision to Verne Gagne. In 1950, he broke into the business under the guidance of Alphonse Bisignano, and although he was primarily known as a Central States guy, he also found success in Minneapolis and Amarillo. He won an abundance of championships during his career, including the AWA World Tag Title three times and the North American belt in West Texas. In 1963, he took over the Kansas City booking office from Orville Brown and, with his partners, ruled cities in Kansas, Iowa, and Missouri. He was elected president of the National Wrestling Alliance six times and was an influential member of the organization during the 1980s. After leaving the promotional side of wrestling behind in 1989, he became a security guard at The Woodlands racetrack in Kansas City, and passed away in October 2014 at the age of ninety.

Born:	June 3, 1905
Height:	6'0"
Weight:	225
Real Name:	Edward Nicholas George Jr.
Parents:	Edward and Sarah George
Wife:	Joanne George
High School:	Canisius High School (NY)
Colleges:	St. Bonaventure College, University of Michigan
Amateur Titles:	AAU Title (1928–29) (HWT)
Military:	United States Navy (WWII)
Trained by:	Fred Moran
Promoted:	Buffalo, New York (1947–55)
Career Span:	1929–42
Died:	September 18, 1985, Fort Lauderdale, FL 80 years old

George, Ed Don

Titles Won:	4
Days as World Champion:	1,194 (not counting European reign)
Age at first World Title Win:	25
Best Opponents:	Jim Londos, Gus Sonnenberg, Henri DeGlane
Halls of Fame:	5

    The fourth place freestyle wrestler in the 1928 Olympics in Amsterdam was Ed Don George, a man who'd go on to grapple as a pro for thirteen years. Son of a Wyoming County, New York farmer, George demonstrated the class of a future Hall of Famer in that time, and won the World Heavyweight Championship four times. He was turned onto the business by New York neighbor Jack Albright, and with a push from the powerful Paul Bowser syndicate, George ended the reign of Gus Sonnenberg for his first AWA World Title on December 10, 1930. He was double-crossed by Ed Lewis on April 13, 1931 and lost the championship, but regained it on February 9, 1933 from another Olympian, Henri DeGlane. For more than two years, George remained titleholder, finally losing the crown to Danno O'Mahoney on June 30, 1935. In Paris, he beat Al Perreira for a European claim to the title in 1937. Once his active career ended, he promoted a circuit out of Buffalo that included a dozen cities and influenced many careers, including those of Johnny Barend and Mark Lewin.

Born:	January 3, 1918
Height:	5'8 ½"
Weight:	190
Real Name:	William Charles Goelz
Parents:	Leroy and Anna Goelz
High School:	Senn High School (IL)
Military:	United States Army (WWII)
Identities:	Stan Pesek
Finisher:	Stepover Toehold
Tag Team:	The G-Men w/ Johnny Gilbert
Career Span:	1936–71
Died:	November 20, 2002, Port Charlotte, FL 84 years old

Titles Won:	16
Best Opponents:	Verne Gagne, Gypsy Joe, Al Williams

Goelz, Billy

Chicago mainstay Billy Goelz was a wrestler for more than thirty-five years, first as an amateur in the city parks system and then as a professional. The son of a fireman, Goelz learned the trade from the legendary Lou Talaber, and began wrestling as a teenager. At 190 pounds, he was a stellar junior heavyweight. He reigned as the Midwest champion of that division for most of the 1946–55 time periods and, in July 1948, was acknowledged as the National Wrestling Alliance World Junior Heavyweight Champion when the expanded union was formed. Goelz was also instrumental in the office of promoter Fred Kohler, working as a matchmaker and trainer, and owned a piece of the business. Always well-liked by fans for his clean and scientific grappling skills, Goelz lived in Fox Lake most of his life, where he and his wife Ruth raised five children. Wrestling his last match in 1971, Billy retired to Florida, where he passed away in 2002 at the age of eighty-four.

Born:	March 24, 1915
Height:	5'9"
Weight:	220
Real Name:	George Raymond Wagner
Parents:	Howard and Bessie Wagner
High School:	Milby Senior High School (TX)
Trained by:	Sam Menacker
Nickname:	The Toast of the Coast
Valets:	Jeffries, Cheri LaMonte, Jeeves
Career Span:	1932–62
Died:	December 26, 1963, Los Angeles, CA 48 years old

Titles Won:	12
Days as World Champion:	97
Age at first World Title Win:	35
Best Opponents:	Billy Watson, The Destroyer, Lou Thesz
Halls of Fame:	4

Gorgeous George

With a style that has often been imitated, but never duplicated, Gorgeous George led a wrestling revolution and was an American entertainment legend. For years, he sauntered to rings around North America, his wavy blond hair uniquely nurtured, and his overwhelming arrogance a thorn in the sides of audiences. He provided the sport a stunningly crafted performance that had been seen in the act of a few other grapplers, but in smaller doses. George packaged all of it up and created the ultimate "bad guy," a villain who wore extravagant robes and spent at least fifteen minutes on his ring entrance, complete with music—just enough to grind into the nerves of fans. He was accompanied by an annoying valet, handed out "Georgie" pins (bobby pins), and even sprayed the ring area with his special perfume, all of which were electrifying to those who witnessed the spectacle. Gorgeous George forged a new style of wrestling heel that has since become textbook.

Despite his effeminate gimmick, George was no pushover. He'd endured a tough childhood and legitimately wrestled at the Houston YMCA and at an area carnival. At fifteen years of age, he worked as an attendant at a filling station and helped his struggling parents financially, then suffered the loss of his mother two years later. Around that same time, he was supplementing his income as a part-time grappler. He weighed only 165 pounds when he began appearing on a secondary pro circuit around Houston, and was notably popular because of his rapid maneuvers and clean style. He toiled as a journeyman before finding success in Oregon, a territory that specialized in non-heavyweight wrestlers, and won a number of regional championships. As early as 1940, he used the nickname "Gorgeous," but the actual gimmick of "Gorgeous George" wasn't perfected until about six years later.

Los Angeles wrestling fans saw him transition into a superstar in 1948. His cunning ring act lured many new enthusiasts to venues, and after he was seen on TV, he became the most talked-about performer in the industry. It wasn't long before he took his show on the road, crisscrossing the US and cementing his place as a premier box office attraction. His exceptionally high level of showmanship made purists cringe, but George was part of the ever-changing wrestling atmosphere, and the dynamics of performers were becoming more outrageous. Fans responded, which, in turn, gave those in the business more motivation to continue raising the bar. He lived his ring character, legally changing his name to "Gorgeous George," and harbored some serious personal problems that weighed heavily on his health. His 1963 death wasn't a shock to people who knew the extent of his issues, but he was fondly remembered throughout wrestling and by the universe of fans who treasured their memories of the influential "Human Orchid."

Photo Courtesy of Pete Lederberg—plmathfoto@hotmail.com

Born:	January 15, 1930
Height:	5'11"
Weight:	225
Real Name:	Edward Gossett
Parents:	Jess and Velma Gossett
Wife:	Lucille Gossett
Identities:	Rip Rogers
Career Span:	1948–80
Died:	January 21, 1985, Beach Park, FL 55 years old

Titles Won:	35
Days as World Champion:	70
Age at first World Title Win:	33
Best Opponents:	Great Malenko, Johnny Valentine, Lou Thesz
Halls of Fame:	4

Graham, Eddie

Tennessee roughneck Eddie Gossett became a professional wrestler in 1948 and remained involved in the sport until his death in 1985. He was a hard-fighting brawler and constantly on the most hated list after adopting the name, "Eddie Graham," one half of the infamous Graham Brothers tag team than began in 1958. However, he became a hero in Florida, which would be his home promotion for decades, and owned part of the exciting territory alongside his mentor, "Cowboy" Luttrall. In 1970, Luttrall retired, and Graham became the main operator in the region, running shows from Jacksonville to the Caribbean. Graham was also an influential member of the National Wrestling Alliance, and was elected president twice. He was a successful wrestling trainer, and his son Mike was one of his finest students.

Born:	January 11, 1921
Height:	5'9"
Weight:	195
Real Name:	Salvador Guerrero Quesada
Family:	Father of Chavo, Eddie, Hector, and Mando Guerrero, grandfather of Chavo Guerrero Jr., brother-in-law of Enrique Llanes
Wife:	Herlinda Yanez Guerrero
Trained by:	El Indio Mejia, Diablo Velasco
Identities:	Joe Morgan
Nickname:	Storm Bird
Finisher:	Gory Special, Camel Clutch
Promoted:	El Paso, Texas (1967–75, 1977)
Career Span:	1937–76
Died:	April 17, 1990, El Paso, TX 69 years old

Titles Won:	10
Best Opponents:	Rey Mendoza, Jack O'Brien, Tarzan Lopez
Halls of Fame:	1

Guerrero, Gory

Gory Guerrero began wrestling professionally as a teenager in Mexico and was involved in the sport as a competitor for nearly forty years. He was also the patriarch of the Guerrero clan, as his four sons and grandson followed him into the business. Gory was born in Ray, Arizona, where his father worked in a copper mine, and grew up partly in Los Angeles and in Mexico. He joined a local gym in Guadalajara, which is where he launched his wrestling career, fast becoming a sensation. Initially capturing the Mexican Welterweight and Middleweight Titles, he followed up with a victory over Tarzan Lopez for the World Middleweight Championship in 1946 and held the belt for two years. In 1951, he debuted in West Texas, where he won over the hearts and minds of local fans. His quickness and unabashed athleticism would become staples of the territory, and fans appreciated his technical ring work. He held the NWA World Light Heavyweight Title for over five years during the 1960s, and was one of the most popular luchadores in the United States.

Born:	February 16, 1924
Height:	6'2"
Weight:	230
Real Name:	Raymond Fred Gunkel
Parents:	Peter and Agnes Gunkel
College:	Purdue University
College Ach.:	Two-Time All-American (1947–48)
Amateur Ach.:	Two-Time National AAU Champion (1947–48) (HWT)
Trained by:	Billy Thom
Career Span:	1948–72
Died:	August 1, 1972, Savannah, GA 47 years old

Titles Won:	33
Best Opponents:	Lou Thesz, Verne Gagne, Fred Blassie
Halls of Fame:	2

Gunkel, Ray

The son of a Chicago police officer, Ray Gunkel was an exemplary genuine wrestler, winning two National AAU championships as a heavyweight and narrowly missing a berth on the 1948 US Olympic team. A dual-sport athlete (football and wrestling) out of Purdue University, Ray made his pro grappling debut in June 1948, and received expert mentorship from Billy Thom and Lou Thesz. Briefly managed by ex-boxing champion Jack Dempsey, Gunkel was one of the most heralded wrestlers of the post-war rookie class, and he lived up to the hype in the ring. In 1953, his "shooting" capabilities came in handy when booking agent Morris Sigel of Houston used him as a "policeman" during the heated promotional war, and he reigned as state champion for over fourteen months. Later in the decade, Gunkel planted roots in Georgia, and won the Southern Title seven times. He owned a percentage of the territory until his death, which occurred shortly after a match with Ox Baker in Savannah in 1972. He was only forty-seven years old.

Born:	April 20, 1914
Height:	6'1"
Weight:	230
Real Name:	Clifton Orville Lowell Gustafson
Parents:	Charles and Gurina Gustafson
Wife:	Helene Gustafson
High School:	Gonvick High School (MN)
College:	University of Minnesota
College Ach.:	Big Ten Heavyweight Title (1937), Two-Time All-American (1937–38)
Amateur Title:	National AAU Title (1938) (UNL)
Trained by:	Tony Stecher
Career Span:	1938–49
Died:	July 19, 2000, Bemidji, MN 86 years old

Gustafson, Cliff

Titles Won:	2
Days as World Champion:	389
Age at first World Title Win:	33
Best Opponents:	Bronko Nagurski, Sandor Szabo, Joe Pazandak

Often obscured by the more highly publicized wrestling champions of his day, Cliff Gustafson was a talented amateur and pro grappler, and one of the few men in history to retire as World Champion. A graduate of the University of Minnesota, he captured Big Ten Heavyweight honors in 1937, and won a National AAU championship in 1938. He studied pro wrestling under Tony Stecher in Minneapolis and, by the end of 1939, was already being touted as a future titleholder. Billy Sandow, his manager, declared that Gustafson could beat both Lou Thesz and Ray Steele in the same evening—an extraordinary feat if accomplished—but the matches were never staged. Everette Marshall said that Cliff was as "strong as a cockeyed bull," and pundits were predicting great things for the up-and-comer. In the 1940s, he obtained Ed "Strangler" Lewis as a mouthpiece, and the latter put him over with the press. On April 22, 1947, he beat Sandor Szabo in Minneapolis for the localized "National Wrestling Association" World Title, but lost it back two months later. Gustafson regained the belt on June 22, 1948, and retired as champion on May 21, 1949, a rare honor that most wrestlers don't get to accomplish.

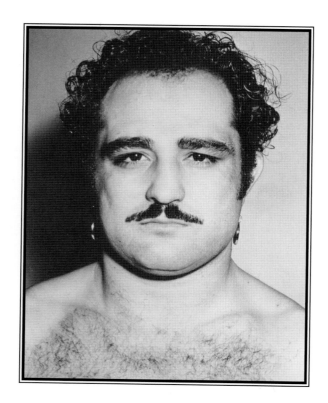

Photo Courtesy of the Wrestling Revue Archives—
www.wrestleprints.com

Born:	August 18, 1915
Height:	5'10"
Weight:	185
Real Name:	Ferdinand Carmen Muccioli
Parents:	Giuseppe and Livia Muccioli
Managed by:	Lorraine Dorsetti (wife)
Career Span:	1936–61
Died:	February 1986, Glendale, AZ 70 years old

Titles Won:	7
Days as World LHW Champion:	278
Age at first World LHW Title Win:	37
Best Opponents:	Billy Goelz, Verne Gagne, Pat O'Connor

Gypsy Joe

"Globetrotter" Gypsy Joe told the press that he was from Romania, but really hailed from Niagara Falls, Ontario, Canada. He initially wrestled as "Joe Dorsetti," which was in sync with his Italian heritage. However, he adopted the gypsy gimmick and, along with his wife, wore customized costumes to highlight his new background. Ever colorful, Joe wrestled a rougher style than most fans liked, and occasionally needed police protection away from the ring; but he never failed to be entertaining. He won the National Wrestling Alliance World Light Heavyweight crown from Johnny Balbo on November 5, 1952, in Des Moines, and held it until the following August, dropping the belt to Frank Stojack in Spokane. Joe also held an array of championships around the Great Lakes and, in 1948, captured the Pacific Coast Light Heavyweight crown in Oregon. Joe lived in Milwaukee most of his career, and retired to Arizona, where he died in 1986 at the age of seventy.

Born:	May 3, 1915
Height:	5'9"
Weight:	215
Real Name:	Stewart Edward Hart
Parents:	Edward and Elizabeth Hart
Military:	Canadian Navy (1942–46)
Amateur Titles:	Canadian Amateur Wrestling Title (1940) (191)
Trained by:	Jack Taylor
Career Span:	1946–79
Died:	October 16, 2003, Calgary, Alberta 88 years old

Titles Won:	2
Best Opponents:	Lou Thesz, Pat O'Connor, Fritz Von Erich
Halls of Fame:	4

Hart, Stu

In the basement of his Calgary home, Stu Hart trained many future wrestling legends, ranking him among the most influential mentors in the sport's history. If a wrestler wanted to learn about legitimate submissions, and if they had the guts, they'd enter Hart's "Dungeon," and would receive the workout of their lives. Hart himself learned how to wrestle the hard way, stretched beyond the normal limits at the YMCA in his hometown of Edmonton, and carried his knowledge to a Canadian amateur championship in 1940. After service in the navy, he joined the pro circuit around New York City, where he met his soon-to-be wife, Helen. They had twelve children together, among them Bret and Owen Hart, and settled in Calgary. Hart bought the local promotion from Larry Tillman in 1951, and operated Stampede Wrestling until 1984. He passed on his wrestling wisdom to his sons and the likes of Chris Jericho, Chris Benoit, Luther Lindsey, and numerous others. His impact was felt around the world as his pupils went out and entertained millions, and in 2014, he was honored by induction into the Professional Wrestling Hall of Fame.

Born:	July 12, 1925
Height:	6'0"
Weight:	225
Real Name:	Lawrence Roy Heffernan
Parents:	Lawrence and Ida Heffernan
Trained by:	Lawrence Heffernan
Promoted:	International Promotions (1975–77) (Australia)
Career Span:	1945–71
Died:	September 24, 1992, Sydney, Australia 67 years old

Titles Won:	22
Days as World Champion:	Unknown (1968)
Best Opponents:	Dick Hutton, Antonino Rocca, Don Leo Jonathan
Halls of Fame:	2

Heffernan, Roy

Roy Heffernan, half of the legendary tag team of The Fabulous Kangaroos, was from New South Wales, Australia, the son of "Hugo the Strongman," an extraordinary weightlifter and staunch disciplinarian. His father's real name was Lawrence Heffernan, a railroad porter and part-time wrestler. Roy began lifting weights at an early age, and was taught many grappling tricks by his father. He eventually turned pro and, by 1950, was known as "Mr. Australia" for his excellent physique and speedy mat work. That same year, he challenged Australian champion Al Costello, his future partner in the Kangaroos. It wasn't until seven years later that their partnership was actually formed in Canada, and the tandem became a sensation across North America. They headlined everywhere, drawing tens of thousands in some places, and won a plethora of championships. Among them were World Titles in Florida and California, the US Tag Title three-times in the northeast for Capitol Wrestling, and the International belts, which were carried overseas to Japan. Also in Japan, as a singles competitor, Heffernan was acknowledged as the TWWA World Heavyweight champion briefly in 1968. The influential work of the Kangaroos set a new template for teams to follow, and promoters realized that there was a ton of money to be made off the right combination of grapplers.

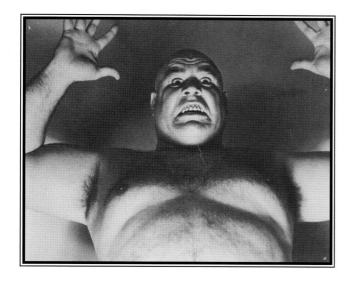

Photo Courtesy of the Pfefer Collection, Department of Special Collections, University of Notre Dame

Born:	October 19, 1903
Height:	6'3"
Weight:	365
Real Name:	Karl Erik Tore Johansson
Parents:	Karl and Lovissa Johansson
Wife:	Greta Johnson
Identities:	King Kong
Career Span:	1932–54
Died:	May 12, 1971, San Fernando, CA 67 years old

Johnson, Tor

Titles Won:	None known
Best Opponents:	Bill Longson, Buddy Rogers, Antonino Rocca
TV Appearances:	Over 10
Movies:	32

Cult film icon Tor Johnson was a journeyman wrestler for more than twenty years. During his extensive international travels, he headlined in many towns, including Boston and Toronto, and his massive size struck a chord with audiences. With his face contorted to express his dramatic fury, Johnson was an imposing character on the mat and had surprisingly good conditioning—even wrestling a ninety-minute match in 1937. Initially, Johnson tried his hand at boxing, but his huge bulk was much more appreciated on the wrestling mat. In the late 1940s, he worked as a member of the Jack Pfefer troupe, using the name "Super Swedish Angel." He was a performer in more than thirty films during his Hollywood career, and gained a legion of admirers. Among his appearances were for director Edward D. Wood Jr., known for his own unique brand of horror flicks. Johnson portrayed Lobo in Wood's 1955 film *Bride of the Monster*, and Inspector Clay in his 1959 movie *Plan 9 from Outer Space*. A Halloween mask in his likeness was a bestseller for years. Johnson wrestled his last match in 1954, and died in 1971.

Born:	April 29, 1931
Height:	6'6"
Weight:	315
Real Name:	Don Leo Heaton
Parents:	Jonathan and Leona Heaton
Wife:	Rosie Heaton
High School:	Cedar City High School (UT)
College:	Branch Agricultural College
Military:	United States Navy (1949–56)
Trained by:	Brother Jonathan
Identities:	El Diablo, El Loco
Nickname:	Sonny, Mormon Giant
Finisher:	Mormon Sickle, Mormon Swing
Career Span:	1950–80

Titles Won:	49
Days as World Champion:	Over 1,203
Age at first World Title Win:	24
Best Opponents:	Bruno Sammartino, Verne Gagne, Karl Gotch
Halls of Fame:	3

Jonathan, Don Leo

With the agility of a cruiserweight, the colossal Don Leo Jonathan never failed to surprise fans and foes alike. He was one of four children born to Mormon parents, and a second generation grappler from Hurricane, Utah. He was groomed to follow in his father, Brother Jonathan's footsteps from an early age, and his gymnastic background rounded out his athletic dexterity. When he finally stopped growing, he was 6'6", and weighed more than 300 pounds of pure muscle. He headlined all over the wrestling landscape from Madison Square Garden to the Olympic Auditorium and acted in the capacity of an aggressive and villainous heel and a popular babyface. Jonathan was also a nice guy outside the ring with an endearing love for the outdoors. Success in the ring came relatively early for him, as promoters were quick to utilize him in top positions. In early 1951, he held the Rocky Mountain Tag Team Title with his father, and then captured the regional single's championship from Joe Bennicasa on February 21, 1951.

Like his father, he served in the Navy, and upon returning to the circuit, won titles all over the wrestling map. North of the border, Jonathan won the Canadian Tag Title eighteen times. In 1955, he beat Pat O'Connor and Yvon Robert for two different runs with the Montreal version of the world championship. He beat Pepper Gomez for the Texas Title in 1957, and would regain the belt three years later from Torbellino Blanco. In Nebraska, he won the local World Title with a victory over Dr. X on January 7, 1961. The masked man won a rematch on March 2, but Don regained the title on April 7. He held the title until September 16, when Verne Gagne beat him in a special No DQ bout. In 1962, Jonathan was recognized as the World

Champion of the American Wrestling Alliance, a circuit of promoters which included Jim Barnett, Johnny Doyle, and Roy Shire. He lost the title to Karl Gotch on September 11, 1962. In 1969, he teamed with Antonio Pugliese to hold the IWA World Tag Team Title on two occasions during a tour of Australia.

Photo Courtesy of the Collection of Libnan Ayoub

Born:	June 23, 1901
Height:	6'0"
Weight:	230
Real Name:	Andrew Lutzi
Wife:	Frances Jones
Military:	United States Army Air Corps (WWII)
Identities:	John Paul Jones
Promoted:	Atlanta, Georgia (1944–84)
Career Span:	1922–44
Died:	April 17, 1988, Atlanta, GA 86 years old

Titles Won:	At least 3
Best Opponents:	Joe Stecher, Jim Londos, Ed Lewis
Halls of Fame:	1

Jones, Paul

Long before he was acknowledged as the heart of Atlanta's professional wrestling scene, Paul Jones was the Pride of Houston, a scientific flash who represented everything good about the sport. He was born in Saratov, Russia and grew up in Lincoln, Nebraska, wrestling at a local YMCA and gaining amateur honors as both a light heavyweight and heavyweight. He received unparalleled training from Clarence Eklund at the latter's Wyoming farm and, after competing under his real name, adopted the guise, "Paul Jones" while in Texas in 1923. In Houston, he was the central hero, and claimed the Southern Title after downing Charles Rentrop. He had a strong run in Los Angeles between 1926 and 1929, but returned to Houston, where he was an assistant in the office of Morris Sigel. When the opportunity to take over the Atlanta promotion came up in January 1944, he jumped at it, and remained a pivotal figure for four decades.

Born:	April 22, 1921
Height:	5'8"
Weight:	210
Real Name:	Hisao Martin Tanaka
Family:	Father of Pat and Jimmy Tanaka
Finishers:	Sleeperhold, Clawhold, Judo chop
Career Span:	1944-71
Died:	June 30, 1991, Las Vegas, NV 70 years old

Titles Won:	35
Best Opponents:	Ray Gunkel, Verne Gagne, Killer Kowalski

Keomuka, Duke

Duke Keomuka drew intense heat in the years following World War II, as fans angrily reacted to his clever jiu-jitsu and Judo tactics in the ring. Although most press reports stated that he was from Honolulu, Keomuka was born in San Joaquin County, California, the son of Japanese parents. After service in the Merchant Marines, he joined the wrestling circuit and spent his first years in the northeast, battling all the big names from Brooklyn to Philadelphia. In 1948, using his real name, he won the Hawaii Heavyweight championship, but made his biggest splash in Texas, where he captured the state title six times between 1951 and 1960, defeating the likes of Ray Gunkel, Cyclone Anaya, and Pepper Gomez. In 1961, a reporter from Galveston, Texas, wrote that Keomuka was "one of the most controversial figures to ever appear in Texas wrestling," and noted that his "flagrant roughness" was the reason Duke was stripped of the Texas Title several years earlier. In Florida, he captured the World Tag Team Title four times with Hiro Matsuda. Keomuka and Matsuda also had interest in the Tampa office from 1985 to 1987.

Born:	July 15, 1909
Height:	6'0"
Weight:	420
Real Name:	Emile George Zeimes
Identities:	Emile Czaja
Career Span:	1936–69
Died:	May 15, 1970, Singapore
	60 years old

Titles Won:	9
Best Opponents:	Hamida Pahalwan, Aslam Pahalwan, Lou Thesz

King Kong Czaja

Born in Brasov, Romania, King Kong was the preeminent big man of his day; a wrestler whose reputation preceded him in his international travels. He was, however, much more than a hulking figure. He was an aggressive and talented athlete, and opponents were easily worn down by his strength and size. King Kong wrestled his way from Germany to Australia, and in Tokyo, he matched up against Rikidozan for the initial JWA All Asia Heavyweight Title on November 22, 1955, but was defeated. He also battled legends Lou Thesz and Bert Assirati and set an attendance record in India against Hamida Pahalwan with as many as 200,000 fans seeing their 1945 bout at Lahore. King Kong was one of the greatest box office attractions in the history of professional wrestling.

Photo Courtesy of Dan Westbrook

Born:	July 6, 1920
Height:	5'10"
Weight:	220
Real Name:	Arpad Sandor Kovacs
Trained by:	Stu Hart
Identities:	Mike Kovacs
Career Span:	1946–72
Died:	June 30, 2004, Vancouver, B.C. 83 years old

Titles Won:	5
Best Opponents:	Don Leo Jonathan, Karl Gotch, Antonino Rocca

Kovacs, Sandor

Sandor Kovacs, a Hungarian athlete, migrated with his family to Canada around 1930, and he picked up amateur wrestling while in the navy. In 1946, he ventured to the US with Stu Hart, his mentor, and joined the booking office of "Toots" Mondt. In the years that followed, he wrestled all over North America, and displayed a fine arsenal of scientific abilities. A sportswriter in Indiana stated that Kovacs was "rated as the greatest Hungarian wrestler of modern times," and complimented his "timing, speed, and aggressiveness" on the mat. In 1955, Sandor teamed with Johnny Barend to capture the Hawaii Tag Team championship, and won both the International TV Tag Title with Lord James Blears and the Pacific Coast Tag belts with Enrique Torres the following year. Yearning to enter the promotional side of the business, he became a promoter in Rochester, New York, for a time in 1960, but later bought the Vancouver booking office with Gene Kiniski, organizing shows across British Columbia.

Born:	October 13, 1926
Height:	6'7"
Weight:	270
Real Name:	Edward Vladimar Spulnik
Parents:	Anthony and Marie Spulnik
Wife:	Theresa Kowalski
High School:	W.D. Lowe Secondary School (Windsor, Ontario)
College:	Assumption University
Military:	Canadian Army
Trained by:	Lou Thesz, Ed Lewis
Identities:	Masked Destroyer, Executioner I
Finisher:	Stomach Claw, Kneedrop
Career Span:	1948–87
Died:	August 30, 2008, Malden, MA 81 years old

Kowalski, Wladek "Killer"

Titles Won:	45
Days as World Champion:	Around 3,621
Age at first World Title Win:	25
Best Opponents:	Yvon Robert, Buddy Rogers, Lou Thesz
Halls of Fame:	4

In 1948, a young man from Windsor, Ontario broke into pro wrestling, effectively beginning a legendary career. He was known at the time as "Ed Kowalski," but later assumed the more familiar name "Killer Kowalski," who was a megastar around the world and terrorized fans and foes alike. The twenty-two-year-old had already served in the military, played organized rugby with the Windsor Rockets, and tested his heart in pro boxing. With that background under his belt, and with the guidance of Bert Rubi of Detroit, he was prepared to gain the knowledge necessary to traverse the wrestling ring. Within two years, the sport was taken by storm, initially by "Tarzan" Kowalski, and then by the famed "Killer," initially adopting the latter designation while in Texas in the summer of 1950. He was seen as a vicious and cruel wrestler, out to maim opponents with no fear of anyone, and promoters pushed him into contests against their best workers, including important matches against NWA World Champion Lou Thesz.

Outside of the ring, Thesz had an influential role in Kowalski's career, to the point in which he had a say where and when he was booked. Thesz may have also been responsible for helping Kowalski navigate into Montreal, the site of many of Kowalski's greatest victories. In the Quebec province, Kowalski was recognized as World Champion twelve times, and feuded with the best in the business. Practically every great wrestler of the era came through Montreal to face him, and he welcomed each of them with intensive punishment.

On November 21, 1962, he took a one-fall victory from NWA World Champion Buddy Rogers after Rogers suffered a legit broken ankle, and assumed his schedule as a defending title claimant. His title was unified with Thesz in February 1963 at Houston. Kowalski was also world champion a number of times in Australia and won an abundance of other titles throughout his career. He retired from active competition in 1975 and opened a wrestling school, where he trained many current superstars, including future Hall of Famer, Triple H.

Photo Courtesy of the Pfefer Collection, Department of Special Collections, University of Notre Dame

Born:	January 3, 1903
Height:	6'0"
Weight:	240
Real Name:	Nicholas Kwariani
Parents:	Nestor and Caserines Kwariani
Career Span:	1928–53
Died:	February 1980, New York, NY 77 years old

Titles Won:	None known (claimed Russian Title in 1929)
Best Opponents:	Jim Londos, John Pesek, Orville Brown

Kwariani, Kola

The bulky, bald man who instigated a memorable brawl in the 1956 Stanley Kubrick film *The Killing* was none other than Kola Kwariani. Kwariani had been part of the wrestling scene in the US since 1928, and was a Greco-Roman grappler in his native Russia before that. He was an intimidating figure, and his calculating mind made him a gifted chess player. On April 21, 1931, he wrestled World Champion Jim Londos in the main event of the very first Chicago Stadium grappling program, a show that drew over 17,000 people. Although Kola was defeated in two-straight falls, he put up a strong fight in a bout lasting over an hour. When he wasn't actively touring North America, he was traveling around the world, entertaining audiences, and on the lookout for potential talent. In Argentina, he discovered Antonino Rocca, and toured for years as his road agent. At various times he was involved in the New York City office, working with Joe "Toots" Mondt and the Johnston clan. Kwariani, who spoke half a dozen languages, was badly beaten outside of a chess club in Manhattan in 1980, and died a short time later.

Born:	August 20, 1920
Height:	6'5"
Weight:	270
Real Name:	Athol Alfred Layton
Military:	Australian Army (1943–46)
Identities:	Ty Layton
Career Span:	1949–76
Died:	January 18, 1984, Toronto, Ontario 63 years old

Titles Won:	8
Best Opponents:	Billy Watson, The Sheik, Lou Thesz

Layton, Lord Athol

A tall, former amateur boxer, Lord Athol Layton was born and reared in Australia. He entered pro wrestling while in Singapore in 1949, and was known as "Ty Layton" of California. He migrated to the UK, and then to Canada where he wrestled for Frank Tunney in Toronto. By that time, he adopted the "Lord" gimmick, and was claiming to be a man of class and royalty from England. For the next twenty-plus years, he drew outstanding crowds, particularly in Toronto against Billy Watson and The Sheik. In Detroit, as a fan favorite, he beat Dick the Bruiser for the United States Heavyweight Title on August 4, 1962. He would lose the belt to Fritz Von Erich in June 1963, only to regain it a month later. Von Erich dethroned him a final time on October 19, 1963. Layton worked as a studio television commentator in Detroit, a role that often saw him drawn into the physical combat, and built toward highly successful arena shows. He remained in that role through the mid-1970s, initially on CKLW and later on WXON. He also performed similar duties in Cleveland and Toronto. Well-respected throughout the business, he died in January 1984 at the age of sixty-three.

Born:	June 8, 1909
Height:	5'9"
Weight:	215
Real Name:	Michele Leone
Parents:	Giovanni and Anna Leone
Wife:	Billie Leone
Trained by:	Michele Leone (uncle)
Finishers:	Bearhug, Roman neckbreaker
Career Span:	1933–56
Died:	November 26, 1988, Los Angeles, CA 79 years old

Titles Won:	At least 5
Days as World Champion:	546
Age at first World Title Win:	41
Best Opponents:	Lou Thesz, Antonino Rocca, Enrique Torres

Leone, "Baron" Michele

Michele Leone was a Herculean performer during the early days of television, and the medium helped transform him from journeyman to superstar. On the many telecasts out of Los Angeles, Leone regularly showcased his affable personality and was striking as the "Baron," an Italian nobleman. He worked the ring like a master and turned many heads during his colorful out-of-the-ring interview segments that glorified his heelish characteristics. No one took him too seriously, and he was a rare breed who carried a strong fan base despite his "bad guy" image. Arriving in Los Angeles in 1949, he quickly rose to main event status at the Olympic Auditorium, and won both the World Junior and Heavyweight championships. On May 21, 1952, he was booked into a title vs. title confrontation against NWA World Titleholder Lou Thesz, a bout that drew wrestling's first $100,000 gate. Leone was defeated, and also lost a rematch in Hollywood in 1953. In August of that year, Leone captured the NWA World Junior Title and reign until April 11, 1955, when he lost the belt to Ed Francis. Not much later, he retired to a quiet life in Santa Monica.

Photo Courtesy of the Collection of Libnan Ayoub

Levin, Dave

Born:	October 31, 1913
Height:	5'11"
Weight:	200
Real Name:	George William Wenzel
Parents:	George and Elizabeth Wenzel
Wife:	Virginia Wenzel
Trained by:	Herb Freeman, Bobby Managoff Sr.
Nickname:	Butcher Boy
Finishers:	Flying tackle, Airplane Spin
Career Span:	1934–58
Died:	February 1, 2004, Oceanside, CA 90 years old

Titles Won:	At least 14
Days as World Champion:	Over 325 (excluding several Pfefer claims which may have amounted to more than a year)
Age at first World Title Win:	22
Best Opponents:	Buddy Rogers, Orville Brown, Dean Detton

An underrated superstar, Dave Levin was the prince of the traveling Jack Pfefer tribe and a claimant to the world heavyweight championship at least nine times during his long career. Born in New York City, he was scouted by Pfefer and trained at George Bothner's famous gym. An ex-butcher, Levin was very popular and his worldwide notoriety increased measurably when he beat Ali Baba by DQ on June 13, 1936, winning the World Title. He added to his laurels by defeating Vincent Lopez on August 19, 1936, for recognition in California, giving him the strongest claim in the country, but lost the title to Dean Detton on September 28. The following January, Levin sustained rope burns in a match that developed into blood poisoning and nearly took his life. He needed seventeen blood transfusions, and was away from the ring for more than a year. In 1944, he won both the NWA and MWA World Heavyweight belts and was often recognized by Pfefer as the titleholder. He settled in Southern California, where he remained a fixture until the late 1950s.

Born:	April 18, 1934
Height:	4'3"
Weight:	92–130
Real Name:	Lionel W. Giroux
Parents:	Lucien and Lucille Giroux
Trained by:	Jack Britton, Sky Low Low
Career Span:	1950–87
Died:	December 4, 1995, St. Jerome, Quebec 61 years old

Titles Won:	At least 2
Days as World Champion:	Unknown, claimed title for years
Age at first World Title Win:	Around 23
Best Opponents:	Sky Low Low, Tom Thumb, Pee Wee James
Halls of Fame:	2

Little Beaver

   The little people of professional wrestling were a well-known and popular attraction in arenas across North America beginning in the late 1940s. Known for its fast-paced and sometimes comical style, the distinctive brand featured a range of colorful performers, one being Lionel Giroux, better known to fans as Little Beaver. Recruited into the business after receiving advice from Quebec mat legend Yvon Robert, the fifteen-year-old Giroux joined the troupe of Jack Britton and soon fascinated the public with his athletic skill. Wearing stylish Indian attire, he ran around the ring with impressive agility and reportedly patterned his techniques after high-flyer Antonino Rocca. Often billed as the World Midget Champion, he wrestled all over the globe between 1950 and the 1970s. He returned to the ring in 1987, for a mixed six-man tag team match at WrestleMania III, and his team triumphed before nearly 80,000 fans. However, he suffered a back injury during the fracas and his career officially ended. Out of the ring he was an entrepreneur, and operated a restaurant in Montreal which he ran for years. Notably, of his nine siblings, he was the only little person. Little Beaver was inducted into the Professional Wrestling Hall of Fame in 2003.

Photo Courtesy of Scott Teal/Crowbar Press

Born:	June 8, 1906
Height:	6'2"
Weight:	235
Real Name:	Willard Rowe Longson
Parents:	George and Alice Longson
Married to:	Althea Graves Longson
High School:	Granite High School (UT)
Amateur Ach.:	Intermountain AAU Wrestling Title (1928, 1931) (HWT)
Identities:	The Purple Shadow, Superman II
Finisher:	Piledriver, Atomic Drop
Career Span:	1931–60
Died:	December 10, 1982, St. Louis, MO 76 years old

Titles Won:	13
Days as World Champion:	1,935
Age at first World Title Win:	35
Best Opponents:	Lou Thesz, Billy Watson, Yvon Robert
Halls of Fame:	3

Longson, Bill

"Wild" Bill Longson was as wild as they came; a master of mayhem and the definitive wrestling champion of the 1940s. He was the glue that held professional wrestling together in many parts of the United States during World War II, and was a consistent drawing card. Additionally, he was the first major heel to reign as the heavyweight titleholder, a job he performed well. He also had the talent to be able to work as a hero when his opponent was more hated than he was. The diversity of Longson came out as a young athlete in Salt Lake City, Utah, where he participated in football in high school, then joined the renowned Deseret Gymnasium, where he was instructed in wrestling by coach John Anderson. Longson was also on the boxing squad, winning the 1927 Intermountain AAU Heavyweight medal. No doubt influenced by the number of amateurs to become pros in the area, including Dean Detton, Longson earned his first paycheck for grappling at Salt Lake's McCullough's Arena on April 17, 1931, losing to Al Newman in twenty-one minutes.

A few months later, Longson boxed an exhibition against the former World Champion Jack Dempsey, but his real future was as a battler on the wrestling mat. Using his size to direct the tempo of matches, he was able to punish opponents with a variety of holds and maul them by resorting to unscrupulous tactics, which was fast becoming a needed ingredient in pro wrestling. Before he really got going, Longson suffered a broken back in a match against Man Mountain Dean in San Francisco in early 1937 and doctors predicted he'd never wrestle again. Longson was determined to return, and he did with a vengeance, capturing the Pacific Coast Heavyweight Championship three separate times. His remarkable comeback continued after relocating to the St. Louis area, where on February 19, 1942 at the Municipal Auditorium in St. Louis,

Longson beat Sandor Szabo and won the World Heavyweight Title, recognized by the National Wrestling Association.

Dethroned by Yvon Robert in Montreal on October 7, 1942, Longson regained the belt with a one-fall victory over Bobby Managoff in St. Louis on February 19, 1943. From that point on, he'd endure as titleholder for the next four years, an astonishing achievement, but indicative of the great success he was having. Longson was a proven box office success and made lots of money for promoters who used his services at the top of their program. Popular "Whipper" Billy Watson ended his lengthy run on February 21, 1947, beating Longson by disqualification when the latter punched the official. After the match, for good measure, "Wild" Bill socked the referee again—earning him a $50 fine. In St. Louis on November 21, 1947, he captured his third NWA World Title from Lou Thesz, using a reverse leglock to win the match in 25:15, however; Thesz regained the belt in July in Indianapolis. Longson owned points in the St. Louis promotion for years and also did some matchmaking and training of younger athletes looking to break into the business.

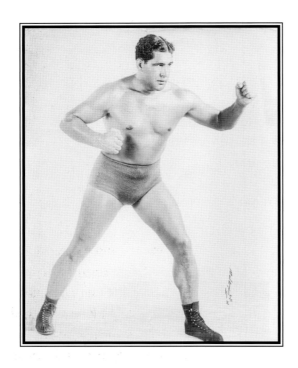

Photo Courtesy of the Collection of Libnan Ayoub

Born:	July 24, 1908
Height:	6'1"
Weight:	225
Real Name:	Daniel Vincente de Vinaspre
High School:	Meridian High School (ID)
College:	University of Idaho
Trained by:	Ed "Strangler" Lewis
Finisher:	Elbow smash
Career Span:	1933-57
Died:	April 13, 1980, San Jose, Costa Rica 71 years old

Titles Won:	At least 5
Days as World Champion:	392
Age at first World Title Win:	27
Best Opponents:	Dean Detton, Ed Lewis, Dave Levin

Lopez, Vincent

A massive international tournament was staged in Los Angeles in 1935, and right from the beginning, Vincent Lopez, an amateur wrestling great who beat Bill Longson for the 1929 Intermountain AAU Title and contended for a spot on the 1932 Olympic team, was a sensation. He was billed as being from Mexico, although he was born in Meridian, Idaho. His parents were from Spain and he was able to appeal to a cross-section of the public. During the tournament, he beat a gaggle of big names, including Chief Little Wolf, Ed Lewis, and Man Mountain Dean in the finals to capture the California version of the World Title on July 24, 1935. Lopez received a special championship trophy the following April, then lost the title to rival title claimant Dave Levin on August 19, 1936. He added three Pacific Coast Championships to his resume and soon became a journeyman, wrestling all over North America until his retirement.

Photo Courtesy of the Collection of Tim Hornbaker

Born:	January 4, 1918
Height:	6'0"
Weight:	235
Real Name:	Robert Manoogian
Parents:	Avak (Robert Sr.) and Azniv Manoogian
Wife:	Eve Manoogian
High School:	Tuley High School (IL)
Career Span:	1937–66
Died:	April 3, 2002, Chicago, IL 84 years old

Titles Won:	15
Days as World Champion:	818
Age at first World Title Win:	24
Best Opponents:	Bill Longson, Yvon Robert, Lou Thesz

Managoff, Bobby Jr.

Second generation superstar Bobby Managoff, Jr. was lightning fast, immensely bright, and managed to know every nook and cranny of the wrestling ring without having exceptional vision. He was born with double cataracts and familiarized himself with the squared circle through endless training, leaving no doubt that he could take care of himself against any opponent. The science of wrestling was something he'd learned from an early age, coached by his father Bob Managoff, a pro grappler as early as 1905 and the man who wrestled famous World Champion Frank Gotch in the infamous bout that saw the latter's leg broken in 1916. Bobby Jr. learned all the holds, the tricks to reverse maneuvers, and had the speed and agility to perform at the highest level. From day one, he was touted as a special athlete, and promoters gave him the room to grow, while at the same time expecting great things from him. Managoff didn't disappoint, and by the time he was twenty-four-years-old, he was ready to be a world champion.

In Houston on November 27, 1942, he beat Yvon Robert to score the National Wrestling Association Championship, and defended it proudly until February 19, 1943, losing a match in St. Louis to "Wild" Bill Longson. The following year, he held the Montreal version of the World Title, a belt he'd win five times in matches against Gino Garibaldi, Joe Savoldi, Yukon Eric, Robert, and Lou Thesz. He'd form a strong relationship with Montreal booker Eddie Quinn and own a percentage of the territory, as well as owning part of the St. Louis territory. Managoff was a regional champion in Texas, California, and Hawaii, and in his off time, he created spectacularly detailed wood carvings as a hobby. Managoff was good friends with Thesz, and their careers paralleled each other in certain respects. He was generally well-liked throughout the profession, and in 2000, was given the Frank Gotch Award by the George Tragos/Lou Thesz Professional Wrestling Hall of Fame.

Born:	November 4, 1905
Height:	6'0"
Weight:	220
Parents:	Claude and Pearl Marshall
Wife:	Harriet Marshall
High School:	La Junta High School (CO)
Trained by:	Mike Howard, Ed "Strangler" Lewis
Finisher:	Airplane Spin
Career Span:	1929–47
Died:	February 10, 1973, Fort Collins, CO 67 years old

Titles Won:	14
Days as World Champion:	1,078
Age at first World Title Win:	29
Best Opponents:	Jim Londos, Ed Lewis, John Pesek
Halls of Fame:	2

Marshall, Everette

Known as the "Pride of the Rockies," Everette Marshall was a top heavyweight grappler who achieved national superstardom very early in his career. At about the time he was celebrating his first anniversary in the business, he was selling out the Olympic Auditorium in Los Angeles, and shortly thereafter, helped draw a $69,000 gate against champion Gus Sonnenberg. It was a remarkable start to an extraordinary career. Marshall was born outside La Junta, Colorado and played football in high school, leading his squad to the 1925 state title. In April 1928, he won a freshman wrestling championship at the University of Iowa and, later that year, he beat a veteran grappler to capture a second school title. During the first part of 1929, he turned pro, and, on May 27, 1929, he defeated Joe Severini for the Rocky Mountain crown. Ed "Strangler" Lewis got wind of the young prodigy and brought him into his fold, expediting his push substantially.

In Los Angeles, Marshall was on course for a match against Sonnenberg and went over many veteran wrestlers, including Lewis himself. On May 5, 1930, Marshall and Sonnenberg drew over 17,000 fans and a gate of $69,745. Marshall remained a top contender to the championship, challenging Jim Londos a number of times, and the two even battled for three hours in 1934 before Marshall was defeated. He won his first World Title in June 1935 and bolstered his national standing with a variety of important victories in several states over the next two years. His biggest victory came over claimant Ali Baba on June 26, 1936. Lou Thesz ultimately beat him for the title on December 29, 1937, but because of his great record, Marshall was again named champion by the National Wrestling Association at its 1938 convention. Incidentally, Thesz was his conqueror this time as well, on February 23, 1939. Marshall wrestled until 1947, and competed mostly in the Central States region so he could tend to his Colorado onion farm.

Born:	July 31, 1918
Height:	6'1"
Weight:	230
Real Name:	Roy Lorne McClarty
Trained by:	Joe Pazandak
Finisher:	Sleeperhold
Career Span:	1948–71
Died:	March 27, 1998, Vancouver, B.C. 79 years old

Titles Won:	At least 7
Best Opponents:	Verne Gagne, Killer Kowalski, Gene Kiniski

McClarty, Roy

Although Roy McClarty played the role of the babyface, popular throughout North America, he was as tough as any down and dirty brawler in the sport. For years he was a defensive specialist in various Winnipeg hockey leagues and was never the kind of guy to back down from a fight. His competitiveness was also on display while as an amateur grappler, and he was a member of the same club as talented George Gordienko. He went pro in 1948, displaying a remarkable confidence. With blond hair and an obviously affable personality, he became a natural favorite of fans and, in 1950, before a Boston audience, married women's wrestler Shirley Strimple in the ring. McClarty, which was also spelled "McClarity" by writers, teamed with Pat O'Connor to capture the World Tag Team Title in 1955 and then with Bobby Bruns to capture the belts in 1956. Roy teamed with Don Leo Jonathan to hold the Canadian Tag championship in 1964. He retired from wrestling in 1971 and became a referee.

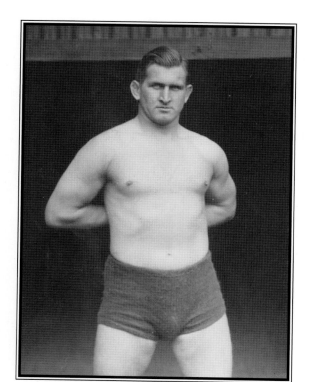

Born:	June 5, 1905
Height:	6'1"
Weight:	230
Real Name:	Earl Gray McCready
Parents:	Elgin and Lillian McCready
High School:	Central Collegiate High School (Regina, Saskatchewan)
College:	Oklahoma A&M
Trained by:	Dan Matheson (Regina YMCA)
Finisher:	Rolling cradle leg submission
Career Span:	1930–55
Died:	December 6, 1983, Edmonds, WA 78 years old

Titles Won:	7
Best Opponents:	Yvon Robert, Billy Watson, Ed Lewis
Halls of Fame:	8

McCready, Earl

Sometimes the best wrestlers are not the ones displaying the most flamboyance. Guys like Earl McCready and Dick Hutton, two of the greatest amateur superstars to ever become professionals, were more stoic and subdued, relying more on genuine athletic abilities than outrageous showmanship. Born in Ontario, Canada, McCready's amateur credentials were unbelievable. He won both Canadian Dominion and the NCAA championship several times over, participated in the 1928 Olympics, and won gold at the 1930 British Empire Games. Once he was a pro, he beat Jack Taylor for the Canadian Title in 1933, and claimed the British Empire championship for most of his career, defending it in Canada, New Zealand, and England. A riveting grappler, he was full of speed, science, and strength, which ultimately made him a feared shooter. In terms of pure wrestling ability, Canada produced no one better than McCready, and Earl has been inducted into eight different halls of fame. These include the National Wrestling Hall of Fame, Canada's Sports Hall of Fame, and the Professional Wrestling Hall of Fame, of which he was inducted in 2016.

Photo Courtesy of Scott Teal/Crowbar Press

Born:	December 10, 1910
Height:	5'11"
Weight:	190
Real Name:	Leroy Michael McGuirk
Parents:	John and Anna McGuirk
High School:	Tulsa Central High School (OK)
Finisher:	Rolling double wrist lock
Promoted:	Tulsa, OK (1958–82)
Career Span:	1932–50
Died:	September 9, 1988, Claremore, OK 78 years old

Titles Won:	At least 6
Days as World Junior Champion:	3,886
Age at first LHW World Title Win:	23
Best Opponents:	Danny McShain, Red Berry, Buddy Rogers
Halls of Fame:	3

McGuirk, Leroy

The prodigious wrestling son of Oklahoma, Leroy McGuirk came up through the amateur ranks like a man on a mission. Learning from extraordinary coaches, he grappled his way to an NCAA championship in 1931. Handicapped by the loss of an eye in a swimming accident when he was young, Leroy studied wrestling with the utmost determination in high school and college—the latter under Ed Gallagher at Oklahoma A&M—and turned pro after failing to repeat as national champion in 1932. Within two years he had captured the NWA World Light Heavyweight Title, and would battle with all comers. Later in the decade, he graduated to the junior heavyweight class and won the National Wrestling Association World Championship from Johnny Swenski on June 19, 1939. He was the face of the division for over ten years, and it wasn't until he was blinded in a car accident in 1950 that his career came to an abrupt end. McGuirk's presence behind the scenes elevated, and he served as a booking agent in Tulsa before taking over the promotional reigns in 1958. He served in that position until the early 1980s. McGuirk passed away on September 9, 1988, at the age of seventy-eight. In 2014, he was inducted into the Professional Wrestling Hall of Fame.

McMillen, Jim

Born:	October 22, 1902
Height:	6'1"
Weight:	220
Real Name:	James W. McMillen
Wife:	Phyllis McMillen
High School:	Libertyville Township High School (IL)
College Ach.:	Two-Time All-American (1922–23), Three-Time letterwinner (1921–23)
Pro Sports:	National Football League—Milwaukee Badgers (1923) National Football League—Cleveland Indians (1923, 1931) National Football League—Chicago Bears (1924–28) (1930–31) (1935)
Military:	United States Navy (1941–45)
Trained by:	Paul Prehn
Career Span:	1925–50
Died:	January 27, 1984, Lake Forest, IL 81 years old

Titles Won:	At least 2
Best Opponents:	Jim Londos, Ray Steele, Dick Shikat

When football star Wayne Munn became wrestling champion in 1925, many other luminaries of the gridiron saw an opportunity to supplement their income by turning to grappling during the offseason. One of them was Jim McMillen, a well-known footballer from the University of Illinois. McMillen captained the 1923 undefeated team that also featured the legendary Red Grange at halfback, and joined the Chicago Bears of the NFL in 1924. Having wrestled in college, he made a flawless leap into pro wrestling the following year and was a prominent challenger to several World Heavyweight champions. His crowning moment was a match against Jim Londos on January 26, 1931, before over 22,000 fans at Madison Square Garden in New York City. Although he lost the bout, it was spectacular showing and a historic turnout. Back home in Illinois, McMillen claimed the state championship until 1937. McMillen was a minority owner of the Chicago Bears and close associate of George Halas, and served as the mayor of Antioch, Illinois, from 1952–58. He passed away in 1984 at eighty-one years of age.

Born:	October 30, 1912
Height:	6'0"
Weight:	190
Real Name:	Woodrow Wilson Shain
Parents:	Charles and Evelina Shain
Wife:	Sallee Lewin McShain
High School:	Glendale High School (CA)
Managed by:	Dick Lane (1937–38)
Career Span:	1933–67
Died:	July 14, 1992, Alvin, TX
	79 years old

Titles Won:	32
Days as World Junior Champion:	637
Age at first World Junior Title Win:	39
Best Opponents:	Red Berry, Leroy McGuirk, Johnny Valentine
Halls of Fame:	2

McShain, Danny

One of the most successful grapplers in history, Danny McShain engaged in mat warfare for over thirty years, and his matches were usually filled with absolute, bloody mayhem. A captivating brawler who punished his opponents with an unmerciful flair, McShain was originally from Little Rock but grew up in Southern California, where he enlisted in the Army as a teenager and learned to box and wrestle at the Los Angeles Athletic Club. Between 1937 and '47, "Dangerous" Danny held the World Light Heavyweight Title more than ten times, and on November 19, 1951, he won the National Wrestling Alliance World Junior Heavyweight belt. He'd carry the prestigious NWA championship for over twenty months until losing it to Baron Michele Leone on August 17, 1953. A legend in the "Lone Star State," McShain was a perennial state champion and defined what it meant to wrestle the brutal "Texas style," which was heavy on violence. He wore extravagant robes to the ring and carried himself with a confident swagger that grinded on fans. After hanging up his gear, McShain worked as a referee, and his presence was a constant reminder of his extraordinary career. He passed away on July 14, 1992, at the age of seventy-nine.

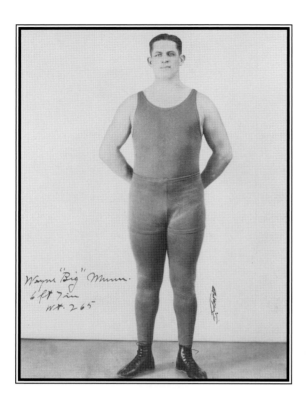

Born:	February 19, 1895
Height:	6'6"
Weight:	260
Real Name:	Wayne H. Munn
Parents:	Bethul and Loretta Munn
Family:	Brother of Glen, Monte, and Wade Munn
High School:	Fairbury High School (NE)
Military:	United States Army (WWI)
College:	University of Nebraska
Pro Sports:	Independent Team—Olson's All-Stars (Sioux City) (1921) National Football League—Kansas City Cowboys (1925)
Trained by:	Ed Lewis, Joe Mondt
Finisher:	Crotch and half Nelson
Career Span:	1924–28
Died:	January 9, 1931, San Antonio, TX 35 years old

Munn, Wayne

Titles Won:	1
Days as World Champion:	97
Age at first World Title Win:	29
Best Opponents:	Ed Lewis, "Toots" Mondt, Stanislaus Zbyszko
Boxing Record:	0-3

In terms of marketing, "Big" Wayne Munn of Jefferson County, Nebraska had three crucial aspects that made him a box office attraction: He was a football standout, had incredible size, and was a rookie sensation when he became a wrestler in 1924, which helped breathe life into a dreary industry. It was exciting to see Munn's newfangled approach to the sport, especially when compared to the monotonous work of many grapplers. Fatigued fans wanted something new; a breath of fresh air, and Munn provided it. On January 8, 1925, with only eleven months of experience, he beat Ed Lewis for the World Heavyweight Title. Immense buzz was created, and Munn's handlers protected him the best they could, building excitement for a financially rewarding rematch against Lewis. On April 15, 1925, however, Stanislaus Zbyszko preyed on Munn's inexperience, double-crossed him in the ring, and took the title in one of history's most infamous moments. In an instant, Munn's stock crashed and his career was never the same.

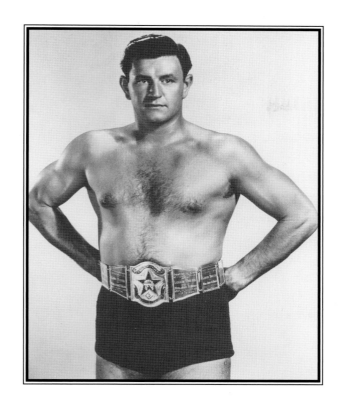

Born:	January 22, 1924
Height:	6'0"
Weight:	220
Real Name:	Harold Calvin Myers
Parents:	William and Sylvia Myers
Wife:	Elaine Myers
High School:	Pickett High School (MO)
Finisher:	Atomic Drop, Shoulder Scissors, Japanese Sleeperhold
Career Span:	1944–75
Died:	May 7, 2007, St. Joseph, MO 83 years old

Titles Won:	32
Days as World Champion:	63
Age at first World Title Win:	23
Best Opponents:	Orville Brown, Lou Thesz, Bob Geigel

Myers, Sonny

A highly decorated regional champion, Sonny Myers was a major fan favorite in the central states territory and, at one point, was so successful on a tour of the "Lone Star State" that pundits began calling him "Mr. Texas." Myers played football at his St. Joseph, Missouri, high school and entered wrestling under the guidance of promoter Gust Karras. Three years after his debut, on November 3, 1947, he beat Orville Brown for the local Iowa version of the National Wrestling Alliance World Title and held it for two months. In June 1951, Myers was nearly killed by an irate fan after a bout in Angleton, Texas, and received an 18-inch knife wound, requiring more than 100 stitches. He rebounded to have the best year of his career in 1952–53, appearing on national TV and wrestling all over the country. Between 1955 and 1964, Myers was embroiled in an ongoing legal fight against the NWA and promoter Pinkie George over a claim that he was a victim of the Alliance's monopolistic practices. There was never a firm resolution to the matter. Wrestling his last match in 1975, Myers became a referee and, that same year, was the third man for Terry Funk's NWA World Title victory over Jack Brisco in Miami, Florida. He returned to promote an indie promotion in St. Joseph in 2000, and passed away seven years later on May 7, 2007.

Nagurski, Bronko

Born:	November 3, 1908
Height:	6'2"
Weight:	230
Real Name:	Bronislau Nagurski
Parents:	Michael and Emila Nagurski
High School:	Bemidji High School (MN)
College:	University of Minnesota
Football Positions:	Tackle, Fullback
Pro Sports:	National Football League— Chicago Bears (1930–37) (1943)
Pro Titles:	NFL World Championship (1932, 1933, 1943)
Career Span:	1933–59
Died:	January 7, 1990, International Falls, MN 81 years old

Titles Won:	7
Days as World Champion:	921
Age at first World Title Win:	28
Best Opponents:	Jim Londos, Lou Thesz, Ray Steele
Halls of Fame:	5

The incredible Bronko Nagurski became a professional wrestler in the 1930s, and supplemented his income on the grappling mat during the football offseason. Born in Canada and trained by Tony Stecher and Henry Ordemann, Nagurski took wrestling very seriously, learning the craft and relying on his strength and agility to beat opponents. However, most people knew him from his role as a member of the Chicago Bears NFL franchise, where he played from 1930 to 1937, and starred at fullback. Wrestling fans were drawn by his magnetism, and his overall name value at the box office motivated promoters to push him to the World Heavyweight Title throne four times, the first time coming on June 29, 1937, when he beat Dean Detton. Nagurski won the prized National Wrestling Association championship twice over Lou Thesz and Ray Steele, and then took a localized claim from Sandor Szabo in Minneapolis in 1948. Nagurski remained prominent into the late 1950s, appearing on TV and maintaining his solid reputation as a tough guy. Well-liked, he wasn't a boisterous self-promoter and achieved fame and fortune in sports like a real gentleman. He made his home in International Falls, Minnesota, and was a charter member of the Pro Football Hall of Fame in 1963, alongside Red Grange, George Halas, and Jim Thorpe.

Photo Courtesy of Scott Teal/Crowbar Press

Born:	September 13, 1927
Height:	6'2"
Weight:	235
Real Name:	Arthur Nelson
Identities:	Art Nielsen, Art Neilson, The Destroyer, The Super Destroyer, The Phantom of the South, Red Raider, Golden Superman, Black Phantom, Avenger, Masked Hox and others
Career Span:	1947–77
Died:	October 28, 1983, Las Vegas, NV 56 years old

Titles Won:	40
Best Opponents:	Pat O'Connor, Dory Funk Sr., Don McIntyre

Nelson, Art

Blond strongman Art Nelson was a masterful performer, having perfected the science of rule-breaking, and was undeniably tough. A Marine veteran, Nelson broke into the sport under Bert Rubi in the Detroit area and was quick to adopt a trademark style. He became a well-known TV star in Chicago during the 1950s, and formed a successful tandem with Reggie Lisowski. The duo beat Bill Melby and Jack Witzig for a claim to the World Tag Team Title on February 13, 1954, and reigned through early 1956. He also had success with faux brother Stan Holek as the "Neilsons," and was a multiple-time World Tag Team titleholder—even winning the IWA belts in Australia with Ray Stevens. In 1957, veteran Virginia promoter Bill Lewis told a reporter: "A lot of [Nelson's] stuff reminded me of Jim Londos in his heyday. [He] will never give a bad performance. He's just that good." Many promoters agreed with Lewis and gave Nelson headliner roles in their territory. From 1947 to '77, Nelson toured the globe and had lengthy runs in the Georgia, Mid-Atlantic, and West Texas regions. Following his death in 1983, he was buried in Memory Gardens Cemetery in Amarillo, Texas.

Born:	June 19, 1924
Height:	6'3"
Weight:	255
Real Name:	Leo Joseph Nomellini
High School:	Crane Technical High School (IL)
College Ach.:	Two-Time All-American (1948–49)
Military:	United States Marine Corps
Pro Sports:	National Football League—San Francisco 49ers (1950–63)
Pro Ach.:	NFL Pro Bowl (10 selections)
Trained by:	Verne Gagne, Joe Malcewicz, Bronko Nagurski
Career Span:	1950–62
Died:	October 17, 2000, San Francisco, CA 76 years old

Nomellini, Leo

Titles Won:	9
Days as World Champion:	115
Age at first World Title Win:	30
Best Opponents:	Lou Thesz, Sandor Szabo, Gene Kiniski
Halls of Fame:	4

Hall of Fame football player Leo "The Lion" Nomellini was also a distinguished pro wrestler. Following a reputable amateur career at the University of Minnesota, where he narrowly missed a Big-Ten mat title in 1950, Nomellini entered the pro ranks under promoter Tony Stecher. Recognizing his football talents, the San Francisco 49ers drafted him with their first round pick in 1950, and he set an NFL record by playing 159 consecutive games, and then retired after 174 straight games in 1963. Nomellini wrestled during the off season and participated in several high profile matches against NWA World Heavyweight Champion Lou Thesz in San Francisco. On March 22, 1955, he beat Thesz, capturing a claim to the NWA Championship, and toured the nation as a titleholder. The controversial situation also saw Thesz retain a claim until the strands were reunited a few months later in St. Louis. Nomellini was a sensational fan favorite on the West Coast and a successful box office attraction. His athleticism and durability were proven commodities in both sports.

Born:	August 22, 1924
Height:	6'1"
Weight:	235
Real Name:	Patrick John O'Connor
Parents:	John and Isabella O'Connor
High School:	Feilding Agricultural High School (N.Z.)
College:	Massey Agricultural College
Amateur Titles:	New Zealand National Title (HWT) (1948–49), British Empire Games (Silver Medal) (1950)
Finisher:	Reverse Rolling Cradle, Spinning Toehold, Sleeperhold
Career Span:	1950–87
Died:	August 16, 1990, St. Louis, MO 65 years old

O'Connor, Pat

Titles Won:	27
Days as World Champion:	1,196
Age at first World Title Win:	29
Best Opponents:	Buddy Rogers, Dick Hutton, Lou Thesz
Halls of Fame:	5

Pat O'Connor was a versatile heavyweight, boasting the intensity, speed, and size to be a thoroughly respected professional wrestler. As he departed the amateur ranks with two national championships and a silver medal in the British Empire Games, representing his home country of New Zealand, he was a highly touted prospect. He was scouted by Joe Pazandak and Butch Levy, and learned much from Verne Gagne and Tony Stecher in Minneapolis. Not wasting any time, O'Connor jumped on the circuit, appearing on national TV programs, and headlining big-time events all over North America. In matches, he applied the knowledge taught by his brilliant instructors, and incorporated his own aggressiveness and the fundamentals he picked up from amateur coaches Don Anderson and Anton Koolman back home in New Zealand. In 1954-1955, he won a slew of championships, including the Montreal World Title.

Many of the straight-laced characteristics Lou Thesz brought to the NWA were also seen in O'Connor, and his powerful backers gave him the time necessary to develop all sides of his wrestling persona, which particularly meant his outward personality, finding a way to connect to audiences and earn a reputation as a box office draw. When O'Connor was selected to replace Dick Hutton as the NWA World Champion, he was expected to improve attendance numbers and generate some excitement after a rough few years. Pinning the regeneration of the sport on the shoulders of one man was unfair, but the NWA's choice of O'Connor was a step in the right direction. On January 9, 1959, he beat Hutton in St. Louis and captured the championship.

Like his predecessors, he went out on tour, crisscrossing the nation, and appearing in cities of all sizes maintaining the prestige of the belt.

In the role of champion, O'Connor was a fan favorite and a heel, performing the necessary deed on any given night, and was very successful at the role. He defended his title against Thesz, Bill Longson, Fred Blassie, Dick the Bruiser, Johnny Valentine, Antonino Rocca, and tons of others, telling a different story in each match and walking from every arena a proud champion. On June 30, 1961, his reign came to an end against Buddy Rogers at Chicago's Comiskey Park in a contest that broke the national gate record, earning more than $120,000. Outside the ring, O'Connor invested in the Kansas City and St. Louis promotions, acting as a matchmaker in both territories simultaneously at certain times. He ended his active career in 1982 during a tour of New Zealand. A champion as an amateur and as a professional, on two continents, O'Connor made a tremendous mark on the business he loved, and influenced actions in front of audiences and behind the scenes for more than thirty years.

The WWE inducted him into its Hall of Fame as part of the inaugural "Legacy" class in 2016.

Photo Courtesy of the Pfefer Collection, Department of Special Collections, University of Notre Dame

Born:	September 29, 1912
Height:	6'2"
Weight:	225
Real Name:	Daniel Aloysius O'Mahony
Military:	Irish Free State Army
Trained by:	Jack McGrath, Fred Moran
Finisher:	Irish Whip
Career Span:	1934–50
Died:	November 3, 1950, Maryborough, Ireland 38 years old

Titles Won:	3
Days as World Champion:	385
Age at first World Title Win:	22
Best Opponents:	Jim Londos, Ed Don George, Ed Lewis

O'Mahoney, Danno

A tall, twenty-two-year-old man arrived at Ellis Island on December 14, 1934 from Ballydehob, County Cork, Ireland. The individual was Danno O'Mahoney, who was entering the country to light the professional wrestling business on fire; and although he claimed to be a farmer, his agricultural days were over—indicated by the rush to get him to the airport that afternoon and onto a private plane to Boston, where he was introduced from ringside at the Garden. The newcomer was pushed to the moon, commencing a win streak that was unparalleled in history, and 195 days after his American landing, O'Mahoney conquered the unbeatable Jim Londos for the World Heavyweight Title. His championship win over the "Golden Greek," along with his victory over Ed Don George, gave him the strongest claim to the heavyweight throne seen in years. O'Mahoney's drawing power in many parts of the country was impressive, and he delivered a fine-tuned performance that wowed audiences.

O'Mahoney, however, was not an established veteran with the tools to protect himself in the ring. Instead, he was a young man with the weight of the world on his shoulders and a humongous target on his back. In a power hungry world, the inevitable happened on March 2, 1936, when Danno was double-crossed at Madison Square Garden by Dick Shikat, and forcibly stripped of his title in a shoot affair. The infamous match had a disillusioning effect on a great portion of the public after leaked information revealed ugly insider truths about the business. Additionally, the double-cross helped to fracture wrestling beyond repair, creating nothing but title claimants and chaos. O'Mahoney continued to wrestle, but his career was never the same. In 1950, after performing in several bouts in the Los Angeles area, he returned to Ireland, and was involved in a serious car accident. He suffered life-threatening injuries, and was taken to Maryborough County Hospital, where he died a short time later.

Photo Courtesy of Pete Lederberg—plmathfoto@hotmail.com

Born:	July 21, 1929
Height:	6'4"
Weight:	245
Real Name:	Robert Dale Orton
Family:	Father of Bob Orton Jr. and Barry Orton, grandfather of Randy Orton
Wife:	Rita Orton
High School:	Wyandotte High School (KS)
Identities:	Rocky Fitzpatrick, The Zodiac
Nickname:	The Big O, Wildcat Orton
Finisher:	Piledriver, Tornado Drop
Career Span:	1949–76
Died:	July 16, 2006, Las Vegas, NV 76 years old

Orton, Bob Sr.

Titles Won:	25
Best Opponents:	Eddie Graham, Hans Schmidt, Bob Ellis

Orville Brown, one of the founders of the National Wrestling Alliance and an influential Central States booking agent, recruited Bob Orton around 1949 and considered him one of the best prospects he'd seen in years. Orton's size and strength made him a natural competitor on the heavyweight circuit, and during the early 1950s, was featured on the DuMont national television program out of Chicago. That kind of exposure opened up many job opportunities across the nation, and Orton went on the road. In the Kansas City territory, he feuded with Pat O'Connor and Sonny Myers, held the local championship several times, and challenged Lou Thesz for the World Title. Bruising opponents unmercifully, Orton was a fearsome grappler, and had plenty of success in New York and Florida, even using a controversial masked Zodiac gimmick. In 1976, he teamed with his son, Bob Jr. to win the Florida Tag Team Championship.

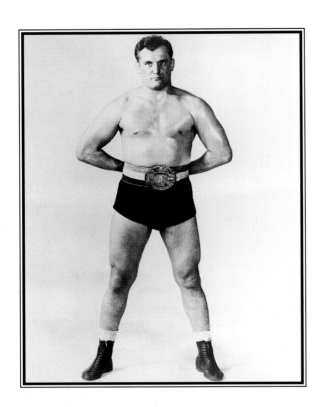

Photo Courtesy of Scott Teal/Crowbar Press

Born:	April 25, 1912
Height:	5'11"
Weight:	210
Wife:	Olga Palmer
High School:	Roosevelt High School (IL)
Colleges:	Crane College, Northwestern University
Trained by:	Lou Talaber
Identities:	George LaMarque, Red Ace, Ace Palmer, George LaMar
Finisher:	Spinning Toe Hold
Career Span:	1936–54
Died:	July 10, 1998, Tucson, AZ 86 years old

Palmer, Walter

Titles Won:	At least 3, claimed a few others
Days as World Champion:	Unknown, maybe as much as several years
Age at first World Title Win:	Around 31
Best Opponents:	Lou Thesz, Ruffy Silverstein, Cyclone Anaya

Walter Palmer was the central babyface in the "Windy City" for a great deal of the 1940s and into the early 1950s, tending to business as the local hero and as a policeman for the territory. Having wrestled since he was in grade school, he gained experience in the parks system and considered training for the Olympics. He was a top contender to the junior light heavyweight title, then, as he gained weight, was billed as the uncrowned heavyweight champion. Based on his outstanding record, including remaining undefeated for several years, he claimed the Chicago World Title and held it multiple times between 1944 and 1949. At one point, he had to give the title up because of a severely broken leg. In 1951, the NWA recognized his career achievements by awarding him a special sportsmanship plaque, declaring him a credit to the sport.

Born:	October 23, 1914
Height:	5'9"
Weight:	230
Real Name:	Joseph Eugene Pazandak
Parents:	Joseph and Caroline Pazandak
High School:	West High School (MN)
Amateur Titles:	Northwest AAU Championship (1935–36)
Military:	United States Army (1941–45)
Identities:	Joe Pazek, The Dark Secret (Masked)
Career Span:	1937–60
Died:	December 2, 1983, Minneapolis, MN 69 years old

Titles Won:	At least 2
Days as "The Champ":	Around 300
Best Opponents:	Verne Gagne, Lou Thesz, Sandor Szabo
Halls of Fame:	1

Pazandak, Joe

A combat veteran, amateur great, and trainer to the stars, "The Champ" Joe Pazandak was an influential and successful wrestler for over twenty years. Guided into the business by Minneapolis promoter Tony Stecher after winning two AAU championships and wrestling at the University of Minnesota, Pazandak was a fundamentally sound heavyweight. He was such an expert that Stecher relied on him to work the territory as a policeman and trainer, coaching dozens of future superstars to include Verne Gagne, Dick the Bruiser, and Roy McClarty. Perhaps his greatest in-ring fame came in Los Angeles as the defender of the TV wrestling jackpot known as "Beat the Champ" beginning in June 1951, and he successfully defended the money against top challengers for more than nine months. He never officially lost the title either, but was stripped of his "championship" in May 1952, when he left the territory. Pazandak also found success in Australia and New Zealand. He retired in 1960, and passed away on December 10, 1983, at sixty-nine years of age.

Born:	April 10, 1925
Height:	6'0"
Weight:	220
Real Name:	Angelo John Poffo
Parents:	Silvio and Egitina Poffo
High School:	Downers Grove North High School (IL)
Trained by:	Lou Talaber, Karl Pojello
Identities:	The Miser, The Question
Finisher:	Neckbreaker
Promoted:	International Championship Wrestling (1978–84)
Career Span:	1949–91
Died:	March 4, 2010, Largo, FL 84 years old

Poffo, Angelo

Titles Won:	10
Best Opponents:	Wilbur Snyder, Dick the Bruiser, Verne Gagne
Halls of Fame:	1

Born into a family of Italian immigrants, Angelo Poffo was raised in the Chicago suburb of Downers Grove and gained a real competitive spirit while serving in the navy. On July 4, 1945, he undertook a challenge of breaking the world record for consecutive sit-ups and accomplished the feat with a total of 6,033, which was seventy-eight more than the previous mark. His achievement was featured in Robert Ripley's cartoon on March 3, 1948. After serving three years in the military, Poffo attended DePaul University where he was a star catcher on the school's baseball team. He also wrestled at the Chicago YMCA and won tournament honors in the 191-pound class. In 1949, he began training to become a professional under Lou Talaber, and launched his career. On December 27, 1958, he beat Wilbur Snyder for the United States Heavyweight Title, and reigned through early May 1959, dropping the belt back to Snyder in Detroit. Poffo was a significant player on the Barnett-Doyle circuit and gained wins from Bob Ellis, Yukon Eric, and Bobby Managoff. A man of convictions, Poffo trained his two sons, Randy Savage and Lanny Poffo, for the pro ring, and spotlighted them in his own promotion, ICW out of Lexington. In 1995, he was inducted into the WCW Hall of Fame.

Born:	November 26, 1917
Height:	5'10"
Weight:	180
Real Name:	Inman Curry Raborn
Parents:	James and Sarah Raborn
Wife:	Doris Raborn
Career Span:	1933–58
Died:	August 31, 1968, Tulsa, OK 51 years old

Titles Won:	At least 6
Days as World LHW Champion:	210
Age at first World LHW Title Win:	24
Best Opponents:	Verne Gagne, Red Berry, Billy Varga

Raborn, Billy

Across North America, Billy Raborn was cheered for his scientific style and blazing fast speed. He was a pure athlete and his masterful wrestling knowledge was on display each time he appeared in the ring. Raborn was from Hephzibah, Georgia, and schooled by southern great Jack Ross prior to his professional debut at sixteen years of age. By 1937, he worked his way up to New York, where he was booked around the circuit by the ever-colorful Jack Pfefer. Gaining great experience and popularity, Raborn found himself booked into a championship bout with National Wrestling Association World Light Heavyweight titleholder Red Berry on August 24, 1942, in Tulsa, Oklahoma. It was the biggest match of his life and a contest he'd win. Billy was world champion through the following March, when, just prior to entering the army, he was defeated by Billy Varga in Hollywood. He also won the Southern, Texas, and Arkansas Junior Titles, plus the Pacific Coast Light Heavyweight belt. Always known as a gentleman, he retired to Cleveland, Oklahoma, where he worked as an insurance agent. Raborn passed away on August 31, 1968, at fifty-one years of age.

Born:	October 8, 1914
Height:	6'0"
Weight:	225
Family:	Older brother of Maurice Robert, father of Yvon Robert Jr.
Wife:	Leona Robert
Finisher:	Rolling short-arm scissors
Career Span:	1932–57
Died:	July 12, 1971, Montreal, Quebec 56 years old

Titles Won:	18
Days as World Champion:	Over 3,336
Age at first World Title Win:	21
Best Opponents:	Lou Thesz, Bill Longson, Sandor Szabo
Halls of Fame:	1

Robert, Yvon

Montreal icon Yvon Robert was a pro grappler by eighteen years of age and a world champion by twenty-one. Originally from Verdun, France, he labored in a lumber camp as a teen and wrestled as an amateur prior to training under Emil Maupas, making his pro debut in 1932. Within two years, he was holding his own against established veterans and was primed to succeed Henri DeGlane as Montreal's leading superstar. On July 16, 1936, he beat Danno O'Mahoney for the first of his fifteen World Heavyweight championships and, over the course of the next twenty years, fought every major name from Lou Thesz to Buddy Rogers. It became a common theme for an American challenger to beat Robert for the local Montreal belt, and then have Yvon regain the title at a later date, of course after building lots of excitement and filling the Forum with adoring fans. On October 7, 1942, he added the National Wrestling Association World Title to his collection with a victory over "Wild" Bill Longson. He was dethroned by Bobby Managoff the next month. Altogether, he was world champion in one shape or form for over 3,300 days, which was the equivalent of nine years. Robert retired in 1957 and passed away in 1971.

Rocca, Antonino

Born:	April 13, 1921
Height:	6'0"
Weight:	225
Real Name:	Antonino Biasetton
Parents:	Antonio and Angelo Basso Biasetton
Wife:	Nellie Biasetton
College:	University of Buenos Aires
Trained by:	The Zbyszko Brothers
Finisher:	Argentine Backbreaker
Managed by:	Joe "Toots" Mondt, Vince McMahon, Fred Kohler
Road Agents:	Kola Kwariani, Harry Lewis
Career Span:	1940–76
Died:	March 15, 1977, New York, NY 49 years old

Titles Won:	8
Days as World Champion:	42
Age at first World Title Win:	31
Best Opponents:	Lou Thesz, Killer Kowalski, Buddy Rogers
Halls of Fame:	4

A cultural icon, Antonino "Argentina" Rocca was the crown prince of pro wrestling for many years. He was the ultimate fan favorite and his enormous appeal transcended ethnic and social barriers during the late 1940s and early 1950s. His array of flashy maneuvers was ideal during the early days of television and helped wrestling attract scores of new viewers. At Madison Square Garden in New York City, there was no end to the support he'd receive in battle against an evil foe, and Rocca usually came out on top, pinning his opponent and leaving the ring as a massive celebration surrounded him. Rocca's superstar status was unmatched, particularly in the northeast, where he was worshipped and he became a household name, recognizable by even the casual observer. He was a likable showman, highly coordinated, acrobatic, and Rocca's fans were pleased by each and every performance.

Legend has it that Rocca was 18 pounds at birth, the sixth child of Italian parents, and migrated to Argentina after two of his brothers ventured there to work in construction. His wrestling debut came as early as 1940, recruited into the business by a veteran named Kola Kwariani, who was always on the lookout for high quality talent. Rocca established himself as a real comer before being brought to Texas by Nick Elitch in 1948. He received a hastened push and won the Texas State Heavyweight Title twice, receiving additional training from Paul Boesch along the way. Already the hottest young commodity in the sport, Rocca was at the heart of a struggle for his contract by promoters hoping to exploit him. The winner was "Toots" Mondt, who used Rocca to rebuild the northeastern circuit and booked him on major television outlets from coast-to-coast. Rocca's transition to full-fledged celebrity was relatively easy, and he met all demands, lived up to expectations, and delivered box office gold wherever he appeared.

From November 1956 to January 1961, Rocca headlined every Madison Square Garden wrestling show, only giving way to the phenomenon of Buddy Rogers. In terms of championships, Rocca didn't need a belt to garner attention, and in spite of that, he still won World Titles in Cleveland and Montreal, and held the United States Tag Team Championship with Miguel Perez in 1957 and 1958. He was featured in the comic book, *Superman* comic book, issue 155 entitled "The Downfall of Superman" in August 1962. Under Vincent J. McMahon, wrestling was evolving in New York, and Rocca and Rogers were both eclipsed by the next superstar attraction, Bruno Sammartino, beginning in 1963. Rocca tried to run opposition to McMahon from Sunnyside Gardens, but couldn't keep pace with his major league rival. During the mid-1970s, he returned to the WWWF as a commentator, and then wrestled in Puerto Rico in 1976. Rocca, who was known for wrestling barefoot, passed away at the age of forty-nine on March 15, 1977 at Roosevelt Hospital.

Photo Courtesy of the Pfefer Collection, Department of Special Collections, University of Notre Dame

Rogers, Buddy

Born:	February 20, 1921
Height:	6'0"
Weight:	235
Real Name:	Herman Karl Rohde
Parents:	Herman and Freda Rohde
Family:	Father of Buddy Rogers Jr.
Identities:	Dutch Rhode, Wally Ward
Nicknames:	Nature Boy, Blond Adonis, Atomic Blond
Finisher:	Figure-four Leglock (Grapevine), Piledriver
Group:	The Mid-Atlantic Death Squad (1979–80)
Managed:	John Studd (1979–80), Jimmy Snuka (1980, 1981–82)
Career Span:	1942–83
Died:	June 26, 1992, Fort Lauderdale, FL 71 years old

Titles Won:	43
Days as World Champion:	Over 1,657
Age at first World Title Win:	26
Best Opponents:	Lou Thesz, Pat O'Connor, Bruno Sammartino
Halls of Fame:	3

Arguably the greatest wrestling villain of all time, Buddy Rogers set a standard so high that only the best of the best could come close. He was a pioneering blond heel that fans loved to hate, and his remarkable run as NWA World Heavyweight Champion between 1961 and 1963 drew millions of dollars. Tapping into the imagination of audiences, he also had his loyalists, but usually his snickering and taunting turned people off—just as he wanted, and Rogers was remarkable in the way he exhilarated arenas. As a performer, he was peerless; and because he was the complete package, Rogers would have been just as big a star today as he was then—perhaps even bigger.

Born in Camden, New Jersey, he was an athlete in high school, and wrestled at a local YMCA with his older brother, John. In November 1939, he joined the Navy, but his father died suddenly a few weeks later, and Buddy was discharged the following March to help his mother. He served as a police officer in Camden, and began moonlighting as a professional wrestler in the beginning of 1942.

Taught by many veterans from the Philadelphia to New York circuits, Rogers learned from the likes of Joe Cox, Fred Grobmier, and the Dusek Brothers, picking up tricks of the trade that are only gained by experience. However, Rogers credited eccentric manager and promoter Jack Pfefer as giving him the push from mediocrity into the spotlight, telling Lester Bromberg of the *New York World Telegram* (3/15/50) that "He made me with the routine, and the costumes." By that time, he'd established himself as one of the premier attractions in the nation. His appearances in St. Louis helped turn the tides in the critical Sam Muchnick-Lou Thesz wrestling war, giving the former the edge and leading to a merger of the two sides. He was featured regularly on TV and claimed to have had "more television exposure than any wrestler in history" between 1947 and 1950. In 1951, incidentally, he broke from Pfefer, ending their long association and, needless to say, the minute manager was immensely bitter because of it.

This didn't matter, because Rogers could write his own ticket into any city he wanted, and promoters beckoned for him because it always meant big money. In the northeast during the late 1950s, Vincent J. McMahon was building an empire that depended on vibrant TV presentations, and bringing Rogers in was a concept that required little thought. His captivating style and overconfidence made him required viewing, and the powers that be crowned him NWA World Champion after he beat Pat O'Connor on June 30, 1961 in Chicago. The championship allure added to his drawing power, and although he was a divisive force within the NWA, he was responsible for boosting the public image of the title after a few less than stellar years. Some wrestlers, however, disliked Rogers' attitude and success. In the dressing room of a Columbus, Ohio arena on August 31, 1962, Rogers was confronted by Bill Miller and Karl Gotch, and the trio had words. The scene escalated into violence and Rogers was left bruised and battered.

A series of mishaps, injuries, and physical ailments plagued Buddy for the rest of his career. Stemming from the Columbus attack, he claimed that he'd developed a speech impediment. After a bout with Bobo Brazil, he reportedly lost forty percent of the vision in one of his eyes. He then broke his arm in Washington and followed that up by breaking his right ankle early in a bout with Killer Kowalski in Montreal . . . unfortunately, the worst was yet to come. In April 1963, Rogers was hospitalized for chest pains, yet no one was positive whether or not he'd suffered a heart attack. Regardless, his health was more important than the business, and he performed all matches in a very restricted capacity. McMahon, at the time, was in the midst of branching out from the NWA, and despite Buddy's loss of the World Title to Lou Thesz on January 24, 1963, he still recognized him as the heavyweight champion. This changed upon news of Rogers' condition, and on May 17, 1963, the "Nature Boy" put McMahon's young star Bruno Sammartino over in less than a minute, and made the latter an instant hero.

Since that time, many rumors have circulated about what Buddy's role in the WWWF might have been had his health improved. There was also some talk that he was going to be a part owner of the organization, although none of this ended up happening. Rogers' attempt to break back into the sport as a promoter in Philadelphia was nixed by state officials, and when he did return to wrestling later in the 1960s, it was far from the heights he once knew. In the late 1970s, he again made a comeback in the Florida and Mid-Atlantic regions, even wrestling "Nature Boy" Ric Flair several times and trading victories. Perhaps his greatest match since 1963 occurred in a sandwich shop in the Fort Lauderdale area in 1989 when Rogers, then sixty-eight, pummeled a thirty-year-old man who was hassling employees. The legend of Buddy Rogers is still strong today through stories, memories, and plenty of wrestling folklore.

Photo Courtesy of the Collection of Libnan Ayoub

Born:	December 28, 1905
Height:	6'3"
Weight:	230
Real Name:	George James Hardison
Parents:	Henry and Mathilda Hardison
Wife:	Mary Andrews Hardison
Trained by:	William O'Connell, Dick Stahl
Identities:	Ras Samara
Career Span:	1934–56
Died:	Unknown

Titles Won:	At least 3, claimed others
Days as World Champion:	Unknown
Age at first World Title Win:	31
Best Opponents:	Lou Thesz, Everette Marshall, Jim Londos

Samara, Seelie

Pioneering African American Seelie Samara was billed as being from Ethiopia, but was actually from Fort Valley, Georgia. To sell his gimmick to the public, promoters created an elaborate story for him, explaining that he had been a bodyguard for Emperor Haille Selassie. In reality, his size and athletic prowess opened doors for him as a boxer, followed then by a pro wrestler as the "Black Demon" in the New England region. Adopting the "Seelie Samara" persona in 1937, he claimed the World Heavyweight Championship of a secondary circuit in Boston. As his ring abilities grew, so did his showmanship, and he was often set up as a headliner. During a successful tour of Australia in 1946, he wrestled before crowds of 11,000 and 12,000 versus Jaget Singh and Jim Londos, respectively. Samara had his last match in 1956, and quietly retired from the wrestling industry.

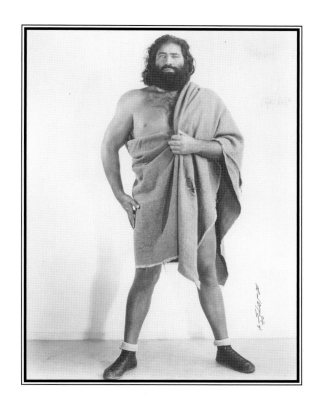

Photo Courtesy of the Pfefer Collection, Department of Special Collections, University of Notre Dame

Born:	March 9, 1900
Height:	6'3"
Weight:	250
Real Name:	Edgar Civil
Military:	United States Army
Identities:	Eddie Civil, Bob Savage
Finishers:	Bearhug
Career Span:	1933–60
Died:	January 7, 1967, Marion County, FL 66 years old

Titles Won:	At least 1
Days as World Champion:	355
Age at first World Title Win:	36
Best Opponents:	Ed Lewis, Danno O'Mahoney, Buddy Rogers
Boxing Record:	8-7
Movies:	1

Savage, Leo

The hillbilly gimmick was trademarked by Leo "Daniel Boone" Savage in 1934, after over a decade as a journeyman boxer. Although he wasn't an upper-crust fighter, he was praised by former heavyweight champion Jack Johnson as the best sparring partner he'd ever had. Originally from Ashland, Kentucky, Savage made the jump from boxing to pro wrestling, reportedly receiving guidance from another boxing legend, Jack Dempsey. In less than two years, he vaulted from virtual obscurity to a popular main eventer, and his powerful bearhug exhibited his immense strength. In St. Louis on March 25, 1936, he proved to be the "popular aggressor" in a bout against the famous Jim Londos, but was conquered by his smaller opponent in just 14:30. Two months later, he was acknowledged as the World Heavyweight champion in Houston after titleholder Danno O'Mahoney ran out on a match against him. Ironically, Savage himself was stripped for the same reason when he failed to wrestle Chief Little Beaver in April 1937. "Whiskers" Savage was a household name in Texas, and because he appealed to the everyman, was a top attraction for many years. He retired from wrestling in 1960.

Born:	April 21, 1914
Height:	5'9"
Weight:	215
Real Name:	Mario Louis Fornini Sr.
Parents:	Felice and Camilla Fornini
Family:	Brother of Lou Farina (Farino)
Military:	United States Coast Guard (WWII)
Nickname:	Granite Chin
Career Span:	1937–70
Died:	September 20, 2013, Parsippany, NJ 99 years old

Titles Won:	At least 5
Best Opponents:	Danny Hodge, Bruno Sammartino, Dory Funk Sr.
Halls of Fame:	3

Savoldi, Angelo

Angelo Savoldi displayed absolute skill and science over a career lasting thirty-three years. For much of that time, he was in the upper echelon of junior heavyweights working the circuit and even those fans who hated his in-ring behavior found it difficult to not appreciate his abilities. Born in Italy, Angelo grew up in Northern New Jersey and quit high school to begin work at a young age. He eventually followed his brother Lou into the wrestling business, and Jack Pfefer bestowed upon him the name "Angelo Savoldi," with the faux lineage that he was a cousin of "Jumpin' Joe" Savoldi. Between 1958 and '64, he won the National Wrestling Alliance World Junior Heavyweight Title five-times, topping Mike Clancy, Dory Funk Sr., Ivan the Terrible, Mike DiBiase, and Hiro Matsuda. Of all his feuds, his most headed was against Danny Hodge. In May 1960, Hodge's father attacked Savoldi in an Oklahoma City ring with a penknife and Angelo necessitated seventy stitches. The incident displayed the intense fervor of spectators during their rivalry. Savoldi was an influential veteran in the budding WWWF during the 1960s and '70s, and promoted his own organization, the ICW in the 1980s. Savoldi died on September 20, 2013, at the age of ninety-nine.

Savoldi, Joe

Born:	March 5, 1908
Height:	5'11"
Weight:	220
Real Name:	Giuseppe Antonio Savoldi Jr.
Parents:	Giuseppe and Celeste Savoldi
Wife:	Lois Savoldi
High School:	Three Oaks High School (MI)
Football Ach.:	Member of the Notre Dame National Champions in 1929 and 1930
Pro Sports:	National Football League— Chicago Bears (1930)
Military:	United States Army (WWII)
Trained by:	Ed Lewis, Joe Mondt
Promoted:	Benton Harbor, Michigan (1946–49)
Career Span:	1931–50
Died:	January 24, 1974, Cadiz, KY 65 years old

Titles Won:	At least 4
Days as World Champion:	136
Age at first World Title Win:	25
Best Opponents:	Jim Londos, Ed Lewis, Jim Browning

Innovator of the flying dropkick, a move that is still a fundamental part of the sport today, Italian-born "Jumpin'" Joe Savoldi was an All-American fullback at the University of Notre Dame under legendary coach Knute Rockne. After being thrown off the squad for getting a divorce, Savoldi briefly played for the Chicago Bears before he was courted into wrestling. With national name recognition, Savoldi used quick, football-like moves on the mat and became very popular. On April 7, 1933, he shockingly beat World Champion Jim Londos in Chicago, taking a pinfall from the previously unbeatable Greek in 26:20. The match was a double-cross, aimed at diminishing the drawing power of Londos, and both wrestlers left the match claiming the title. However, Savoldi's title had narrow support, and he eventually lost it to Jim Browning on June 12, 1933. Savoldi also held the Montreal World Title in 1945. He influenced the careers of Bobo Brazil and Verne Gagne, and taught high school science after retirement.

Born:	September 28, 1915
Height:	5'11"
Weight:	175-230
Real Name:	Francis Scarpa
Parents:	Carmen and Carmilla Scarpa
High School:	East Boston High School (MA)
Identities:	Gino Martinelli
Career Span:	1935–69
Died:	January 25, 1969, Boston, MA 53 years old

Titles Won:	At least 7
Days as World Champion:	639
Age at first World Title Win:	51
Best Opponents:	Killer Kowalski, Bull Curry, Don Leo Jonathan

Scarpa, Frank

East Boston wrestling legend Frank Scarpa had a long and distinguished career. He was trained by amateur great George Myerson after showcasing his sports aptitude as a football player in high school and participated in several Boston Park Department amateur tournaments. In 1934, he won both the wrestling and boxing championships at 175 pounds. Under the name "Manuel Cortez," he was billed as being from Mexico, and used that gimmick for more than twenty years. Popular and aggressive in the ring, he wrestled all the greats of the time and held the Boston area US Title five times. On April 27, 1967, he won a tournament to win the Big Time Wrestling World Heavyweight Title, recognized by Boston promoter Tony Santos, and was presented with the prestigious Ed "Strangler" Lewis belt, valued at $10,000. Scarpa passed away unexpectedly on January 25, 1969, at the age of fifty-three. The night before he had wrestled in North Attleboro and still reigned as champion at the time of his death.

Photo Courtesy of the Pfefer Collection, Department of Special Collections, University of Notre Dame

Born:	February 7, 1925
Height:	6'3"
Weight:	240
Real Name:	Guy R. Larose
Wife:	Monique Larose
Identities:	Roy Asselin
Finisher:	Backbreaker, Piledriver, Neckbreaker, Clawhold
Career Span:	1949–84
Died:	May 26, 2012, Joliette, Quebec 87 years old

Titles Won:	17
Days as World Champion:	Over 302
Age at first World Title Win:	36
Best Opponents:	Verne Gagne, Wilbur Snyder, Edouard Carpentier
Halls of Fame:	2

Schmidt, Hans

Hans Schmidt, the giant Nazi sympathizer, was one of the most hated men in the business. He perfected the performance of German stereotypes, cheated for victories, and criticized fans and opponents, drawing significant heat. Audiences were almost always furious with his actions and cheered wildly for Schmidt's opponent to give him the works. Schmidt was actually Guy LaRose from Joliette, Quebec, a former amateur wrestler who adopted the German gimmick in 1952 upon advice from Boston promoter Paul Bowser. The career choice turned him into a million-dollar draw. In places like New York City, Omaha, Montreal, and Chicago, huge crowds turned out to see him wrestle his dastardly style. The "Teuton Terror" annexed the United States Title from Wilbur Snyder on September 15, 1956, in Chicago, and by May 1957, he'd won the championship a total of four times. He also had five reigns as World Champion in Montreal between 1960 and '66. Schmidt alarmed fans around the world for thirty-five years. He passed away at the age of eighty-seven in 2012. Four years later, he was inducted into the Professional Wrestling Hall of Fame.

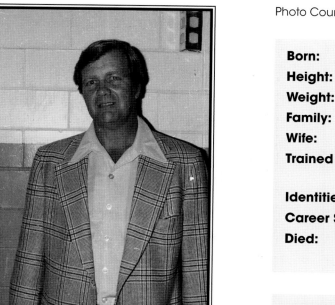

Born:	August 27, 1929
Height:	6'0"
Weight:	230
Family:	Older brother of Sandy Scott
Wife:	Jean Scott
Trained by:	The Dusek Brothers, Pat Murphy, Danno McDonald
Identities:	Benny Becker, The Great Scott
Career Span:	1949–81
Died:	January 20, 2014, Indian Rocks Beach, FL 84 years old

Titles Won:	20
Best Opponents:	Lou Thesz, Gene Kiniski, The Sheik

Scott, George

More committed to athletics at the Hamilton, Ontario, YMCA than to his schooling, George Scott was educated in the ways of pro wrestling and developed one of the sharpest minds in the business. In his extensive travels, he absorbed knowledge like a sponge, learning what worked with audiences and what did not. Born in Scotland, George teamed with his brother Sandy to form a talented duo, and the pair won a number of world, international, and regional titles. Among them were World championships in Australia, Indiana, the Central States, and Mid-Atlantic Regions. In 1963, he teamed with Buddy Austin to capture the Capitol Wrestling version of the US Tag Team Title from Buddy Rogers and Johnny Barend. He also defeated Johnny Valentine for a reign with the Texas Heavyweight Title in 1970. As a matchmaker in the Mid-Atlantic region, he catapulted Ric Flair and Ricky Steamboat into household names. Later on, he served as an influential figure in the WWF, and was a force behind the scenes of the first two WrestleManias. Scott died on January 20, 2014, at the age of eighty-four.

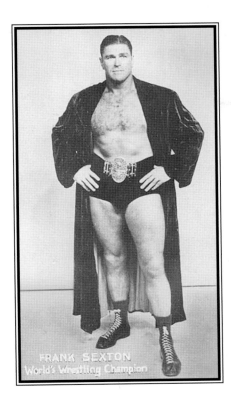

FRANK SEXTON
World's Wrestling Champion

Born:	November 1, 1910
Height:	6'1"
Weight:	230
Real Name:	Francis Paul Sexton
Parents:	James and Elizabeth Sexton
Wife:	Opal Sexton
High School:	Sedalia High School (OH)
Identities:	The Masked Marvel, The Black Panther
Nickname:	The Sedalia Cyclone
Finisher:	Airplane Spin, Giant Swing
Career Span:	1932–55
Died:	November 20, 1991, Columbus, OH 81 years old

Titles Won:	11
Days as World Champion:	1,861, excluding multi-year European claim
Age at first World Title Win:	33
Best Opponents:	Steve Casey, Bill Longson, Jim Londos
Halls of Fame:	1

Sexton, Frank

"Powerhouse" Frank Sexton was one of the longest reigning heavyweight champions at a time in which title switches and championship claimants were plentiful. It was a true testament of his ability to draw fans to arenas during the post-war years and the amount of esteem promoters had for him. A native of Sedalia, Ohio, Sexton was the youngest of eleven children and raised on the family farm. He starred in baseball and basketball in high school, and briefly attended Ohio State before the needs of his family called him back home. He was impressive during a wrestling session at a local circus and broke into pro wrestling under Columbus promoter Al Haft. On the wrestling circuit, he gained lots of experience, and many people whom he impressed along the way called him a future champion. After his breakout year in 1941, Sexton won the Pacific Coast Title in Northern California four times.

Sexton's final reign as Pacific Coast Champion lasted nearly two years. There was no question about it, he was a bonafide superstar and he added to his legacy by winning the Montreal World Title from local favorite Yvon Robert in 1944. In Boston on May 2, 1945, he beat Sandor Szabo for the AWA World Title, and then traded it with Steve Casey in June. Beginning on June 27, 1945 and over the course of the next 1,791 days, Sexton remained titleholder, a crowning achievement in a stellar career. During that run, he never shied away from opponents and met numerous rival champions, unafraid to mix it up in matches that could potentially develop into legitimate contests. He appeared in cities across the United States and included an undefeated tour of Europe, a rarity for most American champions, demonstrating that his claim was truly a "world" championship. In Cleveland on May 23, 1950, Sexton was dethroned by Don Eagle and his spectacular reign came to an end. Upon retirement, he owned and operated a construction company until 1972.

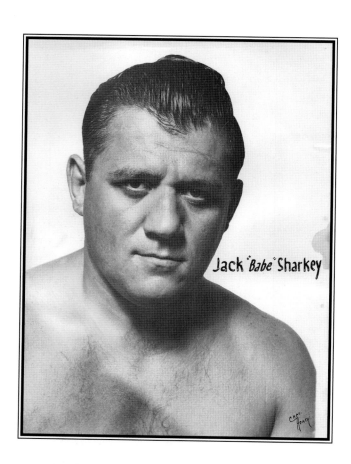

Jack "Babe" Sharkey

Photo Courtesy of John Pantozzi

Born:	November 20, 1912
Height:	6'4"
Weight:	250
Real Name:	Charles Kemmerer
Parents:	Marcus and Katie Kemmerer
High School:	Allentown High School (PA)
College:	Temple University
Pro Sports:	Reading Keys (Independent Pro Football Team) (1935)
Identities:	Tiny Cannon, Hard Boiled Hannigan
Nickname:	Texas
Career Span:	1940–51
Died:	September 25, 1985, Santa Clara, CA 72 years old

Titles Won:	At least 1, claimed another
Days as World Champion:	Over 700
Age at first World Title Win:	31
Best Opponents:	Frank Sexton, Lou Thesz, Ed Lewis

Sharkey, Babe

Lehigh County, Pennsylvania's Charles Kemmerer went from being a relative unknown to a headliner across the country in a very short time. Around 1943, after three years in the business, he adopted the name "Babe Sharkey," and claimed he that was from Texas. He soon gained national notoriety when he boxed Tony Galento in Wilmington, losing in the third round. As a wrestler, Babe was nothing short of spectacular as a heel. He trounced opponents, using his size to dominate matches, and built-up an impressive win streak. On March 7, 1944, he triumphed in a 16-man tournament in Baltimore and a week later, beat Ed "Strangler" Lewis for the vacant World Title, recognized by the Maryland commission. He remained the titleholder until losing to Frank Sexton on January 29, 1946. A few months later, he was again billed as the champion in the Pacific Northwest, but lost his claim to George Becker on September 11 in Portland.

Born:	March 18, 1916
Height:	6'5"
Weight:	265
Real Name:	Benjamin John Sharpe
Parents:	Digby and Margaret Sharpe
High School:	Westdale Secondary School (Hamilton, Ontario)
Olympics:	Rowing (1936) (representing Canada)
Career Span:	1944–62
Died:	November 21, 2001, Palo Alto, CA 85 years old

Titles Won:	27
Best Opponents:	Lou Thesz, Rikidozan, Bobby Managoff
Halls of Fame:	1

Sharpe, Ben

Standing 6'5" and weighing more than 260 pounds, "Big" Ben Sharpe was an outstanding athlete, an Olympic rower in 1936, and Hall of Fame wrestler. One of six children born to a Hamilton, Ontario, detective, Sharpe was six years older than his brother Mike, and began wrestling just prior to service in the Royal Canadian Air Force during World War II. In 1950, Ben and Mike traveled to San Francisco, where their size and overbearing ring presence were valued by promoter Joe Malcewicz. Together they won the local World Tag Team Title eighteen times between 1950 and '59, defeating such teams as Bobo Brazil and Enrique Torres and Primo Carnera and Sandor Szabo. They went to Japan several times and helped spread the American style of grappling to that country. As a singles competitor, Ben won the Hawaii Heavyweight Title from Bobby Managoff in 1953, and carried the Pacific Coast championship twice in 1956 and '59. He retired in 1962 after problems over pay arose with Malcewicz's successor, Roy Shire. The Sharpes were a revolutionary tag team, establishing a high standard for brother duos to come, and were inducted into the Professional Wrestling Hall of Fame in 2010.

Born:	July 11, 1922
Height:	6'6"
Weight:	260
Real Name:	George Edward Sharpe
Parents:	Digby and Margaret Sharpe
High School:	Westdale Secondary School (Hamilton, Ontario)
Career Span:	1945–64
Died:	August 10, 1988, San Joaquin Valley, CA 66 years old

Titles Won:	29
Best Opponents:	Lou Thesz, Killer Kowalski, Bill Longson
Halls of Fame:	1

Sharpe, Mike

The younger of the wrestling Sharpe Brothers, Mike Sharpe was the recipient of several notable pushes as a singles grappler in his career. In the late 1940s, he was a credible heavyweight in Toronto, and then was given matches against NWA World Champion Lou Thesz during his first major US tour. Later on in San Francisco, he captured the Pacific Coast belt four separate times. However, he gained international attention as a tag team competitor with his sibling, Ben, and won eighteen World Tag Team Championships in San Francisco. They were startling figures because of their size, and were vicious in the ring, captivating viewers not only live, but on television. For that reason, Chicago promoter Fred Kohler gave the brothers a spotlight on his prized Saturday night DuMont Network telecast, and the Sharpes beat Billy Darnell and Bill Melby for the World Tag Title on October 17, 1953. Mike also won the International TV and All Asia Tag Team Titles with Zebra Kid and Buddy Austin, respectively. His son, "Iron" Mike, was also a wrestler.

Photo Courtesy of Pete Lederberg—plmathfoto@hotmail.com

Born:	June 9, 1926
Height:	5'11"
Weight:	240
Real Name:	Edward George Farhat Sr.
Parents:	David and Eva Farhat
Family:	Father of Ed George, uncle of Sabu
Wife:	Joyce Fleser Farhat
College:	Michigan State University
Military:	United States Army (WWII)
Identities:	Sheik of Araby
Finisher:	Camel Clutch
Promoted:	Big Time Wrestling (1965–78)
Career Span:	1949–98
Died:	January 18, 2003, Williamston, MI 76 years old

Sheik, The

Titles Won:	30
Days as World Champion:	Over 100
Age at first World Title Win:	41
Best Opponents:	Bobo Brazil, Verne Gagne, Bruno Sammartino
Halls of Fame:	3

Across a career lasting nearly fifty years, the Sheik faced all of the big name wrestlers and tried to gouge out the eyes of each and every one of them. Employing some of the cruelest tactics in pro wrestling history, he defined what it meant to be a roughhouse or extreme grappler. He was the opposite of Lou Thesz and Verne Gagne in terms of wrestling purity, and exemplified violence. In a world that showcased "bad guys," the Sheik was in dire need by promoters all over the world, and he sold plenty of tickets because of his thrilling gimmick. The Shiek broke into the sport under Bert Rubi in Detroit and was trained by Lou Klein. The Sheik immersed himself in his wrestling persona, rarely if ever breaking kayfabe. Fans were often thrown into a fury by his antics, and he never met a foreign object he didn't enjoy brutalizing his ring opponent with. He threw fire in the faces of rivals, bit them, and seemed to revel in being outside the ropes brawling rather than working within the confines of the squared circle.

His hardcore style was still in its infancy, but it was already scary and destructive to anyone who dared to wrestle him. All that being said, the Sheik was an exceptionally successful wrestler, and won titles in many territories. He won the United States belt more than ten times, feuding with the likes of Dick the Bruiser and Bobo Brazil, who was a lifelong adversary. In Montreal, he captured the local World Title three times between 1967 and 1974. With all of the chaos and mayhem came blood, naturally, and the carnage that was created by the Sheik resonated with fans that saw him perform live. Outside the ring, he bought hometown territory of Detroit in 1963 for a reported $50,000. He had a strong working relationship with Frank Tunney in Toronto, where he also worked as a matchmaker. It was in Toronto that he ran up a lengthy win streak, and constantly drew large audiences at the Maple Leaf Gardens. His 2003 passing was noted by the mainstream press and mourned by his longtime fans.

Photo Courtesy of Scott Teal/Crowbar Press

Born:	December 17, 1921
Height:	5'10"
Weight:	200
Real Name:	Roy P. Shropshire
Parents:	William and Amelia Shropshire
Family:	Gimmicked brother of Ray Shire
Wife:	Dorothy Shire
Promoted:	San Francisco, California (1961-81)
Career Span:	1950-61
Died:	September 24, 1992, Sebastopol, CA 70 years old

Titles Won:	At least 7
Best Opponents:	Dory Funk Sr., Frankie Talaber, Joe Scarpello
Halls of Fame:	1

Shire, Roy

Roy Shire lived and breathed wrestling and adhered to the unwritten code of protecting the business for thirty-one years. Two years after he retired, in 1981, he broke kayfabe in a major way, telling the press that he'd prearranged matches for years as a promoter in San Francisco. He talked about blading, the exaggerated effects of in-ring maneuvers, and even lambasted some of his peers. It was an astonishing series of revelations from the Hammond, Indiana product. Shire entered the business in Columbus and toured the country as the "Professor." He claimed to have several college degrees, and usually had a crooked manager helping him. Late in the 1950s, he partnered with a falsified brother named Ray Shire and won a claim to the World Tag Team Title. He invaded the Bay Area in 1961 and garnered a lot of attention. With sound booking, colorful TV programs, and top talent, Shire drove out his competition, and successfully promoted for the next twenty years. Among the highlights of his business was his popular annual 18-man battle royal.

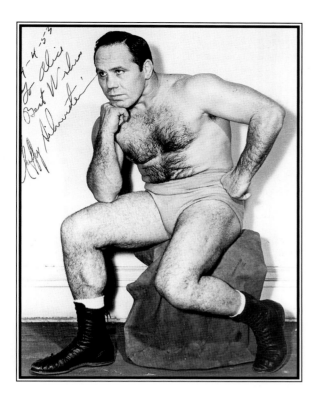

Born:	March 20, 1914
Height:	5'8"
Weight:	220
Real Name:	Ralph Silverstein
Parents:	Benjamin and Pauline Silverstein
High School:	Crane Technical High School (IL)
College:	University of Illinois
College Ach.:	Two-Time Big Ten Wrestling Champion (1935) (175), (1936) (HWT), NCAA Wrestling Title (1935) (175), All-American (1935) (175)
Military:	United States Army (WWII)
Finisher:	Abdominal Stretch
Career Span:	1937–64
Died:	April 5, 1980, Maywood, IL 66 years old

Silverstein, Ruffy

Titles Won:	5
Days as World Champion:	Over 311
Age at first World Title Win:	37
Best Opponents:	Buddy Rogers, Bill Miller, Frankie Talaber

An expert in wrestling fundamentals, straight-laced Ruffy Silverstein won the Illinois State championship in his first pro match, which basically laid the groundwork for a celebrated career. He ultimately won two AWA World Heavyweight Titles in 1951 and '52, and was twice the WLW Television titleholder in Ohio—credentials that added nicely to his Big Ten and NCAA amateur championships. Undefeated for many years, he mostly based his operations out of Columbus and Chicago, where his unparalleled proficiency was featured many times on national television. To many people, Silverstein represented the honest and clean style of pro wrestling, traits that were fast disappearing in a sport demanding chair shots and vast amounts of blood. Incidentally, the moniker "Ruffy" didn't derive from being a rough guy in the ring, but from a pet name his Russian mother had for him when he was a child. He wrestled his final match in 1964, and retired to the Chicago suburbs. He passed away in Maywood, Illinois, on April 5, 1980. He was sixty-six years old.

Born:	March 6, 1898
Height:	5'8"
Weight:	205
Real Name:	Gustave Adolph Sonnenberg
Parents:	Fred and Caroline Sonnenberg
High School:	Marquette High School (MI)
Colleges:	Dartmouth College, University of Detroit
Pro Sports:	National Football League— Columbus Tigers (1923) National Football League— Buffalo All-Americans (1923) National Football League— Detroit Panthers (1925–26) National Football League— Providence Steam Rollers (1927–28, 1930)
Football Ach.:	NFL World Champion (1927–28)
Trained by:	Dan Koloff, John Spellman, Pat McGill, Fred Moran
Career Span:	1928–42
Died:	September 12, 1944, Bethesda, MD 44 years old

Sonnenberg, Gus

Titles Won:	2
Days as World Champion:	718
Age at first World Title Win:	30
Best Opponents:	Ed Lewis, Joe Stecher, Ed Don George
Halls of Fame:	4

The idea of exploiting football players in the world of wrestling was not new when "Dynamite" Gus Sonnenberg entered the business in 1928; but the way he presented himself in the ring revolutionized the concept. Instead of being a lumbering heavyweight with few visible athletic traits, he was quick-moving, crafty, and the originator of the most exciting finisher in sport: the flying tackle. The flying tackle, which saw Sonnenberg hurl himself at his opponent in a spear-like fashion, was extremely flashy, especially when compared to the dull moves usually seen on the pro mat. It was so instrumental to the sport that nearly all wrestlers utilized the move during matches, and it never failed to extract intense audience reaction. The business was rejuvenated by Sonnenberg, almost single-handedly, and on January 4, 1929, he beat Ed

"Strangler" Lewis in two straight falls for the World Heavyweight Title. In that instant, a lightning bolt electrified the entire industry, and Sonnenberg became the most coveted man in wrestling.

A former All-American and coming off a championship season as a member of the Providence Steam Rollers football team, Sonnenberg's lack of size was diminished by his dynamic performance and intensity. His championship reign coincided with a turbulent economic period, but that didn't stop sports fans from being attracted to his unique charisma, and Gus drew outstanding houses throughout the continent. But, with his success came jealousy and controversy. His promotional adversaries branched off and formed their own syndicate, and at one point, Sonnenberg was even attacked by a wrestler representing a rival troupe on the streets of Los Angeles. He reigned as champion until December 1930, then regained the title nine years later, and held it for thirteen more days. During World War II, he served as a physical training instructor at the Great Lakes Naval Center before becoming ill in December 1943. He died of leukemia that following September.

Photo Courtesy of the Collection of Tim Hornbaker

Born:	January 1, 1922
Height:	6'0"
Weight:	225
Real Name:	Eugene Stanley Zygowicz
Family:	Brother of Steve and Loretta Stanlee
Career Span:	1946–65
Died:	September 22, 2005, Redondo Beach, CA 83 years old

Titles Won:	2
Best Opponents:	Antonino Rocca, Buddy Rogers, Lou Thesz

Stanlee, Gene

Gene Stanlee was a popular showman in the early TV era, exhibiting a well-defined body that attracted viewers and a legion of female fans. During World War II, while in the Navy, he performed feats of strength for nearly a million sailors across the Pacific Theater. He was originally from Chicago, the tenth of twelve children, and upon his 1946 discharge from the Navy, he joined the pro wrestling circuit around the Great Lakes area. Stanlee's extraordinary physique was touted in promotions, and he benefited a great deal from joining a major New York booking office that marketed him nationally. Taking the nickname "Mr. America," Stanlee wrestled across the US, and was a top-selling card through the 1950s. He competed less and less, while still technically in his prime, and unceremoniously retired, disappointing his giant block of supporters.

Born:	March 14, 1894
Height:	5'9"
Weight	220
Real Name:	Henry Josef Steinborn
Family:	Father of Henry "Dick" Steinborn
Promoted:	New York City (1948–52) (Manhattan Booking Agency), Orlando, Florida (1953–78)
Career Span:	1922–53
Died:	February 9, 1989, Orlando, FL 95 years old

Titles Won:	None known
Best Opponents:	Ed Lewis, Rudy Dusek, Ray Steele

Steinborn, Milo

Incredible strongman Milo Steinborn was a man who could perform an endless amount of impressive feats. He was a Greco-Roman wrestler and weight-lifter in Europe before landing in the United States after World War I, settling in Philadelphia, where he established three world lifting records. He learned the catch-as-catch-can style from George Bothner and wrestled all of the greats of the era, including Ed "Strangler" Lewis and Jim Londos. He returned to Europe for a tour in 1938–39, and battled the likes of Henri DeGlane, Yvon Robert, and Felix Miquet. Some of his bouts were in the Greco-Roman style. He won a wrestling tournament in Philadelphia in 1944, defeating Michele Leone in the finals. After co-owning part of the New York booking office in the late 1940s and early '50s, he moved to Orlando, Florida, and purchased the promotional rights from Cowboy Luttrall for $1,000. He promoted Orlando from 1953 to '78, and also operated a famous gymnasium at 2371 Orange Street. He died in 1989, at ninety-five years of age.

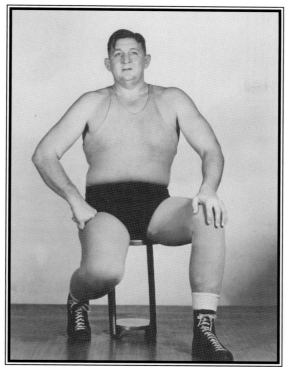

Born:	March 7, 1912
Height:	6'3"
Weight:	300
Real Name:	Robert Otis Stewart
Parents:	John and Susie Stewart
Identities:	Bob Weatherly, Hercules Weatherly, Robert Ashby
Career Span:	1932–54
Died:	October 16, 1970, Austell, GA 58 years old

Titles Won:	1
Days as World Champion:	Around 10
Age at first World Title Win:	26
Best Opponents:	Jim Londos, Yvon Robert, Sandor Szabo

Stewart, Bobby

Throughout his career, the massive Bobby Stewart presented problems for his opponents, and if he didn't break every rule known to mankind during matches, he most certainly tried. He was despised by fans, yet his box office value, especially as the masked Golden Terror, was exceptionally high. Born in Stevenson, Alabama, Stewart lived a mysterious life, and newspaper writers always had trouble accurately reporting on him. In fact, he had a dozen or so hometowns and an abundance of aliases. Little did wrestling fans know that his trouble-making was as legitimate outside the ring as it was inside. His rap sheet was several pages long and he was wanted by the FBI at least two separate times. He also spent time in federal prison from 1956 to 1958 for the transfer of forged checks. Beyond that, there were claims that Stewart's outrageous behavior had gotten him blackballed by promoters. These issues, of course, were years after his superstar status faded. At his height, as the Terror, he briefly held the World championship in Baltimore, and was a constant main event attraction all across North America.

FRANK
STOJACK

Born:	February 11, 1912
Height:	5'10"
Weight:	180
Real Name:	Frank Nickolas Stojack
High School:	Lincoln High School (WA)
College:	Washington State University
Finisher:	Airplane Spin
Career Span:	1935–58
Died:	August 30, 1987, Fox Island, WA 75 years old

Titles Won:	12
Days as World LHW Champion:	At least 1,605
Age at first World LHW Title Win:	41
Best Opponents:	Andy Tremaine, Gypsy Joe, Danny McShain
Halls of Fame:	1

Stojack, Frank

Pacific Northwest luminary Frank Stojack was a tremendous athlete. He wrestled and played football in college, then turning pro in both sports in 1935, breaking into the wrestling business under Charles York in Spokane. The Brooklyn Dodgers signed Stojack in August 1935 and he played twenty-three games over two seasons. Upon returning to the Tacoma region, he continued his wrestling career and played semi-pro football in the Northwest Football League for the Tacoma Columbias (1939) and the Seattle Aero Mechanics (1941). He steadily held the Pacific Coast Junior Heavyweight Title and had big matches against the best in the region. On August 10, 1953, he beat Gypsy Joe for the World Light Heavyweight Title and was recognized by the National Wrestling Alliance, retiring as champion. He served as a Tacoma City Councilman, Tacoma Mayor, Pierce County Sheriff, and Commissioner of the Washington State Athletic Commission between 1950 and 1962.

Born:	October 16, 1906
Height:	6'1"
Weight:	240
Real Name:	Nils Filip Olofsson
Parents:	Alfred and Karolina Olofsson
Trained by:	Charles Hanson
Identities:	Phil Olson, Olaf Swenson
Nickname:	Popeye
Career Span:	1933–52
Died:	February 9, 1974, Myton, UT 67 years old

Titles Won:	At least 2
Days as World Champion:	6
Age at first World Title Win:	37
Best Opponents:	Buddy Rogers, Ed Lewis, Orville Brown
Movies:	1

Swedish Angel, The

On the heels of the sensational rise of "The French Angel," Maurice Tillet, a journeyman worker with unique facial features, was given a second "life" in wrestling. Promoter Jack Pfefer reinvented Olaf Swenson to be "The Swedish Angel," and the latter was a good box office attraction from coast-to-coast during the 1940s. He was a finalist in a championship tournament in Los Angeles in 1942, but was defeated by Rube Wright in the finals. On December 3, 1943, he beat Orville Brown for the Midwest Wrestling Association World Heavyweight championship in Kansas City, but lost it back to Brown less than a week later. In 1946, he conquered the popular Everette Marshall in Denver for the Rocky Mountain championship. Later in the decade, he became a matchmaker in Utah, and then bought out Jim Downing for the local promotion. The Angel ran the territory until December 1952, when he sold the business to Dave Reynolds. He passed away in 1974 at the age of sixty-seven.

Born:	January 4, 1906
Height:	6'1"
Weight:	225
Real Name:	Sandor Varga Szabo
Wife:	Lillian Szabo
Finisher:	Giant Swing
Career Span:	1930–61
Died:	October 13, 1966, Los Angeles, CA 60 years old

Titles Won:	43
Days as World Champion:	Around 1,773, including overlapping reigns
Age at first World Title Win:	35
Best Opponents:	Jim Londos, Bill Longson, Yvon Robert
Halls of Fame:	2

Szabo, Sandor

Hungarian Sandor Szabo, a multi-time world heavyweight champion, was a dexterous grappler, successful in drawing heat from audiences as well as applause. In the ring, he combined speed with smarts, and was a compelling box office attraction throughout his long career. Szabo was a preeminent superstar all over North America, particularly during World War II, when he reigned as the world champion of both the NWA and AWA, plus in the realms of several independent state commissions. Born in Kassa, Czechoslovakia, he came to the US after a successful amateur career as a Greco-Roman wrestler, and was still learning the American catch-as-catch-can trade when he debuted in 1930. On the northeastern circuit, he was an appealing young athlete and challenged Jim Londos for the heavyweight crown on a number of occasions. While he was making headway in New York, Szabo's real taste of fame and glory came in Northern California, where in 1937, he won the first of thirteen Pacific Coast Heavyweight championships.

The biggest win of Szabo's career occurred on June 5, 1941 in St. Louis when he beat Bronko Nagurski for the National Wrestling Association World Heavyweight Title. He held the belt until losing a February 1942 match to Bill Longson. In March 1944, he conquered The Golden Terror in Boston to win the "Duration" World Title, which was implemented after the rightful champion, Steve Casey, went off to serve in the Army. Later that year, he beat Yvon Robert to strengthen his claim and remained champion until suffering a loss to Casey on April 4, 1945. Szabo was able to win a rematch from Casey on April 25, 1945, and won the AWA World Title, but lost it to Frank Sexton the following week. In addition, Szabo was backed as champion in Minnesota four times between 1944 and 1948. A resident of Los Angeles, Szabo was an important figure in the local office for many years, training young grapplers, booking, and refereeing matches. Outside of the ring, Szabo was a talented swimmer and was well-liked and respected by his peers.

Born:	July 17, 1912
Height:	5'11"
Weight:	215
Parents:	Louis and Elizabeth Talaber
High School:	Lane Tech High School (IL)
Trained by:	Lou Talaber
Career Span:	1936–64
Died:	September 7, 1994, Frankfort, IL 82 years old

Titles Won:	20
Best Opponents:	Buddy Rogers, Don Eagle, Bill Miller

Talaber, Frankie

During the astronomical boom period created by the television medium in the early 1950s, Frankie Talaber was a leading star in the Columbus, Ohio, territory and an influential matchmaker. A product of Chicago, Frankie learned all the fundamentals from his father, Lou, who was a former middleweight champion, and captured the Central AAU wrestling title as an amateur. He elevated his showmanship and went pro in 1936. Four years later, he won a claim to the World Junior Heavyweight crown in Detroit, and then the following year, started a run in Ohio by winning the first of ten MWA World Junior championships. He was also a multiple-time light heavyweight titleholder. In addition to his work as a matchmaker, Talaber was an influential trainer in Al Haft's famous Columbus gymnasium and was a longtime favorite of crowds throughout the region. Frequently featured on television, Frankie feuded heavily with Buddy Rogers, Don Eagle, Great Mephisto, Oyama Kato, and Roy Shire, and operated a restaurant in downtown Columbus, where many wrestlers spent their free time. Talaber retired from the ring in 1964.

Born:	April 24, 1916
Height:	6'1"
Weight:	235
Real Name:	Aloysius Martin Thesz
Parents:	Martin and Katherine Thesz
Finisher:	Thesz Press, STF
Trained:	Mark Fleming
Career Span:	1934–90
Died:	April 28, 2002, Orlando, FL 86 years old

Titles Won:	26
Days as World Champion:	5,591 (excluding TWWA claim)
Age at first World Title Win:	21
Best Opponents:	Bill Longson, Verne Gagne, Buddy Rogers
Halls of Fame:	9

Thesz, Lou

As the National Wrestling Alliance unified promoters and booking offices in the late 1940s and into the early 1950s, the sport was facing many major changes. Television was providing a unique outlet for wrestling personalities, giving Gorgeous George and other colorful grapplers a platform to go through their motions of performance. On the other end of the spectrum, representing the NWA and the wrestling business as a whole was a dignified and straight-laced heavyweight champion named Lou Thesz. Thesz was the equivalent to the number one athlete in any other sport, called the "Babe Ruth of Wrestling" by one sportswriter, and heroically carried the weight of the NWA on his back. By refusing to play into the regular stereotypes that accompanied pro wrestling, Thesz commanded and received respect. Thus, the business benefited from having a champion of his caliber. With him, there was reason to believe that the best man was truly the world titleholder.

During Thesz's career, maintaining the illusion of wrestling's realness was the top priority for everyone involved. Thesz personally preserved that with his seriousness and legitimacy. Fans could plainly see it, writers understood it, and promoters coveted it. With all his success, the path to wrestling immortality wasn't cut in stone for Thesz. Over a career lasting fifty-six years, he earned everything that has been said about him. He was born in the Austrian community of Banat, Michigan, the son of hardworking parents, and grew up in St. Louis. Having attained the bug for wrestling from his father, Martin, who'd wrestled Greco-Roman in his youth, Lou worked out in local gymnasiums and became adept to the catch-as-catch-can style. His size and strength stood out on the semi-pro circuit in East St. Louis, and with formal training under Joe Sanderson and George Tragos, he was headed for bigger and better things.

Thesz's discipline for the fundamentals was ungodly. Instead of fixating on being the best grimacing heel, he worked on shooting and hooking opponents, training as if he was going to participate in square matches instead of exhibitions. He impressed promoters in the Central States before going out to San Francisco, where he was schooled by Ad Santel, who furthered his development measurably. By 1937, Thesz, after only three years in the business, was ready for a substantial push by his hometown promoter, Tom Packs, and on December 29, he beat Everette Marshall for the World Title. Rather than getting a real shot to display his talents as champion, Thesz was only a temporarily titleholder, losing the heavyweight crown to Steve Casey on February 11, 1938 in Boston. A victim of the sport's politics, he was quickly learning how to avoid being pushed around by promoters behind-the-scenes. He didn't want to be a pawn of greedy businessmen and wanted more control in the direction of his career.

On February 23, 1939, he returned to the heavyweight throne, topping Hall of Fame footballer Bronko Nagurski for the National Wrestling Association World Title in Houston. He reigned through June, and that following year, he won the Montreal version of the World championship. During the war, he worked as a shipbuilder before entering the Army in January 1945 and wrestled when he could, maintaining his impeccable conditioning. He regained the NWA World Title in 1947, then again in 1948, but his real power came from ownership in the valuable St. Louis office, which came when Packs retired in June 1948. Thesz also assumed control of the NWA championship, allowing him to dictate who was going to hold it and for how long. He topped Bill Longson on July 20, 1948 for the belt, and settled in as the king, a role he'd play for the next eight years. In November 1949, the National Wrestling Alliance put their recognition behind him, giving Thesz the strongest claim to the championship in the world.

Thesz traveled extensively across a well-defined thirty-plus territory landscape and defined what it meant to be a reputable and esteemed titleholder. Demonstrating amazing stamina, he traversed the United States, Canada, Mexico, Cuba, and Hawaii, and successfully defended his title against every notable wrestler in the business. Controversial matches with Leo Nomellini and Edouard Carpentier purposely tainted his title run, executed to make money at the box office, but Thesz remained effective as a draw. Thesz ultimately lost the NWA Title to Dick Hutton on November 14, 1957, ending his lengthy run, and, having already sold out of St. Louis, was ready to control his own destiny as an independent grappler. By 1963, with the membership of the National Wrestling Alliance falling apart, there was a desperate need for stability in the wrestling ranks. The influential St. Louis booker Sam Muchnick coordinated Thesz's return to the throne, and on January 24, 1963 in Toronto, Lou beat Buddy Rogers for the NWA belt, his sixth world title.

Thesz was responsible for helping the NWA return to prominence between 1963 and 1966, and the organization's footing was much more stable when he lost the championship to Gene Kiniski on January 7, 1966 than when he started his run. In the years that followed, he maintained a full-time schedule for some years before slowly scaling back. Although he was getting older, his name recognition still sold tickets, and he was unwilling to give up the sport he loved. Thesz had his final match in Japan on December 26, 1990 against his protégé, Masa Chono. Chono won with an STF, a move Thesz made famous over the years. Over the course of his long career, he traveled an estimated sixteen million miles across the globe and participated in upwards of 6,000 matches. He was a heavyweight champion at twenty-one years of age and lastly, at sixty-two. Thesz's legacy as a wrestler and as an emissary for the sport left an indelible mark, and his influence is still being felt in the sport today.

In 2016, he was inducted into the WWE Hall of Fame as part of the inaugural "Legacy" class.

Born:	October 23, 1903
Height:	5'9"
Weight:	275
Real Name:	Maurice Marie Joseph Tillet
Military:	French Navy
Career Span:	1937–54
Died:	August 4, 1954, Chicago, IL 50 years old

Titles Won:	3
Days as World Champion:	745
Age at first World Title Win:	36
Best Opponents:	Steve Casey, Bill Longson, Yvon Robert
Halls of Fame:	1

Tillet, Maurice

Of all the sports, only in the world of professional wrestling can a man with an advance billing of the "Ugliest Man on Earth" become a top gate attraction and superstar. Additionally, Maurice Tillet was called grotesque, bizarre, and a monster, which were endearing selling points to the wrestling crowd. Tillet was said to be the closest scientists had found to a Neanderthal, possessing a freakish looking head and powerfully built body. The son of French parents, Tillet was born in St. Petersburg, Russia, and was discovered in Singapore by a well-traveled Lithuanian wrestler named Karl Pojello around 1937. Pojello and Tillet immediately bonded and traveled to France, where the latter launched a successful run of 180 victories. Featured by *Life Magazine* and other mainstream press, Tillet was fast becoming wrestling's hottest commodity. People wanted to see his unique appearance in person and they surely weren't disappointed.

Keenly intelligent and with Pojello there to handle unscrupulous promoters, Tillet wasn't robbed regularly as other attractions like Primo Carnera and Antonino Rocca were. He was smartly pushed to the apex of Bowser's AWA, winning the heavyweight title from Steve Casey on May 13, 1940 and holding the title for two years. In that time, he conquered the likes of Bobby Managoff, Frank Sexton, Gus Sonnenberg, Ed "Strangler" Lewis, and many others who were considered the best in the business. Tillet used his amazing strength and signature bearhug to put opponents out, and his sound in-ring performance marginalized the freak factor as his only selling point to a certain degree. For two weeks in 1944, he reigned a second time as AWA World Champion after defeating Casey in San Francisco. Tillet, the "French Angel," spawned a host of other "Angels," that would roam the wrestling landscape, but none were as distinct as the original. He passed away only hours after his longtime friend, Pojello, died, with his grief obviously overcoming him.

Born:	July 25, 1922
Height:	6'1"
Weight:	230
Parents:	Alfonso and Pomposa Torres
Trained by:	Benny Ginsberg
Career Span:	1946–68
Died:	September 10, 2007, Calgary, Alberta 85 years old

Titles Won:	42
Days as World Champion:	1,442
Age at first World Title Win:	24
Best Opponents:	Fred Blassie, Lou Thesz, Gene Kiniski
Halls of Fame:	2

Torres, Enrique

In 1946, booker Johnny Doyle touted young Enrique Torres as the greatest Mexican grappler since Vincent Lopez, and Torres quickly lived up to the hype. Within months of his pro debut, he won the local World Heavyweight Championship on December 11, 1946, from George Becker in Los Angeles. He perpetuated a clean style in the ring, using dropkicks and flying maneuvers, and was extremely popular wherever he traveled. Born in Santa Ana, California, Torres was the oldest of six children, and his two younger brothers, Ramon and Alberto, also became grapplers. In addition to his nearly four-year reign as World Champion in Los Angeles, where he held the Pacific Coast Heavyweight Title, he was a part of a number of tag team championships in San Francisco and Georgia. The Torres Brothers, in various combinations of the trio, were highly successful all over North America as well. Enrique wrestled actively through 1968, when he retired from the business. He later settled in Calgary, Alberta, where he passed away on September 10, 2007.

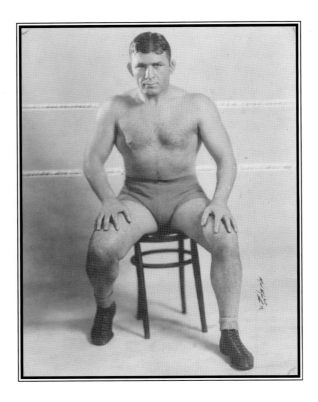

Born:	March 14, 1897
Height:	5'9"
Weight:	215
Parents:	William and Stavroula Tragos
Amateur Ach.:	National AAU Title (1919) (158), Indiana State AAU Title (1921) (175)
Trained by:	George Pinneo
Identities:	George Kondylis
Career Span:	1922–50
Died:	September 5, 1955, St. Louis, MO 58 years old

Titles Won:	1
Best Opponents:	Ed Lewis, Ray Steele, Dick Shikat

Tragos, George

Eighty years ago, it was quite common for promoters to covet genuine wrestling "shooters" to humble the overconfident, punish the unruly, and test the greenhorns who wanted in to the business. In St. Louis, the promoter utilized the expertise of George Tragos, a world-class catch-as-catch-can wrestler, and Tragos not only acted as a training partner for every big name that entered the city, but tutored up-and-comers like Lou Thesz and Fred Blassie. With family in Chicago, Tragos migrated from Greece in 1910, and was a pivotal member of the Gary, Indiana, YMCA, winning several AAU honors. He was also affiliated with the 1920 Greek Olympic wrestling team, although he didn't place. Settling in Missouri around 1922, he became a grappling coach at the University of Missouri at Columbia and began wrestling pro, winning the state heavyweight championship. Even though he weighed between 165 and 175 pounds, Tragos beat larger foes with regularity, and was known for his staunch training discipline. He wrestled out of St. Louis most of his career, but occasionally toured the east. Today, in memory of his varied contributions to the sport, an Iowa wrestling Hall of Fame bears his name alongside his most famous student, Lou Thesz.

Born:	September 19, 1928
Height:	6'2"
Weight:	235
Real Name:	John Theodore Wisniski
Family:	Father of Greg Valentine
Wife:	Sharon Valentine
High School:	Tahoma High School (WA)
Identities:	Jimmy Valentine, Rocky Valentine, The Big O
Nickname:	The Blond Bombshell, Honest, The Blond Jet
Finisher:	Backbreaker
Career Span:	1947–75
Died:	April 24, 2001, Near River Oaks, TX 72 years old

Valentine, Johnny

Titles Won:	64
Days as World Champion:	Over 140
Age at first World Title Win:	34
Best Opponents:	Lou Thesz, Buddy Rogers, Killer Kowalski
Halls of Fame:	5

As the television era courted an avalanche of colorful pretenders in the late 1940s, pro wrestling was running out of hard-nosed athletes who thought, behaved, and performed like wrestlers of old. Johnny Valentine filled the growing void, entering the sport with the knowledge and physicality of a veteran. Taught the traditional ways of the mat by two aging former champions, Stanislaus and Wladek Zbyszko, he was a stark contrast to those wrestlers who placed an emphasis on the dramatic side of the profession. A product of a broken Hobart, Washington home, Valentine began his training as a teenager and quickly absorbed the fundamentals. He also toughened his mind and body to not only dish out punishment, but to be able to take it. In 1947, he went to South America to make his professional debut, and traveled throughout Argentina, the Caribbean, and Florida. When he was ready, he returned to the US, quickly becoming a valuable box office commodity, and won regional championships nearly everywhere he went.

Able to wrestle technically and brawl until the last man was standing, Valentine had bloody feuds with Wahoo McDaniel, Great Malenko, and The Sheik that are embedded in wrestling lore. Never needing a gimmick to get over, he propelled himself into the top tier through hard work and dedication to the sport. Fans understood that when Valentine was coming to town, regardless of his opponent, they were going to get a sincere effort, sometimes in both science and brutality. He won the NWF World Heavyweight Title twice as well as the Montreal World crown. In the northeast, he teamed with Buddy Rogers, Bob Ellis, and Antonio Pugliese to capture the US Tag Team Title. He held three different versions of the US Heavyweight

Title, the Texas championship seven times, and the Missouri State belt. Valentine's career came to an abrupt end in October 1975, when he was involved in a plane crash in North Carolina. At the time, he was still acknowledged as one of the toughest wrestlers in the world.

Born:	January 10, 1919
Height:	5'11"
Weight:	210
Real Name:	William Varga
Family:	Son of "Count" Joseph Varga
Wife:	Rosabelle Varga
High School:	Hollywood High School (CA)
Finisher:	Abdominal Stretch
Career Span:	1940–67
Died:	January 11, 2013, Burbank, CA 94 years old

Titles Won:	9
Best Opponents:	Red Berry, Danny McShain, Joe Scarpello
Movies:	12
TV Appearances:	Over 10

Varga, Billy

   Lauded by fans everywhere for his clean and scientific style, "Count" Billy Varga was a second-generation grappler originally from Cleveland, but spent most of his pro career wrestling in the Southern California area. His father, Joe, began teaching him the art of catch-as-catch-can grappling when he was just five years old. Billy spent a number of years as an amateur, then turning professional in 1940. On December 1, 1941, he won the World Light Heavyweight Title from Red Berry in Hollywood, and held it for three weeks. He captured it again two years later and, in 1945, he won the World Junior belt in Columbus, Ohio. Varga was one of the most popular wrestlers in the business and held the American championship for upwards of ten years, retiring as champion in the late 1960s. He appeared as the ring announcer in the classic film *Raging Bull* in 1980. Billy passed away a day after his ninety-fourth birthday on January 11, 2013, in Burbank, California.

Born:	April 22, 1912
Height:	6'1"
Weight:	225
Real Name:	Raymond Henry Villmer
Parents:	Fred and Rose Villmer
Military:	United States Navy (WWII)
Finisher:	Back Drop, Jackknife
Career Span:	1935–65
Died:	January 9, 2005, Tallahassee, FL 92 years old

Titles Won:	11
Best Opponents:	Buddy Rogers, Bill Longson, Lou Thesz

Villmer, Ray

Ray Villmer grew up in De Soto, Missouri, but wrestled out of St. Louis. The son of a railroad switchman, Ray gave up on furthering his education after attending St. Francis de Sales school, and worked as a freight handler in a warehouse. He played baseball and, in working to keep in condition during the winter, began training as a wrestler under John Anderson. He also worked out with professionals Ray Steele and Ed "Strangler" Lewis at St. Louis's famed Business Men's Gym. He turned pro himself in 1935 and, by the early 1940s, was a challenger to the World Heavyweight Title. Always ready to brawl, Villmer used his athleticism to prevail in matches throughout the territorial system. In describing him, sportswriter Robert Morrison, in 1941, wrote: "Villmer is a thick-necked, large-featured specimen of muscular development," and noted that he was "quite unassuming in manner." Villmer wrestled from coast to coast and won a variety of regional honors, including the Central States, Southern, and Florida Heavyweight Titles. Villmer retired to Florida, ending his three-decade career, and passed away in 2005.

Photo Courtesy of the Pfefer Collection, Department of Special Collections, University of Notre Dame

Born:	August 12, 1912
Height:	5'10 ½"
Weight:	230
Real Name:	Edward Ebner Virag
Wife:	Marguerite Virag
Military:	United States Army (1943–45)
Finisher:	Full Nelson Suplex, Halsch Lock
Career Span:	1936–51
Died:	October 20, 1951, near Kozani, Greece 39 years old

Titles Won:	2
Days as World Champion:	1,482
Age at first World Title Win:	29
Best Opponents:	Roy Dunn, Lou Thesz, Everette Marshall

Virag, Ed

Born in Budapest, Hungary, Ed Virag was an amateur wrestler of note, and placed first in the 1935 European championships in the freestyle division. He competed as a light heavyweight in the 1936 Olympics, but did not place. Turning professional soon thereafter, Virag ventured to the United States, became a citizen, and married a girl from Minnesota. During the 1940s, he scored victories over many well-known wrestlers, including ex-champions Ed "Strangler" Lewis, Wladek Zbyszko, and Everette Marshall. On April 27, 1942, he defeated Roy Dunn for a claim to the regional National Wrestling Alliance World Heavyweight championship, and traded the belt with John Grandovich later in the year. During World War II, Virag served in the army and beat Fred Devine—the "Duration" titleholder—after his discharge in 1945. He would end up losing his NWA Title in a unification match against Orville Brown in November 1946. Able to speak six different languages, Virag was killed in an auto wreck while traveling en route to Athens, Greece, in 1951. He was buried in a Protestant Cemetery at Salonikia.

Born:	June 25, 1915
Height:	6'1"
Weight:	230
Real Name:	William John Potts
Parents:	John and Alice Potts
Family:	Father of Phillip Watson (Billy Watson Jr.)
Trained by:	Phil Lawson
Finisher:	Irish Whip, Canadian Avalanche
Career Span:	1936–71
Died:	February 4, 1990, Orlando, FL 74 years old

Titles Won:	33
Days as World Champion:	302
Age at first World Title Win:	31
Best Opponents:	Lou Thesz, Bill Longson, Yvon Robert
Halls of Fame:	3

Watson, Billy

Wrestling legend "Whipper" Billy Watson was a hero of immense proportions in Ontario and throughout most of Canada. From the moment he debuted in Toronto on October 3, 1940 until his last bout there on November 28, 1971, he always gave fans something to cheer about, with his matches usually full of intense drama and colorful athleticism. The East York product initially gained experience while in England, and by the time of his first match in Toronto, he was ready to set the wrestling world ablaze. Claiming the Canadian and British Empire championships at different times, Watson became the centerpiece of Toronto's grappling scene, and promoter Frank Tunney specifically brought in heel after heel to declare war on him—maintaining his status as the hottest ticket in town. Watson made history when, on February 21, 1947, he beat "Wild" Bill Longson for the National Wrestling Association World Heavyweight Title. He held the belt through April 25, when he lost the prize to the great Lou Thesz.

Some years later, on March 15, 1956, he ended the seven-plus year reign of Thesz as National Wrestling Alliance World Champion when ex-boxing champion Jack Dempsey as special guest referee counted the latter out after more than thirty minutes and declared Watson the new king. While an amazing victory for Watson, Thesz was able to regain the title in November. In addition to his star qualities on the mat, he was a successful businessman, selling branded items featuring his name, and was invested in the Toronto and St. Louis promotions, including briefly in Seattle. On November 30, 1971, he was forced to retire from the ring after being hit by a car.

During his life, he dabbled in politics and was gracious with his time when it came to charities. He was not the kind of guy to walk by a child asking for an autograph, and if there were dozens of kids, he wouldn't leave until he'd signed them all. Watson's legacy goes well beyond the wrestling ring, and those who were touched by his kindness still remember him fondly today.

Photo Courtesy of Scott Teal/Crowbar Press

Born:	December 19, 1902
Height:	5'10"
Weight:	185
Real Name:	Roy Edward Welch
Parents:	Edwin and Birdie Welch
Trained by:	Edwin Welch, Cal Farley, Dutch Mantell
Family:	Brother of Herb, Lester, and Jack Welch
Career Span:	1929–59
Died:	September 27, 1977, Trenton, TN 74 years old

Titles Won:	At least 6
Best Opponents:	Joe Gunther, Ike Chacoma, Tex Riley

Welch, Roy

A skilled athlete, animal handler, matchmaker, and promoter, Roy Welch wore many hats in the world of wrestling during a career that lasted over forty years. Originally from Sallisaw, Oklahoma, he was the oldest of four wrestling brothers and first gained fame as a light heavyweight in Oklahoma and Texas during the early 1930s. He toured many territories as the trainer of Ginger, a 350-pound wrestling bear, and claimed titles in both the light heavyweight and junior heavyweight divisions. Along with business partner Nick Gulas, Welch controlled wrestling in over three dozen cities and booked a couple hundred grapplers at a time between the 1940s and his death in 1977. His son Buddy Fuller and grandsons Robert and Ron Fuller also wrestled professionally.

Born:	July 27, 1910
Height:	6'2"
Weight:	230
Real Name:	Marvin Louis Westenberg
Parents:	August and Louise Westenberg
High School:	Lincoln High School (WA)
College:	University of Washington
Career Span:	1930–50
Died:	August 20, 1978, Pierce County, WA 68 years old

Titles Won:	At least 1
Days as World Champion:	14
Age at first World Title Win:	28
Best Opponents:	Steve Casey, Yvon Robert, Ed Don George

Westenberg, Marvin

Westenberg was a twenty-year wrestling veteran, a heavyweight championship claimant, and a minority owner of a major promotion during his career. Originally from Tacoma, Westenberg broke into the sport in early 1930, and found a strong mentor in Paul Bowser of Boston, where he first appeared in 1932. Under the guise of "The Shadow" and wearing a mask, he conquered the unbeatable Steve "Crusher" Casey on March 2, 1939, and won the AWA World Heavyweight Title—becoming the first masked wrestler to hold such a prestigious title. His reign only lasted two weeks, when he lost a rematch to Casey. For a time during his career, Westenberg was part owner of the Boston wrestling office, the location of his most important matches. In 1950, he suffered a serious head injury during a bout that prematurely and unfortunately ended his time on the mat. He returned to his native Washington and passed away in 1978, at sixty-eight years of age.

Born:	November 6, 1907
Height:	6'2"
Weight:	265
Real Name:	Reuben Haz Wright
Family:	Brother of Jim Wright
Career Span:	1932–61
Died:	November 9, 1983, Klamath County, OR 76 years old

Titles Won:	At least 2
Days as World Champion:	Unknown
Age at first World Title Win:	34
Best Opponents:	Ed Lewis, Everette Marshall, Sandor Szabo
Halls of Fame:	1

Wright, Rube

Big Rube Wright didn't follow in his father's footsteps by joining the clergy, but instead spent his time as a young man at the Hollywood Athletic Club. He was from Brown County, Texas, but grew up in Southern California and debuted after four years of amateur wrestling in 1932. A New Jersey sportswriter wrote that Wright looked "more like a matinee idol than a wrestler," but his appearance was deceiving. Rube was a legitimate tough guy and was unafraid to mix it up in the ring, the gym, or on the streets. In 1941, though, he battled Ruffy Silverstein in what was alleged to be a shoot match in St. Louis, and Rube was disqualified in 13:28 after he was found "absolutely defenseless" against the skill of his opponent. The next year, he won an international tournament in Los Angeles and a claim to the World Heavyweight Title, backed by Jack Pfefer. Wright also spent a number of years as wildman "Lu Kim," a wrestler claiming Manchuria as his homeland. Mostly acknowledged as a journeyman, he retired from the mat in 1961, and died in 1983.

Photo Courtesy of the Pfefer Collection, Department of Special Collections, University of Notre Dame

Born:	March 10, 1898
Height:	5'11"
Weight:	225
Real Name:	Lee Arlo Wykoff
Parents:	Charles and Ethel Wykoff
College Ach.:	All-Kansas Football Honors (1920, 1922–23)
Pro Sports:	National Football League—St. Louis All-Stars (1923)
Identities:	Big Bad Wolf (Masked)
Finisher:	Stepover toehold
Career Span:	1925–47
Died:	April 30, 1974, Kansas City, KS 76 years old

Titles Won:	5
Days as World Champion:	Around 282
Age at first World Title Win:	43
Best Opponents:	Ed Lewis, Orville Brown, Everette Marshall

Wykoff, Lee

A scientifically skilled grappler from Osborne, Kansas, Wykoff made his mark from coast to coast and was legitimately feared for his exceptional shooting skills. He attended Washburn College in Topeka, where he earned a wide amount of respect for his athletic prowess on the football field. In the years that followed, he built his strength while working for the Missouri Pacific Railroad, and by 1926, he was traveling around the Central States as a professional wrestler. Finding that it was valuable to work the role of a heel during matches, Wykoff displayed rough tactics during tours of the east, and was a policeman for champion Everette Marshall in 1936. On August 13 of that year, he faced Ed Lewis in an infamous shoot match in New York. Their affair was marred by lengthy rest holds and tiresome inactivity and ended in a draw when both were counted out after more than two hours. In 1940, he won an international tournament in Los Angeles, and held claims to the World Title in the Kansas City region prior to retiring in 1947.

Born:	March 12, 1923
Height:	5'6"
Weight:	145
Real Name:	Johnnie Mae Young
Parents:	John and Lillian Young
High School:	Sand Springs High School (OK)
Trained by:	Billy Wolfe
Career Span:	1941–2010
Died:	January 14, 2014, Columbia, SC 90 years old

Titles Won:	4
Best Opponents:	Mildred Burke, June Byers, Nell Stewart
Halls of Fame:	2

Young, Mae

A pioneering, Hall of Fame wrestler, Mae Young entertained audiences from 1941 until her last appearance on WWE-TV in 2013. To put that into perspective, she began grappling professionally prior to the attack on Pearl Harbor, and wrestled in nine different decades. From the small town of Wekiwa, just west of Tulsa, Oklahoma, Young was the last of seven siblings, the daughter of a carpenter, and was taught how to wrestle by her brothers. She grappled on the boys' team in high school and made the acquaintance of women's wrestling impresario Billy Wolfe. Mae toured the world and was one of the toughest female grapplers in the business. She even demonstrated her indomitable spirit and toughness, at seventy-seven, when she was put through a table by the Dudley Boys on *Raw*, and partook in wild storylines—like giving birth to a hand—all for the profession she loved. In celebration of her ninetieth birthday, Mae appeared on *Raw* in March 2013, and was presented with a special Divas championship belt in honor of her legendary career. She passed away on January 14, 2014, leaving fans to remember her great contributions to the sport.

Born:	April 22, 1916
Height:	6'1"
Weight:	275
Real Name:	Erick Holmback
College:	Washington State University
Finisher:	Backbreaker
Career Span:	1946–65
Died:	January 16, 1965, Bartow County, GA 48 years old

Titles Won:	6	
Days as World Champion:	266	
Age at first World Title Win:	33	
Best Opponents:		Killer Kowalski, Verne Gagne, Lou Thesz

Yukon Eric

Holmback was born in Monroe, Washington. He was the son of a logger and excelled in football as an adolescent, and spent much of his time weightlifting. Following a stint in the Army during World War II, he decided to become a wrestler and went pro. With an astonishing chest expansion measuring upward of 65 inches, he was initially billed as "The Chest," but matchmaker Al Mayer dubbed him "Yukon Eric," a lumberman from Alaska. In possession of a powerful bearhug, Eric toured extensively, winning the Montreal World Title over Bobby Managoff in 1950. On October 15, 1952, he suffered the loss of part of his cauliflower ear during a match with Killer Kowalski at the Montreal forum. He was rushed to the hospital and had surgery to repair the damage, and the event only served to strengthen their enduring feud. In Jacksonville on January 24, 1963, he teamed up with Don Curtis to win the World Tag Team Title from the Kangaroos. Eric was a popular superstar wherever he appeared, and the audience always left knowing they'd gotten their money's worth.

Born:	February 28, 1908
Height:	6'0"
Weight:	230
Real Name:	Theodore Vetoyanis
Parents:	Gust and Demitra Vetoyanis
Wife:	Babe Didrikson Zaharias
Trained by:	Milo Steinborn
Career Span:	1929-48
Died:	May 22, 1984, Tampa, FL 76 years old

Titles Won:	Claimed at least 2
Best Opponents:	Jim Londos, Ray Steele, Joe Stecher
Halls of Fame:	1

Zaharias, George

A product of Pueblo, Colorado, Zaharias was often known as a "bad guy" in the ring; but outside of the squared circle, he was very personable and popular among his peers. Today, people tend to associate the name "Zaharias" with the world renowned golfer, Mildred "Babe" Didrikson, who was George's wife from 1938 until her death in 1956. George and his two brothers, Chris and Tom and his nephew, Babe, were collectively known as the "Cripple Creek Terrors," and created chaos throughout the wrestling world. In addition to claiming the Colorado State Title, he was deemed the local successor to World Heavyweight Champion Danno O'Mahoney in January 1936 by a group of cynical sportswriters. He promoted the Olympic Auditorium in Los Angeles and in Denver before leaving wrestling for the greener pastures of golf courses throughout the globe.

III. Heroes and Villains Wage War in the Sacred Territories

Pro Debut Between 1951 and 1975

Spurred on by the exposure of television, professional wrestling's esteem increased measurably in the early 1950s, and many viewers were fascinated by the colorfulness of its performers. The creation and expansion of the monopolistic National Wrestling Alliance helped streamline championships and made it easy for wrestlers to travel within its huge web of territories. Later in the decade, the Department of Justice found the NWA's ruthless actions with regard to outsiders to be illegal, and brought the hammer down—stopping short, though, of forcing the coalition of promoters to break up. The AWA and WWWF were established in the years that followed, and with the NWA, were collectively known as the "Big Three." The trio of organizations were the most noteworthy in the business for the next couple of decades.

The sport benefited greatly from a stream of credible amateurs who decided to turn pro. Former NCAA champions Verne Gagne, Dick Hutton, and Danny Hodge each made an impact soon after their debuts, and the likes of Jack Brisco followed in the mid-1960s. To the public, these individuals were shining examples of the genuine athletic marvels performing on a nightly basis around the country—and not all wrestlers were beastly figures with little to no legitimate sports ability. The varied gimmicks, particularly the behemoths, did make things lively and sometimes the crazier the worker, the more money it drew. For example, the maniacal Sheik displayed his riotous behavior across the globe and fans knew that when he was on the card, plenty of mayhem was to be expected. A mixture of authentic wrestlers and untamed brawlers gave the business a nice balance.

At the top of the heavyweight class, Bruno Sammartino, Gene Kiniski, and Dory Funk Jr. were fitting titleholders, and their multi-year reigns were nothing but successful. In terms of box office attractions, there was no one who quite matched up with the 6'11", 400-plus-pound Andre the Giant, and the "Eighth Wonder of the World" made a real impact wherever he traveled. Behind the scenes,, promoters Sam Muchnick and Vincent J. McMahon provided instrumental leadership that resonated throughout wrestling, and although the overall popularity waned at times, the territorial system thrived for the most part across North America. Likewise in Japan and Mexico, and with an abundance of superstars constantly touring and logical booking that made sense to enthusiasts, wrestling's reach continued to grow.

The squared circle was the center of attention in arenas around the globe, and grappling provided a nice escape from the cultural and social turmoil that people were dealing with on a daily basis. Into the 1970s, wrestling was facing some serious new challenges, particularly when confronted with the retirement or deaths of many older promoters who were the backbone of the territories. There was also the cable television factor, which made it easier for rival wrestling operations to present their brand in opposing regions. These critical avenues would soon be exploited by an enterprising third-generation promoter, and professional wrestling was never going to be the same.

Abdullah the Butcher

Born:	January 11, 1941
Height:	6'1"
Weight:	360
Real Name:	Larry Paul Shreve
Parents:	George and Martha Shreve
Nicknames:	The Sudanese Madman, Madman from the Sudan, The Black Wizard
Finisher:	Elbowdrop
Career Span:	1966–2010

Titles Won:	45
Days as World Champion:	235
Age at first World Title Win:	31
Best Opponents:	The Sheik, Carlos Colon, Dusty Rhodes
Managers:	Over 25
Halls of Fame:	2

Long before being "extreme" was all the rage, there were only a few mat men with a penchant for hardcore violence and a longing for bloodshed. At the top of that short list was Abdullah the Butcher; a hefty, fork-wielding superstar from Windsor, Ontario who broke into the sport under the supervision of Detroit promoters Jack Britton and Bert Rubi. Initially known as "Zelis Amara," he adopted the "butcher" gimmick while wrestling in Vancouver in 1967, and regularly sent crowds into a panic with his out-of-control behavior, which failed to play by any of the old catch-as-catch-can rules. Abdullah was crafty in using Taekwondo martial arts, a style that he earned a seventh-degree black belt in, even though he weighed over 350 pounds. An international phenomenon, Abdullah held the WWC World Title in Puerto Rico, the PWF World Title in Japan, and the NWF World Title in the United States at different points in his over forty years in the business. One way or another, his matches were always memorable, and fans knew around the world knew that if Abby was heading toward them with fork in hand, it was best to flee in the opposite direction. In 2011, he was inducted into the WWE Hall of Fame.

Born:	September 15, 1953
Height:	5'11"
Weight:	275
Real Name:	Keith A. Franke
Parents:	Kenneth and Kay Franke
Wife:	Bea Franke
High School:	Kenmore East High School (NY)
Trained by:	Fred Atkins
Nickname:	Adorable, The Golden Boy
Finisher:	DDT
Tag Team:	The East-West Connection w/ Jesse Ventura
Career Span:	1974–88
Died:	July 4, 1988, near Lewisporte, Newfoundland 34 years old

Adonis, Adrian

Titles Won:	8
Days as World Champion:	96
Age at first World Title Win:	29
Best Opponents:	Bob Backlund, Roddy Piper, Hulk Hogan

Adrian Adonis was a colorful wrestling personality with an incredible abundance of talent. Unusually nimble for his size, he competed in the 250-pound division while as a high school amateur grappler. He used his weight to his advantage once he turned pro, but it was also problematic when his weight reached over 300 pounds. He wrestled under the name "Keith Franks" in many territories prior to taking on the Adonis guise, which he adapted while wrestling in Georgia in 1978. During his stint in the AWA, he formed a successful alliance with Jesse "The Body" Ventura, and the two were awarded the World Tag-Team Title when the champs failed to appear for a defense in Denver on July 20, 1980. Adonis, wrestling in San Antonio in 1983, captured the SCW World Title, and, while in Japan a short time later, began teaming with Dick Murdoch. Adonis and Murdoch won the WWF World Tag-Team Title from Tony Atlas and Rocky Johnson in April 1984, and held the belts until January 21, 1985, when they lost to Mike Rotundo and Barry Windham. Adonis tragically lost his life when he was in a car accident en route to a show in Newfoundland in 1988.

Photo Courtesy of the Wrestling Revue Archives—
www.wrestleprints.com

Born:	November 21, 1943
Height:	6'2"
Weight:	325
Real Name:	Afa Amituanai Anoai
Parents:	Amituanai and Tovale Anoai
Trained by:	Peter Maivia, Kurt Von Steiger, Rocky Johnson, Jerry Monti
Finisher:	Samoan Drop
Career Span:	1971–94

Titles Won:	19
Best Opponents:	Andre the Giant, Hulk Hogan, Bob Backlund
Halls of Fame:	2

Afa

The brothers that made up the Hall of Fame Wild Samoans tag team performed with a brutal urgency in the ring, appearing to have absolutely no other mission in life than assaulting their opponents and forcing them to concede. Afa, one of eleven children born in American Samoa, served in the marines and was influenced to join by watching fellow Samoan Chief Peter Maivia wrestle in San Francisco. He immediately turned pro and then spent time mentoring his younger brother, Sika, and the two rampaged around the world, winning nineteen championships together. While in the WWF, they won the World Tag-Team Title three times between 1980 and 1983, defeating Ivan Putski and Tito Santana, Tony Garea and Rene Goulet, and the Strongbows. Later, in the 1990s, Afa managed the Headshrinkers. Throughout his career—and continuing after retirement from active wrestling—Afa has trained many well-known stars for the ring. Among them were Yokozuna, Rikiski, Billy Kidman, and Batista. Another prominent student was actor Mickey Rourke in advance of his performance in the 2008 film *The Wrestler*. Afa and Siki were inducted into the WWE Hall of Fame in 2007, and the Wild Samoans Pro-Wrestling Training Center continues to teach youngsters in Florida to this day.

Born:	October 4, 1939
Height:	6'0"
Weight:	230
Real Name:	Eugene Avon Anderson
Parents:	Royal and Pauline Anderson
High School:	South St. Paul High School (MN)
College:	North Dakota State College
Managed:	Jimmy Snuka (1979–80), Ray Stevens (1980), Hussein Arab (1980), Masked Superstar (1980), Ivan Koloff (1981)
Career Span:	1961–85
Died:	October 31, 1991, Charlotte, NC 52 years old

Titles Won:	27
Best Opponents:	Verne Gagne, Ricky Steamboat, Ric Flair
Halls of Fame:	1

Anderson, Gene

The famous Minnesota Wrecking Crew which was made up of Gene and Ole Anderson, won more than twenty championships between 1968 and 1981, establishing themselves as one of the best tandems in wrestling history. Gene was the only true "Anderson" in the hard-nosed clan of "siblings," which included Lars and Ole, and later Arn. Like Ole, he was from Ramsey County, Minnesota, and was a talented amateur grappler. Trained by the famous Verne Gagne, Anderson became a pro in 1961. Starting his career in the AWA, California, and Tennessee, he then moved on to have a prolonged career in the Mid-Atlantic territory in 1966. Teamed with Lars, the Andersons fought all the popular duos in very violent scraps, with Ole joining them two years later. Gene and Ole won the World Tag-Team Title seven times, plus a multitude of belts for the Crocketts and in Georgia. Of the two, Gene was the more reserved personality, but didn't hold back once he got in the ring. Outside of the squared circle, Anderson also worked as a matchmaker, trainer, and manager. His son, Brad, became a pro wrestler as well, and held the PNW Tag Team Title in 1991.

Born:	September 22, 1942
Height:	6'1"
Weight:	256
Real Name:	Alan Robert Rogowski
Parents:	Robert and Georgiana Rogowski
High School:	Alexander Ramsey High School (MN)
College:	University of Colorado
Groups:	The Four Horsemen (1985–86, 1990, 1993)
Tag Teams:	The Minnesota Wrecking Crew w/ Gene Anderson
Career Span:	1967–90

Titles Won:	48
Best Opponents:	Antonio Inoki, Ricky Steamboat, Dusty Rhodes
Halls of Fame:	2
Published Books:	1

Anderson, Ole

The Anderson name has been synonymous with pro wrestling excellence since the 1960s, and Ole Anderson was not only one-half of the famous brother duo that ruled the tag team ranks, but was a member of the legendary Four Horsemen. From Roseville, Minnesota, he was an athlete in high school and college, served in the Marines, and went through the grueling training camp of Verne Gagne. He debuted as "Rock Rogowski," and was a tough competitor, wrestling throughout the AWA region until June 1968, when he departed for the Mid-Atlantic area, and adopted the name "Ole Anderson." He teamed with his "brothers," Gene and Lars Anderson, and had a thirteen-year run with Gene as his partner. The Andersons captured the World Tag-Team Title seven times, the Mid-Atlantic championship five, and the Georgia Title on six occasions. Ole also held the Georgia Tag-Team Title an additional eleven times with six different partners (Jacques Goulet, Lars Anderson, Ivan Koloff, Stan Hansen, Ernie Ladd, Jerry Brisco). Behind the scenes, he was a first-rate matchmaker for the Crocketts, in Georgia, and for WCW. His son Bryant was also a wrestler, and competed in SMW and WCW in the 1990s.

Andre the Giant

Born:	May 19, 1946
Height:	6'11"
Weight:	520
Real Name:	Andre Rene Roussimoff
Parents:	Boris and Marian Roussimoff
Trained by:	Frank Valois, Edouard Carpentier
Identities:	Monster Eiffel Tower, Giant Machine
Nicknames:	The Eighth Wonder of the World, The Battle Royal King
Tag Teams:	The Mega Bucks w/ Ted DiBiase, The Colossal Connection w/ Haku
Managed by :	Bobby Heenan, Ted DiBiase
Personal Managers:	Frank Valois, Frenchy Bernard, Tim White
Career Span:	1964–92
Size Notes:	Andre's height was commonly inflated to 7'4" during his career; he was also reported to have had a size 24 shoe, a 71" chest, a 21" Bicep, and a 24" neck.
Died:	January 27, 1993, Paris, France 46 years old

Titles Won:	6
Days as World Champion:	0
Age at first World Title Win:	41
Best Opponents:	Hulk Hogan, Antonio Inoki, El Canek
Halls of Fame:	4
TV Appearances:	Over 10
Movies:	4

In and out of the ring, Andre the Giant was a superstar beyond words. His dominance as a performer, his humongous size and power, and the way he commanded the squared circle made him a peerless professional wrestler. At a weight that fluctuated upwards of more than 500 pounds, and at a height of 6'11", Andre was the largest man on the circuit. Whereas it might seem that someone of that bulk would be immobile, he was agile and athletic, being able to perform dropkicks and other impressive maneuvers. Andre had normal sized parents, but by the age of twelve, he was growing at a rate more in tune with his grandfather, who stood more than seven feet tall. A poor child from the Grenoble area of France, Andre was discovered at a local gym and brought to Paris, where he debuted as a wrestler in 1964. As he developed as a grappler, he toured Europe, and his reputation spread like wildfire. Soon after, he met Frank Valois, an influential Montreal wrestler, who taught a great deal to him.

In 1970, he went to Japan as "Monster Rousimoff," and traveled to the US in the summer of 1971 under the guise, "Jean Ferre." He wrestled all over Canada, as well as for the AWA, but his life changed forever when Valois steered him toward cunning WWWF promoter, Vincent J. McMahon. McMahon knew how to maximize his potential, booking Andre throughout the world, and never in one territory too long. Thus, it kept his act fresh, and fans were always left in awe by his bigger-than-life appearance. Prior to the 1975 NFL season, the Washington Redskins expressed interest in Andre, but nothing more than publicity came from it. A year later, he beat boxer Chuck Wepner by count out in a special mixed match-up at Shea Stadium. When Vincent K. McMahon expanded the WWF into a national organization, Andre was a central part of the promotion. He beat Big John Studd in a $15,000 bodyslam match at the first WrestleMania, and was victorious in a battle royal at the second.

Andre turned heel against the popular Hulk Hogan in 1987, took Bobby Heenan as his manager, and went into the highly-anticipated WrestleMania III as Hogan's biggest WWF World Title threat to date. Before over 70,000 fans, Andre put Hogan over, helping catapult the latter into another league of superstardom, and was a remarkable passing of the symbolic torch. Andre finally beat Hogan on February 5, 1988, and won the WWF belt, but controversy saw the championship declared vacant. Andre held the WWF World Tag-Team Title with Haku from 1989-1990, but toned back his schedule, wrestling mainly in Japan after that. While in France for his father's funeral, Andre passed away at the age of forty-six. A&E ran a feature *Biography* on Andre, which was one of the highest rated shows in that program's history. Stories of his amazing consumption of beer, which was more than 100 bottles and up to 7,000 calories in a single day, are still marveled at. The "Boss," as he was known, was the first man inducted into the WWF Hall of Fame in 1993.

In 2014, the WWE instituted a special battle royal for the "Andre the Giant Memorial Trophy" at its annual WrestleMania event. Cesaro was the first ever winner of the trophy, followed by The Big Show in 2015, and Baron Corbin at WrestleMania 32 in 2016.

Born:	September 1940
Height:	6'3"
Weight	240
Real Name:	Spiridon Manousakis
Parents:	Stauros and Konstantina Manousakis
Identities:	Arion Manousakis
Career Span:	1965–85

Titles Won:	13
Days as World Champion:	320
Age at first World Title Win:	24
Best Opponents:	Jack Brisco, Killer Kowalski, Bruno Sammartino

Arion, Spiros

An international superstar, Spiros Arion was born in Egypt to Greek parents and migrated to Athens as a teenager, where he excelled in the Greco-Roman form of wrestling. Naturally charismatic and physically powerful, he trained to become a pro grappler and made an early mark on European mats, often billed as the "son" of his mentor, veteran Andreas Lambrakis. In 1965, he went to Australia and became one of the most popular wrestlers of the era. Arion won the IWA World Heavyweight Title five times and the Austra-Asian crown three times. Upon his arrival in the US in 1974, he toured the WWWF and had a successful series against World Champion Bruno Sammartino at Madison Square Garden. Arion had partnered with Sammartino years earlier to capture the US Tag-Team Title, a belt he held twice.

Born:	October 3, 1939
Height:	6'0"
Weight:	230
Real Name:	Joseph Melton James Jr.
Parents:	Joseph and Rebekah James
Wife:	Gail James
High School:	Sprayberry High School (GA)
Military:	United States Marine Corps
Identities:	The Bullet
Career Span:	1966–2010

Titles Won:	61
Best Opponents:	Jack Brisco, Terry Funk, Ric Flair
Halls of Fame:	1

Armstrong, Bob

In 2011, forty-five years after his pro debut, "Bullet" Bob Armstrong is still appearing in professional wrestling matches. The father of a quartet of wrestlers and the 1967 NWA Rookie of the Year, Armstrong has been a longtime fan favorite and a perennial champion. He played high school football in his hometown of Marietta, Georgia, and became a fireman at the Fair Oaks station. A dedicated weightlifter, he was convinced to try his hand at grappling by local promoter, Elmo Chappell. Across the southeast, and wherever he traveled, he flourished, winning an extensive list of championships that included the North American, Southern, and Southeastern heavyweight crowns. Additionally, he was a matchmaker in the Georgia and Gulf Coast territories. In SMW and USWA, he acted as the commissioner, and was in an on-screen position of power in TNA in 2002. Armstrong remains semi-active on the indie circuit and was inducted into the WWE Hall of Fame in 2011. His four sons, Scott, Brad, Steve, and Brian, also had successful careers on the mat.

Born:	August 28, 1938
Height:	6'1"
Weight:	230
Real Name:	Joseph Hamilton
Parents:	Orville and Faye Hamilton
High School:	Benton High School (MO)
Trained by:	Larry Hamilton, Mike DiBiase
Identities:	Jody Hamilton, Mighty Bolo, The Flame
Career Span:	1956–88

Titles Won:	61
Best Opponents:	Jack Brisco, Harley Race, Dusty Rhodes
Halls of Fame:	3

Assassin, The

In 1961, the Assassin appeared for the first time in Georgia, and wrestling fans were not too thrilled by his overt rule-breaking style. Under the mask he was Joseph "Jody" Hamilton, the younger brother of Larry Hamilton. Like his sibling, Joe played football in high school and was an amateur boxer in his hometown of St. Joseph. The Hamiltons were successful in tag-team matches, but Joe, as the Assassin, would become an international sensation. Along with Tom Renesto as the second masked Assassin, Hamilton toured the globe and won many tag-team championships, including world titles in Australia, Georgia, and Florida. He was the main trainer at the WCW Power Plant and was inducted into the WCW Hall of Fame in 1994, as well as also running the Deep South promotion until it closed its doors in 2007. Six years later, the Assassins were inducted into the Professional Wrestling Hall of Fame. Hamilton's son, Nick Patrick, was a referee in both WCW and WWE.

Born:	April 23, 1954
Height:	6'2"
Weight:	297
Real Name:	Anthony Gerald White
High School:	Patrick Henry High School (VA)
Bodybuilding Ach.:	Mr. Southern Hemisphere (1978), WBBG Pro Mr. USA (1979), and numerous other titles
Trained by:	Gene and Ole Anderson, Larry Sharpe
Identities:	The Black Atlas, Black Superman
Nickname:	Mr. USA, Mr. Universe
Finisher:	Powerslam, Full Nelson, Bearhug
Managed:	Mark Henry (2008–09)
Career Span:	1975–2009

Titles Won:	18
Halls of Fame:	2
Published Books:	1

Atlas, Tony

The widespread popularity and amazing strength of Tony Atlas made him a bright prospect when he debuted in 1975. Formerly a bodybuilder, Atlas heeded the advice of George and Sandy Scott to become a grappler. From Roanoke, Virginia, Atlas appeared all over the Mid-Atlantic region and into Georgia, and won many local championships. In 1979, in addition to winning the title of "Mr. USA," he joined the WWF, and his incredible physique and likeability got him over with fans just like it had in the south. He beat Hulk Hogan at Madison Square Garden in 1981, and two years later, won the WWF World Tag-Team Title with Rocky Johnson. Atlas also won championships in World Class, IWCCW, the CWA, and the WWC in Puerto Rico, but personal troubles ended up hurting his career. He returned to the WWF in 1991 as "Saba Simba," but it was short-lived. His off-camera struggles were featured on MTV's *True Life: I'm a Pro Wrestler*, a reality show that was initially broadcast in 1999. In 2006, he was inducted into the WWE Hall of Fame.

Atlas returned to the WWE in 2012 under a Legends contract and two years later, his autobiography, entitled Atlas: *Too Much…Too Soon*, was published by Crowbar Press.

Photo Courtesy of Scott Teal/Crowbar Press

Born:	February 27, 1929
Height:	6'2"
Weight:	240
Real Name:	Wesley Austin Rapes
Parents:	William and Jewel Rapes
Career Span:	1956–77
Died:	August 13, 1981, San Joaquin County, CA 52 years old

Titles Won:	15
Days as World Champion:	196 (excluding any claim in 1962)
Age at first World Title Win:	37
Best Opponents:	Buddy Rogers, Lou Thesz, Rikidozan

Austin, Buddy

Buddy Austin, an arrogant heel, was an international terror of wrestling rings. Crowds generally reacted loudly to his riotous antics, especially if he was giving one of their favorites a rough going over. He grew up in Fulton County, Georgia, and learned the elementary methods of being a ruthless rule-breaker from a veteran of that style, Roy Graham. During his twenty-plus year career, he feuded with the best in the business, including Bruno Sammartino, Buddy Rogers, Rikidozan, and Fred Blassie. Austin won titles in the US, Australia, and Japan and was a three-time WWA World Heavyweight champion in Los Angeles. In late 1962, after National Wrestling Alliance World champion "Nature Boy" Buddy Rogers was injured in a real world accident in Montreal, promoters for Capitol Wrestling billed Austin as a title claimant, and asserted that Austin put Rogers out of action. To emphasize his violent and aggressive approach to the mat, Austin was nicknamed "Killer," and his piledriver was one of the most feared finishers of his time. Buddy, who legally changed his name to "Austin Wesley Rogers," retired in 1977, and passed away four years later at the age of fifty-two.

Born:	April 20, 1927
Height:	6'1"
Weight:	250
Real Name:	Wadi Youssef Ayoub
Trained by:	Tom Lurich, Chief Little Wolf, Jim Deakin
Career Span:	1953–75
Died:	September 29, 1976, Australia 49 years old

Titles Won:	3
Best Opponents:	Dara Singh, King Kong, George Gordienko

Ayoub, Wadi

An impressive athlete with widespread popularity, Sheik Wadi Ayoub wrestled around the world, and it wasn't uncommon for tens of thousands to be in attendance for his matches. He began as an amateur Greco-Roman grappler in his native Lebanon, and, in 1951, moved to Australia, where he decided to go pro. Training extensively, he was a genuine force to be reckoned with on the mat, and proceeded to wrestle the best the sport had to offer throughout the South Pacific, India, and Europe. In 1965, Ayoub won a competitive Middle East tournament and was billed as the uncrowned world champion two years later in Singapore. He displayed his strength in a victory over King Kong for the Orient championship and also held the All-Asian belt.

Baba, Shohei

Born:	January 23, 1938
Height:	6'10"
Weight:	320
Real Name:	Shohei Baba
Parents:	Kazuo and Mitsu Baba
Wife:	Motoko Baba
High School:	Niigata Prefectural Sanjo Industry High School (Japan)
Trained by:	Rikidozan, Fred Atkins
Owned:	All-Japan Pro Wrestling Co., Ltd. (October 1972-January 1999)
Career Span:	1960–99
Died:	January 31, 1999, Tokyo, Japan 61 years old

Titles Won:	24
Days as World Champion:	3,866
Age at first World Title Win:	35
Best Opponents:	The Destroyer, Jack Brisco, Billy Robinson
Tournament Wins:	16
Halls of Fame:	2

The legendary Shohei "Giant" Baba of Sanjo, Japan was a world renowned in-ring performer, known for his mammoth build, and an influential promoter. During the 1970s and 1980s, American fans were accustomed to reading about Baba's three NWA World Title victories in magazines, but there was much more to his legacy that went unrevealed by those kayfabe driven sources. Specifically, how his popularity kept wrestling hot following the stabbing death of Rikidozan, and his role as founder of All-Japan Pro Wrestling, one of the premier grappling institutions. A former baseball player for the Yomiuri Giants, Baba was courted into the business by Rikidozan and debuted in 1960. He toured the US extensively early in his career, headlining some of the biggest venues from coast to coast, and faced off against Bruno Sammartino and Buddy Rogers while both were world champions. After several years of international touring, Baba returned to Japan and assumed a leadership role after Rikidozan died in 1963.

As a member of the Japan Wrestling Association, Baba won the International championship on three occasions and was victorious in the World League tournament six times. In October 1972, he formed All Japan, as well as an important relationship with many American promoters. He also joined the NWA, which kept a free-flowing stream of imported talent for his company. On December 2, 1974, he dethroned Jack Brisco and became the first Japanese grappler to hold the NWA World Title. Baba reigned for only a week, but he won the belt a second time from Harley Race on October 31, 1979, and then captured his third title on

September 4, 1980, again from Race. As a mentor, Baba influenced the careers of superstars Jumbo Tsuruta, Toshiaki Kawada, and Mitsuharu Misawa, and maintained the success of All Japan until his death in 1999. Giant Baba was a cherished wrestling icon and his gentlemanly spirit will be remembered forever.

Photo Courtesy of Pete Lederberg—plmathfoto@hotmail.com

Backlund, Bob

Born:	August 14, 1949
Height:	6'1"
Weight:	230
Real Name:	Robert Lee Backlund
Parents:	Normal and Bernice Backlund
Wife:	Corrine Backlund
High School:	Princeton High School (MN)
College:	North Dakota State University
Trained by:	Terry Funk, Danny Hodge
Finisher:	Cross face chicken wing, German suplex
Managed:	The Sultan (1997), Kurt Angle (2000)
Career Span:	1973–2007

Titles Won:	12
Days as World Champion:	2,086
Age at first World Title Win:	28
Best Opponents:	Billy Graham, Antonio Inoki, Harley Race
Halls of Fame:	3
Published Books:	1

The ultimate baby face, Bob Backlund was World Heavyweight champion for a total of 2,086 days over four different reigns. He's remembered mostly for his quality work as the technically proficient hero in the WWF from 1978 to 1983. A product of Princeton, Minnesota, Backlund was a grappler in high school and college and won NCAA Division II honors in 1971 at 190 pounds. He trained under Eddie Sharkey and made his professional debut in 1973. Early in his career, Backlund worked his way through many different National Wrestling Alliance territories and learned from guys like Danny Hodge and Terry Funk as he developed his ring skills and confidence as a professional. By 1977, he was considered one of the best up-and-comers, and impressed the hierarchy of the World Wide Wrestling Federation. Backlund's clean-cut appearance, amateur background, and popularity edged him into a unique position as top challenger to Billy Graham's World Title only weeks after beginning a tour of the northeastern region.

Wrestling fans were shocked, yet pleased, to hear that he dethroned the notorious "Superstar" Graham on February 20, 1978 in New York. In Japan, he was defeated by Antonio Inoki on November 30, 1979, but Inoki vacated the championship shortly thereafter and Backlund won a bout over Bobby Duncum to begin his second reign. The title was held up after a bout with Greg Valentine on October 19, 1981, and Backlund was victorious in the rematch. He overcame the challenges of Ivan Koloff, Ken Patera, George Steele, Peter Maivia, and many other big names throughout his years as titleholder. Finally, he was met with defeat on December 26, 1983 when his manager, Arnold Skaaland, tossed a towel into the ring, signifying his submission while locked in the Iron Sheik's camel clutch. Backlund had a strong showing at the 1993 Royal Rumble, and, on November 23, 1994, he turned in a heel performance to beat Bret Hart for his fourth WWF Title, though lost the belt three days later to Diesel. In 2000, Backlund ran for Congress in Connecticut and returned to the ring with appearances for TNA and the WWE in 2007.

Backlund was inducted into the WWE Hall of Fame in 2013, and two years later released his autobiography, *Backlund: From All-American Boy to Professional Wrestling's World Champion.* He returned to the WWE again in 2016 as a life coach for wrestler Darren Young.

Born:	April 19, 1934
Height:	6'5"
Weight:	330
Real Name:	Douglas Allan Baker
High School:	West Waterloo High School (IA)
Trained by:	Bob Geigel, Pat O'Connor, Buddy Austin
Managed by:	The Grand Wizard, Sir Oliver Humperdink
Managed:	The Russian Brute, The Nightstalker, Mark Callous
Career Span:	1964–88
Died:	October 20, 2014, Hartford, CT 80 years old

Titles Won:	25
Days as World Champion:	497
Age at first World Title Win:	40
Best Opponents:	The Sheik, Carlos Colon, Bruiser Brody
Halls of Fame:	1
Movies:	3

Baker, Ox

The potent Heart Punch was the dreaded finisher of Ox Baker, a former amateur grappler and boxer from Waterloo, Iowa. Baker participated in several Golden Gloves championships and, in February 1964, won the Des Moines heavyweight crown. Soon after, Baker became a pro wrestler on the Central States circuit and capitalized on his impressive size and unique look to become an unforgettable villain. In 1974, he beat Bob Ellis for the WWA World Title and also held the WWC World Championship in Puerto Rico. Baker won belts in a number of territories from New Zealand to Los Angeles. In 1981, he appeared as the character "Slag," in the film *Escape from New York.*

Born:	August 11, 1934
Height:	5'8"
Weight:	145
Real Name:	Mary Ann Kostecki Weaver
Parents:	Frank and Clara Kostecki
High School:	Rosati Kain High School (MO)
Nickname:	Wow Girl
Career Span:	1954–74
Died:	May 13, 2008, Mint Hill, NC 73 years old

Titles Won:	6
Days as World Champion:	Around two years
Age at first World Title Win:	27
Best Opponents:	June Byers, Fabulous Moolah, Cora Combs
Halls of Fame:	3

Banner, Penny

Penny Banner was a credit to professional wrestling; a heroine who overcame obstacles and demonstrated the utmost bravery to become a sensational grappler. An athlete in high school, she was a waitress at the Arabian Lounge in St. Louis when convinced by promoter Sam Muchnick to try her hand at wrestling. With knowledge of judo, she ventured to Columbus, Ohio, where she trained for her 1954 debut. Before the end of her first year as a pro, she was already chasing World Champion June Byers. Banner teamed with Betty Joe Hawkins, Bonnie Watson, and Lorraine Johnson to capture the tag team championship, and, in August 1961, she beat Theresa Theis in Angola, Indiana to become the initial AWA Women's World Champion. She wed wrestler Johnny Weaver and competed across North America into the 1970s. At the 1995 Senior Olympics, she won a silver medal in the 50-meter butterfly event and won another silver two years later in the discus event. She remained one of the more enjoyable personalities in the business until her 2008 passing.

Bearcat Wright

Born:	January 13, 1932
Height:	6'6"
Weight:	265
Real Name:	Edward Michael Wright
Parents:	Edward and Lillian Wright
High School:	Omaha South High School (NE)
Boxing Trainers:	Bearcat Wright, Ralph Hayes
Finisher:	African Cannonball
Career Span:	1952–75
Died:	August 28, 1982, Tampa, FL 50 years old

Titles Won:	19
Days as World Champion:	199
Age at first World Title Win:	29
Best Opponents:	Killer Kowalski, Buddy Rogers, Johnny Valentine
Boxing Record:	8-0

In 1932, shortly after his newborn son Edward Michael Wright was born, noted African American boxer Bearcat Wright told an Omaha sportswriter that he would steer his child away from the fighting business. He was only somewhat successful. "Junior" Bearcat was a Golden Gloves boxer and won all eight of his professional fights before cutting his career short to become a pro wrestler in January 1952. Tall and powerful, Wright was a popular matman, and his box office appeal was most impressive in 1960 when he headlined at stadiums in Chicago and Washington, D.C., drawing 26,000 and 16,000 respectively in bouts against Killer Kowalski and Buddy Rogers. On April 4, 1961, he beat Kowalski for a claim to the World Title in Boston and won the WWA belt on August 23, 1963 in Los Angeles. Wright also won the IWA Championship in Australia in August 1966. Wright was a pivotal black wrestler during a time in which the industry was still trying to completely eradicate racial barriers and was a significant influence on many fans.

Born:	February 19, 1948
Height:	6'4"
Weight:	295
Real Name:	John William Minton
Family:	Father of Chip Minton
High School:	Butler High School (PA)
Identities:	Captain USA, Masked Superstar II
Groups:	The Mid-Atlantic Death Squad (1979–80)
Career Span:	1972–90
Died:	March 20, 1995, Burke, VA 46 years old

Big John Studd

Titles Won:	15
Days as World Champion:	5
Age at first World Title Win:	35
Best Opponents:	Andre the Giant, Hulk Hogan, Bruiser Brody
Halls of Fame:	3
Movies:	8

The powerful and intimidating Big John Studd had the stature to stand toe-to-toe with Andre the Giant and Hulk Hogan and was always considered one of the best big men in the industry. He was a basketball star in high school and spent a lot of time on his family's Butler County, Pennsylvania, farm. Trained by Killer Kowalski, he debuted as "Chuck O'Connor" in 1972 in the northeast and donned a mask as one of the Executioners a few years later, teaming with Kowalski and Nikolai Volkoff in defenses of the WWWF Tag Team Title. In 1977, he adopted the "Big John Studd" gimmick and was managed by Gary Hart in memorable matches against the Von Erichs and others in Dallas. He won the American Heavyweight belt, and, among his other achievements, were the North American and Canadian Titles. In 1989, he eliminated Ted DiBiase to win the second ever WWF Royal Rumble. He worked with George Scott in the latter's NAWA promotion in 1990 and was a successful businessman prior to his death in 1995.

Photo Courtesy of the Collection of Tim Hornbaker

Born:	October 14, 1935
Height:	6'3"
Weight:	260
Real Name:	John Mortl Lanzo
High School:	DeLaSalle High School (MN)
College:	University of Minnesota
Identities:	Jack Lanza, Gino Lanza, The Texan
Career Span:	1962–85

Titles Won:	10
Best Opponents:	Jack Brisco, Fritz Von Erich, Johnny Valentine
Halls of Fame:	2

Blackjack Lanza

The Blackjacks were a Hall of Fame tag team in the 1970s, and won world titles in the WWA and WWWF. The pair, made up of Blackjack Lanza and Blackjack Mulligan, shared a common characteristic: both were relentless heels with a shared appetite for brawling and rough tactics. Lanza grew up in Minneapolis, and started in the business as a protégé of Verne Gagne. His longtime gimmick, however, claimed Albuquerque as his hometown, and he was known as the "Cowboy." The Blackjacks won the WWWF World Tag Title in August 1975, and remained titleholders through the first week of November, until losing the straps to Louis Cerdan and Parisi. Lanza was managed by Bobby Heenan for several years and, partnered with Bobby Duncum, won the AWA World Tag Team Title from Dick the Bruiser and The Crusher in July 1976. They reigned for nearly a full year, until dropping the belts to Jim Brunzell and Greg Gagne in July 1977. After his retirement, he worked for the WWE behind-the-scenes as an agent and producer, and the Blackjacks were inducted into the WWE Hall of Fame in 2006.

Born:	November 25, 1941
Height:	6'6"
Weight:	235
Real Name:	Robert Deroy Windham
Parents:	W.R. and Nadine Windham
Family:	Father of Barry and Kendall Windham
High School:	Ector High School (TX)
Trained by:	Joe Blanchard
Identities:	Bob Windham, Big Machine
Finisher:	Clawhold, Boston Crab
Owned:	A percentage of the Amarillo promotion (1978–80)
Career Span:	1969–93
Died:	April 7, 2016, Tampa, FL 74 years old

Blackjack Mulligan

Titles Won:	18
Days as World Champion:	Around 380
Age at first World Title Win:	39
Best Opponents:	Verne Gagne, Bruno Sammartino, Fritz Von Erich
Halls of Fame:	2

Some wrestlers take a direct path to professional wrestling, but for Blackjack Mulligan, his Hall of Fame career came after playing two other sports and serving in the Marines. In high school at Odessa, Texas, he was a star basketball player and his awesome height was a great advantage. Following four years in the service, he was recruited to Texas Western College, where he played football. In 1966, he nearly made the New York Jets squad and played a few years in the Texas Football League. Mulligan, in 1969, debuted in wrestling, and was named the 1970 AWA Rookie of the Year. He officially took the "Blackjack Mulligan" moniker in 1971 during a run in the WWWF. While in the WWA, that same year, he began teaming with Blackjack Lanza, and in 1975, the duo won the WWWF Tag Team Title. For a majority of the 1975 to 1982 time-frame, he was a main star in the Mid-Atlantic region and feuded with Ric Flair, Ricky Steamboat, and Mr. Wrestling. In that territory, he won the US Title three times.

In 2006, Mulligan and his Lanza were inducted into the WWE Hall of Fame.

Born:	January 22, 1954
Height:	5'11"
Weight:	225
Real Name:	Tully Arthur Blanchard
Parents:	Joe and Jackie Blanchard
High School:	Churchill High School (TX)
Colleges:	Southern Methodist University, West Texas State University
Trained by:	Joe Blanchard
Identities:	The Midnight Stallion
Finisher:	Slingshot Suplex
Tag Teams:	The Dynamic Duo w/ Gino Hernandez, The Brain Busters w/ Arn Anderson
Career Span:	1974-2008

Blanchard, Tully

Titles Won:	28
Best Opponents:	Magnum T.A., Wahoo McDaniel, Dusty Rhodes
Halls of Fame:	2

Four Horsemen alumni Tully Blanchard was a confident and slick performer. He could wrestle scientifically, brawl, and integrate high levels of psychology into his matches, making him one of the truly must-see grapplers of the 1980s. His father, Joe, was a well-known wrestler, and his biggest influence growing up. Tully was a star high school and collegiate quarterback, and wrestled during the off season. The same speed and cleverness that had helped him shine on the field were among his outstanding qualities on the mat. He held the SCW Championship eleven times and, after joining Jim Crockett Promotions, won the TV Title twice. He also captured the US belt from Magnum T.A. and the World Tag Team Title on two occasions. Along with partner Arn Anderson, he went to the WWF and won tag title gold there as well. He went into semi-retirement, and made sporadic appearances, including a run in 1998 with Barry Windham as NWA Tag champs. He devoted his life to religion and acts as a preacher for prison inmates.

Blanchard, in 2012, was inducted into the WWE Hall of Fame beside the other members of the Four Horsemen: Ric Flair, Arn Anderson, Barry Windham, and James J. Dillon. Two years later, his daughter Tessa made her professional wrestling debut and is currently one of the brightest up-and-comers on the indie circuit.

Bockwinkel, Nick

Born:	December 6, 1934
Height:	6'1"
Weight:	245
Real Name:	Nicholas Warren Bockwinkel
High Schools:	Canoga Park High School (CA), Jefferson Union High School (CA)
Colleges:	Valley Junior College, University of Oklahoma
Military:	United States Army
Trained by:	Warren Bockwinkel, Lou Thesz, Wilbur Snyder
Identities:	Dick Warren, Nick Warren, Nick Bock, Roy Diamond, The White Phantom
Managed by:	Bobby Heenan
Career Span:	1954-93
Died:	November 14, 2015, Las Vegas, NV 80 years old

Titles Won:	30
Days as World Champion:	2,990
Age at first World Title Win:	40
Best Opponents:	Verne Gagne, Lou Thesz, Curt Hennig
Halls of Fame:	3

A calculating and intellectual wrestler, Nick Bockwinkel was the definitive heavyweight champion heel of the 1970s. He stepped free of the tag team division to rule the AWA World Title from 1975 to 1980 for a total of 1,714 straight days, after dethroning the pride of the AWA, Verne Gagne. The son of wrestler Warren Bockwinkel, he was originally from St. Louis and attended several high schools while touring with his father—Jefferson Union High in the San Francisco area being one of them. While in school, he was a star fullback and earned an outstanding player trophy in 1953. An opportunity to continue his football success in college was sidelined because of injury, and in 1954, he made his professional wrestling debut in Southern California. Warren was entirely supportive of his son's athletic endeavors and coached him in all aspects of the mat, teaching him the technical skills that would serve him exceptionally well throughout his career.

Bockwinkel was a receptive student, even before he entered the business, learning the ins and outs of the road while traveling with his father and wrestler Yukon Eric. In the ring, he was able to adapt to the various styles of opponents and create his own sequence of maneuvers that were very popular. He toured the Great Lakes area, the Jim Barnett circuit, Pacific Northwest, and Hawaii, as well as also appearing in Japan. In 1969, he made a sharp change to his act, emphasizing a rule-breaking attitude that rubbed many fans the wrong way. Initially developing his newfound role in Georgia, Bockwinkel carried the disposition to Minneapolis and the AWA, where he really made his mark. He teamed with the talented Ray Stevens to capture the World Tag Team Championship four times between 1972 and 1974, and on November 8, 1975 in St. Paul, he dethroned Gagne for the AWA World Heavyweight belt, initiating an exciting era for the promotion.

Bockwinkel was a distinctive champion, traveling throughout the US and into Canada. He successfully defended his title against Billy Robinson, The Crusher, Edouard Carpentier, Maurice Vachon, and other big names. Gagne finally was able to regain the title at Chicago's Comiskey Park on July 18, 1980, ending Bockwinkel's lengthy run. When Gagne retired in May 1981, Bockwinkel was awarded the belt because he was the number one contender, and in 1982, he traded the belt with Otto Wanz. On February 22, 1984, he lost the title to Jumbo Tsuruta. He was awarded his fourth AWA championship after Stan Hansen failed to defend on June 29, 1986 and Bockwinkel held it until losing a bout to Curt Hennig the following May. He wrestled his last match for the AWA in 1987 and came out of retirement in late 1990 to battle Masa Saito in Japan. Three years later, he drew with Dory Funk Jr. at WCW's Slamboree event. Bockwinkel also acted as WCW commissioner from 1994 to 1996.

Born:	August 6, 1948
Height:	6'1"
Weight:	248
Real Name:	Adolfo Bresciano
Wife:	Diane Bresciano
Nicknames:	The World's Strongest Man
Finisher:	Bearhug
Tag Team:	The Italian Connection w/ Gino Brito
Career Span:	1971–92
Died:	March 11, 1993, Laval, Quebec 44 years old

Titles Won:	17
Best Opponents:	Harley Race, Ric Flair, Nick Bockwinkel

Bravo, Dino

Powerhouse Dino Bravo found success in the wrestling ring as both a fan favorite and as an arrogant heel. He was a Canadian legend, although relocated from Italy, and based out of Montreal, where he learned a diverse repertoire of maneuvers from Gino Brito and Edouard Carpentier. Bravo was agile enough to pull off fast-paced moves, charismatic in revving up audiences, and impressively strong—able to bench over 600 pounds. On May 5, 1976, he teamed with Mr. Wrestling to win the NWA World Tag Team Title from the Andersons and two years later, he captured the WWWF Tag Team belts with Dominic DeNucci. In

Montreal, between 1980 and 1985, he won the Canadian Heavyweight Championship six times and was immensely popular. He returned to the WWF, turned heel, and hooked up with Frenchy Martin and Jimmy Hart. In 1990, he was a top rival for Hulk Hogan. Sadly, in March 1993, he was shot to death in his Quebec home and his murder spawned heavy speculation to his ties to the illegal cigarette business.

Photo Courtesy of Pete Lederberg—plmathfoto@hotmail.com

Born:	September 21, 1941
Height:	6'1"
Weight:	225
Real Name:	Freddie Joe Brisco
Parents:	Floyd and Iona Brisco
Wife:	Jan Brisco
High School:	Blackwell High School (OK)
HS Ach.:	Oklahoma State Wrestling Champion (1958–60)
College:	Oklahoma State University
College Ach.:	NCAA Wrestling Title (1965) (191)
Identities:	Tiger Brisco, The Masked Okie
Finisher:	Figure-four leglock
Career Span:	1965–85
Died:	February 1, 2010, Tampa, FL 68 years old

Brisco, Jack

Titles Won:	53
Days as World Champion:	866
Age at first World Title Win:	31
Best Opponents:	Dory Funk Jr., Harley Race, Terry Funk
Halls of Fame:	4

The epitome of class and honor, Jack Brisco represented everything good about the business and particularly what was expected from a premier claimant to the World Heavyweight Title. There was no outrageous flamboyance or arrogance when it came to Brisco. He stuck to his pure athleticism in the ring, applying knowledge from his amateur days and throwing back the clock to an era in which fundamentals were the keynote to success. Brisco was respected by all corners of the industry and fans cheered on his efforts as he played by the rules and dismantled roughnecks with technical savvy. He was considered more of a "real" wrestler than his colorful counterparts, and was compared to legends and fellow NWA World Champions Lou Thesz and Dick Hutton. Like Hutton, Brisco was from Oklahoma, where he excelled in high school and collegiate wrestling and learned the essentials from Leroy McGuirk in Tulsa. Brisco was an NCAA champion and that distinction meant credibility in pro wrestling, regardless of his experience.

Beginning in 1965, Brisco proceeded along the circuit, learning the craft and helping support his family. He landed in Florida three years later and political cards were played by influential members of the National Wrestling Alliance in support of his candidacy for World Champion. After some wrangling and an injury to the heavyweight titleholder, Dory Funk Jr., a planned bout between Funk and Brisco that would see the latter win the championship was scrapped. Instead, Funk lost the title to Harley Race, and Brisco wrestled the belt away from Race on July 20, 1973 in Houston, becoming only the second man to have won both the NCAA and NWA titles in their career, with Hutton being the first. While in Japan in December 1974, Brisco lost the NWA Title to Giant Baba, but regained it back a week later. Finally, on December 10, 1975, he dropped the belt to Terry Funk in Miami Beach. His two reigns were saturated with spectacular matches across the grappling landscape, and, as the hero, he never failed to live up to his advance billing.

Brisco won the Missouri, Florida, Southern, Mid-Atlantic, and a number of other championships during his illustrious career. He also formed the famous Brisco Brothers tag team with his younger sibling, Jerry, and the two dominated competition for years. They won the NWA World Tag Team Title, plus belts in Florida, Georgia, and Puerto Rico. The Briscos were also part owners in the Georgia territory until selling out in 1984. They wrestled for a time in the WWF prior to Jack retiring in 1985, and when Brisco walked away, he walked away for good. His history was completely captured in his 2004 autobiography, *Brisco*, and he's been honored by several Halls of Fame. Recognized as one of the best the sport's ever seen, Brisco carried himself as a champion inside the ring and out, and was a true gentleman, a characteristic that contrasted very conspicuously against the murky backdrop of professional wrestling.

Born:	September 19, 1946
Height:	6'0"
Weight:	210
Real Name:	Floyd Gerald Brisco
Parents:	Floyd and Iona Brisco
Family:	Father of Wes Brisco
High School:	Stillwater High School (OK)
College:	Oklahoma State University
Identities:	Gerald Brisco
Career Span:	1967–2000

Titles Won:	43
Best Opponents:	Dory Funk Jr., Harley Race, Jerry Lawler
Halls of Fame:	2

Brisco, Jerry

The talented Jerry Brisco teamed with his brother, Jack to win the World Tag Team Championship on three separate occasions between 1983 and 1984, and engaged in rough battles with the teams of Jay Youngblood and Ricky Steamboat and Wahoo McDaniel and Mark Youngblood. They discarded their usual hero roles to portray the "bad guys" across the Mid-Atlantic region and had a memorable run. Jerry, who was the younger of the two siblings, learned the ropes from Jack and entered the pro ranks in 1967 after several years of amateur grappling. In addition to his success as a tag team wrestler, Jerry won many singles titles and held the NWA World Junior Title in 1981. He had a backstage role with the WWF when, in 1998, he stepped back in front of the camera as one of Vince McMahon's faithful "stooges," along with Hall of Famer Pat Patterson. In 2000, he won the Hardcore Title twice and, along with Jack, was honored by induction into the WWE Hall of Fame.

Born:	October 16, 1938
Height:	5'11"
Weight:	255
Real Name:	Robert Harold Brown
Identities:	Bobo Brown
Finisher:	Backbreaker, Legdrop
Career Span:	1960–96
Died:	February 5, 1997, Kansas City, MO 58 years old

Titles Won:	68
Best Opponents:	Harley Race, Dory Funk Jr., Bruiser Brody

Brown, Bob

A top-notch heel for decades, "Bulldog" Bob Brown grew up in Winnipeg, where he was a star amateur heavyweight grappler at the Westbrook Athletic Club. He found his first pro success competing under the auspices of the Madison Wrestling Club, and won both the heavyweight and tag team championship on multiple occasions. Forming a lifelong friendship with Bob Geigel, he ventured to the latter's hometown of Kansas City, where the duo captured the North American Tag Title five times. Known for his riotous behavior, Brown became a legend in the Central States territory, capturing the local heavyweight title twenty-one times between 1968 and '87. Among his title feuds were against Harley Race, Bob Sweeten, Bob Slaughter, and the Assassin. He also booked the territory for owners Geigel and Pat O'Connor in the 1980s. In 1989, Brown partnered with his nephew Kerry Brown to win the International Tag Team belts in Calgary. After retirement, he worked at the Woodlands Racetrack in Kansas City as a security guard alongside Geigel and former rival Mike George. Although a heel in the ring, Brown was always charitable and fondly remembered by his friends after his 1997 death.

Bruiser Brody

Born:	June 14, 1946
Height:	6'4"
Weight:	275
Real Name:	Frank Donald Goodish
Wife:	Barbara Goodish
High School:	Warren High School (MI)
College:	West Texas State University
Pro Sports:	Texas Football League—San Antonio Toros (1968)
	Continental Football League—Mexico Golden Aztecs (1969)
	Continental Football League—West Texas Rufneks (1969)
	National Football League—Washington Redskins (1970) (camp)
	Continental Football League—Fort Worth Braves (1970)
	Canadian Football League—Edmonton Eskimos (1971)
Trained by:	Jack Adkisson, Buck Robley
Identities:	Red River Jack
Nicknames:	The Hammer, King Kong
Career Span:	1974–88
Died:	July 17, 1988, Bayamon, Puerto Rico 42 years old

Titles Won:	30
Days as World Champion:	301
Age at first World Title Win:	33
Best Opponents:	Ric Flair, Harley Race, Antonio Inoki
Halls of Fame:	3

A one-of-a-kind wrestling performer, Bruiser Brody was a frightful sight for the unprepared viewer. He was an extraordinary brawler, taking violence to another level, and his great size and athletic ability added unique aspects to his colorful persona. Crowds around the world were captivated by his matches and he was known as an "outlaw" backstage for his shrewd business perspective. He was rarely without championship gold around his waist: In Indiana, he captured the WWA World Title, and won the AJPW International championship three times in Japan and the AJPW Tag Team Title with both Jimmy Snuka and Stan Hansen.

He also held numerous regional belts in Texas, Florida, and the Central States. During his career, he had memorable feuds with Abdullah the Butcher, Dick the Bruiser, The Von Erichs, and Jumbo Tsuruta. On July 16, 1988, prior to a show in Bayamon, Puerto Rico, he was stabbed by a fellow wrestler, Jose Huertas Gonzales, and died the following day. His life story has been told in two published biographies.

Born:	August 13, 1949
Height:	5'10"
Weight:	230
Real Name:	James Ewald Brunzell Jr.
High School:	White Bear Lake High School (MN)
College:	University of Minnesota
Football:	Manitowoc County Chiefs— Central Football League (1971)
Finisher:	Dropkick
Career Span:	1972–94

Titles Won:	9
Best Opponents:	Ric Flair, Jumbo Tsuruta, Ray Stevens

Brunzell, Jim

"Jumping" Jim Brunzell was an energetic and clean-cut wrestling hero. He was a football star in high school and college and was trained by the legendary Verne Gagne. Teamed with Verne's son Greg Gagne as the Hi-Flyers, Brunzell won the AWA World Tag Team belts on July 7, 1977 from Bobby Duncum and Blackjack Lanza. They reigned a second time from 1981 to 1983 after dethroning Adrian Adonis and Jesse Ventura. He also formed a popular tandem with Brian Blair in the WWF, known as the Killer Bees. As a singles performer, Brunzell held the Mid-Atlantic championship twice in 1979-1980. At the UWF Beach Blast show in 1991, Brunzell and Blair reunited to beat The Power Twins and Brunzell retired from the sport a few years later.

Born:	June 19, 1952
Height:	6'0"
Weight:	235
Real Name:	Felipe Estrada
Trained by:	Felipe Ham Lee
Identities:	El Canek, Principe Azul, El Principe Maya
Career Span:	1972–Present

Canek

Titles Won:	20
Days as World Champion:	Over 7,000
Age at first World Title Win:	26
Best Opponents:	Lou Thesz, Vader, Andre the Giant
MMA Record:	1-0
Halls of Fame:	1

Powerful heavyweight Canek wrestled all the greats from Lou Thesz to Andre the Giant and was admired all over the globe. In the tradition of Mexico's finest lucha libra heroes, he wore colorful masks and attire and was the backbone of the Universal Wrestling Association since its inception. Canek reigned as UWA World Heavyweight Champion fifteen times between 1978 and 2004, dethroning Thesz for his first claim and also beating the likes of Tiger Jeet Singh, Riki Choshu, Tatsumi Fujinami, and Vader. He furthered his legacy in Japan as part of a talent agreement with Antonio Inoki's New Japan Pro Wrestling promotion and received worldwide attention for bodyslamming and pinning Andre the Giant. Many recognizable names went to Mexico to face him before stunning crowds, including Hulk Hogan, Billy Robinson, and Inoki himself. On June 18, 2004, he lost the UWA Title for the final time to Dr. Wagner Jr. in Mexico City. Canek still wrestles from time to time, continuing to add chapters to his legendary career.

Born:	July 17, 1926
Height:	5'9"
Weight:	225
Real Name:	Edouard Wieczorkwicz
College:	University of Sorbonne
Identities:	Eduardo Wiecezorski, Eddie Wiecz
Nicknames:	The Flying Frenchman
Career Span:	1952–87
Died:	October 30, 2010, Montreal, Quebec 84 years old

Titles Won:	15
Days as World Champion:	Around 2,090
Age at first World Title Win:	30
Best Opponents:	Lou Thesz, Fred Blassie, Killer Kowalski
Halls of Fame:	3

Carpentier, Edouard

The lively acrobatics of Antonino Rocca initiated a trend in professional wrestling that was also capitalized on by the popular Edouard Carpentier of France. Carpentier, a former gymnast, was an innovator in the way he used a wide variety of tumbling maneuvers, displaying his amazing athleticism and craftiness. Standing about 5'9", he was one of the smaller grapplers, but he made up for his lack of stature with his quick feet and intellect. Carpentier matched up well with all the great monster heels of the time and his classy personality made him a ring idol for fans throughout the world. As a teen, he displayed extraordinary courage while fighting with the French Resistance and excelled on the rings and the trampoline, earning a spot as an alternate with the French national gymnastics squad at the 1948 Olympics. He trained for the mat under Henri DeGlane and launched his professional career in Europe. A few years later, he was scouted by Yvon Robert and debuted in Montreal in April 1956.

Carpentier had no trouble adapting to the flashy North American style of wrestling and to the fame that came very easily to him. He succeeded Robert as the top draw in Montreal, drawing huge crowds to the Forum and the baseball stadium during the summers, and fought heated contests against Killer Kowalski, Gene Kiniski, and Buddy Rogers. The match he's most remembered for, however, was his disqualification win over NWA World champion Lou Thesz on June 14, 1957 in Chicago, which saw him proclaimed as the new titleholder. Unbeknownst to fans, the title switch was a political ploy to split the championship while Thesz was overseas, allowing NWA members to book him on the circuit in the interim. A squabble between promoters disintegrated the strategy a few months later, but Carpentier was a trooper and went about his business in rings all across North America in spite of the political shenanigans happening around him.

When Thesz eventually returned from his tour, he lost his official National Wrestling Alliance World Title lineage to Dick Hutton; but by that point, Carpentier was seen as a more valuable champion in terms of ticket sales. The one thing that Carpentier did not have was an out-of-control ego and he was willing to help a number of promoters across the nation establish new title lineages based on his 1957 win over Thesz. It began on May 3, 1958 in Boston when Carpentier dropped the championship to Killer Kowalski. A few months later in Omaha, he lost his title again to Verne Gagne on August 9, 1958. Finally, he was acknowledged as champion in Los Angeles in 1961 until being defeated by Fred Blassie on June 12, 1961 before 13,000 fans at the Sports Arena. In Montreal, he was a five-time champion and held tag team titles with both Bob Ellis and Bruno Sammartino. Carpentier was a strong mentor to many wrestlers and was credited with bringing Andre the Giant to North America from France.

Photo Courtesy of Dr. Mike Lano—Wrealano@aol.com

Born:	December 3, 1951
Height:	6'0"
Weight:	245
Real Name:	Mitsuo Yoshida
College:	Senshu University
Olympics:	Freestyle Wrestling (1972) (Representing South Korea) (DNP)
Trained by:	NJPW Dojo, Masa Saito
Finisher:	Lariet
Career Span:	1974–2015

Titles Won:	13
Days as World Champion:	Around 792
Age at first World Title Win:	30
Best Opponents:	Antonio Inoki, Tatsumi Fujinami, Keiji Mutoh
Halls of Fame:	1

Choshu, Riki

Riki Choshu was a preeminent figure inside the squared circle and out, wrestling countless great matches during his thirty-six year career and assisting in the charge of New Japan Pro Wrestling as a booker as it skyrocketed to record success during the 1990s. Additionally, his invasion of All-Japan in 1984 set off a dynamic feud and garnered a lot of worldwide attention. Choshu, as a singles competitor, has won three IWGP Titles, initially defeating Salman Hashimikov for the championship on July 12, 1989, as well as also dethroning Vader and Tatsumi Fujinami. Between 1988 and 1997, he held the IWGP Tag Team Title three times with partners, Masa Saito, Takayuki Iizuka, and Kensuke Sasaki, and in 1996, he won the G-1 Climax Tournament. Outside NJPW, he won the UWA World Title from Canek in Mexico in 1982 and captured the PWF World Title from Stan Hansen on April 5, 1986. He remained with New Japan from 1987 until 2002, and then operated the promotions Riki Pro and Lock Up. He was still semi-active as of 2010.

Colon, Carlos

Born:	July 18, 1948
Height:	5'10"
Weight:	245
Real Name:	Carlos Edwin Colon Gonzalez
Family:	Father of Carlito, Primo, and Stacy Colon
Wife:	Nancy Colon
Trained by:	Red Beard
Identities:	Chief White Feather, Prince Kahulia
Finisher:	Figure-four leglock
Promoter:	World Wrestling Council (1974–Present) (Puerto Rico)
Career Span:	1966–2014

Titles Won:	68
Days as World Champion:	491
Age at first World Title Win:	34
Best Opponents:	Ric Flair, Harley Race, Terry Funk
Halls of Fame:	2

A wrestling legend from Santa Isabel, Puerto Rico, Carlos Colon grew up in New York City. He was one of seven children and was influenced by the excitement of grappling throughout the area. Colon joined a gym frequented by legends Miguel Perez and Antonino Rocca, and learned the pro style, debuting on the circuit in 1966. He worked his way across the US to California, and had extended stays in Montreal and the northeast. He returned to Puerto Rico and launched the WWC with Victor Jovica in January 1974. Blending native workers with talent from around the world, Colon's WWC has been a hotbed for action, and he reigned as Universal champion twenty-six times, battling the likes of Abdullah the Butcher, Dory Funk Jr., and Ron Garvin. His long-running war with Abdullah is among the greatest feuds in wrestling history and perhaps the most violent. Colon was also a top challenger to NWA champions Harley Race and Ric Flair, and even pinned the latter in 1983, but was never acknowledged as an official titleholder.

In 2014, Carlos was enshrined in the WWE Hall of Fame and his sons Carlito (Carly) and Primo (Eddie), plus his nephew Epico (Orlando) inducted him. His daughter Stacy is also a professional wrestler.

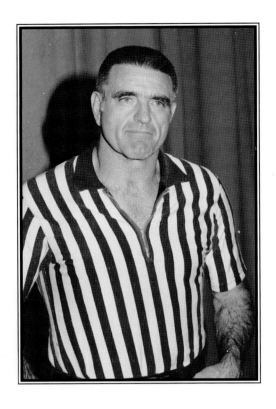

Curtis, Don

Born:	May 22, 1927
Height:	5'11"
Weight:	220
Real Name:	Donald Bain Beitelman
Parents:	Thomas and Helen Beitelman
Wife:	Dotty Curtis
High School:	Riverside High School (NY)
Trained by:	Lou Thesz
Identities:	Don Lutz
Finisher:	Sleeperhold
Career Span:	1951–72
Died:	March 6, 2008, Jacksonville, FL 80 years old

Titles Won:	14
Best Opponents:	Lou Thesz, Johnny Valentine, Gene Kiniski
Halls of Fame:	2

A longtime crowd pleaser, Don Curtis was a superb athlete from Buffalo and had a long, successful career on the mat. While still a teenager, he served in the Navy on two submarines, the USS. *Skipjack* and the USS. *Entemedor*, attending the University of Buffalo upon his discharge. He was a standout football player in college, but it was his lightning moves as an amateur grappler that caught the eye of area promoter Ed Don George. He wrestled for six years under his real name, competing at length in the South Pacific, and debut in West Texas in January 1957, where he debuted under the guise, "Don Curtis." He formed a renowned tag team with Mark Lewin, also of Buffalo, and won a number of championships in the Northeast and Florida. Altogether, Curtis won the World Tag Team Title five times and also reigned as the Southern champion. During the 1960s, he became an NWA-affiliated promoter in Jacksonville, but broke from the Tampa office in 1981 and formed an indie promotion, Sun Belt Wrestling.

Born:	April 7, 1932
Height:	6'1"
Weight:	245
Real Name:	Eduardo Ramon Rodriguez
Wife:	Cheryl Rodriguez
Identities:	Lalo Rodriguez, Caribs Hurricane, Ciclon Negro
Career Span:	1956–84
Died:	February 20, 2013, Melbourne, FL 80 years old

Titles Won:	33
Best Opponents:	Dory Funk Jr., Terry Funk, Ricky Steamboat

Cyclone Negro

Venezuelan Cyclone Negro was an extraordinarily hard-hitting competitor, a standout against all types of foes, and a hardcore brawler. During his twenty-eight years on the mat, his time in West Texas in the early 1970s was the finest representation of his fierceness, and his battles against Dory Funk Sr. and his sons Dory Jr. and Terry remain legendary. Initially a boxer, it was once alleged that he fought future World Champion Floyd Patterson in the Pan-American Games in the early 1950s, and was defeated. However, he'd gain international fame as a pro wrestler, touring the US, Canada, Europe, Australia, and Japan. In Texas, he held both the state heavyweight and tag team titles simultaneously, and gained similar success in territory after territory, winning regional belts in Puerto Rico, California, and Florida. In 1974, he won the first of five International Titles. Whether it was a straight match, a no-rules brass knuckles bout, or a brutal Texas Death Match, Cyclone Negro was a hearty battler, and fans always got their money's worth with him on the bill. He retired in the 1980s and settled to Florida, where he passed away on February 20, 2013, at the age of eighty.

Born:	June 15, 1932
Height:	6'2"
Weight:	260
Real Name:	Domenic D. Nucciarone
Trained by:	Tony Lanza, Jack Britton
Identities:	Masked Marvel, Dominic Bravo
Finisher:	Airplane Spin
Career Span:	1958–2012

Titles Won:	21
Days as World Champion:	Around 340
Age at first World Title Win:	32
Best Opponents:	Killer Kowalski, Ray Stevens, Waldo Von Erich
Halls of Fame:	2

DeNucci, Dominic

The immensely popular and influential Dominic DeNucci wrestled for three decades and left a dent wherever he appeared. Originally from Campobasso, Italy, he was an amateur Greco-Roman wrestler as a youth and turned professional in 1958, wrestling as the "Masked Marvel" in Montreal. For several years he performed as one-half of the Bravo Brothers with Dino Bravo, and then took the DeNucci name. He captured the US Championship in San Francisco, the NWF Title, and the IWA World Heavyweight crown in Australia four times between 1964 and '70, winning over Killer Kowalski, Ray Stevens, and King Curtis Iaukea. He also teamed with Bruno Sammartino to hold the WWWF International Tag Title in 1971, and with partners Victor Rivera, Pat Barrett, and Dino Bravo as WWWF World Tag champions. Upon retirement, he opened a wrestling camp in Freedom, Pennsylvania, where he mentored the likes of Mick Foley and Shane Douglas. In April 2012, during a Wrestle Reunion show in Toronto, DeNucci returned to the ring, teaming with Douglas to beat Lord Zoltan and Shawn Blanchard. His longtime friend, Bruno Sammartino was in his corner for the bout. In 2012, DeNucci was inducted into the Professional Wrestling Hall of Fame.

© Dan Westbrook

Born:	July 11, 1931
Height:	5'11"
Weight:	230
Real Name:	Richard John Beyer
Family:	Father of Kurt Beyer
Wife:	Wilma Beyer
High School:	Seneca Vocational High School (NY)
Amateur Title:	Niagara District AAU Wrestling Title (1952) (HWT)
Military:	United States Army
Trained by:	Bill Miller, Ray Stevens, Dick Hutton
Finisher:	Figure-four leglock
Career Span:	1954–93

Titles Won:	24
Days as World Champion:	470
Age at first World Title Win:	31
Best Opponents:	Fred Blassie, Rikidozan, Shohei Baba
Halls of Fame:	4

Destroyer, The

A white mask concealed the identity of the "Intelligent, Sensational" Destroyer as he toured the world and earned recognition as a living legend of the wrestling mat. He was technically sound, entertaining, and a box office smash wherever he traveled. Known outside the ring as Dick Beyer of Buffalo, he earned accolades for football and wrestling at Syracuse University and was guided into business by Ed Don George. In 1962, he adopted the "Destroyer" gimmick in Southern California and debuted in Japan the following year, garnering huge TV ratings for his match against Rikidozan. He was a huge attraction in the Los Angeles area, and won the WWA World Title three times. In 1968, he held the AWA World Title for a few weeks under the name, "Dr. X," while wearing a black mask. He wrestled his final bout in Japan in 1993, and taught education in Akron, New York. The Destroyer holds the distinction of having wrestled icons Gorgeous George and Rikidozan in their final matches.

DiBiase, Ted

Born:	January 18, 1954
Height:	6'2"
Weight:	245
Real Name:	Theodore Marvin DiBiase Sr.
Parents:	Mike and Gladys "Helen" DiBiase
Family:	Father of Mike, Brett, and Ted DiBiase Jr.
High Schools:	Creighton Prep (NE), Willcox High School (AZ)
Identities:	The Saint
Finisher:	Powerslam, Million Dollar Dream Sleeperhold
Groups:	The Rat Pack (1982–83), The Million Dollar Corporation (1994–95), The New World Order (1996–97)
Tag Teams:	The Mega Bucks w/ Andre the Giant, Money Inc., w/ Irwin R. Schyster
Career Span:	1975–2007
Website:	www.milliondollarman.com

Titles Won:	30
Best Opponents:	Randy Savage, Jack Brisco, Ric Flair
Wrestlers Managed:	16
Halls of Fame:	3

During the 1980s, few wrestlers had innate talent superseding that of Ted DiBiase. Both his mother, Helen Hilde, and adopted father, Mike DiBiase, were pro grapplers, and the business was in his blood. He spent a lot of time during his youth in Amarillo growing up in a wrestling town, and was heavily influenced by the Funk family. After his father's sudden death, he finished high school in Arizona and earned many accolades for his football prowess. After high school, DiBiase attended West Texas State and began training to be a pro wrestler with Terry and Dory Funk Jr. mentoring him. In the Mid-South territory, he garnered his first notable success, winning the North American Title. Two years later, he went to St. Louis and captured the prestigious Missouri championship. In 1987, he entered the WWF and adopted the gimmick "Million Dollar Man," claiming that "everyone has a price." DiBiase's powerful promos sold the unique character and he would often pay off spectators to perform embarrassing feats to earn cash.

In early 1988, he hired Andre the Giant to win the WWF World Title for him, and a controversial match on the *Main Event* against Hulk Hogan ended with Andre winning the belt—and DiBiase taking over as champion immediately afterward. Officials declared the title vacant, and at WrestleMania IV, DiBiase was in contention for the championship, but lost in the tournament finals to Randy Savage. Between 1992 and 1993, DiBiase held the WWF Tag Team belts three times with Irwin R. Schyster (IRS). DiBiase also had success in Japan, winning the PWF Tag Team Title twice in 1987 and the AJPW Unified World Tag Team Title in 1993. DiBiase often wore his custom Million Dollar Belt, a prize that demonstrated his riches. A serious neck injury ended his active career, but he remained involved in the WWF and WCW from outside the squared circle. In 2010, he was inducted into the WWE Hall of Fame.

Photo Courtesy of the Collection of Tim Hornbaker

Born:	June 27, 1929
Height:	6′1″
Weight:	260
Real Name:	William Franklin Afflis
Parents:	William and Margaret Afflis
Family:	Father of Michelle Replogle, father-in-law of Spike Huber
Wife:	Louise Afflis
High School:	Lafayette High School (IN)
Colleges:	Purdue University, University of Nevada
Trained by:	Leo Nomellini, Verne Gagne, Joe Pazandak
Finisher:	Stomach claw
Promoted:	World Wrestling Association (Indiana) (1964–88)
Career Span:	1954–88
Died:	November 10, 1991, Largo, FL 62 years old

Dick the Bruiser

Titles Won:	57
Days as World Champion:	Over 2,300
Age at first World Title Win:	34
Best Opponents:	Wilbur Snyder, Bob Ellis, Bruiser Brody
Halls of Fame:	4

No matter if it was singles or tag team wrestling, Dick the Bruiser was going into the ring for a fight. A brawler of the highest degree, Bruiser took the action from pillar to post and did everything in his power to cripple his opponent. The style he employed riled up crowds and his aggressiveness was as fierce as a tiger going after prey. He was hard-hitting and his roughness earned him as many cheers as it did jeers throughout his legendary career. His personality was also very apparent when he'd counteract howling from the audience with his own, often comical, posturing.

Dick the Bruiser was a standout football player in high school and college, and was drafted by the Green Bay Packers in 1951. He played forty-eight games over the next four years, and then hung his cleats up for wrestling boots and dedicated his life to grappling. Between 1957 and 1963, he won the United States Heavyweight Title thirteen times and engaged in many violent and bloody matches with Wilbur Snyder and Bob Ellis.

Bruiser formed a Hall of Fame tag team with Crusher Lisowski, and they won the AWA World Tag Team Title five times and the WWA championship six. They also captured gold while in Japan in 1969. As a singles competitor, Bruiser beat Fred Blassie for the WWA World Title in 1965, and took the championship back to Indianapolis, where he formed the World Wrestling Association, a regionally-based promotion. Late in 1965, he teamed with Snyder to buy the Chicago territory, expanding their business significantly. Bruiser would win the WWA Title ten times during his time on the mat and promoted shows throughout Indiana, Illinois, and Michigan, as well as in St. Louis, where he won the Missouri Title three times. One of Bruiser's most noteworthy incidents occurred in 1963, when he brawled with football star Alex Karras in the latter's Detroit bar. It was a chaotic scene that promoted a future mat showdowns perfectly.

The WWA folded in 1988, and Bruiser retired from active wrestling. Two years later, he returned to St. Louis and the Kiel Auditorium to perform special guest referee duties for a bout between NWA World Champion Sting and The Black Scorpion during Starrcade 1990. Of course, Bruiser was drawn into the action, much to the delight of the crowd, and Sting prevailed over his masked challenger, who was revealed to be Ric Flair. In November 1991, Bruiser passed away at the age of sixty-two. A detailed biography about his life, entitled *Bruiser: The World's Most Dangerous Wrestler*, was released in 2016, written by Richard Vicek and published by Crowbar Press.

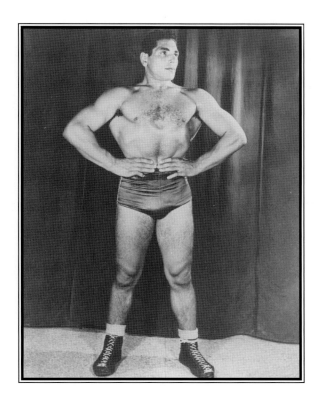

Born:	November 8, 1926
Height:	6'2"
Weight:	250
Real Name:	Ilio P. DiPaolo
Wife:	Ethel DiPaolo
Trained by:	Joe "Toots" Mondt, Dick Beyer
Career Span:	1951–65
Died:	May 10, 1995, Buffalo, NY
	68 years old

Titles Won:	8
Best Opponents:	Gene Kiniski, Don Leo Jonathan, Buddy Rogers
Halls of Fame:	2

DiPaolo, Ilio

A popular hero and genuinely great guy, Ilio DiPaolo was a class act in a tough profession. He rose above the demoralizing aspects of the business to shine in every way possible, inside the ring and out. Originally from Introdacqua, Italy, DiPaolo was scouted by Joe "Toots" Mondt in Venezuela, and arrived in the US on July 31, 1951. Soon thereafter, he found a permanent home in the Buffalo area, where he married the daughter of promoter Pedro Martinez. He won over audiences with his strength and likeable personality and formed popular tag teams with Bruno Sammartino, Sandor Szabo, and Billy Watson. In Canada, he was a six-time tag team champion and also found success during tours of Texas, California, and Japan. He opened a restaurant in Blasdell, New York and formed close bonds with many members of the Buffalo Bills football team. For his community leadership, he was named "Citizen of the Year" for 1978 in Blasdell and honored by the Professional Wrestling Hall of Fame with the New York State Award.

Born:	February 1, 1935
Height:	5'9"
Weight:	220
Real Name:	Dorrel Dixon
Trained by:	Rafael Salamanca
Nicknames:	El Gigante de Ebano (The Ebony Giant), Black Bullet
Finisher:	Jamaican Flying Bodyblock, Dropkick
Career Span:	1955–83

Titles Won:	11
Days as World Champion:	35
Age at first World Title Win:	28
Best Opponents:	Buddy Rogers, Lou Thesz, Duke Keomuka

Dixon, Dory

The "Calypso Kid," Dory Dixon was a Jamaican transplant to Mexico, competing as a weightlifter when he was scouted by promoter Salvador Lutteroth who encouraged him to become a professional wrestler. Quickly gaining a widespread following, he defeated Al Kashey for the NWA World Light Heavyweight Championship on February 13, 1959, in Mexico City, and reigned for over a year. Dixon was defeated for the coveted belt by Ray Mendoza in September 1959. Shortly thereafter, he began to tour the Texas circuit, and twice won the state heavyweight title, winning over Waldo Von Erich in 1961 and Jack Dalton in 1962. Dixon won numerous regional titles and was always a solid challenger for the touring NWA World Heavyweight champion. On March 28, 1963, he beat "Nature Boy" Buddy Rogers for the WWWA World Heavyweight Title in Cleveland, though he'd end up losing the belt to Karl Von Hess in early May 1963. Exceptionally conditioned and quick on his feet, Dixon was an excellent box office attraction throughout his career, which ended during the 1980s. He became a pastor in Mexico and continues to teach young people about health and fitness to this day.

Born:	October 24, 1943
Height:	5'7"
Weight:	215
Real Name:	William Cruickshanks
Family:	Father of Jamie Dundee
Identities:	Sir William Dundee
Nickname:	Superstar
Finisher:	Flying Press, Sleeperhold
Managed:	Lord Steven Regal (1993–94)
Career Span:	1967–Present

Titles Won:	63
Days as World Champion:	44
Age at first World Title Win:	36
Best Opponents:	Jerry Lawler, Dutch Mantel, Billy Robinson
Published Books:	1

Dundee, Bill

A charismatic grappling legend, Bill Dundee was a bright spot in the Memphis Territory for decades. Born in Scotland, he migrated to Australia in 1961, and worked in a circus as a trapeze artist. He debuted as a local grappler in 1967, and then came to the US eight years later alongside George Barnes, wrestling throughout the Mid-America territory. Over the course of his career, he held more than sixty championships, including the Continental Wrestling Association World Heavyweight Title in 1980. Dundee teamed with Jerry Lawler to win the AWA World Tag championship twice in 1987, and, in February 1995, beat Lawler for the USWA Unified World Title in Memphis. He would end up losing the belt to Razor Ramon in April. He was the AWA Southern titleholder nine times, and carried the USWA Tag Title with his son Jamie in 1996. Also, for a time, he worked as the manager of Lord Steven Regal in World Championship Wrestling, using the name "Sir William." Dundee's autobiography was released in 2011.

Born:	December 5, 1958
Height:	5'8"
Weight:	225
Real Name:	Thomas Billington
Other Sports:	Boxing
Trained by:	Ted Betley, Stu Hart
Career Span:	1975-96

Titles Won:	24
Best Opponents:	Tiger Mask, Tatsumi Fujinami, Randy Savage
Halls of Fame:	2

Dynamite Kid, The

The influential Dynamite Kid was heralded around the world for his stunning moves, quickness in the ring, and overall technical abilities; with that skill set, he was considered one of the best wrestlers of his era. From Goldborne in Lancashire, England, he won championships in his native country, Canada, Japan, and the US In February 1984, he beat The Cobra for the WWF Junior Heavyweight Title. Later in the year, Dynamite joined the WWF full-time, forming a popular tag team with cousin Davey Boy Smith, known as the British Bulldogs. The Bulldogs annexed the World Tag Team Title from Brutus Beefcake and Greg Valentine at WrestleMania 2 on April 7, 1986. Later that year, Dynamite suffered a devastating injury and needed surgery to have two discs removed from his back. He displayed his fortitude in returning to the ring to lose the belts to the Hart Foundation in January 1987. He wrestled his last match on October 10, 1996 in Tokyo, competing in a six-man tag team bout along with fellow legends Mil Mascaras and the original Tiger Mask, his greatest opponent.

Born:	December 27, 1946
Height:	6'2"
Weight:	300
Real Name:	William Reid Eadie
High School:	Brownsville High School (PA)
Trained by:	Newton Tattrie, Boris Malenko
Identities:	The Medic, Bolo Mongol, Super Machine, Ax, Axis
Career Span:	1972–2012

Titles Won:	31
Days as World Champion:	Unknown
Age at first World Title Win:	37
Best Opponents:	Rick Steamboat, Andre the Giant, Wahoo McDaniel
Halls of Fame:	2

Eadie, Bill

Track sensation Bill Eadie grew up south of Pittsburgh and attended West Virginia University. He graduated from a wrestling school taught by Newton Tattrie and partnered with his mentor as the Mongols, which made the rounds from the WWWF to the IWA. In 1976, he became the Masked Superstar in the Mid-Atlantic region and displayed his versatile style. His effective interview segments were also a sight to behold, and the Superstar wowed fans from Charlotte to Tokyo with his ring mastery. He claimed the IWA World Title during the summer of 1984 and held the National Heavyweight crown three times. Eadie formed the successful Demolition tag team with Barry Darsow, as Ax and Smash, respectively, and won a trio of WWF World Tag Team Championships between 1988 and 1990. Through 2012, Eadie continued to make appearances on the indie circuit, and two years later the Masked Superstar was inducted into the Professional Wrestling Hall of Fame. In 2015, the Cauliflower Alley Club honored Demolition with its first ever CAC Tag Team Award at its annual celebration in Las Vegas.

Born:	March 15, 1929
Height:	6'3"
Weight:	240
Real Name:	Robert Al Ellis
Parents:	John and Rose Ellis
High School:	San Angelo High School (TX)
Identities:	Bob Elliott
Finisher:	Bulldog Headlock
Career Span:	1956–78

Titles Won:	25
Days as World Champion:	Over 340
Age at first World Title Win:	35
Best Opponents:	Buddy Rogers, Dick the Bruiser, The Sheik
Halls of Fame:	1

Ellis, Bob

The tall "Cowboy" from San Angelo, Bob Ellis was a popular brawler, and his toughness was on display every time he stepped through the ropes. He boxed as an amateur and played both high school and college football, the latter for McMurry College after service in the army. After finishing college, Ellis was signed to play football by the Philadelphia Eagles in 1954. He was unimpressed with the money and returned to San Angelo, where he operated a gym. Around 1955, he received a tip from Pepper Gomez about a wrestling school in California, and ventured westward to learn the ropes from veteran Sandor Szabo. Ellis made his pro debut the following year, and by 1958, was already a box office sensation. He engaged in many violent matches with Dick the Bruiser and beat the latter three separate times for the US Title. Buddy Rogers was another important rival, and Ellis contended for the NWA Championship in the early 1960s. In 1964, he beat the Destroyer in California for the WWA World Title and, in 1973–74, won the WWA (Indiana) World Championship twice. Ellis was a headliner nearly everywhere he appeared, including Madison Square Garden and the Olympic Auditorium in Los Angeles. Ellis turned eighty-seven years of age in March 2016.

Born:	June 26, 1930
Height:	5'10"
Weight:	230
Real Name:	Henry Leonard Faggart
Parents:	Lewis and Delma Faggart
Family:	Brother of Sonny Fargo
Nicknames:	Wildman, Fabulous
Career Span:	1951–99
Died:	June 24, 2013, China Grove, NC 82 years old

Titles Won:	60
Days as World Champion:	Around 1,550
Age at first World Title Win:	30
Best Opponents:	Jerry Lawler, Gene Kiniski, Bruno Sammartino
Halls of Fame:	3

Fargo, Jackie

The legendary Jackie Fargo of China Grove, North Carolina, was a talented wrestler and performer. He was a top box office attraction for years, and was always known to offer a superb interview. Picking up wrestling as a youngster at a Goldsboro YMCA, he entered the business in the early 1950s and found a niche as an ultra-confident and strutting heel. He formed a successful tag team with faux brother Don Fargo (Don Kalt), and the pair drew huge at Madison Square Garden in New York. For most of the 1961–66, he claimed the World Heavyweight Title of Jack Pfefer's troupe, and in Houston, Pfefer put up a $50,000 offer for a unification bout between Fargo and NWA World titleholder Lou Thesz. Even with a decent amount of publicity, the big match never happened. Fargo was a legend in Memphis, where he dominated headlines for years. He mentored and feuded with Jerry Lawler, and was a perennial champion throughout his career. Fargo passed away two days shy of his eighty-third birthday in 2013 and, the next year, was inducted into the Professional Wrestling Hall of Fame.

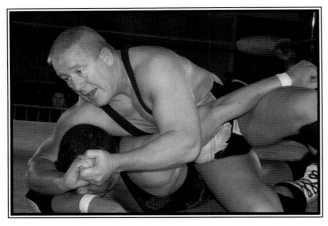

Born:	October 20, 1958
Height:	5'10"
Weight:	235
Real Name:	David John Finlay
Identities:	Belfast Bruiser, Fit Finlay
Finisher:	Celtic Cross
Career Span:	1974–2012

Finlay, Dave

Titles Won:	26
Best Opponents:	Chris Benoit, Booker T, William Regal

The no-nonsense Dave Finlay was a longtime student of amateur wrestling in his Northern Ireland hometown. Taught by his father, Dave Sr., Finlay excelled on the mat, and it wasn't before long that he combined a deep scientific knowledge of the catch-as-catch-can style with his own innate, old-fashioned toughness. He won middleweight, light heavyweight, and heavyweight championship honors in Europe prior to making his WCW debut in 1995. Initially using the name "The Belfast Bruiser," he gained more fame as "Fit Finlay," and beat Booker T for the WCW World TV Title in 1998. He joined the WWF in 2001, and was an influential coach to many up-and-comers. While on *Smackdown*, he won the United States Heavyweight Title in the summer of 2006 at the age of forty-seven, and remained an important figure in the organization until leaving the WWE in 2011. After making a number of appearances on the indie circuit, he returned to the WWE in 2012 as a producer. That same year, his son, David Finlay Jr., made his professional wrestling debut.

Flair, Ric

Born:	February 25, 1949
Height:	6'1"
Weight:	240
Real Name:	Richard Morgan Fliehr
Parents:	Richard and Kathleen Fliehr
Family:	Father of David and Reid Flair
High School:	Wayland Academy (WI)
College:	University of Minnesota
Trained by:	Verne Gagne, Billy Robinson
Nicknames:	Nature Boy®, Naitch, Slick Ric
Finisher:	Figure-four leglock
Groups:	The Four Horsemen (1986–89, 1990–91, 1993, 1996–98), The Millionaires Club (2000), Team Package (2000), The Magnificent Seven (2000–01), Evolution (2003–05), Fortune (2010–11), Immortal (2011)
Managed:	Hunter Hearst Helmsley (2002–03), Batista (2002–03)
Career Span:	1972–2011

Titles Won:	44
Days as World Champion:	3,721
Age at first World Title Win:	32
Best Opponents:	Ricky Steamboat, Harley Race, Randy Savage
Managers:	9
Halls of Fame:	7

Every generation has a "greatest wrestler," and Ric Flair is arguably the best seen by wrestling fans in the last fifty years. He was a masterful grappler—full of charisma, arrogance, and technical savvy, and was normally on the top of his game when delivering an enthusiastic promo or wrestling an important contest. His matches were always entertaining and it didn't matter if he was facing a comparable athlete or a dead weight, Flair could always make the bout interesting. His pacing and style, which set a standard for others to emulate, was extraordinary. At his height as the NWA World Heavyweight Champion, he'd wrestle more than 20-times a month, sometimes twice in a single day, and never missed a beat—performing well above his peers in an industry that respected his dedication and the honor he brought to the mat. Flair would wear his extravagant robes, strut around the ring, and wrestle like there was no tomorrow, leaving an indelible mark on audiences around the world.

Flair is a twenty-time World Heavyweight Champion, having won the National Wrestling Alliance World Title ten times between 1981 and 1993, the WWF World Title twice in 1992, and the WCW World Title eight times between 1991 and 2000. Those honors are emblematic of a surefire Hall of Famer, and he's since been enshrined in five separate institutions. The journey from motivated upstart to wrestling's "God" was winding, and it almost ended before it got started when he was nearly killed in a plane crash on October 4, 1975 on a flight from Charlotte to Wilmington, North Carolina. By this juncture, he'd graduated from the famous wrestling school of Verne Gagne and jumped from the AWA to Crockett promotions in the Mid-Atlantic territory and was establishing himself as a real up-and-comer. The accident broke Flair's back and immediate reports were that he would never wrestle again.

Defying the odds, he returned in late January 1976 and continued his ascent to the top of the sport. Flair waged a long feud with Wahoo McDaniel, which saw them battle in many brutal and bloody matches. During his early years, he learned a great deal from veterans Rip Hawk, Johnny Valentine, and Tim Woods, and formed a successful tag team with Greg Valentine. Impressing the leaders of the National Wrestling Alliance, Flair was soon supported as a candidate for the heavyweight belt, and at thirty-two years of age, on September 17, 1981, he beat Dusty Rhodes for his NWA World Title in Kansas City. He immediately assumed a hectic schedule, wrestling throughout the globe and taking on a wide variety of competitors. After 631 days on top, Flair lost the belt to Harley Race in St. Louis on June 10, 1983. In the main event of the first Starrcade, Flair regained the belt in a special cage match.

The next seven years was a remarkable time for professional wrestling and for Flair. He was considered the opposite of Hulk Hogan, as Ric was the more finely-tuned grappler who appealed more to the serious wrestling enthusiast. During that time, he won the NWA World Title five additional times, beating both Race and Rhodes again, Kerry Von Erich, Ron Garvin, and Ricky Steamboat. He led the illustrious Four Horsemen, headlined Starrcade events, and proved his durability an endless amount of times. In 1989, he had two classic feuds against Steamboat and Terry Funk, and battled an old rival, Lex Luger all over the map the following year. Sting beat him for the NWA championship on July 7, 1990, but Flair regained it at the Meadowlands in East Rutherford, New Jersey on January 11, 1991, making him an eight-time titleholder. Flair also traded the crown with Tatsumi Fujinami before departing for WCW during that summer.

The WWF was his next stop, and on January 19, 1992, he entered the Royal Rumble at number three and remained in the bout for more than an hour. He outlasted his competitors to win the event and the vacant World Title. Flair became the second man in history to have won the NWA and WWF Titles after the original "Nature Boy," Buddy Rogers. He ended up losing the title to Randy Savage at WrestleMania, but regained it from him on September 1 of that year. Finally, he dropped the belt to Bret Hart at a house show in Saskatoon, Saskatchewan on October 12. In 1993, he returned to WCW and won his tenth and final NWA World championship from Barry Windham. On December 27, 1993 in Charlotte, he defeated Vader for the WCW World Title and a few months later, he resumed his longstanding feud with Steamboat. On July 17, 1994, he lost his title to the newly arriving Hulk Hogan.

Seven years later, after many memorable performances, Flair matched up against one of his greatest rivals, Sting, on the emotional final episode of WCW *Nitro* in March 2001. Their bout was acknowledged as a fitting farewell to the promotion. Flair appeared in the WWF before the year was out, and engaged in a war for control of the organization with Vince McMahon as a purported co-owner. They took their bad blood into the ring at the Royal Rumble, which saw Flair win a street fight, but McMahon won a bout later on for full ownership. In 2003, he joined a group known as Evolution along with Triple H, Batista, and Randy Orton. On December 14, 2003, he captured the World Tag Team Title with Batista and regained the belts from Rob Van Dam and Booker T for a second reign as champion. At Unforgiven on September 18, 2005, he beat Carlito for the Intercontinental Championship. His reign lasted until February 20, 2006, when he lost a bout to Shelton Benjamin on *Raw*. Flair also teamed up with Roddy Piper to win the World Tag Team Title from the Spirit Squad in November 2006, but they lost the belts a week later in England.

A decree was made announcing that the next match Flair lost would force his retirement and "Naitch" did his best to remain active against many tough opponents. On March 30, 2008 in Orlando, he met his match, Shawn Michaels, and was defeated. The crowd and his peers the next night on *Raw* all gave him the respect he deserved. He remained employed by the promotion through the summer of 2009, and then left for greener pastures. Flair joined a tour led by Hulk Hogan in Australia later in the year and debuted for TNA on January 4, 2010. He began to mentor a younger crop of grapplers starting with A.J. Styles and later named his group, Fortune. Appropriately, Flair wrestled his final match in TNA against his longtime rival, Sting, in September 2011. He departed the promotion the next year and returned to WWE, where he served in a variety of roles. Beginning in 2013, shortly after her pro debut, Flair acted as a manager for his daughter Charlotte. She captured the WWE Divas championship in September 2015, and Flair continued to appear by her side.

The WWE has honored Flair with two separate inductions into its Hall of Fame; the first in 2008, recognizing his legendary solo career, and in 2012 as a member of the illustrious Four Horsemen. Flair has been inducted into five other distinct halls of fame, including the Professional Wrestling Hall of Fame (2006) and the Thesz-Tragos Hall of Fame in Iowa (2013). Regardless of his on-camera responsibility, Flair continues to live up to his trademark style and not only entertains people with his "styling and profiling," but reminds enthusiasts of what he's given to the sport over the last forty-plus years. And his faithful fans know that few individuals in history have been more dedicated to pro wrestling than the "Nature Boy."

Fujinami, Tatsumi

Born:	December 28, 1953
Height:	6'1"
Weight:	200–235
Family:	Father of Leona Fujinami
Trained by:	Antonio Inoki, Karl Gotch
Identities:	Dragon Fujinami
Nickname:	The Dragon
Finisher:	Dragon Sleeper, Dragon Suplex
Trained:	Numerous athletes including Osamu Nishimura
Career Span:	1971–Present

Titles Won:	21
Days as World Champion:	887
Age at first World Title Win:	34
Best Opponents:	Riki Choshu, Vader, Antonio Inoki
Halls of Fame:	2

A superb technical wrestler who, in February 2011, celebrated his fortieth anniversary in the business, Tatsumi Fujinami is credited with helping launch the junior heavyweight revolution in Japan. He was a pioneering figure in New Japan Pro Wrestling and was with the company when it started in 1972, being trained extensively by the legendary duo of Antonio Inoki and Karl Gotch. Fujinami took what he learned and spawned many classic matches throughout the course of his great career. On May 8, 1988, he won the vacant IWGP championship over Big Van Vader at Ariake Coliseum in Tokyo and wrestled a no-contest against Riki Choshu on May 27, which held up the title. Fujinami won the rematch on June 24, winning his second IWGP Title. On December 9, 1988, he beat Kerry Von Erich in a controversial IWGP-WCCW World Title unification match. A serious back injury forced him to surrender the IWGP Title in April 1989, but he bounced back to win his third championship on December 26, 1990 over Choshu.

In early 1991, Fujinami traded the IWGP belt with Vader, and then beat Ric Flair for the NWA World championship at the Tokyo Dome on March 21, 1991. The switch was never recognized in the US, but a rematch was staged on May 19, 1991 with Flair regaining the NWA crown. His longtime rival, Choshu, ended his reign as IWGP champion in January 1992. In 1993, Fujinami won the G-1 Climax Tournament and captured his fifth IWGP Title from Shinya Hashimoto in April 1994. It would be four years before he would win his sixth and final IWGP championship, on April 4, 1998, defeating Kensuke Sasaki during Inoki's retirement show. Between 1985 and 2001, he held the IWGP Tag Team Title four times with partner Kengo Kimura. Outside the ring, Fujinami worked as a booker and president for New Japan and was involved with the organization until 2006. On February 5, 2011, he wrestled Mil Mascaras to a ten-minute draw on a IGF show promoted by Inoki.

Born:	February 3, 1941
Height:	6'2"
Weight:	235
Real Name:	Dory Earnest Funk Jr.
Parents:	Dory and Dorothy Funk
Wife:	Marti Funk
High School:	Canyon High School (TX)
College:	West Texas State University
Trained by:	Dory Funk Sr.
Identities:	The Outlaw (Masked), Hoss Funk
Finisher:	Spinning Toehold
Managed:	Jesse Barr, Adam Windsor
Career Span:	1963–2015
Website:	www.dory-funk.com

Funk, Dory Jr.

Titles Won:	44
Days as World Champion:	Over 1,660
Age at first World Title Win:	22
Best Opponents:	Jack Brisco, Harley Race, Gene Kiniski
Halls of Fame:	8
Movies:	2, plus a few documentaries

History was made on the evening of February 11, 1969 at the Armory in Tampa when Dory Funk Jr. forced champion Gene Kiniski to submit to his spinning toe-hold and won the NWA World Heavyweight Title. He won the most coveted championship in the business, and a belt that his father, Dory Sr. had chased for years. Funk would endure as champion for 1,563 days, the second longest reign the National Wrestling Alliance history. During that time, he met all contenders and performed admirably throughout the world. After an incredible run, he was finally beaten by Harley Race on May 24, 1973. Funk won regional championships throughout the NWA, from Florida to Japan, and teamed with his brother Terry to capture the AJPW International and World Tag Team Titles. They also won the Real World tournament in 1977, 1979, and 1982. Dory wrestled Terry on April 30, 1981 in Japan after being named International champion, and he came out victorious after a fifty-four minute match.

It may be hard to conceive, but Dory was actually a claimant to the World Heavyweight Title less than three months into his professional career. Ironically, the title victory also came at the expense of Gene Kiniski on March 28, 1963 in Amarillo. This version of the title, however, was regionally based, and was later merged with Lou Thesz's NWA championship. As a rookie, Funk was already conditioned enough to wrestle a broadway with Verne Gagne and challenge Thesz. He was a versatile athlete, and the family tradition of wrestling was carried forward to great success. Long affiliated with All-Japan Pro Wrestling,

Funk acted as a booker for the promotion and did the same in Florida for a period. The Funk Brothers sold their interest in the Amarillo promotion in 1980 and he wrestled his last match in Japan in 2008. Dory operates the famous Funking Conservatory wrestling school in Ocala, Florida, where he's coached some of the best and brightest.

Photo Courtesy of Pete Lederberg—plmathfoto@hotmail.com

Funk, Terry

Born:	June 30, 1944
Height:	6'1"
Weight:	235
Real Name:	Terry Dee Funk
Parents:	Dory and Dorothy Funk
Family:	Brother of Dory Funk Jr.
Wife:	Vicki Funk
High School:	Canyon High School (TX)
Colleges:	Cisco Junior College, West Texas State University
Trained by:	Dory Funk Sr.
Identities:	Chainsaw Charlie
Nicknames:	Hardcore Legend
Finisher:	Piledriver, DDT, Spinning Toehold
Owned:	A percentage of the Amarillo promotion (1967–78)
Career Span:	1965–2015

Titles Won:	57
Days as World Champion:	724
Age at first World Title Win:	31
Best Opponents:	Ric Flair, Harley Race, Dusty Rhodes
Halls of Fame:	11
TV Appearances:	Over 20
Movies:	10, plus 7 documentaries
Published Books:	1

Terry Funk's love and passion for the wrestling business was apparent in every match he participated in, beginning in 1965 and continuing through 2015, where at seventy-one years of age, still gave it his all for the entertainment of fans.t The "Funker" grew up around the business, watching intently as his father Dory Funk Sr. did battle week after week at the Sports Arena in Amarillo. Terry, along with his brother, Dory Jr., not only also became pro wrestlers, but established themselves as legends in their own distinctive ways. For Terry, it was a natural affinity toward work as a tremendously brutal heel, drawing the anger from crowds and laying down the groundwork for the hardcore style that has become a significant part of the industry. He has held numerous wrestling championships across the globe, but perhaps his greatest accomplishment was winning the National Wrestling Alliance World Heavyweight Title in 1975, an honor that his brother also achieved six years earlier.

Hailing from the Double Cross Ranch near Canyon, Texas, Funk played football at West Texas State, and his anticipated wrestling debut came in December 1965. The lessons of the Amarillo territory were vast, and included old-fashioned, no-holds-barred brawling. Terry was a quick learner and an enthusiastic competitor, displaying his fierceness in violent matches. He also knew the fundamentals that benefited him his entire career. In February 1973, he won the Missouri Heavyweight Title in St. Louis, and two years later, he won the Mid-Atlantic version of the US Heavyweight Title in a tournament. On December 10, 1975, at the Miami Beach Convention Center, he beat Jack Brisco for the NWA World Title, stunning the 5,000 fans in attendance. Funk remained champion until February 6, 1977 in Toronto, when he was defeated by Harley Race at Maple Leaf Gardens. Race preyed on Funk's injured knee and won the match with an Indian Deathlock in 14:10.

The Funk Brothers were also quite successful as a tag team, capturing the International Tag Team Title on several occasions, winning the AJPW Real World Tag Tournament three times in 1977, 1979, and 1982, and the WWC World Tag Team Title twice in Puerto Rico. Funk won a number of regional championships; the USWA and ECW World Heavyweight Titles, and the WCW US Title in 2000. He had a memorable feud against Ric Flair in 1989 and great matches against Harley Race, Dusty Rhodes, Cactus Jack, and Sabu. He was instrumental in helping ECW gain notoriety and was the poster child for what it really meant to be "hardcore." His dedication to that "anything goes" style earned him respect from yet another generation of fans and influenced many of his fellow wrestlers. Although he's had a number of retirement matches, Funk has never completely walked away from the sport. He teamed with brother Dory in October 2013, with Tommy Dreamer in November 2013, and wrestled longtime rival Jerry Lawler in October 2015. The latter match, which occurred in Jackson, Tennessee, ended with Lawler winning by disqualification. Honored by eleven different Halls of Fame, Terry Funk has been an icon for decades, and will continue to set the standard for professionalism both in and away from the squared circle.

Born:	November 27, 1948
Height:	6'1"
Weight:	220
Real Name:	Gregory Allan Gagne
High School:	Mound High School (MN)
College:	University of Wyoming
Finisher:	Sleeperhold
Career Span:	1973–91

Titles Won:	4
Best Opponents:	Nick Bockwinkel, Curt Hennig, Larry Zbyszko

Gagne, Greg

Popular second-generation grappler Greg Gagne was not even a year old when his famous father, Verne, wrestled in his first pro match. For the next forty years, he was surrounded by the sport—from the promotional side of the AWA to his own in-ring career. He was a talented quarterback in school and was trained by his father and Billy Robinson for his 1973 professional wrestling debut. Along with Jim Brunzell, he formed the babyface tag team The Hi-Flyers and won the AWA World belts on two occasions. The first victory came on July 7, 1977, over Blackjack Lanza and Bobby Duncum. They held the straps for over a year, until losing the title to Pat Patterson and Ray Stevens. Gagne and Brunzell regained the championship in mid-1981, and dominated challengers for another two years, finally succumbing to the Sheiks in June 1983. In 1987–88, Gagne also won the AWA International TV Title twice, and remained a main figure in the promotion until it went out of business in the early 1990s. He worked for WCW and the WWE behind the scenes and had an influential effect on many careers. In 2006, he inducted his father into the WWE Hall of Fame.

Photo Courtesy of Pete Lederberg—plmathfoto@hotmail.com

Born:	September 25, 1952
Height:	5'11"
Weight:	230
Real Name:	James Williams
High School:	Leto High School (FL)
Trained by:	Joe Scarpa
Finisher:	DDT
Career Span:	1969–99

Titles Won:	26
Best Opponents:	Ric Flair, David Von Erich, Rick Martel
Halls of Fame:	1

Garvin, Jimmy

"Gorgeous" Jimmy Garvin's entertaining personality was always on display when he entered the ring. He was an engaging heel while touring with Precious on his arm, and also as a member of the Fabulous Freebirds. A talented amateur grappler in Tampa, Garvin broke into the business as the manager of Terry Garvin, and, under the name "Beau James," worked as a second for Ray Stevens. While in the Dallas territory during the 1980s, he captured the American Heavyweight Title four different times and feuded heavily with Kevin Von Erich and Chris Adams. In 1985, he partnered with Steve Regal to upset The Road Warriors for the AWA World Tag Team championship. They would never lose the belts in the ring, as officials claimed they were dethroned by Curt Hennig and Scott Hall in Albuquerque in January 1986. Along with Michael Hayes as a member of the Fabulous Freebirds, Garvin won the NWA and WCW World Tag Team Titles in 1989 and '91, respectively. The Freebirds, including Terry Gordy and Buddy Roberts, were inducted into the WWE Hall of Fame in 2016, and Garvin and Hayes were present in Dallas to accept the honor.

Photo Courtesy of Pete Lederberg—plmathfoto@hotmail.com

Born:	March 30, 1945
Height:	5'10"
Weight:	230
Real Name:	Roger Barnes
Family:	Stepfather of Jim Garvin
Trained by:	Pat Girard, Tony Santos Pro-Wrestling Camp
Identities:	Mr. Eau Gallie, Miss Atlanta Lively
Nickname:	Hands of Stone, One Man Gang
Finisher:	Indian Death Lock, Garvin Stomp
Career Span:	1962–2011

Titles Won:	35
Days as World Champion:	62
Age at first World Title Win:	42
Best Opponents:	Ric Flair, Randy Savage, Tully Blanchard

Garvin, Ronnie

"Rugged" Ronnie Garvin of Quebec was a distinguished grappler for more than thirty-five years, displaying his toughness with his hands and feuding with the best in the business. He shocked the world on September 25, 1987 when he beat "Nature Boy" Ric Flair for the coveted NWA World Heavyweight Title. The victory, which came in Detroit, was inside of a steel cage, and Garvin reigned for sixty-two days, losing the belt back to Flair at Starrcade on November 26. Without question, that was the defining moment of his career, but Garvin won a number of regional championships in Florida, Georgia, and Tennessee, and formed a successful tag team with his "brother," Terry Garvin. He retired from the ring in 1999 and has occasionally worked as a referee for various indies. Nowadays, Garvin can be found in the cockpit of planes, as he is an accomplished pilot.

Photo Courtesy of Scott Teal/Crowbar Press

Born:	April 21, 1927
Height:	5'9"
Weight:	225
Real Name:	Joseph Serapio Palemino Gomez Jr.
Parents:	Joseph and Maria Gomez
Wife:	Bonnie Gomez
High School:	Roosevelt High School (CA)
Trained by:	Miguel Guzman
Finishers:	Stomach Claw, Airplane Spin
Career Span:	1953–82
Died:	May 6, 2004, Oakland, CA 77 years old

Titles Won:	50
Days as World Champion:	154
Age at first World Title Win:	48
Best Opponents:	Lou Thesz, Buddy Rogers, Pat O'Connor

Gomez, Pepper

The "Man with a Cast Iron Stomach" was known to audiences as Pepper Gomez, a heroic superstar who fought the wrestling wars for twenty-nine years. Born in Los Angeles, Gomez was the son of a plumber, and an athletic standout in high school and college. In 1950, the same year he was starring as a fullback at Los Angeles City College, he won "Mr. Muscle Beach" at Santa Monica for his impressive strength. Over the next six years, he participated in no less than thirteen amateur bodybuilding tournaments and was featured on the covers of *Strength & Health* and *Muscle Power*. Ed "Strangler" Lewis aided in his becoming a wrestler, and Gomez had no trouble finding a large base of fans throughout the country. He won the Texas State Title a total of fifteen times, the United States Title in California, and the WWA World Title in 1975. Feats like having a car drive over his midsection proved without a doubt that he had a "cast iron stomach." Gomez passed away on May 6, 2004, at the age of seventy-seven.

Born:	April 23, 1961
Height:	6'4"
Weight:	285
Real Name:	Terry Ray Gordy Sr.
Parents:	Billy and Mildred Gordy
Family:	Father of Terry Gordy Jr., uncle of Richard Slinger
High School:	Rossville High School (GA)
Trained by:	James Kyle, Archie Gouldie, Afa
Identities:	Terry Mecca, Terry Meeker, Mr. Wrestling, The Executioner
Nicknames:	Bamm Bamm
Finisher:	Powerbomb
Career Span:	1974-2001
Died:	July 16, 2001, Soddy Daisy, TN 40 years old

Gordy, Terry

Titles Won:	37
Days as World Champion:	176
Age at first World Title Win:	25
Best Opponents:	Jumbo Tsuruta, Mitsuharu Misawa, Giant Baba
Halls of Fame:	2

An agile 6'4" grappler with natural abilities, Terry Gordy was a well-rounded performer and a headliner around the world. He grew up in Rossville, Georgia and had the size and athletic competency to become a professional wrestler at the age of thirteen, initially working for his uncle's promotion. In 1978, he formed the legendary Freebirds with Michael Hayes, and, along with Buddy Roberts, won the World Six-Man Tag Team Title five times between 1982 and 1986, brutally feuding with the Von Erich Family. On May 30, 1986, Gordy beat Jim Duggan in a tournament final for the initial UWF World Heavyweight Title. While in Japan, he became the first foreigner to capture the coveted All-Japan Unified Triple Crown when he beat Jumbo Tsuruta in 1990. Gordy teamed with Stan Hansen to win the AJPW World Tag Team Title twice and with Steve Williams five times. He was a powerful, yet intelligent grappler, who was able to perform moves like a running dropkick with ease. At one point, he was among the best in the world.

In 2016, Gordy and his Freebird mates, were inducted into the WWE Hall of Fame, and his son Ray was on hand to accept on his behalf.

Born:	June 4, 1937
Height:	6'6"
Weight:	350
Real Name:	Robert James Marella
Family:	Father of Joey Marella
High School:	Jefferson High School (NY)
College:	Ithaca College
Trained by:	Pedro Martinez, Stu Hart
Finisher:	Airplane Spin
Owned:	A minority share in the Capitol Wrestling Corporation
Career Span:	1960–87
Died:	October 6, 1999, Mooresville, NJ 62 years old

Gorilla Monsoon

Titles Won:	7
Days as World Champion:	35
Age at first World Title Win:	30
Best Opponents:	Bruno Sammartino, Bill Miller, Bobo Brazil
Managers:	2
Halls of Fame:	3

The affable and insightful voice behind WWF programming during the 1980s and 1990s, Gorilla Monsoon was a talented Greco-Roman wrestler while in college, and during the summer of 1959, he toured with the national squad overseas. After turning pro, he was billed as being from Manchuria and was a convincing challenger to WWWF champion Bruno Sammartino. He also teamed with Killer Kowalski to lift the US Tag Team Title from Brute Bernard and Skull Murphy. During a tour of Australia in 1968, Monsoon won the IWA World Title from Spiros Arion, and held the WWA World Tag Team Title twice in Indiana. In 1976, he made national news when he bodyslammed boxing legend Muhammad Ali. Away from the ring, he participated in many hilarious and sometimes oddball skits with Bobby Heenan on USA Network's *Prime Time Wrestling*. His straight-laced commentary worked perfectly alongside pro-heel talkers, Heenan and Jesse Ventura, and earned a spot in the WWF Hall of Fame in 1994.

Born:	August 3, 1924
Height:	6'1"
Weight:	235
Real Name:	Karl Charles Istaz
Trained by:	Billy Riley
Identities:	Karl Krauser
Finisher:	Atomic Suplex
Career Span:	1953–82
Died:	July 28, 2007, Tampa, FL 82 years old

Titles Won:	5
Days as World Champion:	Over 727 (NJPW Real World Title claim is of unknown length)
Age at first World Title Win:	38
Best Opponents:	Antonio Inoki, Lou Thesz, Don Leo Jonathan
Halls of Fame:	3

Gotch, Karl

A student of the legendary "Snakepit" gymnasium in Wigan, England, Karl Gotch went on to become an astonishingly talented professional grappler. In fact, he was almost too much of an expert to be a pro wrestler in a world of flashy gimmicks and high drama. He was more in the league of a great Olympic champion, and had the ferociousness to beat nearly every opponent he stepped in the ring against. Born in Antwerp, Belgium, Gotch began wrestling at nine years of age, and was a perennial amateur champion. He represented Belgium in the 1948 Olympics in both the freestyle and Greco-Roman events, but did not place. By 1960, he was competing on the North American pro circuit and held the Ohio-based AWA World Title for nearly two years. Always displaying amazing scientific prowess, he earned international praise, particularly while in Japan, and trained many athletes in the pure art of submission grappling.

Born:	June 7, 1943
Height:	6'3"
Weight:	270
Real Name:	Eldridge Wayne Coleman
Wife:	Valerie Coleman
High School:	North Phoenix High School (AZ)
Pro Sports:	American Football League—Houston Oilers (1966)
Finisher:	Bearhug
Managed:	Don Muraco (1987–88)
Career Span:	1970–87

Titles Won:	12
Days as World Champion:	383
Age at first World Title Win:	31
Best Opponents:	Bruno Sammartino, Bob Backlund, Harley Race
Halls of Fame:	3

Graham, Billy

Displaying the frame of a bodybuilder, "Superstar" Billy Graham was a remarkable athlete and box office attraction. He was originally from the Phoenix area, where he was a track and field standout, specializing in the discus and shot put. Additionally, he boxed and participated in competitive arm wrestling. Already 6'3" and 200 pounds by the time he was fifteen, Graham was successful in every endeavor, even capturing the 1961 "Mr. Arizona" title for his impressive physique. In 1969, he was trained by Stu Hart in Calgary, and a year later, he adopted the signature "Graham" name while in Los Angeles—becoming a "brother" of Dr. Jerry Graham. Seven years later, he ended Bruno Sammartino's second run with the WWWF Heavyweight Title on April 30, 1977. He toured successfully as champion until February 20, 1978, when Bob Backlund beat him for the belt at Madison Square Garden. As a flamboyant grappler, Graham was outstanding and he established the standard for future muscle-bound heels to emulate.

Born:	December 16, 1931
Height:	6'0"
Weight:	275
Real Name:	Jerry Martin Matthews (legally changed to Jerry M. Graham)
Parents:	John and Mary Graham
Military:	United States Army (1947–48)
Groups:	The Stable of Champions (1963–65)
Career Span:	1952–93
Died:	January 24, 1997, Glendale, CA 65 years old

Titles Won:	13
Days as World Champion:	Unknown, briefly claimed in 1960
Age at first World Title Win:	28
Best Opponents:	Antonino Rocca, Bruno Sammartino, Bobo Brazil
Halls of Fame:	1

Graham, Dr. Jerry

The one and only Dr. Jerry Graham was a chaotic figure inside and outside of the squared circle. He lived a life full of wrestling success, yet was troubled in his personal life to the extent that he had numerous run-ins with the law. He entered the Army at fifteen years of age in June 1947 and served with the 82nd Airborne Division at Fort Bragg as the driver for the famed General James Gavin. He returned to Phoenix, where he grew up, and participated in local athletics before being scouted and trained by Jim Londos. Large physically, Graham developed into a crafty worker, and was known as the wrestling hypnotist, claiming to own several college degrees, but was known to employ his own brand of psychology to manipulate both opponents and audiences. In 1958, he formed a punishing brother duo with Eddie Graham and won the US Tag Team Title four times. Some type of controversy usually followed Graham wherever he went, and he wrestled into the 1990s on a part-time basis around Los Angeles. His legacy as an enjoyable villain is still celebrated today.

Born:	February 5, 1940
Height:	6'2"
Weight:	290
Real Name:	James Grady Johnson
Parents:	James and Grace Johnson
Identities:	Pretty Boy Calhoun, Pretty Boy Floyd, Mighty Yankee, El Lobo
Career Span:	1961–2001
Died:	June 23, 2006, Milledgeville, GA 66 years old

Titles Won:	22
Days as World Champion:	86
Age at first World Title Win:	25
Best Opponents:	Lou Thesz, Bruno Sammartino, Dusty Rhodes

Graham, Luke

The unpredictable Dr. Jerry Graham located a wrestler in 1963 that enjoyed chaos and carnage almost as much as he did. That man was Luke Graham, his "brother" in an ever-growing clan of talented rulebreakers. Appropriately nicknamed "Crazy," Luke was from Union Point, Georgia, and wrestled around the southeast under a variety of gimmicks. The Grahams entered WWWF territory in 1964 and captured the US Tag Team championship. A year later, in Los Angeles, Luke beat Pedro Morales for the WWA World Title, and won belts in Hawaii, Puerto Rico, and across the territorial system. In 1971, he was crowned, along with Tarzan Tyler, as the initial WWWF World Tag Team Champions, and it was claimed they beat Dick the Bruiser and The Sheik in a tournament in New Orleans, though the tournament never happened. Graham and Tyler held the championship until December 1971, when they were defeated by Rene Goulet and Karl Gotch in New York. Graham's antics drove audiences wild, and he always provided a colorful show worth watching. He passed away on June 23, 2006, at sixty-six years of age.

Born:	January 7, 1949
Height:	5'11"
Weight	225
Real Name:	Salvador Guerrero III
High School:	Burges High School (TX)
College:	University of Texas
Trained by:	Gory Guerrero
Career Span:	1970–2011

Titles Won:	48
Best Opponents:	Dory Funk Jr., Harley Race, Roddy Piper

Guerrero, Chavo Sr.

The first of four wrestling sons born to Gory Guerrero, Chavo Guerrero Sr. was an accomplished amateur grappler in El Paso. He went pro in 1970, initially using the name "Gory Jr.," but soon adopted the name that would carry him to international fame. In 1975, he had a breakout year in Los Angeles. The popular athlete won the Jules Strongbow Scientific trophy and the Americas Heavyweight and Tag Team belts. Over the next five years, he won the Americas championship seventeen times, defeating the likes of Roddy Piper, Ernie Ladd, and Dory Funk Jr. On February 11, 1977, he beat Alfonso Dantes for the NWA World Light Heavyweight crown, the same title his father held back in the 1960s. Chavo would hold the belt twice in 1977, losing it the final time back to Dantes in April. In May 2004, as "Chavo Classic," he won the WWE Cruiserweight belt, taking the strap from his own son, Chavo Jr., on *Smackdown*.

Born:	April 1, 1931
Height:	6′3″
Weight:	250
Parents:	Orville and Faye Hamilton
High School:	Benton High School (MO)
Identities:	Rocky Hamilton, The Missouri Mauler, Casey McShain
Career Span:	1951–80
Died:	July 20, 1996, St. Joseph, MO 65 years old

Titles Won:	22
Best Opponents:	Jack Brisco, Gene Kiniski, Dory Funk Jr.

Hamilton, Larry

St. Joseph, Missouri, was a hotspot for professional wrestling under promoter Gust Karras for forty years, and among the latter's greatest protégés was Larry Hamilton. Hamilton was captain of his high school football team, a talented amateur boxer, and a top grappling prospect when he made his debut in 1951. He was physically big, and his oversized presence made him a natural heel, which Hamilton developed over the course of his career. By the late 1950s, he was a major personality. He flourished in tag teams with his younger brother Jody and Tom Renasto while headlining across North America. As a singles competitor, he won both the Central States and Nebraska State Titles under his own name, but transitioned to the "Missouri Mauler," and the new gimmick spawned even greater success. The Mauler won the Southern Heavyweight crown in both the Mid-Atlantic region and in Florida, the American championship in Texas, and a number of other belts. Hamilton retired in 1980, and passed away at the age of sixty-five in 1996.

Born:	August 29, 1949
Height:	6'3"
Weight:	320
Real Name:	John Stanley Hansen II
Parents:	John and Nella Hansen
Wife:	Yumi Hansen
HS Ach.:	All-State Football Player (1966–67)
College Ach.:	Letterman (1968–70), Team captain (1970)
Trained by:	The Funk family
Nicknames:	The Lariet, The Badman from Borger
Finisher:	Lariet Clothesline, Brazos-Valley Backbreaker
Tag Team:	The Superpowers w/ Vader
Career Span:	1973–2000

Hansen, Stan

Titles Won:	37
Days as World Champion:	1,846
Age at first World Title Win:	34
Best Opponents:	Kenta Kobashi, Jumbo Tsuruta, Mitsuharu Misawa
Halls of Fame:	4

Hard-striking Stan Hansen was a brutally tough wrestler and an international legend. Engaging in mat battles for twenty-seven years, with over 120 tours of Japan, he was an aggressive competitor and unleashed awesome blows that could cut down even the largest foe. His brawling skills were intense, and the cowboy hat and tobacco dripping from his mouth added to his mystique. No one was safe around him and his career was full of memorable matches and championship victories. He was a high school football standout for the Las Cruces Bulldogs under coach Ed Boykin and was awarded the Prep All America Football Award. He continued his exceptional football career as a linebacker at West Texas State and had a tryout with the Baltimore Colts in July 1971, but was cut the following month. Hansen broke into the business, learning from many ring veterans in the Amarillo area, and visited a few territories before working for All-Japan for the first time in 1975.

Managed by Fred Blassie, Hansen turned up in the WWWF the following year and broke Bruno Sammartino's neck with his lariat clothesline on April 26, 1976 at Madison Square Garden. The angle built up to their June 25, 1976 bout at Shea Stadium, where an estimated 32,000 fans turned out to see Sammartino exact revenge—and that's exactly what happened. On February 8, 1980, Hansen beat Antonio Inoki for the NWF belt and three years later, topped Shohei Baba for the PWF championship, becoming the only man to have beaten both Japanese legends for titles. He made Rick Martel submit to capture the AWA World Heavyweight Title on December 29, 1985 and held the coveted AJPW Unified Japanese Triple Crown four times. During his career, he had memorable matches with Jumbo Tsuruta, Terry Funk, Genichiro Tenryu, and Hulk Hogan, and formed a vicious tag team with Bruiser Brody. From 2001 to 2007, he acted as the PWF Commissioner for All-Japan, adding another dimension to his wrestling resume.

Photo Courtesy of the Collection of Libnan Ayoub

Hard Boiled Haggerty

Born:	April 2, 1925
Height:	6'1"
Weight:	265
Real Name:	Donald Joseph Stanisauske (changed to Stansauk, then to Haggerty)
Parents:	Joseph and Josie Stanisauske
High School:	Franklin High School (CA)
Colleges:	Texas Christian University, Denver University
Military:	United States Navy (WWII)
NFL Draft:	Detroit Lions (1950) (18th Round) (226)
Pro Sports:	National Football League— Green Bay Packers (1950–51)
Trained by:	Danny Loos, Tom Zaharias
Identities:	Don Sparrow, Mr. M, The Masked Executioner
Finisher:	Clawhold
Career Span:	1951–69
Died:	January 27, 2004, Malibu, CA 78 years old

Titles Won:	22
Days as World Champion:	Unknown
Age at first World Title Win:	31
Best Opponents:	Verne Gagne, Fred Blassie, Gene Kiniski
TV Appearances:	Around 30
Movies:	Over 20

Recognizable Hollywood actor Don Haggerty was known by a variety of names throughout his life. In the ring, he was the most famous as the third "Hard Boiled Haggerty," a villain of the highest order, who wreaked havoc throughout the territories from the early 1950s until the late 1960s. One of his crowning achievements occurred in 1956 when he beat Killer Kowalski for the World Heavyweight Title in Montreal. The youngest of six children, Haggerty grew up in Los Angeles, took drama classes in high school and college, and developed the range of his characters in the squared circle—snarling at opponents and crowds, and drawing the ire of everyone who saw him wrestle. Wearing a trademark mustache, he performed in more than twenty films and made dozens of TV appearances. He was also a longstanding member of the Cauliflower Alley Club.

Photo Courtesy of Pete Lederberg—plmathfoto@hotmail.com

Haystacks Calhoun

Born:	August 3, 1934
Height:	6'2"
Weight:	600
Real Name:	William D. Calhoun
Career Span:	1956–80
Died:	December 7, 1989, McKinney, TX 55 years old

Titles Won:	4
Best Opponents:	Buddy Rogers, Johnny Valentine, Bruno Sammartino
Movies:	1

In 1989, professional wrestling lost a true great: the giant Haystacks Calhoun of McKinney, Texas. Calhoun, a world-renowned hero of the industry, was recognized in the mainstream for his appearances on *The Tonight Show* and *Art Linkletter*, and his awesome 600 pounds were carried well inside of the squared circle. He entered the mat field in 1956 as Billy "The Blimp" Calhoun, but soon adopted the moniker, "Country Boy Calhoun," and took Count Pietro Rossi as his manager. "Haystacks" was his guise by 1958 and after many successful performances throughout the east, he was highly sought after by promoters and television producers. Calhoun won the WWWF Tag Title in 1973 with Tony Garea and kept up his popular act until 1980. His overalls, horseshoe, and bare feet were trademarks of the legendary big man.

Born:	January 29, 1936
Height:	6'0"
Weight:	275
Real Name:	Lawrence Henry Hennig Jr.
Parents:	Lawrence and Gertrude Hennig
Wife:	Irene Hennig
Family:	Father of Curt and Jesse Hennig
High School:	Robbinsdale High School (MN)
HS Ach.:	Minnesota High School State Wrestling Title (1954) (HWT)
Nicknames:	Pretty Boy
Career Span:	1957–85

Titles Won:	10
Best Opponents:	Verne Gagne, Nick Bockwinkel, Dory Funk Jr.
Halls of Fame:	1

Hennig, Larry

Over a career lasting nearly thirty years, Larry "The Axe" Hennig proved time and again that he was one of the roughest men in the business and not someone who could be pushed around. He was a high school wrestling champion at Robbinsdale High, just outside Minneapolis, and his diverse knowledge of holds combined with his size made him a feared battler. Schooled by two of the best professional coaches in the business, Verne Gagne and Joe Pazandak, he made his debut in 1957 and went on to capture the AWA World Tag Team championship on four occasions. Hennig teamed with Duke Hoffman to win a tournament for the vacant title on January 15, 1962, but his most successful partnership came with Harley Race. The duo dethroned the legendary Bruiser and Crusher on January 30, 1965, traded the belts with Crusher and Gagne, and then triumphed over Bruiser and Crusher for the final time in 1967. His son, Curt Hennig, would also have a great wrestling career. In fact, when Curt was honored for a posthumous induction into the WWE Hall of Fame in 2007, Larry was on hand to accept in his honor. Larry's grandson, Curtis Axel, is a current WWE superstar as well. In 2006, Larry was inducted into the Thesz-Tragos Hall of Fame, and was honored with the Iron Mike Mazurki Award by the Cauliflower Alley Club in 2015.

Born:	July 7, 1932
Height:	6'2"
Weight:	315
Real Name:	Alfonso Carlos Chicarro
Identities:	Pepe Cortes, Hercules Romero, Raoul Romero, Mighty Hercules
Career Span:	1955–71
Died:	July 24, 1971, Near St. Cloud, MN 39 years old

Titles Won:	At least 4
Days as World Champion:	Over 14 (unknown time for 1964 claim in Europe)
Age at first World Title Win:	Around 32
Best Opponents:	Killer Kowalski, Hans Schmidt, Nick Bockwinkel

Hercules Cortez

Entering the sport in his native country of Spain, Hercules Cortez toured the world, and his remarkable strength made a real impression on the fans of North and South America, Asia, and Australia. Cortez benched over 540 pounds and demonstrated his power in the ring on a nightly basis. In 1958, he appeared throughout the northeastern US as "Pepe Chicharro," and also used the name "Claude Dassary" in Canada. In 1958, he was a popular challenger to Killer Kowalski's World Title in Montreal, and the latter, incidentally, was the man who ended Cortez's reign as IWA World Champion in Australia in 1965. Cortez teamed with Red Bastien to win the AWA World Tag Title in 1971 and was still champion when he tragically lost his life in a car accident.

Hodge, Danny

Born:	May 13, 1932
Height:	6'0"
Weight:	215
Real Name:	Daniel Allen Hodge
Parents:	William and Hazel Hodge
Wife:	Dolores Hodge
High School:	Perry High School (OK)
HS Ach.:	Oklahoma State High School Wrestling Title (1951) (165)
Amateur Titles:	Three-Time National AAU Champion (1953–54, 1956) (174) (Freestyle), National AAU Champion (1956) (174) (Greco-Roman)
Military:	United States Navy (1951–53)
Trained by:	Leroy McGuirk, Ed Lewis
Career Span:	1959–76
Magazine Cover:	*Sports Illustrated* (April 1, 1957)

Amateur Titles:	12
Titles Won:	16
Days as World Junior Champion:	4,176
Days as World HWT Champion:	Unknown (TWWA World Title in 1968)
Age at first Junior Title Win:	28
Best Opponents:	Angelo Savoldi, Hiro Matsuda, Lou Thesz
Boxing Record:	7-2
Halls of Fame:	6

The remarkable Danny Hodge was arguably, pound-for-pound, the most skilled professional wrestler in history. He was an extraordinary athlete, winning Olympic honors as a wrestler, a national boxing championship, and for seventeen years, traveled the highways and byways as one of the most acclaimed pros in the industry. Hodge, from just outside Perry, Oklahoma, won nearly every amateur match he participated in from 1952 to 1957, including both Olympic Games during that period and during his stretch at the University of Oklahoma, with his losses being counted on a single hand. His amateur achievements began in junior high school when he took the Oklahoma State title in 1948 at 145 pounds, then won the high school championship in 1951. While in the Navy, he qualified and participated in the 1952 Olympic Games, but placed 5th overall. He then won Big Seven and NCAA Titles from 1955 to 1957, going undefeated all through college, and captured the silver medal at the 1956 Olympics.

Hodge was not done showing the world the limits of his athletic prowess and entered the sport of boxing. He proceeded to go undefeated as an amateur, winning regional honors, and then taking to the National Golden Gloves heavyweight championship in March 1958. His impressive foray into boxing continued as he stepped into the pro ring three months later and was victorious. Over the next ten months, he won seven additional fights, and only losing two. Promoter Leroy McGuirk was instrumental in getting Hodge to shift to pro wrestling and he made his debut later in 1959. During his career, he captured the NWA World Junior Heavyweight Title six times with wins over Angelo Savoldi, Sputnik Monroe, Hiro Matsuda, and others, and displayed his ring mastery and unnatural strength against opponents of all sizes. On March 15, 1976, he was injured in a car accident, and his days as a wrestler came to an end. If wrestling was decided by legitimate means, Hodge would've been an unconquerable force at his weight.

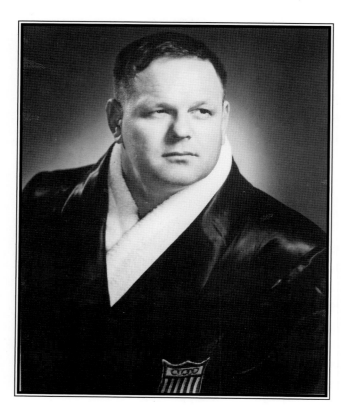

Photo Courtesy of the Collection of Tim Hornbaker

Born:	October 4, 1923
Height:	6'1"
Weight:	285
Real Name:	Richard Heron Avis Hutton
Parents:	Bailey and Gladys Hutton
High School:	Daniel Webster High School (OK)
College:	Oklahoma A&M University
College Ach.:	Three-Time NCAA Heavyweight Wrestling Champion (1947–48, 1950), Four-Time All-American (1947–50)
Military:	United States Army (WWII)
Trained by:	Leroy McGuirk, Ed Lewis
Nickname:	Cowboy
Finisher:	Abdominal Stretch
Career Span:	1953–64
Died:	November 24, 2003, Tulsa, OK 80 years old

Hutton, Dick

Titles Won:	7
Days as World Champion:	421
Age at first World Title Win:	34
Best Opponents:	Lou Thesz, Pat O'Connor, Billy Watson
Halls of Fame:	3

Terrifically gifted, Dick Hutton of Oklahoma was as fierce and competitive in the world of pro wrestling as he was in the amateur ranks. A veteran of the 1948 Olympics and winner of three NCAA titles, he was seen as a potential future champion from day one. Low-key in terms of flamboyance, he let his aptitude speak for itself and his profound knowledge of the pure form of catch-as-catch-can grappling earned him the utmost respect from fans and peers. After only four years in the business, he defeated Lou Thesz for the NWA World Heavyweight Title on November 14, 1957, and displayed poise much greater than his experience. Facing many obstacles as titleholder, including a decline of wrestling's popularity in many territories, Hutton performed commendably as the straight-laced champion, but altogether, his reign lacked any overly defining moments. He met his match on January 9, 1959, and lost the NWA Title to Pat O'Connor in St. Louis. Upon retiring from wrestling, he was inducted into a handful of Halls of Fame, one of them being the National Wrestling Hall of Fame in Stillwater, Oklahoma.

Photo Courtesy of the Collection of Libnan Ayoub

Born:	September 15, 1937
Height:	6'3"
Weight:	350
Real Name:	Curtis Piehau Iaukea III
High School:	Punahou School (HI)
Identities:	Chico Garcia, King Curtis
Career Span:	1959–79
Died:	December 4, 2010, Honolulu, HI 73 years old

Titles Won:	29
Days as World Champion:	Around 296
Age at first World Title Win:	30
Best Opponents:	Mark Lewin, Johnny Valentine, Ray Stevens
Halls of Fame:	1

Iaukea, Curtis

Curtis Iaukea was a highly-touted football player at the University of California, Berkeley, and played three seasons in the Canadian Football League. While in the San Francisco area, he broke into pro wrestling and learned much from ex-footballers Leo Nomellini and Don Manoukian. He returned to his native Hawaii and was a key superstar in Honolulu throughout the 1960s. It was only natural that he'd also venture to Australia, where he became a household name, and won the IWA World Heavyweight Championship four times between 1967 and 1970. Two years later, he teamed with Baron Mikel Scicluna for the WWWF World Tag Team Title. Iaukea portrayed a cruel rule-breaker throughout his career, and when he dropped his 350-pound Hawaiian Splash, it usually marked the end for opponents. His son Rocky also made a career as a pro wrestler.

Born:	February 20, 1943
Height:	6'3"
Weight:	230
Real Name:	Kanji Inoki
Parents:	Sajiro and Fumiko Inoki
Identities:	Tokyo Tom
Nickname:	Moeru Toukon
Tag Team:	B-I Cannon w/ Shohei Baba
Owner:	New Japan Pro Wrestling Co., Ltd. (1972–2005)
Promoter:	Tokyo Pro Wrestling (1966–67) (w/ Toyonobori), New Japan Pro Wrestling (1972–89), Universal Fighting-arts Organization (1998–2002), Inoki Genome Federation (2007–Present)
Career Span:	1960–98
Website:	www.antonio-inoki.com

Inoki, Antonio

Titles Won:	23
Days as World Champion:	1,031 (not counting time as Real World Champion)
Age at first World Title Win:	29
Best Opponents:	Karl Gotch, Stan Hansen, Riki Choshu
Tournament Wins:	17
MMA Record:	16-1, 3 Draws
Halls of Fame:	6

Perhaps no single man has been more influential in professional wrestling on a worldwide scale than Antonio Inoki. He was an admired wrestler for thirty-eight years, taking on the best in the business and beating the likes of Andre the Giant, Ric Flair, Stan Hansen, Hulk Hogan, Vader, and Sting. Adding credibility to the profession by his willingness to participate in legitimate contests against athletes from other sports, Inoki went to a fifteen-round draw against boxing legend Muhammad Ali in 1976. Outside the ring, he founded New Japan Pro Wrestling, a hugely successful promotion, and was crucial in the presentation of wrestling in places like the Soviet Union and North Korea, where it had rarely been seen. In fact, Inoki's appearance in the latter country drew the largest single attendance for a wrestling show ever—at a reported 190,000 people for his April 29, 1995 bout against Flair in Pyongyang. Rightfully enshrined in a number of Halls of Fame, Inoki is the standard-bearer for pro wrestling excellence.

The pupil of the legendary Rikidozan, Inoki made his pro debut the same day his longtime rival Giant Baba did in 1960 and toured the US early in his career. Late in the 1960s, after his first attempt to run his own organization ended, Inoki rejoined the Japan Pro Wrestling Association (JWA) and formed a successful tag team with Baba. In late 1971, he departed from the promotion and again went out on his own, kick-starting New Japan on March 6, 1972 in Tokyo. He headlined the inaugural show and lost to Karl Gotch. In December 1973, he beat Johnny Powers for the NWF World Heavyweight Title, a championship that would become the primary belt for NJPW until the early 1980s. Inoki would have four reigns as titleholder. He formed a strong relationship with the WWF and captured the heavyweight title of that promotion with a win over Bob Backlund on November 30, 1979 in Tokushima.

Inoki was also recognized as WWF World Martial Arts Heavyweight Champion and held the belt for nearly twelve years straight from 1978 to 1990. New Japan implemented the International Wrestling Grand Prix tournament and Inoki was knocked out in his finals match against Hulk Hogan on June 2, 1983 at Tokyo's Sumo Hall in an unscripted finish. In 1984, he beat Hogan to win the event and repeated the next three years. He vacated the IWGP championship in 1988 and made sporadic ring appearances after that. His "Final Countdown" series of matches led to his ultimate retirement on April 4, 1998 in Tokyo before an estimated 70,000 at the Tokyo Dome. He wrestled and beat Don Frye in his final match as two of his biggest rivals, Backlund and Muhammad Ali watched on. He sold his interest in New Japan in 2005 and two years later, he founded Inoki Genome Federation (IGF). A recognized icon throughout the industry, Inoki has been honored by the WCW, WWE, and Professional Wrestling Halls of Fame.

Photo Courtesy of Pete Lederberg—plmathfoto@hotmail.com

Born:	September 9, 1945
Height:	6'0"
Weight:	260
Real Name:	Hossein Khosrow Vaziri
Amateur Ach.:	National AAU Greco-Roman Title (1971) (180)
Identities:	Ali Vaziri, Great Hussein, Colonel Mustafa
Groups:	The Triangle of Terror (1990–91)
Managed:	Sgt. Slaughter (1990–91), The Sultan (1997)
Career Span:	1973–2010

Titles Won:	16
Days as World Champion:	28
Age at first World Title Win:	38
Best Opponents:	Bob Backlund, Hulk Hogan, Ricky Steamboat
Halls of Fame:	2

Iron Sheik, The

In recent years, the wildly outspoken Iron Sheik has candidly voiced his opinion about pro wrestling on a slew of popular radio shows, revealing a side of his personality that many people did not know. He was much more identifiable by his work in the ring, an occupation he'd undertaken since 1973, and as an amateur before that. The Sheik's longtime pro-Iran gimmick and rulebreaking were real attention-getters, and he could turn a crowd against him within seconds. A former National AAU Champion while a member of the Minnesota Wrestling Club, he was trained by Verne Gagne and gained his greatest fame when he beat Bob Backlund for the WWF World Title on December 26, 1983 in New York City. He was an interim champion, losing the belt to Hulk Hogan on January 23, 1984. At WrestleMania X-Seven, Sheik won a special gimmick battle royal, and was inducted into the WWE Hall of Fame in 2005.

Photo Courtesy of Dr. Mike Lano—Wrealano@aol.com

Born:	August 24, 1944
Height:	6'2"
Weight:	255
Real Name:	Wayde Bowles
Trained by:	Billy Watson, Bobo Brazil
Identities:	Sweet Ebony Diamond
Career Span:	1965–2008

Titles Won:	33
Best Opponents:	Nick Bockwinkel, Billy Graham, Harley Race
Halls of Fame:	1

Johnson, Rocky

A boxer-turned-wrestler, "Soulman" Rocky Johnson launched his wrestling career in his native Nova Scotia in 1965 and wrestled across Canada in his first year. Four years later, he worked his way into California, where he became a household name in Los Angeles and San Francisco. He beat Paul DeMarco for the US Title, and held the World Tag Team Championship three times with Pat Patterson. Johnson won state heavyweight titles in Texas, Georgia, and Florida, and other regional titles all over the map. In 1983, he teamed with Tony Atlas for the WWF World Tag Team Title. With wife Ata, the daughter of Peter Maivia, he had a son named Dwayne, better known to wrestling fans as The Rock. He was inducted into the WWE Hall of Fame in 2008.

Born:	June 28, 1942
Height:	6'0"
Weight:	230
Real Name:	Alfred Morris Frederick
Parents:	Daluck and Jessie Frederick
High School:	Thomas Jefferson High School (TX)
Nickname:	Number One
Career Span:	1964–91

Titles Won:	33
Best Opponents:	Jack Brisco, Dory Funk Jr., Ric Flair

Jones, Paul

Having participated in Golden Gloves boxing for years, Paul Jones of Port Arthur, Texas, was very adept to the squared circle and easily made the transition to wrestling in 1964 through promoter Morris Sigel in Houston. He learned the ropes from veteran Paul Boesch and made successful tours of Hawaii, Japan, and Australia before landing in the Mid-Atlantic territory, where he won a cache of championships. He held the United States Heavyweight Title twice and the World Tag Title six-times with partners Baron Von Raschke, Masked Superstar, Wahoo McDaniel, and Ricky Steamboat. He also had some of the greatest matches of his career against the likes of Johnny Valentine, Terry Funk, and Jack Brisco. During his stay in Florida, he took his state championship belt and threw it off a Tampa bridge in one particularly hot angle. In the 1980s, he became a manager and seconded the likes of the Assassins and Warlord and Barbarian. Jones retired from the wrestling business in 1991.

Born:	January 23, 1957
Height:	5'7"
Weight:	165
Real Name:	Patricia Seymour Schroeder
High School:	Riverdale High School (FL)
Nickname:	Hawaiian Princess
Tag Team:	The Glamour Girls w/ Judy Martin
Career Span:	1975–2004

Titles Won:	12
Days as World Champion:	506
Age at first World Title Win:	28
Best Opponents:	Chigusa Nagayo, Madusa, Wendi Richter
Halls of Fame:	2

Kai, Leilani

Internationally known for her competitive spirit and skilled offensive ring attack, Leilani Kai was a world champion in the WWF and NWA. She grew up on the west coast of Florida and idolized great women grapplers Penny Banner and Ann Casey. At the age of seventeen, she attended the Fabulous Moolah's Columbia, South Carolina school, and was trained by Moolah's cadre, a group of experienced workers that included Susan Green. Kai was given a Hawaiian heritage and toured the world with Moolah's troupe. On February 18, 1985, she beat Wendi Richter for the WWF Women's World Title and holds the distinction of going into the first WrestleMania as the defending champion—although she lost the belt to Wendi Richter. Kai formed a championship tag team with Judy Martin and held the NWA Women's World Title for over a year in 2003-2004. Leilani was inducted into the Professional Wrestling Hall of Fame in 2016.

Born:	September 10, 1951
Height:	6'0"
Weight:	235
Real Name:	Stephen Paul Keirn
Parents:	Richard and Hazel Keirn
High School:	Robinson High School (FL)
Identities:	Doink the Clown
Nickname:	The Gator
Owner:	Florida Championship Wrestling (2007–Present)
Career Span:	1972–2007

Titles Won:	58
Best Opponents:	Harley Race, Bret Hart, Terry Funk

Keirn, Steve

Tampa product Steve Keirn was friends with Mike Graham in his youth and entered the business under the tutelage of Mike's legendary father Eddie Graham and Hiro Matsuda. He won numerous championships and was named NWA Rookie of the Year in 1974. In 1986 and 1987, he won the US Tag Team Title twice with Stan Lane as a member of the Fabulous Ones, and in 1989 he procured the PWF Heavyweight belt from Kendall Windham. Keirn took out a license to hunt alligators in Florida and after he joined the WWF in 1991, he took on a gimmick that played off that theme, known as "Skinner." Since the late 1980s, he's run a wrestling school in one form or fashion. For a time, it was known as the "Pro Wrestling School of Hard Knox," but now it is "Florida Championship Wrestling," a WWE Developmental territory. Graduates have included current WWE superstars Ted DiBiase Jr., Drew McIntyre, and Jack Swagger.

Born:	April 26, 1931
Height:	6'1 ½"
Weight:	270
Real Name:	Herbert Alan Gerwig
Trained by:	The Sheik, The Dusek Brothers
Finisher:	Brainbuster
Managed by:	Bobby Heenan
Career Span:	1955–82
Died:	November 10, 2011, Dallas, TX 80 years old

Titles Won:	31
Days as World Champion:	54
Age at first World Title Win:	36
Best Opponents:	Dory Funk Jr., Jack Brisco, Dusty Rhodes
Halls of Fame:	1

Killer Karl Kox

Killer Karl Kox held a master's degree in crowd psychology, and his ability to effectively rile up audiences was second to none. He grew up in Baltimore, and played football for the Security Athletic Club in his teens. In 1955, following service in the marines, he was taken under the wing of a local grappler named Fred Bozic in Cleveland. For the next six years, he wrestled under his given name and then embraced the Kox gimmick in the early 1960s. He was an imposing heel, demonstrating his fine ring work and toughness all over the US, Japan, and Australia. In the "Land Down Under," he captured the IWA World Heavyweight Title three times in 1968 and '69, defeating Mario Milano twice and also Bob Ellis. He was a regional champion in Florida, Texas, and Georgia, and held both the North American and National Titles. Kox passed away on November 10, 2011, at the age of eighty. Two years later, he was inducted into the Texas Wrestling Hall of Fame.

Kiniski, Gene

Born:	November 23, 1928
Height:	6'3"
Weight:	250
Real Name:	Eugene Nicholas Kiniski
Parents:	Nicholas and Julia Kiniski
Family:	Father of Kelly and Nick Kiniski
High School:	St. Joseph's High School (Edmonton, Alberta)
Amateur Titles:	Canadian AAU Wrestling Title (1947–48) (1952), AAU Title (1951)
Pro Sports:	WIFU—Edmonton Eskimos (1949, 1951–53)
Identities:	Gene Kelly, The Mighty Canadian, Crimson Knight II
Nicknames:	Big Thunder, Canada's Greatest Athlete, Canadian Avalanche
Finisher:	Backbreaker
Owned:	A percentage of Northwest Wrestling Promotions (w/ Al Tomko)
Career Span:	1952–92
Died:	April 14, 2010, Blaine, WA 81 years old

Titles Won:	52
Days as World Champion:	Over 1,650
Age at first World Title Win:	28
Best Opponents:	Lou Thesz, Verne Gagne, Bruno Sammartino
Halls of Fame:	6
Movies:	3

In terms of wrestlers on the pro circuit, Gene Kiniski was the cream of the crop; a perennial champion with an expressive personality, and a favored headliner throughout the world. Born in Lamont, Alberta, Canada, he grew up in Edmonton, where he was a standout amateur wrestler and football player. While attending the University of Arizona, he met promoter Rod Fenton, and the latter was eager to turn the big tackle into the next big grappling superstar. Kiniski had viable options to play pro football, but was found that the money in wrestling was better. He was aggressive in the ring and the kind of man who could chain together an endless amount of holds or brawl until the mat was red with blood. In June 1957, he conquered Edouard Carpentier for the Montreal World Title, and on July 11, 1961, he went over Verne Gagne for the AWA World championship in Minneapolis. Kiniski was also regularly a champion in Toronto and booked as a title claimant in West Texas in 1962.

Versus Bruno Sammartino, Kiniski was spectacular and narrowly missed winning the WWWF World championship in 1964—actually carrying the belt for a short time after one controversial match. All of these accomplishments were setting the table for his greatest triumph on January 7, 1966 when he beat Lou Thesz for the National Wrestling Alliance World Heavyweight Title in St. Louis. For three years, he exceeded expectations by meeting all comers and upholding the dignity of the prized championship. His list of challengers reads like a Hall of Fame roster and include such luminaries as Bobo Brazil, Fritz Von Erich, Dick the Bruiser, Billy Watson, and Johnny Valentine. In November 1968, he became the first NWA Champion to defend the title in Los Angeles in more than a decade. Dory Funk Jr. was the man to finally dethrone him, on February 11, 1969, in Tampa. Outside the ropes, Kiniski was well-liked throughout the industry, and he had his final match in 1992.

Born:	August 15, 1942
Height:	5'10"
Weight:	250
Real Name:	Oreal Donald Perras
Parents:	William and Blanche Perras
Wife:	Renae Perras
Identities:	Orwell Paris, Jim Parris, Red McNulty
Finisher:	Bearhug, clothesline
Career Span:	1965–99
Website:	www.ivankoloff.com

Titles Won:	45
Days as World Champion:	Over 170
Age at first World Title Win:	25
Best Opponents:	Bruno Sammartino, Pedro Morales, Verne Gagne
Halls of Fame:	2

Koloff, Ivan

Rulebreaking legend, Ivan Koloff had a storied career, and in 2011 was honored for induction into the Professional Wrestling Hall of Fame. It was recognition for years of hard work, battering opponents, and using his chain to brand foes with the famous stamp of the "Russian Bear." He was from the Ottawa Valley area of Ontario, not Moscow as it was usually claimed, and raised on a dairy farm. He was trained by an old grappler named Jack Wentworth and took the name "Ivan Koloff" while in Montreal in 1968. He scored a historic upset over Bruno Sammartino on January 18, 1971 at Madison Square Garden—ending Sammartino's seven-year-plus reign as WWWF World Champion. Ivan was dethroned by Pedro Morales a few weeks later. He headlined everywhere, and held the Mid-Atlantic version of the World Tag Team Title four times, as well as winning other numerous regional titles. In contrast to his wildman image, Koloff has always been a charitable and religious man outside the ring.

Ladd, Ernie

Born:	November 28, 1938
Height:	6'9"
Weight:	310
Real Name:	Earnest Lawrence Ladd
High School:	Wallace High School (TX)
College:	Grambling State University
Drafted by:	San Diego Chargers (AFL) (15th Round)
Pro Sports:	American Football League—San Diego Chargers (1961–65) American Football League—Houston Oilers (1966) American Football League—Kansas City Chiefs (1967–69)
Football Ach.:	AFL All-Star (1962–65)
Trained by:	Hardy Kruskamp, Dick Beyer, Fred Blassie
Nicknames:	The Big Cat
Finisher:	The Taped Thumb
Career Span:	1963–88
Died:	March 10, 2007, Franklin, LA 68 years old

Titles Won:	27
Days as World Champion:	43
Age at first World Title Win:	33
Best Opponents:	Bruno Sammartino, Fred Blassie, Lou Thesz
Halls of Fame:	6

Pro football's powerful lineman Ernie Ladd made a substantial contribution to wrestling for two decades, crushing foes with his strength and endlessly entertaining audiences. He was born in Louisiana, but reared in Orange County, Texas, and amazed football coaches all the way into the AFL in 1961. While playing for San Diego, he was approached to try his hand at wrestling, and agreed to give it a shot under promoter Hardy Kruskamp. Ladd, who reportedly made $13,000 a year in the AFL, doubled his salary in the ring and eventually quit the gridiron altogether. As an intimidating heel, Ladd was very successful on both coasts, and throughout the territorial system, winning the Mid-South North American championship five times between 1978 and 1984 and the NWF North American Title. Ladd had notable feuds with Dusty Rhodes and Andre the Giant and was, in the 1960s, a competitive eater—able to put away an unbelievable amount of food.

Lawler, Jerry

Born:	November 29, 1949
Height:	5'11"
Weight:	230
Real Name:	Jerry O'Neil Lawler
Parents:	Jerome and Hazel Lawler
Family:	Father of Brian Christopher and Kevin Christian, cousin of Carl Fergie and Wayne Ferris
High School:	Treadwell High School (TN)
College:	Memphis State University
Trained by:	Jackie Fargo
Finisher:	Piledriver, Fistdrop from the Second Rope
Tag Teams:	The Outlaws w/ Jim White, The Heavenly Bodies w/ Don Greene
Owned:	A percentage of the Memphis territory (1983–97)
Career Span:	1970–Present

Titles Won:	over 160
Days as World Champion:	2,275
Age at first World Title Win:	29
Best Opponents:	Jack Brisco, Curt Hennig, Bret Hart
Halls of Fame:	3

Many wrestlers through the ages have called themselves "King," but no man has worn the crown like Jerry Lawler. He has been involved in wrestling for the last forty-one years and has established himself as an icon in Memphis and throughout the WWE universe. In fact, he's wrestled as late as 2011, even competing against fellow broadcaster Michael Cole at WrestleMania XXVII on April 3, 2011. Perhaps Lawler's most notable feud was against comedian Andy Kaufman, which garnered mainstream attention in 1982. Their war of words became physical during an episode of *Late Night with David Letterman*, and the question of whether it was real or scripted remained for years. Lawler appeared as himself in the 1999 Kaufman biopic *Man on the Moon*, finally revealing that their "conflict" had been completely worked. Synonymous with wrestling in the "Music City," Lawler was the focal point of grappling on Monday nights at the Mid-South Coliseum since achieving his initial main event there in 1973.

In matches that were both scientific and violent, and in passionate feuds that meant something to fans, Lawler was worshipped to no end. He was champion most of his active career and may have held more titles than any single grappler in history. That includes the Southern belt forty-one times between 1974 and 1987 and the Unified World Title twenty-seven times between 1988 and 1997. He also held the CWA and AWA

World Heavyweight Titles, the latter came as a result of a victory over Curt Hennig on May 9, 1988. The next day, the Memphis *Commercial Appeal* newspaper reported the news on its front page, representative of the local esteem showered upon him. As a commentator on WWE's *Raw*, he has been able to interject his decades of wrestling experience into the weekly storylines, showing his intellect and sense of humor. A talented artist, Lawler has also been an influential member of the community, and has donated lots of his personal time to charity.

Photo Courtesy of Pete Lederberg—plmathfoto@hotmail.com

Born:	March 16, 1937
Height:	5'11"
Weight:	235
Real Name:	Mark W. Lewin
Trained by:	Ed Don George, Danny McShain
Identities:	The Purple Haze
Nicknames:	Maniac
Finisher:	Sleeperhold
Career Span:	1953–87

Titles Won:	37
Days as World Champion:	Around 220
Age at first World Title Win:	29
Best Opponents:	Dusty Rhodes, Lou Thesz, Terry Funk
Halls of Fame:	1

Lewin, Mark

Versatile Mark Lewin was the younger brother of Donn and Ted, the sons of a Buffalo jeweler. He became a pro wrestler as a teenager in Southern California and was a longtime idol to fans. Along with Don Curtis, he formed a Hall of Fame tag team and held the United States Tag Team championship in the northeast. In 1963, he adopted the mannerisms of a ring "bad guy," while remaining a fan favorite in some locations, including Australia, where he was a two-time IWA World Champion. Lewin also captured the WWA World Heavyweight Title with a victory over Lou Thesz in Los Angeles. Lewin's most memorable heel persona was the "Purple Haze," an exponent of sheer violence and madcap behavior.

Born:	August 29, 1933
Height:	6'1"
Weight:	245
Real Name:	Dale Folsom Lewis
High School:	Rib Lake High School (WI)
College:	University of Oklahoma
Trained by:	Verne Gagne
Identities:	Dr. Blood, Masked Medic I
Career Span:	1961–79
Died:	August 31, 1997, Deschutes County, OR 64 years old

Titles Won:	19
Best Opponents:	Dory Funk Jr., Jack Brisco, Tim Woods
Halls of Fame:	1

Lewis, Dale

Looking at his outstanding amateur credentials, one would guess that "Professor" Dale Lewis had wrestled from a young age . . . however, that is a false assumption. Lewis actually played basketball at his Wisconsin high school and didn't begin grappling until joining the marines. He earned a berth on both the 1956 and 1960 US Olympic squads as a Greco-Roman competitor, but didn't place in either tournament. He added two Big Eight and NCAA heavyweight titles to his profile while at the University of Oklahoma, and became a pro in 1961 after studying under Verne Gagne in Minnesota. Later that year, he won the AWA World Tag Team belts with Pat Kennedy. Additionally, he held state championships in Nebraska, Florida, and Georgia, and captured both the United National and Southern Heavyweight crowns. Lewis passed away on August 31, 1997, at sixty-four years of age. In 2007, he was inducted into the Tragos-Thesz Hall of Fame in Iowa.

Born:	December 30, 1924
Height:	5′7″
Weight:	235
Real Name:	Luther Jacob Goodall
Parents:	Luther and Ruby Goodall
Wife:	Gertrude Lindsay Goodall
High School:	Booker T. Washington High School (VA)
College Ach.:	All-CIAA (1948–49)
Trained by:	Al Haft Gym trainers, Jack Ganson
Nicknames:	Juice, Bronze Bomber
Career Span:	1951–72
Died:	February 21, 1972, Charlotte, NC 47 years old

Lindsay, Luther

Titles Won:	19
Days as World Champion:	Unknown
Age at first World Title Win:	Around 29
Best Opponents:	Lou Thesz, Dick Hutton, Buddy Rogers
Halls of Fame:	2

An exceptionally talented wrestler, Luther Lindsay was not only respected for his athletic abilities, but was admired for his kind personality. He is one of those guys in wrestling history who you never hear anything negative about—and was a definite legend on all accounts. Born in Norfolk, Virginia, he was a star football player in high school, and joined the Army in June 1943. While in Italy, he saved the life of a fellow soldier in a swimming mishap and earned the Soldier's Medal. Between 1947 and 1949, he played football at Hampton Institute in Virginia and, in 1950, he had a stint as a pro with the Jersey City Giants. Mentored by Jack Ganson, Lindsay broke into pro wrestling and his skills were lauded by fellow grapplers, promoters, and the press. He conquered prejudices as he went forward, and worked his way up the card to title matches against NWA champion Lou Thesz, and performed spectacularly. He also won regional titles in Portland, Honolulu, and Calgary. Lindsay passed away after a match in Charlotte in 1972.

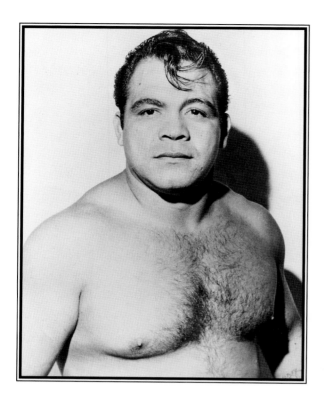

Born:	December 12, 1935
Height:	6'0"
Weight:	245
Real Name:	Guadalupe Garcia Robledo
Family:	Husband of Jean Lothario, father of Pete Lothario
Identities:	Jose Garcia, El Gran Lothario
Finisher:	Knockout Punch, Abdominal Stretch
Career Span:	1959–85

Titles Won:	36
Best Opponents:	Johnny Valentine, Boris Malenko, Dory Funk Jr.

Lothario, Jose

Acknowledged as the man who helped shape "Icon" Shawn Michaels into a superstar, Jose Lothario was a talented and engaging grappler himself through a career lasting more than thirty-five years. He was scientifically knowledgeable, but also a cunning brawler, and competed in some hardcore matches for the Texas and Florida Brass Knuckles championships. A boxer before he became a wrestler, Lothario was originally from Mexico and settled in San Antonio, where he had two children with his wife Betty Jean. Lothario participated in many interesting feuds and won regional titles all over the United States, including the Texas State Title six times, as well as also capturing the world tag team belts in Florida and San Francisco. In 1997, Lothario appeared on WWF telecasts in Michaels' corner and feuded with manager Jim Cornette.

Born:	August 20, 1940
Height:	5'10"
Weight:	220
Real Name:	Kenneth Lucas
High School:	Mesa High School (AZ)
Trained by:	Lu Kim, Al Pago Pago, Art Nelson, Sputnik Monroe
Finisher:	Sleeperhold
Career Span:	1959–98
Died:	August 6, 2014, Pensacola, FL 73 years old

Titles Won:	104
Best Opponents:	Jack Brisco, Harley Race, Ric Flair

Lucas, Ken

Ken Lucas was a superstar throughout the territorial system and a popular champion from West Texas to the Gulf Coast. Born in Pittsburgh but raised in Mesa, Arizona, he was a talented and disciplined athlete, entering the wrestling trade at the age of nineteen after working with many well-known grapplers. He began an impressive career that saw him win over 100 championships and battle the best in the business. He laid roots in the Pensacola region and captured eleven Gulf Coast Heavyweight Titles. He also held the US Junior belt and regional straps in the Central States, Tampa, and Tennessee. Lucas teamed with Dennis Hall and Kevin Sullivan to become World Tag Team Champion as well. He was a top-tier wrestler and influenced peers and fans across the US. Lucas retired from the wrestling business in 1998 and passed away at the age of seventy-three in August 2014.

Born:	April 6, 1937
Height:	5'10"
Weight:	235
Real Name:	Peter Fanene-Maivia
Parents:	Alfred and Peke Fanene
Wife:	Ofelia Maivia
Trained by:	Steve Rickard
Identities:	Peter Fanene Anderson
Finisher:	Samoan Stump Puller
Promoted:	Honolulu, Hawaii (1979–82)
Career Span:	1960–82
Died:	June 13, 1982, Honolulu, HI 45 years old

Titles Won:	15
Best Opponents:	Billy Graham, Bob Backlund, Pat Patterson
Halls of Fame:	2
Movies:	2

Maivia, Chief Peter

"High Chief" Peter Maivia was a preeminent wrestler from Western Samoa, supremely powerful, energetic, and full of charisma. He followed in the footsteps of Alo Leilani and Prince Maiava, two Samoan grapplers who went on to earn international recognition, and earned a name for himself in New Zealand before landing in United Kingdom in 1963. After developing his abilities on the rough English scene, he went to San Francisco, where he teamed with Pepper Gomez to win the World Tag Team Championship. He'd hold the straps four times in total, also teaming with Pat Patterson and Ray Stevens, as well as being the leading challenger to the local US champion. During his career, he headlined at the Olympic Auditorium and Madison Square Garden. In 1979, he bought the NWA rights to Hawaii and promoted until his death in 1982. Maivia helped launch the Samoan wrestling revolution, and he had ties, bloodline or otherwise, to dozens of other wrestlers, including his grandson, The Rock.

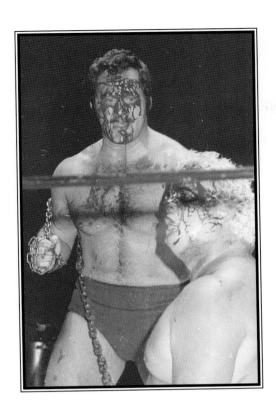

Born:	July 8, 1933
Height:	5'10"
Weight:	235
Real Name:	Larry Simon
Family:	Father of Dean and Joe Malenko
Identities:	Larry "Crusher" Dugan
Nicknames:	Professor
Career Span:	1955–80
Died:	September 1, 1994, Tampa, FL 61 years old

Titles Won:	21
Best Opponents:	Eddie Graham, Johnny Valentine, Wahoo McDaniel

Malenko, Boris

The Great Malenko was truly a terrorizing matman with incredible psychological powers. He was a proficient talker who made the bitter feuds he was involved in always sound legitimate, as if he really hated his opponents. His war with Eddie Graham in Florida was the model for viciousness, and every step of the way, in every city they worked the angle, it appeared to be genuine. Malenko did the same thing throughout his career, regardless of the gimmick he used, but as Boris Malenko, the Russian heel, he was masterful. He was originally from Irvington, New Jersey, where he learned the ropes at a local YMCA and trained with a number of talented coaches. He used numerous identities to include Otto Von Krupp, a Nazi sympathizer, and found his greatest fame as Malenko. Settling in Tampa, he was the mainstay bad guy, luring foes into violent Russian Chain matches and regularly winning regional titles. Malenko later opened up a wrestling school and taught many future stars, including both his sons, Marc Mero, and Barry Horowitz.

Born:	November 29, 1949
Height:	5'11"
Weight:	240
Real Name:	Wayne Maurice Keown
Identities:	Uncle Zebakiah (Zeb)
Groups:	Lawler's Army (1977)
Tag Teams:	The Kansas Jayhawks w/ Bobby Jaggers, The Desperados w/ Black Bart and Deadeye Dick
Managed:	Justin Bradshaw, The Blu Brothers
Career Span:	1973–Present
Website:	www.dutchmantell.com

Titles Won:	47
Days as World Champion:	Over 85
Age at first World Title Win:	47
Best Opponents:	Jerry Lawler, Randy Savage, Bill Dundee
Published Books:	2

Mantell, Dutch

Sporting a distinctive look, capable of being a pivotal player in front of the camera and behind the scenes, and always an entertaining storyteller, "Dirty" Dutch Mantell has been a standout member of the wrestling community since 1973. A Vietnam veteran, Mantell was an outstanding brawler and a legend in Tennessee, where he won the Mid-America Title upwards of fourteen times. Also influential in the careers of Steve Austin and The Undertaker, Mantell has written two autobiographies full of wonderful stories, and his insightful perspective of the business is a quality rarely seen. These reasons are why he's been successful as a creative player in the IWA and TNA, and widely respected by his peers. Mantell operated a wrestling school in Nashville, known as the "University of Dutch," and joined the WWE in 2013 as "Zeb Colter." He managed several grapplers, including Jack Swagger and Alberto Del Rio, through 2015, and was released in May of the following year.

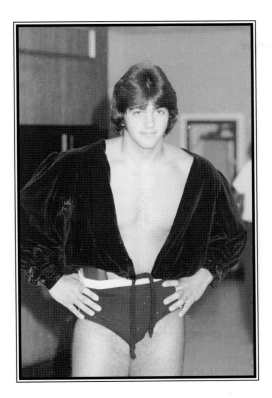

Born:	March 18, 1956
Height:	6'0"
Weight:	230
Real Name:	Richard Vigneault
Parents:	Fernand and Evelyne Vigneault
Family:	Brother of Michel Martel, uncle of Kevin Martel
Trained by:	Michel Martel
Finisher:	Boston Crab
Tag Teams:	The Can-Am Connection w/ Tom Zenk, The Strike Force w/ Tito Santana
Career Span:	1973–98

Titles Won:	20
Days as World Champion:	595
Age at first World Title Win:	28
Best Opponents:	Ric Flair, Nick Bockwinkel, Stan Hansen
Halls of Fame:	1

Martel, Rick

Rick Martel of Quebec City, Quebec played a variety of roles during his lengthy career on the wrestling mat. From his run as the smiling babyface with the science and strength to uphold the credibility of the AWA World Heavyweight Title, to the arrogant heel known as "The Model," Martel was successful, delivering countless entertaining matches and promos. His AWA Title win was, without question, his defining moment, occurring on May 13, 1984 when he took the strap off Jumbo Tsuruta in St. Paul. In the WWF, he held the World Tag Team Title three times, twice with Tony Garea in the early 1980s and again with Tito Santana beginning on October 27, 1987 when the duo beat The Hart Foundation. As a cunning rule-breaker, he had an intense feud with Jake Roberts after he temporarily blinded the latter with the cologne he usually doused the ring with. In 1998, he appeared in WCW and won the TV Title from Booker T, but lost a rematch at SuperBrawl VIII. That same year, he suffered an injury that forced him to retire from the mat for good.

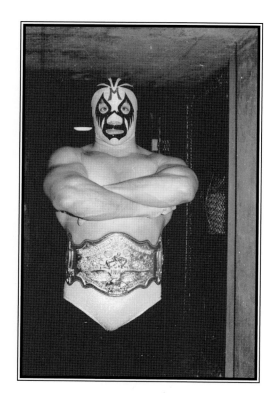

Born:	July 15, 1942
Height:	5'11"
Weight:	245
Real Name:	Aaron Rodriguez
Family:	Brother of El Sicodelico and Dos Caras
Trained by:	Diablo Velasco
Nickname:	The Man of 1,000 Masks
Finisher:	Flying Bodypress
Career Span:	1964–Present

Titles Won:	17
Days as World Champion:	Over 14,000 (and counting)
Age at first World Title Win:	32
Best Opponents:	Black Gordman, The Destroyer, Canek
Halls of Fame:	4
Movies:	21

Mascaras, Mil

In wrestling history, there were individuals who were at the forefront of popularizing particular styles and in-ring methods that would later become commonplace. Mexican wrestler Mil Mascaras was the leader of an international revolution which saw audiences around the world accept and embrace the lucha libra style—and all of the high flying and athleticism that came along with it. His explosion on the US scene in Los Angeles in 1968, then Texas in 1970, and Japan a year later was remarkable, and he was a unique trendsetter, indoctrinating fans worldwide to his quickness and aerial attack. His influence was immense, impacting fans who watched him and future wrestlers who wanted to emulate him. A regional champion in Los Angeles and Texas, Mascaras also was a World Heavyweight Champion in Mexico and for the upstart IWA indie promotion in 1975, still holding the IWA belt today. Additionally, Mascaras is a film icon in Mexico and continues to wrestle from time to time, further building upon his legacy.

Born:	July 22, 1937
Height:	5'11"
Weight:	220
Real Name:	Yasuhiro Kojima
Wife:	Judy Matsuda
Identities:	Ernest Kojima, Suhiro Kojima, The Great Matsuda
Finisher:	Sleeperhold, Judo Chop
Owned:	A percentage of Championship Wrestling from Florida (1985–87)
Career Span:	1957–90
Died:	November 27, 1999, Tampa, FL 62 years old

Titles Won:	18
Days as World Junior Champion:	387
Age at first World Title Win:	26
Best Opponents:	Danny Hodge, Lou Thesz, Jack Brisco

Matsuda, Hiro

Technical wrestling wonder Hiro Matsuda was universally respected across the industry and left a considerable imprint on the business. He was born in Yokohama, Japan, was trained under the celebrated Rikidozan, and spent time in Peru and Mexico prior to making his debut in the United States in the summer of 1961. Known as a Judo specialist, he wrestled as "Kojima Saito" in Texas and was renamed "Hiro Matsuda" by Bobby Bruns while in the Central States. He then went to Tampa, which would become his home base, and worked the Florida circuit, regularly teaming up with Duke Keomuka. On July 11, 1964, he beat a man who he'd have some of his most competitive matches against, Danny Hodge, for the first of two NWA World Junior Titles. The second reign began in June 1975 when he vanquished Ken Mantell. Matsuda came out of retirement to face Osamu Kido on December 26, 1990 in Japan. As a trainer, Matsuda schooled scores of future legends to include Hulk Hogan, Ron Simmons, and Lex Luger.

McDaniel, Wahoo

Born:	June 19, 1938
Height:	5'11"
Weight:	260
Real Name:	Edward Hugh McDaniel
Parents:	Hugh and Catherine McDaniel
High School:	Midland High School (TX)
College:	University of Oklahoma
AFL Draft:	Los Angeles Chargers (1960)
Pro Sports:	American Football League—Houston Oilers (1960) American Football League—Denver Broncos (1961–63) American Football League—New York Jets (1964–65) American Football League—Miami Dolphins (1966–68)
Trained by:	Balk Estes, Johnny Heidman
Finisher:	Indian Deathlock, Double Underhook Suplex
Career Span:	1962–96
Died:	April 18, 2002, Houston, TX 63 years old

Titles Won:	39
Days as World Champion:	21
Age at first World Title Win:	35
Best Opponents:	Johnny Valentine, Billy Graham, Ric Flair
Halls of Fame:	3
NFL Games:	105

"Chief" Wahoo McDaniel was a powerful force on the wrestling circuit; superbly popular and undeniably tough. He could mix it up with the best in the business and brawl until the sun came up, all for the sake of earning a victory—or just giving the audience a good show. A dual-sport athlete, McDaniel was a standout football player, playing for the legendary Bud Wilkinson at Oklahoma, and then becoming a star in the American Football League. Around 1960, he was contacted by an old acquaintance named Balk Estes, who was also from the "Sooner State," and asked whether he wanted to give pro wrestling a try. McDaniel compared the potential earnings to be made in wrestling to what he was bringing in from football and noticed that some wrestlers made considerably more. He decided to jump into the grappling world on the trail of Estes' boss, Jim Barnett of Indianapolis, and began touring during the off season. His Indian heritage—part Chickasaw and part Choctaw—being a major part of his wrestling persona.

Sporting a headdress, performing a war dance, and delivering tomahawk chops to his opponents, Wahoo was a box office draw wherever he traveled. He had extended stays in the WWWF and AWA, plus Texas, Florida, and the Mid-Atlantic territory. On November 9, 1973 in Japan, he beat Strong Kobayashi for the IWA World Heavyweight Title, and then lost it back to the latter on November 30 of the same year. McDaniel made his home in Charlotte and was an icon for the Crocketts, winning numerous championships and feuding with the likes of Ric Flair and Roddy Piper. As the king of the Indian strap match and a hardcore warrior, he engaged in brutally violent and bloody matches, but never tarnished his image as the hero. Fans knew what to expect from him, and McDaniel lived up to expectations, dishing out punishment to the rule-breakers fans loved to hate. He held the World Tag Team Title three times in the Mid-Atlantic region and the US belt a total of five times. He racked up numerous other regional titles and continued to wrestle through 1996.

Photo Courtesy of the Collection of Tim Hornbaker

Miller, Dr. Bill

Born:	June 5, 1927
Height:	6'5"
Weight:	275
Real Name:	Dr. William Merritt Miller, D.V.M.
Parents:	Dale and Dorothy Miller
High School:	Fremont High School (OH)
College:	Ohio State University
College Ach.:	Big Ten Heavyweight Wrestling Title (1950–51), All-American Wrestler (1951)
Military:	United States Navy (WWII)
Trained by:	Ruffy Silverstein
Identities:	Dr. X, Mr. M, Crimson Knight
Finisher:	Neck stretcher, backbreaker
Career Span:	1951–76
Died:	March 24, 1997, Reynoldsburg, OH 69 years old

Titles Won:	10
Days as World Champion:	1,108
Age at first World Title Win:	24
Best Opponents:	Verne Gagne, Bruno Sammartino, Ruffy Silverstein
Halls of Fame:	4

Only weeks after his successful collegiate wrestling career came to an end, "Big" Bill Miller was in a professional ring getting paid for grappling on the Ohio circuit by booker Al Haft. His debut occurred in April 1951, and before the end of the summer, Haft's massive wrestling prodigy was claiming the AWA World

Heavyweight Championship and appearing on national television across the ABC network. It was a remarkable push, but Haft felt Miller's potential needed to be tapped immediately, as the former two-time Big Ten Heavyweight Champion had the word "superstar" written all over him. And Miller lived up to expectations, winning the Nebraska World Title, the coveted AWA World Title in Minneapolis in 1962, as well as capturing the IWA World Championship in Japan in 1971. Miller nearly annexed Bruno Sammartino's WWWF World belt on numerous occasions and their feud was very popular, of course, with Miller wearing the badge of the hated heel. Miller's brother Danny was also a professional wrestler for many years.

Photo Courtesy of Scott Teal/Crowbar Press

Born:	March 17, 1930
Height:	6'4"
Weight:	360
Real Name:	Edward S. Cholak
Parents:	Steve and Mary Cholak
Wife:	Arlene Cholak
High School:	Chicago Vocational High School (IL)
Military Sports:	All-Navy Boxing and Wrestling Heavyweight Champion (1952)
Identities:	The Golden Terror
Nicknames:	Golden, Yukon
Known for:	Wearing a moose head to the ring; his moose call
Career Span:	1953–87
Died:	October 31, 2002, Hammond, IN 72 years old

Moose Cholak

Titles Won:	At least 6
Days as World Champion:	25
Age at first World Title Win:	33
Best Opponents:	Verne Gagne, Fred Blassie, Dick the Bruiser

A much-talked-about fixture on the Chicago amateur sports scene, super heavyweight Edward Cholak competed successfully for years as both a boxer and a wrestler. The son of Yugoslavian parents, he played freshman football at Wisconsin, and then joined the Navy, where he continued to demonstrate his toughness as a fighter. In 1952, he even advanced to the finals of National AAU boxing qualifiers. Cholak also appeared on the nationally televised program "Meet the Champ." A short time later, he was scouted by Don Eagle and trained to be a pro wrestler. He adopted the "Moose" gimmick, claiming to be from a fictitious town in Maine, but it was in his legit hometown of Chicago where he was recognized as IWA World Champion in 1963. He also held the WWA World Tag Team Title three times in Indiana, twice with Wilbur Snyder and once with Paul Christy.

Born:	October 22, 1940
Height:	5'11"
Weight:	235
Real Name:	Pedro A. Morales
Wife:	Karen Morales
Trained by:	Barba Roja
Identities:	Johnny Como
Finisher:	Dropkick, Boston Crab
Career Span:	1959–87

Titles Won:	24
Days as World Champion:	1,452
Age at first World Title Win:	24
Best Opponents:	Bruno Sammartino, Fred Blassie, Don Muraco
Halls of Fame:	2

Morales, Pedro

Renowned fan favorite Pedro Morales is a surefire Hall of Famer, a man who headlined steadily on both coasts, and accomplished goals that few peers have ever been able to duplicate. He was a hearty competitor, full of charisma, and extremely popular with people from many different backgrounds. A native of Culebra, Puerto Rico, Morales finished high school in Brooklyn and picked up wrestling at a local YMCA. He entered the business at seventeen years of age and, by 1960, he was traveling between the United States and Canada full time, wrestling steadily and learning the ropes from many established grapplers. In the northeast, his background was marketed specifically to lure Puerto Rican fans to the arena, and, to a lesser degree than Miguel Perez and Antonino Rocca, was responsible for doing so. He continued to build upon his ring talents and popularity in the Los Angeles area in 1965, and only a few months after arriving in the territory, he beat The Destroyer for the WWA World Heavyweight Title, starting the first of his two reigns.

On February 8, 1971, Morales made history when he dethroned the hated Ivan Koloff for the WWWF World Heavyweight Title at Madison Square Garden and held the title for over 1,000 days. He successfully defended it against some of the toughest heel challengers in the business, and it was commonplace to see over 19,000 fans at the Garden when he was at the top of the bill. After such a long and distinguished time as champion, Stan Stasiak finally ended his run on December 1, 1973. Some years later, Morales teamed with Bob Backlund to win the WWF World Tag Team Title and stopped Ken Patera for the Intercontinental belt, becoming the first man in organization history to hold the World, Tag Team, and Intercontinental Titles. In 1981, he traded the latter championship with Don Muraco, and lost the belt a final time to Muraco on January 22, 1983. Along with his WWF titles, Morales was also a four time co-holder of the WWA World Tag Team Title. Morales engaged in his final match in 1987.

Born:	May 4, 1935
Height:	5'10"
Weight:	250
Real Name:	Harry W. Fujiwara
Trained by:	Nick Bockwinkel
Career Span:	1962–96

Titles Won:	21
Best Opponents:	Pat Patterson, Bob Backlund, Ricky Steamboat
Halls of Fame:	1

Mr. Fuji

A proponent of tossing salt into the eyes of foes and utilizing his walking cane as a weapon, Mr. Fuji was a prominent wrestler and manager for three decades. He entered the business in his native Hawaii, although billed from Japan, and devised his own trademark heel characteristics, which came to be quite successful across the globe. He won championships in Hawaii, New Zealand, Australia, and the United States, including the WWWF World Tag Team Title—becoming the first team to not only repeat, but three-peat as champions with Professor Tanaka in the 1970s. Fuji took to managing in the WWF, leading Demolition and Yokozuna to world titles. He retired to Tennessee and was inducted into the WWE Hall of Fame in 2007.

Born:	August 7, 1942
Height:	5'11"
Weight:	245
Real Name:	Masanori Saito
College:	Meiji University
Olympics:	Freestyle Wrestling (1964) (Representing Japan) (7th Place)
Identities:	Masa Saito
Managed by:	Captain Lou Albano (1981–82), Masao Hattori (1983)
Finisher:	Saito Suplex
Career Span:	1965–99

Titles Won:	25
Days as World Champion:	57
Age at first World Title Win:	47
Best Opponents:	Antonio Inoki, Jack Brisco, Hulk Hogan

Mr. Saito

The famed Mr. Saito was an aggressive rule-breaker with a wide range of offensive weapons. His chops and suplexes were very effective and, many times, opponents on the receiving end of his arsenal appeared to be in serious pain. A former two-time Japanese national amateur champion and Olympic veteran, Saito formed a successful tag team in the World Wrestling Federation with Mr Fuji, winning the tag title twice. In addition, he captured championships in Florida, Alabama, Los Angeles, San Francisco, and Vancouver, and was a two-time IWGP World Tag champion for New Japan. Mr. Saito made history on February 10, 1990, in Tokyo, where he beat Larry Zbyszko for the AWA World Heavyweight championship. Zbyszko would regain the belt on April 8, 1990, at SuperClash IV. Later that year, he teamed with The Great Muta in WCW's special Pat O'Connor Memorial Tag Team Tournament at Starrcade 1990. They progressed to the finals, but were defeated by the Steiner Brothers. Saito retired from wrestling in 1999.

Born:	September 10, 1934
Height:	6'0"
Weight:	230
Real Name:	John Francis Walker
Wife:	Olivia Walker
College:	University of Hawaii
Trained by:	Tony Morelli, Pat O'Connor
Identities:	The Grappler
Career Span:	1956–2007

Titles Won:	51
Best Opponents:	Harley Race, Jack Brisco, Masked Superstar
Halls of Fame:	2

Mr. Wrestling II

The hooded hero, Mr. Wrestling II began his career as the contortionist Johnny Walker, a man who could escape any hold, and dubbed the "Rubberman." He grew up in Hawaii, the son of a sailor, and was involved in many sports while in high school. By the time he donned the white mask as a partner to the original Mr. Wrestling (Tim Woods), Walker had appeared all over North America and was well known for his athletic prowess. Since he was such a strong competitor, he was a natural for Woods' partner, and the two won the state tag team title on several occasions. As singles performer, he won the Georgia Heavyweight Title a total of ten times, and his most high-profile fan was none other than President Jimmy Carter. He feuded with many big-named superstars, challenged Jack Brisco and other NWA World Champions, and solidified himself as one of the greatest ever in the territory. He was also a spectacular draw in Florida, Alabama, and Tennessee, and won the Mid-South North American Title in 1984.

Born:	September 10, 1949
Height:	6'3"
Weight:	250
Real Name:	Donald T. Muraco
High School:	Punahou High School (HI)
College:	Glendale Junior College
Identities:	Dr. X, Magnificent M
Finisher:	Reverse Piledriver
Career Span:	1969–2005

Titles Won:	16
Best Opponents:	Pedro Morales, Nick Bockwinkel, Hulk Hogan
Halls of Fame:	2

Muraco, Don

Most WWE fans today associate "The Rock" with Dwayne Johnson, but years before, Don Muraco of Hawaii used that moniker, and was exceptionally successful with it. Also known as "Magnificent" Muraco, he was a clever heel, utilizing strength, psychology, and was adept at the often forgotten form of telling a story in the ring. In 1967, he won a high school wrestling championship and trained at Dean Ho's gym, working out with many talented pros—with Lord James Blears being his greatest mentor. Named AWA Rookie of the Year, Muraco toured the territories and was a strong challenger for Bob Backlund's WWF crown before winning the Intercontinental Title from Pedro Morales in 1981. Muraco lost and regained the Intercontinental belt from Morales prior to losing it to Tito Santana in February 1984. In July 1985, he won the first King of the Ring tournament and had well-received feuds with Ricky Steamboat and Hulk Hogan. Muraco was also a leading veteran in the budding ECW promotion that started out of Philadelphia.

Born:	August 16, 1946
Height:	6′2″
Weight:	265
Real Name:	Hoyt Richard Murdoch Jr.
Family:	Son of Hoyt "Frankie" Murdoch, nephew of Cecil "Farmer Jones" Murdoch
High School:	Caprock High School (TX)
Trained by:	Frankie Murdoch, Dory Funk Sr.
Identities:	Ron Carson, The Invader, The Tornado, Tornado Murdoch, Black Ace
Finisher:	Brainbuster
Tag Teams:	The Texas Outlaws w/ Dusty Rhodes
Career Span:	1967–96
Died:	June 15, 1996, Amarillo, TX 49 years old

Murdoch, Dick

Titles Won:	44
Best Opponents:	Harley Race, Ric Flair, Antonio Inoki
Managers:	8
Halls of Fame:	2
Movies:	4

Dick Murdoch of Canyon, Texas was a versatile athlete, but mostly remembered for being a ruthless, brawling heel. It was a role he performed well; drawing the ire of audiences and making fans believe that all of the violence they were witnessing was all too real. Wild disregard of all rules were commonplace in his matches, and Murdoch delivered thunderous blow after thunderous blow to his opponents, drawing blood, and never missing a beat as he pummeled foes into submission. Murdoch gained initial fame as a tag team partner of Dusty Rhodes in the late 1960s and early 1970s, and the pair captured championships in several territories. In the Mid-South region, he was a four-time North American champion and in St. Louis, the city he was born in, he won the Missouri crown three times. A regular in Japan and Puerto Rico, Murdoch also teamed with Adrian Adonis to capture the WWF Tag Team Title in 1984. He appeared in WCW in 1991 along with Dick Slater as one of the Hardliners, and was part of the WWF's 1995 Royal Rumble.

Born:	October 25, 1957
Height:	5'9"
Weight:	215
Trained by:	Giant Baba at AJPW Dojo
Identities:	Mr. Onita, The Great Nita
Nickname:	Namida no Karisuma (Charisma of Tears)
Finisher:	Thunder Fire Powerbomb
Promoted:	Frontier Martial-Arts Wrestling (1989–95)
Career Span:	1974–Present

Onita, Atsushi

Titles Won:	16
Days as World Champion:	Over 641
Age at first World Title Win:	33
Best Opponents:	Tarzan Goto, The Sheik, Hayabusa
Halls of Fame:	1

In the early 1990s, many wrestling fans around the world heard stories of violent barbed-wire death matches taking place in Japan, but couldn't fathom the logistics of such a brutal contest taking place in their own squared circle. The man behind the innovative bouts was Atsushi Onita, a former high-flyer turned extreme warrior. Onita founded the FMW promotion in 1989 and launched a crusade against fundamental catch wrestling, turning the sport onto its head by engaging in bloody no-rope barbed wire bouts with explosions, electricity, and even fire. His ring wars against Tarzan Goto, The Sheik, Genichiro Tenryu, and Hayabusa were extraordinary for the amount of punishment the grapplers would take, and Onita, as the hero, would put his body on the line night after night in ways that made him almost appear supernatural. FMW drew huge crowds during its heyday and fans in all corners of the world wanted to see Onita's chaotic matches as a testament to his inventive style and charisma. Outside of the ring, Onita was also involved in Japanese politics.

Photo Courtesy of Pete Lederberg—plmathfoto@hotmail.com

Born:	November 10, 1950
Height:	6'1"
Weight:	235
Real Name:	Robert Keith Orton
Parents:	Robert and Rita Orton
Wife:	Elaine Orton
High School:	Ruskin High School (MO)
Finisher:	Superplex
Career Span:	1972–2009

Titles Won:	23
Best Opponents:	Harley Race, Ric Flair, Bob Backlund
Halls of Fame:	1

Orton, Bob Jr.

An amateur background added to the knowledge taught by Jack Brisco, Hiro Matsuda, and the wrestling crew in Tampa provided "Cowboy" Bob Orton with the skills needed to handle just about any wrestling situation. A second-generation grappler, Orton went to Florida to learn the trade, initially working as a referee. He developed his in-ring and interview skills, and teamed with his tough father, Bob Sr., to capture the Florida Tag Team Championship in 1976. Orton had success as a singles grappler, winning regional titles, and then teaming up with Don Kernodle for the NWA World Tag Team belts in 1984. While a member of the WWF, he challenged both Bob Backlund and Hulk Hogan for the heavyweight title, and acted as a bodyguard for Roddy Piper. He also participated in the main event of the initial WrestleMania. One of his memorable gimmicks was wearing an arm cast to the ring and using it as a weapon during bouts. He returned to the WWE to assist his son Randy in his feud with The Undertaker and still occasionally wrestles on the indie circuit.

Born:	November 6, 1943
Height:	6'0"
Weight:	265
Real Name:	Kenneth Wayne Patera
Parents:	Frank and Dorothy Patera
High School:	Cleveland High School (OR)
Pan-Am Games:	4 Gold Medals (1971) (weightlifting)
Trained by:	Verne Gagne
Finisher:	Swinging Neckbreaker, Swinging Full Nelson
Tag Teams:	The Olympians w/ Brad Rheingans, The Sheiks w/ Jerry Blackwell
Career Span:	1972–92

Titles Won:	16
Best Opponents:	Andre the Giant, Nick Bockwinkel, Hulk Hogan

Patera, Ken

The ultra-competitive Ken Patera was one of five children born to a Portland baker and, like his three brothers, participated in multiple sports during his youth. At Portland State College, and later Brigham Young University, he established many records and was highly decorated in the shotput event. As a weightlifter, he won a number of AAU Titles, and at the 1970 tournament, he set four national records. In 1972, Patera became the first American to lift more than 500 pounds in the clean and jerk. That same year, he participated in the Olympics, but failed to place. Scouted by Verne Gagne, Patera dropped weight to become a wrestler, and was known as a charismatic heel on the AWA and NWA circuits. While wrestling the WWWF territory, he had many key matches against champions Bruno Sammartino and Bob Backlund, and was the second man to ever hold the Intercontinental Title, as well as also holding the AWA World Tag Team and Missouri State Championships. His 1977 third place showing in the World's Strongest Man competition is still occasionally broadcast on TV.

Born:	January 19, 1941
Height:	6'1"
Weight:	240
Real Name:	Pierre Clermont
Identities:	Lord Patrick
Nickname:	Killer, Pretty Boy
Groups:	The Corporation (1998–99)
Tag Team:	The Blond Bombers w/ Ray Stevens
Career Span:	1960–2000

Titles Won:	35
Best Opponents:	Ray Stevens, Bob Backlund, Gene Kiniski
Halls of Fame:	2

Patterson, Pat

Pat Patterson's behind-the-scenes influence helped develop many careers in the WWE and his creative mind established trademark concepts that the organization still uses, including the design of the Royal Rumble match. Before Patterson settled into a backstage role, he was a colorful and successful in-ring performer. Trained by Pat Girard at the latter's Rachel Street wrestling school in Montreal, Patterson worked in New England and in the Pacific Northwest early in his career. While wrestling in the San Francisco territory, he became a major star, capturing the local US Title five times, the World Tag Team title nine times, and won the annual 18-man battle royal in 1975 and 1981. On June 19, 1979, he beat Ted DiBiase for the North American Championship, which was soon renamed the WWF Intercontinental Title. Nearly twenty years later, in June 2000, Patterson won the WWF Hardcore Title and was known as one of Vince McMahon's "stooges." He's served as a close advisor to McMahon and was inducted into the WWE Hall of Fame in 1996.

Born:	April 17, 1954
Height:	6'2"
Weight:	245
Real Name:	Roderick George Toombs
Wife:	Kitty Toombs
Trained by:	Tony Condello, Stu Hart
Identities:	The Masked Canadian
Nicknames:	Rowdy, Rowdy Scot, Hot Rod
Finisher:	Sleeperhold
Tag Team:	The Dream Team w/ Greg Valentine
Managed:	Paul Orndorff (1984), David Shultz (1984), Sean O'Haire (2003)
Career Span:	1973–2011
Died:	July 31, 2015, Hollywood, CA 61 years old

Piper, Roddy

Titles Won:	35
Best Opponents:	Hulk Hogan, Bret Hart, Greg Valentine
Halls of Fame:	3
TV Appearances:	over 30
Movies:	37
Published Books:	1

The rowdy one, Roddy Piper was always exceptionally unrestrained, straying far from the playbook—and rulebook for that matter. He was brutally honest and often funny in his rants, laying it out for the public to consume and driving up the intensity going into his next match. His outrageousness was the reason why he was loved and hated at the same time, and he was never at a loss for words. On those rare occasions when enough was said, he would let his fists do the talking, as he was always ready for a brawl. Billed as being from Glasgow, Scotland, he was originally from Saskatchewan and was raised in Winnipeg. He represented Windsor Park Collegiate at the Manitoba High School wrestling championships and won the 165-pound title in March 1971. Under the guidance of promoter Tony Condello, Piper broke into the business in 1973, and bounced around the Canadian independents with appearances for Verne Gagne in Minneapolis—including an early match against the future "Nature Boy" Ric Flair.

Breaking out into a star in Los Angeles, he feuded heavily with hero Chavo Guerrero and won the Americas championship five times. He left his mark in the Pacific Northwest before venturing east to the Mid-Atlantic territory, and was drawing intense heat everywhere he appeared. Piper's ability to inflame audiences was a promoter's dream. He won the US Title twice for Crockett Promotions, and then jumped to the WWF in 1984. At the first WrestleMania, he partnered with Paul Orndorff in a losing effort against

Hulk Hogan and Mr. T. That following year, he fought Mr. T. in a boxing match at WrestleMania 2 and was disqualified in the fourth round. His antics and violent behavior made feuds with Hogan and Jimmy Snuka exciting, and was responsible for helping bolster the WWF's exposure during a critical time in its history. In 1987, he retired to focus on his budding acting career, but returned to the ring two years later to feud with Rick Rude and Bad News Brown.

Piper won his first WWF championship when he captured the Intercontinental Title on January 19, 1992 from The Mountie, but ended up losing it to Bret Hart at WrestleMania VIII. Over the course of the next few years, he made sporadic appearances for the WWF and WCW. In the main event of Starrcade 1996, he beat Hollywood Hogan with a sleeperhold and three years later, toppled Hart for the US Title with help from comedian Will Sasso. Piper retired again in 1999, but later worked as a WCW official. In March 2003, he made his WWE homecoming, smashing Hogan with a pipe during the latter's bout with Vince McMahon at WrestleMania XIX, and then made an appearance for NWA-TNA, where he delivered an infamous shoot-style rant against Vince Russo. In 2005, he was inducted into the WWE Hall of Fame and has made a number of appearances for the promotion, including wrestling a handicap bout at WrestleMania XXV against Chris Jericho. Piper continued to make appearances for the WWE several times a year, and always drew a huge ovation from the fans. He passed away suddenly in July 2015, at the age of sixty-one, and the wrestling world mourned the loss of one of the greatest in its history.

Photo Courtesy of the Collection of Tim Hornbaker

Born:	March 20, 1943
Height:	6'4"
Weight:	245
Real Name:	Dennis Waters
Trained by:	Jack Wentworth
Identities:	Lord Anthony Lansdowne
Nickname:	Blond Adonis, Blond Bombshell
Finisher:	Powerlock
Managed by:	Bobby Davis
Career Span:	1963–82

Titles Won:	14
Days as World Champion:	Over 324
Age at first World Title Win:	27
Best Opponents:	Antonio Inoki, Bruno Sammartino, Johnny Valentine

Powers, Johnny

In the summer of 1964, a blond-haired newcomer named Johnny Powers, reportedly fresh from a stint in Hawaii, appeared in the WWWF territory and challenged World Heavyweight Champion Bruno Sammartino. It was a remarkable ascension for the twenty-one-year-old Powers, who'd only made his pro debit the year before in the Detroit area. Originally from Hamilton, Ontario, Powers was incredibly strong, standing 6'4", and made the perfect foil for Sammartino. Powers went on to become a major superstar in the NWF, a territory extending from Cleveland to Buffalo, and held both their World and North American belts. He was also involved on the promotional side of both the NWF and the IWA, which was an indie promotion that ran between 1975 and 1978.

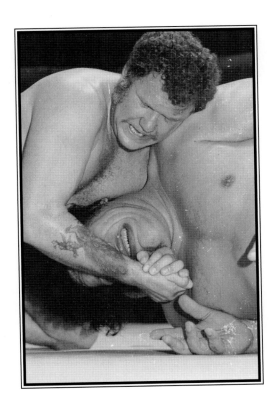

Photo Courtesy of Pete Lederberg—plmathfoto@hotmail.com

Born:	April 11, 1943
Height:	6'1"
Weight:	250
Real Name:	Harley Leland Race
Parents:	Jay and Mary Race
High School:	Quitman High School (MO)
Identities:	Jack Long, The Great Mortimer
Nicknames:	Handsome, Mad Dog
Finisher:	Indian Deathlock, Suplex
Managed:	Lex Luger (1991–92), Mr. Hughes (1991–92), Big Van Vader (1991–95), The Super Invader (1993), Yoshi Kwan (1993), Steve Austin (1994)
Promoted:	World League Wrestling (WLW) (1999–Present)
Career Span:	1960–93

Race, Harley

Titles Won:	44
Days as World Champion:	Around 1,976
Age at first World Title Win:	30
Best Opponents:	Dory Funk Jr., Jack Brisco, Ric Flair
Halls of Fame:	7

Incredibly tough and intimidating, Harley Race was the classic professional wrestler in a day and age of corny gimmicks and characters. He was a solid force to be reckoned with, capable of dealing with a brawler in the same manner he'd take care of a technician: dismantling both with his power and skills. His overriding knowledge of holds and psychology gave him an advantage over his foes in the ring, but more importantly, put him in a place to be eternally successful in a business that coveted ring warriors of his ilk. In an era in which the National Wrestling Alliance World Heavyweight Championship was considered the most prestigious wrestling title in the business, Race won the belt not once, but eight different times. There is nothing more that needs to be said to affirm his Hall of Fame career. For some wrestlers, wearing the NWA belt even a few days was the high point of their career, but for Race, he stood tall as champion for 1,800 days.

Guided into the profession by St. Joseph promoter Gust Karras, Race studied the finer points of the art from old-school masters Stanislaus and Wladek Zbyszko, who had a farm in nearby Savannah, Missouri. Put through the wringer, Race was taught many lessons that were no longer commonplace among wrestlers because the sport had evolved with an emphasis on color instead of fortitude, which actually worked to give Race an advantage in terms of in-ring confidence. His core toughness and size made him unafraid of anyone in the ring, regardless of their reputation, and he was never unwilling to match up in a legitimate fight. Debuting as a teenager, Race suffered a career setback after being injured in a serious car accident after only a year in the business. He never gave up on trying to return to the ring, and set off on a whirlwind tour that took him all over the wrestling landscape. He was impressive in the ring and earned the respect of many influential NWA bookers who'd later support his candidacy for the World Title.

In Minneapolis, he formed a successful tag team with Larry Hennig and beat Bruiser and Cruiser for the AWA World Title, the first of three championship reigns, on January 31, 1965. Basing his operations in the Central States territory, Race won the regional heavyweight title nine times and the Missouri belt seven. His biggest achievement, however, occurred on May 24, 1973, setting off his decade-long relationship with the NWA World Heavyweight Title. That very first win came at the expense of Dory Funk Jr. with Race taking two of three falls. Even with it being a big win for his career, Race was only a transitional titleholder the first time around, losing the belt to Jack Brisco on July 20, 1973. That wasn't the case for his second reign. He dethroned Terry Funk on February 6, 1977 and remained champion for over two years, reportedly making over 700 successful title defenses. Race embodied the spirit of all his predecessors, fulfilling the rigorous demands of the NWA, and maintained the worldwide esteem for both the organization and the title itself.

Race went everywhere and met everyone, even battling WWWF champions Billy Graham and Bob Backlund in title vs. title contests. He was finally defeated by Dusty Rhodes on August 21, 1979, but regained the title five nights later. The next three title losses saw Race regain the belt within a week or less, including twice in Japan against Giant Baba. Race's seventh NWA Title victory came on June 10, 1983 against Ric Flair, and it was considered historic at the time because he was supposedly beating Lou Thesz's record six reigns as champ; Thesz, truth be told, was only a three-time wearer of the Alliance crown. In 1984, Race and Flair traded the belt once more, making Race an eight-time titleholder. A few years later, he became the "King" of the WWF after winning a King of the Ring tournament outside Boston. He later managed Lex Luger and Vader to gold in WCW, but unfortunately broke his hip in a car accident in 1995, which officially ended his active career. He currently runs a wrestling school in Eldon, Missouri, which he's been doing since 1999 and has taught many future pros the ropes.

Born:	October 12, 1945
Height:	6'2"
Weight:	275
Real Name:	Virgil Riley Runnels Jr.
Parents:	Virgil and Katherine Runnels
High School:	Johnston High School (TX)
College:	West Texas State University
Pro Sports:	Continental Football League— Hartford Charter Oaks (1967)
Identities:	Dusty Runnels, The Midnight Rider, The Midnight Cowboy
Tag Teams:	The Texas Outlaws w/ Dick Murdoch, The Superpowers w/ Nikita Koloff
Promoted:	Turnbuckle Championship Wrestling (2000–03)
Career Span:	1967–2007
Died:	June 11, 2015, Orlando, FL 69 years old

Rhodes, Dusty

Titles Won:	57
Days as World Champion:	107
Age at first World Title Win:	33
Best Opponents:	Ric Flair, Harley Race, Randy Savage
Halls of Fame:	4

The legendary "American Dream," Dusty Rhodes was beyond popular during the height of his career. He was an icon, a naturally charismatic wrestling sensation that fought the good fight against heels from coast to coast. He'd verbally connect to the audience in promos, then play out a back-and-forth storyline in the ring, and rebound to grab the attention of all watching going into his finisher, the Bionic Elbow. He was an incredible lure to the box office throughout his time on the mat and his popularity is certainly on par with any of the other major stars of his era.

An actor in his high school drama club, Rhodes was a capable performer and confident in front of large crowds. After receiving words of encouragement from Fritz Von Erich, attending the Santos wrestling school in Boston, and learning from Joe Blanchard in San Antonio, Dusty was ready to make an impact on the business . . . and he did. Within his first year, he was already a headliner. Teaming with "Tornado" Dick Murdoch, he won a number of tag team championships as a rule-breaking heel.

Rhodes and Murdoch made a lot of noise in Toronto, Detroit, and Florida during their tenure together. In 1974, Dusty turned fan favorite in Florida and rampaged through the territory, building an army of supporters. Within a short time, there was no bigger superstar in the southeast. Rhodes kept the momentum going across other areas of the NWA, and his regular guy image was extraordinarily popular and was billed as the common man. Proven to be a box office success, he rose right to the top of the business and pinned Harley Race at the famous Armory in Tampa to capture the National Wrestling Alliance World Heavyweight Title on August 21, 1979. He had a matinee program in Jacksonville on August 26, and then appeared in Orlando at night, where he lost the belt in a rematch against Race. Rhodes became a two-time NWA Champion on June 21, 1981, winning again from Race, this time at the Omni in Atlanta. His reign lasted until September 17, when he lost a bout to his longtime foe, Ric Flair, in Kansas City.

During the 13th show of the Great American Bash tour, Rhodes captured his third NWA World Title from Flair in a cage match on July 26, 1986 in Greensboro. Flair regained the title on August 9, pinning Dusty while Rhodes was locked in a figure-four. Over the course of his career, Rhodes held many other championships, including two versions of the US Title. In the Mid-Atlantic region, he worked as part of the behind-the-scenes staff as a booker where he had some of his most memorable moments. He feuded with Tully Blanchard over the TV Title, was double-crossed by the Road Warriors, and teamed with Nikita Koloff to win the second annual Jim Crockett Sr. Memorial Tag Team Tournament on April 11, 1987. They were victorious over Blanchard and Lex Luger and dedicated their win to the injured Magnum T.A. Dusty was a persistent challenger to Flair's crown, and they headlined Starrcade in both 1984 and 1985. In April 1988, he was stripped of the US Title after attacking Jim Crocket with a baseball bat.

Shortly after Starrcade in 1988, Rhodes returned to Florida and launched the PWF, a short-lived regional promotion with lofty aspirations. In 1989, he entered the WWF and Vince McMahon pushed Dusty's "son of a plumber" image, and the former NWA champion was decked out in polka dot attire. Although he gained a large following, Rhodes remained in the middle of the card and had strong feuds with Randy Savage and Ted DiBiase. It was during his war with the "Million Dollar Man" that Dusty's son, Dustin, was introduced to the national audience. Both father and son ended up in WCW, where Dustin found much success and Dusty worked as a commentator. In September 1994, Rhodes came out of semi-retirement to team with his son and the Nasty Boys against the members of Colonel Parker's group in a War Games event. Rhodes would eventually make Parker submit to a figure-four and give his team the victory. A few years later, he shocked his followers by turning on Larry Zbyszko and joining the New World Order.

In 2000, he established an indie promotion known as Turnbuckle Championship Wrestling, which ran shows across the south. Many big name stars appeared for the promotion and Rhodes often laced up his boots and returned to the ring. His final stint in WCW came at its final pay-per-view on March 18, 2001 in Jacksonville. Dusty teamed with Dustin to beat Ric Flair and Jeff Jarrett.

An ironic fact: Rhodes was at Jim Crockett's first pay-per-view of Starrcade 1987 and WCW's last PPV, Greed. On January 8, 2003, Rhodes reunited with the Road Warriors in TNA in Nashville, and worked an angle with Nikita Koloff the following week. Between 2005 and 2015, he made a number of appearances on WWE television, and was a major force behind-the-scenes at NXT. Rhodes also had the honor of inducting the Funk Brothers and Eddie Graham into the WWE Hall of Fame, where he himself was enshrined by his sons Dustin and Cody in 2007. Dusty passed away in June 2015, at the age of sixty-nine. His legacy will never be forgotten.

Rich, Tommy

Born:	July 26, 1956
Height:	6'0"
Weight:	245
Real Name:	Thomas Richardson
Trained by:	Dick Steinborn, Jerry Jarrett, Jerry Lawler
Finisher:	Sleeperhold, Thesz Press
Groups:	The York Foundation (1991–92)
Tag Teams:	The Fabulous Ones w/ Eddie Gilbert
Managed by:	Jimmy Hart, Jackie Fargo, Paul E. Dangerously, Alexandria York
Managed:	The FBI (1997–98)
Career Span:	1974–Present

Titles Won:	58
Days as World Champion:	4
Age at first World Title Win:	24
Best Opponents:	Harley Race, Jerry Lawler, Buzz Sawyer
Halls of Fame:	1

"Wildfire" Tommy Rich was one of the biggest names in the sport in the 1970s and 1980s. He was immensely popular, a "wide-eyed Southern boy" with charisma and appeal that never failed to pack arenas. A high school athlete from Hendersonville, Tennessee, Rich grew up around wrestling and committed himself to the business at the age of eighteen. Quickly embraced by fans throughout the region, he was steadily pushed by promoters, winning numerous championships, and eventually capturing the biggest prize of them all: the National Wrestling Alliance World Heavyweight Title. The victory came on April 27, 1981 at the Civic Center in Augusta, Georgia, when he pinned Harley Race in 27:22, making him the youngest NWA champion at that point. Although he was champion for only four days, losing it back to Race on May 1 in Gainesville, Rich had made history with it being a crowning achievement on a celebrated career. To this day, Rich makes independent appearances and can still light up an audience with his magnetism.

Photo Courtesy of Dan Westbrook

Born:	November 14, 1924
Height:	5'10"
Weight:	235
Real Name:	Mitsuhiro Momota
Family:	Father of Mitsuo Momota
Finisher:	Sleeperhold
Promoted:	Japan Wrestling Alliance (JWA) (1953–63)
Career Span:	1951–63
Died:	December 15, 1963, Tokyo, Japan 39 years old

Rikidozan

Titles Won:	13
Days as World Champion:	119
Age at first World Title Win:	37
Best Opponents:	Lou Thesz, Masahiko Kimura, Fred Blassie
Tournament Wins:	5
Halls of Fame:	2

Regarded as the "Father of Japanese Professional Wrestling," Rikidozan was originally from Korea and spent five years as a Sumo wrestler beginning in 1946. He spent some time working in construction at the Tachikawa Air Base before taking part on a show featuring a band of American wrestlers trying to build interest in the Western style of wrestling. The date was October 28, 1951, and Rikidozan made his debut, wrestling Bobby Bruns to a draw. Bruns, incidentally, had been his trainer, and was the liaison for the tour for Honolulu promoter Al Karasick, who had membership in the National Wrestling Alliance. Rikidozan was said to have dropped as much as six inches off his waist and had learned a great deal about the profession in a short amount of time. The appearance of an Asian grappler on the program was a welcomed sight, and from that point forth, he was more responsible for the spread of American wrestling in Japan than anyone else.

In 1952, Rikidozan appeared in Honolulu and then toured California, losing very few singles matches. Although he initially worked as a fan favorite, he altered his persona and became a heel, drawing the ire of fans with his illegal tactics. In Japan, however, Rikidozan was entirely popular. In fact, he helped foster the wrestling revolution in that country, propelling the sport into the public's eye. On December 22, 1954, he beat Masahiko Kimura to win the initial Japanese Heavyweight Title, winning the match by knockout. His televised matches drew record numbers and there was no debate who the most popular wrestler in the country was. He added to his fame with a victory over Lou Thesz for the International Title and also beat Fred Blassie for the WWA World Heavyweight crown in March 1962. On December 8, 1963, Rikidozan was stabbed in the left side of his abdomen at the New Latin Quarter club in Tokyo. The thirty-nine-year-old international wrestling celebrity died a week later of peritonitis at Sanno Hospital.

Born:	May 30, 1955
Height:	6'5"
Weight:	250
Real Name:	Aurelian Jake Smith, Jr.
Family:	Son of Grizzly Smith, stepbrother of Sam Houston and Rockin' Robin
Trained by:	Grizzly Smith
Nickname:	The Snake
Groups:	The Legion of Doom (1983–84)
Managed by:	Paul Ellering
Snake's Names:	Damian, Lucifer
Career Span:	1975–2014

Titles Won:	14
Best Opponents:	Ted DiBiase, Rick Rude, Randy Savage
Halls of Fame:	1

Roberts, Jake

Second generation star Jake Roberts of Cooke County, Texas was a colorful performer and the man who put the DDT finisher on the map. A cunning ring psychologist, he intimidated foes with his snake-like tactics, and the literal snake he carried to the ring added to his mystique. He was a capable heel and fan favorite and wore both hats while in the NWA, WWF, and WCW during the 1980s and 1990s. Roberts was a convincing brawler, and he had memorable feuds with Ricky Steamboat, Rick Rude, and Ted DiBiase. At one juncture, the massive wrestler Earthquake purportedly squashed his snake in a controversial angle that horrified witnesses—but really caused no harm to the animal. Roberts won the SMW heavyweight title in 1994, made occasional showings for ECW, and also wrestled in Great Britain and Mexico. Roberts reemerged in the WWF briefly in 1996 and in recent years has appeared for numerous indie organizations and for TNA. He retired from the ring in January 2011, but returned to make several indie appearances through 2014.

His out-of-the-ring trials were spotlighted in the documentary *Beyond the Mat*, which came out in 1999. In 2014, Roberts was inducted into the WWE Hall of Fame.

Born:	September 18, 1938
Height:	5'11"
Weight:	235
Real Name:	William Alfred Robinson
Nickname:	Man of 1000 Holds
Finisher:	Double Arm Suplex
Career Span:	1958–92
Died:	March 3, 2014, Little Rock, AR
	75 years old

Titles Won:	18
Days as World Champion:	Over 719
Age at first World Title Win:	30
Best Opponents:	Antonio Inoki, Verne Gagne, Jumbo Tsuruta
Halls of Fame:	4

Robinson, Billy

Billy Robinson was a legendary catch-as-catch-can grappler. Influenced by his father and uncle, who were both boxers, he was instilled with a toughness at an early age and progressed through the amateur ranks in Britain, winning the national light heavyweight wrestling title in 1957. He trained for years at Billy Riley's infamous "Snake Pit" in Wigan, learning from some of the masters of the pure catch style. In addition to Riley, Robinson worked out with brothers Billy Joyce and Joe Robinson, Ernie Riley, and Jack Dempsey. He'd later beat trainer Joyce for the British championship in 1967. On December 19, 1968, he won a tournament in Japan for the initial IWA World Title and also teamed with Verne Gagne and The Crusher to hold the AWA Tag Title. During the 1970s, Robinson was one of the trainers at Gagne's wrestling school, coaching scores of future superstars. At one time, he was considered to be the best wrestler in the world, and his combination of science, strength, and unyielding ferociousness made him a dangerous and successful competitor.

Born:	May 24, 1931
Height:	6'0"
Weight:	220
Real Name:	Enrique Gregory Romero
Trained by:	Diablo Velasco, Dory Funk Sr.
Finisher:	Cannonball
Career Span:	1954–83
Died:	January 15, 2006, Amarillo, TX 74 years old

Titles Won:	31
Best Opponents:	Dory Funk Sr., Gene Kiniski, Mike DiBiase

Romero, Ricky

For three decades, "Rapid" Ricky Romero was an undeniably popular hero of the wrestling world, being universally well-liked in and out of the ring. Originally from San Bernardino, California, Romero competed for several years under his real name, and his quickness and enthusiasm were keys to his success. He found a home in the Amarillo region and became a legend, winning the North American and Rocky Mountain Titles and often teaming with Dory Funk Sr. as the North American Tag Team champs. Romero, who played baseball when he was young, was a perfect foil to the heels in the territory and had the kind of charisma that people gravitated toward. His sons, Steve, Mark, and Chris were also grapplers, known professionally as the Youngbloods.

Photo Courtesy of Scott Teal/Crowbar Press

Born:	June 9, 1929
Height:	6′2″
Weight:	225
Real Name:	Jean Rougeau
Parents:	Armand and Albina Rougeau
Family:	Nephew of Eddie Auger, brother of Jacques Rougeau
High School:	Catholic High School (Montreal)
Trained by:	Eddie Auger, Yvon Robert
Promoted:	International Wrestling Association (IWA) (1964–75)
Career Span:	1952–71
Died:	May 25, 1983, Montreal, Quebec 53 years old

Rougeau, Johnny

Titles Won:	At least 8
Days as World Champion:	Over 725
Age at first World Title Win:	32
Best Opponents:	Killer Kowalski, Hans Schmidt, Ivan Koloff

Quebec legend Johnny Rougeau was influenced by professional wrestling early on his life, particularly by his uncle Edouard Auger, who'd turned to the grappling trade to earn a living in the late 1940s. Add the fact that the province was full of opportunities on a large scale at the Montreal Forum or on a secondary circuit, made becoming a wrestler was an easy choice for Rougeau after his goal of becoming a hockey player didn't pan out. Being a natural athlete, he took to wrestling easily, and by the summer of 1953, he'd defeated Harry Madison for the Canadian Junior Heavyweight Title. The following year, he dropped the championship and became a heavyweight. The popular hometown boy was an exciting part of the wrestling bill for Eddie Quinn's productions, and the latter brought in scores of top heels to wage war. Between 1965 and 1970, he won the International World Title six times and retired on August 2, 1971 to focus on his Laval Nationals Junior Hockey team, as well as to promote wrestling and boxing.

Born:	July 21, 1935
Height:	5'9"
Weight:	215
Real Name:	Nelson Combs
Career Span:	1955–89
Died:	February 3, 2002, Mooresville, NC 66 years old

Titles Won:	17
Best Opponents:	Lou Thesz, Antonio Inoki, Dory Funk Sr.
Halls of Fame:	1

Royal, Nelson

Kentucky born Nelson Royal was a spectacular junior heavyweight wrestler and was a multi-time world champion. He studied under the legendary Indian grappler, Don Eagle, traveling with the "Chief" in 1955. By 1962, in Texas, he had developed a "Sir Nelson Royal" gimmick that claimed he was an aristocrat from England. Often aiming at the ire of the crowd, he even worked with a valet named Jeeves, which drove fans mad. Royal won many regional tag team championships in West Texas, Los Angeles, Pacific Northwest, and Mid-Atlantic territories, and held the NWA World Junior Title four times between 1976 and 1988. Royal, well-liked throughout the business, influenced many careers as a trainer and owned a western store in Mooresville, North Carolina.

Born:	October 6, 1935
Height:	5'10"
Weight:	265
Real Name:	Bruno Laopardo Franceso Sammartino
Parents:	Alfonso and Emilia Sammartino
Family:	Father of David Sammartino
Trained by:	Rex Perry, Ace Freeman
Finisher:	Bearhug, Backbreaker
Career Span:	1959–87

Titles Won:	9
Days as World Champion:	4,040
Age at first World Title Win:	27
Best Opponents:	Killer Kowalski, Bill Miller, Gene Kiniski
Halls of Fame:	6

Sammartino, Bruno

The "Living Legend" Bruno Sammartino is arguably the most important wrestler in World Wrestling Entertainment history. A case can be made that if it wasn't for the success of Sammartino as an outstanding fan favorite and box office attraction during the early days of the promotion, the WWE wouldn't be what it is today. His value to Vincent J. McMahon in the 1960s and 1970s cannot be measured. Audiences throughout the world treasured his magnetism and were brought to their feet as he stood toe to toe with the most vile rule-breakers in the industry. Fans wholeheartedly embraced McMahon's formula of importing in the biggest and baddest heels to challenge Sammartino, and Bruno, month after month and year after year, knocked them all back one at a time. The drama of each feud may have changed slightly, but the blueprint was written in stone, and Sammartino's ability to rise above each individual test only brought him closer to the people who were devoted to cheering him.

Born in Abruzzi, Italy, he developed his frame into that of a power-lifter and worked out at local Pittsburgh gyms with University of Pittsburgh wrestling coach Rex Perry, learning the finer points of amateur wrestling. His eagerness to excel was a selling point for Rudy Miller, an old wrestling promoter and manager, who scouted Sammartino for McMahon and brought him into the Capitol Wrestling fold in 1959. Green all over, Sammartino entered pro wrestling with an exceptional look and natural appeal, and McMahon found developing him into a fan favorite quite easy. Within a short time, however, there was some friction in Sammartino's northeastern run, and he ventured to Toronto, where his climb to the top of the wrestling rankings continued. Promoters and managers sought his contract with vigor, but McMahon pulled Sammartino back into the fold, setting the stage for the biggest match of Bruno's young career.

On May 17, 1963 at Madison Square Garden, 19,000 fans watched Sammartino crush the "Nature Boy" Buddy Rogers, the renowned champion and icon in less than a minute and win the WWWF World Heavyweight Title. The commanding victory pushed Sammartino into another realm of popularity, kick-starting his championship reign with flavor. The Sammartino era of dominance began that night, and McMahon wasted no time in lining up a stable of heels to push his young star to the limit. Guys like Dr. Bill Miller, Gene Kiniski, Fred Blassie, Gorilla Monsoon, Bill Watts, Waldo Von Erich, Stan Hansen, and Killer Kowalski all seemed like potential successors, and many times appeared to be the cusp of winning the prized championship. But Sammartino rebounded with Herculean strength, powering out the doldrums to pin his rivals. His knack for surviving perilous situations never got old, and his popularity was sustained throughout the northeastern territory for well over a decade.

Remarkably, Sammartino remained champion for more than 2,800 days and gave the WWWF major credibility against the NWA and AWA. When it was finally time to go in another direction, Ivan Koloff beat him for the title on January 18, 1971. A few years later, Sammartino was called upon again by McMahon to lead his company, and on December 10, 1973, he beat Stan Stasiak for his second WWWF World Championship. Bruno carried the belt until April 30, 1977, when he dropped the strap to Billy Graham in Baltimore. He wrestled into the 1980s, even appearing in a battle royal at WrestleMania 2, and has since been honored for induction into several Halls of Fame. He established a high standard for heroes in the WWF/WWE, which Hulk Hogan, Bret Hart, The Rock, and John Cena had to follow and emulate, of course in their own individual ways. Sammartino laid the groundwork for each and every one of them, and was honored by induction into the WWE Hall of Fame in 2013.

Savage, Randy

Born:	November 15, 1952
Height:	6'1"
Weight:	235
Real Name:	Randy Mario Poffo
Parents:	Angelo and Judith Poffo
High School:	Downers Grove North High School (IL)
Pro Sports:	Minor League Baseball—In system for the St. Louis Cardinals, Cincinnati Reds, and the Chicago White Sox (1972–75)
Trained by:	Angelo Poffo
Identities:	The Spider, The Executioner, The Destroyer, The Graduate, Mr. Madness
Nicknames:	Rotten, Macho King
Finisher:	Flying Elbowdrop
Career Span:	1973–2004
Died:	May 20, 2011, Seminole, FL 58 years old

Titles Won:	20
Days as World Champion:	Over 1,060
Age at first World Title Win:	26
Best Opponents:	Ricky Steamboat, Ric Flair, Hulk Hogan
Halls of Fame:	2
TV Appearances:	Over 15
Movies:	3

One of the most entertaining and influential wrestlers of the last thirty years, "Macho Man" Randy Savage has seen and done it all. He's delivered excellent matches, won World Titles, and established a legacy that is still fondly remembered by his conglomerate of fans. The son of wrestler Angelo Poffo, Randy was born in Columbus and grew up in the Chicago suburbs, where he was an outstanding baseball player in high school. After bouncing around the farm systems of several pro teams, he became a pro wrestler in 1973 under a mask. He wrestled in a number of territories to include Florida, Alabama, Detroit, and Toronto, and in 1977, he adopted the name "Randy Savage" upon the recommendation of Ole Anderson in Atlanta. Angelo and his two sons, Randy and Lanny, launched their own promotion, International Championship Wrestling in 1978 and it was known as an "outlaw" organization because it operated outside the global sphere of the National Wrestling Alliance.

A month after Randy beat his brother Lanny for the ICW World Heavyweight Title in July 1979, the Poffos filed a $2.4 million federal antitrust suit against nine wrestling promoters to include Jerry Jarrett, Nick Gulas, Verne Gagne, and Jim Barnett. The Poffos claimed that the rival promoters prevented them from talent, blacklisted them, and damaged them financially. The ICW pushed forward and remained a strong independent force until 1983. Savage toured Puerto Rico and the Tennessee area before landing a job with the WWF. Appearing with his wife Elizabeth, who he married in 1984, he feuded with Bruno Sammartino, George Steele, and Ricky Steamboat. He beat Tito Santana for the Intercontinental Title on February 8, 1986, but lost it to Steamboat in a classic at WrestleMania III. During the summer of 1987, Savage became a fan favorite and won that year's King of the Ring tournament in September. At WrestleMania IV, he toppled four opponents in another tourney to win the vacant WWF World Heavyweight Title.

Jealousy over Elizabeth broke up the "Mega Powers" tag team he had formed with Hulk Hogan, and the two feuded until April 2, 1989 at WrestleMania V, when Hogan beat him for the belt. Now a rule-breaker, Savage partnered up with "Sensational" Sherri Martel and beat Jim Duggan to become "King" of the WWF. Three years later, he once again became World champion with a victory over Ric Flair at WrestleMania VIII, but lost it back to Flair that September. Savage divided his time as a wrestler and commentator until leaving the WWF in November 1994. Only weeks later, he emerged in WCW, which had signed Hogan earlier in the year and once again feuded with Flair. He won the three-ring, 60-man battle royal known as "World War III" and captured the vacant WCW World Title on November 26, 1995. Flair beat him for the belt at Starrcade in December, but Savage regained it on January 22, 1996 with some unexpected help from Arn Anderson.

Flair beat Randy again on February 11 at SuperBrawl, this time in a cage match. On April 19, 1998 in Denver, Savage dethroned Sting for the WCW Title at Spring Stampede with interference from both Hollywood Hogan and Kevin Nash. The next day at the World Arena in Colorado Springs, Hogan defeated him and took the WCW Title. He had another single-day reign as titleholder beginning on July 11, 1999, when he won the title during a tag team match with Sid Vicious against champion Nash and Sting. Hogan again ended his title run the next day on *Nitro*. In 2002, Savage appeared in the box office hit *Spider-Man* as Bone Saw McGraw. He was also in several programs including *Mad About You; Baywatch; Arli$$, Walker, Texas Ranger; and Nikki*. To those outside of the wrestling world, Savage was known as the spokesman for Slim Jim. Other than a few appearances in TNA in 2004, Savage remained retired for the last decade of his life. He died tragically in a car accident in May 2011 at the age of fifty-eight. In 2015, Randy was inducted into the WWE Hall of Fame.

Born:	August 27, 1948
Height:	6'6"
Weight:	290
Real Name:	Robert Rudolph Remus
Parents:	Rudolph and Florence Remus
High School:	Eden Prairie High School (MN)
Identities:	Bob Slaughter, Super Destroyer Mark II
Finisher:	Cobra Clutch
Groups:	Sgt. Slaughter's Army (1982–83), The Triangle of Terror (1990–91), The Corporation (1998)
Career Span:	1974–2011

Sgt. Slaughter

Titles Won:	13
Days as World Champion:	64
Age at first World Title Win:	42
Best Opponents:	Bob Backlund, Hulk Hogan, Ric Flair
Halls of Fame:	2

Sgt. Slaughter was an extraordinary wrestling hero; a man who transcended the business with his immense popularity and becoming the real life inspiration for a G.I. Joe character. He grew up in Minnesota and served in the Marines prior to learning the ropes at Verne Gagne's camp in Chanhassen. In 1974, he made his debut and toured several territories as "Bruiser" Bob Remus. He gained success in the Central States and the WWF, and beat Ricky Steamboat for the vacant US Title in the Mid-Atlantic region on October 4, 1981. A few years later, he became one of the most admired and recognizable pro wrestlers in the world. He promoted American patriotism and chants of "USA" were commonplace during his matches. That changed in 1990 when his character supported Iraq during the first Gulf War, and in January 1991, he beat the Ultimate Warrior for the WWF World Title. He regained his fan support and worked numerous roles in the WWE, including as commissioner and wrestled on *Raw* as recently as July 2011.

© Dan Westbrook

Born:	May 16, 1921
Height:	5'9"
Weight:	230
Real Name:	Robert Kinji Shibuya
Parents:	Kinkichi and Kura Shibuya
Trained by:	Tetsuo "Rubberman" Higami
Identities:	Mr. Hito
Career Span:	1952–75
Died:	May 3, 2010, Hayward, CA 88 years old

Titles Won:	22
Best Opponents:	Ray Stevens, Pepper Gomez, Dory Funk Jr.
Movies:	3
TV Appearances:	3

Shibuya, Kinji

Fondly remembered for his ruthless style inside the ring and his gentlemanly attitude out, Kinji Shibuya was a multitalented athlete. He was a standout high school and collegiate football player, starting guard at the University of Hawaii, and was convinced by Honolulu promoter Al Karasick to give pro wrestling a shot. He traveled across North America and developed a strong heel persona while in Minneapolis that helped him become a top box office attraction in the Bay Area in the 1960s and 1970s. Until his retirement in 1974, he drew extraordinary heat from crowds and knew how to push the right buttons to attain a powerful reaction. Shibuya held the San Francisco version of US Title and World Tag Team championship three times each.

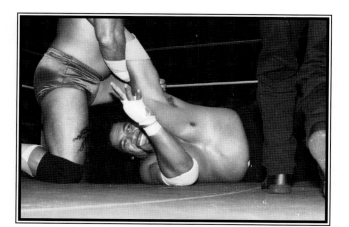

Born:	April 5, 1945
Height:	6'2"
Weight:	315
Real Name:	Leati Sika Anoai
Parents:	Amituanai and Tovale Anoai
Trained by:	Afa Anoai, Jerry Monti, Stu Hart
Career Span:	1973–2006

Sika

Titles Won:	19
Best Opponents:	Hulk Hogan, Bob Backlund, Jimmy Snuka
Halls of Fame:	2

In 1973, Sika joined his older brother Afa in the professional wrestling business, and the two, known as The Wild Samoans, were a dominant tag team, winning over a dozen regional championships. While in the World Wrestling Federation they won the World Tag Title three times and established a standard for teamwork and timing. As mammoth heels, they were intimidating to the utmost degree, and their coordinated attacks not only left welts on opponents, but made an indelible mark on audiences across the globe. In recognition of their achievements, the Samoans were inducted into the WWE Hall of Fame in 2007 and the Professional Wrestling Hall of Fame in 2012. Siki's son, Leati Joseph "Joe" Anoai, also became a pro wrestler, making his debut in 2010. Two years later, he debuted on the WWE's main roster, using the name "Roman Reigns," and was part of a devastating combination known as "The Shield." Reigns went onto win the 2015 Royal Rumble, and has captured the WWE World Heavyweight championship on three occasions.

Photo Courtesy of Pete Lederberg—plmathfoto@hotmail.com

Born:	May 19, 1951
Height:	6'1"
Weight:	240
Real Name:	Richard Van Slater
High School:	Robinson High School (FL)
College:	University of Tampa
Trained by:	Hiro Matsuda, Eddie Graham, Jack Brisco
Career Span:	1972-96

Titles Won:	42
Days as World Champion:	391
Age at first World Title Win:	43
Best Opponents:	Ricky Steamboat, Ric Flair, Jack Brisco

Slater, Dick

Tampa roughneck Dick Slater was part of an exciting new crop of young talent coming out of the area in the early 1970s; a group that included Mike Graham, Steve Keirn, and later, his college wrestling teammate, Paul Orndorff. With nicknames like "Unpredictable" and "Dirty," Slater was a prototypical brawling heel, but that style mixed with his amateur background made him a standout. He was just as successful as his contemporaries, winning the Missouri Title from Jack Brisco in 1977 and the US Heavyweight belt from Greg Valentine in 1983. He formed a brutal team with Dick Murdoch known as the "Hardliners," and also teamed with Bunkhouse Buck to win the WCW Tag Team Title in 1995. He also held the IWA World Title for over a year in Japan.

Born:	May 18, 1943
Height:	6'0"
Weight:	235
Real Name:	James William Reiher
Family:	Father of Jimmy Snuka Jr., Tamina Snuka
Trained by:	Frankie Laine, Danny Hodge
Identities:	Jimmy Kealoha, Great Snuka, Lani Kealoha
Groups:	The Mid-Atlantic Death Squad (1979–80)
Tag Team:	The South Pacific Connection w/ Ricky Steamboat
Career Span:	1970–2009

Titles Won:	34
Best Opponents:	Bob Backlund, Don Muraco, Ricky Steamboat
Halls of Fame:	2

Snuka, Jimmy

Seared into the minds of wrestling fans forever is the moment that Fiji Islander Jimmy Snuka launched himself from the top of a Madison Square Garden cage toward a prone WWF champion, Bob Backlund. The June 28, 1982 incident was one of the most dramatic moments in wrestling history, climaxing when Backlund moved at the last moment. Unfortunately for many other wrestlers on different occasions, they didn't have the luxury of moving out of the way, and Snuka landed his "Superfly" splash in spectacular fashion, putting them down for the count. With bodybuilder looks and stunning ring aerodynamics, Snuka proved to be one of the most popular wrestlers in the world throughout his career. He accompanied main eventers Hulk Hogan and Mr. T to the ring at the first WrestleMania in 1985 and returned to battle Chris Jericho in a handicap match at WrestleMania XXV in April 2009. He was known for wrestling barefoot, and won regional championships in the Mid-Atlantic, Georgia, and Pacific Northwestern territories.

In 2015, the seventy-one-year-old Snuka was arrested for the 1983 death of his girlfriend, Nancy Argentino, which occurred after a wrestling event in Allentown, Pennsylvania. Charged with third-degree murder and involuntary manslaughter, he was found to be mentally incompetent to stand trial in June 2016.

Snyder, Wilbur

Born:	September 15, 1929
Height:	6'2"
Weight:	235
Real Name:	Wilbur E. Snyder
Parents:	Firman and Lola Snyder
High School:	Van Nuys High School (CA)
College:	University of Utah
Pro Sports:	National Football League—Los Angeles Rams (1950–51) WIFU—Edmonton Eskimos (1951–53) Canadian Football League—Edmonton Eskimos (1952–53)
Trained by:	Sandor Szabo
Finisher:	Cobra Twist
Tag Team:	The Young Lions w/ Bobo Brazil
Career Span:	1953–83
Died:	December 25, 1991, Pompano Beach, FL 62 years old

Titles Won:	45
Days as World Champion:	Around 205
Age at first World Title Win:	29
Best Opponents:	Dick the Bruiser, Hans Schmidt, Verne Gagne

In 1953, the Southern California booking office revealed their newest superstar: an ex-football player named Wilbur Snyder. The fresh-faced giant of an athlete was an instant hit, and video of his matches circulated around the country, earning him a universe of fans who hoped to see him appear live. His legitimate football experience helped cement his push from promoters who sought such credentials in their advertising, and Snyder's charisma and physical ability pushed him over the top. He had two high-profile TV matches with NWA champion Lou Thesz in 1954, which helped expedite his path to superstardom. He would capture the US Heavyweight Title no less than eleven times, the WWA World championship in Indiana, and the World Title in Omaha. In 1964, he partnered with Dick the Bruiser to purchase the Indianapolis promotion and the two launched the successful World Wrestling Association. Snyder remained an important member of the wrestling community, particularly throughout the Midwest, until his retirement in 1983.

Born:	March 24, 1940
Height:	6'4"
Weight:	270
Real Name:	Donald Delbert Jardine
Identities:	Sonny Cooper, Super Destroyer
Career Span:	1955–85
Died:	December 16, 2006, Wetaskiwin, Alberta 66 years old

Titles Won:	41
Days as World Champion:	35
Age at first World Title Win:	29
Best Opponents:	Lou Thesz, Harley Race, Fritz Von Erich

Spoiler, The

In 1955, the wrestling world was invaded by a New Brunswick teenager with the size and athletic coordination to match up against any of the decorated veterans. Taught by veterans Emile Dupre and "Whipper" Billy Watson, Jardine was quickly elevated to featured programs at major arenas in Canada. In the years that followed, he won the Nebraska Title and the World Tag Team belts with Dutch Savage under his real name, then donned a mask in Dallas in the summer of 1967, becoming the frightful Spoiler. From there on, he was an unstoppable heel and captured an abundance of state and regional championships; and in 1969, he held the IWA World Title in Australia for a little more than a month. While in the WWF, he reigned as the National champion after the Georgia promotion was purchased in 1984. Exceptionally influential, aspects of his ring style were adopted by other superstars—including by The Undertaker, who still uses the top-rope walking he learned from Jardine.

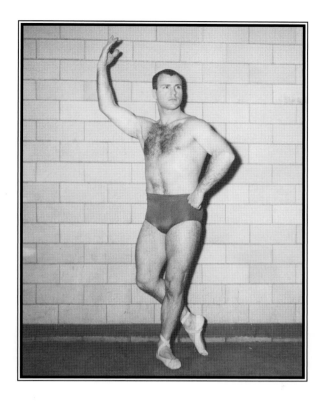

Born:	1932
Height:	5'9"
Weight:	191
Real Name:	Bernard Herman
Parents:	Joseph and Margy Herman
Family:	Brother of Mark Starr
High School:	Soldan-Blewett High School (MO)
College:	Purdue University
Trained by:	Joe Herman
Career Span:	1952–74
Died:	September 20, 2014, London, England 83 years old

Titles Won:	3
Best Opponents:	Antonino Rocca, Gorgeous George, Fred Blassie

Starr, Ricki

A ballet performer and wrestler, Ricki Starr pranced around the ring in pink shoes and displayed an outstanding combination of athleticism and showmanship. Even though he had a background in dance, Starr was no slouch in terms of wrestling ability. In fact, he showed well in three National AAU tournaments from 1949 to '51, and was a disciplined student of the sport in his hometown of St. Louis. He learned from his father, an ex-wrestler, and made his debut in Texas in 1952. By the end of the decade, he was one of the biggest attractions in the sport, exceptionally popular, and headlined all over the United States. He spent a majority of the 1960s and '70s in Europe, and the popular grappler eventually retired to London, where he maintained a quiet life outside of the spotlight he once commanded. Starr passed away on September 20, 2014, at the age of eighty-three.

Born:	April 13, 1937
Height:	6'6"
Weight:	280
Real Name:	George Emile Stipich
Trained by:	Yvon Robert
Identities:	Stan Stasiak Jr.
Nicknames:	Stan the Man, Crusher
Career Span:	1958–84
Died:	June 19, 1997, Portland, OR 60 years old

Titles Won:	29
Days as World Champion:	18
Age at first World Title Win:	33
Best Opponents:	Pedro Morales, Don Leo Jonathan, Bruno Sammartino
Halls of Fame:	1

Stasiak, Stan

Wrestling fans everywhere were saddened when mammoth heel Stan Stasiak dethroned the popular Pedro Morales for the WWWF Heavyweight Title on December 1, 1973 in Philadelphia. But for Stasiak, it was a defining moment in a career lasting twenty-six years. While it was an epic moment for him personally, he was only an interim champion, losing the title to Bruno Sammartino at Madison Square Garden nine days later. Well known throughout the Northeastern circuit, in Texas, and in the Portland territory, Stasiak was a powerhouse heel and his devastating heart punch was a frightening finisher. In Australia in 1970, he held the IWA World Heavyweight Title and captured the Pacific Northwest Title six times. Although he was occasionally billed as the son of the original Stanley Stasiak from the 1920s and 1930s, he had no relation. He passed away in June 1997 at the age of sixty. His son Shawn also became a professional wrestler.

Born:	May 4, 1934
Height:	6'0"
Weight:	225
Real Name:	Samuel Kauaawa Mokuahi Jr.
High School:	Roosevelt High School (HI)
Trained by:	Lou Thesz
Career Span:	1956–78
Died:	May 2, 2006, Honolulu, HI
	71 years old

Titles Won:	23
Best Opponents:	Don Leo Jonathan, Giant Baba, Gene Kiniski

Steamboat, Sam

The immensely popular Sam Steamboat was a longtime hero of fans throughout the territorial system, and particularly in his native Hawaii. In high school and at Weber College in Utah, he was a talented lineman in football and NWA champion Lou Thesz was credited with discovering him. In Texas and the Mid-Atlantic region, he was commonly seen battling the crooked villains, but he gained his biggest fame in Florida. He teamed with Eddie Graham to win the World Tag Team Title three times in the "Sunshine State," and captured the belts two additional times with Jose Lothario and Ronnie Etchison. Steamboat and Graham were also champions in Georgia and Florida. In Hawaii, he held the state championship twice and the North American crown on four occasions.

Photo Courtesy of Pete Lederberg—plmathfoto@hotmail.com

Born:	April 16, 1937
Height:	6'2"
Weight:	285
Real Name:	William James Myers
Trained by:	Bert Rubi, Gino Brito
College:	Michigan State University
Identities:	The Student (masked)
Groups:	The Oddities (1998)
Career Span:	1963–2000
Website:	www.georgesteele.com

Titles Won:	2
Best Opponents:	Bruno Sammartino, The Sheik, Gorilla Monsoon
Halls of Fame:	3

Steele, George

George "The Animal" Steele was a memorable character of the wrestling ring. As his nickname implied, he acted much like an untamed beast, creating carnage wherever he appeared. Steele would take time out of a match to chew on a nearby turnbuckle or blast his foes with a foreign object. When he wasn't an unabashed wildman performing his gimmick, he was calm, articulate, and demonstrated his level of education. In fact, he was a teacher for more than twenty years, only wrestling part-time for the extra money. Originally from Michigan, Steele entered the WWWF and was a strong challenger to Bruno Sammartino's World Title in the late 1960s. He is often remembered for his wanton displays of affection toward Miss Elizabeth in the WWF in the late 1980s. Steele even appeared in film, performing the role of Tor Johnson in the Tim Burton classic, *Ed Wood*. Retired to Cocoa Beach, Florida, he still makes the occasional wrestling appearance as a manager.

Born:	September 28, 1933
Height:	6'1"
Weight:	220
Real Name:	Richard Steinborn
Family:	Brother-in-law of Jerry Oates
Trained by:	Milo Steinborn
Identities:	Dickie Gunkel, Mr. High, Mr. Wrestling, White Knight
Career Span:	1951–84

Titles Won:	34
Days as World Champion:	7
Age at first World Title Win:	29
Best Opponents:	Buddy Rogers, Lou Thesz, Killer Kowalski

Steinborn, Dick

Started in the pro ring at seventeen years of age, Dick Steinborn, the son of strongman Milo Steinborn, was destined for greatness; and during his three-decade career, he won championships in at least nine different territories. A former amateur grappler, he was a legitimate force to be reckoned with on the mat, and crowds applauded his ring work in every city he wrestled. Steinborn toured the US endlessly and also worked Puerto Rico, Canada, and Australia. In 1962, he teamed with Doug Gilbert to win the AWA World Tag Team belts and the following year he briefly wore the Georgia version of the World Heavyweight crown, as well as also holding the Southern and Texas Titles.

Stevens, Ray

Born:	September 5, 1935
Height:	5'11"
Weight:	235
Real Name:	Carl Raymond Stevens
High School:	North High School (OH)
Trained by:	Bill Miller, Buddy Rogers, Roy Shire
Identities:	Ray Shire
Tag Team:	The Blond Bombers w/ Pat Patterson
Career Span:	1952–88
Died:	May 3, 1996, Fremont, CA 61 years old

Titles Won:	41
Days as World Champion:	Unknown
Age at first World Title Claim:	26
Best Opponents:	Bruno Sammartino, Pepper Gomez, Bob Ellis
Halls of Fame:	2

A football player in high school, Ray Stevens got the attention of influential promoter Al Haft and made his wrestling debut in Columbus. He was touted as a future superstar in his rookie year, and lived up to all expectations. He morphed into "The Crippler," an influential heel grappler, and teamed with faux brothers Roy Shire and Don Fargo. He was briefly billed as the world champion in Los Angeles in 1961, and six years later, defeated Bruno Sammartino by countout in San Francisco to claim the WWWF World Title. Aside from all of his singles achievements, Stevens was one of the most successful tag team wrestlers of all time. He won World Titles with Shire, Nick Bockwinkel, Pat Patterson, Peter Maivia, and others. His "Bombs Away" kneedrop from the top rope was a stunning finisher that always had devastating results. With all of his talents as a wrestler, Stevens never rose above being willing to help younger wrestlers, and lived life to the fullest. For a period in wrestling history, arguably, there was no better pro in the business than Ray Stevens.

Born:	October 26, 1949
Height:	5'11"
Weight:	250
Real Name:	Kevin Francis Sullivan
Family:	Brother of David Sullivan, ex-husband of Woman
College:	Boston University
Identities:	Kevin Caldwell, Lucifer, The Taskmaster
Nicknames:	Games Master
Groups:	The Varsity Club (1988–89, 1999), Sullivan's Slaughterhouse (1990) Dungeon of Doom (1994–95)
Tag Team:	Butch Cassidy and the Sundance Kid w/ Mike Graham
Managed:	The Purple Haze (1983–84), Elijah Akeem (1983), Kareem Muhammad (1983), Buzz Sawyer (1984), The Lock (1984), Fallen Angel (1984), Oliver Humperdink (1984), Billy Graham (1984), Mike Davis (1984), The Aug (1984), The Chairman of the Board (1984), Kharma (1984), Jim Duggan (1984), Angel Vachon (1984), Abdullah the Butcher (1990), Cactus Jack (1990), Black Blood (1991), Zodiac (1994–95), Meng (1995), Kamala (1995), Barbarian (1995), The Giant (1995), The Shark (1995)
Career Span:	1970–2009

Titles Won:	32
Best Opponents:	Dusty Rhodes, Chris Benoit, Mick Foley

Sullivan, Kevin

A popular fan favorite, a hated heel, and a creative force behind the scenes, Kevin Sullivan has done it all in the world of professional wrestling. Mostly remembered for his "Prince of Darkness" role that had him leading a pack of Satan worshippers, Sullivan began his career in 1970 after being trained in the Boston area by Ron Hill. He ventured through the Southeastern territories, getting over with crowds, and his stock continued to rise while in the WWWF. Sullivan turned his image around during the early 1980s and, as a commandant of a possessed group of souls, he earned widespread recognition for his gimmick. Sullivan, with his painted face and live snakes, entered a longtime war with hero Dusty Rhodes in Florida, and their matches were full of brutality and bloodshed. In 1997 and again in 2000, he worked as a booker for WCW, and later for the short-lived XWF. Since his retirement, he has operated Froggy's Fitness gym with his wife in the Florida Keys.

Born:	January 6, 1930
Height:	6'1"
Weight:	270
Real Name:	Charles J. Kalani
High School:	Iolani High School (HI)
Colleges:	Weber Junior College, University of Utah
Military:	United States Army (1955–66)
Career Span:	1966–80
Died:	August 22, 2000, Lake Forest, CA 70 years old

Titles Won:	30
Days as World Champion:	92
Age at first World Title Win:	36
Best Opponents:	Bruno Sammartino, Pedro Morales, Fritz Von Erich
TV Appearances:	Over 15
Movies:	22

Tanaka, Professor Toru

Professor Tanaka, in addition to being a well-known heel grappler with a menacing presence, was a recognizable actor, having performed in over thirty TV and film projects. Originally from Hawaii, he attended college in Utah, and was a football All-American honorable mention in 1951 as an offensive guard and kicker. He briefly boxed professionally, but his heavyweight stature didn't equate to immediate success. He worked as a policeman in Honolulu, and in the summer of 1954, he was given a tryout with the San Francisco 49ers. With knowledge of martial arts, Tanaka was often billed as a Japanese karate expert on the wrestling circuit. It didn't matter that he wasn't Japanese, but that he filled an important role as an Asian "bad guy" and intimidated crowds with his size wherever he appeared. He won two IWA World Titles in Australia and four WWWF Tag Team Titles with partners Mitsu Arakawa and Mr. Fuji. In 1987, he appeared in the film, *The Running Man*, starring Arnold Schwarzenegger, performing the role of stalker, Subzero.

Born:	April 6, 1927
Height:	6'2"
Weight:	240
Real Name:	Camille Tourville
Parents:	Amedee and Esmeralda Tourville
High School:	Montreal High School
Trained by:	Manuel Cortez, Edouard Carpentier, Dr. Bill Miller
Career Span:	1956–82
Died:	December 24, 1985, Laurentides Park, Quebec 58 years old

Titles Won:	22
Days as World Champion:	42
Age at first World Title Win:	36
Best Opponents:	Lou Thesz, Bruno Sammartino, Verne Gagne

Tarzan Tyler

The youngest of eight children, Tarzan Tyler was born and raised in the Montreal area, and played football in high school. With expert coaching, he became a grappler under the alias, "Tarzan Tourville," until adopting his more famous name in 1961. He spent a considerable amount of time in Florida and feuded with Jack Brisco and Bob Orton over the Southern and Florida State championships. While wrestling in Atlanta in 1963, he captured the localized version of the world title twice with victories over Eddie Graham and Dick Steinborn. In 1971, he teamed with Luke Graham to hold both the WWWF International and WWWF World Tag Team Titles, becoming the first tandem to be recognized as the latter. He was also a top challenger to champions Bruno Sammartino and Pedro Morales. After his retirement, he managed King Tonga and Masked Superstar in the Montreal promotion, and in 1985, he was killed in a car accident with two others following a wrestling show in Chicoutimi.

Born:	October 28, 1940
Height:	5'10"
Weight:	220
Real Name:	Leslie Alan Malady
High School:	Central High School (OH)
Career Span:	1960–80

Titles Won:	15
Best Opponents:	Danny Hodge, Hiro Matsuda, Don Curtis
Halls of Fame:	1

Thatcher, Les

Personable Les Thatcher was still a teenager when he left his Cincinnati home for Boston to train at promoter Tony Santos' wrestling camp. He was successful across the circuit, winning an assortment of regional championships and earning the NWA Rookie of the Year trophy in 1967. In November 1968, he teamed with Dennis Hall to win the World Tag Team belts and became a serious contender to the NWA World Junior Title. Thatcher hung up his boots to work as an announcer, promoter, and booker, and was also an influential trainer at a camp he operated in Ohio. Many superstars have a wealth of knowledge today because of the lessons they learned from Thatcher, and his contributions to the sport will continue to be seen for many years to come.

Photo Courtesy of Pete Lederberg—plmathfoto@hotmail.com

Born:	January 30, 1924
Height:	6'4"
Weight:	255
Real Name:	Arthur Thomas
Parents:	Alfred and Jessie Thomas
High School:	Madison Vocational School (WI)
Finisher:	Bearhug
Career Span:	1957–87
Died:	March 20, 2003, Fitchburg, WI 79 years old

Titles Won:	7
Days as World Champion:	56
Age at first World Title Win:	48
Best Opponents:	Buddy Rogers, Johnny Valentine, Killer Kowalski
Halls of Fame:	1

Thomas, "Sailor" Art

African American superstar, "Sailor" Art Thomas was the hero to legions of fans over a career lasting twenty-six years. He was born in Arkansas and raised in Madison, Wisconsin, working at the Northland Greyhound garage when he joined the Merchant Marines in 1944. Devoted to weightlifting, he added 25 pounds of muscle mass by 1950, and was one of the most talked-about bodybuilders in the state. Thomas performed public demonstrations of strength, participated in competitions, and caught the eye of promoter, Jimmy Demetral, who tutored him in the art of wrestling. Shortly after his debut, he was booked along the major Kohler-McMahon circuit from Chicago into the northeast, and his imposing size and personality got him over with audiences in cities big and small. He went to war with the likes of Buddy Rogers and The Sheik, and maintained his credibility as a potential champion, even winning a claim to the WWA World Title in the Midwest in 1972. Known as a class act, Thomas left a lasting impression on those who saw him in the ring. In 2016, he was inducted into the WWE Hall of Fame as part of the inaugural "Legacy" class.

Born:	April 29, 1935
Height:	5'9"
Weight:	225
Real Name:	Leslie Thornton
Identities:	Henri Pierlot, Checkmate
Career Span:	1957–90

Titles Won:	17
Best Opponents:	Ricky Steamboat, Tiger Mask, Tatsumi Fujinami
Halls of Fame:	1

Thornton, Les

The Florida territory was honored by the presence of a man dubbed "The Professional" in 1983; an individual who featured an endless array of submission holds, counters, and exemplified technical savvy in the ring. He was Les Thornton of Salford, Lancashire, England, a former amateur boxer and graduate of Billy Riley's "Snake Pit." Thornton, by that time, had won the NWA World Junior Heavyweight Championship four times and competed around the globe, from Calgary to Sydney. Legend has it that he turned the tables on hooker Stu Hart during one of the latter's well-known stretching sessions. Thornton was a masterful grappler, and fans were treated to his excellent athletic performances until his retirement in 1990.

Born:	April 3, 1944
Height:	6′3″
Weight:	260
Real Name:	Jagjit Singh Hans
Family:	Father of Tiger Ali Singh
Finisher:	Cobra hold
Career Span:	1965–97

Titles Won:	15
Days as World Champion:	Over 325
Age at first World Title Win:	30
Best Opponents:	Antonio Inoki, The Sheik, Terry Funk

Tiger Jeet Singh

Tiger Jeet Singh of India relocated to Ontario and debuted at Toronto's Maple Leaf Gardens as an understudy of Fred Atkins, who doubled as his interpreter. Singh and Atkins, playing the roles of the heels, formed a successful tag team in 1966. The following year, Singh dethroned Johnny Valentine for the US Heavyweight Title. Singh, in Japan, kick-started a feud with Antonio Inoki, and it garnered huge attention for the sport and his career. A wild man comparable to The Sheik and Abdullah the Butcher, he wrestled many gory matches in the hardcore style and won championships in Australia and Mexico. In the latter country, he was a two-time UWA World Champion, defeating El Canek and Inoki in 1980.

Born:	April 5, 1931
Height:	6'2"
Weight:	245
Identities:	The Coach
Tag Teams:	The Canadian Wrecking Crew w/ Chris Tolos, Big and Little Murder w/Jack McDonald
Managed:	Cactus Jack (1991), Bob Orton Jr. (1991), Mr. Perfect (1991), The Beverly Brothers (1991)
Career Span:	1953–92
Died:	May 29, 2009, Los Angeles, CA 78 years old

Tolos, John

Titles Won:	50
Best Opponents:	Fred Blassie, Killer Kowalski, Victor Rivera
Halls of Fame:	1

Known as the "Golden Greek," John Tolos was a fantastically talented wrestler, combining a sincere wrestling ability with the personality traits that made him a superstar. Originally from Hamilton, Ontario, he and his older brother Chris trained at a local YMCA under pro wrestler "Wee" Willie Davis in the early 1950s. Within a short period of time, the Tolos Brothers were headlining throughout North America; and by the end of the decade, were appearing on the biggest stage in all the land, Madison Square Garden. They were villainous yet multi-faceted, and delighted as many fans as they repelled. Their toughness was spelled out on the foreheads of their opponents and they collected championship belts in several territories. As a singles wrestler, John was just as successful, winning the Americas Heavyweight Title nine times in the Los Angeles territory. His bloody feud with Fred Blassie culminated in a $142,000 box office gate in 1971. Other matches against Victor Rivera, Rocky Johnson, and the Sheik are still fondly remembered.

Born:	March 25, 1951
Height:	6'3"
Weight:	260
Real Name:	Tomomi Tsuruta
High School:	Hikawa High School (Japan)
College:	Chuo University
Olympics:	Greco-Roman Wrestling (1972) (Representing Japan) (7th Place)
Career Span:	1973–99
Died:	May 13, 2000, Philippines 49 years old

Titles Won:	33
Days as World Champion:	659
Age at first World Title Win:	32
Best Opponents:	Mitsuharu Misawa, Genichiro Tenryu, Riki Choshu
Tournament Wins:	7
Halls of Fame:	2

Tsuruta, Jumbo

Born in Yamanashi, Tsuruta was a Japanese amateur wrestling great and Olympian. He was guided into the professional ranks by Giant Baba and trained extensively under the Funk Brothers. In Amarillo on March 24, 1973, he made his debut, launching a hall-of-fame career that lasted nearly twenty-six years. Tsuruta was a fan favorite for a majority of his career, earning the respect of his peers and people across the globe. Highly decorated and still celebrated, he is on a very short list for best wrestler of the 1980s, winning the AWA World Heavyweight Title from Nick Bockwinkel on February 22, 1984 and the initial AJPW Unified Triple Crown in April 1989 with a defeat over Stan Hansen. During the early 1990s, his matches with Mitsuharu Misawa were considered some of the best in the business. He also formed legendary tag teams with Genichiro Tenryu and Yoshiaki Yatsu.

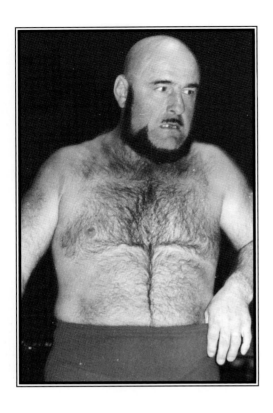

Born:	September 14, 1929
Height:	5'7"
Weight:	235
Parents:	Ferdinand and Marguerite Vachon
Family:	Brother of Paul and Vivian Vachon, uncle of Luna Vachon
Trained by:	Frank Saxon, Jim Cowley
Finisher:	Piledriver, Backbreaker
Career Span:	1952-86
Died:	November 21, 2013, Omaha, NE 84 years old

Titles Won:	34
Days as World Champion:	785
Age at first World Title Win:	34
Best Opponents:	Verne Gagne, Dick the Bruiser, The Crusher
Halls of Fame:	4

Vachon, Maurice

Successful amateur and pro wrestler, "Mad Dog" Maurice Vachon was a six-time World Heavyweight Champion. One of thirteen children born in Quebec, he trained at the Central YMCA in Montreal with brothers Paul, Guy, and Regis. Maurice made the national squad going to the 1948 Olympics and placed seventh at 174 pounds. As an amateur, Vachon collected a number of honors, including the 1950 British Empire middleweight crown. He turned pro in 1952, and was known for his shaved head and distinct beard. On May 2, 1964, he beat Verne Gagne for the AWA World Title, the first of five reigns for him between 1964 and 1967. Along with his brother Paul, he won the AWA Tag Team Title in 1969 from Bruiser and Crusher, and they remained champs until 1971. Vachon surprised many when he teamed with Gagne, his longtime archenemy, to win the AWA belts from Pat Patterson and Ray Stevens. He also held regional championships in Texas, Georgia, and Pacific Northwest.

Born:	September 20, 1950
Height:	6'0"
Weight:	245
Real Name:	John Anthony Wisniski
Identities:	Johnny Fargo, John Fargo, Hiroshima Joe, Johnny Valentine Jr.
Finisher:	Figure-four leglock
Career Span:	1970–2015

Titles Won:	38
Best Opponents:	Roddy Piper, Ric Flair, Tito Santana
Halls of Fame:	4

Valentine, Greg

Greg "The Hammer" Valentine was a talented and successful second generation wrestler. As the son of Johnny Valentine, Greg possessed many of the qualities his father had made famous, and was a hard-hitting rule-breaker with trademark blond hair. He debuted in Canada after training under Stu Hart and developed further under the guidance of The Sheik in Detroit. In 1979, he was a top challenger to Bob Backlund's WWF Title and nearly won the belt on several occasions. He had a vicious feud with Roddy Piper in the Mid-Atlantic territory and held the US crown twice and the World Tag Team Title four times. Back in the WWF, he captured the Intercontinental Title from Tito Santana in 1984 and wore the tag team belts with Brutus Beefcake. In 1989-1990, he had a memorable war with Ronnie Garvin and formed a comical team with the Honky Tonk Man, known as Rhythm and Blues. In 2009, he suffered a serious injury at a Chicago independent show and only occasionally wrestles today. The WWE inducted him into its Hall of Fame in 2004.

Born:	August 6, 1942
Height:	6'2"
Weight:	270
Real Name:	James Harold Fanning
High School:	Hammond Technical High School (IN)
Identities:	Jim Vallen, Jimmy Valentine, Charlie Brown
Nicknames:	Handsome
Career Span:	1964–2015

Titles Won:	29
Days as World Champion:	Around 21 (WWA reign unknown length)
Age at first World Title Win:	Around 32
Best Opponents:	Jerry Lawler, Johnny Valentine, Jack Brisco
Halls of Fame:	1
Published Books:	2

Valiant, Jimmy

Entertaining for many reasons, Jimmy Valiant was an unorthodox performer and his style was unique all to himself. Needless to say, there was never a dull moment around him; from his days as one-half of the Valiant Brothers to his time as the popular "Boogie Woogie Man," he was a superstar who exuded charisma. From Hammond, Indiana, he was trained by Frank Zela, and took the name "Valiant" in Dallas in 1970. He partnered with John L. Sullivan, who became "Johnny Valiant," and the rule-breaking "brother" duo won championships across the US On May 8, 1974, they won the WWWF World Tag Team Title under the guidance of Lou Albano, and held the belts for over a year. Valiant was also a World champion in the WWA and USWA. The Valiants were inducted into the WWF Hall of Fame in 1996.

Ventura, Jesse

Born:	July 15, 1951
Height:	6'3"
Weight:	245
Real Name:	James George Janos
Parents:	George and Bernice Janos
High School:	Roosevelt Senior High School (MN)
College:	North Hennepin Community College
Military:	United States Navy (1969–73) (SEALs)
Trained by:	Eddie Sharkey
Nickname:	The Body
Career:	1975–84

Titles Won:	7
Best Opponents:	Bob Backlund, Andre the Giant, Hulk Hogan
Halls of Fame:	1
Movies:	16
TV Shows:	2
Published Books:	10

A colorful athlete and television commentator, Jesse "The Body" Ventura left an indelible mark on the world of professional wrestling. In recent years, however, he's been committed to another realm of the sometimes unbelievable: American politics. Nowadays, most people have forgotten that he was even a wrestler at all, but his fans still enjoy the memories of him strutting around the ring—everlastingly confident—wearing his trademark feather boa. He was a multiple-time regional champion and one of his greatest moments came when he won the AWA World Tag Team Title on July 20, 1980 as part of the East-West Connection with Adrian Adonis. Ventura was physically imposing, using his brute strength to batter opponents, and was a top-notch brawler. Ventura and Adonis were champions for almost a year, losing the straps to Greg Gagne and Jim Brunzell on June 14, 1981. In the WWF, he was a serious challenger to Bob Backlund's heavyweight championship.

Ventura rechanneled his energy behind the microphone, where he was truly gifted. His ability to commentate added a unique spice to even the most ordinary bouts, and his chemistry alongside Gorilla Monsoon and Vince McMahon was extraordinary. Mostly pro rule-breaker, Ventura's quick wit and unconventional statements were sometimes out-and-out hilarious, especially with Monsoon and McMahon playing the straight man. Featured on *Saturday Night's Main Event* and WWF pay-per-views until 1990, Ventura spent some time in WCW, and appeared in a number of popular movies as an actor, including *The Running Man* and *Predator*. In 1991, Ventura was elected the mayor of Brooklyn Park, Minnesota, and became the 38th Governor of Minnesota in 1998 as a Reform Party Candidate. He made several wrestling appearances, and worked as a broadcaster for the short-lived XFL. Since then, he's been all over the media map, discussing politics and other important issues of the day. He's also written several books, including *Don't Start the Revolution Without Me!*, *American Conspiracies*, and *63 Documents the Government Doesn't Want You to Read* to name a few.

Born:	October 14, 1946
Height:	6'4"
Weight:	290
Real Name:	Josip B. Peruzovic
Trained by:	Stu Hart, Newton Tattrie
Identities:	Joe Peruzovic, Bepo Mongol, Executioner, Boris Breznikov
Finisher:	Bearhug
Tag Teams:	The Mongols w/ Geto Mongol (Newton Tattrie), The Executioners w/ Killer Kowalski and Big John Studd, The Bolshevicks w/ Boris Zukhov
Career Span:	1967–2006

Titles Won:	8
Best Opponents:	Bruno Sammartino, Hulk Hogan, Sgt. Slaughter
Halls of Fame:	1

Volkoff, Nikolai

A Yugoslavian weightlifter before turning pro wrestler, Volkoff reportedly once bench-pressed 500 pounds. He teamed with several partners to win the WWWF Tag Team Title, among them Geto Mongol, Masked Executioners (Killer Kowalski and Big John Studd), and the Iron Sheik. Around 1974, Volkoff was a strong challenger to Bruno Sammartino's WWWF heavyweight belt. Known for his anti-American gimmick, Volkoff regularly sung the Russian National Anthem before matches. That persona changed during the first Gulf War in 1990-1991 as a counter to Sgt. Slaughter, turning rule-breaker. Volkoff became an ardent US supporter, and at the 1990 Survivor Series, led the popular team of Tito Santana and the Bushwhackers against Slaughter's Mercenaries. In the mid-1990s, he was lured into the Million Dollar Corporation and put into awkward and embarrassing situations by the group's rich manager, Ted DiBiase. Volkoff was inducted into the WWE Hall of Fame in 2005.

Born:	August 16, 1929
Height:	6′5″
Weight:	275
Real Name:	Jack Barton Adkisson
Parents:	Benn and Coren Adkisson
Wife:	Doris Smith Adkisson
Pro Sports:	American Football League— Dallas Texans (early 1950s)
Trained by:	Stu Hart
Nickname:	The Claw, Teutonic Terror
Finisher:	The Clawhold, Prussian Drop
Owned:	Southwest Promotions, Inc. (1966–87)
Career Span:	1953–84
Died:	September 10, 1997, Lake Dallas, TX 68 years old

Von Erich, Fritz

Titles Won:	36
Days as World Champion:	67
Age at first World Title Win:	32
Best Opponents:	Verne Gagne, Johnny Valentine, Lou Thesz
Halls of Fame:	4

The Von Erich legacy in wrestling was initiated by Jack Adkisson of Dallas, Texas, and remained strong for the next four decades. Graduating from Crozier Tech High School, Adkisson excelled in football and track. He went on to attend Southern Methodist University and gained a reputation as one of the nation's finest young football stars. In 1953, he made his Dallas Sportatorium wrestling debut, and within two years, was fully engaged in the business, even adopting a lifelong moniker that would impact his entire family and a nation of fans. Adkisson took the name "Fritz Von Erich," capitalizing on the anti-German sentiment after the war. It wasn't long before he was among the most hated wrestlers in the business. With impressive size and strength, he was a premier headliner throughout the territorial system, and seen as a menace to every regional and world heavyweight championship he challenged.

On July 27, 1963, he beat Verne Gagne for both the AWA and Nebraska World Heavyweight Titles. Three years later, he opened Southwest Promotions, Inc, an NWA affiliate, and promoted the Dallas region until December 1987. He would win the American Heavyweight Title, the main belt of the territory, a total of fifteen times, battling the likes of Johnny Valentine, The Great Malenko, Bruiser Brody, and Ox Baker. A feud with manager Gary Hart's stable gained Von Erich fan support in 1967, ending his long run as a rule-breaker. Von Erich also held the US and North American Titles. Fritz trained his five sons for the wrestling ring and they each made their debuts between 1976 and 1990. Four of them would pass away at a young age, and in 1997, Adkisson was buried next to his sons in Grove Hill Memorial Park in Dallas County. "Beloved Father" was carved onto his plot, as was the name he made famous, "Fritz Von Erich." In 2009, the entire Von Erich family was inducted into the WWE Hall of Fame.

Photo Courtesy of the Collection of Libnan Ayoub

Born:	October 2, 1933
Height:	6'1"
Weight:	250
Real Name:	Walter Paul Sieber
Trained by:	Red Garner
Identities:	Kurt Von Sieber, Baron Von Sieber, Wally Sieber
Career Span:	1954–79
Died:	July 5, 2009, Kitchener, Ontario 75 years old

Titles Won:	16
Days as World Champion:	174
Age at first World Title Win:	38
Best Opponents:	Killer Kowalski, Bruno Sammartino, Destroyer
Halls of Fame:	1

Von Erich, Waldo

For fans of wrestling's popular heroes, it was bad enough when there was one "Von Erich" roaming the countryside—but in 1958, a second appeared, and was similarly committed to causing mayhem. Waldo Von Erich was really not from Germany as his gimmick implied, but rather from Toronto; and together, the Von Erichs were masters of disaster, winning championships in the Mid-Atlantic and Dallas territories. Waldo, on his own, won the NWF World Heavyweight crown twice, the Canadian championship, and the Texas State belt. During a tour of Australia, he captured the IWA World Tag Title, and not only won the U.S Tag belts while in the WWWF with Gene Kiniski, but was a leading challenger to Bruno Sammartino's World championship.

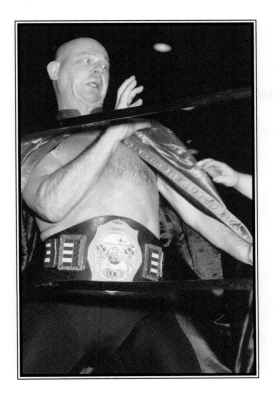

Born:	July 30, 1940
Height:	6′2″
Weight:	250
Real Name:	James Donald Raschke
High School:	Omaha North High School (NE)
HS Ach.:	Nebraska State Wrestling Title (1958) (HWT)
College:	University of Nebraska
College Ach.:	Big Eight Heavyweight Title (1962)
Olympics:	Qualified for the 1964 US Olympic Wrestling Team (injured)
Military:	United States Army (1963–65)
Nickname:	The Teuton Terror, The Clawmaster
Managed:	The Powers of Pain (1988)
Career Span:	1966–93

Von Raschke, Baron

Titles Won:	21
Days as World Champion:	Over 1,004
Age at first World Title Win:	27
Best Opponents:	Verne Gagne, Dick the Bruiser, Edouard Carpentier
Halls of Fame:	4

Master of the clawhold, Baron Von Raschke was originally from Omaha, Nebraska, not Germany, as his gimmick indicated. He was an amateur Greco-Roman sensation, winning the bronze at the World championships in 1963, and a year later, while in the Army, he took home an Interservice title. His size and proven ability were significant factors in his warm reception into pro wrestling, and Verne Gagne took the lead in giving Von Raschke the tools he'd need to be successful. Adopting a pro-German attitude, he was immensely hated throughout the grappling community. In November 1967, he beat Edouard Carpentier for a claim to the World Title in Montreal. He would win the WWA World Championship three times, and annexed numerous other belts in the AWA and NWA. Von Raschke is enshrined in several different wrestling Halls of Fame, recognizing his remarkable career as an amateur and pro.

Born:	June 13, 1943
Height:	6′2″
Weight:	360
Nicknames:	Big, King, Bulldog
Finisher:	The Steamroller
Promoted:	Catch Wrestling Association (CWA) (1977–2000)
Career Span:	1970–90

Titles Won:	5
Days as World Champion:	4,015
Age at first World Title Win:	34
Best Opponents:	Antonio Inoki, Andre the Giant, Nick Bockwinkel

Wanz, Otto

Many fans were taken aback by the news that Otto Wanz had dethroned Nick Bockwinkel in St. Paul for the AWA World Heavyweight Title on August 29, 1982. The shock was mostly because Wanz was relatively unknown in the United States, but in his native country of Austria, he was a legend. A former amateur boxing champion, Wanz was awesomely powerful, able to tear a phone book in half, and his giant size made him an imposing figure of the squared circle. Only holding the title for a few months, Wanz dropped the AWA Title back to Bockwinkel on October 9, 1982 in Chicago. He was also a four-time CWA World Champion, defeating Jan Wilkens, Don Leo Jonathan, and Bull Power (Vader) twice. He retired as champion in 1990.

Watts, Bill

Born:	May 5, 1939
Height:	6′3″
Weight:	275
Real Name:	William Frederick Watts Jr.
Parents:	William and Emma Watts
High School:	Putnam City High School (OK)
College:	University of Oklahoma
Pro Sports:	American Football League—Houston Oilers (1961) United Football League—Indianapolis Warriors (1962) National Football League—Minnesota Vikings (1963)
Trained by:	Leroy McGuirk
Career Span:	1961–93

Titles Won:	25
Best Opponents:	Bruno Sammartino, Harley Race, Lou Thesz
Halls of Fame:	3

The bruising "Cowboy" Bill Watts of Tulsa was a stellar wrestler and one tough customer. He followed up college and professional football with a lengthy career as a grappler, and had the size and grit to be a real success. Only a few years after his debut, he stormed through the northeast territory and was a vicious contender to Bruno Sammartino's WWWF Title—as the two drew huge numbers at Madison Square Garden. He won many regional titles and was a perennial North American champion. Behind the curtain, Watts was a matchmaker for his mentor Leroy McGuirk and, in 1979, branched off to form Mid-South Sports, which staged shows in Louisiana, Oklahoma, and Mississippi. A creative booker, he emphasized the importance of youthful talent on his shows, and pushed Steve Williams, Junkyard Dog, Jim Duggan, and Ted DiBiase early in their careers. Later on, he worked for WCW from 1992-1993. The WWE honored his career by inducting him into its Hall of Fame in 2009. His son Erik was also a wrestler.

Woods, Tim

Born:	July 28, 1934
Height:	6'0"
Weight:	230
Real Name:	George Burrell Woodin
High School:	Ithaca High School (NY)
College:	Michigan State University
College Ach.:	Two-Time Big Ten Wrestling Champion (1958) (177), (1959) (HWT)
Amateur Titles:	Two-Time AAU National Wrestling Champion (1955, 1957)
Career Span:	1962–84
Died:	November 30, 2002, Charlotte, NC 68 years old

Titles Won:	24
Best Opponents:	Maurice Vachon, Blackjack Mulligan, Jack Brisco
Halls of Fame:	1

Ithaca's wrestling sensation, Tim "Mr. Wrestling" Woods, influenced a generation with his talent and popularity as a masked superstar. An amateur grappler in high school, Woods attended a handful of colleges from Cornell to Oklahoma A&M, and landed at Michigan State, where he won two Big-Ten championships, also placing second in the 1958 and 1959 NCAA tournaments. He began his pro career under the guidance of Bert Rubi in Detroit, wrestling as "Tim Woodin" in 1962. In the years that followed, he appeared throughout the territorial system, and his amateur background served him well. The arrival of "Mr. Wrestling" was a landmark for pro wrestling, and Woods' career vaulted to new highs—particularly in the southeast. He held the United States, Southern, and Georgia Heavyweight Titles, and nearly lifted the AWA World Heavyweight crown from Maurice Vachon in January 1966. He also won the Georgia Tag belts with Mr. Wrestling II three times. In 2001, he was inducted into the Tragos/Thesz Hall of Fame.

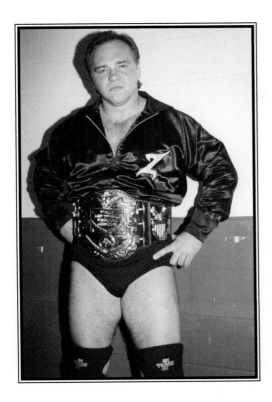

Born:	December 5, 1953
Height:	5'11"
Weight:	245
Real Name:	Larry Whistler
Family:	Son-in-Law of Verne Gagne
College:	University of Pittsburgh
Trained by:	Newton Tattrie
Finisher:	Bearhug, Boston Crab
Groups:	The Dangerous Alliance (1992)
Tag Team:	The Enforcers w/ Arn Anderson
Career Span:	1972–2015

Titles Won:	15
Days as World Champion:	865
Age at first World Title Win:	35
Best Opponents:	Bruno Sammartino, Mr. Saito, Curt Hennig
Halls of Fame:	1

Zbyszko, Larry

Technically savvy with personality to spare, Larry Zbyszko was a cool, calculating heel and held the AWA World Heavyweight Championship twice. Originally from the Pittsburgh area, he stunned many fans when he turned on his mentor, Bruno Sammartino, leading to a historic feud. The payoff was huge, and over 40,000 fans witnessed their steel cage showdown in Shea Stadium on August 9, 1980, with Sammartino winning the match. In 1983, he "purchased" the National Title from Killer Brooks and won the Western States Heritage belt from Barry Windham in 1988. Zbyszko won his first AWA belt when he survived a battle royal on February 7, 1989 and held the crown for more than a year. He traded the title with Mr. Saito, and was the final AWA champion as the promotion folded in 1991. While with WCW, he worked as a TV commentator and won both the World Tag Team Title with Arn Anderson, as well as the TV Title. In 2008, he held the AWA Superstars of Wrestling World championship and still makes appearances across the US. Zbyszko was welcomed into the WWE Hall of Fame in 2015, and appropriately, Bruno Sammartino was the one to induct him. Larry's son Tim is also a pro wrestler, having made his debut in 2012.

IV. New Legends Are Born: From Hulking Up to the G.T.S.

Pro Debut Between 1976 and Present

The ever-changing wrestling environment kept creative minds on their feet, and the wrestlers themselves had to adapt and adjust their ring personas to keep things fresh. A sudden heel turn for a renowned fan favorite was commonplace, or vice versa, and the flip was a spark enough to recharge an entire territory; of course, depending on the wrestler. Dusty Rhodes and Bob Backlund were among the most favored heroes of the late 1970s, and in the opposite corner were guys like Harley Race, Bruiser Brody, and a relative newcomer to the industry, the "Nature Boy" Ric Flair. Ultra arrogant with ring skills and personality to match, Flair was the standard bearer for technically proficient wrestlers and wore the NWA World Heavyweight championship ten times between 1981 and 1993. In recent years, Flair has performed many different roles in both the WWE and TNA, and is nearing his 40th anniversary in the business.

One of the most influential actions taken by any single individual involved with pro wrestling occurred during the first half of the 1980s, when Vincent Kennedy McMahon began a revolutionary raid on the traditional territories. His World Wrestling Federation (WWF) launched a campaign to "go national," and used television to garner local and national exposure for his creative cast of wrestlers. Directly opposing many old school promoters who were having a tough time upgrading their businesses to fit the times, McMahon's efforts made great headway, and in some places, he bought the entire territory to secure future dominance. Although he was following in the footsteps of his grandfather Jess and father Vincent J. in becoming a promoter, McMahon was doing things that no one had ever attempted before, and he was either going to sink or swim. Needless to say, he found a way for his company to not only survive, but thrive.

Incorporating and utilizing key talent was another major factor in McMahon's push. In addition to Andre the Giant, the Junkyard Dog, Randy Savage, and Roddy Piper, the WWF had the sport's biggest attraction, mega superstar in Hulk Hogan. Coming off a memorable role in *Rocky III* and a stint in the AWA, Hogan was as important to wrestling's remarkable growth as McMahon was, and his popularity was simply stunning. Arenas everywhere exploded on his arrival and as McMahon launched a blitz on the mainstream, annual WrestleMania events and regular pay-per-views, Hogan was the key to his success. World Championship Wrestling (WCW), which was spawned by Jim Crockett Promotions in the Mid-Atlantic region, was the WWF's main competition, and their head-to-head rivalry lasted until 2001 when WCW was purchased by McMahon.

Today, McMahon's World Wrestling Entertainment (WWE) is a publicly traded company that is broadcast in over 145 countries and is the clear leader in the industry. The wrestlers of the WWE continue to build upon the tradition that Bruno Sammartino, Hogan, and their peers established, and current stars

John Cena, CM Punk, and Triple H are as popular as ever. Other promotions like TNA and ROH offer an alternative product and the motivated young blood in pro wrestling are itching to show their talents to possibly one day solidify their place amongst the *Legends of Pro Wrestling*.

Photo Courtesy of Dr. Mike Lano—Wrealano@aol.com

Born:	October 4, 1969
Height:	6'5"
Weight:	350
Real Name:	Christopher J. Park
High School:	St. Joseph High School (OH)
College:	Ohio University
Trained by:	Roger Ruffin
Identities:	Original Terminator, Justice, King of Pain, Stone Mountain
Nickname:	The Monster
Finisher:	Black Hole Slam
Career Span:	1995–Present

Titles Won:	21
Days as World Champion:	56
Age at first World Title Win:	37
Best Opponents:	Sting, Kurt Angle, A.J. Styles

Abyss

Known as "The Masked Monster," the sizable Abyss has been a top star in TNA for years. With a willingness to engage in violent matches with bizarre stipulations, he has given his all to the wrestling business and taken wild bumps in bouts that featured thumbtacks and barbed wire. A football player in high school and college, Abyss made a name for himself in Puerto Rico and joined TNA full time in 2003. He engaged in some memorable mat wars against greats like Sabu and Mick Foley, and won the NWA World Title from Sting on November 19, 2006, yet lost the belt to Christian Cage the following January. In 2010, he formed a pact with Hulk Hogan and made a run for TNA champion Rob Van Dam's belt, but was unsuccessful. Known as an intimidating force, he even carried around a board with nails jutting out from all sides, which he referred to as "Janice." In 2011, he captured the TNA TV and X-Division championships and was a member of Hogan's Immortal group. He revealed a more passive persona with the character "Joseph Park," and claimed to be Abyss's brother in 2012–13. A few years later, he joined "Decay," and teamed with Crazzy Steve to win the TNA World Tag Title in March 2016.

Born:	February 10, 1955
Height:	6'1"
Weight:	230
Real Name:	Christopher Adams
Trained by:	Shirley Crabtree
Tag Teams:	The Dynamic Duo w/ Gino Hernandez
Trained:	Steve Austin, Khris Germany
Career Span:	1978–2001
Died:	October 7, 2001, Waxahachie, TX 46 years old

Titles Won:	25
Days as World Champion:	73
Age at first World Title Win:	31
Best Opponents:	Kerry Von Erich, Ric Flair, Jimmy Garvin

Adams, Chris

"Gentleman" Chris Adams was a world-class judo expert (along with his brother Neil), and won many championships in his native England. He switched gears to become a wrestler in 1978, and toured through several regions before finding a regular spot in the Dallas territory. Teaming up with Gino Hernandez, he captured the American Tag championship on two occasions, and feuded with Jimmy Garvin over the American singles belt in 1983 and '84, winning it three-times. He won the belt a fourth time from Kerry Von Erich in February 1985. On July 4, 1986, he beat Rick Rude for the WCWA World Heavyweight championship, and reigned through the middle of September, giving up his claim when he left World Class. The owner of an impressive superkick, Adams also held the Americas championship in Southern California. He spent time in the UWF, GWF, NWA, and WCW during the 1980s and '90s and, after opening up a wrestling school in Texas, mentored a young "Stone Cold" Steve Austin. In fact, Austin was his first graduate. He was embroiled in legal difficulties before passing away on October 7, 2001, at the age of forty-six.

Born:	September 20, 1958
Height:	6'1"
Weight:	245
Real Name:	Martin Anthony Lunde
Parents:	Gary and Bobbie Lunde
High School:	East Rome High School (GA)
College:	Floyd Junior College
Nicknames:	The Enforcer, Double A
Finisher:	DDT
Groups:	Stud Stable (1983), The Legion of Doom (1983), The Four Horsemen (1986–89, 1990–91, 1993, 1996–97), The Dangerous Alliance (1992)
Tag Teams:	The Brain Busters w/ Tully Blanchard, The Enforcers w/ Larry Zbyszko
Career Span:	1982–97

Anderson, Arn

Titles Won:	15
Best Opponents:	Ric Flair, Great Muta, Barry Windham
Halls of Fame:	1

Always cool under pressure, Arn Anderson was a diabolical heel and the backbone of the Four Horsemen, an elite group of wrestlers during the 1980s and '90s. In the ring, it appeared that he was intent on hurting opponents and every move that he made was well thought out in advance. Anderson grew up in Rome, Georgia, and wrestled during his youth, as well as also playing organized baseball and football. Through weight-lifting and rigorous exercise, he increased his size from under 180 pounds to upwards of 230, and trained to be a wrestler under Ted Allen of Cartersville, Georgia. He spent time wrestling in Alabama, where he was known as the masked Super Olympia, and then the Mid-South, before becoming an "Anderson," a well-known family of grapplers, in the Mid-Atlantic territory. With Ole Anderson, he won the National Tag Team Title in 1985 and joined the dominant Horsemen. Arn won the NWA World Tag Title twice with Tully Blanchard and then won the WWF World Tag Team Title in 1989, as well as holding the NWA/WCW World TV Title on four different occasions. In 1997, he had neck surgery and announced his retirement from the sport. For a number of years, Anderson has worked for the WWE as a producer on *Raw*, and was inducted into the organization's Hall of Fame in 2012, alongside his Four Horsemen teammates.

Angle, Kurt

Born:	December 9, 1968
Height:	6'1"
Weight:	232
Real Name:	Kurt Steven Angle
Parents:	David and Jacqueline Angle
Family:	Brother of Eric Angle
High School:	Mt. Lebanon High School (PA)
High School Ach.:	Pennsylvania State Wrestling Title (1987)
College Ach.:	Two-Time NCAA Heavyweight Wrestling Champion (1990, 1992)
College Record:	116-10-2
Trained by:	Dory Funk Jr. and Dr. Tom Prichard
Finisher:	Olympic Slam, Anklelock Submission
Groups:	Team Angle (2002–03), Angle Alliance (2007–08), Main Event Mafia (2008–09)
WWF Debut:	November 14, 1999, Detroit, MI, Survivor Series (TV Debut)
TNA Debut:	October 19, 2006, Orlando, FL, Interview Segment
Career Span:	1998–Present

Titles Won:	20
Days as World Champion:	1,083
Age at first World Title Win:	31
Best Opponents:	Chris Benoit, Shawn Michaels, Brock Lesnar
Halls of Fame:	8

Olympic gold medalists are an extreme minority in professional wrestling with only a handful of grapplers ever earning top honors, which include Robin Reed, Russell Vis, John Spellman, Henri DeGlane, and Johan Richthoff. Of this elite grouping of superstar athletes, only one heavyweight with an Olympic gold medal in the freestyle event has transcended the amateur ranks and become a top pro grappler . . . and that is Kurt Angle. Angle, hailing from the suburbs of Pittsburgh, has been a premier superstar since his debut in 1998, initially for the WWF and currently for TNA. He is a twelve-time World champion and participated in many incredible and unforgettable matches. The same determined spirit that carried him through the Olympic experience has pushed him to the heights of pro wrestling, and there have been very few grapplers of his caliber on the trail—and that includes all of history.

Angle's outstanding amateur accomplishments began in high school, where he won a state title in 1987, and then captured a Junior National championship that same year. He went on to Clarion University, and captured two NCAA Titles and added the World Title in 1995. At the 1996 Olympic Games in Atlanta, Angle advanced to the 220-pound freestyle finals despite a severe neck injury and beat Abbas Jadidi of Iran, taking a referee's decision to win the gold medal. While his world-class amateur record didn't guarantee that he'd be a great pro wrestler, Angle adjusted without a problem and was seen to be a natural performer when he debuted for the WWF in 1999. He built a respectable undefeated streak and quickly won both the European and Intercontinental titles. Angle was victorious in the 2000 King of the Ring and headlined his first pay-per-view event in August 2000 at SummerSlam. Finally, only about a year after his first televised showing, Angle beat The Rock on October 22, 2000, and won his first WWF World Title.

Aside from his in-ring work, Angle displayed plenty of personality, particularly when matched with Steve Austin, and the two had some humorous moments before entering into a bloody feud. On September 23, 2001, in his hometown of Pittsburgh, he won his second WWF Title in a grueling bout against Austin, and after the win, members of his family celebrated in the ring with him. Angle was drafted to *Smackdown* and had a long war with Edge. With some outside help from Brock Lesnar, he pinned Big Show for his third WWE championship on December 15, 2002. The anticipated Angle-Lesnar feud soon started thereafter. Often helped by his "Team Angle" partners, Charlie Haas and Shelton Benjamin, Angle remained the champ, going into WrestleMania XIX on March 30, 2003, but lost the belt to Lesnar. At Vengeance on July 27, he beat Lesnar and Big Show in a three-way bout for his fourth and final WWE Title, but was defeated a second time by Lesnar in a memorable Iron-Man bout in September of that year.

Over the next few years, he served as *Smackdown* General Manager, feuded with the likes of Eddie Guerrero, and had a classic WrestleMania match against Shawn Michaels in 2005. Following a run as World Champion in early 2006 and a stint in ECW, he jumped to TNA in October 2006. He won the TNA championship on May 13, 2007 over champion Christian Cage and Sting, but because of the controversial finish, the championship was declared vacant. Angle won it again in a King of the Mountain bout on June 17, 2007, and before the end of the month, had added the IWGP championship to his list of credentials with a victory over Lesnar in Tokyo. In August 2007, he topped Samoa Joe and captured both the TNA X-Division and World Tag-Team Titles, meaning that he held four separate championships at the same time. The two latter belts were lost at No Surrender and Sting won the TNA World Title on October 14, 2007. Angle defeated Sting in a rematch and took the belt back on *Impact* later in the month.

Neck problems were still hampering him, but Angle proved to be a relentless warrior and was fully dedicated to pro wrestling—often working through the pain. On June 21, 2009, he won his fourth TNA World championship over champion Mick Foley, A.J. Styles, and Samoa Joe. A leading fan favorite through 2010 and into 2011, he engaged in a lengthy feud with Jeff Jarrett, and his ex-wife Karen was part of the storyline. However, he turned heel by joining Immortal and beat Sting for his fifth TNA World Title in August 2011. He dropped the belt to James Storm two months later. Angle was inducted into the TNA Hall of Fame in 2013 and, the next year, was recognized as the "Executive Director of Wrestling Operations." He won his sixth TNA World Title in early 2015, but lost it in the middle of the year to Ethan Carter III. For several months he engaged in a "Farewell Tour" of TNA, and departed the promotion in March 2016. Since then, he's been active on the indie circuit, despite rumors of an eventual return to the WWE.

Born:	September 12, 1960
Height:	6′1″
Weight:	285
Real Name:	Joseph Michael Laurinaitis
Parents:	Joseph and Lorna Laurinaitis
Family:	Brother of Johnny Ace and The Terminator
Wife:	Julia Laurinaitis
High School:	Irondale High School (MN)
College:	Moorehead State College
Finisher:	Doomsday Device w/ Hawk
Groups:	The Legion of Doom (1983–84), LOD 2000 (1998)
Career Span:	1982–2012

Titles Won:	21
Best Opponents:	Ric Flair, Dusty Rhodes, Arn Anderson
Halls of Fame:	3
Published Books:	1

Animal

A twenty-two-year-old Minneapolis power-lifter entered the wrestling profession in 1982 under the guidance of Eddie Sharkey and adopted the signature name, "Animal," while in Georgia along with his friend, Hawk. The two debuted as the "Road Warriors," and were highly influential because of their outstanding display of strength and ferociousness, as well as their intimidating look. In fact, there was no team similar anywhere else in the world. They were the first duo to capture the AWA, NWA, and WWF World Tag Team Titles, and reigned as the AJPW champions in Japan in 1987-1988. All tag teams during the 1980s and 1990s were compared to the Warriors, and their iconic role in history has earned them a spot in several Halls of Fame. In 2001, Animal returned to WCW and challenged Scott Steiner for the World Title. He was also briefly a member of the Magnificent Seven group. Since Hawk's passing in 2003, Animal has appeared in the WWE and TNA in smaller capacities, and in 2011, released his autobiography. His son James is a pro football player for the St. Louis Rams. The Road Warriors were honored for induction into the WWE Hall of Fame in 2011.

Born:	April 15, 1978
Height:	5'9"
Weight:	215
Real Name:	Daniel Healy Solwold Jr.
High School:	West High School (WI)
College:	Winona State University
Identities:	Austin Starr
Career Span:	2000–Present

Titles Won:	12
Days as World Champion:	419
Age at first World Title Win:	26
Best Opponents:	Samoa Joe, CM Punk, Jerry Lynn

Aries, Austin

One of the most talented performers in the ring today, Austin Aries garnered national attention when he energized the X-Division in TNA in 2011 with his slick maneuvers, flashy style, and cocky attitude. It actually marked his second stint in the promotion, but after two ROH World Title reigns and an endless string of top performances in bouts around the world, Aries was ready to make a serious impact. The former baseball pitcher from Waukesha, Wisconsin, broke into the business with friend Justin Leeper, training under Eddie Sharkey in 2000, and garnered considerable success for Ring of Honor out of Philadelphia. With years of experience behind him and moves like the pendulum elbow and brainbuster—plus a wealth of submission holds—Aries advanced to the X-Division championship and held it for nearly 300 days. In July 2012, he beat Bobby Roode for the TNA World Heavyweight Title, and later teamed with Roode to capture the TNA World Tag Title. Between 2011 and '15, he held the X-Division belt a total of six times. Aries left TNA in mid-2015, and later signed with the WWE, making his on-air debut for NXT in early 2016. It is just a matter of a time before he joins the main roster and makes an impact, just like he did previously in ROH and TNA.

Born:	June 15, 1962
Height:	6'0"
Weight	225
Real Name:	Robert Bradley James
Parents:	Joseph and Gail James
Family:	Brother of Scott, Steve, and Brian Armstrong
High School:	Wheeler High School (GA)
Trained by:	Bob Armstrong
Identities:	Mr. R., Fantasia, Arachnaman, Mr. K., B.A., Buzzkill
Groups:	No Limit Soldiers (1999)
Tag Teams:	The Lightning Express w/ Tim Horner, White Lightning w/ Tim Horner
Career Span:	1980–2012
Died:	November 1, 2012, Kennesaw, GA 50 years old

Armstrong, Brad

Titles Won:	26
Best Opponents:	Ric Flair, Ted DiBiase, Brian Pillman

Talented Brad Armstrong may never have reached his full potential in the wrestling business. He was a celebrated teenage rookie, a second generation star, and there were many high expectations for the Marietta, Georgia athlete. Throughout the southeast, he was adored by fans, and his quickness and mat knowledge were second to none. As he was gaining his wrestling experience, he teamed up many times with his father, Bob Armstrong. In January 1984, he won the National Heavyweight championship under the masked "Mr. R" guise, and then regained it from the Spoiler to begin a second reign. He also captured the MSWA North American Title that year, and along with Tim Horner, won the UWF World Tag-Team Title in 1987. Armstrong captured the WCW World Light Heavyweight Title in 1992, and while in that promotion, he used a variety of gimmicks to include a masked heel, Badstreet, and The Candyman, a hero who gave candy out to ringside youngsters. In 2006, he worked for the revived ECW, and also wrestled for a number of indie promotions. Armstrong passed away suddenly in November 2012, at the age of fifty.

Austin, Steve

Born:	December 18, 1964
Height:	6'2"
Weight:	240
Real Name:	Steven James Williams
Parents:	Kenneth and Beverly Williams
High School:	Edna High School (TX)
Colleges:	Wharton Junior College, North Texas State University
Finisher:	Stone Cold Stunner, Stun-Gun Suplex off Ropes, Million Dollar Dream
Managed by:	Jeannie, Lady Blossom, Paul E. Dangerously, Col. Robert Parker, Harley Race, Ted DiBiase
Career Span:	1989–2003

Titles Won:	20
Days as World Champion:	529
Age at first World Title Win:	33
Best Opponents:	Bret Hart, The Rock, Triple H
Halls of Fame:	3
TV Appearances:	over 80
Movies:	15

One of wrestling's greatest all-time attractions, "Stone Cold" Steve Austin ruled the industry during the prime of his career, pushing the envelope of showmanship and delivering record box office and merchandise sales. Although he hung up his boots in 2003, Austin continues to appear on WWE programming in various capacities, as well as in feature films as an action star. His biting personality still captures the attention of audiences and his calculating behavior and beer drinking are still staples of his popular act. During the late 1990s, his rise to prominence helped the WWF shift momentum in the all-important Monday night ratings battle with WCW, and eventually overtook its rivals completely. Austin's image as the unpredictable "Texas Rattlesnake" and his crusade against his crooked boss, Vince McMahon, which the everyman could relate to, pushed him into a spot that no other wrestler in history ever reached, including Hulk Hogan.

A football player in high school and college, he graduated from Chris Adams' wrestling school, and began his career in 1989 at the famed Sportatorium. He wrestled on a circuit between Dallas and Memphis for the USWA before joining WCW in 1991, and won the TV Title from Bobby Eaton within a few short days of his debut. Known as "Stunning" Steve Austin, he was managed by Lady Blossom and feuded with Dustin Rhodes and Barry Windham. He was a nice fit in Paul E. Dangerously's heel faction, The Dangerous Alliance, and went on to form the Hollywood Blonds, arguably the best tag team in the business, with Brian Pillman. In late

1993, he beat Rhodes to capture the WCW US Title and reigned for eight months. He dropped the belt to Ricky Steamboat on August 24, 1994, but regained it a few weeks later by forfeit when the latter was injured and unable to defend at Fall Brawl. Austin, however, was immediately thrust into a bout with newcomer Jim Duggan, who pinned him in less than a minute.

A triceps injury kept Austin off the mat and he was subsequently let go from WCW. Austin reemerged in ECW and displayed a newfound attitude that lashed out at his former employers. His shoot-style promos were raw and realistic, and with the platform to speak his mind, Austin did so without restraint. The wrestling world took notice, and on December 18, 1995, he made his first showing for the WWF at a TV Taping. Austin was managed by Ted DiBiase and known as "The Ringmaster," which emphasized his technical skills. He also used the "Million Dollar Dream" sleeper as his finisher, but the gimmick didn't last long. By June 1996, he had evolved into "Stone Cold," a wrestler whose aggressiveness and independence were earning as many cheers as boos. He spoke his mind in interviews, displaying his outward anger toward rivals, and utilized the easily applied Stunner as his finisher. His catchphrases caught on with crowds, and his popularity increased measurably within a short amount of time.

Austin entered a feud with Bret Hart that dominated 1997, and their submission match at WrestleMania 13 was historic. The spectacular back-and-forth contest saw Austin win the crowd's favor with an admirable performance, but lost when he passed out to the pressure of a sharpshooter. The war against Hart continued, and was brutally violent at times. That August, he won the Intercontinental belt from Owen Hart, but suffered a serious neck injury in the match and later vacated the title. He beat Owen again in November, but lost the title a month later to Rocky Maivia Jr. In early 1998, he confronted ex-boxing champion Mike Tyson, who was named the special enforcer for Austin's match against Shawn Michaels at WrestleMania XIV. At that show, Austin pinned his foe and captured his first WWF World Title. In the weeks that followed, his private war against Vince McMahon escalated, and on April 13, 1998, their face-off helped *Raw* beat WCW's *Nitro* in the ratings for the first time since the summer of 1996.

Between January and October 1998, Austin participated in ten straight pay-per-view main events, from special referee to defending as World Champion. He lost his WWF championship to Kane on June 28, 1998, but regained it the next night. On September 27, he was defeated again by both Kane and The Undertaker in a controversial finish that left the title vacated. He entered the 1999 Royal Rumble at number one and McMahon was the second entrant. Shockingly, both were still there at the end, and McMahon scored the victory. They fought in a cage match in February with the winner going to headline at WrestleMania. Austin was victorious in a bloody match after the Big Show interfered. In Philadelphia at WrestleMania XV, he won his third WWF Title from The Rock. He traded the belt with The Undertaker, and then lost it in a three-way bout to Mankind on August 22, 1999. In November of that year, Austin stepped away from the business to have major surgery on his neck and remained away until September 2000.

Austin had a significant feud with Triple H and then won his fifth WWF Title at WrestleMania X-Seven, defeating The Rock. He then turned heel and formed a surprising alliance with Triple H and McMahon. On October 8, 2001, Austin won his sixth and final WWF belt, defeating Kurt Angle. That December, he was dethroned by Chris Jericho. He had a memorable battle with Booker T in a California grocery store, and made the word "What" into a popular catchphrase that is still relevant today. Austin participated in his final match at WrestleMania XIX, losing an epic battle to The Rock. Since that time, in addition to his work as an actor, he's been active as a guest referee, host, and in various other capacities on WWE telecasts. In 2009, he was inducted into the WWE Hall of Fame and, in 2011, was involved in the revived *Tough Enough* series. He reemerged at WrestleMania XXX and 32, and during the latter event in 2016, delivered his popular stunner to Xavier Woods of The New Day. Despite being off the mat for more than a decade, the always unruly Austin remains to be one of the most celebrated personalities in wrestling and fans continue to beckon for one more match.

Photo Courtesy of Dr. Mike Lano—Wrealano@aol.com

Born:	September 4, 1977
Height:	5'9"
Weight:	270
Real Name:	Kia Michelle Stevens
High School:	Carson High School (CA)
Trained by:	Jesse Hernandez, All-Japan trainers
Identities:	Amazing Kong, Kharma
Career Span:	2002–Present

Titles Won:	13
Days as World Champion:	943
Age at first World Title Win:	26
Best Opponents:	Ayako Hamada, Aja Kong, Gail Kim

Awesome Kong

Awesome Kong is a multiple-time world champion and one of the fiercest women's competitors in the business. Originally from Carson, California, she became a professional in 2002 and, two years later, won the WWWA World Title in Tokyo. In 2007, she held both the AWA Superstars of Wrestling and NWA Women's World championships simultaneously. That same year, she debuted in TNA and won the TNA Knockouts Title twice in 2008, defeating Gail Kim and Taylor Wilde. Awesome Kong lost the belt for the final time in April 2009 to Angelina Love. She also captured the TNA Women's Tag Title with Hamada. In 2010, she signed a deal with World Wrestling Entertainment, but only competed in one match over the next two years, and that was at the 2012 Royal Rumble, where she became the third female wrestler ever to participate in the bout. She returned to TNA for another run until her February 2016 departure. Powerful and intelligent, Awesome Kong continues to wrestle on the indie circuit and there is little doubt that more success is in her future.

Photo Courtesy of Dr. Mike Lano—Wrealano@aol.com

Born:	January 24, 1965
Height:	6'6"
Weight:	290
Real Name:	Michael Lee Alfonso
High School:	King High School (FL)
Nickname:	Mullet
Finisher:	Awesome Bomb
Career Span:	1989–2006
Died:	February 17, 2007, Tampa, FL 42 years old

Titles Won:	12
Days as World Champion:	840
Age at first World Title Win:	30
Best Opponents:	Masato Tanaka, Taz, Hayabusa

Awesome, Mike

Incredibly strong, Mike Awesome performed a number of unbelievable moves for a man of his size, and flattened many opponents with his devastating top-rope splash and powerbomb. Awesome played football in high school and entered the sport under the tutelage of Steve Keirn in his hometown of Tampa, Florida. Overseas, in Japan, he wrestled as "The Gladiator" and won the FMW Independent World Title from Kanemura in 1996. On September 19, 1999, he won a three-way bout over champion Taz and Masato Tanaka for the ECW World Heavyweight Title. He would trade it with Tanaka, his longtime rival, in December 1999, and entered 2000 wearing the belt. Soon, however, he signed with World Championship Wrestling, and ECW officials worked out a backstage deal for Taz, then with the WWF, to return to the promotion and beat Awesome for the title. That's exactly what occurred on April 13, 2000. A prominent name in WCW's final months, Awesome joined the WWF in 2001, and won the Hardcore Title, becoming the first of the "invading" WCW employees to win a WWF belt. He also appeared for All-Japan, MLW, and TNA before retiring in 2006.

Photo Courtesy of Dr. Mike Lano—Wrealano@aol.com

Born:	October 22, 1943
Height:	6'2"
Weight:	260
Real Name:	Allen James Coage
High School:	Thomas A. Edison High School (NY)
Other Sports:	Fifth degree black belt in Judo, second degree black belt in Aikido
Judo Ach.:	1970 Judo Grand Champion, *Black Belt* magazine Judo Player of the Year (1970, 1977)
Pan-Am Games:	Judo (1967) (Gold Medal), Judo (1975) (Gold Medal)
Trained by:	Antonio Inoki, Stu Hart
Identities:	Buffalo Allen
Finisher:	Ghetto Blaster
Career Span:	1978–99
Hall of Fame:	Judo Hall of Fame—Inducted in 1990
Died:	March 6, 2007, Calgary, Alberta 63 years old

Titles Won:	13
Best Opponents:	Bret Hart, Hulk Hogan, Antonio Inoki
Halls of Fame:	1

Bad News Allen

By the time Bad News Allen became a pro wrestler in the late 1970s, he was already a world-class athlete. He'd won an Olympic medal and appeared in competitions around the world, demonstrating his talent and dexterity in Judo. Allen began his whirlwind Judo training around 1964 and took to it naturally, despite not being an athlete in high school. He was from Queens, New York, and labored as a baker to pay his bills as he advanced into national tournaments. He captured four AAU championships, and then won the bronze medal at the 1976 Olympics. Two years later, he debuted as a wrestler and based on his Judo discipline and profound toughness, he carried with him an aura of distinction that rookies rarely saw. He won a number of titles in Calgary, Florida, California, and Hawaii, and, under the name "Bad News Brown," was a threat to Hulk Hogan's WWF Title in 1989. He also feuded with Roddy Piper, culminating in their infamous match at WrestleMania VI. He continued to appear on the mat sporadically through 1999.

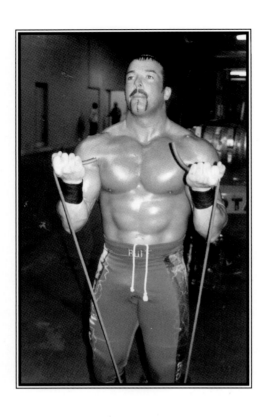

Born:	January 10, 1970
Height:	6'1"
Weight:	235
Real Name:	Marcus Alexander Bagwell
High School:	Sprayberry High School (GA)
Trained by:	Steve Lawler
Identities:	Fabulous Fabian, The Handsome Stranger
Finisher:	Buff Blockbuster
Career Span:	1990–Present

Titles Won:	21
Best Opponents:	Roddy Piper, Lex Luger, Dallas Page

Bagwell, Marcus

In the five years prior to joining the New World Order (NWO) in 1996, Marcus Bagwell was a popular hero. In a way, he represented the next generation of WCW superstars and won the World Tag Team Title on four occasions, twice with The Patriot and once with 2 Cold Scorpio and Scotty Riggs. Bagwell of Marietta, Georgia, adopted a more arrogant gimmick while as a member of the NWO, known as "Buff Bagwell," and teamed with Scott Norton as "Vicious and Delicious." Narrowly escaping a career-ending neck injury, Bagwell returned to the ring and won the WCW World Tag Team Title a fifth time with Shane Douglas in 2000. He wrestled briefly for the WWF in 2001, and outside several TNA appearances, he's been a mainstay on the indie circuit.

Born:	September 1, 1961
Height:	6'3"
Weight:	350
Real Name:	Scott Charles Bigelow
High School:	Neptune High School (NJ)
Identities:	Crusher Yurkof
Nickname:	The Beast from the East
Finisher:	Greetings from Asbury Park
Groups:	The Triple Threat (1997–98), The New Jersey Triad (1999)
Career Span:	1985–2006
Died:	January 19, 2007, Hudson, FL 45 years old

Titles Won:	13
Days as World Champion:	45
Age at first World Title Win:	36
Best Opponents:	Taz, Bret Hart, Rob Van Dam
MMA Record:	0-1
Movies:	5

Bam Bam Bigelow

Respected for his toughness and appreciated for his personable attitude, Bam Bam Bigelow was a frightening looking wrestler. His tattooed cranium was a daunting sight to fans as he approached the ring, but Bigelow was a kindhearted man and a genuine hero. In July 2000, he risked his life to save several children from a dangerous brush fire and suffered burns over 40 percent of his body. Originally from Neptune, New Jersey, he wrestled as an amateur in high school and finished with a 26-1 record as a senior. He graduated from Larry Sharpe's Monster Factory and debuted at Studio 54 in New York City in 1985. Ten years later, he wrestled his biggest match against Hall of Fame linebacker Lawrence Taylor at WrestleMania XI, gaining tremendous national exposure. Bigelow's distinctive look and impressive agility made him a star across the globe and he captured titles in many promotions. In 1997, he beat Shane Douglas for the ECW World Heavyweight belt and also held the IWGP Tag and WCW World Tag Team Titles.

Barrett, Wade

Born:	August 10, 1980
Height:	6'5"
Weight:	260
Real Name:	Stuart Alexander Bennett
High School:	Llanishen High School (Cardiff, Wales)
Trained by:	Jon Richie, Al Snow
Identities:	Stu Sanders
Finisher:	Wasteland
Career Span:	2004–Present

Titles Won:	4
Best Opponents:	John Cena, Randy Orton, Sheamus

For months, in 2010, a group of newcomers known as the Nexus ran rough shot over the WWE. Perpetrating acts of violence on popular stars such as John Cena, the rogue band gained real traction and its leader, Wade Barrett, was pegged to be the next big thing. Barrett, a youthful athlete from Great Britain, was only six years into his pro career and had trained in WWE developmentals since 2007. His ability to deliver promos advanced the important feud against Cena, which dominated headlines until December. In March 2011, he won his first of five Intercontinental championships with a victory over Kofi Kingson. Additional title victories came over Ezekiel Jackson, Miz, and Dolph Ziggler, and Barrett held the belt the final time in 2015. He used the name "Bad News Barrett" before winning the 2015 King of the Ring tournament, and from that point became "King Barrett." He joined the League of Nations with Sheamus, Alberto Del Rio, and Rusev, and remained a mid-carder until his May 2016 departure from the WWE.

Born:	January 18, 1969
Height:	6'5"
Weight:	275
Real Name:	David Michael Bautista Jr.
Parents:	David and Donna Bautista
High School:	Wakefield High School (VA)
Trained by:	Wild Samoan School, WCW Power Plant, WWE Ohio Valley Territory
Identities:	Kahn, Leviathan, Deacon Batista
Finisher:	Batista Bomb
Groups:	Evolution (2003–05)
WWE Debut:	May 9, 2002, Bridgeport, CT, Taped *Smackdown*
Career Span:	1999–2014
Website:	www.demon-wrestling.com

Batista

Titles Won:	11
Days as World Champion:	544
Age at first World Title Win:	36
Best Opponents:	The Undertaker, Triple H, John Cena
TV Appearances:	over 15
Movies:	18

In professional wrestling, Batista rose to the pinnacles of World Wrestling Entertainment, and now is on his way to conquering Hollywood with roles in a number of popular mainstream movies. His development as a wrestler was astronomically fast and, in just three years, he catapulted from the bodyguard for Reverend D-Von to the top spot in the WWE, ultimately winning the World Heavyweight Title from Triple H at WrestleMania 21 in 2005. Carrying his 290-pound muscular frame with intensity, charisma, and confidence, he reigned as champion for nine months, and was only knocked from his perch after suffering an injury in early 2006. At the 2006 Survivor Series, he beat Booker T for his second World Title, but was unsuccessful at WrestleMania 23, losing the belt to the Undertaker in Detroit. Batista won his third World championship from The Great Khali at Unforgiven in September 2007, but was dethroned by Edge in December at Armageddon.

On October 26, 2008, he won his fourth and final World championship from Chris Jericho, but lost it back to the former champ a short time later. During the summer of 2009, he took a cage match victory over Randy Orton and won the WWE Title, but had to vacate it again because of an injury. Batista went over John Cena for the WWE Championship a second time on February 21, 2010, when he took advantage of Cena moments after he'd retained his belt in an Elimination Chamber match. Cena would end up regaining the strap at WrestleMania XXVI. Batista retired from wrestling a few weeks later, but made his WWE return in 2014.

He won the Royal Rumble for a second time (first time in 2005) and advanced to WrestleMania, where he competed in a three-way bout against WWE World champion Randy Orton and the eventual winner, Daniel Bryan. Batista again left the WWE in mid-2014, and has since appeared in the films *Guardians of the Galaxy* and *Spectre*, with many other high-profile projects in the works.

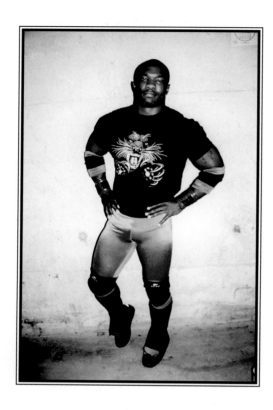

Born:	July 9, 1975
Height:	6'2"
Weight:	245
Real Name:	Shelton James Benjamin
High School:	Orangeburg-Wilkinson High School (SC)
HS Ach.:	Two-Time State Wrestling Champion
JC Ach.:	1996 NJCAA Collegiate Champion (HWT)
College Ach.:	Two-Time NCAA Division I All-American
Trained by:	Ohio Valley trainers
Nickname:	The Gold Standard
Finisher:	450 Splash
Tag Teams:	Minnesota Stretching Crew w/ Brock Lesnar
Career Span:	2000–Present
Titles Won:	13
Best Opponents:	Shawn Michaels, Triple H, Chris Jericho

Benjamin, Shelton

Although amateur and professional wrestling great Shelton Benjamin never broke into a headliner role in the WWE, he demonstrated that he was of a rare breed of high-flying scientific grapplers. He was a standout Intercontinental Champion, which he held three times, and also reigned as the US Titleholder for eight months. A product of the University of Minnesota and the teachings of J. Robinson, Benjamin broke into the business in 2000 and made his WWE TV debut in August 2002. He joined Charlie Haas as a member of Team Angle and won the WWE Tag Team Title twice. On October 19, 2004 in Milwaukee, he beat Chris Jericho for his first Intercontinental Championship and also took title victories from Ric Flair and Rob Van Dam. He captured the US Title from Matt Hardy on July 20, 2008 and retained the belt through March 2009. Benjamin left the WWE in April 2010 and has appeared in Puerto Rico for the WWC and also for Ring of Honor. He reunited with Haas to win the ROH World Tag Title in April 2011. He also ventured to Japan for NJPW and Pro Wrestling Noah, where he currently appears as "Shelton X. Benjamin."

Benoit, Chris

Born:	May 21, 1967
Height:	5′10″
Weight:	225
Real Name:	Christopher Michael Benoit
Parents:	Michael and Margaret Benoit
High School:	Archbishop O'Leary High School (Edmonton, Alberta)
Trained by:	Stu Hart and the Hart Brothers (Dungeon)
Identities:	The Pegasus Kid, Wild Pegasus
Nicknames:	The Crippler, Canadian Crippler
Finisher:	Flying Headbutt, German Suplex, Crippler Crossface
Groups:	The Four Horsemen (1995–98), The Revolution (1999), The Radicals (2000)
Career Span:	1985–2007
Died:	June 24, 2007, Fayetteville, GA 40 years old

Titles Won:	32
Days as World Champion:	155
Age at first World Title Win:	32
Best Opponents:	Bret Hart, Kurt Angle, Chris Jericho
Halls of Fame:	2

In the wrestling ring, few were better than Chris Benoit. His sound technical abilities made him the favorite of scores of fans throughout the world, but his actions in June 2007 demolished the respect people had for him and turned a influential life and career into one of horror. There is no getting past the fact that he killed his wife Nancy and seven-year-old son Daniel and all of his mat achievements are secondary to the sad truths of reality. The character of "Chris Benoit," a wrestler, who fans appreciated for his enthusiasm to the craft, always maintained a stoic personality and wrestled with a particular grit that few peers shared. He won world titles in WCW and the WWE, and engaged in many well-received bouts. At times, he was considered to be one of the best in the world. Prior to taking his own life on June 24, 2007, he murdered his wife and son in their suburban Atlanta home, and left the wrestling world in utter disbelief. To this day, it is still hard to comprehend what he did, and the perspective of his rightful place in pro wrestling history will forever be debated.

Born:	May 2, 1963
Height:	6'6"
Weight:	325
Real Name:	Ray Washington Traylor
Parents:	Ray and Maryland Traylor
Wife:	Angela Traylor
High School:	Paulding County High School (GA)
Trained by:	Ted Allen, Mickey Henry
Identities:	The Boss, The Guardian Angel, Big Bubba
Finisher:	Sidewalk Slam
Career Span:	1985–2004
Died:	September 22, 2004, Acworth, GA 41 years old

Big Bossman, The

Titles Won:	6
Days as World Champion:	83
Age at first World Title Win:	23
Best Opponents:	Hulk Hogan, Rick Rude, Vader
Halls of Fame:	1

Known by a variety of names, The Big Bossman was a sizable wrestler with outstanding athletic abilities. He made a dent in the profession shortly after his pro debut in Crockett Promotions as "Bubba Rogers," and won the UWF World Title from One Man King in April 1987. In the WWF, he adopted the name, "Big Bossman," and was purported to be a prison guard from Cobb County, Georgia. He partnered with One Man Gang, now known as Akeem, as the Twin Towers, and had a memorable *Saturday Night's Main Event* bout against Hulk Hogan and Randy Savage in 1989 that caused the latter duo to break up. In 1993, he joined WCW and remained there for five years, feuding with the members of the NWO late in his run. He rejoined the WWF in 1998 as a member of the Corporation and won the World Tag Team Title with Ken Shamrock, as well as winning the Hardcore belt four separate times. After leaving the promotion in 2003, he was a dedicated member of the Paulding County, Georgia community, and devoted lots time to charities and other causes. Bossman was inducted into the WWE Hall of Fame in 2016, and the honor was accepted by his wife, Angela, and two daughters.

Born:	February 14, 1971
Height:	6'7"
Weight:	480
Real Name:	Nelson Lee Frazier Jr.
High School:	Eastern Wayne High School (NC)
Identities:	Nelson Knight, King V
Career Span:	1991–2013
Died:	February 18, 2014, Memphis, TN 43 years old

Big Daddy Voodoo

Titles Won:	12
Best Opponents:	The Undertaker, Big Show, Kane
Movies:	2

Full of charisma, agile, and, not to mention weighing a monstrous 400-plus pounds, Big Daddy Voodoo is known by a variety of names, but is still the same powerful wrestler that has entertained audiences since the early 1990s. Taught by the famed Gene Anderson, Big Daddy of Goldsboro, North Carolina wrestled in the PWF and USWA, until he debuted in the WWF as "Mabel," along with "Mo," as the tag team, Men on a Mission, in 1993. The duo briefly held the World Tag Team Title during a tour of England in March 1994. Since then, he's undergone several gimmick changes, including "Viscera" and "Big Daddy V." Among his other honors are victories in the 1995 King of the Ring tournament and the WWC Universal championship in Puerto Rico. For a number of years, Big Daddy was a force on the indie circuit. Unfortunately, he passed away on February 14, 2014, at the age of forty-three.

Born:	February 8, 1972
Height:	7'0"
Weight:	450
Real Name:	Paul Donald Wight Jr.
Parents:	Paul and Dorothy Wight
High School:	Wyman King Academy (SC)
Finisher:	Chokeslam
Tag Team:	ShowMiz w/ The Miz
Groups:	The Dungeon of Doom (1995–96), New World Order (1996, 1997), The Union (1999), New World Order (2002)
Career Span:	1994–Present

Big Show, The

Titles Won:	21
Days as World Champion:	348
Age at first World Title Win:	23
Best Opponents:	Brock Lesnar, John Cena, Hulk Hogan
TV Appearances:	over 30
Movies:	9

When The Big Show was twelve years of age, he already stood 6'4" and was still growing. Today, he measures around the seven foot mark and weighs more than 400 pounds. In terms of size, he is this generation's Andre the Giant, and has thrived in the industry since 1995 with explosive charisma and impressive agility. An all-around athlete in high school, he was recruited by colleges around the nation and decided that he wanted to play basketball for Wichita State. He spent his freshman year at Northern Oklahoma Junior College and had a good season, making the All-Division first team, and then transferring to Wichita the following year. However, the death of his father and the departure of his coach made things rough on him, and he only averaged two points a game. He finished up at Southern Illinois and returned to Wichita, where he held down a number of different occupations, including as a club bouncer. He met Hulk Hogan at a charity event and, with the prospect of wrestling full time, attended WCW's Power Plant in Atlanta.

Using the name "The Giant," Show beat Hulk Hogan by DQ and won the WCW World Title on October 29, 1995. The belt was stripped from him on November 6 and declared vacant due to the controversy of his match with Hogan. He regained the title on April 22, 1996 when he beat Ric Flair on *Nitro* and was champion until August 10, suffering a loss to Hogan. Before departing WCW in early 1999, he also held the WCW World Tag Team Title twice with partners Sting and Scott Hall. Defecting to the WWF, he made a high-profile debut on February 14, 1999 during Vince McMahon's cage match with Steve Austin. He feuded with Mankind and teamed with The Undertaker to win the WWF Tag Team Title twice. Show was a late substitution for the injured Steve Austin in a three-way bout against champion

Triple H and The Rock on November 14, 1999, and ended the night as the new WWF World titleholder. His first reign ended on January 3, 2000 when he lost a bout to Triple H on *Raw*.

Show beat Brock Lesnar to win his second WWF Title on November 17, 2002, and Kurt Angle took the strap at Armageddon the following month. In October 2003, he won the US Title from Eddie Guerrero, and partnered with Kane in 2005 to hold the World Tag Team Title for five months. The ECW World Title was the prize for his July 4, 2006 win over Rob Van Dam, and the conquest made him the first man to capture a WWE, WCW, and ECW belt. He participated in a boxer vs. wrestler match against the 5'8" Floyd Mayweather Jr. at WrestleMania XXIV, and was defeated after the latter employed the use of brass knuckles. Since that time, he won tag team championships with Chris Jericho, The Miz, and Kane, and in 2011, he found himself in an increasingly violent war with the powerful Mark Henry—one that left him injured for several months. In December, he finally gained revenge on Henry, winning the World Title, but only to lose it to Daniel Bryan moments later after the latter cashed in his Money in the Bank briefcase.

In 2012, Big Show beat Cody Rhodes for the Intercontinental championship, and after losing the belt back to the latter, went over Sheamus for the World Heavyweight Title in October. His reign lasted into January 2013, and ended during a bout against Alberto Del Rio. Big Show remained a solid fixture in the WWE in the years that followed, and at WrestleMania 31, he won the second annual Andre the Giant Memorial Battle Royal.

Photo Courtesy of Dr. Mike Lano—Wrealano@aol.com

Born:	March 1, 1965
Height:	6'3"
Weight:	250
Real Name:	Booker Tio Huffman
Parents:	Booker and Rosa Huffman
High School:	Yates High School (TX)
Trained by:	Scott Casey
Identities:	G.I. Bro, Kole
Finisher:	Spinaroonie into an Axe-Kick, Book End, Missile Drop Kick
Groups:	The New Blood (2000), The Alliance (2001), New World Order (2002)
Tag Teams:	The Black Bombers w/ Stevie Ray, The Ebony Experience w/ Stevie Ray, The Harlem Heat w/ Kane
Career Span:	1989–2015
Wrestling School:	Pro Wrestling Academy (2005-Present) (Houston)
Website:	www.bookertonline.com

Booker T

Titles Won:	40
Days as World Champion:	379
Age at first World Title Win:	35
Best Opponents:	Chris Benoit, The Rock, Kurt Angle
Halls of Fame:	1

Booker T was long acknowledged as underrated, a potential superstar in a brother tandem with Stevie Ray—together known as Harlem Heat. In the late 1990s, he began to come into his own, revealing the depth of his abilities as a charismatic and entertaining grappler. His series with Chris Benoit in 1998 solidified his status as an up-and-comer and made naysayers believers. Finally, in 2000, he entered the upper echelon of WCW, winning the World Heavyweight Championship four times. Houston's Booker T hasn't looked back since, and has consistently been a leading figure in the industry. A student of Ivan Putski's wrestling school; he wrestled for the Dallas-based GWF prior to landing in WCW in 1993. Along with his brother Stevie Ray, Booker was a mainstay in the tag team division for years, feuding with the Nasty Boys, Public Enemy, and the Outsiders. On December 29, 1997, he beat Disco Inferno for the first of six WCW World TV Title victories and was a pointed moment in his career as a singles performer.

WCW was in complete turmoil in 2000, but one of the more responsible and appreciated decisions was the long awaited push of Booker T. During a controversial Bash at the Beach show on July 9, 2000, he pinned Jeff Jarrett and captured his first WCW World Heavyweight Title. Later that summer, he traded the title with Kevin Nash, and then lost the belt to Vince Russo on September 25 during *Nitro*. Russo vacated the championship and Booker won his third WCW Title on October 2 in a special four-corner "San Francisco 49er" bout. Late in November, Scott Steiner won the championship, but Booker regained it during the final edition of *Nitro* in March 2001; and was also the WCW US Champion during that time. Booker T emerged on WWF TV a few months later, and was still acknowledged as the WCW champion. He was quickly involved in feuds with the promotion's best, including Steve Austin, The Rock, The Undertaker, and Kurt Angle, and was an important figure in the Alliance vs. WWF war.

In 2002, he formed a comical team with Goldust, and the duo won the World Tag Team Title. Booker T won the Intercontinental Title from Christian, and also feuded with John Cena and Chris Benoit over the US Title. On May 21, 2006, he beat Bobby Lashley to win the King of the Ring tournament, and two months later, pinned Rey Mysterio for the World Title. He feuded with Batista, successfully repelling his challenge until the latter won the belt at the 2006 Survivor Series. In October 2007, Booker T joined TNA, where he was recognized as the Legends Champion. He joined a stable of grapplers known as the Main Event Mafia along with Sting, Scott Steiner, and Kevin Nash, and teamed with Steiner to capture the TNA World Tag Team Title. He remained in the promotion for two years and toured the indies until returning to the WWE at the 2011 Royal Rumble. In the years that followed, Booker worked as a commentator on *Smackdown* and *Raw*, plus acted as a trainer for the *Tough Enough* reality series. He wrestled occasionally, and appeared as the General Manager for *Smackdown* in 2012. The following year, he was inducted into the WWE Hall of Fame.

Born:	August 1, 1972
Height:	6'1"
Weight:	260
Real Name:	Devon Hughes
Wife:	Yessenia Hughes
High School:	New Rochelle High School (NY)
Trained by:	Johnny Rodz
Identities:	Deacon, D-Von Dudley
Finisher:	3D w/ Bubba Ray Dudley
Groups:	The Alliance (2001), Front Line (2008–09), EV 2.0 (2010)
Wrestling School:	Team 3D Academy in Kissimmee, FL
Career Span:	1992–Present

Brother Devon

Titles Won:	27
Best Opponents:	Eddie Guerrero, Rob Van Dam, Taz
Halls of Fame:	1

Amassing a collection of twenty-three World Championships with partner Brother Ray, Brother Devon is one of the most prolific tag team grapplers of the modern era. Their combined achievements will never be duplicated, as well as their finely tuned cooperation in the ring, which set the standard for teamwork. Team 3D, also known as the Dudley Boys, were intense brawlers, doling it out as good as they could take it, and always taking it to the extreme. The duo first teamed in ECW and captured the World Tag Team Title eight times. They debuted in the WWF in 1999 and participated in the two famous WrestleMania TLC matches in 2000 and 2001. Feuding with the Hardys and Christian and Edge, they won the WWF Tag Team belts six times by the end of 2001. Before departing the promotion in 2005, the Dudleys added to their championship totals, winning the World Tag Team title twice more and the WWE Tag Team Title once. They turned up in TNA, and have been there ever since. In addition to their TNA and NWA title victories, they won the IWGP belts twice in 2009. As a singles competitor, Devon captured the TNA Television Championship on two occasions in 2012. With Brother Ray, he was inducted into the TNA Hall of Fame in 2014 and, the following year, reemerged in the WWE as the "Dudleys."

Born:	May 22, 1981
Height:	5'9"
Weight:	195
Real Name:	Bryan Danielson
High School:	Aberdeen High School (WA)
College:	Grays Harbor College
Trained by:	Tracey Smothers, William Regal
Identities:	American Dragon
Finisher:	Dragon Suplex, Cobra Clutch
Career Span:	1999–2016

Titles Won:	20
Days as World Champion:	475
Age at first World Title Win:	24
Best Opponents:	Samoa Joe, Austin Aries, Takeshi Morishima
Published Books:	1

Bryan, Daniel

As the captain of the insanely popular "Yes" Movement, Daniel Bryan earned a new level of respect and fame across professional wrestling. Already known for his tremendous ring proficiency, he garnered a cult-like following, always living up to the hype. A product of Aberdeen, Washington, he trained at Shawn Michaels' school in San Antonio, and further developed at MCW in Memphis and at the Inoki Dojo in Los Angeles. He was a legend on the indie circuit and featured prominently on Ring of Honor shows beginning in 2002. In 2005, he beat James Gibson for the ROH World Title and held the title until December 2006. He joined the WWE in 2010, and was initially part of the NXT organization. But soon, he took the US championship from The Miz, and in July 2011, won the *Smackdown* Money in the Bank ladder match, earning a future World Title shot. Bryan announced that he'd cash in his briefcase at WrestleMania, but instead capitalized on the battered new champion Big Show in December, winning the belt.

Bryan's reign ended at WrestleMania on April 1, 2012, losing in just 18 seconds to Sheamus, but his rise to the top levels of superstardom didn't miss a beat. The fans decided over and above any specific push by WWE management that he was their hero and reacted positively to just about everything he did. "Yes" chants were explosive, and Bryan began to edge into popular culture. On August 18, 2013, he beat John Cena for his first WWE World Title, but lost it the same evening after Randy Orton cashed in his MITB contract. But Bryan won the belt again in September before the title was declared vacant because of controversy. Orton captured the title in a rematch in October, and Bryan started a grueling path to WrestleMania XXX. At that event, on April 6, 2014, he beat Orton and Batista in a three-way bout, and won the championship in glorious fashion. However, he was forced to vacate two months later because of a real world neck injury.

Bryan's three WWE title reigns equaled just 65 days, but to the fans, he was still the most popular force in the organization. He returned later in 2014 and appeared at the 2015 Royal Rumble, but he was no longer part of the organization's main event picture. He captured the Intercontinental Title at WrestleMania 31, but was again forced to step away from the sport due to continued injuries. On February 8, 2016, he announced his retirement from active wrestling in an emotional speech on *Raw*, and thanked the fans for their eternal support. He expected to remain an ambassador to the WWE and with his wife, wrestler Brie Bella, planned to start a family.

Photo Courtesy of Dr. Mike Lano—Wrealano@aol.com

Born:	July 14, 1971
Height:	6'3"
Weight:	295
Real Name:	Mark Lomonica
High School:	Half Hollow Hills High School (East) (NY)
Trained by:	Sonny Blaze
Identities:	Bubba Ray Dudley, Brother Ray
Finisher:	3D w/ D-Von Dudley, Bubba Bomb
Groups:	Alliance (2001), Front Line (2008–09), EV 2.0 (2010)
Wrestling School:	Team 3D Academy in Kissimmee, FL
Career Span:	1991–Present

Bully Ray

Titles Won:	32
Best Opponents:	Brock Lesnar, Chris Jericho, A.J. Styles
Halls of Fame:	1

In 2010, the former Brother Ray emerged as "Bully Ray," a powerful and intimidating heel who used his size to dominate smaller competitors. The new gimmick was a refreshing turn for the ex-member of Team 3D and put a temporary hold on the long-running tag team with Brother Devon. Also known as the Dudleys, Ray and Devon established themselves as legends, winning twenty-three World Titles in the US and Japan in ECW, the WWE, and NJPW. They were also two-time holders of the tag title in TNA, the organization they've been affiliated with since 2005. Gaining their initial fame in ECW, the Dudleys were famous for putting rivals through tables, and no one was safe from their Dudley Death Drop. Their success continued in the WWF beginning in 1999, and they participated in two classic Tables, Ladders, and Chairs bouts at WrestleMania. Team 3D broke up in 2010 when Bully Ray attacked his longtime partner and began an impressive singles run. He joined Immortal and feuded with Mr. Anderson and Abyss in 2011. In 2013, he captured the TNA World Heavyweight Title on two occasions, defeating Jeff Hardy and Chris Sabin, and was inducted into the TNA Hall of Fame in 2014. Bully Ray and Devon returned to the WWE as the "Dudleys" in 2015, and continue to wreak havoc in the tag team division to this day.

Candido, Chris

Born:	March 21, 1972
Height:	5'8"
Weight:	225
Real Name:	Christopher B. Candito
Family:	Brother of Johnny Candido
High School:	Red Bank Catholic High School (NJ)
Colleges:	Wellesley College, University of Tennessee
Trained by:	Larry Sharpe
Identities:	Skip
Nicknames:	Suicide Blond, Hard Knox, No Gimmicks Needed
Tag Teams:	The Suicide Blonds w/ Johnny Hot Body, The Bodydonnas w/ Zip
Groups:	Triple Threat (1996–98, 2000)
Career Span:	1986–2005
Died:	April 28, 2005, New Brunswick, NJ 33 years old

Titles Won:	24
Days as World Champion:	97
Age at first World Title Win:	22
Best Opponents:	Cactus Jack, Sabu, Terry Funk
Halls of Fame:	1

On April 28, 2005, Chris Candido, a gifted yet underrated wrestler, died in New Brunswick, New Jersey. He had participated in a tag team cage match for TNA only days before, and his unexpected passing shocked his peers and fans throughout the world. The Edison native was a veteran of many years of ring combat, and was the grandson of Chuck Richards, a former WWWF grappler. Candido competed all over the indie circuit and for major promotions, the WWF, WCW, and ECW. On November 19, 1994, he became the youngest NWA World Heavyweight Champion in history when, at twenty-two years of age, he beat Tracey Smothers in the finals of a tournament. He lost the title a few months later, on February 24, 1995, to Dan Severn. While in the WWF and ECW, he won World Tag Team Titles and held the XPW World Championship in 2000. In addition to his sound wrestling abilities, Candido was a mentor for many grapplers behind the scenes. His longtime partner and manager, Tammy, was inducted into the WWE Hall of Fame in 2011.

Born:	April 23, 1977
Height:	6'1"
Weight:	240
Real Name:	John Felix Anthony Cena
Parents:	John and Carol Cena
High School:	Cushing Academy (MA)
Football Ach.:	NCAA Division III 1st Team All-American (1998), Freedom Football Conference All Star (1998), Captain of the football team
Finisher:	Protobomb, Attitude Adjustment
Career Span:	2000–Present

Titles Won:	22
Days as World Champion:	1,163
Age at first World Title Win:	27
Best Opponents:	Shawn Michaels, CM Punk, Triple H
TV Appearances:	Over 50
Movies:	14
Halls of Fame:	1

Cena, John

Mega superstar John Cena gets plenty of heat from audiences across the WWE Universe, but no one can doubt his status as the organization's franchise wrestler. His likeable personality, enthusiasm for the sport, and commitment to an endless number of charities and the military make him the kind of hero that a promotion can be built around. In the ring, Cena has constantly overcome the odds to prevail. It doesn't matter who his opponent is, he's able to display wit in promos and sharpness in the ring. While some fans are hoping for a revitalization of the Cena "character," preferably by him turning heel, John serves the greater good as a smiling babyface, and continues to appear in mainstream roles as a one-of-kind ambassador for the WWE. The West Newbury, Massachusetts, native was an All-American football player at Springfield College, and a product of the Ultimate University wrestling school in Southern California. As "Prototype," he won the UPW heavyweight crown in April 2000.

Featured in a cable documentary about wrestling, Cena gained some early publicity and the attention of the WWE. He graduated from Ohio Valley and worked his way onto the main roster in June 2002. Before the end of the year, he developed a new image, a hip-hop gimmick, complete with in-ring rap performances and inspired wrestling gear. The role received mixed reviews, but Cena stuck to his guns and continued to add dimensions to his ring work and outward presentation. He beat the Big Show at WrestleMania XX for the US Heavyweight crown and would win the title two additional times in 2004. He also switched gears by taking time off to film, *The Marine*, in which he had a leading role. Cena was garnering steam and ready to break into a headliner role in the organization. At WrestleMania 21, on April 3, 2005, he beat JBL for his first WWE Championship, and soon introduced his famous spinning belt. For the remainder of the year, Cena remained champion, fighting off challenger after challenger.

Edge ended his reign as champion when he cashed in his Money in the Bank contract after Cena retained in a tough Elimination Chamber bout on January 8, 2006; Although Cena regained the belt at the Royal Rumble. On April 2, 2006, he forced Triple H to submit to retain at WrestleMania 22 and remained champion until June, when Rob Van Dam dethroned him in New York City. Cena won the WWE Title for a third time from Edge at Unforgiven, winning a TLC bout. This started an amazing reign as titleholder, which lasted more than a year and was the longest in the WWE since Hulk Hogan's first run. At WrestleMania 23, he beat Shawn Michaels to retain the championship in a classic bout and also warded off The Great Khali and Randy Orton in defenses. Unfortunately, he suffered a real-life injury in October and was stripped of the belt. Cena came back before he was expected at the 2008 Royal Rumble in the 30th spot, and eliminated Triple H to win the event. However, he wasn't able to win back the WWE Title at No Way Out or WrestleMania.

During the summer of 2008, he teamed with Batista to win the World Tag Team Title, and then feuded with the latter. A neck injury sidelined him again, but Cena returned with a vengeance at the Survivor Series, defeating Chris Jericho for his first World Heavyweight Title. Edge stripped him of the belt, but Cena regained it at WrestleMania XXV. Edge got the last word at Backlash, again defeating him in a Last Man Standing affair. Cena defeated Orton for the WWE championship on September 13, 2009, but Orton regained it less than a month later. They met again at Bragging Rights in a 60-minute Iron Man bout, which Cena won, and began his fifth reign as a WWE titleholder. Sheamus beat him in December 2009 in a tables match, but Cena won over Triple H for the Irish grappler's belt at February's Elimination Chamber show. There was no time for a celebration because Batista stepped into an impromptu bout and beat him for the belt in less than a minute. Cena beat Batista for the WWE Title at WrestleMania on March 28, 2010.

The year marked a long feud with Nexus, a band of upstarts looking for recognition in the WWE. Cena prevailed, as expected, and extracted revenge from its leader, Wade Barrett. In May 2011, he won the WWE championship for the eighth time when he beat The Miz and engaged CM Punk in an engrossing feud that summer. He added two additional WWE championship wins over Rey Mysterio and Alberto Del Rio, the triumph over the latter being his record-setting tenth title victory. At WrestleMania XXVIII, he was beaten by The Rock in a high-profile main event, but rebounded to defeat his foe a year later at the same event. With his win came his eleventh WWE championship. After losing the belt to Daniel Bryan at SummerSlam, Cena went out of action with an arm injury.

Returning on October 27, 2013, he went over Albert Del Rio for the World Title, but lost a unification bout against WWE Champion Randy Orton in December. He feuded with the Wyatt Family and with Kevin Owens over the United States championship in the following months, but went out of action again in a shoulder injury in early 2016. With mainstream television appearances and a recognizable persona, Cena continues to be the "face" of World Wrestling Entertainment. He's made over 500 wishes through the Make-A-Wish Foundation, and it's proof he lives the hero character just as much outside the ring as he does in.

Born:	September 17, 1963
Height:	6'0"
Weight:	235
Real Name:	Masahiro Chono
Trained by:	NJPW Dojo, Lou Thesz, Stu Hart
Nickname:	Mr. August
Finisher:	STF
Groups:	New World Order (1997–98)
Career Span:	1984–2012

Chono, Masa

Titles Won:	13
Days as World Champion:	209
Age at first World Title Win:	24
Best Opponents:	Riki Choshu, Shinya Hashimoto, Kensuke Sasaki
Halls of Fame:	1

A celebrated grappler who established himself in Japan and the United States, Masa Chono was actually a member of the NWO in both countries during its peak run. He was also the last man to wrestle the famous Lou Thesz. Chono has an astonishing list of accomplishments under the banner of New Japan Pro Wrestling, winning the IWGP Title from Tatsumi Fujinami on August 8, 1998 and the IWGP Tag Team belts seven times with partners Hiroyoshi Tenzan and Keiji Mutoh. He also proved victorious in the G-1 Climax World Tournament five times and won the vacant NWA World Heavyweight Title with a tourney win over Rick Rude in 1992, but would lose the title to Mutoh on January 4, 1993 in Tokyo. Early in his career, while wrestling for Bob Geigel in the Central States, he beat Mike George on February 26, 1988 to capture the WWA World Title in St. Joseph, although George regained the belt on March 17. Chono officially left New Japan in early 2010 and made appearances for a number of different promotions. However, he returned for New Japan's 40th Anniversary program on April 20, 2012, teaming with Akira and Hiro Saito in a loss to Tatsumi Fujinami, Riki Choshu, and Tiger Mask I.

Christian

Born:	November 30, 1973
Height:	6'1"
Weight:	225
Real Name:	William Jason Reso
High School:	Orangeville District Secondary School (Ontario)
College:	Humber College
Trained by:	Ron Hutchison
Identities:	Christian Cage, Conquistador I
Nickname:	Canadian Rage, Captain Charisma
Finisher:	The Impaler, Frog Splash
Tag Teams:	Hard Impact w/ Edge, Suicide Blonds w/ Edge
Groups:	Thug Life (1997), Revolution X (1998), The Brood (1999), The Un-Americans (2002)
Career Span:	1995–2014

Titles Won:	24
Days as World Champion:	522
Age at first World Title Win:	32
Best Opponents:	Kurt Angle, Chris Jericho, Edge
TV Appearances:	1
Movies:	2

Fierce, skilled, and wildly entertaining, Christian carried a lethal combination of characteristics that firmly solidified his place among the top heavyweights in the sport. Between 2006 and '14 he won six World championships in TNA and the WWE, and established himself as a main event player. Often compared to his longtime tag team partner, Edge, Christian has defined himself individually, and worked hard to achieve his own level of success. Three years after his pro debut, he went to Florida to train with the legendary Dory Funk Jr., and made his debut in the WWF in 1998, along with Edge. Their longtime friendship translated to perfect compatibility in the ring, and Christian and Edge formed an incomparable tag team. They captured the tag team championship seven times, winning two WrestleMania TLC matches, and setting an early course for superstardom. Christian defined himself as a singles competitor and had a memorable feud with Chris Jericho in 2004.

In November 2005, he joined TNA and captured the NWA World Heavyweight Title from Jeff Jarrett on February 12, 2006. He lost the belt back to Jarrett in June in a King of the Mountain match. After successfully turning heel, he beat Abyss and Sting in a three-way bout for his second NWA championship on

January 14, 2007. He ended up losing the belt to Kurt Angle in May of that year. In 2009, Christian returned to the WWE and won the first of two ECW World Titles from Jack Swagger. An injury sidelined him, but he rebounded to help Edge in the latter's war with Alberto Del Rio. When Edge retired in April 2011, Christian faced Del Rio for the vacant World Title and, on May 1, captured the championship. Two days later, he lost it to Randy Orton. Christian and Orton traded the belt again during the summer. Slowed by injuries, Christian wrestled his final match in 2014 and is currently appearing with Edge in their own WWE Network program, appropriately named *The Edge and Christian Show.*

Photo Courtesy of Mike Mastrandrea

Born:	October 26, 1978
Height:	6'1"
Weight:	220
Real Name:	Phillip Jack Brooks
High School:	Lockport High School (IL)
Trained by:	Danny Dominion, Ace Steel, Kevin Quinn
Finisher:	GTS (Go to Sleep), Anaconda Vice
Groups:	Straight Edge Society (2009–10), New Nexus (2011)
Career Span:	1998–2014

Titles Won:	28
Days as World Champion:	427
Age at first World Title Win:	26
Best Opponents:	Samoa Joe, John Cena, The Undertaker

CM Punk

For a time during the 2010s, CM Punk was reputed to be the "Best in the World," and may just have been. Demonstrating his exceptional versatility time and time again, he proved a dominant figure in World Wrestling Entertainment. His ingenuity inside the ring and out, and the way he connected with audiences was extremely rare and, in 2011, his popularity skyrocketed to astronomical proportions. His credo was "straight-edge" all the way, refraining from the purported ills of society, and had two X-marks on his taped hands to represent his ideology. Having grown up in a suburb of Chicago, he attended a local wrestling school, and debuted in 1998. Punk's experience in martial arts, plus his athleticism makes for an entertaining show when he steps into the ring, and his personality-driven character completes the package. While working the independent circuit , he won the IWA Mid-South Title on five occasions between 2000 and 2004, beating Eddie Guerrero and A.J. Styles for two of his reigns. He also had lengthy feuds with Chris Hero and Colt Cabana that garnered a lot of buzz.

In the Ring of Honor promotion, he wrestled classic matches against Raven and Samoa Joe, including two sixty-minute draws against the latter in 2004. Despite his effort, he never overcame Joe for the ROH World Championship, but did beat Austin Aries for the belt on June 18, 2005. He dropped the title in August and went to Ohio Valley, a WWE developmental promotion. Punk beat Bret Albright for the local heavyweight title, and then debuted for the ECW brand in mid-2006, initiating a long win streak. He chased John Morrison for the ECW World Title, finally beating him on September 1, 2007, but lost it to Chavo Guerrero Jr. in January 2008. At WrestleMania XXIV, he prevailed in an electrifying Money in the Bank ladder match. Three months later, on June 30, he watched as World Champion Edge was brutally beaten by Batista, and smartly cashed in his contract, capitalizing on the moment, and pinning Edge for the title.

At WrestleMania XXV, he won his second straight Money in the Bank ladder match, and on June 7, 2009, he cashed it in again at an opportune time, pinning Jeff Hardy after the latter's grueling match against Edge. In 2011, Punk was back at the top of his game and was outstanding in explosively candid promo segments that appealed both to the "smart" audience and the mainstream wrestling public. Even the non-wrestling sports community took notice of his dynamic performances. Punk beat Cena for the WWE Title on July 17, 2011 in a classic match, was stripped after apparently leaving the promotion, then beat Cena again to unify the two strands at SummerSlam. However, he was attacked by Kevin Nash after the bout, and then dropped the belt to Alberto Del Rio, who cashed in his MITB contract. On November 20, 2011, Punk forced Del Rio to submit, and regained the WWE championship. He ended the year still on top, and was constantly at odds with interim *Raw* General Manager John Laurinaitis.

In 2012, he repelled the challenges of Dolph Ziggler, Chris Jericho, Mark Henry, Daniel Bryan, John Cena, and Ryback, and held the WWE championship until January 27, 2013, when he was defeated by The Rock. His reign was the longest since 1988. At WrestleMania 29, he attempted to end The Undertaker's streak, but was unsuccessful in his endeavor. CM Punk made appearances in the WWE through 2013, but left the organization the next year under a cloud of mystery. Unhappy with a number of things, Punk walked away from wrestling altogether and signed a deal with Ultimate Fighting Championship (UFC) in December 2014. He went into heavy training but, as of May 2016, hadn't officially competed in a bout. Fans eagerly anticipate his UFC debut and continue to wonder whether he'll ever return to wrestling again.

Born:	May 29, 1973
Height:	6'1"
Weight:	220
Real Name:	Steven Eugene Corino
Family:	Brother of Allison Danger, father of Colby Corino
High School:	Perkiomen Valley High School (PA)
Trained by:	Tom Brandi
Finisher:	Old School Expulsion Neckbreaker, Northern Lights Bomb
Career Span:	1994-Present

Corino, Steve

Titles Won:	79
Days as World Champion:	974
Age at first World Title Win:	27
Best Opponents:	Samoa Joe, Shinya Hashimoto, Dusty Rhodes

Leader of the "old school" revolution, Steve Corino has wrestled, toured, and represented a previous generation of pro grappling better than most of his contemporaries. He has over seventy-five wrestling championship victories, including the NWA and ECW World Heavyweight Titles. Born in Canada, Corino was raised in Trappe, Pennsylvania, northwest of Philadelphia, and entered the profession in 1994. Under 200 pounds, Corino was at a disadvantage early on, trying to wedge himself into a sport that spotlighted mostly behemoths; but he was persistent, and worked into contention for the ECW Title. On November 5, 2000, he beat Justin Credible to capture the ECW Title. The following April, he won the NWA belt from Mike Rapada, etching his name into the title lineage of many of the legends he admired. Corino remains a favorite wherever he appears, and if he continues at this rate, he'll have won more than 100 titles before he retires.

Born:	March 24, 1970
Height:	5'11"
Weight	220
Real Name:	Daniel Christopher Covell
Parents:	Charles and Marcia Covell
Wife:	Lisa Covell
High School:	Pine Forest High School (NC)
Trained by:	Sam DeCero, Mike Anthony and Kevin Quinn
Identities:	Conquistador I, Curry Man, Suicide
Finisher:	Last Rites
Career Span:	1993–Present

Titles Won:	37
Days as World Champion:	182
Age at first World Title Win:	34
Best Opponents:	A.J. Styles, Samoa Joe, Kurt Angle
Halls of Fame:	1

Daniels, Christopher

Wrestling fans who appreciate athleticism, daring acrobatics, and technical savvy respect the work and dedication of Christopher Daniels. A product of Fayetteville, North Carolina, Daniels graduated with a degree in theater from Methodist College in 1991. He attended Chicago's Windy City Pro Wrestling School and made his debut as a grappler in 1993. Since then, he has since won over thirty championships across the Continental US, Puerto Rico, England, and Japan. Daniels has also won the TNA X-Division belt four times, the NWA World Tag Team Title six times, and held the ROH World Television crown from 2010–11. In January 2011, he made his return to TNA and aligned himself with the members of Fortune. He later formed a championship tag team with Frankie Kazarian, and the two captured two TNA and ROH World Tag Titles. Known as the "Fallen Angel," Daniels has consistently been among the best pro wrestlers on the circuit and continues to shine regardless if he's working an indie show before a few hundred or in a championship match on pay-per-view. His value as a wrestler is appreciated by his peers, audiences across the globe, and by promoters who benefit from booking him.

Born:	October 6, 1959
Height:	6'2"
Weight:	260
Real Name:	Barry Alan Darsow
Parents:	Melvin and Adeline Darsow
Family:	Father of Dakota Darsow
High School:	Robbinsdale High School (MN)
Identities:	Zar, Krusher Darsow
Tag Team:	The Mongolians w/ Gor
Career Span:	1983-2012

Titles Won:	14
Best Opponents:	Randy Savage, Chris Benoit, Bob Backlund

Darsow, Barry

Teamed with Bill Eadie, Barry Darsow formed one of the most notable tag teams of the 1980s, Demolition. Darsow was "Smash," while Eadie was known as "Ax," and the pair won the WWF World Tag Team Title on three occasions. Their first reign lasted sixteen months, from March 1988 to July 1989. A product of Minnesota, Darsow played hockey in his youth and attended the camp of Eddie Sharkey after a few of his friends became pro wrestlers. Early in his career, he toured New Zealand as one of the Mongolians, and late in 1984, joined the Koloffs, Ivan and Nikita, as Russian "Krusher Khrushchev." He defended the NWA Tag Team Title, which the Koloffs had won previously, and also teamed with Ivan to capture the US Tag Team belts. While in the WWF, following his run as a member of Demolition, he worked as the "Repo Man," and then as "Blacktop Bully" in WCW. At the Uncensored 1995 show, he wrestled Dustin Rhodes in the back of a moving truck. He's since reunited with Eadie on the indie circuit and is a successful businessman in Minnesota.

Born:	May 25, 1977
Height:	6'5"
Weight:	260
Real Name:	Alberto Rodriguez
Family:	Son of Dos Caras, nephew of Mil Mascaras
Trained by:	Dos Caras, FCW trainers
Identities:	Dos Caras Jr.
Finisher:	Cross Armbar submission
Career Span:	2000–Present

Titles Won:	3
Days as World Champion:	617
Age at first World Title Win:	30
Best Opponents:	John Cena, Edge, Ultimo Guerrero
MMA Record:	9-5

Del Rio, Alberto

Many fans throughout the WWE Universe were pleasantly surprised that relative newcomer Alberto Del Rio won the 2011 Royal Rumble in Boston. A former amateur from Mexico, he was indisputably talented and his gimmick as an arrogant heel exhibited his charisma perfectly. His ring entrance saw him drive out in an expensive automobile and his own personal ring announcer alerted the audience of his arrival. For a number of years, he wrestled Greco-Roman for the Mexican national team and debuted as a pro in 2000, following in the footsteps of his father, Dos Caras. On July 8, 2007, he beat Universo 2000 for the CMLL World Heavyweight Title and held the belt until December 2008. He went to Florida Championship Wrestling after signing a deal with the WWE and debuted in August 2010, engaging in an early feud with Rey Mysterio Jr. After the Rumble, he continued his winning ways, adding *Raw*'s Money in the Bank contract, and then captured the WWE championship twice between August and October 2011.

Alberto also captured the World championship twice in 2013, defeating The Big Show and Dolph Ziggler. During the summer of 2014, he departed the WWE and made appearances for AAA, WWC, and ROH, using the name "El Patron Alberto." Among his honors during this time-frame was the AAA Mega championship. In 2015, he joined Lucha Underground before returning to the WWE in October 2015. He won the US Heavyweight Title and joined a new faction known as the "League of Nations." Alberto was looking to work his way back into the World Title picture in 2016 and, considering his abilities on the mat, it is pretty certain he will do so as the year progresses.

Born:	April 11, 1978
Height:	6'0"
Weight:	225
Real Name:	Elijah Burcks
High School:	Frank H. Peterson Academies of Technology (FL)
Identities:	Elijah Burke
Career Span:	2003–Present

Titles Won:	1
Best Opponents:	Chris Benoit, CM Punk, Kurt Angle

Dinero, D'Angelo

A completely multi-dimensional wrestler with lots of potential, D'Angelo Dinero is one of the best current TNA superstars never to win a championship in the promotion. He's demonstrated skill behind the microphone and fluidity on the mat, and it seems like just a matter of time before he fights his way into the upper echelon of the promotion. Originally from Jacksonville, Florida, Dinero served as a corrections officer and boxed as an amateur before going to Louisville to train at Ohio Valley. While in the WWE from 2006-2008, he formed a partnership with Sylvester Terkay and nearly won the ECW championship on several occasions. After jumping to TNA, he prevailed in the 8 Card Stud Tournament in February 2010 and feuded with Samoa Joe and Brother Devon. "The Pope" left TNA in January 2013, only to return two years later. He acts as a commentator for the organization to this day.

Born:	November 21, 1964
Height:	6'0"
Weight:	240
Real Name:	Troy Shane Martin
Parents:	George and Louise Martin
Wife:	Carla Martin
High School:	New Brighton Area High School (PA)
College:	Bethany College
Trained by:	Dominic DeNucci
Identities:	Troy Orndorff, Dean Douglas
Finisher:	Pittsburgh Plunge, The Franchiser
Groups:	Triple Threat (1997–98), The Revolution (1999), The New Blood (2000)
Tag Team:	The Dynamic Dudes w/ Johnny Ace
Career Span:	1982–Present

Douglas, Shane

Titles Won:	21
Days as World Champion:	Around 1,000
Age at first World Title Win:	29
Best Opponents:	Terry Funk, Taz, Justin Credible

The "Franchise" Shane Douglas helped launch a revolution in 1994 when he denounced the NWA World Title and proclaimed himself the inaugural champion of "Extreme Championship Wrestling." It was a defining moment for the business as a whole and helped usher in a new era that influenced both the WWF and WCW. Douglas was a fan of wrestling as a young man and helped stage benefit grappling programs in his hometown of New Brighton, Pennsylvania while still in high school. By the mid-1990s, he was an experienced pro and the commanding figure behind ECW's rise to prominence. He held the ECW championship four times, feuding with the likes of Terry Funk and The Sandman, and always delivered heated promos, especially when he ranted about Ric Flair. At the tail end of WCW's run, Douglas won the World Tag Team and US crowns. He competed for TNA in the beginning of 2003, and made his final showing in 2009. He's wrestled all over the indie map, and has won many belts to include the MLW and XPW World Titles.

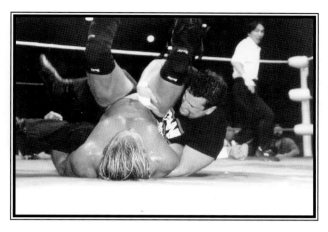

Dreamer, Tommy

Born:	February 13, 1970
Height:	6'2"
Weight:	245
Real Name:	Thomas James Laughlin
Parents:	John and Susan Laughlin
Wife:	Trisa Laughlin
High School:	Iona Preparatory School (NY)
College:	Iona College
Trained by:	Johnny Rodz
Identities:	T.D. Madison
Finisher:	DDT
Career Span:	1989–Present

Titles Won:	29
Days as World Champion:	49
Age at first World Title Win:	30
Best Opponents:	Raven, Rob Van Dam, A.J. Styles
Halls of Fame:	1

Tommy Dreamer is as passionate about pro wrestling as anyone involved in the sport today. His enthusiasm for the business is apparent every time he steps into the ring. Also known as the "Innovator of Violence," Dreamer displayed just how hardcore he was in August 1994 during a Singapore caning session by the Sandman. He was the heart and soul of ECW and only left the promotion because it was sold in 2001. During his nine-year stay with the organization, he won the World Tag Team Title three times, and then on April 22, 2000, he beat Taz for the ECW World Heavyweight Title. After ECW folded in early 2001, Dreamer traveled to Ontario and won the vacant BCW Can-Am Heavyweight Title over Rhino and Scott D'Amore. He joined the WWF in 2001 and remained involved with the organization through January 2010. While apart of the ECW "brand extension," he regained the ECW World Title. He emerged in TNA and was a member of the EV 2.0 troupe, then begrudgingly joined Immortal in 2011. His run in TNA ended later that year, and he started his own organization, the House of Hardcore, in 2012. Dreamer returned to the WWE in 2015, and continues to make appearances into 2016.

Duggan, Jim

Born:	January 14, 1954
Height:	6'3"
Weight:	280
Real Name:	James Edward Duggan
Wife:	Deborah Duggan
High School:	Glens Falls High School (NY)
HS Ach.:	New York State High School Wrestling Title (1973) (250)
Pro Sports:	National Football League—Atlanta Falcons (1977–78) (injured) Canadian Football League—Toronto Argonauts (1979)
Finisher:	Three-Point Football Stance into Clothesline
Groups:	Team Canada (2000)
Career Span:	1979–Present

Titles Won:	9
Days as World Champion:	Unknown
Age at first World Title Win:	50
Best Opponents:	Randy Savage, Ted DiBiase, Rick Rude
Halls of Fame:	2

The epitome of wrestling hero, "Hacksaw" Jim Duggan charged up audiences like few others, his explosive charisma inspiring chants of "USA," and his magnetism radiating to all corners of arenas. A high school wrestler and football star, he was a starting offensive lineman at SMU as a freshman, and was the team captain in 1976. He was trained by Jack Adkisson in Dallas and made his professional debut in 1979. A few years later, he formed the Rat Pack with Ted DiBiase and Matt Borne in the Mid-South territory, and then turned fan favorite in 1983. One of his first big title victories occurred when he defeated Buzz Sawyer for the North American crown in 1986. In the WWF, he won the very first Royal Rumble on January 24, 1988, and beat Haku to become "King" in April 1989. While as a part of WCW, Duggan pinned Steve Austin in 27 seconds for the US Title on September 18, 1994. Six years later, he found the WCW TV belt in the trash and held it for nearly two months. He's appeared in the WWE many times since 2005, maintaining his popularity, and was inducted into the WWE Hall of Fame in 2011.

Photo Courtesy of Pete Lederberg—plmathfoto@hotmail.com

Eaton, Bobby

Born:	August 14, 1958
Height:	6'0"
Weight:	235
Real Name:	Bobby Lee Eaton
High School:	Lee High School (AL)
Wife:	Donna Eaton
Trained by:	Tojo Yamamoto
Identities:	Earl Robert Eaton
Finisher:	Alabama Jam (Flying Legdrop)
Groups:	The Dangerous Alliance (1991–92)
Tag Teams:	The Jet Set w/ George Gulas, Bad Attitude w/ Steve Keirn, The Blue Bloods w/ Lord Steven Regal
Career Span:	1976–2015

Titles Won:	43
Days as World Champion:	7
Age at first World Title Win:	22
Best Opponents:	Ric Flair, Billy Robinson, Jerry Lawler
Managers:	9
Halls of Fame:	1

Highly respected by wrestling fans and peers alike, "Beautiful" Bobby Eaton of Huntsville, Alabama was the backbone of two versions of the famed Midnight Express tag team. He originally teamed with Dennis Condrey under the guidance of Jim Cornette, and beat the Rock and Roll Express for the NWA World Tag Team Title in 1986. The second incarnation saw Eaton partnered with another talented heel, Stan Lane, and this duo won the vacant US Tag Team Title in a tournament. On September 10, 1988, while still holding the US Title, they beat Arn Anderson and Tully Blanchard to win the World Tag Team straps. As a singles competitor, Eaton held the CWA World Title in 1980 and won the Mid-America belt eleven times between 1979 and 1983. In 1991, he captured the WCW TV Title and had an impressive, high-profile televised match against NWA champion Ric Flair. Eaton's son Dylan became a pro wrestler in 2006 and the two teamed up on several occasions.

Edge

Born:	October 30, 1973
Height:	6'4"
Weight:	240
Real Name:	Adam Joseph Copeland
High School:	Orangeville District Secondary School (Ontario)
College:	Humber College
Trained by:	Sweet Daddy Siki, Ron Hutchison, Dory Funk Jr.
Identities:	Adam Impact, Sexton Hardcastle, Damon Stryker
Nickname:	Rated R Superstar
Finishers:	Edgecution, Downward Spiral, Spear
Tag Teams:	Sex and Violence w/ Joe Legend, Hard Impact w/ Christian, Suicide Blonds w/ Christian, Rated-RKO w/ Randy Orton
Groups:	Thug Life (1997), The Brood (1999), La Familia (2007–08)
Career Span:	1992–2011

Titles Won:	35
Days as World Champion:	548
Age at first World Title Win:	32
Best Opponents:	The Undertaker, John Cena, Chris Jericho
Managers:	4
Movies:	4
TV Appearances:	1
Halls of Fame:	1

Eight days after successfully turning back the top contender to his World Heavyweight Title at WrestleMania XXVII, Edge announced his retirement from pro wrestling on *Monday Night Raw* on April 11, 2011. The decision, made on the recommendation of his doctor, shocked fans everywhere and effectively ended his nineteen-year career at the age of thirty-seven. Since breaking out of the independents for the WWF in 1998, Edge has been a significant player, winning more than thirty championships, including eleven World Titles. His cunning personality and skillful ring work made him a headline performer, and the angles he worked and the feuds he engaged in were some of the most memorable in recent years. Destined to be a WWE superstar, Edge had dreams of wrestling in high school and pursued training at a Toronto-area camp.

He made his debut on the Canadian independent circuit and toiled away for the next six years before landing a full-time gig with the WWF. His childhood friend, Christian, also joined the promotion, and the two joined the Brood along with Gangrel in 1999.

The tag team made up of Edge and Christian was uniquely special, providing a high-flying and fast-paced style that matched well with two of the other dominant squads of the period: The Hardy Brothers and the Dudley Boys. They engaged in a "Tables, Ladders, and Chairs" contest against their two rivals at WrestleMania on April 2, 2000 in Anaheim and won the lively match to capture the WWF World Tag Team Title for the first time. Over the next year, Edge and his partner won the championship five more times, and captured their seventh tag team title at WrestleMania X-Seven in Houston, once again defeating the Hardys and Dudleys in a dangerous, but exciting TLC bout. The adjustment to singles competition was easy for Edge and he won the King of the Ring tournament in 2001, as well as feuding with his former partner, Christian. He captured the US Heavyweight Title from Kurt Angle, and unified it with the Intercontinental championship at the Survivor Series on November 18, 2001.

In 2002, he formed successful tag teams with Hulk Hogan and Rey Mysterio Jr., winning the WWE Tag Team Title with both partners, and a neck injury forced him from the ring in early 2003. At WrestleMania 21, he won the initial Money in the Bank match, guaranteeing him a future World Title shot. That contract was cashed in on January 8, 2006 in Albany following champion John Cena's successful title defense in an Elimination Chamber bout. Edge capitalized on Cena's condition, and scored the pinfall for his first WWE championship. He'd end up losing it back to Cena at the Royal Rumble, but would regain it later in the year from Rob Van Dam. In 2007, he won the World Heavyweight Title after cashing in his second Money in the Bank contract and beating The Undertaker. That time around, he had to vacate the title because of another injury. He formed an on-screen relationship with Vickie Guerrero, the *Smackdown* General Manager, and benefited from her influence over the brand.

Edge was a five-time World Heavyweight Champion by the end of April 2009, having won the belt from Batista, Undertaker, Jeff Hardy, and John Cena. His relationship with Guerrero finally soured, but a legitimate injury forced him out of action yet again during the middle of 2009. When he returned in January 2010, he came back with a vengeance, and won the Royal Rumble. It took him until December to win his sixth World Title in a TLC match over champion Kane, Alberto Del Rio, and Rey Mysterio. Guerrero stripped away his belt, but Edge regained it later in the same night from Guerrero's new cohort, Dolph Ziggler, capturing his record seventh World Title on February 15, 2011. He survived the Elimination Chamber, and then beat Del Rio at WrestleMania, all leading up to an unexpected announcement. Edge was suffering from spinal stenosis and, to prevent further injury, retired from the business as the reigning world champion. Edge was inducted into the WWE Hall of Fame in 2012, and made a number of appearances on WWE-TV in the years that followed. In 2016, his comedy program, *The Edge and Christian Show*, debuted on the WWE Network.

Born:	June 7, 1965
Height:	6'3"
Weight:	270–290
Real Name:	Michael Francis Foley
Parents:	John and Beverly Foley
Wife:	Colette Foley
High School:	Ward Melville High Scholl (NY)
College:	State University of New York College at Cortland
Identities:	Jack Foley, Jack Manson, Dude Love, Cactus Jack, Mankind
Finisher:	Double-arm DDT, Mandible Claw
Groups:	Sullivan's Slaughterhouse (1990), The Corporation (1999), EV 2.0 (2010)
Tag Team:	The Rock and Sock Connection w/ The Rock
Career Span:	1986–2015

Titles Won:	28
Days as World Champion:	110
Age at first World Title Win:	33
Best Opponents:	The Undertaker, The Rock, Shawn Michaels
Halls of Fame:	1
TV Appearances:	Over 25
Movies:	3
Published Books:	10
Halls of Fame:	2

Foley, Mick

Mick Foley took a unique route to becoming an international wrestling celebrity, a path that he forged through years of hard work. He overcame unfavorable odds, including promoters who didn't see the marketability in his ring persona, and set himself apart by always giving 100 percent of his body to a match. The reckless character that he turned into inside the ring never held back. His bumps were outrageously solid every time, and fans could see the legitimacy of his passion for the business. While other wrestlers have longevity on Foley, few could say that they gave as much as he did across the length of his career. Foley's matches were more like wrestling stunt shows with no regulator to limit the risks. He was a brawler on par with the "Hardcore Legend," Terry Funk, and adept to the psychological side of wrestling, getting feuds and angles over by talking on the microphone. Foley had a continued presence in TNA and the WWE in 2011, and his ability to sell major storylines is still very strong.

Trained by Dominic DeNucci, Foley wrestled in the USWA and WCW early in his career, and received his most significant push in 1992-1993 when he feuded with Ron Simmons, Sting, and Vader. During one Atlanta show in April 1993, Foley was powerbombed on the floor of the arena and knocked out, setting up a long-running amnesia skit that saw him wandering aimlessly around Cleveland, lost. The angle displayed more of his personality and exhibited another dimension of his character. His mystique grew further when he lost part of his right ear during a bout in Germany against Vader on March 16, 1994—but yet continued to wrestle. He appeared in ECW later that year, and electrified the not-so-easily impressed Philadelphia audience in battles with The Sandman and Terry Funk, and took his rivalry with Funk to Japan, where he met the "Funker" in the finals of the IWA King of the Death Match tournament. Foley won that wild exploding barbed-wire bout. In early 1996, he began a new phase in the WWF as "Mankind."

Entering into a lengthy war with The Undertaker, Foley gave forth a monumental effort during their June 28, 1998 Hell in a Cell match, and his actions defied believability. He took two huge falls from the top of the 16-foot cage, and continued to fight until being chokeslammed on tacks, and finally tombstoned. Foley's ungodly commitment to the sport was evident, and made him an enormous superstar. From there, he won the WWF World Heavyweight Title three times and released his autobiography, which not only became a *New York Times* bestseller, but revolutionized the wrestling book business. He stepped away from the mat in 2000, but returned often to perform roles in both the WWE, and later TNA. Throughout this time, he's penned two additional autobiographies, three children's books, and two novels. On April 19, 2009, he returned to the ring to beat Sting for the TNA World Title and was positioned as the "network consultant" in 2011, but left the promotion before the angle got off the ground. He soon rejoined the WWE, and wrestled a number of times during 2012. The following year, he was inducted into the WWE Hall of Fame. At WrestleMania 32 in 2016, he made a special appearance alongside fellow legends Steve Austin and Shawn Michaels.

Photo Courtesy of Pete Lederberg—plmathfoto@hotmail.com

Born:	July 19, 1958
Height:	5'11"
Weight:	225
Real Name:	Ruben Chalker Cain Jr.
Family:	Younger brother of Ricky Gibson
Trained by:	Ricky Gibson
Promoter:	Pro Wrestling Connection (Northport, AL)
Career Span:	1976–Present

Gibson, Robert

Titles Won:	47
Best Opponents:	Ric Flair, Paul Orndorff, Ricky Morton
Halls of Fame:	2

The dynamic Rock and Roll Express made up of Robert Gibson and Ricky Morton was an explosively popular tag team in the 1980s and remains so to this day. They captured the hearts of young wrestling fans that admired their quick moves and likeable personalities, and won the NWA World Tag Team Title seven times between 1985 and 2000. Gibson grew up in Pensacola, Florida, and learned the trade from his older brother, Ricky. On July 9, 1985, the Express won their very first NWA championship from Ivan Koloff and Krusher Khrushchev, and over the next six years, they had memorable feuds with the Midnight Express and Four Horsemen. While in the Smoky Mountain territory between 1992 and 1994, the pair won the tag team belts ten times, and later in the decade, made appearances in the WWF as part of an NWA "invasion." In South Korea, they won their seventh NWA Title on April 12, 2000 over Steven Dunn and Jackie Fulton. Gibson continues to wrestle, reforming the famous Express with Morton on occasion.

Gilbert, Eddie

Born:	August 14, 1961
Height:	5'10"
Weight:	220
Real Name:	Thomas Edward Gilbert Jr.
Parents:	Thomas and Peggy Gilbert
Family:	Grandson of Arlie Gilbert, brother of Doug Gilbert
High School:	Lexington High School (TN)
College:	Kennesaw State College
Nicknames:	Hot Shot, King Edward
Groups:	Hyatt and Hotstuff Incorporated (1986–87), The First Family (1989)
Tag Teams:	The Fabulous Ones w/ Tommy Rich
Managed:	Jerry Bryant (1985), Playboy Frazier (1985), Mike Sharpe (1985), Dutch Mantell (1985), The Nightmare (1985), Sting (1986), Rick Steiner (1987–88)
Career Span:	1979–95
Died:	February 18, 1995, San Juan, Puerto Rico 33 years old

Titles Won:	29
Days as World Champion:	137
Age at first World Title Win:	30
Best Opponents:	Jerry Lawler, Terry Funk, Tiger Mask
Managers:	13
Halls of Fame:	1

As a young man, Eddie Gilbert possessed the kind of brilliant wrestling mind only associated with well-traveled veterans. His innovative concepts were utilized throughout his career, giving promoters a charismatic wrestler in the ring and a superior asset behind the scenes. A third-generation grappler from Lexington, Tennessee, Gilbert entered the business as a seventeen-year-old prodigy, having studied under his father, Tommy, with the duo teaming together many times. In 1980, he formed a popular tandem with Ricky Morton, and in 1982, was a star on the rise in the WWF. He bounced back from a broken neck sustained in a car accident and had a good run in the Memphis territory. While in the UWF, he won the tag team title with Sting in 1986, and partnered with Rick Steiner to capture the NWA US straps three years later. Among his other accomplishments were winning the USWA World Title on four occasions and the GWF North American crown. Gilbert was an influential creative force in nearly every territory he worked in from 1986 until his unfortunate death in 1995.

Born:	December 27, 1966
Height:	6'2"
Weight:	285
Real Name:	William Scott Goldberg
Parents:	Jed and Ethel Goldberg
Wife:	Wanda Goldberg
High School:	Tulsa Edison High School (OK)
NFL Draft:	Los Angeles Rams (1990) (11th Round) (301)
Pro Sports:	World League—Sacramento Surge (1992) National Football League— Atlanta Falcons (1992–94) (14 games)
Career Span:	1997–2004
Website:	www.billgoldberg.com

Goldberg, Bill

Titles Won:	5
Days as World Champion:	258
Age at first World Title Win:	31
Best Opponents:	Hulk Hogan, Triple H, Brock Lesnar
TV Appearances:	Over 25
Movies:	12

In seven years, Bill Goldberg made a sincere impression on the world of pro wrestling. He ascended the ranks like a bolt of lightning, bringing an intensity and determination that was unmatched, and achieved World championships in both WCW and the WWE. His popularity during his undefeated streak, which lasted through 173 matches, was enormous, and considering he was basically just a rookie, was simply remarkable. Throngs of fans chanted "Goldberg" as he approached the ring, and his matches were usually very quick, ending with a tremendous spear and jackhammer that planted his foe squarely on his back for the pinfall. The power displayed by the ex-football player was immense, and his streak was one of the hottest things in the sport in 1997-98. Goldberg grew up in Tulsa, the youngest of four siblings, and attended the

University of Georgia, where he shone on the football field as a defensive tackle. He logged 121 tackles his senior year and was drafted by the Los Angeles Rams in 1990 as the 301st pick (11th round).

An injury during preseason temporarily halted his football career, and the Rams cut him. But Goldberg rebounded to play in the World League, and then three seasons with the Atlanta Falcons. In 1997, he entered the WCW Power Plant, and made his debut in July of that year. He rapidly gained a following, as fans were fascinated by his enthusiasm and invincibility. Week after week, he demolished opponents with a certain ease, and as his unbeaten streak grew, as did his popularity. Before long, he was receiving the loudest reaction of anyone on the WCW roster. There was no denying it—Goldberg was a phenomenon. He won the US crown in April 1998, and a few months later, on July 6 at the Georgia Dome in Atlanta, he beat Hollywood Hogan for the World Heavyweight Title before more than 39,000 fans. His famous streak came to an odd end at Starrcade 1998 in a controversial match against Kevin Nash that saw a taser play a part in the finish. Missing months due to injury, he returned in late 1999, feuding with Bret Hart.

The remainder of Goldberg's stay in WCW was turbulent to say the least, and included a brief stint as a heel. His final showing came on January 14, 2001 in a tag team match with Dwayne Bruce against Lex Luger and Buff Bagwell. The stipulation was if Goldberg's team lost, he'd be forced to retire. They indeed were defeated, and he never returned to WCW. In March 2003, he entered the WWE and debuted the night after WrestleMania XIX. He made his mark by spearing the Rock on *Raw*. On August 24, 2003, he nearly won the World Title from Triple H in an Elimination Chamber bout, and finally succeeded in doing so at Unforgiven on September 21. He remained the World Champion until December 14, 2003, when he lost the title back to Triple H in a three-way contest that also involved Kane. Goldberg won his final match against Brock Lesnar at WrestleMania XX and retired from the business. He has since acted as a commentator for MMA programs and appeared in several films. In 2010, he was featured on *Celebrity Apprentice*.

Born:	October 20, 1970
Height:	5'10"
Weight:	220
Real Name:	Salvador Guerrero IV
Trained by:	Chavo Guerrero
Identities:	Lieutenant Loco, Kerwin White
Finisher:	Tornado DDT, Frog splash
Tag Team:	Los Guerreros w/ Eddy Guerrero
Career Span:	1994–Present

Titles Won:	11
Days as World Champion:	68
Age at first World Title Win:	37
Best Opponents:	Eddie Guerrero, Rey Mysterio Jr., Chris Benoit

Guerrero, Chavo Jr.

Talented third-generation wrestler, Chavo Guerrero Jr. is the son of Chavo Sr. and the grandson of Gory Guerrero. He started out in Mexico and Japan, finally gaining traction in WCW, winning the World Cruiserweight championship twice. For awhile, he carried around a toy horse, known as "Pepe," and regularly got on the nerves of his uncle, Eddie Guerrero. The Guerreros formed a winning tag team in the WWE, capturing the Tag Team Title twice in 2002-2003, and Chavo added four WWE Cruiserweight Titles to his resume. On January 22, 2008, he beat CM Punk for the ECW World Heavyweight Title, but lost it two months later at WrestleMania to Kane. Chavo departed from the WWE in June 2011 and went to Puerto Rico, where he soon won the WWC Caribbean Title. Guerrero emerged in TNA, where he formed a partnership with Hernandez and won the TNA World Tag Team Championship on two occasions. In 2014, he entered the new Lucha Underground organization and held the Gift of the Gods championship briefly in January 2016.

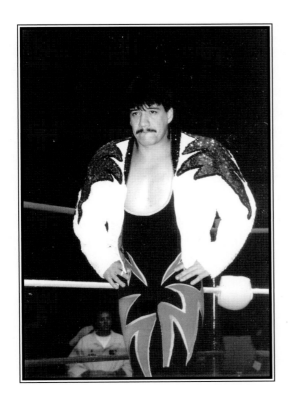

Born:	October 9, 1967
Height:	5'8"
Weight:	220
Real Name:	Eduardo Gory Guerrero
Wife:	Vickie Guerrero
High School:	Jefferson High School (TX)
Identities:	Magic Mask, Black Tiger, Eddie Guerrero
Nickname:	Latino Heat
Groups:	Los Gringos Locos (1994), Latino World Order (1998), The Filthy Animals (1999–2001), The Radicals (2000)
Tag Team:	Los Guerreros w/ Chavo Guerrero Jr.
Career Span:	1987–2005
Died:	November 13, 2005, Minneapolis, MN 38 years old

Guerrero, Eddie

Titles Won:	21
Days as World Champion:	133
Age at first World Title Win:	36
Best Opponents:	Dean Malenko, Rey Mysterio Jr., Chris Benoit
Halls of Fame:	3

The entertaining personality of Eddie Guerrero was a shining spot in wrestling, and he could always be counted on for an excellent match or amusing promo. His well-rounded abilities set him apart from his peers and his sudden 2005 death shocked the industry. There was no replacing a guy like Guerrero, who was finally hitting his stride in the WWE and getting his due in main events after years of hard work. The mainstream wrestling public had only been aware of his outstanding wrestling since 1995 when he debuted for WCW and made regular appearances on *Nitro*. Prior to that, however, he'd displayed the same heightened level of performance in Mexico, Japan, and ECW. The youngest son of wrestling superstar Gory Guerrero, Eddie grew up surrounded by wrestling in El Paso. Not only did his father wrestle and promote matches, but his three brothers, Chavo, Mando, and Hector, also entered the profession. Eddie was nineteen years younger than his oldest sibling, Chavo, and was heavily influenced by seeing his family perform.

His turn on the mat came in 1987 when he became a pro, and Guerrero spent his earliest years working in Mexico and Japan. In 1995, he was a fixture in the Philadelphia-based ECW promotion, and his unbelievable string of matches with Dean Malenko were among the best in the business at the time. He entered WCW and beat Dallas Page in a tournament final for the vacant US Title on December

29, 1996. Guerrero also held the Cruiserweight title, but never broke through to the top level of the promotion's hierarchy—and WCW politics were to blame. In one emotional *Nitro* segment, he claimed Eric Bischoff was holding him back, and many people were left to wonder how much of the speech was true. After suffering serious injuries in a car accident, Guerrero ended up leaving WCW for the WWF in January 2000 and took a commanding share of the spotlight upon arrival. He'd have stints as Intercontinental and European champion, and held the WWE Tag Team Title with nephew Chavo Guerrero Jr. and Tajiri.

Guerrero won the US Title in the finals of a tournament on July 27, 2003, defeating Chris Benoit, and was champion until October. The biggest win of his career came on February 15, 2004 in San Francisco, when he pinned Brock Lesnar for the WWE Heavyweight Title after landing his patented frog splash. A month later at WrestleMania XX in New York City, he retained his belt over Kurt Angle in a memorable twenty-one-minute contest. Guerrero held back the challenge of John "Bradshaw" Layfield until losing the championship to him in a Texas Bullrope match on June 27, 2004 at the Great American Bash. A regular on *Smackdown*, Guerrero teamed with Rey Mysterio to win the WWE Tag Team Title from the Bashams in February 2005, and then engaged in a personal war with Mysterio, even claiming to be the father of Rey's son. After several classic TV matches, Mysterio beat him for custody on August 21, 2005 at SummerSlam. The eternally charismatic Guerrero passed away in a Minneapolis hotel room on November 13, 2005.

Photo Courtesy of the Wrestling Revue Archives—
www.wrestleprints.com

Haku

Born:	February 10, 1959
Height:	6'1"
Weight:	295
Real Name:	Tonga Uliuli Fifita
Parents:	Kelepi and Atiola Fifita
Wife:	Dorothy Fifita
Trained by:	Shohei Baba, Genichiro Tenryu
Identities:	Prince Tonga, King Tonga, Meng
Finisher:	Savate Kick, Tongan Death Grip
Tag Team:	The Islanders w/ Tomah, The Colossal Connection w/ Andre the Giant, The Faces of Fear w/ The Barbarian
Career Span:	1978–Present
Titles Won:	20
Best Opponents:	Dino Bravo, Hulk Hogan, Sting

The formidable Haku is not the kind of guy you wanted to run into in an alley on a dark evening. Luckily for anyone who actually met him, Haku is a nice, quiet, family man currently living in Florida. With that said, he's been more than successful in convincing the wrestling public that he's the opposite—a monster heel looking to demolish his rivals with his brute strength. The former Sumo wrestler from the Island of Tonga learned the profession while in Japan in the late 1970s, and traveled the globe honing his craft. He was given the title of WWF "King" after Harley Race was injured in 1988, and teamed with Andre the Giant to win the promotion's World Tag Team Title in late 1989. While in WCW, he was pushed as an unstoppable force and made it to the finals of the US title tournament in 1995, but eventually lost to Sting. He held the WLW Title twice in 2000 and the WCW Hardcore belt in January 2001. Every now and then, Haku still appears on the indie circuit.

Hall, Scott

Photo Courtesy of Dr. Mike Lano—Wrealano@aol.com

Born:	October 20, 1958
Height:	6'6"
Weight:	285
Real Name:	Scott Oliver Hall
High School:	American High School (Munich, Germany)
College:	St. Mary's College
Trained by:	Hiro Matsuda, Barry Windham
Identities:	Starship Coyote, Diamond Studd
Nicknames:	Magnum
Finisher:	Diamond Death Drop, The Razor's Edge
Groups:	New World Order (1996–99, 2002)
Tag Teams:	The American Starship w/ Eagle (Dan Spivey), The Outsiders w/ Kevin Nash
Career Span:	1984–Present
Titles Won:	19

Days as World Champion:	28
Age at first World Title Win:	36
Best Opponents:	Shawn Michaels, Bret Hart, Steve Austin
Halls of Fame:	1

Impressively built and full of charisma, Scott Hall performed in many entertaining contests during the 1990s. His ladder match against Shawn Michaels at WrestleMania X set the standard for all ladder matches to be compared, and had a significant role in the New World Order angle in WCW. In recent years, his life has been plagued by personal trials and tribulations that have kept him from a major role in pro wrestling and gotten him headlines for more dire reasons. Hall's contributions to the sport are considerable, and it is easy to remember him with his toothpick, parading around the squared circle as the Miami "Bad Guy," Razor Ramon. The son of a military father, Hall lived in many places when he was young, including Germany, Florida, and southern Maryland. He received his training in Tampa and entered the business, attaining his earliest fame in the AWA when he teamed with Curt Hennig to win the World Tag Team Title in 1986. He bounced around the business, working for WCW in 1991, and then was hired by the WWF.

As "Razor Ramon," Hall received a nice push, winning the vacant Intercontinental Title on September 27, 1993. On March 20, 1994, he beat Shawn Michaels to unify the latter's claim with his own, in a spectacular ladder match at WrestleMania. In 1995, he became the first three-time Intercontinental Champion, and followed up by winning his fourth in October over Dean Douglas. He left the WWF for WCW in 1996, initiating the NWO angle with his May 27, 1996 appearance on *Nitro*. A short time later, he was joined by his friend Kevin Nash and Hollywood Hogan, and the NWO turned the promotion on its head. Hall and Nash captured the WCW Tag Team Title five times between 1996 and 1999, and in 1997, he eliminated The Giant to win the World War III event. Hall briefly wrestled for the WWF again in 2002 and later worked for TNA, teaming with Nash to wear the World Tag Team Title in 2010. He often appears for various independent promotions. In 2014, he was inducted into the WWE Hall of Fame.

Photo Courtesy of Bill Stahl

Born:	August 31, 1977
Height:	6'0"
Weight:	210
Real Name:	Jeffrey Nero Hardy
Parents:	Claude and Ruby Hardy
High School:	Union Pines High School (NC)
Identities:	Willow the Whisp, The Willow, Wolverine, Conquistador I
Nickname:	Charismatic Enigma
Finisher:	Swanton Bomb
Groups:	Team Xtreme (2000–02), Immortal (2010–11)
Career Span:	1993–Present

Hardy, Jeff

Titles Won:	31
Days as World Champion:	172
Age at first World Title Win:	31
Best Opponents:	The Undertaker, Rob Van Dam, CM Punk

Jeff Hardy brings many things to a wrestling match, including impressive ring savvy and mind-blowing high spots. His athleticism ranks among the best in the grappling world, and has carried him to main event status. Through his dedication to the business, magnetic personality, and unique appearance, he's acquired a legion of steady followers. His popularity has made it easy for the WWE and TNA to push him to the top level of their promotions, and Hardy has captured five heavyweight championships in those two organizations since 2008. The son of a tobacco farmer, Hardy grew up in the small town of Cameron, North Carolina, and was a fan of pro wrestling at a young age. Along with his older brother, Matt, he constructed a makeshift wrestling environment in their backyard, which included a trampoline, and practiced acrobatic moves incessantly. He was just sixteen years of age when he received his first preliminary match for the WWF in May 1994, but it would be four years before he received a full-time contract.

The brothers received further training in Florida by the legendary Dory Funk Jr., and then came onto the WWF scene, albeit their push was slow at first. When it was time for them to shine, they did, particularly in big matches at WrestleMania that featured tables, ladders, and chairs. The TLC matches were spectacular displays of risky maneuvers that continuously set the bar higher and higher. There were no limits to what Jeff would do in the ring, above it from atop a tall ladder, or diving to the arena floor. The Hardys had a lot of success in tag team matches, winning a combined seven championships, and feuded heavily with Christian and Edge and the Dudleys. In 2001, as a singles performer, Hardy won the Intercontinental and Hardcore Titles, and was involved in a number of different angles before his sudden departure in 2003. During the middle of 2004, he resurfaced in TNA and challenged Jeff Jarrett for the NWA World Title.

Hardy made his way back to the WWE in 2006 and captured the Intercontinental Title three additional times. On December 14, 2008, he won a three-way match to win Edge's WWE Title, but lost it back to the latter at the Royal Rumble after his brother Matt interfered on behalf of his opponent. That led to a sibling rivalry, in which both brothers scored victories. Jeff beat Edge on June 7, 2009 for the World Title, but was the victim of CM Punk cashing in his Money in the Bank contract, and immediately lost the belt. The next month, Hardy regained the title, but Punk won it back at SummerSlam. He rejoined TNA in January 2010 and won the vacant World Title at Bound for Glory with help from Hulk Hogan and Eric Bischoff. As the heel, he'd trade the title with Mr. Anderson before fading from the active roster after a controversial appearance at Victory Road in March 2011, in which his main event match against Sting lasted less than two minutes. Hardy returned to TNA in August, and sought forgiveness for his actions from his peers and the fans.

The fans did forgive him. Hardy won his third TNA World Heavyweight Title with a defeat of Austin Aries on October 14, 2012. He held the championship into March 2013, but lost the belt in a cage match against Bully Ray. The Hardy Brothers reformed their famous tag team and won the TNA World Tag straps in March 2015, but vacated the belts two months later after Jeff suffered a broken leg. Jeff needed months to recover and returned to TNA in early 2016.

Born:	September 23, 1974
Height:	6'1"
Weight:	235
Real Name:	Matthew Moore Hardy
Parents:	Claude and Ruby Hardy
High School:	Union Pines High School (NC)
Trained by:	Dory Funk Jr.
Identities:	Surge, Conquistador II
Finisher:	Twist of Fate
Groups:	Team Xtreme (2000-02)
Career Span:	1992–Present

Titles Won:	21
Days as World Champion:	127
Age at first World Title Win:	33
Best Opponents:	Edge, The Undertaker, Booker T
TV Appearances:	9

Hardy, Matt

An exciting grappler from Cameron, North Carolina, Matt Hardy teamed with his brother Jeff to form one of the most spectacular tag teams of this generation. The Hardys have come a long way since their days training on a backyard trampoline when they were kids, ascending up to the main stages of pro wrestling. They've defied the odds in the ring, leaping from turnbuckles and ladders, and constantly putting their bodies on the line. Together, they won the WWE World Tag Team Title six times and the WCW Tag Team belts once. After the Hardys went their own ways, Matt demonstrated that he was not to be pigeonholed as strictly a mid-card tag team worker, and stood out when he used the "Matt Hardy: Version 1.0" gimmick in 2002. He held both the US and ECW World Titles, prevailing in a championship scramble bout in 2008 for the latter title and holding the belt for several months. In 2011, he debuted in TNA as a heel member of Immortal. Of his time in TNA, Matt enjoyed his greatest singles achievement when he won a three-way bout for the World Heavyweight Title in October 2015. The championship was vacated within days, but Hardy beat Ethan Carter III for his second TNA title on January 8, 2016. Hardy lost it for the final time in mid-March 2016, when Drew Galloway scored a victory. Along with Jeff, Matt also held the TNA World Tag Team belts in 2015.

Hart, Bret

Born:	July 2, 1957
Height:	5'11"
Weight:	235
Real Name:	Bret Sergeant Hart
Parents:	Stu and Helen Hart
Family:	Brother of Bruce, Dean, Keith, Owen, Ross, Smith, and Wayne Hart, brother-in-law of Davey Boy Smith and Jim Neidhart
High School:	Ernest Manning High School (Calgary)
College:	Mount Royal College
Nicknames:	The Hitman
Finisher:	Sharpshooter
Groups:	The Hart Foundation (1997-98), New World Order (1998), NWO 2000 (1999–2000)
Career Span:	1978-2011
Website:	www.brethart.com

Titles Won:	32
Days as World Champion:	710
Age at first World Title Win:	35
Best Opponents:	Steve Austin, Shawn Michaels, Owen Hart
Halls of Fame:	5
TV Appearances:	Over 20
Documentaries:	7
Published Books:	1

The "Excellence of Execution," Bret Hart was a preeminent superstar, one of the greatest Canadian wrestlers in history, and enormously popular throughout the world. Born into the business as the son of Stu Hart, Bret learned how to grapple in the basement of the Hart family home, known as the "Dungeon." The painstaking lessons he endured fostered a deep respect for the business and a laundry list of admirable qualities that he carried with him throughout his entire career. He broke free from a reputation as being strictly a tag team wrestler through hard work and consistently delivered first-class performances on the mat. The WWF recognized that he was ready for a substantial singles push, and Hart was capable of matching up against anyone in the promotion. Between 1991 and 1997, he was the backbone of the WWF, and won five World Titles, defining what it meant to be a traditional champion in a new era of wrestling shenanigans. Hart's smooth, calculating maneuvers set the standard very high for others to emulate.

The education Hart received from his father made his progression into the sport easy, and he stood out as an amateur in high school and college, even winning a Calgary city championship in 1974. Four years later, he made his pro debut, and was heavily influenced by wrestlers Mr. Hiro and Mr. Sakurada. He toured Puerto Rico, Amarillo, and Georgia in his first two years in the pro ranks, and feuded with the likes of Norman Frederick Charles III, Marty Jones, and Dynamite Kid in Calgary. He also teamed with brothers Keith and Bruce. From 1980 to 1982, he won the regional North American Title five times and had some grueling bouts with Leo Burke and Bad News Allen. Hart participated in a WWF Junior Title tournament for New Japan Pro Wrestling in early 1984 and teamed with Hulk Hogan on a few occasions. His explicit knowledge of technical wrestling drew the attention from WWF officials.

During the summer of 1984, Hart made his WWF debut and worked steadily as a preliminary grappler, often using a sleeperhold as a finisher. His role in the promotion was mainly undefined until becoming part of a heel tag team with Jim Neidhart known as the Hart Foundation, managed by Jimmy Hart in March 1985. This was the central position he'd play for the next six years, although his talents would shine in the occasional one-on-one match. The Hart Foundation won the WWF Tag Team Title twice, the first in 1987 from the British Bulldogs, and the second in 1990 from Demolition. Hart went out on his own in 1991 and took the WWF by storm. He had two reigns as Intercontinental champion and wrestled a dynamic match against his brother-in-law Davey Boy Smith at SummerSlam in London on August 29, 1992 in which the latter captured the championship before 80,000 fans. Two months later, Hart dethroned Ric Flair for his first WWF World Title, and was champion until a loss to Yokozuna at WrestleMania IX.

On March 20, 1994, Hart beat Yokozuna for his second WWF championship, and participated in some of the most talked-about matches of the year against his brother, Owen. He'd lose the belt to Bob Backlund in November, but would regain it a year later from Diesel. At WrestleMania XII, he lost the title to Shawn Michaels in sudden death of an Iron Man match. Hart violently feuded with Steve Austin, and their explosive WrestleMania 13 submission match ended when "Stone Cold" passed out while in the sharpshooter. Hart's actions during the match drew the ire of fans, which led to his condemnation of US audiences, effectively turning him heel—but maintaining his popularity north of the border. He reformed the pro-Canada Hart Foundation and, on August 3, 1997, beat The Undertaker for his fifth and final WWF Title. With his future in the promotion in doubt, Hart and Vince McMahon haggled over a match that would see Bret lose the belt to Michaels on November 9, 1997 at the Survivor Series in Montreal.

However, Hart didn't want to lose the belt in Canada, and went into the match believing that he'd drop the title on a later date. McMahon didn't want Hart appearing on WCW TV with the WWF belt, and had the referee call for the bell seconds after Michaels applied a sharpshooter. This event became known as the infamous "Montreal Screwjob." Hart departed the WWF for WCW, and over the next three years won the World Title twice, the US crown four times, and had memorable matches against Chris Benoit and Dallas Page. A concussion received during a match forced him into semi-retirement in January 2000. Two years later, Hart suffered a stroke after a bicycle accident and displayed an inspiring amount of courage in the recovery process. He made his WWE return as a wrestler in 2010, battling McMahon at WrestleMania XXVI, and beat The Miz for the US Title. Hart dedicated his life to the business, understood the art of pro wrestling, and was a tremendous credit to the sport.

Hart, Owen

Born:	May 7, 1965
Height:	5'10"
Weight:	225
Real Name:	Owen James Hart
Family:	Brother of Bret, Bruce, Dean, Keith, Ross, Smith, and Wayne Hart, brother-in-law of Davey Boy Smith and Jim Neidhart
High School:	Ernest Manning High School (Calgary)
College:	University of Calgary
Trained by:	Stu Hart
Identities:	The Avenger
Nicknames:	The Rocket
Groups:	The Hart Foundation (1997–98), The Nation of Domination (1998)
Tag Teams:	High Energy w/ Koko B. Ware, The New Foundation w/ Jim Neidhart
Career Span:	1986–99
Died:	May 23, 1999, Kansas City, MO 34 years old

Titles Won:	13
Days as World Champion:	14
Age at first World Title Win:	28
Best Opponents:	Bret Hart, Shawn Michaels, Davey Boy Smith
Halls of Fame:	1

The youngest child of Stu and Helen Hart, Owen was an undeniable wrestling talent, able to match holds on the mat or scale the top rope and fly through the air. His repertoire of maneuvers was endless, and during his time in the industry, he played many roles. Unfortunately, there was one role in particular, a revisited gimmick from the past with a non-wrestling related stunt for an entrance, which ultimately cost him his life. Initially wanting to become a physical education teacher, Hart followed his brothers into the sport, in the footsteps of his father, Stu, and was a hot prospect in the latter's Calgary promotion. He displayed advanced skills for someone so young, and annexed regional gold. In 1988, he went to Japan and did the same, pinning Hiroshi Hase in Sendai for the IWGP Junior Heavyweight Title. Owen also debuted for the WWF as the masked "Blue Blazer," which was a tough character to sell to the audience.

It really wasn't until he turned on his brother Bret and became a heel in 1994 that his stock in the WWF really began to rise. At WrestleMania X, Owen pinned his sibling and became a top contender for the World Title. A few months later, he won the King of the Ring tournament, and declared himself the "King of Harts." He received a title shot against Bret at SummerSlam and the two wrestled a thirty-three-minute classic with Bret retaining the belt. In 1995, he teamed with the massive Yokozuna to capture the WWF Tag Team Title and won the belts again with Davey Boy Smith (also known as the British Bulldog, and Owen's brother-in-law) the following year. Hart became a double-champion on April 28, 1997, when he beat Rocky Maivia Jr. for the Intercontinental Title. On May 23, 1999, Owen was booked in a match against The Godfather at Kansas City's Kemper Arena, and was going to make an elaborate entrance via the rafters above the ring. When his harness failed to hold him, he fell more than 70-feet to the ring below, and was fatally injured. His death left a hole in the industry that still hasn't healed.

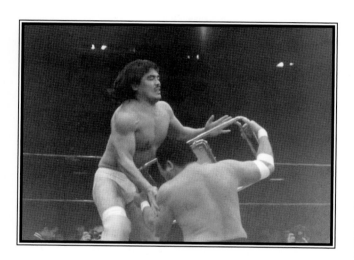

Photo Courtesy of Dr. Mike Lano—Wrealano@aol.com

Hase, Hiroshi

Born:	May 5, 1961
Height:	6'0"
Weight:	225
College:	Senshu University
Olympics:	Greco-Roman Wrestling (1984) (Representing Japan) (9th Place)
Amateur Titles:	Two-Time World Freestyle Wrestling Champion
Trained by:	Riki Choshu, Stu Hart
Finisher:	Northern Lights Suplex
Tag Team:	The Viet Cong Express w/ Fumihiro Niikura
Career Span:	1986–2006

Titles Won:	8
Days as World Champion:	8
Age at first World Title Win:	32
Best Opponents:	Tatsumi Fujinami, Kenta Kobashi, Keiji Mutoh
Halls of Fame:	2

Olympian Hiroshi Hase was well-respected throughout the world for his technical abilities and has been a politician in Japan for the last sixteen years. With his stellar amateur background, his future was bright as he entered the business in 1986 and excelled as expected. He won the IWGP Junior Heavyweight Title twice, and then formed a successful tag team with Kensuke Sasaki. On November 1, 1990, they won the IWGP Tag

Team Title from Keiji Mutoh and Masa Chono. The duo lost the belts in December of that year to Hiro Saito and Super Strong Machine, but regained it from them in March 1991. Hase and Sakaki went head to head with the WCW champion Steiner Brothers on March 21 and lost the IWGP straps. Hase also won the IWGP belts with Mutoh as his partner on two occasions; as well as beating Rick Rude on March 16, 1994 to win the WCW International World Title, with Rude regaining the title eight days later. In 1995, he was elected to the Japanese House of Councilors, and from 2007 to 2013, served as the chairman of the PWF. Hase was named to the cabinet of the Japanese Prime Minister in 2015.

Photo Courtesy of Dr. Mike Lano—Wrealano@aol.com

Born:	July 3, 1965
Height:	6'0"
Weight:	290
Family:	Father of Daichi Hashimoto
Identities:	Hashif Khan, Shogun
Finisher:	Jumping DDT
Promoted:	Zero-One (2001–05)
Career Span:	1984–2004
Died:	July 11, 2005, Yokohama, Japan 40 years old

Hashimoto, Shinya

Titles Won:	11
Days as World Champion:	1,307
Age at first World Title Win:	28
Best Opponents:	Keiji Mutoh, Tatsumi Fujinami, Masa Chono
Halls of Fame:	3

On July 11, 2005, pro wrestling lost a genuine legend in Shinya Hashimoto, who died at forty-five years of age. The exciting ring warrior had thrilled fans across the globe since his debut in 1984 and accumulated a spectacular list of achievements. Hashimoto was much more dedicated than the average grappler; fine-tuning his skills early in his career under the guidance of the great Antonio Inoki. He then toured the US and Canada, where he picked up additional knowledge from Stu Hart and Brad Rheingans, two of the best teachers in the sport. It's no coincidence that Hashimoto was a great wrestler as he had put in the time learning the trade, both the fundamentals and the electrifying maneuvers that would make him popular with crowds. He won the IWGP Heavyweight Title on three occasions between 1993 and 1997, and on October 13, 2001, he captured the NWA World Championship. Two years later, he became the fourth man in history to win both the IWGP and Triple Crown Titles when he beat Keiji Mutoh for the latter.

Born:	January 26, 1958
Height:	6'3"
Weight:	277
Real Name:	Michael James Hegstrand
Parents:	Arthur and Margaret Hegstrand
Wife:	Dale Hegstrand
High School:	Patrick Henry High School (MN)
Trained by:	Eddie Sharkey
Identities:	Hawk Warrior
Finisher:	Doomsday Device w/ Animal
Groups:	LOD 2000 (1998)
Tag Teams:	The Hell Raisers w/ The Power Warrior
Career Span:	1983–2003
Died:	October 19, 2003, Indian Rocks Beach, FL 45 years old

Hawk

Titles Won:	22
Days as World Champion:	196
Age at first World Title Win:	34
Best Opponents:	Ric Flair, Keiji Mutoh, Masa Chono
Halls of Fame:	5

The international tag team scene was reinvigorated by The Road Warriors, made up of two friends from the Minneapolis area who were known to fans as Hawk and Animal. With spiked shoulder pads, intimidating haircuts and face paint, the duo actually appeared like warriors. Hawk grew up on the north side of Minneapolis, played football in high school, and was a devoted weightlifter. Along with Animal, he trained to be a grappler, and then proceeded to Georgia, where he joined Paul Ellering's Legion of Dome in 1983. During the summer of 1984, Hawk and Animal won the AWA World Tag Team Title and held the belts for over a year. They had a similar run in Japan with the AJPW International Tag Team Title as well. On October 29, 1988, they beat The Midnight Express for the NWA World Tag Team Title and in August 1991, they became the first team to hold the AWA, NWA, and WWF belts when they toppled The Nasty Boys at SummerSlam. Hawk also teamed with Kensuke Sasaki to capture the IWGP Title twice and held the CWA World Title in 1992.

Born:	March 29, 1959
Height:	6'1"
Weight:	240
Real Name:	Michael Joseph Seitz
Trained by:	Afa
Identities:	Doc Hendrix
Nickname:	Pretty Boy, P.S. (Purely Sexy)
Finisher:	DDT
Music:	Lead vocalist on the album *Off the Streets*, including the song "Badstreet USA."
Career Span:	1977–2001

Titles Won:	25
Best Opponents:	Bruiser Brody, Kerry Von Erich, Rick Martel
Halls of Fame:	2

Hayes, Michael

Wrestler and rock musician, Michael Hayes of Pensacola, Florida, entered the wrestling profession when he was still a teenager, gaining experience along the Mississippi circuit and early on in Germany. In late 1978, he bonded with another young athlete, Terry Gordy, and the two formed the basis for what would become the renowned Fabulous Freebirds. They garnered initial accolades while in the Mid-America territory and had many tough matches, among such legends as Jerry Lawler and Bill Dundee. While in the Mid-South territory in 1980, the duo added a third member, Buddy Roberts. In December 1982, in Dallas, the fabled Freebirds-Von Erich feud commenced and lasted years. Later in the decade, Hayes turned fan favorite and won the US belt from Lex Luger. He also reformed the Freebirds with Jimmy Garvin and captured the World Tag Team Title in 1989 and again in 1991. He remained in WCW until 1993, then joining the WWF as a commentator. His backstage duties increased until he was head of the creative team for *Smackdown* in 2006.

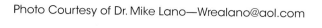

Born:	July 12, 1974
Height:	5'10"
Weight:	195
Real Name:	Gregory Shane Helms
High School:	East Wake High School (NC)
Trained by:	Hardy Boys, WCW Power Plant
Nicknames:	The Show, Serial Thriller, Sugar
Finisher:	Chokeslam
Career Span:	1991–Present

Titles Won:	20
Best Opponents:	The Rock, Rey Mysterio Jr., Ric Flair

Helms, Gregory

Under a mask as the wrestling superhero "The Hurricane," Shane Helms earned widespread popularity. His sound ring work balanced out his character, and he was involved in many comical skits and entertaining matches. Hailing from Smithfield, North Carolina, he broke into regional independents as a teenager and got his first big break as a member of 3-Count in WCW. Days before the promotion folded, he won the Cruiserweight Championship, and took the belt with him to the WWF. He reigned as titleholder two additional times, including a reign that lasted more than a year, as well as teaming with Kane and Rosey to win the World Tag Team Title. He left the WWE in 2010 and rejoined the indie circuit where he first got his start. In 2015, he joined TNA and currently works in a backstage role.

Hennig, Curt

Born:	March 28, 1958
Height:	6'2"
Weight:	235
Real Name:	Curtis Michael Hennig
Parents:	Lawrence and Irene Hennig
Family:	Father of Michael McGillicutty and Amy Hennig
Wife:	Leonice Hennig
High Schools:	Robbinsdale High School (MN), Saguaro High School (AZ)
Colleges:	Normandale Community College, University of Minnesota
Trained by:	Verne Gagne, Larry Hennig
Groups:	The Four Horsemen (1997), New World Order (1997–98)
Career Span:	1981–2003
Died:	February 10, 2003, Brandon, FL 44 years old

Titles Won:	15
Days as World Champion:	373
Age at first World Title Win:	29
Best Opponents:	Bret Hart, Ric Flair, Nick Bockwinkel
Halls of Fame:	3

A profoundly scientific wrestler, Curt Hennig was admired by peers and fans alike for his adroit mat techniques. He was a first-rate grappler, gifted in the fundamentals and owning the right kind of mannerisms to get a crowd going. The son of Larry Hennig, Curt was destined for ring greatness, and since he grew up in the Minneapolis area, it was only fitting that he'd first become a superstar in the AWA, and on May 2, 1987, he defeated Nick Bockwinkel for the AWA World Championship. He held the title for a year and a week, until losing it to Jerry Lawler on May 9, 1988. In the WWF, he became known as "Mr. Perfect," a gimmick that he performed flawlessly, and beat Tito Santana for the first of two Intercontinental Titles on April 23, 1990. A back injury slowed his career, but he had a respectable run in WCW, where he won the US and World Tag Team Titles with Barry Windham. He also had a string of success while wrestling on the indie circuit. Hennig had a second stint in the WWF and a run in TNA before his premature death in 2003.

Henry, Mark

Born:	June 12, 1971
Height:	6'3"
Weight:	375
Real Name:	Mark Jerrold Henry
Parents:	Ernest and Barbara Henry
High School:	Silsbee High School (TX)
Olympics:	Weightlifting (1992—Barcelona) (10th Place) Weightlifting (1996—Atlanta) (14th Place)
Trained by:	Stu Hart
Nicknames:	World's Strongest Man, Sexual Chocolate
Finisher:	Powerslam
Groups:	Nation of Domination (1998)
Career Span:	1996–Present

Titles Won:	3
Days as World Champion:	161
Age at first World Title Win:	37
Best Opponents:	Randy Orton, Big Show, The Undertaker
Halls of Fame:	3
Moves:	1

Prematurely born, Mark Henry grew to immense proportions, weighing 340 pounds while in high school. When he joined the US weightlifting team, he was literally the biggest thing to hit the sport in decades. By nineteen years of age, he was considered a world-class lifter, and coaches marveled at his natural ability. Henry was more than just a mass of muscle; he was coordinated, flexible, and supremely athletic, able to slam dunk a basketball and capable of doing a split. He underachieved at the 1992 and 1996 Olympics, but took three medals—including a gold in the snatch event—at the 1995 Pan American Games. Signed to a ten-year contract by the WWF in 1996, Henry joined the Nation of Domination and participated in an odd angle with Mae Young, which saw the latter give birth to a hand. Winner of the 2002 Arnold Strongman Competition, Henry beat Kane for the ECW Title in June 2008, and instituted his own "Hall of Pain" in 2011 en route to winning the World Heavyweight Title from Randy Orton at the September pay-per-view. He lost the championship three months later to The Big Show at TLC in Baltimore. In 2012, he was inducted into the International Sports Hall of Fame.

Hogan, Hulk

Born:	August 11, 1953
Height:	6'7"
Weight:	302
Real Name:	Terry Gene Bollea
Parents:	Peter and Ruth Bollea
Family:	Uncle of Horace Boulder
Wife:	Jennifer Bollea
High School:	Robinson High School (FL)
Colleges:	St. Petersburg Junior College, University of South Florida
Identities:	The Super Destroyer (Masked), Terry Boulder, Sterling Golden
Nicknames:	The Hulk, The Hulkster, Immortal
Finisher:	Big foot leading into the legdrop
Tag Teams:	The Mega Powers w/ Randy Savage, The Mega Maniacs w/ Brutus Beefcake, The Monster Maniacs w/ Randy Savage
Groups:	New World Order (1996–99) (2002), The Millionaires Club (2000), Immortal (2010–11)
Managed by:	Billy Spears, Fred Blassie, Johnny Valiant, Elizabeth, Jimmy Hart
Career Span:	1977–2012
Website:	www.hulkhogan.com

Titles Won:	16
Days as World Champion:	3,362
Age at first World Title Win:	30
Best Opponents:	Randy Savage, Andre the Giant, Sting
Halls of Fame:	3
TV Appearances:	Over a hundred, including several TV series
Movies:	16
Published Books:	2

In wrestling history, only a handful of individuals have had the capability to step into influential roles and single-handedly broker revolutionary periods that affect an entire business. Hulk Hogan was one of those people, ascending into the national limelight in 1984 with his signature blond hair, bronze coloring, and massive build; immediately capturing the imaginations of the young and old. His free-flowing charisma attracted immense attention for the World Wrestling Federation, which was in the process of launching a national campaign on the sacred territories, and his role as the captain of the grapplers helped the promotion achieve goals that were once deemed unattainable. Hogan spearheaded an amazing crusade to expand the WWF into the first nationally-functioning promotion to endure the many pitfalls of such an endeavor. It also allowed the organization to transition into a culture of pay-per-view and mass marketing, and ultimately, enormous financial success.

Hogan's rise to iconic status went hand-in-hand with the growth of the WWF, and his box office power during those pivotal years was astonishing. Born in Georgia, Hogan grew up in Port Tampa, Florida, and was interested in baseball and music early in life. The exciting pro wrestling scene in the area caught his eye as a kid, and he attended local shows where he caught the attention of the Brisco Brothers. Hogan's impressive size got him in the front door of a local wrestling school, and his commitment to the craft was sincerely tested after Hiro Matsuda broke his leg during his initial workout. But Hogan was resolute, making his debut in 1977, and wrestling along the Florida circuit—competing under a mask as the "Super Destroyer" at times. Two years later, he went to New York for an impressive run as a heel in Vincent J. McMahon's WWF and adopted the name, "Hulk Hogan." His first stint in the WWF placed him in matches against Andre the Giant and his appearances at Madison Square Garden garnered international attention.

Overseas for New Japan Pro Wrestling, Hogan won the initial IWGP tournament and both teamed and opposed the legendary Antonio Inoki. He also went toe-to-toe with Sylvester Stallone in the film *Rocky III* as the mammoth "Thunderlips," and his performance left an imprint on audiences worldwide. Hogan was simply bigger than life, and his two-year tour of the Minneapolis-based AWA ended in late 1983 without the anticipated championship win over Nick Bockwinkel for the World Title. Instead, he took advantage of a job offer for Vincent K. McMahon, the son of his former boss and the enthusiastic new leader of the WWF. In less than a month in the organization, Hogan beat The Iron Sheik on January 23, 1984 and won the WWF World Heavyweight crown. The "Hulkamania" era was officially launched, and Hogan was the right man in the right place at the right time. Crowds loved him, and his promos, ring work, and overall mannerisms won over a whole generation of wrestling fans.

Hogan was the central character of McMahon's operations as the WWF expanded nationally, implementing an annual WrestleMania event, as well as semi-regular pay-per-view shows. At the box office, he was unrivaled as a draw, and Hogan remained the undefeated champion until 1988. At WrestleMania V, a year later, he regained the belt with a win over Randy Savage, and in 1990, he grappled fellow fan favorite, The Ultimate Warrior, in a rare losing effort. He'd return to the top spot at WrestleMania VII, defeating Sgt. Slaughter, and by 1993, he was a five-time WWF World Champion. In June 1994, he signed a deal with WCW, and debuted on July 17, 1994 to capture the World Title from Ric Flair. WCW followed the WWF blueprint by relentlessly pushing Hogan, and his reign as champion lasted until October 29, 1995 when he was defeated by The Giant by DQ. In 1996, he shocked the industry by turning heel, becoming "Hollywood Hogan," and a member of the New World Order.

The NWO was a band of rebellious heels intent on causing problems within WCW, and the angle developed perfectly, helping the promotion maintain an advantage over the WWF in the ratings war. Hogan was always a main figure in the storyline, winning and losing the World Title and feuding with the likes of Roddy Piper, Lex Luger, and Sting. In 1998, he lost the championship to the undefeated Bill Goldberg at the Georgia Dome before more than 41,000 fans. The stability of the promotion began to dwindle and Hogan left under odd circumstances following the controversial Bash at the Beach pay-per-view on July 9, 2000 . . . he'd never return to WCW. Two years later, he resurfaced in the WWF and had a memorable match against The

Rock at WrestleMania X-8 before a rowdy crowd of Hogan supporters. On April 21, 2002, he beat Triple H for his sixth WWE World Championship but lost it the following month to The Undertaker.

Hogan faced off and beat Randy Orton at SummerSlam on August 20, 2006, and toured Australia in 2009, where he feuded with Ric Flair. On January 4, 2010, he debuted for TNA and was working with Eric Bischoff to change the creative focus of the promotion. He took Abyss under his wing and worked a number of angles, including one in which he took over ownership of TNA from Dixie Carter. Outside the ring, he appeared in thirty-five episodes of the VH1 reality show entitled *Hogan Knows Best*, featuring his then-wife Linda and two children from 2005 to 2007. Over the next couple years, he faced many harrowing personal trials, documented in his second book *My Life Outside the Ring*, and a 2010 A&E special *Finding Hulk Hogan*. He has since made a number of TV appearances, including on *American Idol*.

In 2012, Hogan served as TNA General Manager and eventually left the promotion in October 2013. He made his return to the WWE a few months later. He appeared at WrestleMania XXX and the WWE honored him with a special "Hulk Hogan Appreciation Night" at Madison Square Garden in 2015. However, he departed the organization during the summer in the midst of controversy. In 2015 and into 2016, he was also involved in a lawsuit against Gawker, which received mainstream attention. Despite his out-of-the-ring challenges, his wrestling fanbase—the fanbase that grew up with him—will never forget what he's given to the business. And they will welcome his WWE return with another mind-blowing ovation.

Photo Courtesy of Dr. Mike Lano—Wrealano@aol.com

Honky Tonk Man, The

Born:	January 25, 1953
Height:	6'1"
Weight:	265
Real Name:	Roy Wayne Farris
Family:	Cousin of Jerry Lawler
High School:	Central High School (TN)
Trained by:	Herb Welch
Nickname:	The Greatest Intercontinental Champion of All-Time
Finisher:	Swinging Neckbreaker
Tag Team:	Rhythm and Blues w/ Greg Valentine
Career Span:	1977–Present
Website:	www.honkytonkman.net

Titles Won:	26
Best Opponents:	Ricky Steamboat, Randy Savage, Dusty Rhodes
Halls of Fame:	1

A thoroughly entertaining wrestler, The Honky Tonk Man has made a career out of wearing jumpsuits, riding around in pink Cadillacs, and strumming guitars—much like another Tennessee icon, Elvis. His gimmick as a "musician" and grappler carried him to the longest reign in WWF Intercontinental Title history, a total of 454 days, and to center stage at WrestleMania. Born in Bolivar, Tennessee, he was a weightlifter at Memphis State and initially wanted to be a teacher. He coached high school athletics for two years before attending a wrestling camp in Dyersburg. He quickly found out that there was much more money to be made as a grappler than as a teacher, and began wrestling full time. On June 2, 1987, he beat Rick Steamboat for the Intercontinental Title and remained titleholder until August 29, 1988, when he lost it to the Ultimate Warrior in twenty-eight seconds. He performed a song at WrestleMania VI and often worked as a WWF commentator during the 1990s. He still wrestles on the indie circuit today.

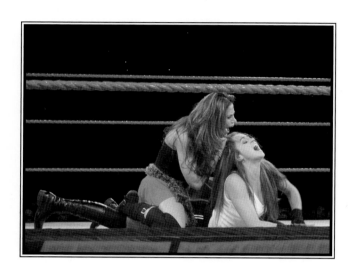

Photo Courtesy of Dr. Mike Lano—Wrealano@aol.com

Born:	August 31, 1979
Height:	5'4"
Weight:	130
Real Name:	Mickie Laree James
High School:	Patrick Henry High School (VA)
Trained by:	Dory Funk Jr., Ohio Valley trainers
Identities:	Alexis Laree
Career Span:	1999–Present

James, Mickie

Titles Won:	16
Days as World Champion:	496
Age at first World Title Win:	26
Best Opponents:	Trish Stratus, Tara, Madison Rayne

Currently one of the most talented and enthusiastic performers in women's wrestling, Mickie James of Virginia represents "Hardcore Country" in mind, body, and spirit. Her determination to rank among the best in the sport was second to none, and she graduated out of the indies and Ohio Valley to become a feature grappler in the WWE. Between 2006 and 2010, James held the WWE Women's championship on five occasions, and also captured the Divas Title from Maryse in 2009. The following year she turned up in TNA and won the Knockouts belt twice in 2011, from Madison Rayne and Winter. James captured the belt a third time on May 23, 2013, with a victory over Velvet Sky. In 2015, she joined the Global Force Wrestling (GFW) promotion. She also wed fellow wrestler, Magnus. When she is not wrestling, James has entertained audiences with her country singing.

Born:	February 3, 1962
Height:	5'11"
Weight:	220
Real Name:	Frederick Martin Jannetty
High School:	Hardware High School (GA)
Trained by:	The Oates Brothers
Identities:	Martin Oates
Finisher:	Showstopper
Tag Teams:	The Uptown Boys w/ Tommy Rogers, The New Rockers w/ Leif Cassidy
Career Span:	1984–Present

Titles Won:	16
Best Opponents:	Shawn Michaels, Steve Austin, Kurt Angle

Jannetty, Marty

Rocker Marty Jannetty grew up in Columbus, Georgia and entered the business in 1984. While working in the Central States, he befriended Shawn Michaels and the two formed a remarkably compatible tag team able to perform colorful spots and garner loud crowd reactions—especially from younger fans. As the Midnight Rockers, they won the AWA World Tag Team Title in 1987. The following year, they jumped to the WWF, where their popularity intensified, but were obscured by the larger teams in the promotion. In October 1990, they won the tag team title from the Hart Foundation, but the belts were returned to the latter on a technicality and the duo parted ways in 1991. On May 17, 1993, Jannetty captured Michaels' Intercontinental Title in a classic match on *Raw*. The following January, Marty and the 1-2-3 Kid won the WWF Tag Team Title. Jannetty has made a number of appearances for the WWE throughout the years, including a match on *Raw* against The Miz in October 2009; a bout he lost. He is still a regular on the indie scene.

Jarrett, Jeff

Born:	July 14, 1967
Height:	5'10"
Weight:	230
Real Name:	Jeffrey Leonard Jarrett
Parents:	Jerry and Deborah Jarrett
Trained by:	Jerry Jarrett, Tojo Yamamoto
Identities:	The Blue Blazer
Nicknames:	Double J, The Chosen One
Finisher:	The Stroke, Figure-four leglock
Groups:	The Four Horsemen (1997), New World Order 2000 (1999–2000), The New Blood (2000), The Magnificent Seven (2000–01), Planet Jarrett (2005), Immortal (2010)
Owner:	J Sports & Entertainment (2002) (partner with Jerry Jarrett), TNA Entertainment, LLC (2002–Present) (minority shareholder)
Career Span:	1986–Present

Titles Won:	74
Days as World Champion:	1,620 (and counting)
Age at first World Title Win:	26
Best Opponents:	Kurt Angle, Booker T, Sting
Halls of Fame:	1
Movies:	4

Wrestling has come very naturally to Jeff Jarrett, a third-generation grappler. Simply, his work over the last twenty-five years has been Hall of Fame quality, particularly when he's drawing the ire from just about everyone with his overwhelmingly heelish attitude. His ability to grind into the minds of wrestling fans catapults him to the head of the class in terms of wrestling psychology. It is hard not to lambaste his overly cocky persona and his brash and arrogant remarks. But his in-ring wrestling is textbook, covering many fundamental bases. Where his size could've been a handicap, Jarrett perfected the mental game and that, along with his admirable wrestling skills, have carried him to great success. In fact, he won World championships in WCW, WWA, USWA, AAA, and TNA, the latter being the National Wrestling Alliance title.

The grandson of Eddie Marlin and son of Jerry Jarrett, Jeff became a wrestler in 1986 and appeared in the CWA and USWA, where he amassed a full resume of championship victories. In 1993, he arrived in the WWF and received national exposure for the first time in his career. He was a perennial Intercontinental Champion and developed his heel country singer gimmick, much to the dismay of crowds. He used a guitar as a weapon, smashing it over the heads of foes, for which he drew a lot of heat. Jarrett jumped to WCW for a year term in 1996-1997, but then returned to the WWF. Finally, in 1999, he departed the WWF for the final time, burning a bridge in the process, and went to WCW, where he'd stay until the promotion was sold. It was during that period that he'd ascend to the World Heavyweight Title, initially winning a tournament for the vacant strap in April 2000. Over the next few months, he lost and re-won the WCW belt three additional times. When WCW closed up shop, Jarrett had to look for opportunities other than the WWF for work.

Teaming with his father, Jerry, a veteran promoter, Jarrett established Total Nonstop Action in 2002. The new promotion was based out of Nashville, and was positioned to assume the number two promotional role in the US with a weekly pay-per-view offering. On November 20, 2002, he beat Ron Killings for his first NWA World Title. Over the next four years, he'd win the belt five more times. Jarrett engaged in a heated ring war with Kurt Angle, and the feud was given an extra boost of symbolism when Angle's ex-wife Karen married Jarrett, and the real life relationship was turned into a wrestling storyline involving Kurt. Jarrett returned to the title picture, this time in Mexico, when he won the AAA World Title on June 18, 2011, from El Zorro. His reign lasted 274 days, ending on March 18, 2012 when he was defeated by El Mesias. That year, he also appeared in the film *Spring Breakers*. Still enterprising, he founded Global Force Wrestling in 2014 and scheduled shows in 2015 and '16. Jarrett was honored by TNA by induction into its Hall of Fame.

Jericho, Chris

Born:	November 9, 1970
Height:	5'10"
Weight	225
Real Name:	Christopher Keith Irvine
Parents:	Edward "Ted" and Loretta Irvine
High School:	Westwood Collegiate (Winnipeg)
College:	Red River Community College
Identities:	Super Liger
Nicknames:	Lionheart, Y2J, Living Legend
Finisher:	The Lion Tamer, Walls of Jericho, Lionsault
Tag Teams:	Sudden Impact w/ Lance Storm, The Thrillseekers w/ Lance Storm
Career Span:	1990–Present
Website:	www.chrisjericho.com

Titles Won:	37
Days as World Champion:	219
Age at first World Title Win:	30
Best Opponents:	Shawn Michaels, Steve Austin, The Rock
Halls of Fame:	1
TV Appearances:	over 50
Movies:	3
Published Books:	3

A versatile entertainer, Chris Jericho can safely be called the "King of All Media" when it comes to professional wrestlers. He broached the usually impenetrable wall from wrestling into the mainstream media by performing on the wildly popular television show *Dancing with the Stars*, appeared in several films, wrote two successful books, and tours as the lead singer of a rock band, Fozzy. On top of all that, he's been an influential figure in wrestling for the last fifteen years, initially gaining rave reviews for his cruiserweight showings in WCW to becoming the first grappler to win the undisputed WWF World Heavyweight Title. Behind the microphone, he's delivered top-notch promos, setting himself apart from his peers, and it didn't matter if he was invoking the name "Bore-us" Malenko or going off on a tangent on Shawn Michaels, he always gained an intense fan reaction. This combination of being able to convey psychologically stimulating promos with his abundance of mat talent makes him a superstar in every sense of the word.

Jericho emulated his father, renowned NHL player Ted Irvine, by playing hockey in high school, but followed his interest in wrestling to the Hart Brothers camp in Calgary, where he was extensively trained. Physically able to perform high-flying maneuvers that few others could, he was very impressive from an early age, and gained experience in Japan and Mexico—two places that allowed the quicker non-heavyweights to thrive. It also gave him an opportunity to gain further experience before entering the US indie scene in SMW, then in Philadelphia, for ECW. He advanced to WCW in 1996 and would remain in the promotion for three years. Despite his best efforts, he couldn't break out of the middle of the card, but distinguished himself as a four-time Cruiserweight champion and TV titleholder in 1998. He'd proven his value, and the WWF was ready to exploit his talents where WCW had failed to do so.

By the latter stages of 2001, Jericho had already won the WWF Intercontinental Title four times, plus the European and Hardcore championships. He defeated The Rock for the WCW World Heavyweight Title on October 21, 2001, and was soon entered in a four-man tournament to determine an undisputed titleholder on December 9, 2001. That night, Jericho unexpectedly went over both The Rock and Steve Austin and won the championship. Elevated to another plateau of wrestling success, Jericho went into WrestleMania X-8 as the defending champion, but lost the title to Triple H. Jericho feuded with the likes of Rob Van Dam and Christian over the Intercontinental Title, and also battled Shawn Michaels and Goldberg. In August 2005, he left the promotion to focus on his band and reemerged in November 2007—appearing to not have missed a step. Jericho did battle with Randy Orton and JBL prior to kick-starting his longtime rivalry with Michaels. Jericho also won the Intercontinental Title two more times, giving him nine reigns in total.

Six years had passed since Jericho last held the Undisputed World Title, and on September 7, 2008, he prevailed in a championship scramble match and captured the belt once again. He lost it to Batista on October 26, 2008, but regained it eight days later. John Cena ended his reign on November 23. In February 2010, he won the World Title for a third time, but lost it to Jack Swagger in March. He left the WWE again during the summer and participated in ABC's *Dancing with the Stars* in 2011, teaming with Cheryl Burke, and placing 7th. He returned to the WWE in January 2012, and enjoyed a part-time schedule for the next four years, wrestling some of the year, and touring with his band for the remainder. He engaged in feuds with CM Punk and AJ Styles, and continued to deliver high-performance matches that only someone with his level of veteran skill could. He will eventually be honored among the other legends in the WWE Hall of Fame.

Born:	December 12, 1952
Height:	6'3"
Weight:	275
Real Name:	Sylvester Ritter
High School:	Bowman High School (NC)
College:	Fayetteville State University
College Ach.:	All-CIAA (1975), All-NAIA (1975)
Pro Sports:	Ohio Valley Panthers (1975)
Trained by:	Sonny King
Identities:	Leroy Rochester, Big Daddy Ritter
Groups:	Dudes with Attitudes (1990)
Career Span:	1976–93
Died:	June 2, 1998, Near Forest, MS 45 years old

Junkyard Dog

Titles Won:	20
Days as World Champion:	21
Age at first World Title Win:	39
Best Opponents:	Ric Flair, Harley Race, Ted DiBiase
Halls of Fame:	2

One of the greatest stars of the "Rock and Wrestling" era, Junkyard Dog was extraordinarily popular, arguably second only to Hulk Hogan in the 1985-1987 time frame. A former footballer, he received NFL tryouts with Houston and Green Bay, and made headway in his quest to play for the Packers, but was sidelined when he suffered a serious knee injury. In November 1976, he made his pro wrestling debut in Batesboro, South Carolina as part of the Southern Wrestling Association. He shuffled around the territories before landing in the Mid-South promotion for Bill Watts. It was there that he adopted his trademark gimmick as "JYD," and set a course for success. Entering the ring to "Another One Bites the Dust," he danced around the ring, and then preceded to headbutt and power-slam his opponents into submission. In addition to winning the Wrestling Classic tournament, the first pay-per-view in WWE history, he held the North American Title and USWA Unified World belt.

Born:	April 26, 1967
Height:	6'8"
Weight:	320
Real Name:	Glenn Thomas Jacobs
Wife:	Crystal Jacobs
High School:	Bowling Green High School (MO)
Identities:	Bruiser Mastino, Doomsday, Dr. Isaac Yankem
Finisher:	Chokeslam, Reverse Piledriver
Groups:	The Corporation (1998–1999)
Tag Team:	The Brothers of Destruction w/ The Undertaker, The Dynamic Duo w/ Al Snow
Career Span:	1992–Present

Titles Won:	19
Days as World Champion:	246
Age at first World Title Win:	31
Best Opponents:	The Undertaker, Steve Austin, Shawn Michaels
Movies:	5

Kane

The "Big Red Machine" Kane was never really burned in a fire, nor is he related in any way to The Undertaker. Glenn Jacobs is the man who portrays the unstoppable monster, and the success of the gimmick pushed him straight to the upper echelon of the WWF. Before turning to wrestling, the Pike County, Missouri athlete played basketball at Northeast Missouri State, establishing school records for field goal percentage for a single year and career. He was also a notable offensive lineman in football, but a knee injury caused him to fail his physical with the Chicago Bears in 1991. Within two years, Jacobs had made the decision to become a professional wrestler, relocated to Tampa to train with the Malenkos, and even made his first showing on national television as enhancement talent for WCW. He bounced around the independents before finding stable work for Smoky Mountain Wrestling in Tennessee as "Unibomb." An early WWF run as a psychotic dentist (Isaac Yankem, DDS) was unremarkable.

The immensely powerful Kane debuted at the WWF's Badd Blood pay-per-view in St. Louis on October 5, 1997, going to the ring with Paul Bearer to confront his "brother," the Undertaker during the latter's Hell in the Cell bout against Shawn Michaels, with Kane's interference costing the Undertaker the match. The feud between the "siblings" lasted for several years. On June 28, 1998, he beat Steve Austin and captured the WWF World Heavyweight Title— undoubtedly his most important career achievement to date. He lost the belt back to Austin the next night on *Raw*. Despite his English degree, Kane's verbal promos were limited because of the role he played, but ended up developing more over time. He won the Intercontinental

Title twice, beating Triple H and Chris Jericho for the championship, and had lots of success as a tag team wrestler. He captured the World Tag Team Title nine times with various partners, including Mankind, The Undertaker, X-Pac, and Big Show. In June 2003, he finally unmasked—showing the world that he really wasn't disfigured.

Throughout his tenure in the WWE, Kane has participated in a few bizarre angles. One of them was the Katie Vick necrophilia storyline in 2002, and another was his "relationship" with Lita in 2004. He outlasted his foes in a special battle royal prior to the Wrestlemania XXIV broadcast, and then beat Chavo Guerrero Jr. in eight seconds for the ECW World Title. In July 2010, he won the Money in the Bank ladder match and, later in the night, cashed it in and went over Rey Mysterio Jr. for the World Title. His victory came in less than a minute. Kane remained champion until December, finally succumbing to Edge in a four-way bout. In 2011, he reformed a tag team with Big Show and won the WWE Tag Team Title. Kane also formed a successful tag team with Daniel Bryan known as "Team Hell No." The duo beat Kofi Kingston and R-Truth for the WWE Tag championship on September 16, 2012, and held the belts for 245 days. They were finally stopped by The Shield in May 2013. Kane became a member of The Authority in 2013, and served as the group's "Director of Operations."

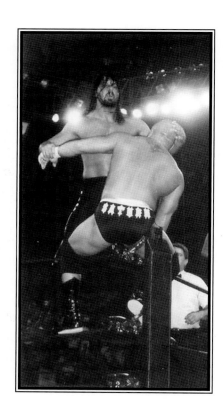

Photo Courtesy of Dr. Mike Lano—Wrealano@aol.com

Kanyon, Chris

Born:	January 4, 1970
Height:	6'3"
Weight:	250
Real Name:	Christopher Klucsarits
Parents:	Jack and Barbara Klucsarits
High School:	Archbishop Molloy High School (NY)
College:	University of Buffalo
Trained by:	Pete McKay, Afa, Fabulous Moolah
Career Span:	1992–2010
Died:	April 2, 2010, Sunnyside, NY 40 years old

Titles Won:	4
Best Opponents:	Dallas Page, Booker T, Mike Awesome
Movies:	2

Full of personality and potential, Chris Kanyon was a bright spot on the WCW roster during its final years, and carried his talent over to brief runs in the WWF. He grew up in Queens, New York, and was physically adept to play a number of sports because of his size and agility. Interested in pro wrestling, he attended the WCW Power Plant, and became known as "Mortis," managed by James Vandenberg. Later in his career, he gained attention as a member of the Jersey Triad with Dallas Page and Bam Bam Bigelow. Kanyon engaged in an entertaining war with Page, and adopted some of the latter's ring traits, including use of the "Kanyon Cutter," which he employed on many unsuspecting people—in a humorous way. He held the US and Tag Team Titles in the WWF, but was plagued by injuries for most of his time there. He wrestled for indie promotions until 2010, the last appearance several months before he took his own life. His candid autobiography was released in 2011.

Photo Courtesy of Dr. Mike Lano—Wrealano@aol.com

Born:	December 8, 1963
Height:	5'11"
Weight:	230
Trained by:	Shohei Baba, Genichiro Tenryu
Identities:	Kio Kawata, The Black Mephisto
Nickname:	Dangerous K
Finisher:	Powerbomb
Career Span:	1982–2010

Titles Won:	18
Days as World Champion:	912
Age at first World Title Win:	30
Best Opponents:	Mitsuharu Misawa, Kenta Kobashi, Stan Hansen
Tournament Wins:	7
Halls of Fame:	1

Kawada, Toshiaki

A five-time All-Japan Unified Triple Crown Champion, Toshiaki Kawada was long the backbone of the promotion, even remaining steadfast after nearly all other wrestlers abandoned ship in 2000. He displayed unreal strength in title victories over Steve Williams, Mitsuharu Misawa, Keiji Mutoh, and reigned supreme in a tournament for the vacant title on September 6, 2003. Two of the reigns, ironically, were ended prematurely because of injuries. Kawada formed a legendary tag team with Akira Taue, and the pair held the AJPW Tag Team Title on six occasions. Once the All-Japan roster left to form Pro Wrestling NOAH under Misawa's leadership in 2000, Kawada and his remaining cohorts entered an interpromotional rivalry with New Japan—a long-awaited concept that helped keep AJPW alive. For a time in 2005, Kawada appeared for HUSTLE, but returned to All-Japan the next year. On October 24, 2009, he beat Masato Tanaka for the Zero-One World Heavyweight Championship, and reigned until April 11, 2010.

Born:	February 20, 1977
Height:	5'4"
Weight:	125
High School:	York Memorial Collegiate Institute (Toronto)
College:	University of Toronto
Identities:	La Felina
Career Span:	2000–Present

Kim, Gail

Titles Won:	5
Days as World Champion:	161 (and counting)
Age at first World Title Win:	26
Best Opponents:	Awesome Kong, Mickie James, Trish Stratus

Awesomely talented, Gail Kim's athleticism radiates each time she steps through the ropes. Trained by Ron Hutchinson in her hometown of Toronto, she won the WWE Women's belt in her first televised match in the promotion on June 30, 2003. Kim beat out nine others for the initial TNA Women's Title on October 14, 2007, and regained it upon her return to the organization with a win over Velvet Sky on November 13, 2011. Over the next four years, she won the championship three additional times, beating out champions ODB, Angelina Love, and Brooke. She also teamed with Madison Rayne to win the TNA Knockouts Tag Team belts. As a heel or fan favorite, she delivers top-notch ring performances, displaying the veteran qualities that make her one of the best women grapplers in the world today.

Born:	November 7, 1955
Height:	6'3"
Weight:	425
Real Name:	Christopher Alan Pallies
High School:	Washington Township High School (NJ)
Trained by:	Larry Sharpe
Identities:	Chris Canyon, Big Daddy Bundy, Boom Boom Bundy
Finisher:	Atlantic City Avalanche
Groups:	The Legion of Doom (1983–84), Million Dollar Corporation (1994–95)
Career Span:	1982–2007

Titles Won:	13
Best Opponents:	Hulk Hogan, Andre the Giant, The Undertaker
Movies:	2

King Kong Bundy

Once you saw King Kong Bundy in person or on TV, you never forgot the image. The bald behemoth weighing more than 400 pounds with the fear-inducing scowl on his face was a terror of the wrestling ring, splashing victims into temporary comas, and demanding referees count to five for pinfalls instead of the customary three. Little did many fans know was that the "King" had a great sense of humor and has often performed as a stand-up comedian. A funny and light-hearted personality was far from the man crowds saw in feuds with the Von Erichs and Hulk Hogan, particularly in the run up to WrestleMania 2, which Bundy co-headlined with the latter in 1986. He was ferocious in squash matches on TV, and footage of him manhandling opponents was either comical or frightening, depending on whom you asked. He was a regular on the indie circuit before returning to the WWF in 1995. In reruns, fans can still catch Bundy's two appearances on *Married . . . with Children*; particularly the episode in which he pulverizes "Bud Bundy" in a wrestling exhibition.

Born:	August 14, 1981
Height:	6'1"
Weight:	225
Real Name:	Kofi Sarkodie-Mensah
High School:	Winchester High School (MA)
College:	Boston College
Finisher:	Trouble in Paradise
Career Span:	2006–Present

Titles Won:	7
Best Opponents:	Chris Jericho, Jack Swagger, Kane

Kingston, Kofi

Supremely athletic and overwhelmingly popular, Kofi Kingston's progression as a pro wrestler has been nothing but remarkable. Since his debut in 2006, he's won three United States and four Intercontinental championships and, as a tag team performer, has added four WWE and one World Tag Title. Born in Ghana, West Africa, Kingston attended high school in Winchester, Massachusetts, and collected over 100 victories as an amateur grappler. He learned the fundamentals from Mike Hollow and Killer Kowalski, then worked out at the Deep South and Ohio Valley WWE developmental organizations before his 2008 ECW debut. Later that year, he won the Intercontinental belt from Chris Jericho and gained additional title victories from Drew McIntyre and Dolph Ziggler. His first two US Title wins came at the expense of MVP and Sheamus and, in 2008, he held the World Tag belts with CM Punk. In 2014, he formed "The New Day" with Xavier Woods and Big E, and captured the WWE World Tag Title on two occasions. He was also champion with partners Evan Bourne and R-Truth.

Born:	March 27, 1967
Height:	6'2"
Weight:	250
High School:	Fukuchiyama High School (Japan)
Trained by:	Shohei Baba, Dory Funk Jr.
Nickname:	Orange Crush
Finisher:	Brainbuster
Career Span:	1988–2013

Titles Won:	17
Days as World Champion:	431
Age at first World Title Win:	29
Best Opponents:	Mitsuharu Misawa, Jun Akiyama, Stan Hansen
Tournament Wins:	8
Halls of Fame:	1

Kobashi, Kenta

Over the last twenty years, few wrestlers have engaged in as many instant classics as Kenta Kobashi of Japan. He's been a walking highlight reel, famously displaying his fine ability to tell a story in the ring, and working terrifically performed matches that resonate with fans across the world. His influence has been global, and only injuries could keep him away from the ring he's graced with his pure athleticism since 1988. A three-time AJPW Triple Crown Champion, Kobashi defeated Akira Taue for his first reign on July 24, 1996, and then Mitsuharu Misawa for his second in January 1997. During his third run as champion in 2000, he joined a group led by Misawa, leaving All-Japan to form Pro Wrestling NOAH, and effectively vacated his title. He won the Global Honored Crown from Misawa on March 1, 2003 in Tokyo and held the respected title for more than two years In that time, his high level of performance was unrelenting, and Kobashi participated in some of the best matches anywhere in the world.

Born:	March 9, 1959
Height:	6'2"
Weight:	250
Real Name:	Nelson Scott Simpson
Parents:	Paige and Olive Simpson
High School:	Robbinsdale High School (MN)
Colleges:	Golden Valley Junior College, Moorhead State University
Trained by:	Eddie Sharkey, Ivan Koloff
Identities:	Mr. Wrestling IV
Nickname:	The Russian Nightmare
Finisher:	Russian Sickle
Career Span:	1984-92
Website:	www.nikitakoloff.com

Koloff, Nikita

Titles Won:	7
Best Opponents:	Magnum T.A., Ric Flair, Lex Luger
Halls of Fame:	1

Wrestling was impacted by a Lithuanian nightmare in 1984 when powerful Nikita Koloff began to come into his own in the Mid-Atlantic region. A truly feared competitor, he was billed as the nephew of Ivan Koloff, and teamed with his uncle and Don Kernodle as part of the World Six-Man Tag Team Champions. However, in reality, young Nikita was from Robbinsdale, Minnesota, and had been a football player throughout high school and college. The Koloffs also reigned as World Tag Team titleholders twice in 1985 and 1986. Remarkably strong, Nikita was a gifted personality in a colorful industry, and his best-of-seven series against Magnum T.A. for the US Title is still talked about today. After Magnum was injured in a car accident, Koloff turned fan favorite and teamed up with Dusty Rhodes to win the Crockett Cup Tag Team Tournament in 1987—dedicating the win to their fallen comrade. He retired a year later, but came back in 1991 to feud with Lex Luger and Sting in WCW before his career was ended after suffering a serious neck injury.

Konnan

Born:	January 6, 1964
Height:	5'11"
Weight:	235
Real Name:	Charles R. Ashenoff
High School:	Southwest Miami Senior High School (FL)
Trained by:	Rey Mysterio Sr., Negro Casas, Super Astro
Identities:	El Centurion, Max Moon, Konnan el Barbaro
Nickname:	K-Dogg
Finisher:	Tequila Sunrise, 187—Cradle DDT
Groups:	Los Gringos Locos, New World Order (Black and White) (1997–98), New World Order (Wolfpack) (1998), The Filthy Animals (1999–2001), Authentic Luchadores (2003), 2 Live Kru (2003–05), La Legion Extranjera (2006–11)
Career Span:	1988–2012

Titles Won:	17
Days as World Champion:	Over 295
Age at first World Title Win:	27
Best Opponents:	Cien Caras, Perro Aguayo, Ric Flair
Halls of Fame:	1

Exploding on audiences with outstanding charisma and the ability to rap, Konnan was a multitalented performer and a favorite everywhere he went. He was born in Cuba and raised in South Florida, served in the Navy, and broke into the business in early 1988. He had the size and athletic skill set to stand out very quickly and was a major star in Mexico during the early 1990s. Huge crowds saw him feud with Perro Aguayo and Cien Caras, and on June 9, 1991, he beat the latter to capture the CMLL World Title, and was also a headliner in the newly founded AAA promotion in 1993. In 1996, he entered WCW and quickly won the US Title. He built a faithful following and was standout member of the NWO Wolfpack and Filthy Animals. Behind the microphone, he was always a great promo man, letting it fly off the cuff and giving the fans what they wanted to hear. He wrestled in TNA from 2003 to 2007 but was sidelined because of health issues. He rejoined AAA in Mexico for several years and currently is a member of the Lucha Underground promotion.

Born:	September 1, 1961
Height:	6'0"
Weight:	235
Real Name:	William Ensor
Trained by:	Boris Malenko
Identities:	Buddy Roop
Finisher:	Superplex
Managed by:	Jim Cornette, General Skandor Akbar, James J. Dillon, Peaches
Career Span:	1979–2010
Died:	June 22, 2015, Chilhowie, VA 53 years old

Titles Won:	36
Best Opponents:	Shawn Michaels, Ric Flair, Jerry Lawler
Halls of Fame:	3

Landel, Buddy

Similar to his "Nature Boy" counterparts, Buddy Landel was a blond and arrogant grappler with respectable mat abilities. From Knoxville, Tennessee, where he was a natural athlete in high school, he was destined for great things in 1985 when he was fired from Jim Crockett Promotions because of his outside-the-ring problems. Despite his personal issues, he won more than thirty wrestling titles to include the NWA National, USWA, SMW, and WWC North American Heavyweight belts. In 1991, he nearly squared off against Buddy Rogers in New Jersey, but the match was cancelled. Landel was terrific in promos and many of his interviews are must-see classics.

Photo Courtesy of Pete Lederberg—plmathfoto@hotmail.com

Born:	August 5, 1953
Height:	6′1″
Weight:	225
Real Name:	Wallace Stanfield Lane
High School:	Page High School (NC)
College:	East Carolina University
Career Span:	1978–2008

Titles Won:	39
Best Opponents:	Dusty Rhodes, Jimmy Garvin, Dutch Mantel
Halls of Fame:	1

Lane, Stan

Trained by Ric Flair, Stan Lane of Greensboro initially worked as "Stan Flair," and also adopted the trademark "Nature Boy" moniker. He teamed with Steve Keirn to form the Fabulous Ones, winning the US Tag Team Championship twice in 1986 and then reunited to capture the USWA World Tag Team Title in 1991. Lane also joined Bobby Eaton as a member of the famed Midnight Express, managed by Jim Cornette. The duo won the US Title three times, and the World Tag Team belts in 1988. Later on, he partnered with Tom Prichard as the Heavenly Bodies and won the SMW Tag Team Title five times. Always displaying a good repertoire of moves, Lane has returned to the ring several times over the years, appearing at reunion shows alongside Eaton and Cornette.

Born:	December 27, 1969
Height:	5'10"
Weight:	180
Real Name:	Joan Marie Laurer
Parents:	Joseph and Janet Laurer
High School:	Penfield High School (NY)
College:	University of Tampa
Nicknames:	Ninth Wonder of the World, Amazon
Finisher:	Pedigree
Magazine Covers:	*Playboy* (November 2000), *Playboy* (January 2002)
Career Span:	1995–2016
Died:	April 20, 2016, Redondo Beach, CA 46 years old

Laurer, Joanie

Titles Won:	5
Days as World Champion:	214
Age at first World Title Win:	31
Best Opponents:	Chris Jericho, Jeff Jarrett, Masa Chono
TV Appearances:	Over 20, including recurring roles on several reality programs
Movies:	10

The spirited Joanie Laurer resurfaced in big-time pro wrestling in May 2011, after a long hiatus of reality TV appearances and personal struggles, and her fans couldn't have been happier. Trained by Killer Kowalski, she initially entered the World Wrestling Federation in 1997 as "Chyna," and was a bodyguard for Triple H. She joined the infamous DeGeneration X and became the first woman to hold the WWF Intercontinental Title, a feat she repeated two additional times. At WrestleMania X-Seven, she defeated Ivory for the WWF Women's Title. After leaving the WWF in 2001, she wrestled for New Japan and lost to Masa Chono on October 14, 2002, at the Tokyo Dome. Her return to wrestling for TNA alongside Kurt Angle in 2011 created a lot of interest, but lasted only one match. Widely influential, Joanie's size always set her apart in a world of divas and knockouts, and she remained one of the most recognizable women grapplers in the business until her sudden death on April 20, 2016, at the age of forty-six.

Born:	November 29, 1966
Height:	6'6"
Weight:	285
Real Name:	John Charles Layfield
Parents:	Richard Lavelle and Mary Layfield
High School:	Sweetwater High School (TX)
College:	Abilene Christian University
College Ach.:	1st team All-American (1989), 2nd team All-American (1988), 1st team All-Conference (1988, 1989)
Pro Sports:	National Football League—Los Angeles Raiders (1990) (camp) World League—San Antonio Riders (1991)
Identities:	Justin Hawk, John Hawk, Blackjack Bradshaw, JBL
Finisher:	Clothesline from Hell
Groups:	The Ministry of Darkness (1999), The Cabinet (2004–05)
Career Span:	1992–2014

Layfield, John "Bradshaw"

Titles Won:	30
Days as World Champion:	280
Age at first World Title Win:	37
Best Opponents:	Eddie Guerrero, John Cena, The Undertaker
Published Books:	1

A towering figure, John Layfield was a WWE superstar from 1996 until 2009 and graduated from the tag team division to reign as the heavyweight champion for nine months. He played offensive tackle in high school and college, and learned the ropes from Brad Rheingans. In 1995, he captured the North American belt from Kevin Von Erich, and the next year debuted in the WWF as "Justin Bradshaw." He partnered with Faarooq as the Acolytes and they won the World Tag Team Title three times between 1999 and 2001. Their often comical performances displayed Layfield's wit and diversified his on-air role. He won the Hardcore Title seventeen times and added the WWE Heavyweight Title to his resume with a victory over Eddie Guerrero in June 2004. He remained champ until the following April, losing to John Cena at WrestleMania 21. He retired from the business in 2009, and was a prominent figure on cable TV as a financial analyst. Two years later, JBL resurfaced in the WWE, making various appearances before settling into a more permanent role as a commentator. He also returned to the ring during the Royal Rumble in 2014.

Photo Courtesy of Dr. Mike Lano—Wrealano@aol.com

Born:	April 21, 1957
Height:	6'3"
Weight:	270
Real Name:	Edward Harrison Leslie Jr.
Wife:	Barbara Leslie
High School:	Robinson High School (FL)
Identities:	Ed Boulder, Dizzy Hogan, Ed Hogan, The Butcher, The Man with No Name, The Zodiac, The Booty Man, The Disciple, Brute Force
Groups:	Dungeon of Doom (1995), OWN (1998)
Tag Teams:	The Dream Team w/ Greg Valentine, The Mega Maniacs w/ Hulk Hogan
Career Span:	1979–Present

Titles Won:	8
Best Opponents:	Curt Hennig, Randy Savage, Hulk Hogan

Leslie, Ed

Ed Leslie was a high school friend of Hulk Hogan and broke into the business under his pal's wing in the late 1970s. He achieved a great deal of superstardom using the name "Brutus Beefcake" in the WWF. The Tampa product was initially a heel and co-held the WWF Tag Team Title with Greg Valentine. But it was his tour as the "Barber" that carried him to immense popularity, and by 1990, he was one of the top fan favorites in the organization. His specialty was putting an opponent out with his sleeperhold, and then cutting his downed foe's hair. Leslie was challenging for Intercontinental belt when he was nearly killed in a freak parasailing accident. Proving doctors wrong, he not only made a comeback, but teamed with Hogan at WrestleMania IX. He'd also headline Starrcade 1994 in a bout against Hogan—which he lost. Leslie used an abundance of gimmicks while in WCW, and has wrestled on the indie circuit ever since. His fine showmanship and likable personality have been a staple in the business for over thirty years.

Lesnar, Brock

Born:	July 12, 1977
Height:	6'3"
Weight:	265
Real Name:	Brock Edward Lesnar
Parents:	Richard and Stephanie Lesnar
High School:	Webster High School (SD)
College:	Bismark State
College Record:	106-5
Trained by:	WWE Ohio Valley Trainers, Scott LeDoux (MMA), Greg Nelson (MMA)
Nickname:	The Next Big Thing
Finisher:	F-5
WWF Debut:	March 18, 2002, Montreal, Quebec, *Raw*
Tag Team:	The Minnesota Stretching Crew w/ Shelton Benjamin
Career Span:	2000–Present

Amateur Titles:	5
Titles Won:	7
Days as World Champion:	984
Age at first World Title Win:	25
Best Opponents:	Kurt Angle, The Undertaker, The Rock
MMA Record:	6-3
Days as UFC Champion:	707
Halls of Fame:	1

Looking back at wrestling history, it's hard to find someone comparable to Brock Lesnar. The massive South Dakotan is the embodiment of exceptional genetics and intense discipline, and his success as a professional wrestler and MMA fighter put him in a category all by himself. In the worked environment of wrestling, he performed flawlessly, winning world titles in the United States and Japan. He then crossed over to the legitimate combat sport, mixed martial arts, where he proved that he was the real deal—a world-class battler with the heart and ability to become heavyweight champion in that realm, too. Lesnar has cultivated all the tools necessary to stand out in any endeavor he chooses to undertake, and when he made his return to pro wrestling in 2012, he quickly reclaimed a spot among the best in the business. Not only did he regain the WWE World Title, but he ended the most famous streak in pro wrestling—that being The Undertaker's WrestleMania win streak.

A wrestler in high school, Lesnar learned from coach John Schiley, and with two consecutive third-place finishes at the state tournament, he was not recruited to a major university, and instead landed at Bismarck Junior College. It was there that he won his first significant amateur title, taking the NJCAA championship as a heavyweight in 1998, then proceeded to the University of Minnesota, where he won an NCAA championship in 2000. Lesnar opted not to pursue an Olympic medal and signed with the WWF, making his debut in August 2000. He quickly outgrew his environment in the developmental promotion, and was on the fast track to glory by the summer of 2002, winning the King of the Ring tournament. On August 25, 2002, he became the youngest man in history to win the WWE Title when he beat The Rock for the belt at SummerSlam. His reign was disrupted on November 17 when his manager Paul Heyman turned on him, and allowed The Big Show to capture the championship.

Now a fan favorite, Lesnar prevailed at the Royal Rumble and wrestled another former NCAA champion, Kurt Angle, at WrestleMania XIX on March 30, 2003. The hugely anticipated match was full of high drama, and at one crucial moment, Brock sailed from the top rope attempting a dangerous shooting star press—and narrowly missed serious injury. Lesnar pulled through and won his second WWE championship. His feud with Angle continued that summer and they traded the title again. Their September 16, 2003 Iron Man match was a classic and saw Lesnar with five falls to his opponent's four. After losing to Goldberg at WrestleMania in 2004, he departed from the promotion and announced his intentions to play in the NFL. He played some preseason ball, but was cut by the Minnesota Vikings in August. Lesnar returned to wrestling for NJPW and won the IWGP Title in a three-way match against Masa Chono and Kazuyuki Fujita on October 8, 2005 at the Tokyo Dome.

While overseas, he made many successful showings, but was stripped of the title during the summer of 2006. Incidentally, he kept the belt and defended it against Kurt Angle on June 29, 2007 in what would be his final pro wrestling match to date, with Angle winning by submission. The options for Lesnar were wide open, and it was initially believed he'd return to wrestling in some capacity, but he instead announced his intentions to participate in mixed martial arts. He trained to diversify his fighting skills, and prepared for his June 2007 debut in Los Angeles, where he beat Min-Soo Kim. He lost his second match to Frank Mir, but rebounded to stop Heath Herring and then Randy Couture for the UFC Heavyweight Title on November 15, 2008. Following intensive recovery after a serious illness, Lesnar beat Shane Carwin, and then lost his title to Cain Velasquez on October 23, 2010 in Anaheim. In late December 2011, he retired from MMA after a first round loss to Alistair Overeem at UFC 141.

Lesnar resumed his pro wrestling career in April 2012, picking up Paul Heyman as a mouthpiece, and established his dominance early on. He broke the arm of Triple H and then beat the latter at SummerSlam on August 19. After a several month break, he returned again in early 2013, and battled Triple H again at WrestleMania 29. This time, Brock was defeated. Exactly a year later, at WrestleMania XXX on April 6, 2014, he defeated The Undertaker, ending the latter's win streak at 21. Four months later, he captured the WWE World Title from John Cena. Lesnar retained the belt going into WrestleMania 31, but lost a three-way bout when Seth Rollins pinned Roman Reigns and dropped the championship. At WrestleMania 32 in 2016, he went over Dean Ambrose in a special no-holds barred street fight. All things considered, it is clear Lesnar will remain a pivotal member of the WWE Universe well into the future. But even if he decides to hang up his boots tomorrow, his legacy in wrestling is well established.

Born:	November 10, 1964
Height:	5'7"
Weight:	215
Real Name:	Keiichi Yamada
Trained by:	NJPW Dojo including Tatsumi Fujinami, Stu Hart
Identities:	Fuji Yamada
Finisher:	Liger Bomb, Shooting Star Press
Career Span:	1984–Present

Liger, Jushin

Titles Won:	33
Days as IWGP Junior Champion:	2,245
Age at first IWGP Junior Win:	24
Best Opponents:	Great Sasuke, El Samurai, Ultimo Dragon
Tournament Wins:	9
Halls of Fame:	1
MMA Record:	0-1

Japanese marvel, Jushin "Thunder" Liger has been a leader of the wrestling high-flier community since the 1980s. His epic aerial display and athleticism carried him to world championships in Japan, the United States, Mexico, and Great Britain, and a record eleven IWGP Junior Titles. Always heroically performing risky maneuvers, Liger made a real impact on WCW fans in 1991, and has returned to the US to wrestle many times. Originally from Hiroshima, he entered the business in 1984 and adopted the "Jushin Liger" character five years later for New Japan. He won his first IWGP Junior Championship from Hiroshi Hase on May 25, 1989 in Osaka. In the years following, he would win the belt from Naoki Sano, The Pegasus Kid, and two times from Norio Honaga. On December 25, 1991, he beat Brian Pillman for the WCW World Light Heavyweight Title, but lost it back to the latter on February 29, 1992. Their remarkable feud continued at the very first edition of *Nitro* in 1995, with Pillman winning that round.

On January 4, 1993, Liger beat Ultimo Dragon at the Tokyo Dome for his sixth IWGP Junior Title. He won his seventh before 64,000 on January 4, 1996 from Koji Kanamoto. A year later, Liger beat Dragon for the J-Crown Octuple Championship, which included his eighth IWGP Junior Title. Over the next two years, he won the belt from Shinjiro Ohtani and Kendo Ka Shin before Juventud Guerrera ended his reign on WCW *Nitro* on November 29, 1999. It was the first time the IWGP Junior Title changed hands outside of Japan. Guerrera was injured in the contest and unable to defend the title a week later in Milwaukee. Psicosis was allowed to defend against Liger and lost the championship. It was his eleventh and final IWGP Junior Title victory. Over the last decade, he's continued to make the rounds, appearing in TNA, ROH, and in Mexico. At this point, he is only building upon his incredible record and showing younger fans what their older counterparts already knew about his legendary status.

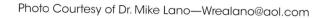

Born:	April 14, 1975
Height:	5'7"
Weight:	135
Real Name:	Amy Christine Dumas
High School:	Lassiter High School (GA)
Trained by:	Leilani Kai, Dory Funk Jr.
Identities:	Miss Congeniality, Angelica
Career Span:	1998–2006

Titles Won:	4
Days as World Champion:	160
Age at first World Title Win:	25
Best Opponents:	Trish Stratus, Victoria, Ivory
Halls of Fame:	1

Lita

Sporting reddish hair and an affinity for extreme spots, Lita stood out from most of the women grapplers on the WWE roster. She regularly performed the moonsault and top-rope huracanrana, and her athleticism made her highly popular with fans. Lita began her career in Mexico and worked in ECW in 1999, just prior to entering the WWF. She initially appeared at the side of Esse Rios, but was mostly known for her strong bond with the Hardy Boys. She won the Women's Title from Stephanie McMahon in August 2000 and also beat Trish Stratus and Mickie James for the belt. She lost the title for the last time on November 26, 2006, to James, in what was her retirement match, and decided to focus on her music career. In 2014, she was inducted into the WWE Hall of Fame, recognizing her outstanding innovation and influence in the ring, and also returned to perform in several behind-the-scenes and on-camera roles.

Luger, Lex

Born:	June 2, 1958
Height:	6'5"
Weight:	275
Real Name:	Lawrence Wendell Pfohl
High School:	Orchard Park High School (NY)
College:	University of Miami
Pro Sports:	Canadian Football League— Montreal Alouettes (1979–81) National Football League— Green Bay Packers (1982–83) (camp) United States Football League— Jacksonville Bulls (1983) United States Football League— Tampa Bay Bandits (1984) United States Football League— Memphis Showboats (1984–85)
Finishers:	Torture Rack Backbreaker "Rebel Rack," Forearm Smash, Piledriver
Tag Teams:	The Allied Powers w/ Davey Boy Smith, Totally Buff w/ Buff Bagwell
Career Span:	1985–2006

Titles Won:	18
Days as World Champion:	242
Age at first World Title Win:	33
Best Opponents:	Ric Flair, Hulk Hogan, Sting
Managers:	8

With a bodybuilder physique, three-time World Heavyweight Champion Lex Luger was a pivotal player in wrestling for over two decades. He was pushed right from the beginning, shown by his Southern Title victory over Wahoo McDaniel only nineteen days after his pro debut. He had the size and strength to become a superstar, and promoters gave him the platform to sink or swim. Luger had winning potential, stepped up to the plate, and delivered a home run—successfully transitioning from the football field to the pro mat. The wise Hiro Matsuda and Bob Roop gave him the tools he needed to measure up to the hype, and he was capable, even as a rookie, of delivering a performance that the fans reacted positively to. As his stock rose, he joined the Four Horsemen and won the US Heavyweight belt, the first of four title victories, from Nikita Koloff at the 1987 Great American Bash. At the initial Clash of the Champions, he teamed with Barry Windham to capture the World Tag Team Title, but his partner turned on him a month later.

Throughout 1988, he chased NWA champion Ric Flair and came close to winning the belt innumerable times, but one technicality or another prevented him from walking away as the new titleholder. He beat

Windham for the US Title at the Chi-Town Rumble on February 20, 1989, and, incidentally, Chicago was always billed as Luger's hometown, although he was really from upstate New York. After trading the belt back and forth with Freebird Michael Hayes, Luger began a seventeen-month reign as US Champion. It took Stan Hansen, a former AWA World Champion, to dethrone him at Halloween Havoc on October 27, 1990. On July 14, 1991, he won the WCW World Heavyweight Title, turning heel in the process, and took Harley Race as his manager. He ended up losing the crown to Sting the following February. Shortly thereafter, he left WCW to participate in the short-lived World Bodybuilding Federation, and, in 1993, he entered the WWF as "The Narcissist," an egotistical rule-breaker.

Fans took to Luger after he bodyslammed the humongous Yokozuna on the USS. *Intrepid*, and while Luger rose to the top of the promotion, even co-winning the 1994 Royal Rumble, he never won gold in the WWF. On September 3, 1995, Luger worked a WWF house show, and the very next night, he appeared on WCW's first showing of *Nitro*. Luger's unexpected arrival brought a sense of spontaneity to *Nitro* that would linger for years. He won his second WCW Title from Hollywood Hogan on August 4, 1997, but lost it back to the latter five days later. In late 2002, he beat Sting for the vacant WWA World Title on a pay-per-view from Scotland, and reigned for a week before Sting won in a rematch. He went into semi-retirement and made varied showings for TNA between 2003 and 2006. In 2007, he suffered a spinal stroke that left him paralyzed. He has slowly recovered his ability to walk, and has devoted himself to the Christian religion, publicly speaking out against drug abuse.

Lynn, Jerry

Born:	June 12, 1963
Height:	5'10"
Weight:	215
Real Name:	Jeremy Clayton Lynn
High School:	Woodcrest Baptist Academy High School (MN)
Trained by:	Eddie Sharkey, Brad Rheingans
Identities:	Mr. J.L.
Nickname:	Dynamic, The New F'n Show
Finisher:	Cradle Piledriver
Career Span:	1990–2013

Titles Won:	Over 50
Days as World Champion:	106
Age at first World Title Win:	37
Best Opponents:	Rob Van Dam, A.J. Styles, Lance Storm
Halls of Fame:	1

A talented grappler from Minneapolis, Jerry Lynn was the World Heavyweight Champion twice in his career, and merits the respect he now receives wherever he appears on the circuit. With a background in gymnastics, Lynn was quick to grasp the wrestling trade, and bore all the characteristics of a future champion. His first significant milestone occurred at ECW's Anarchy Rules on October 1, 2000, when he beat Justin Credible for the World Title. While in the WWF, he won the light heavyweight championship and became a two-time NWA World Tag Team titleholder in TNA. Lynn also captured the prized X-Division belt twice. In Australia, on May 21, 2003, he won a tournament for the WWA International Cruiserweight Title. More recently, on April 3, 2009, Lynn topped Nigel McGuinness for the ROH World Heavyweight crown. He remained champion until June 13, 2009, when he lost the title to Austin Aries.

Born:	June 11, 1959
Height:	6'1"
Weight:	240
Real Name:	Terry Wayne Allen
Wife:	Courtney Allen
High School:	Norfolk Collegiate High School (VA)
College:	Old Dominion University
Trained by:	Buzz Sawyer, Eddie Graham
Nickname:	Tenacious
Finisher:	Belly-to-belly suplex
Career Span:	1981–86

Titles Won:	11
Best Opponents:	Nikita Koloff, Tully Blanchard, Ric Flair

Magnum T.A.

Terry Allen had noticeable magnetism that radiated outward and, to promoters, it meant money. It is hard to ignore a young athlete in the world of wrestling with superstar qualities. Fans who were privy to the outward expression of his innate talents, supported him thoroughly, and made him the hero of the day. A 1977 VISWA amateur wrestling champion in high school, Allen took the name "Magnum T.A." while in the Mid-South region, and received a mighty push for the Crocketts a short time later. He won the US Title on March 23, 1985, and traded the belt with Tully Blanchard. His second reign came to an abrupt end after he punched NWA President Bob Geigel and was stripped of the title. The title was put up in an exciting best-of-seven series between Magnum and Nikita Koloff, ending on August 17 when Koloff won his fourth match and the championship. On October 14, 1986, Magnum was severely injured in a car accident, and the career of the twenty-seven-year-old with the immensely bright future ended far too prematurely.

Malenko, Dean

Born:	August 4, 1960
Height:	5'9"
Weight:	220
Real Name:	Shelly Dean Simon
Family:	Brother of Joe Malenko
Wife:	Julie Simon
High School:	Jesuit High School (FL)
Identities:	Dean Solkoff, Cyclope
Nicknames:	Iceman
Finisher:	Texas Cloverleaf
Groups:	The Four Horsemen (1998–99), The Revolution (1999), The Radicals (2000)
Career Span:	1979–2001

Titles Won:	13
Best Opponents:	Eddie Guerrero, Chris Benoit, Chris Jericho
Halls of Fame:	1

Dean Malenko, the son of the Great Malenko, and an enthusiastic student of the legendary ring master, Karl Gotch, earned the nickname "Man of 1,000 Holds" because of his endless repertoire of grips and methodical techniques. His knowledge of submissions and ability to down rivals with legitimate skills also warranted the moniker, "Shooter." There was never a question about his talent, but promoters were hesitant to use such a mild-mannered spokesman in a world of cockiness and brash attitudes. Simply, Malenko let his athletic prowess speak for itself, and finally, in 1995, he began to gain national attention in WCW. He held the US Title and the World Cruiserweight Championship four times. He jumped to the WWF and became the first man to have held both the WWF Light Heavyweight and WCW Cruiserweight Titles when he captured the former championship from Esse Rios during *Raw* in March 2000. After his retirement in 2001, he was hired by the WWE as an agent.

Born:	February 8, 1958
Height:	5'7"
Weight:	130
Real Name:	Sherry Lynn Russell Schrull
Nicknames:	Scary, Sensuous, Queen
Career Span:	1980–2006
Died:	June 15, 2007, McCalla, AL 49 years old

Titles Won:	6
Days as World Champion:	Over 926
Age at first World Title Win:	27
Best Opponents:	Fabulous Moolah, Candi Devine, Rockin' Robin
Wrestlers Managed:	23
Halls of Fame:	4

Martel, Sherri

The tough "Sensational" Sherri Martel, born and reared in Alabama, had a Hall of Fame career. She was initially a wrestler, trained by the Fabulous Moolah, and won the AWA World Title from Candi Devine on September 28, 1985. Two additional reigns followed, and Martel distinguished herself with her aggressiveness and outgoing personality. In the summer of 1987, she entered the WWF, where she won the WWF Women's Title from her old coach, Moolah, and reigned as champion for over a year. After Wrestlemania V, she joined Randy Savage, aiding in his victory over Jim Duggan for the title of "King" of the WWF, and becoming known as "Sensational Queen" Sherri. Martel and Savage feuded with Sapphire and Dusty Rhodes in 1990, and lost a mixed tag bout at WrestleMania VI when the latter duo received outside help from Miss Elizabeth. In the years that followed, she also acted in a managerial-type role for Ric Flair, Shawn Michaels, Shane Douglas, and Harlem Heat.

Born:	July 9, 1960
Height:	6'0"
Weight:	235
Real Name:	Marc Eric Mero
Parents:	Harold and Diane Mero
High School:	Liverpool High School (NY)
Family:	Brother of Joel Mero
Nicknames:	Marvelous, Wildman
Finisher:	Knockout Punch
Managed by:	Teddy Long, Sable
Career Span:	1991–2005
Website:	www.championofchoices.org

Titles Won:	4
Best Opponents:	Steve Austin, Triple H, Brian Pillman

Mero, Marc

In 1979, a young man from Liverpool, New York was looking to stay in shape during the hockey off season, and met Ray Rinaldi, the coach of the North Area Athletic Club. Rinaldi convinced the talented athlete, Marc Mero, to step into a boxing ring, and Mero agreed. In 1980, he won a gold medal in the Empire Games and took a victory in the Golden Gloves tournament the following year. Mero's pro boxing aspirations were sidetracked by an injury, and he took a chance at wrestling instead, training under the Malenkos in Tampa. He was hired by WCW and became known as "Johnny B. Badd," incorporating some boxing into his grappling repertoire. He won the World TV Title on three occasions between 1994 and 1996, and, after jumping to the WWF, captured the Intercontinental belt on September 23, 1996. After the Chris Benoit murder-suicide, Mero spoke out about the industry and today aspires to empower people to make positive life choices through his organization, Champion of Choices.

Born:	February 9, 1963
Height:	5'9"
Weight:	145
Real Name:	Debra Ann Miceli
High School:	Robbinsdale High School (MN)
Trained by:	Eddie Sharkey, Brad Rheingans
Finisher:	German Suplex (bridge)
Groups:	The Dangerous Alliance (1991–92), Team Madness (1999)
Career Span:	1985–2001
Website:	www.madusa.com

Titles Won:	8
Days as World Champion:	Over 1,349
Age at first World Title Win:	24
Best Opponents:	Sherri Martel, Wendi Richter, Bull Nakano
Halls of Fame:	1

Miceli, Madusa

Born in Italy and raised in the Minneapolis area, the talented Madusa Miceli was a prominent wrestler for over fifteen years, capturing world championships in the AWA, WWF, WCW, and in Japan. She was a relentless worker, dedicating herself to the business after trying her hand at modeling and nursing, and was tough to the bone. She beat Candi Devine to capture the vacant AWA Women's World Title on December 27, 1987. Miceli then went overseas to wrestle for All-Japan and won the IWA World Title on two occasions in 1989, the second reign lasting until 1991. As Alundra Blayze, she captured the reactivated WWF World Title in a tournament final over Heidi Lee Morgan on December 13, 1993. She held it two additional times before appearing on WCW *Nitro* and dumping the belt in a trash can on December 18, 1995. In 1999, she held the WCW Cruiserweight Championship and retired from wrestling in 2001 to focus on her new career as a monster truck driver. It didn't take her long to find success in that realm as well. In 2015, Madusa was inducted into the WWE Hall of Fame.

Michaels, Shawn

Born:	July 22, 1965
Height:	6'0"
Weight:	225
Real Name:	Michael Shawn Hickenbottom
Parents:	Richard and Carole Hickenbottom
High School:	Randolph High School (TX)
College:	Southwest Texas State University
Nicknames:	The Heartbreak Kid
Finisher:	Sweet Chin Music (Superkick)
Groups:	D-Generation X (1997–98, 1999, 2006, 2009) The Corporation (1998-1999), New World Order (2002)
Managed by:	Sherri Martel, Luna Vachon, Jose Lothario
Promoted:	Texas Wrestling Alliance (2000) (San Antonio, Texas)
Career Span:	1984-2010

Titles Won:	22
Days as World Champion:	424
Age at first World Title Win:	30
Best Opponents:	Bret Hart, The Undertaker, Scott Hall
Halls of Fame:	2
Published Books:	2

By surveying the nicknames bestowed upon the shoulders of the great Shawn Michaels, you get the feeling that he is a well-respected guy in the wrestling industry. He's known as the "Showstopper," the "Icon," and "Mr. WrestleMania," and these descriptive monikers weren't done flippantly—but very astutely. Michaels has been one of the most influential and successful wrestlers of the last quarter century. He's had innumerable outstanding matches and constantly performed brilliant maneuvers with excellent timing. Michaels was committed to greatness, and in time, fans came to expect nothing less from him. He was born on a military installation southeast of Phoenix, the son of a decorated Air Force officer, and moved a number of times during his youth. In 1973, his father, Col. Richard Hickenbottom became commander of the 47th Air Base Group at Laughlin near Del Rio, Texas, and the family relocated again.

From a very sports-oriented family, Michaels took part in track events and was a standout on the Memorial Lobos football squad of the Val Verde Pee Wee Football League while in Del Rio. After his father was transferred to Randolph Air Force Base outside of San Antonio, he earned a reputation as a defensive marvel in high school, and in 1982, performed a wrestling skit with a friend at a talent show that suggested his real goal of becoming a pro grappler. Michaels was influenced by television broadcasts of Southwest Championship Wrestling and sought out legend Jose Lothario for training, becoming a pro at the age of nineteen. He spent his rookie season in the Mid-South territory for Bill Watts, then toured Kansas and the AWA, establishing himself as an up-and-comer with Marty Jannetty in a lightning quick tag team known as the Midnight Rockers. The Rockers were able to mix science with high-flying, and were idols to kids, possessing the right kind of look to draw the interest of younger audiences.

The appeal of Michaels and Jannetty was an attractive quality to promoters, and they received a push in the AWA to the top of the tag team ranks. On January 27, 1987, the Rockers beat Buddy Rose and Doug Somers for the World Tag Team Title and were champions through May 25, when they were defeated by Soldat Ustinov and Boris Zukhov. Later that year, they had an exceptionally brief stay in the WWF, and then turned up in the CWA before regaining the AWA World Tag Team Title in late December 1987, by beating the Original Midnight Express. When the WWF came calling again in 1988, they were ready embrace the new adventure. Although the promotion had a heavy tag team field, the Rockers found their place, winning over fans, and extended their popularity from coast to coast. It was clear that Michaels had singles potential, and in December 1991, after five years together, he turned on his partner, and attacked Jannetty. To mark the occasion, he threw the latter through a glass window on an edition of the "Barber Shop."

On October 27, 1992, Michaels beat Davey Boy Smith for the first of three Intercontinental Title reigns. Full of charisma and portraying a character as arrogant as could be, Michaels went a long way in a short period of time in establishing himself as a potential future World Champion. At WrestleMania X, he wrestled a classic ladder match against Razor Ramon, proceeded to win the 1995 and 1996 Royal Rumbles, then beat Bret Hart on March 31, 1996 to capture his first WWF World Heavyweight Title. Michaels lost the belt to Sid Vicious on November 17, but regained it on January 19, 1997. The belt was later declared vacant after Michaels suffered an injury. On November 9, he rebounded to challenge Hart in what is commonly known as the Montreal Screwjob match. Michaels won the controversial bout and his third WWF Title. 1997 was also the year that saw D-Generation X formed by Michaels, Triple H, Chyna, and Rick Rude, and the group established itself the rebellious backbone of the promotion.

Michaels lost the WWF Title to "Stone Cold" Steve Austin on March 29, 1998 at WrestleMania XIV and retired from the business to nurse a seriously injured back suffered earlier in the year. Back home in Texas, he operated a wrestling school and made sporadic appearances in the WWF, including as commissioner in late 1998 and as a member of DX in 1999. In 2000, he briefly made a comeback for his San Antonio promotion, and it wasn't until June 2002 that he returned to the WWF as a full-time competitor. He feuded heavily with his former DX partner Triple H and won the World Title on November 17, 2002 at Madison Square Garden in an elimination chamber bout, beating "The Game" in the finals. A month later, he lost the belt to Triple H at Armageddon. Michaels also went to war against Chris Jericho, who he beat at WrestleMania XIX. A year later, he came up short in a three-way match against Triple H and Chris Benoit at WrestleMania XX, which Benoit won and captured the World Title.

On July 4, 2005, Michaels attacked Hulk Hogan, setting up a dream match for many fans at SummerSlam on August 21. The bout went more than twenty-one minutes before Hogan scored the win. Michaels beat Vince McMahon in a no-holds barred match at WrestleMania 22 and was unable to win the WWE Title from John Cena at WrestleMania 23 on April 1, 2007. He did force Ric Flair into retirement at WrestleMania XXIV on March 30, 2008 with his win. Staying on top of the sport, he feuded with Randy Orton and Chris Jericho again, maintaining his bigger-than-life presence in storylines, but went down in defeat against his old rival The Undertaker on April 5, 2009 at WrestleMania XXV in Houston. Later that year, he teamed with Triple H to win the WWE Unified Tag Team Title. With his own career on the line, Michaels tackled The Undertaker again at WrestleMania XXVI, and was defeated, ending his career. He was inducted into the WWE Hall of Fame in 2011, and although his active career was over, Michaels was a prominent figure on WWE programming in the years that followed. On hand for special ceremonies and announcements, and also performing his patented superkick when needed, he always added an additional spark to whatever event he appeared. In 2016, he joined fellow legends Mick Foley and Steve Austin at WrestleMania 32.

Photo Courtesy of Dr. Mike Lano—Wrealano@aol.com

Born:	June 18, 1962
Height:	6'1"
Weight:	245
High School:	Ashikaga-kodai High School (Japan)
Trained by:	Shohei Baba, Dick Beyer, La Fiera
Identities:	The Kamikaze, Tiger Mask II
Nickname:	Untouchable
Finisher:	Emerald Flowsion
Owned:	Pro Wrestling NOAH (2000–09)
Career Span:	1981–2009
Died:	June 13, 2009, Hiroshima, Japan 46 years old

Titles Won:	20
Days as World Champion:	1,799
Age at first World Title Win:	30
Best Opponents:	Toshiaki Kawada, Kenta Kobashi, Stan Hansen
Tournament Wins:	8
Halls of Fame:	1

Misawa, Mitsuharu

Five days before his 47th birthday, wrestling legend Mitsuharu Misawa wrestled his final match in Hiroshima, Japan, participating in a tag team event. The routine situation turned tragic when Misawa was rendered unconscious following a move and later passed away. He'd been a recognized icon around the world for his superlative performances in matches, and was a leader during the wrestling boom of the 1990s. A former amateur wrestler, Misawa trained in the All-Japan dojo and was a noteworthy junior heavyweight, winning the NWA International Junior Title over Kobayashi in August 1985. For six years he used the Tiger

Mask gimmick and unmasked in May 1990 as part of a major push he was set to receive. Misawa competed in a number of spectacular bouts and held the AJPW Unified Triple Crown five times, carrying the promotion's banner and elevating the international repute for its main championship to immense proportions.

Among his title victories came over Stan Hansen (twice), Kenta Kobashi (twice), and Vader. His final win came on May 2, 1999 against the latter at the Tokyo Dome before an estimated 65,000 fans, during the Shohei "Giant" Baba Memorial Show. After the death of his mentor, Misawa became the President of All-Japan, a role he performed until May 2000 when disagreements with members of the company's management saw him ousted. Misawa founded Pro Wrestling Noah, a new organization, a short time later. In the finals of a 16-man tournament, Misawa beat Yoshihiro Takayama for the initial Global Honored Crown World Heavyweight Title on April 15, 2001 in Tokyo. He would hold the championship two additional times. Misawa was a special breed of professional wrestlers, naturally capable of raising his game to the level of legends, and delivering extraordinary matches that will be heralded forever.

Photo Courtesy of Mike Mastrandrea

Born:	October 8, 1980
Height:	6'1"
Weight:	230
Real Name:	Michael Gregory Mizanin
Parents:	George and Barbara Mizanin
High School:	Normandy High School (OH)
Trained by:	UPW trainers, Bill DeMott, Al Snow
Identities:	The Calgary Kid (masked)
Nickname:	The Most Must-See WWE Champion in History
Finisher:	Skull-Crushing Finale
Tag Team:	ShowMiz w/ The Big Show
Career Span:	2003–Present

Titles Won:	10
Days as World Champion:	160
Age at first World Title Win:	30
Best Opponents:	John Cena, Randy Orton, Daniel Bryan
Movies:	8

Miz, The

A number of reality TV entertainers have tried to cross over to wrestling, and many were put off by the difficulty of the transition. The Miz not only made the leap successfully, but rose to the top of the WWE to become a superstar. His dedication to the craft shows in his smooth ring work and his personality displayed behind the microphone. These traits accelerated his push and climaxed when he won the WWE

Championship in 2010. From Parma, Ohio, The Miz participated in a number of sports while in high school, and attended Miami University until auditioning for the 10th season of the popular reality show, *The Real World* on MTV. During that program, viewers actually witnessed the first incarnation of "The Miz" character, and in the succession of reality programs that followed, his athleticism was displayed in physical exhibitions. He attended the UPW wrestling camp and participated in the WWE's 2004 Tough Enough series, but lost in the finals to Daniel Puder.

Despite the result, The Miz still found himself in the WWE developmentals. Learning from many skilled trainers, he sharpened his ring knowledge and formed a dynamic team with John Morrison. The duo held both the WWE and World Tag Team Titles between 2007 and 2009. In the years that followed, he captured the US Heavyweight Title twice and the Intercontinental Title on five occasions. He also won the 2010 Money in the Bank ladder match and cashed it in to face Randy Orton on November 22, 2010, where he won the WWE championship. Miz retained his title over John Cena at WrestleMania XXVII in what was the biggest match of his career, but lost it to the latter less than a month later. Miz formed successful tag teams with R-Truth and Damien Mizdow and, in 2016, he was joined in the WWE by his wife Maryse.

Photo Courtesy of George Tahinos

Born:	September 10, 1976
Height:	6'9"
Weight:	320
Real Name:	Matthew Thomas Morgan
Parents:	William and Patricia Morgan
Wife:	Larissa Morgan
High School:	Fairfield High School (CT)
Colleges:	Monmouth University, Chaminade University
Finisher:	Hellevator
Groups:	Fortune (2010)
Career Span:	2002–2015

Titles Won:	6
Best Opponents:	Kurt Angle, Samoa Joe, A.J. Styles

Morgan, Matt

Athletically gifted and immense in size, "The Blueprint" Matt Morgan has come close to becoming a TNA World Champion on a number of occasions. His ring weaponry is as punishing as it gets, and his Carbon Footprint finisher looks as if it will knock the head off his foe. A basketball player in high school and college, Morgan finished up his schooling in Hawaii, and trained at Ohio Valley, a WWE Developmental in Louisville. In 2004-2005, he reigned as OVW Heavyweight Champion on two occasions and had a brief run on the main WWE roster. Morgan debuted in TNA during the summer of 2007 as a bodyguard for Jim Cornette. He teamed with Hernandez to win the World Tag Team Title on January 17, 2010, but his partnership ended violently with Morgan injuring his teammate. From there on, he was the sole defender of the belts, and it was a solid gimmick while it lasted. An injury sidelined him in 2011, but he returned to feud with Samoa Joe, and then won the TNA World Tag Team Title with rival, Crimson. Morgan retired from the wrestling business in 2015.

Photo Courtesy of Dr. Mike Lano—Wrealano@aol.com

Born:	March 6, 1971
Height:	6'2"
Weight:	240
Real Name:	Sean Allen Morley
High School:	Markham District High School (Ontario)
Trained by:	Ron Hutchison, Dewey Robertson, Dory Funk Jr., Tom Prichard
Identities:	Scott Borders, Steel, Sean Morgan, The Big Valbowski
Nickname:	The Pornstar
Groups:	The Right to Censor (2000)
Career Span:	1995–Present

Titles Won:	14
Days as World Champion:	Around 136
Age at first World Title Win:	26
Best Opponents:	The Rock, Mankind, Steve Austin

Morley, Sean

A talented and colorful wrestler, Morley is widely known as "Val Venis," for his controversial pornstar gimmick in the WWF. Originally from Oakville, Ontario, he wrestled all over the world from Japan to England, and won the CMLL World Heavyweight Title from Rayo de Jalisco in April 1997 in Mexico City. While in the WWF, he won the Intercontinental Championship on two occasions, beating Ken Shamrock on February 14, 1999 for his first reign and then beating Rikishi on July 4, 2000 for his second. He also held the European belt and the World Tag Team Title with Lance Storm. Many of the outside-the-ring segments he participated in drew fire from conservative groups, especially when off-color jokes were made about his "occupation" in the adult industry. In 2002-2003, he served as the "Chief of Staff" on *Raw* under general manager Eric Bischoff. Morley left the WWE in 2009, toured New Japan, and then appeared on Hulk Hogan's tour of Australia. He briefly worked for TNA in early 2010, and then returned to WWE as a "producer."

Photo Courtesy of Mike Mastrandrea

Born:	October 3, 1979
Height:	6'1"
Weight:	220
Real Name:	John Randall Hennigan
Parents:	Brian and Karen Hennigan
High School:	Palos Verdes Peninsula High School (CA)
Trained by:	Trainers from SPW, Tough Enough, and Ohio Valley
Identities:	Johnny Blaze, Johnny Spade, Johnny Nitro
Finisher:	Starship Pain
Tag Team:	MNM w/ Joey Mercury
Career Span:	2003-Present

Titles Won:	10
Days as World Champion:	69
Age at first World Title Win:	27
Best Opponents:	Rey Mysterio Jr., Jeff Hardy, The Miz

Morrison, John

A product of Palos Verdes in the Los Angeles area, John Morrison wrestled through high school and was a film major at the University of California. He attended a wrestling camp before landing a spot as a cast member of Tough Enough III, and his previous training as a gymnast and in martial arts worked in his favor throughout the series. Morrison displayed the heart and agility of a pure athlete, and won the competition along with Matt Cappotelli on January 23, 2003. He was ushered to the WWE Developmental territory, Ohio Valley, and there formed MNM with Joey Mercury and Melina. The trio had an organic compatibility that led them to *Smackdown* in 2005—and three reigns as WWE Tag Team champs. As a singles grappler, he won the Intercontinental belt three times before winning the ECW

World Heavyweight crown in June 2007. Known for his exaggerated ring entrances, Morrison also formed a successful tag team with The Miz, holding the World Tag Team Title in 2008–09. He departed the WWE in late 2011. Morrison joined Lucha Underground in 2014 as "Johnny Mundo," and has appeared in independent promotions across the world. Without a doubt, he is one of the best grapplers in the United States today not signed with the WWE.

Born:	September 21, 1956
Height:	5'11"
Weight:	225
Real Name:	Rickey Wendell Morton
Parents:	James and Lucille Morton
Trained by:	Paul Morton
Identities:	Richard Morton
Groups:	The York Foundation (1991–92)
Finisher:	Diving Crossbody
Career Span:	1978–Present

Titles Won:	83
Days as World Champion:	189
Age at first World Title Win:	35
Best Opponents:	Ric Flair, Brian Pillman, Jushin Liger
Halls of Fame:	4

Morton, Ricky

An entertaining high-flyer, Ricky Morton was a member of one of the most successful and influential tag teams of all time, the Rock and Roll Express. Since his debut in the late 1970s, he has been a perennial fan favorite and has showcased a wealth of athletic maneuvers, with his patented dropkick being considered textbook. Originally from Tennessee, Morton joined Robert Gibson to form the Rock and Roll Express around 1983, and the duo were the youthful idols for scores and scores of fans in the expanding Jim Crockett promotional territory. Between 1985 and 1987, they won the NWA World Tag Team belts four times, and would later capture numerous other championships, including ten Smoky Mountain titles. In 1991, he turned heel and joined the York Foundation, becoming known as "Richard Morton." For a majority of the last twenty years, he's been a favorite on the independent circuit, and in March 2011, won the AIWF World Heavyweight Title from Jimi Love in a cage match. Three years later, in January 2014, he beat Chase Owens for the NWA World Junior Heavyweight Title, but lost a rematch in March.

Born:	March 6, 1976
Height:	6'2"
Weight:	230
Real Name:	Kenneth C. Anderson
Parents:	James and Sheryl Holmes
Wife:	Shawn Anderson
High School:	Washington High School (WI)
Trained by:	Eric Hammers, Michael Krause
Identities:	Two Rivers Jack, Kamikaze Ken, Ken Kennedy
Finishers:	Mic Check, Green Bay Plunge
Career Span:	1999–Present

Titles Won:	15
Days as World Champion:	64
Age at first World Title Win:	34
Best Opponents:	Sting, The Undertaker, Shawn Michaels
Movies:	2

Mr. Anderson

In today's wrestling environment, personality is as important as in-ring abilities, and when a special performer can combine a variety of mat styles and an outgoing attitude that connects with audiences, they usually are on the fast track to superstardom. Ken Anderson of Two Rivers, Wisconsin demonstrated these rare qualities and shot to the top of the ranks as "Mr. Kennedy" in the WWE, and is now one of the top grapplers in TNA. His sense of humor and poise in front of crowds developed in high school, where he was involved in drama and broadcasted his school's basketball games. After graduation, he served in the Army before attending the camp of Brad Rheingans. He followed standard protocol for newcomers in the business by touring the indie scene, honing his techniques, until 2005 when he entered the Ohio Valley WWE developmental territory. He made it to *Smackdown*, and exploited a colorful gimmick that had him making his own ring introductions on a house microphone dropped down from the rafters.

An injury slowed his rise, but by the summer of 2006, he was clearly heading toward bigger and better things. He captured the US Title and feuded with The Undertaker, Bobby Lashley, and Batista, even challenging the latter for the World Title at the 2007 Royal Rumble. On April 1, 2007, he emerged victorious in the Money in the Bank ladder match, earning a future World Title shot, but lost the opportunity to Edge. Injuries continued to haunt Anderson and many fans were disappointed when they heard he was released from the WWE in May 2009. He toured Australia later in the year, and in January 2010, he found a new home in TNA. A year into his stint in the promotion, he overcame Matt Morgan and World Heavyweight Champion Jeff Hardy in the same night to annex the TNA belt on January 9, 2011. His reign came to an end at the next pay-per-view, on February 13, 2011, when Hardy regained the title. On June 12, 2011, he captured the TNA World Title a second time from Sting at Slammiversary. Sting won a rematch in July. Anderson later joined the heel group, Aces and Eights.

Born:	December 23, 1962
Height:	6'1"
Weight:	240
Trained by:	Hiro Matsuda
Identities:	The White Ninja, Super Black Ninja
Nickname:	Pearl of the Orient
Finisher:	Moonsault, Cork Screw Elbow
Groups:	The J-Tex Corporation (1989–90), New World Order (1997), The Dark Carnival (2000)
Career Span:	1984–Present

Titles Won:	26
Days as World Champion:	1,833
Age at first World Title Win:	29
Best Opponents:	Shinya Hashimoto, Yuji Nagata, Genichiro Tenryu
Tournament Wins:	14
Halls of Fame:	1

Mutoh, Keiji

When Keiji Mutoh as the Great Muta arrived in WCW in 1989, many new fans were exposed to the Japanese style of grappling, and were enthralled by his unique abilities. His colorful face paint, green mist, and moonsault made watching wrestling on TBS even more interesting and added a unique dynamic to WCW that the WWF couldn't claim. It has been more than twenty years since that initial showing, and Mutoh has firmly established his legacy as an international superstar. After studying Judo in his youth, Mutoh attended the New Japan wrestling school, and wrestled in Texas and Florida before arriving in WCW under the management of Gary Hart. In September 1989, he won the World TV Title from Sting. Back in Japan, he won the first of four IWGP Titles from Riki Choshu on August 16, 1992, and remained champion for more than a year. On January 4, 1993, he added the NWA World crown to his list of achievements, defeating Masa Chono at the Tokyo Dome.

Mutoh's second IWGP run began on May 3, 1995 when he went over Shinya Hashimoto and his third reign started when he conquered Scott Norton on January 4, 1999. Genichiro Tenryu ended the latter reign on December 10, but that loss was avenged on June 8, 2001 when Mutoh won the AJPW Unified Triple Crown from Tenryu, becoming the third man in history to hold both the Triple Crown and IWGP Titles. Mutoh transferred his base of operations completely to All Japan and won the Triple Crown twice more, the final time on September 28, 2008 with a win over Suwama in Yokohama. That same year, Mutoh also regained the IWGP Title with a victory over Shinsuke Nakamura, and held both championships simultaneously. Mutoh appeared a number of times in the US, including for WCW and TNA. In mid-2013, he left All-Japan to form his own organization, Wrestle-1. A legendary competitor and athlete, Mutoh influenced a generation of fans across the globe.

Photo Courtesy of Bill Stahl

Mysterio, Rey Jr.

Born:	December 11, 1974
Height:	5'6"
Weight:	175
Real Name:	Oscar Gutierrez
Parents:	Roberto and Maria Gutierrez
Family:	Nephew of Rey Misterio Sr.
Wife:	Angelica Gutierrez
High School:	Montgomery High School (CA)
Trained by:	Rey Misterio, Super Astro, La Gacela, Cavellero 2000
Identities:	El Colibri, Green Lizard
Finisher:	619, Diving hurricanrana
Groups:	Latino World Order (1998), The Filthy Animals (1999–2001)
Career Span:	1989–Present

Titles Won:	35
Days as World Champion:	140
Age at first World Title Win:	31
Best Opponents:	Eddie Guerrero, Dean Malenko, Shawn Michaels
Halls of Fame:	3

In the case of Rey Mysterio, Jr., his astounding athleticism has been rewarded with international popularity. He's certainly earned the support of the thousands of fans who cheer him relentlessly on any given night by performing an intriguing array of high-risk maneuvers, taking the breath away from witnesses of his speed and agility. His innovative style differs greatly from his ring competitors, setting him far apart from the competition. Add the fact that he is about a foot shorter than many WWE superstars, and wears a colorful mask; Mysterio is truly a one-of-a-kind pro wrestler. His explosive charisma and multitalented physical abilities have demonstrated time after time that his size is not a handicap. In fact, he takes advantage of the differences in size, and really helped shatter the myth that smaller wrestlers couldn't rise to the top of the heavyweight ranks and be world champions. It is well understood that Mysterio can beat any wrestler in the WWE, regardless of the size difference. His underdog status is a treasured part of the promotion.

Mysterio is an immense hero and his trademark masks are worn by people of all ages. Having debuted as a young teenager, he was a confirmed veteran by the time he entered WCW in 1996. He bedazzled viewers with his acrobatics and his presence was a considerable boost to the cruiserweight division. His match on the program was often the most talked about, and he had many outstanding contests against Chris Jericho, Dean Malenko, and Billy Kidman. In 2002, he signed with the WWE and captured the tag team title with partners Edge, Rob Van Dam, Eddie Guerrero, and Batista. Following Guerrero's death in 2005, Mysterio dedicated many of his victories to his fallen friend. At the 2006 Royal Rumble, he overcame great odds after entering the ring at number two and remained at the end only to win the event. A few months later at WrestleMania, he beat Randy Orton and defending titleholder Kurt Angle to win the World Heavyweight Championship. It was a glorious moment for Rey and his legion of fans, shared in the ring by Eddie Guerrero's widow Vickie and brother Chavo.

Mysterio was dethroned by King Booker on July 23, 2006, after Chavo turned on him. Over the next couple of years, he was haunted by injuries, but remained in the hunt for championship gold. On June 20, 2010, he prevailed over CM Punk, Big Show, and champion Jack Swagger to win his second World Title. Mysterio retained against Swagger on July 18, 2010, only to see Kane cash in his Money in the Bank briefcase and pin him for the belt in less than a minute. On July 25, 2011, he beat Miz in a tournament final to win the vacant WWE Title, but lost it the same night to John Cena. Mysterio left the WWE in 2015, and has since appeared in AAA and Lucha Underground.

Nash, Kevin

Born:	July 9, 1959
Height:	6'11"
Weight:	325
Real Name:	Kevin Scott Nash
High School:	Aquinas High School (MI)
Identities:	Steele, Oz, Vinnie Vegas
Nicknames:	Big Daddy Cool, Big Sexy
Finisher:	Jackknife Powerbomb
Groups:	New World Order (1996–99, 2002) (Black and White/Wolfpack), The Millionaires Club (2000), The Natural Born Thrillers (2000), Kings of Wrestling (2004), Main Event Mafia (2008–09)
Tag Teams:	The Master Blasters w/ Steele, The Vegas Connection w/ Dallas Page, The Insiders w/ Dallas Page
Managed by:	The Great Wizard
Career Span:	1990–2014

Titles Won:	21
Days as World Champion:	456
Age at first World Title Win:	35
Best Opponents:	Bret Hart, Shawn Michaels, The Undertaker
Halls of Fame:	1
Movies:	16

Kevin Nash was an original member of the New World Order, and led a ground-breaking "invasion" of WCW that was full of colorful angles and what appeared many times to be kayfabe-breaking in-ring promos. His ability to deliver powerful, personality-driven verbal segments was always important to the development of feuds, and once in the ring, he dominated opponents with his massive size. With deliberate and crushing maneuvers, he was effective in establishing himself as one of the best big men in the business. Nash was from the Detroit suburbs and attended the University of Tennessee, where his sport of choice was basketball. He played pro ball in Europe, but a leg injury cut his experience short, and served in the Army after his playing days. Trained for wrestling by Jody Hamilton at the WCW Power Plant, Nash entered the promotion using a variety of less-than-stellar gimmicks. He was reinvented when he went to the WWF in 1993, becoming "Diesel," a bodyguard for Shawn Michaels.

At the 1994 Royal Rumble, his potential was showcased when he eliminated seven competitors and went on to win the Intercontinental, Tag Team, and WWF World Heavyweight Championships. The latter was captured from Bob Backlund on November 26, 1994, at a house show at Madison Square Garden. For 358 days, he remained titleholder, and finally lost his grip on the belt to Bret Hart at the 1995 Survivor Series. Nash returned to WCW six months later, but unlike his first run in the promotion, this time history was going to be made. Along with Scott Hall and Hulk Hogan, Nash formed the rebellious NWO, initiating a tremendously successful period for the organization. In fact, the New World Order was a golden concept that has since been often imitated, but never duplicated. Together, Nash and Hall were known as the "Outsiders" and won the WCW Tag Team Title five times. Between 1998 and 2000, he also won the WCW World Title five times and held the distinction of ending Bill Goldberg's long winning streak.

A brief tour of the WWE, where the NWO was briefly reformed, concluded in 2003, and Nash joined TNA in November 2004. He partnered with Scott Hall and Jeff Jarrett as the Kings of Wrestling, but continued health problems put a damper on any sustained effort. He preyed on members of the popular X-Division in April 2006, and later advised Kurt Angle and his wife as "Dr. Nash." He feuded with Angle, but the two ultimately banded together as part of the Main Event Mafia in 2008. On July 19, 2009, he beat A.J. Styles for the TNA Legends belt, and in May 2010, he captured the TNA Tag Team Title with Hall. The following January, he reemerged in the WWE at the Royal Rumble, and participated in a unique three-way feud involving Triple H and CM Punk during the Fall. Many insider shoot references were used in promo segments between Nash and Punk, and Nash brutalized both rivals in deliberate attacks. He lost a sledgehammer ladder match to Triple H at the TLC pay-per-view on December 18, 2011. Nash was inducted into the WWE Hall of Fame in 2015.

Photo Courtesy of Dr. Mike Lano—Wrealano@aol.com

Born:	February 8, 1955
Height:	6'1"
Weight:	280
Real Name:	James Henry Neidhart
High School:	Newport Harbor High School (CA)
College:	UCLA
Identities:	Who (Masked)
Finisher:	Anvil Flattener
Career Span:	1979-Present

Titles Won:	12
Best Opponents:	Steve Austin, Triple H, Curt Hennig
Halls of Fame:	1

Neidhart, Jim

A product of Southern California, Jim Neidhart was a shot put expert in school. He attended the training camp of the Dallas Cowboys in 1978, but only to be cut after three weeks. Taught by Stu Hart, Neidhart married his mentor's daughter and formed a famous tag team with his brother-in-law, Bret Hart. The Hart Foundation, as they were known, won the WWF World Tag Team Title twice, and Neidhart backed Hart during the reformation of the group in 1997. Possessing a trademark goatee, Neidhart was known for his high-energy interviews, and was aggressive in the ring. He also wrestled for WCW, and his daughter Natalya currently works for the WWE.

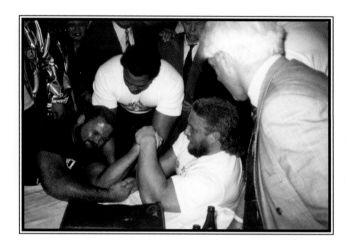

Norton, Scott

Born:	June 15, 1958
Height:	6'3"
Weight:	360
Real Name:	Scott Michael Norton
High School:	Patrick Henry High School (MN)
College:	Anoka-Ramsey Community College
Trained by:	Brad Rheingans, Verne Gagne
Nickname:	Flash
Finisher:	Powerbomb, Shoulder Breaker
Tag Teams:	Jurassic Powers w/ Hercules Hernandez, Fire and Ice w/ Ice Train,
Career Span:	1989–2012

Titles Won:	7
Days as World Champion:	126
Age at first World Title Win:	40
Best Opponents:	Great Muta, Vader, Eddie Guerrero

A former bouncer and construction worker from Minneapolis, Scott Norton won innumerable championships in arm-wrestling competitions. In 1986, he beat the 600-pound Cleve Dean for the International Arm-Wrestling Title. Part of that tournament was filmed in association with Sylvester Stallone's film about the sport, *Over the Top*, which Norton was briefly featured. Extremely powerful, Norton bench-pressed in excess of 650 pounds. He held the coveted IWGP Title twice in Japan, and teamed with Tony Halme and Hercules Hernandez for reigns as IWGP Tag Team Champion. While in WCW, he formed the team "Vicious and Delicious" with Buff Bagwell and was also an intimidating member of the New World Order. Norton has occasionally returned to the mat on independent programs and often works as a bodyguard.

One Man Gang

Born:	February 12, 1960
Height:	6'8"
Weight:	450
Real Name:	George Anthony Gray
High School:	Dorman High School (SC)
Trained by:	Joe Gilbert, Jerry Bragg
Identities:	Crusher Broomfield, Blue Avenger
Nickname:	The African Dream
Finisher:	Big Splash
Managed by:	Jim Holliday, General Skandor Akbar, James J. Dillon, Sir Oliver Humperdink, Jim Cornette, Gary Hart, Slick
Career Span:	1977–2009

Titles Won:	12
Days as World Champion:	161
Age at first World Title Win:	26
Best Opponents:	Steve Williams, Bruiser Brody, Hulk Hogan

An impressively-sized man named George Gray began training to be a pro wrestler before he was out of high school, taking part in athletic programs coordinated by Joe Gilbert in the Spartanburg, South Carolina area around 1977. Along with Gilbert, Gray tutored others, and then became a wrestler on a small-time circuit under the banner of the "Independent Wrestling Association," appearing under his real name. He went to Georgia, Florida, Texas, and the Mid-South territories, winning championships and solidifying his stature as one of the best big men in the sport. He took the name "One Man Gang" and cruised to the UWF World Title on November 9, 1986 by forfeit over Terry Gordy. In the WWF, he became known as Akeem and formed the Twin Towers with the Big Bossman. On December 27, 1995, he beat Kensuke Sasaki for the WCW US Title and was one of the competitors in the gimmick battle royal at WrestleMania in 2001. After going into semi-retirement, he worked as a prison guard in Louisiana.

Born:	October 29, 1949
Height:	5'11"
Weight:	250
Real Name:	Paul Parlette Orndorff Jr.
Parents:	Paul and Eileen Orndorff
Family:	Brother of Terry Orndorff
High School:	Brandon High School (FL)
College:	University of Tampa
Tag Team:	Pretty Wonderful w/ Paul Roma
Career Span:	1976–2000

Titles Won:	18
Best Opponents:	Hulk Hogan, Ricky Steamboat, Ted DiBiase
Halls of Fame:	4

Orndorff, Paul

A pivotal player in the wrestling business during the 1980s and 1990s, "Mr. Wonderful" Paul Orndorff was an accomplished football player in high school and college. In addition to racking up yardage on the field as a running back, he was successful in the discus and shot put events. In 1973, he was drafted in the 12th round by the New Orleans Saints, but after leaving camp in July, there were already reports circulating that he was considering wrestling. Orndorff instead signed with the Chicago Bears in 1974, then the Jacksonville Express of the World Football League in 1975. Finally, he became a grappler after training in Tampa under Eddie Graham and Hiro Matsuda. He made the rounds of the southeastern territories of the NWA, winning championship gold wherever he went. In the Mid-Atlantic region, he teamed with Jimmy Snuka for the World Tag Team Title and captured the National Heavyweight crown three times in Georgia.

The always entertaining Orndorff went to the WWF and was a challenger to Hulk Hogan's heavyweight title in 1984. He co-headlined the first WrestleMania with Roddy Piper against Hogan and Mr. T, and in August 1986, his match against Hogan drew over 70,000 to a stadium in Toronto. After a layoff of several years, he became one of the Dudes with Attitudes in WCW in 1990, and feuded with the Four Horsemen. On March 2, 1993, he beat Erik Watts in a tournament for the vacant WCW World TV Title. He also teamed with Paul Roma to capture the WCW World Tag Team Title on two occasions. Orndorff participated in a number of feuds and angles until injuries caught up with him, forcing him to retire. For years, he was a trainer at the WCW Power Plant and coached many future superstars. At the 2000 Fall Brawl pay-per-view, he came out of inactivity to wrestle, but injured his neck delivering his patented piledriver. The WWE honored Orndorff by inducting him into its Hall of Fame in 2005.

Born:	April 1, 1980
Height:	6'4"
Weight:	245
Real Name:	Randal Keith Orton
Parents:	Robert and Elaine Orton
Family:	Grandson of Bob Orton Sr.
High School:	Hazelwood Central High (MO)
Trained by:	Bob Orton Jr., WWF Developmental Territories (OVW)
Nickname:	The Legend Killer
Finisher:	Full Nelson Slam, Wheelbarrow Suplex, RKO
Groups:	Evolution (2003)
Career Span:	2000–Present

Titles Won:	13
Days as World Champion:	558
Age at first World Title Win:	24
Best Opponents:	John Cena, Triple H, The Undertaker
Movies:	1

Orton, Randy

The Orton name has been synonymous with wrestling for more than sixty years. Today, Randy Orton is thrilling audiences much like his father and grandfather had decades before. Fans have watched his progression from preliminaries to winning the WWE championship eight times and the World Heavyweight belt four—and his ring demeanor and physical skills are as sharp as anyone in the industry. Orton was popular in the role of a babyface, but was even more hated as a heel, working his gimmick to perfection and drawing the ire of international viewers. It wasn't long before he was out from under the shadow of his father, Bob Orton Jr., and grandfather Bob Orton Sr., making history. His feuds with Triple H, John Cena, and The Undertaker were stunningly violent, and Orton demonstrated his versatility time after time. Being able to apply an RKO in a flash is one of his trademarks, leaving his foes—and sometimes friends—out for the count.

A product of St. Louis, Orton made an impressive WWE TV debut on April 25, 2002 and was initially established as a crowd favorite. Soon, though, he turned his back on the fans and became a member of Evolution with Triple H, Batista, and Ric Flair. On December 14, 2003, he began a seven-month reign as Intercontinental titleholder after a victory over Rob Van Dam. A month after losing the belt, he raised the bar to another level when he beat Chris Benoit for the World Heavyweight Title at SummerSlam. It was an achievement, at twenty-four-years-old, that few wrestlers accomplish in their entire careers. Orton proved he was the real deal and the future of pro wrestling. He wanted to add to his credentials by ending The Undertaker's streak at WrestleMania 21, but was turned away. He faced another legend, Hulk Hogan, on August 20, 2006, and was also defeated. Following a run as tag champion with Edge and a feud with DX, Orton reestablished himself as a top contender to the WWE championship.

On October 7, 2007 at No Mercy, he was awarded the vacant championship because titleholder John Cena had been injured. However, that same night, he was defeated by Triple H and lost the belt, only to regain it in the main event, which was a rough Last Man Standing match. In the months following, he held off challenges from Shawn Michaels and Jeff Hardy, and then faced off with Cena and Triple H at WrestleMania on March 30, 2008—a match he won. A month later at Backlash, Orton lost the belt to Triple H. He recovered from a broken collarbone and formed Legacy with Cody Rhodes and Ted DiBiase, two other multi-generational stars, and the trio created plenty of havoc. Orton won the 2009 Royal Rumble, but couldn't take a WrestleMania victory from Triple H. He did leave a six-man match on April 26, 2009 with the WWE championship when the stipulation allowed the title to change hands. He would end up trading it with Batista, and often relied on his Legacy mates to interfere when the chips were down.

Before the end of 2009, he also traded the title back and forth with Cena, winning a Hell in a Cell match on October 4, 2009 in Newark. Cena won an iron-man match at Bragging Rights, taking a firm hold on the WWE Title. Orton, on September 19, 2010, won his sixth WWE Title by winning a six-man elimination contest at Night of Champions, and was successful in defenses against Sheamus and Wade Barrett. He was able to get by Barrett in a grueling affair on November 22, 2010, then forced into a second defense when The Miz cashed in his "Money in the Bank" briefcase and pinned him. In 2011, he went to *Smackdown* following WrestleMania and had a long and intense feud with Christian, winning the World Heavyweight Title twice. Mark Henry proved to be his fiercest challenger, and downed Orton at Night of Champions for the belt. Orton traded victories with Wade Barrett in a feud that remained hot through the end of the year.

On August 18, 2013, Orton pulled a shocker by cashing in his Money in the Bank contract and defeating newly crowned champion Daniel Bryan for the WWE Title. It was Randy's seventh championship win. Soon thereafter, he was backed by the newly created "Authority," a heel combination of Triple H and Stephanie McMahon. Orton lost the belt back to Bryan a month later, but regained it in October. On December 15, 2013, he went over John Cena to unify the WWE and World Heavyweight championships, creating a singular WWE World Title. He would ultimately lose the belt to Bryan at WrestleMania XXX in April 2014. Knocked out of action in 2015 because of a shoulder injury, he missed WrestleMania 32 in 2016, but was expected to return during the summer.

Page, Dallas

Born:	April 5, 1956
Height:	6'5"
Weight:	245
Real Name:	Page Joseph Falkinburg, Jr.
Parents:	Page and Sylvia Falkinburg
Family:	Husband of Kimberly
High School:	Point Pleasant High School (NJ)
Colleges:	Ocean County College, Coastal Carolina College
Trained by:	WCW Power Plant, Jake Roberts
Groups:	The Diamond Exchange (1988, 1991), The Millionaires Club (2000), The Alliance (2001)
Tag Teams:	The Vegas Connection w/ Vinnie Vegas, The New Jersey Triad w/ Bam Bam Bigelow and Chris Kanyon, The Insiders w/ Kevin Nash
Managed:	Bad Company (1988–89), Diamond Studd (1991), The Fabulous Freebirds (1991), Badstreet (1991)
Career Span:	1991–2005

Titles Won:	12
Days as World Champion:	29
Age at first World Title Win:	43
Best Opponents:	Sting, Randy Savage, Curt Hennig
Movies:	14

"Diamond" Dallas Page was a major success in WCW, winning the World Heavyweight Title for the first time six days after his 43rd birthday on April 11, 1999. The triumphant victory came over Ric Flair during a four-way match at Spring Stampede, and was a defining moment in his rise to superstardom. Originally from Point Pleasant, New Jersey, Page began as a manager and TV announcer in the AWA, claiming to have been a rich diamond miner from South Africa. Fans loved to hate his arrogance, and Page continued that theme when he migrated to WCW as the manager of the Fabulous Freebirds. In 1991, he made his pro debut as a wrestler at thirty-five years of age, and for several years, he toiled around the promotion as an enhancement performer. He got a break in 1995 with mid-card feuds against Johnny B. Badd and Jim Duggan, and slowly won over fans with his likeable attitude and popular Diamond Cutter finisher.

Page was also involved in a number of angles and feuds that crossed over into the mainstream. During his feud with Raven, their hatred for one another boiled over onto the set of *MTV Live*, and involved a stop sign. In 1998, he teamed with basketball star Karl Malone and Jay Leno at separate pay-per-view events, garnering lots of attention for WCW and for Page himself. He'd also later figure into the David Arquette angle, rounding out his celebrity association in the ring.

After winning the WCW World Title in 1999, he was defeated by Sting on April 26, only to regain it the same night by outlasting Sting, Bill Goldberg, and Kevin Nash in a four-corners match. On April 16, 2000, he advanced to the finals of a week-long tournament for the vacant WCW Title, but came up short against Jeff Jarrett. Eight days later, he beat Jarrett for his third WCW championship in a cage match. Page would also team with Nash to capture the WCW World Tag Title on two occasions.

Between 1999 and 2001, Page was involved in wars with Scott Steiner, Ric Flair, Mike Awesome, and Kanyon. Once WCW was sold to the WWF, he joined the latter organization as a heel, and during the summer of 2001, he appeared in a mystery stalker angle involving The Undertaker's wife Sara. "DDP" teamed with Kanyon to win the WWF World Tag Team Title from The APA on August 7, 2001. They would hold the championship until August 19 when they lost a WWF Tag vs. WCW Tag unification cage match to Kane and The Undertaker. On January 29, 2002, Page beat Christian for the WWF European Title. Bothered by injuries, Page retired in June 2002, and returned briefly in 2005. All during his tenure as a wrestler, he was committed to helping others, teaching kids about dyslexia and acting as a role model. In recent years, he's created a "Yoga for Regular Guys" fitness program and has pursued film roles.

Pillman, Brian

Born:	May 22, 1962
Height:	5'10"
Weight:	225
Real Name:	Brian William Pillman
High School:	Norwood High School (OH)
College:	Miami University (OH) (Grad. 1983)
College Ach.:	All-American, Mid-American Conference Football Defensive Player of the Year (1983)
Football Position:	Defensive Lineman, Linebacker
Pro Sports:	National Football League—Cincinnati Bengals (1984) Canadian Football League—Calgary Stampeders (1986)
Identities:	The Yellow Dog (Masked)
Nicknames:	Flyin'
Finisher:	Flying Dropkick, Crossbody from the Top Rope
Career Span:	1986–97
Died:	October 5, 1997, Bloomington, MN 36 years old

Titles Won:	7
Best Opponents:	Steve Austin, Lex Luger, Jushin Liger
Halls of Fame:	1

As an inspiring high-flyer or an off-the-cuff heel, Brian Pillman was a thrilling superstar, creating all kinds of buzz and memorable moments. Pillman was an undrafted free agent signed by the Cincinnati Bengals in 1984, playing six games, and won the NFL's Ed Block Courage Award overcoming long odds. After his career was sidetracked because of injury, Pillman went to Calgary and trained to be a wrestler in the famous Hart Dungeon, then wrestled throughout the Stampede territory. In 1989, he turned up in WCW, where his aerial attack earned him a strong following. Along with Tom Zenk, he captured the US Tag Team Title and won a tournament over Richard Morton for the initial WCW Light Heavyweight crown. His astounding series of matches against nimble Jushin Liger altered the way many Americans viewed non-heavyweight workers, and are still fondly talked about today. Pillman, in 1993, formed the Hollywood Blonds with Steve Austin, and duo won the WCW and NWA World Tag Team Titles.

Before the Blonds fully hit their stride, Pillman suffered an injury, only to return as a babyface later in the year to feud with Austin. He joined the Four Horsemen and became more and more unpredictable in and out of the ring. In promos, he made cryptic comments and defined what it meant to be a "Loose Cannon," which became his nickname. Things came to a head at SuperBrawl on February 11, 1996 when he told "booker-man" Kevin Sullivan that he respected him and left the ring. Fans were left to wonder how much of it was a work and how much was real. Pillman left WCW for a brief stint in ECW, then signed with the WWF, but a car accident and ankle injury put him out of action. He still knew how to make things exciting, particularly as he resumed his feud with Austin—spawning their infamous "gun incident" on *Raw* after Austin broke into his Cincinnati home. On the morning of the 1997 Bad Blood pay-per-view, Pillman passed away of arteiosclerotic heart disease and tributes were held on both *Raw* and WCW *Nitro*.

Photo Courtesy of Dr. Mike Lano—Wrealano@aol.com

Born:	October 16, 1973
Height:	6'0"
Weight:	225
Real Name:	Peter Joseph Polaco
Wife:	Jill Polaco
High School:	Holy Cross High School (CT)
Finisher:	That's Incredible
Career Span:	1992–Present

Polaco, Pete

Titles Won:	20
Days as World Champion:	260
Age at first World Title Win:	26
Best Opponents:	Jerry Lynn, Shane Douglas, Tommy Dreamer

   As the "Portuguese Man 'o War," Aldo Montoya, Pete Polaco was a masked fan favorite with a flashy array of dropkicks. As Justin Credible, he was a cane-wielding heel and ECW World Champion. What his ring name is doesn't necessarily matter, but what does is that he's been on top of his game for nearly twenty years. A soccer player in school, Polaco trained in Calgary under the Harts and Lance Storm, and spent a good chunk of the 1990s with the WWF as Montoya. He debuted in ECW in 1997 and defeated Tommy Dreamer for the World Title on April 22, 2000. He ruled the promotion until October 1 when Jerry Lynn won the belt. Teaming with his former mentor, Storm, he formed the Impact Players, and won the ECW World Tag Team Title twice in 2000. He affiliated himself with the Alliance upon his return to the WWF in 2001 and, between May and July 2002, won the WWE Hardcore crown eight times. Since then, he's appeared for ROH and a host of other organizations, and wrestled at TNA's Hardcore Justice in 2010.

Born:	October 28, 1973
Height:	6'2"
Weight:	250
Real Name:	Hassan Assad
Trained by:	Norman Smiley, Soulman Alex G
Identities:	Antonio Banks
Career Span:	2002–Present

Porter, Montel Vontavious

Titles Won:	6
Best Opponents:	Chris Benoit, Kane, Matt Hardy

A product of the Miami area, MVP joined the WWE developmental system in 2005 and debuted on *Smackdown* during the summer of 2006. As part of his gimmick, he was touted as a coveted sports star, and he really had the athletic ability to match the hype. He won the United States Heavyweight Championship from Chris Benoit on May 20, 2007 and held it with distinction until the following April. He also reigned as the WWE Tag Team Champion with his perennial rival, Matt Hardy. In late 2010, he departed the WWE and joined New Japan Pro Wrestling. He was victorious in a tournament for the initial IWGP Intercontinental belt on May 15, 2011. MVP turned up in TNA in 2014.

Born:	September 8, 1964
Height:	6'1"
Weight:	235
Real Name:	Scott Levy
High School:	Lake Worth High School (FL)
College:	University of Delaware
Trained by:	Larry Sharpe, Jake Roberts
Identities:	Scotty the Body, Scott Anthony
Finisher:	Evenflow DDT
Groups:	The Flock (1997–98), The Alliance (2001), Sports Entertainment Xtreme (2003), The Gathering (2003)
Career Span:	1988–Present
Website:	www.theraveneffect.com

Raven

Titles Won:	57
Days as World Champion:	614
Age at first World Title Win:	31
Best Opponents:	Tommy Dreamer, Rhino, Dallas Page
Halls of Fame:	2

Raven was wrestling's symbolic representative to the grunge era, a brooding intellect, yearning for respect and admiration. Verbally gifted, he expressed himself in ways other wrestlers couldn't, making feuds seem much more personal, and adding a unique element to the wrestling world. College-educated and owning the discipline of the US Marine Corps, Raven made his bones in Memphis and Portland, and then appeared in WCW as Scotty Flamingo in 1992. Months later, he went to the WWF, where he managed the Quebecers, actually helping them win the WWF World Tag Team Title from the Steiners and Adam Bomb. Then known as Johnny Polo, he displayed his talents behind the microphone as a commentator, and many people were becoming aware of his well-rounded abilities. In 1994, he was back on the indie scene, where he found a new home in Philadelphia working for Extreme Championship Wrestling.

ECW was the launching pad for a new dimension of his wrestling persona, and saw the birth of Raven, an introverted soul searching for purpose. Part of his gimmick was luring weak-minded and lost souls to his camp, almost like a cult leader, and creating a universe that he was the center of. In 1995, he joined Stevie Richards to win the ECW Tag Team Title on two occasions, then toppled The Sandman on January 27, 1996 for the ECW World belt. He then went to WCW, where he beat Dallas Page for the US crown in 1998, and over a two-year period, captured the WWE Hardcore Title twenty-seven times. He also had success in TNA, defeating A.J. Styles for the NWA World Heavyweight Title on June 19, 2005 in a King of the Mountain bout.

In 2010, he was part of the EV 2.0 faction but left TNA before the end of the year. Raven has wrestled all over the world, taking part in violent feuds against Tommy Dreamer, Abyss, and CM Punk, and solidified his standing as a complex mat personality.

Photo Courtesy of George Tahinos

Born:	February 5, 1986
Height:	5'3"
Weight:	125
Real Name:	Ashley Nichole Simmons
High School:	Ridgewood High School (OH)
Trained by:	Jeff Cannon
Identities:	Ashley Lane, Lexi Lane
Career Span:	2005–Present

Titles Won:	7
Days as World Champion:	299
Age at first World Title Win:	24
Best Opponents:	Tara, Mickie James, Angelina Love

Rayne, Madison

Full of personality and a dynamic performer in the ring, Madison Rayne has been one of the standout women's wrestlers over the past decade. She's a five-time TNA Knockout champion, a former member of the illustrious Beautiful People, and has been embroiled in intense feuds with Tara, Angelina Love, and Mickie James. Rayne, who is from West Lafayette, Ohio, began her career in Ohio Championship Wrestling and made her TNA debut in 2009. She initially won the Knockouts belt in April 2010, was awarded her second title that July after a controversial bout with Love, and beat Tara in October 2010 to start her third reign. Her fourth championship victory came in August 2012, when she defeated Miss Tessmacher, but lost a rematch shortly thereafter. Rayne departed TNA in mid-2013, but returned late in the year. She also regained the Knockouts Title with a victory over Gail Kim. In 2015, she married TNA commentator Josh Matthews.

Born:	July 11, 1954
Height:	6'2"
Weight:	265
Real Name:	Bruce Reed
High School:	Warrensburg High School (MO)
College:	Central Missouri State University
Pro Sports:	National Football League— Kansas City Chiefs (late 1970s) (camp)
Nicknames:	Hacksaw
Career Span:	1978–2006

Titles Won:	15
Days as World Champion:	5
Age at first World Title Win:	38
Best Opponents:	Ron Simmons, Ric Flair, Randy Savage

Reed, Butch

Powerfully built and an imposing presence in the ring, Butch Reed was a football star in high school and college in Warrensburg, Missouri. He was recruited into wrestling by Ronnie Etchison and made his debut in 1978. On the NWA circuit, he appeared in a number of territories and received a good push by Bill Watts in the Mid-South region, defeating Dick Murdoch for the North American Title in 1985. He entered the WWF late in 1986, dyed his hair blond, took Slick as his manager, and became known as the "Natural." A few years later, Reed formed a distinguished tag team with Ron Simmons known as Doom, and won the WCW Tag Team Title in 1990. They fended off challenges from the Horsemen and Rock and Roll Express before losing the belts to the Freebirds. In 1992, he beat Junkyard Dog for the USWA Unified World belt and then, in 2001, captured the WLW Title. He was a force on the Midwestern indie circuit until his retirement in 2006.

Born:	May 10, 1968
Height:	6'2"
Weight:	240
Real Name:	Darren Kenneth Matthews
Trained by:	Marty Jones, Bobby Barron
Identities:	Roy Regal, Steve Regal, Lord Steven Regal
Nicknames:	Lord, The Real Man's Man
Finisher:	Regal Stretch
Career Span:	1983–Present

Titles Won:	18
Best Opponents:	Chris Benoit, Ricky Steamboat, Dave Finlay

Regal, William

William Regal is more of a throwback warrior of the ring than a modern villain. His European uppercuts are brutal, and he constantly mixes a technical style with that of a sheer gladiator. Originally from England, he made his mark on the US scene beginning in 1993 by posing as a member of the royal elite in WCW. He won the World TV Title four times and was a member of the Blue Bloods along with "Earl" Robert Eaton and "Squire" David Taylor. In 1998, he entered the WWF, and would later serve as both commissioner and the general manager of *Raw*. He was also the first member of Vince McMahon's infamous "Kiss My Ass" club. Regal formed tag teams with Lance Storm, Eugene, and Tajiri, winning the World Tag Team Title four times and also holding the Intercontinental belt twice. In the years that followed, he performed a variety of roles in the WWE, including as commentator and general manager in NXT. He is also a trainer of the organization's up-and-comers. His trademark facial expressions, mannerisms, and comedic timing make him one of the most entertaining grapplers outside of the ring.

Photo Courtesy of the Collection of George Schire

Born:	December 13, 1953
Height:	6'0"
Weight:	245
Real Name:	Bradley Bert Rheingans
Parents:	Willard and Lois Rheingans
High School:	Appleton High School (MN)
HS Ach.:	Two-Time Minnesota Wrestling Champion (1970–71) (175)
College:	North Dakota State University
College Ach.:	NCAA Division II Champion (1975) (190)
Amateur Titles:	Two-Time Senior Greco-Roman Champion (1977, 1979) (220)
Olympics:	Greco-Roman Wrestling (1976) (220) (4th Place)
Trained by:	Verne Gagne
Tag Team:	The Olympians w/ Ken Patera
Career Span:	1981–95

Titles Won:	2
Best Opponents:	Nick Bockwinkel, Larry Zbyszko, Rick Martel
Halls of Fame:	2

Rheingans, Brad

The superior legitimate wrestling skills owned by Brad Rheingans made him one of the best trainers in the business and many future superstars attended his school to learn the fundamentals. His outstanding amateur background as a Greco-Roman grappler drew the attention of Verne Gagne, who was always on the lookout for talented pure wrestlers. Rheingans was an NCAA champion and two-time member of the US Olympic Team, although he did not compete in 1980 due to the US boycott. He joined Gagne's AWA and was an influential coach to wrestlers Curt Hennig, Vader, and Tom Zenk. On March 25, 1989, he teamed with Ken Patera to win the AWA World Tag Team Title from Bad Company in Rochester. He went out with an injury during the summer and the title was eventually declared vacant. In the early 1990s, he wrestled for New Japan Pro Wrestling and later acted as a special advisor to Antonio Inoki's UFO group.

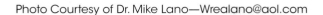

Born:	October 7, 1975
Height:	6'3"
Weight:	270
Real Name:	Terrance Gerin
High School:	Annapolis High School (MI)
Trained by:	Scott D'Amore, Mickey Doyle, Doug Chevalier
Identities:	Terry Richards, Rhino Richards
Groups:	Thug Life, The Alliance
Career Span:	1995–Present

Titles Won:	18
Days as World Champion:	Around 90
Age at first World Title Win:	25
Best Opponents:	Abyss, Christian, Kurt Angle

Rhino

Rhino, an outstanding brawler, was a perfect fit in ECW in 1999. His rough-and-tumble style demonstrated his willingness to battle on the most primitive of levels, leading up to his powerful Gore, a running spear that he drove through opponents. A former amateur wrestler from Dearborn Heights, Michigan, Rhino was trained at the Can-Am Wrestling School in Windsor and grappled for various indie promotions and in Germany prior to landing a spot for ECW. In the years that followed, he won the TV Title twice and captured the World Heavyweight belt from Sandman in 2001. He also wrestled for the WWF prior to suffering a near career-ending neck injury that shelved him for more than a year. In October 2005, while in TNA, he beat Jeff Jarrett for the NWA World Title, and was a member of the ECW reunion group EV 2.0 in 2010. Rhino joined Ring of Honor in 2011 and, several years later, made his return to the WWE.

Born:	June 30, 1985
Height:	6'1"
Weight:	225
Real Name:	Cody Garrett Runnels
Parents:	Virgil and Michelle Runnels
Family:	Brother of Dustin Rhodes
HS Ach.:	Georgia State Wrestling Champion (2003) (189), (2004) (189)
Trained by:	Dusty Rhodes, Al Snow, Bob Holly
Finisher:	Cross Rhodes
Groups:	Legacy (2008–10)
Career Span:	2006–Present

Titles Won:	9
Best Opponents:	Rey Mysterio Jr., Randy Orton, Daniel Bryan

Rhodes, Cody

The naturally charismatic Cody Rhodes began wrestling when he was five years old, and went undefeated as a junior at Lassiter High in Marietta, Georgia, winning two state titles. Joining the family business, he followed his father Dusty and brother Dustin into pro wrestling. Rhodes not only carried on the tradition in name, but in athletic talent, and made a dent early in his WWE career, winning the World Tag Team Title on three occasions with Hardcore Holly and Ted DiBiase Jr. For a time he was a member of the "Legacy" group, later known as "Dashing," but suffered a facial injury in a bout with Rey Mysterio, forcing him to wear a protective mask. He won the first of two Intercontinental championships in August 2011, and would also capture the WWE Tag Title three times with Drew McIntyre and brother Goldust. Cody also used the name "Stardust," a similar gimmick to his brother. Finally, he decided to leave WWE in May 2016, unhappy with his position in the company. Full of potential, his future remains bright.

Born:	April 11, 1969
Height:	6'5"
Weight:	240
Real Name:	Dustin Patrick Runnels
Parents:	Virgil and Sandra Runnels
Family:	Brother of Cody Rhodes
Trained by:	Dusty Rhodes
Identities:	Dusty Rhodes Jr., Marilyn Mansondust, Artist formerly known as Goldust, Dustin Runnels, Seven, Gold Dustin, Black Reign
Nicknames:	The Natural, The Lone Star
Finisher:	Bulldog Headlock
Career Span:	1988–Present

Rhodes, Dustin

Titles Won:	22
Best Opponents:	Rick Rude, Steve Austin, Ricky Steamboat

For many second generation wrestlers, breaking out from underneath the shadow of their fathers is a painstaking chore. Even more difficult is trying to establish an identity enveloped by the shadow of a wrestling legend, and in the case of Dustin Rhodes, he's successfully achieved his own persona separate from his father, Dusty . . . particularly when dressed as Goldust, a strange and complex wrestling gimmick. As Goldust, he bears little resemblance to the ring stylings of his father outside of some of the same maneuvers. Rhodes played football at East Mecklenburg High in Charlotte after transferring from Austin and won his consolation final at the Southwestern 4A state wrestling championships. Seven months later, he turned pro in Florida, and learned a great deal about the business from Dusty. The relationship between father and son has been severely strained at times, yet they've come together to participate in angles and matches in the WWF and WCW.

With partners Ricky Steamboat and Barry Windham, Dustin won the WCW Tag Team Title, and then captured the US Title on January 11, 1993, beating Steamboat in the finals of a tournament. A few years later, he migrated to the WWF and established the "Goldust" character. Flaunting an eccentricity and locked into an identity crisis, Goldust was lavish in his ring introductions and was deliberate in his overly peculiar behavior. Initially disturbing, Goldust became known more for his comedy factor, and annexed the Intercontinental championship three times, also winning the World Tag Team Title with Booker T. Rhodes had two stints in TNA and returned to the WWE after each tour, appearing on *Smackdown* as late as 2010. In December of that year, he suffered a serious shoulder injury that necessitated surgery. His autobiography, *Cross Rhodes*, was released around the same time. Through all of the different gimmicks and personal trials, Rhodes has had a successful career and created a legacy all his own.

Richards, Stevie

Born:	October 9, 1971
Height:	6'1"
Weight:	230
Real Name:	Michael Manna
High School:	Frankford High School (PA)
Trained by:	Mike Sharpe, The Sandman
Identities:	Dr. Stevie
Nickname:	King of Swing
Finisher:	Superkick
Managed by:	Beulah McGillicutty
Managed:	Bull Buchanan (2000–01), The Good Father (2000–01), Ivory (2000–01), Jazz (2002), Victoria (2003)
Career Span:	1992–Present

Titles Won:	38
Best Opponents:	Tommy Dreamer, Sabu, CM Punk

Wrestling favorite Stevie Richards has excelled in the business for nearly two decades, appearing in colorful roles and offering many comedic performances. He's been a hardcore superstar, a member of the Blue World Order, and a lackey for Raven. A product of the Port Richmond section of Philadelphia, Richards gained lots of esteem while working for ECW, teaming with Raven to win the World Tag Team Title on two occasions in 1995. Venturing through the independents, WCW, and the WWF, he gained plenty of ring experience and confidence behind the microphone. As the smug leader of Right to Censor, Richards managed Buchanan and The Good Father to the WWF Tag Team Title in November 2000. Between April and August 2002, he captured the WWF Hardcore Championship a whopping twenty-two times. He also seconded women's champions Jazz and Victoria. While a part of TNA, he became known as Dr. Stevie, feuded with Abyss, and joined the ECW reunion group EV 2.0 in 2010.

Born:	September 8, 1960
Height:	5'9"
Weight:	145
Real Name:	Victoria Lynn Richter
High School:	Bossier High School (LA)
Career Span:	1979-2005

Titles Won:	8
Days as World Champion:	819
Age at first World Title Win:	23
Best Opponents:	Fabulous Moolah, Leilani Kai, Madusa Miceli
Halls of Fame:	2

Richter, Wendi

The first woman to achieve superstar status in Vincent K. McMahon's nationally expanding WWF was Wendi Richter of Bossier City, Louisiana, a supremely popular heroine who was much more than just a pretty face in the ring. She was proficient in actually wrestling, and was able to distinguish herself as a world champion, which she was three times over—twice in the WWF and once in the AWA. Richter was the goddess of the WWF's Rock n' Wrestling era, and appeared both on MTV and in the family friendly cartoon. She was also managed by music icon Cyndi Lauper in 1984-1985. After being double-crossed out of her title by Fabulous Moolah in 1985, she departed the WWF and only returned when she was inducted into the WWE Hall of Fame in 2010.

Photo Courtesy of Dr. Mike Lano—Wrealano@aol.com

Born:	October 11, 1965
Height:	6'1"
Weight	375
Real Name:	Solofa Fatu
High School:	Balboa High School (CA)
Trained by:	Afa
Identities:	Fatu, The Sultan, Kishi
Finisher:	Rikishi Driver
Career Span:	1995–Present

Rikishi

Titles Won:	13
Best Opponents:	Steve Austin, The Rock, Bret Hart
Halls of Fame:	1

A member of the famous Anoai family, Rikishi is the nephew of Samoans Afa and Siki, and cousin of Samu, his longtime tag team partner. His brothers, Jamal and Tonga Kid, were also wrestlers of note. In 1987, along with Samu as the Samoan Swat Team, he appeared all over the globe. They won titles in Puerto Rico and Texas, and, in 1994, captured the WWF World Tag Team Title as the Headshrinkers, managed by Afa and Captain Lou Albano. In 1999, he adopted the Rikishi persona, wearing modified sumo gear, and gained popularity for his dancing in the ring. He was also known for giving rivals the uproarious "Stinkface." He held the Intercontinental Title in 2000 and the World Tag Team Title with Rico two years later. In 2004, he partnered with Scotty 2 Hotty to win the WWE Tag Team Title. He left the WWE that same year. Rikishi was inducted into the WWE Hall of Fame in 2015, and his two sons, Jimmy and Jey Uso, are among the leading tag teams in the organization.

Born:	May 20, 1969
Height:	6'2"
Weight:	230
Real Name:	Brian Girard James
Parents:	Joseph and Gail James
Family:	Brother of Scott, Steve, and Brad Armstrong
Trained by:	The Armstrong Family
Identities:	Brian Armstrong, The Roadie, Jesse James, B.G. James
Career Span:	1993–Present

Titles Won:	23
Days as World Champion:	A few days
Age at first World Title Win:	32
Best Opponents:	Steve Austin, The Rock, Kane

Road Dogg

The youngest son of Bob Armstrong, "Road Dogg" Brian James joined his father and brothers in wrestling after proud service as a Marine during the first Gulf War. He was associated with Jeff Jarrett during his first stint in the WWF, but didn't gain significant status until forming the rogue New Age Outlaws with Billy Gunn. In addition to winning the World Tag Team Title five times, the unruly pair were members of popular anti-establishment group, D-Generation X. As a singles competitor, he captured the Intercontinental Championship from Val Venis in March 1999 and was known for his colorful promos and popular catchphrases. On TNA, he partnered with Ron Killings and Konnan as 3Live Kru and was twice a tag team champion. He also wrestled all over the indie scene, and, in 2001, became the initial WWA World Champion during a tour of Australia. In 2011, he returned to WWE and has worked as a backstage producer for several years.

Born:	May 2, 1972
Height:	6'5"
Weight:	250
Real Name:	Dwayne Douglas Johnson
Parents:	Rocky and Ata Maivia Johnson
High School:	Freedom High School (PA)
HS Ach:	High School All-American Football Player (1989)
College:	University of Miami (FL)
College Ach:	Member of the 1991 National Champions Football Squad
Trained by:	Rocky Johnson
Nicknames:	Brahma Bull, Rocky, The Most Electrifying Man in Sports Entertainment, The People's Champion
Finisher:	Rock Bottom, People's Elbow, Sharpshooter
Tag Team:	The Rock and Sock Connection w/ Mankind
Career Span:	1996–Present

Titles Won:	18
Days as World Champion:	394
Age at first World Title Win:	26
Best Opponents:	Steve Austin, Hulk Hogan, Mankind
Halls of Fame:	1
TV Appearances:	Over 150
Movies:	30

Rock, The

"The Rock" Dwayne Johnson is an internationally recognizable actor and a third generation professional wrestler. His full-time active career lasted only eight years, but during that time he displayed a mastery of performances, connecting to the audience with remarkable flair, and saturating the WWE Universe with entertaining segments. His ability to convert humdrum angles and scenarios into amusing content was uncanny. In the ring, he was just as skilled, appearing in high-tension matches against the likes of Hulk Hogan, Steve Austin, Triple H, and many other big-name superstars. The Rock's catchphrases united audiences as they repeated the sayings along with him, electrifying arenas, and spotlighting his natural charisma. Winning the WWE World Title a total of seven times between 1998 and 2002, The Rock was instrumental in helping the organization win the ratings war against WCW.

Born in Alameda County, California, Johnson was the son of wrestler Rocky Johnson and the grandson of wrestler "High Chief" Peter Maivia, as well as the nephew of Jimmy Snuka. He played football in college at the University of Miami and made the practice squad for the Calgary Stampeders of the CFL. Finding his pursuit of football to be less than desirable, he entered the wrestling business in 1996, touring the USWA out of Memphis as Flex Kavana. Before the end of the year, however, he was on the main stage in the WWF, wrestling as Rocky Maivia Jr., a tribute to his father and grandfather. At the Survivor Series on November 17, 1996, he was the sole survivor for his team, making his first pay-per-view appearance a successful one. In February 1997, he beat Triple H for the Intercontinental Title and joined the Nation of Domination later in the year as a heel. He continued to build momentum in his rise up the bill, and on November 15, 1998, he beat Mankind in the finals of a tournament to win the WWF World Heavyweight Title.

The Rock's first WWF championship win was tainted by a screwy finish, and marked his transition to the "Corporation Champion," a henchman of Vince McMahon. He feuded with Mankind over the belt, and the two traded the title twice. At WrestleMania XV on March 28, 1999, The Rock was unsuccessful in his defense against Steve Austin, and lost the title, leading to him being fired from the Corporation. The angle turned Rock into a fan favorite again, which worked out nicely as he began to achieve some mainstream success. In addition to the release of his autobiography, he appeared as a guest host on *Saturday Night Live.* With help from Austin, Rock regained the WWF Title from Triple H on April 30, 2000, but lost it back to him in an iron-man match on May 21. A month later at the King of the Ring, Rock pinned McMahon in a six-man tag team match, and won his fifth WWF Title. Former Olympian Kurt Angle beat him for the belt, but Rock regained it in February 2001, becoming the first ever six-time champion.

Austin again dethroned Rock at WrestleMania X-Seven, this time with some unexpected outside help from McMahon. Shortly thereafter, he was put out of action in an injury angle, and spent several months filming *The Scorpion King.* The movie was a prequel to *The Mummy,* and a continuation of the story of his character featured in *Mummy Returns,* which opened to a $65 million weekend in May 2001. He returned during the WCW/ECW Invasion and feuded with Booker T. At SummerSlam, he won the WCW World Title and proceeded to trade it with Chris Jericho before dropping it to the latter on December 9, 2001. In what was considered a dream match for many fans, The Rock faced off against Hulk Hogan on March 17, 2002 at WrestleMania X-8 in Toronto, and the 68,237 in attendance chanted feverishly for their heroes in an emotionally charged match. The back-and-forth drama saw Rocky score the pin and take the proverbial torch.

On July 21, 2002, he won his seventh WWF Title, and held it until SummerSlam. The Rock battled Austin at the following WrestleMania, but this time around, he was victorious. Retiring from wrestling to meet the growing demands of his film career, he appeared in twenty movies between 2001 and 2011 and made a few rare appearances on WWE programming. He returned "home" to the promotion on February 14, 2011, and ignited a feud with John Cena. It was announced that he'd be the guest host for WrestleMania, which gave him and Cena the opportunity to escalate their war of words. Finally, the two agreed to face off in the main event of Wrestlemania XXVIII in 2012. In the meantime, Rock and Cena teamed up at the Survivor Series in a win against The Miz and R-Truth, and touted their anticipated match every chance they got.

Finally, after months and months of build-up, Rock beat Cena at WrestleMania in April 2012. He made sporadic appearances in the days and weeks that followed, and returned again on January 27, 2013, to challenge CM Punk for the WWE championship. After a controversial bout, Rock beat Punk and captured his eighth WWE Title and his first in more than a decade. He ultimately lost the belt to Cena in a rematch at WrestleMania 29. The Rock made appearances at WrestleMania XXX, 31, and 32, and at the latter event in April 2016, he defeated Erick Rowan in a spontaneous bout which lasted but six seconds. With his Hollywood career flourishing and his willingness to get back in the ring, all of his fans are content and there is little doubt he will make his presence felt in the WWE well beyond 2016.

Born:	January 1, 1977
Height:	6'0"
Weight:	230
Real Name:	Robert F. Roode Jr.
High School:	Kenner Collegiate High School (Ontario)
Trained by:	Sean Morley
Identities:	Lee Awesome
Groups:	Fortune (2010–11)
Career Span:	1998–Present

Roode, Bobby

Titles Won:	22
Days as World Champion:	66
Age at first World Title Win:	34
Best Opponents:	Kurt Angle, A.J. Styles, James Storm

Bobby Roode of Peterborough, Ontario, realized a dream on October 26, 2011, when he beat James Storm to capture the TNA World championship. A hockey player in his youth, he entered the business in 1998 and worked on the indie scene and in Puerto Rico before joining TNA in 2004. He gained fame with Storm as "Beer Money, Inc.," and won the TNA World Tag Title a total of five times. During a feud with Immortal, his passion for the business was evident in promos, and it was clear he sought success as a singles performer. He won the Bound for Glory series in 2011, and ultimately beat Storm for the World Title. Roode reigned for 256 days, the longest in TNA history, until he lost the belt to Austin Aries in July 2012. In September 2014, he regained the title with a defeat of Lashley, but lost it the following January. After a long stint in the promotion, Roode left TNA in March 2016.

Rotundo, Mike

Born:	March 30, 1958
Height:	6'3"
Weight:	240
Real Name:	Lawrence Michael Rotunda
High School:	Newark Valley High School (NY)
College Ach.:	Four-Time letterwinner in wrestling (1977–79, 1981)
Identities:	Mike Rotunda, Irwin R. Schyster, Michael Wall Street, V.K. Wall Street
Finisher:	Airplane Spin, Stock Market Crash
Groups:	The Varsity Club (1988–89), The Corporation (1994–95), New World Order (1996), The Varsity Club (1999)
Tag Teams:	The Young Lions w/ Barry Windham, The US Express w/ Barry Windham, The US Express w/ Dan Spivey, The Varsity Club w/ Steve Williams, Money Inc. w/ Ted DiBiase
Managed by:	Captain Lou Albano, Ted DiBiase
Career Span:	1981–2008

Titles Won:	18
Best Opponents:	Rick Steiner, Bret Hart, Razor Ramon

An amateur wrestler at Syracuse where he won the Eastern championship as a heavyweight in 1981, Mike Rotundo was lured into pro wrestling by another member of the school's alumni, Dick Beyer, who gained international fame as The Destroyer. After initial success in Florida and becoming known as one of the best young athletes in the business, he headed for the WWF along with tag team partner Barry Windham. Outside the ring, Rotundo married Barry's sister Stephanie. During that first stint in the WWF, Rotundo and Windham won the World Tag Team Title twice, and he'd personally return to the promotion again in the early 1990s to have similar success with Ted DiBiase as his partner, known as Money, Inc. A neck injury a few years later slowed his career, but he'd make appearances in the WWE through 2008, where he works as a road agent. Rotundo is also a successful businessman,, and his two sons, Windham and Taylor, are both pro wrestlers themselves.

Born:	January 19, 1972
Height:	6'1"
Weight:	220
Real Name:	Ronnie Aaron Killings
High School:	Harding High School (NC)
Trained by:	Manny Fernandez
Identities:	Ron Killings, K-Kwik, K-Krush
Finisher:	Hang Time
Groups:	3 Live Kru (2003–05)
Career Span:	1997–Present

Titles Won:	12
Days as World Champion:	119
Age at first World Title Win:	30
Best Opponents:	Chris Jericho, CM Punk, Curt Hennig
Movies:	2

R-Truth

An exciting entertainer from Charlotte, R-Truth became the first African American to win the NWA World Heavyweight Championship when he defeated Ken Shamrock on August 7, 2002. Considering the title had lineage stretching back more than a half century, it was a superb achievement. Two years later, he won the title again in a four-way match. He teamed with pro football player Adam "Pacman" Jones to capture the TNA World Tag Team Title in 2007 and returned to the WWE, where he'd worked earlier in the decade, the following year. He supplemented his wide athletic range with his ability to rap, and his catchy song, "What's Up," inspired lackluster crowds innumerable times. On May 24, 2010, he won the US Title, but lost it a few weeks later on *Raw*. He shocked many by turning heel in April 2011, but his new attitude was gold, especially when he ranted about the "Little Jimmys" in the audience. He also formed a tag team with The Miz.

Rude, Rick

Born:	December 7, 1958
Height:	6'4"
Weight:	246
Real Name:	Richard Erwin Rood
Parents:	Richard and Sally Rood
High School:	Robbinsdale High School (MN)
Trained by:	Eddie Sharkey
Identities:	Halloween Phantom
Nicknames:	Smooth Operator
Finisher:	Reverse Neckbreaker (Rude Awakening)
Groups:	Pringle's Dynasty (1985), The Dangerous Alliance (1991–92), D-Generation X (1997), New World Order (1997–98)
Tag Team:	Ravishing and Raging w/ Manny Fernandez
Managed:	Triple Threat (1997), D-Generation X (1997), Curt Hennig (1997–98)
Career Span:	1982–94
Died:	April 20, 1999, Alpharetta, GA 40 years old

Titles Won:	14
Days as World Champion:	336
Age at first World Title Win:	27
Best Opponents:	Ric Flair, Sting, Ricky Steamboat

"Ravishing" Rick Rude of Minnesota drew immense heat from audiences for his arrogance, and was adept at chastising fans, opponents, and whoever else got in his way. During the late 1980s, he used a gimmick that portrayed him as the ultimate ladies man, often kissing women from the crowd before matches. His colorful personality, chiseled physique, and profound toughness were a grand slam in terms of marketability, making him a top superstar and routine champion. He gained experience and success in many territories, which included Memphis, Dallas, and Tampa, before landing in the WWF in 1987. At the time of his jump to the northeast, he was co-holder of the World Tag Team Title in the Mid-Atlantic region along with Manny Fernandez. Rude entered a heated feud with Jake Roberts after trying to kiss the latter's wife. In 1989, he pinned the unbeatable Ultimate Warrior, with help from his manager Bobby Heenan, to win the Intercontinental Title, and the following year, chased Warrior's World Title.

Rude went to WCW, where he captured the United States belt and enjoyed a fourteen-month reign as titleholder beginning in November 1991. He also won the WCW International World Title three times, first taking the gold belt from Ric Flair on September 19, 1993. In March of the following year, he traded the title with Hiroshi Hase, and then lost it to Sting on April 17, 1994. Before more than 53,000 fans in Japan on May 1, 1994, Rude regained the belt, but suffered a serious back injury that ended his active career. A few years later, he made appearances for ECW and then the WWF, where he was one of the original members of DX, along with Shawn Michaels, Triple H, and Chyna. During a taped edition of *Raw* on November 17, 1997, Rude, sporting a beard, made a showing with his cohorts on an attack of Sgt. Slaughter. That same night, a clean-shaven Rude appeared on WCW's *Nitro*, live from Cincinnati, as a member of the NWO—marking one of the most notable promotional jumps of the Monday Night Wars.

Born:	December 12, 1963
Height:	6'0"
Weight:	220
Real Name:	Terry Michael Brunk
Trained by:	The Sheik
Identities:	Sabu the Elephant Boy
Finisher:	Moonsault, Arabian Facebuster
Career Span:	1985–Present

Titles Won:	37
Days as World Champion:	Around 670
Age at first World Title Win:	30
Best Opponents:	Terry Funk, Shane Douglas, Rob Van Dam
Halls of Fame:	1

Sabu

Sabu, the "Most Homicidal, Suicidal, Genocidal Man in Wrestling," has been at it since 1986. As the nephew of The Sheik, he's lived up to the family reputation of violence and extreme ring methods, including the use of weaponry. He has proven many times over to be indestructible, by performing spectacular maneuvers and working through injuries that would've sidelined a lesser man; even once applying super glue to an open wound as a way to continue participating in the sport he loves. Sabu has combined the terrifying antics of his uncle with a high-flying athleticism that makes him a sight to behold every time he steps through the ropes and into the ring. His stunts, like moonsaulting through empty tables, are always crowd pleasers. Early in his career, after toiling around the Michigan independents, he made appearances in the Memphis-based USWA and Tri-State Wrestling in Philadelphia before going to Japan for FMW.

Two years later, in 1993, Sabu was a major figure in the upstart Philly organization, ECW, which prided itself on a hardcore style of grappling. It was a perfect fit for the daredevil Sabu, who won the ECW Heavyweight belt from Shane Douglas on October 2, 1993, and then the TV Title the following month. On July 23, 1994, Sabu beat Al Snow in a ladder match for the initial NWA World Independent Title. In addition to winning the ECW World Title in 1997, he won an array of honors in Japan to include the IWGP and UWA World Junior Heavyweight championships. He captured the NWA World Title from Mike Rapada in November 2000 and the XPW Title in Los Angeles. He's also appeared for the WWE, WCW, and TNA. In 2010, he appeared at TNA's Hardcore Justice show and was defeated by Rob Van Dam. Sabu was also involved in the Extreme, Version 2.0 angle until being fired after losing a ten-man tag match on November 7 of that year.

Born:	March 17, 1979
Height:	6'3"
Weight:	300
Real Name:	Nuufolau Joel Seanoa
High School:	Ocean View High School (CA)
Trained by:	UIWA's West Coast Dojo—Johnny Hemp, Cincinnati Red
Identities:	King Joe
Nickname:	Samoan Suplexing Machine
Finisher:	Island Driver, Dragon Suplex, Muscle Buster
Career Span:	1999–Present

Samoa Joe

Titles Won:	15
Days as World Champion:	771
Age at first World Title Win:	24
Best Opponents:	Kurt Angle, CM Punk, Kenta Kobashi

Samoa Joe is a highly regarded superstar of Samoan descent. Originally from Orange County, California, Joe has the ability to become world champion in either one of the big two promotions in the near future. A powerful grappler, he mixes strength with ingenuity, and is well-versed in Judo, as well as other martial arts. These aspects make him a dangerous grappler with submission knowledge, and if he's not trouncing an opponent with violent blows, he's got them twisted up and forcing them to tap out. As a child, he performed a Polynesian dance at the opening ceremonies of the 1984 Olympic Games in Los Angeles, and later became a California State Junior Judo Champion. He trained to become a wrestler and one of the major feuds was against John Cena in UPW in 2000. With experience in Japan under his belt, Joe went to the Ring of Honor promotion, and became World Champion on March 22, 2003, with a victory over Xavier.

For the next twenty-one months, Joe reigned as ROH titleholder, successfully defending his belt against some of the best independent grapplers in the world, including Christopher Daniels, CM Punk, and A.J. Styles, though was dethroned by Austin Aries on December 26, 2004. Joe had a memorable bout against Japanese legend Kenta Kobashi when the latter toured the US in 2005. That same year, he made his debut for TNA, winning the Super X Cup tournament and then the first of four X Division titles. In 2006, he was named "Mr. TNA," and continued to battle up the card. On April 13, 2008, Joe beat Kurt Angle for the TNA World Title in a match that he threatened to retire if defeated. Joe survived a lengthy feud with Booker T and the challenge of Angle and Christian and became the first champion to successfully retain in a King of the Mountain bout. He ran into the "Icon," Sting on October 12, 2008 at Bound for Glory and dropped the championship.

Samoa Joe formed a successful tag team with Magnus and captured both the TNA World and GHC (Japan) Tag Team championships in 2012. That same year, he also captured the TNA Television Title. Over the next three years he maintained his status as a role player, but never ascended back to the heavyweight throne. Joe departed TNA in March 2015 and, two months later, turned up in World Wrestling Entertainment's developmental organization, NXT. Unlike many of the upstarts in the promotion, Joe was a battle tested veteran, and he captured the NXT Heavyweight Title from Balor on April 21, 2016.

Photo Courtesy of Pete Lederberg—plmathfoto@hotmail.com

Born:	June 16, 1963
Height:	6'4"
Weight:	245
Real Name:	James Fullington
Family:	Husband of Peaches
High School:	Marple Newtown High School (PA)
Trained by:	Tri-State Wrestling Academy (Larry Winters)
Identities:	Mr. Sandman, Hak
Nickname:	Hardcore Icon
Finisher:	DDT
Career Span:	1989–Present

Titles Won:	16
Days as World Champion:	545
Age at first World Title Win:	31
Best Opponents:	Cactus Jack, Raven, Shane Douglas
Halls of Fame:	1

Sandman, The

The longtime backbone of Extreme Championship Wrestling, The Sandman is known for carrying a Singapore cane and smoking a cigarette while guzzling beer on the way to the ring. It is definitely a unique approach, one that differs greatly from the mat technicians of yesteryear. Sandman represents a generation of extreme competitors, thus dubbed the "Hardcore Icon," a wrestler who will put his body on the line for the sport. During his years in ECW, he had memorable feuds with Shane Douglas, Sabu, and Raven, but his feud with Tommy Dreamer was the most brutal. A football player in high school, Sandman won the first of five heavyweight championships on November 16, 1992 when he beat Don Muraco in Philadelphia. He won his fifth title on January 7, 2001, beating Steve Corino and Justin Credible. Since that time, he's wrestled for both the WWE and TNA, and is still making headlines on the independent scene.

Born:	May 10, 1953
Height:	6'1"
Weight:	230
Real Name:	Merced Solis
Pro Sports:	National Football League—Kansas City Chiefs (1975) Canadian Football League—British Columbia Lions (1976)
Identities:	Richard Blood, El Madator
Nickname:	Chico
Finisher:	Flying-forearm smash, Figure-four leglock
Career Span:	1977–2014

Titles Won:	22
Best Opponents:	Greg Valentine, Randy Savage, Don Muraco
Halls of Fame:	4

Santana, Tito

The multi-sport high school athlete Tito Santana became a star tight end at West Texas State University, playing alongside quarterback Tully Blanchard. Having admired the Funks, he became a wrestler after a stint as a pro football player, and trained under Hiro Matsuda in Tampa. He made the rounds of several territories, and then went to the northeast to work for the WWF, adopting the name "Tito Santana" in the process. On October 22, 1979 in New York, he teamed with powerful Ivan Putski to dethrone the Valiants for the WWF World Tag Team Title, but were later beaten by the Wild Samoans, losing the belts. A popular star, Santana won the Intercontinental Title from Don Muraco in Boston on February 11, 1984, becoming the youngest man to hold the championship. He traded the belt with Greg Valentine, and then was pinned by Randy Savage for the title on February 8, 1986 after the latter used a foreign object.

Santana's unique balance of technical and high-flying skills sustained his status as one of the best wrestlers in the promotion. He teamed with Rick Martel to win the WWF World Tag Team Title from the Hart Foundation on October 27, 1987, and established another internal record by becoming the first wrestler to win both the Intercontinental and tag team titles on two separate occasions. Strike Force lost the belts to Demolition at WrestleMania IV, and Santana feuded with his former partner. On October 14, 1989, Santana won the annual King of the Ring Tournament with a finals victory over Martel. In the vacant Intercontinental Title tournament, Santana made it to the finals in April 1990, only to be beaten by Mr. Perfect. Santana was a longtime member of the WWF Spanish-language commentary team and wrestled occasionally, even appearing for one night on WCW *Nitro* in January 2000. He still makes independent appearances.

Born:	August 4, 1966
Height:	5'10"
Weight:	260
Identities:	Power Warrior
Tag Team:	The Hell Raisers w/ Hawk
Career Span:	1986–2014

Titles Won:	25
Days as World Champion:	894
Age at first World Title Win:	31
Best Opponents:	Kenta Kobashi, Toshiaki Kawada, S. Hashimoto
Halls of Fame:	1
MMA Record:	2-0

Sasaki, Kensuke

Powerhouse Kensuke Sasaki is one of the most decorated wrestlers in Japanese wrestling history. Raised in Fukuoka, he was a student of Riki Choshu, and was also educated in Stu Hart's famed Dungeon in Calgary. He found success with partners Hiroshi Hase and Hawk, winning the IWGP Tag Team Title, and capturing the gold seven times altogether. Sasaki, as a singles wrestler, was even more impressive. He won the IWGP Title five times, the AJPW Unified Triple Crown, and the GHC Heavyweight belt. While in WCW in 1995, he beat Sting for the United States Heavyweight Championship. His wife, Akira Hokuto, was also a professional wrestler.

Severn, Dan

Born:	June 9, 1958
Height:	6'2"
Weight:	250
Real Name:	Daniel DeWayne Severn
Parents:	Marvin and Barbara Severn
High School:	McCloy High School (MI)
College:	Arizona State University
Amateur Titles:	Thirteen-Time National AAU Champion, Junior World Champion (1977), Greco-Roman Wrestling Champion
Trained by:	Al Snow
Finisher:	Armbar Submission
Career Span:	1992–2010

Titles Won:	9
Days as World Champion:	1,559
Age at first World Title Win:	36
Best Opponents:	Ken Shamrock, Owen Hart, The Rock
Halls of Fame:	5
MMA Record:	100-18-7

A world class wrestler and MMA fighter, Dan "The Beast" Severn won the National Wrestling Alliance World Heavyweight Title on two separate occasions, helping the fledging organization regain credibility during its lowest point in history. Severn began wrestling in his youth and won a score of amateur titles. Over a two-year period from 1992-1994, he went into pro wrestling and mixed martial arts. On February 24, 1995, in Erlanger, Kentucky, Severn beat Chris Candido by submission for the NWA World Title on a Smoky Mountain Wrestling program. He went on to win the UFC V tournament on April 7. He was NWA titleholder for 1,479 days, the third longest reign in history, and finally lost the belt to Naoya Ogawa on March 14, 1999. Severn won his second NWA Title from Shinya Hashimoto on March 9, 2002. On May 29, the NWA stripped him of the belt because he was unable to defend at the initial NWA-TNA pay-per-view in June 2002. He remains a trainer and often makes appearances for the Price of Glory promotion in Michigan.

Born:	February 11, 1964
Height:	6'1"
Weight:	230
Real Name:	Kenneth Wayne Kilpatrick
Parents:	Richard and Diane Kilpatrick
High School:	Lassen High School (CA)
Trained by:	Buzz Sawyer, Nelson Royal
Identities:	Wayne Shamrock, Vince Torelli
Nickname:	World's Most Dangerous Man
Career Span:	1990–2004

Titles Won:	4
Days as World Champion:	49
Age at first World Title Win:	38
Best Opponents:	Shawn Michaels, The Rock, Steve Blackman
Halls of Fame:	3
MMA Record:	28-17-2

Shamrock, Ken

With the heart of a champion, Ken Shamrock helped popularize mixed martial arts fighting in the United States and around the world, and was at the core of the UFC when it was lifting off the ground in 1993. His spectacular battles against Royce Gracie and Dan Severn drew an abundance of interest in MMA, and with his UFC 6 victory over the latter, he earned the title of "Superfight Champion." In 1997, he joined the WWF and won the Intercontinental Title. He also was triumphant in the 1998 King of the Ring tournament, and teamed with Corporation ally Big Bossman to capture the WWF World Tag Team Title. In June 2002, he won a battle royal final to become the NWA World Heavyweight king at TNA's initial pay-per-view. Shamrock was inducted into the UFC Hall of Fame in 2003, and returned to MMA for two fights in 2015 and 2016 against Kimbo Slice and Royce Gracie. Both were losses.

Born:	January 28, 1978
Height:	6'6"
Weight:	270
Real Name:	Stephen Farrelly
Trained by:	Larry Sharpe, Jim Molineaux
Identities:	Sheamus O'Shaunessy
Finisher:	Brogue Kick
Career Span:	2002-Present

Titles Won:	6
Days as World Champion:	161
Age at first World Title Win:	31
Best Opponents:	Triple H, John Cena, Randy Orton
Movies:	3

Sheamus

Sheamus might be the first ever Irish-born WWE heavyweight champion, but he's not the first ever Irish claimant to the World Heavyweight Title in the United States. Seventy-four years earlier, Danno O'Mahoney became the undisputed champion and earned that special distinction. O'Mahoney and his famed "Irish Whip" finisher took the industry by storm, much like Sheamus in recent years. By watching him wrestle, it is not shocking that he's already had much success, which includes two reigns as WWE champion and winning the King of the Ring tournament. A former bodyguard for musician Bono, Sheamus attended Larry Sharpe's famed Monster Factory Wrestling School and ventured through a number of independent promotions before landing in the WWE developmental program in Florida. His athletic background, which included rugby, gave him the dexterity and discipline to hurdle the initial obstacles to be a leading wrestler, and he was on the fast track to glory.

Initially turning up on the ECW brand and then graduating to *Raw*, Sheamus won his first WWE Title over John Cena on December 13, 2009, in a tables match. Cena was his second victim as well on June 20, 2010, but he eventually lost the title to Randy Orton on September 19. A few months later, on November 29, 2010, he won the King of the Ring tournament. On March 14, 2011, he won the US Title from Daniel Bryan, and was champ until May 1, 2011, when he lost it to Kofi Kingston. Sheamus went over Bryan again, this time at WrestleMania XXVIII, beating the latter in just 18 seconds to capture the World Heavyweight Title. He'd remain champion through October, dropping the belt to The Big Show. In November 2015, he won his third WWE Title when he cashed in his Money in the Bank contract and beat Roman Reigns. Less than a month later on *Raw*, he lost a rematch and the belt. In 2015 and into 2016, Sheamus was part of a heel group known as the League of Nations.

Born:	May 15, 1958
Height:	6'2"
Weight:	260
Real Name:	Ronald Simmons
High School:	Warner Robins High School (GA)
College Ach.:	Two-Time All-American Football Player (1978-1979)
NFL Draft:	Cleveland Browns (1981) (6th Round)
Pro Sports:	Canadian Football League—Ottawa Rough Riders (1980-1983) United States Football League—Tampa Bay Bandits (1983–85)
Nickname:	All-American
Finisher:	Spinebuster
Groups:	The Ministry of Darkness (1999), The Acolyte Protection Agency (2000)
Career Span:	1986–2010

Simmons, Ron

Titles Won:	9
Days as World Champion:	150
Age at first World Title Win:	34
Best Opponents:	Vader, Butch Reed, Cactus Jack
Halls of Fame:	3

While in college at Florida State University, Ron Simmons of Perry, Georgia was a two-time All American nose guard. His number, 50, was retired by the school, and in 1986, he was inducted into the Seminole Hall of Fame. After playing some pro football, he chose to give wrestling a chance, and trained under Hiro Matsuda before joining the Florida circuit in October 1986. He toured a handful of regions before settling into WCW in late 1989. As part of a masked tag team known as Doom, Simmons and Butch Reed were bent on taking care of the Steiners for Robin Green, also known as Woman. Doom were unmasked at Clash of the Champions X by the Steiners, but rebounded after taking Teddy Long as their manager, and winning the WCW World Tag Team Title. They reigned until February 24, 1991, when they were defeated by the Freebirds. Simmons then turned babyface and feuded with Reed and Long, gaining a large following of fans.

On August 2, 1992 in Baltimore, he beat Big Van Vader to win the WCW World Heavyweight Title, and placed his name among the other great African American champions, including Seelie Samara, Jack Claybourne, Bobo Brazil, and Bearcat Wright. Simmons nearly survived the year with his title intact, but lost a rematch to Vader on December 30, 1992, also in Baltimore. During a tour of Europe, he suffered a broken leg and eventually left WCW. He briefly worked for ECW, but then signed with the World Wrestling Federation and changed his name to Faarooq. He entered the gang wars of 1997 and 1998, joining the Nation of Domination. In 1999, Faarooq formed a successful card-playing tag team with Justin Bradshaw known as the "Acolytes," and were a team for hire, prepared to go wherever the money took them. Simmons made the catchphrase "Damn" a hit, and remained in the WWE until 2009.

Photo Courtesy of Dr. Mike Lano—Wrealano@aol.com

Born:	November 27, 1962
Height:	5'11"
Weight:	260
Real Name:	David Smith
Parents:	Sid and Joyce Smith
Trained by:	Ted Betley
Identities:	Young David
Finisher:	Running Powerslam
Career Span:	1978–2002
Died:	May 18, 2002, Invermere, British Columbia 39 years old

Titles Won:	16
Best Opponents:	Bret Hart, Shawn Michaels, Owen Hart
Halls of Fame:	1

Smith, Davey Boy

The popular "British Bulldog" was from Leeds, England and made his debut in the Calgary promotion as an eighteen-year-old in May 1981. Already owning several years of pro experience and time under the watchful eye of his future father-in-law Stu Hart in the famed "Dungeon," Smith teamed with Hart Brothers Bruce and Bret and his cousin Dynamite Kid. He also won the World Mid-Heavyweight championship in the summer of 1982 and the North American Title twice. Continuing his development in Japan, Smith competed in a junior heavyweight tournament there in 1983 and formed an impressive tag team with Dynamite Kid. Smith and Kid debuted in the WWF in 1984, and two years later, they won the World Tag Team Title. As a singles performer, he beat Bret Hart on August 29, 1992 for the Intercontinental Title before 80,355 fans in London. Extremely built, Smith had a 56" chest and 21" bicep, and trained his son Harry for the ring.

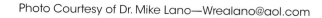

Born:	July 18, 1963
Height:	6'1"
Weight:	230
Real Name:	Allen Ray Sarven
High School:	Lima Senior High School (OH)
Trained by:	Jim Lancaster
Identities:	Steve Moore, Avatar, Shinobi, Leif Cassidy
Nickname:	Simply Sensational
Finisher:	Snow Plow
Groups:	The JOB Squad (1998–99)
Tag Teams:	The Fabulous Kangaroos w/ Denny Kass, The Motor City Hitmen w/ Mickey Doyle, The Dynamic Duo w/ Unibomb
Career Span:	1982–Present

Snow, Al

Titles Won:	41
Best Opponents:	Sabu, Shane Douglas, Chris Benoit

For most of the first decade of Al Snow's wrestling career, he was an underrated talent and ignored by the major promotions. He made some headlines while in SMW around 1994 and had several short stints in the WWF, using different gimmicks, but none were exceptionally notable. In the late 1990s, he began to see his popularity increase, and rightfully so, as part of the JOB Squad. In ECW, the Lima, Ohio product carried a styrofoam mannequin's head as part of his oddball character, which was a home run with audiences. More and more people began learning about Snow and paying closer attention to his talents as a wrestler. In 2001, he gained national attention after appearing as the lead trainer for the WWE's Tough Enough series on MTV, remaining in that role for three seasons. The martial artist was a fixture in the WWE through 2007, winning several titles, and appeared on the independent scene before landing a gig as an agent for TNA in 2010.

Born:	November 1, 1963
Height:	6'3"
Weight:	260
Real Name:	Monty Kip Sopp
High School:	Oviedo High School (FL)
College:	Sam Houston State University
Trained by:	Harris Brothers
Identities:	Kip Winchester, Rockabilly, The Outlaw, Kip James
Nicknames:	Bad Ass, The One
Career Span:	1992–Present

Sopp, Monty

Titles Won:	19
Best Opponents:	Shawn Michaels, Steve Austin, The Rock

Always an entertaining performer, Monty Sopp of Central Florida was a key figure in the WWF's late 1990s resurgence, and was part of both D-Generation X and the New Age Outlaws tag team. Billy Gunn, as he was known, and the Road Dogg, always delivered cutting-edge promos, and the Outlaws' disorderly behavior carried them to five World Tag Team Championships. Sopp also teamed with Bart Gunn and Chuck Palumbo to capture the WWF belts, making him a ten-time titleholder. In 1999, he won the King of the Ring tournament, and beat Eddie Guerrero for the Intercontinental strap the following year. Between 2005 and 2009, he appeared for TNA and made his return to the WWE in 2012, where he worked both in the ring and behind-the-scenes. He was also a *Tough Enough* coach. Currently, Sopp is wrestling on the indie circuit. Considering all of his success, it's hard to believe that Sopp nearly took a different path and devoted his life to the rodeo.

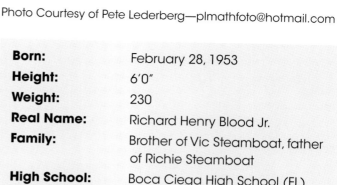

Photo Courtesy of Pete Lederberg—plmathfoto@hotmail.com

Born:	February 28, 1953
Height:	6'0"
Weight:	230
Real Name:	Richard Henry Blood Jr.
Family:	Brother of Vic Steamboat, father of Richie Steamboat
High School:	Boca Ciega High School (FL)
Trained by:	Verne Gagne, The Iron Sheik
Identities:	Sammy Steamboat Jr., Dick Blood, The Dragon
Nicknames:	The Dragon, Steamer
Finisher:	Flying Crossbody
Tag Teams:	The Great Warriors w/ Jay Youngblood, The South Pacific Connection w/ Jimmy Snuka
Career Span:	1976–2009

Steamboat, Ricky

Titles Won:	26
Days as World Champion:	76
Age at first World Title Win:	35
Best Opponents:	Randy Savage, Ric Flair, Rick Rude
Halls of Fame:	3

High-flying and technically proficient, Ricky "the Dragon" Steamboat wrestled in one of WrestleMania's greatest matches in 1987 against Randy Savage. It is still commonly referenced as a classic; full of excitement, drama, and athleticism, which are the aspects that combine to forge a true mat memory. That was a prime example of what Steamboat brought to wrestling, and his matches were constantly heralded for his ability to create powerful exhibitions against even lackluster opponents. A talented sportsman in high school, he attended the grueling wrestling school of Verne Gagne in Minnesota, and made his pro debut in 1976. With a purported relation to former wrestler Sam Steamboat, Ricky's career progressed naturally, and he learned the tough lessons of the business from the ground up, and by the late 1970s, he was a hot commodity in the Mid-Atlantic region for the Crocketts. Steamboat captured the US and Television titles, plus formed a World championship tandem with Jay Youngblood, warring regularly with the Brisco Brothers in 1983.

Owning the distinction of appearing the initial Starrcade and first WrestleMania, Steamboat wrestled in some of the most gripping matches of the 1980s against Ric Flair, defeating the latter for the NWA World Heavyweight Title on February 20, 1989. He was a fighting champion for his seventy-six days as king, and Flair was the only one who could best him, on May 7, 1989. Over the next several years,

LEGENDS OF PRO WRESTLING

he appeared for the WWF and WCW, and won a number of honors while in the latter organization between 1991-1994; among them being the WCW World Tag Team Title with Dustin Rhodes and Shane Douglas. A devastating back injury forced him off the mat, and he made sporadic appearances until joining the WWE as a road agent in 2005. Steamboat returned to the ring to battle Chris Jericho in a special handicap elimination match at WrestleMania on April 5, 2009. Despite a heroic effort, he was defeated. He was also named to the WWE Hall of Fame. Steamboat's energetic ring style will influence professional wrestlers forever.

Photo Courtesy of Pete Lederberg—plmathfoto@hotmail.com

Born:	March 9, 1961
Height:	5'11"
Weight:	245
Real Name:	Robert Rechsteiner
Family:	Older brother of Scott Steiner
High School:	Bay City Western High School (MI)
College:	University of Michigan
College Ach.:	Wrestling Letterman (1981, 1983–84)
Trained by:	Steve Fraser, George Steele, Eddie Sharkey
Groups:	Hyatt and Hot Stuff Incorporated (1986–87), The Varsity Club (1988–89, 1999), The First Family (1989), Dudes with Attitudes (1990), The Magnificent Seven (2000–01)
Career Span:	1984–2013

Titles Won:	27
Best Opponents:	Scott Steiner, Mike Rotundo, Booker T
Halls of Fame:	2

Steiner, Rick

The "Dogfaced Gremlin," Rick Steiner was a powerful wrestling superstar and his version of the clothesline, known as the Steinerline, was one of the most hard-hitting moves in the business. Always wearing his amateur-style head and ear protector during matches, Rick began wrestling with his brother Scott as a kid, and gained formal training in high school and college at the University of Michigan. He initially made a name for himself in the UWF and then joined WCW, where he was part of the Varsity Club with Kevin Sullivan and Mike Rotundo. As a singles competitor, he held the World TV Title, but things really picked up once he began teaming with his brother Scott. The Steiners won seven WCW and two WWF World Tag Team Championships, and added two IWGP Titles to their record while in Japan. They were a perfect mesh of athletes, and their versatile offense was far too much for most opponents.

Few brother duos in history experienced anywhere near their success, but the Steiners ultimately broke up in February 1998. Remaining popular with fans, Rick teamed with Buff Bagwell to win the WCW World Tag Team Title, but after Bagwell turned on him, he picked Kenny Kaos to be his new partner. In 1999, he beat Booker T and Chris Benoit for two separate stints as WCW World TV Champion and captured the United States crown from Shane Douglas in February 2001 before losing it to Booker at the final WCW pay-per-view in March. Rick made numerous TNA appearances, including a reunion of the Steiners in a heated war with Team 3D. Away from the squared circle, he was elected to the Cherokee County, Georgia School Board, and today serves as the chairman after being reelected in 2010. In addition to being an active member of the community, Rick sells real estate.

Photo Courtesy of Pete Lederberg—plmathfoto@hotmail.com

Born:	July 29, 1962
Height:	6'1"
Weight:	255
Real Name:	Scott Carl Rechsteiner
College Ach.:	All-American Wrestler (1986), Wrestling Letterman (1982–83, 1985–86)
College Record:	125-51-2
Trained by:	Don Kent, Dick the Bruiser, Jerry Graham Jr.
Nicknames:	White Thunder, Big Poppa Pump, Big Bad Booty Daddy, Genetic Freak
Finisher:	Steiner Recliner
Groups:	Dudes with Attitudes (1990), New World Order (1998–99, 2000), The New Blood (2000), The Magnificent Seven (2000–01), Main Event Mafia (2008)
Career Span:	1986–2015

Steiner, Scott

Titles Won:	30
Days as World Champion:	Around 584
Age at first World Title Win:	24
Best Opponents:	Booker T, Samoa Joe, Bill Goldberg
Halls of Fame:	2

After years of being part of a legendary brother tag team, Scott Steiner broke free and established himself as one of the most colorful and unpredictable grapplers in the world. His promos are a league apart from his peers, seemingly intermixing kayfabe-breaking commentary with the regular hullabaloo. Upon first glance, you'd suspect he was a nothing more than a bodybuilder because of his mammoth size, but Scott has shown his amazing athleticism throughout his career, particularly early on when the Steiners were dominating competition on both the North American and Asian continents. His pure grappling knowledge was fostered at Western High School in Bay City, Michigan and later at the University of Michigan, where his older brother Rick also wrestled. After becoming an All-American in 1986, Scott turned pro, working for Dick the Bruiser's WWA based out of Indiana. On August 14, 1986, he beat the Great Wojo and captured the promotion's World Heavyweight Title. Scott was only twenty-four years of age.

Three years later in May 1989, Scott joined his brother in WCW, and the two formed a tag team that naturally clicked in the ring. They quickly garnered a following, and upended The Fabulous Freebirds for the NWA World Tag Team Title on November 1, 1989. They feuded with the Andersons, Nasty Boys, and Doom over the course the next year, losing the belts to the latter in May 1990, but winning the US Title from the Midnight Express in August. In 1991, they added to their list of accomplishments by regaining the World Tag Team Title, then beat Hiroshi Hase and Kensuke Sasaki for the IWGP crown. At that point, they held three championships and six belts, simultaneously. A serious bicep injury suffered during the summer of 1991 put Scott on the shelf, but The Steiners returned to regain the WCW and IWGP Titles. The duo also toured the WWF and added two more World Title reigns there, while still making routine trips to Japan. They appeared briefly in ECW before returning to WCW in 1996.

The Steiners feuded with the Road Warriors, Harlem Heat, and The Outsiders, remaining fan favorites through late 1997. In January 1998, Scott turned on Rick at SuperBrawl and joined the NWO. He proceeded to dye his hair blond, concentrate more and more on his physique, and adopted a more punishing ring style. Steiner's volatile interview segments were both vicious and comical, and over the next year and a half, he won the TV and US belts. On November 26, 2000, he won his first major World championship when he beat Booker T for the WCW Title.

After WCW was sold, Steiner appeared in the WWE and feuded with Triple H. Off and on since 2006, he's worked for TNA, and appeared in various capacities—more recently as a fan favorite in January 2011, then as a member of Immortal. Scott's innovative Frankensteiner, imaginative suplexes, and supreme power have set him apart from his peers during a career lasting a quarter of a century. No one quite knows what he will say or do next.

Sting

Born:	March 20, 1959
Height:	6'2"
Weight:	260
Real Name:	Steven L. Borden
High School:	William S. Hart High School (CA)
College:	College of the Canyons
Identities:	Blade Runner Flash
Finisher:	Stinger Splash leading into the Scorpion Deathlock, Scorpion Deathdrop
Groups:	Power Team USA (1985), Hyatt and Hot Stuff, Inc. (1986–87), The Four Horsemen (1990), Dudes with Attitudes (1990), New World Order (Wolfpack) (1998), The Millionaires Club (2000)
Tag Team:	The Blade Runners w/ Rock
Career Span:	1985–2015

Titles Won:	25
Days as World Champion:	1,002
Age at first World Title Win:	31
Best Opponents:	Ric Flair, Kurt Angle, Rick Rude
Halls of Fame:	2

Eternally charismatic, the wrestler known as Sting has enthralled audiences for decades. He was long the backbone of World Championship Wrestling (WCW) and Total Nonstop Action (TNA), and his popularity remained constant throughout the 1990s and 2000s. In 2015, crowds lit up with excitement when Sting finally made his World Wrestling Entertainment debut. And it was a highly-anticipated arrival, years in the making. His jump to the WWE was just what the "Little Stingers" wanted, and he solidified his place as a Hall of Famer. Sting's path to superstardom began in 1985, when he joined Rick Bassman's Power Team USA, and was trained by Bill Anderson and Red Bastien along with Jim Hellwig, the future Ultimate Warrior.

Sting gained experience in the Mid-South and UWF territories, joining Eddie Gilbert's Hyatt and Hot Stuff, Inc.; a group of heels. With the more experienced Gilbert, Sting captured the UWF Tag Team Title on two occasions and feuded with the popular Fantastics. He also partnered with Rick Steiner to win the belts, only to eventually turn fan favorite and feud with Gilbert and Steiner. His transition to a widely acknowledged hero was furthered by his actions on January 26, 1988, when he called out to NWA champion Ric Flair during a Four Horsemen party. When Flair refused to respond and James J. Dillon tossed champagne in his face, Sting gave the latter a splash in the corner. In that instant, he became a huge crowd favorite and was an immediate contender for Flair's NWA World Title. That led to the match that made him a star at Clash of the Champions in March 1988. That night, he held Flair to draw after more than forty minutes, and nearly saw him win the belt.

Over the next two years, he continued to rise up the ladder, winning the TV Title and the Iron Man competition at Starrcade 1989—pinning Flair in the finals. As his destiny to become NWA champion was about to be realized, Sting suffered a ruptured left patella and was out of action for five months. The inevitable was only delayed, and on July 7, 1990 at the Great American Bash, Sting pinned Flair and won the World Title. Flair would regain the championship the following January at a house show in New Jersey. In February 1992, Sting won his first WCW World Title from Lex Luger, and had an ongoing feud with Big Van Vader, which saw the title change hands several times. Hulk Hogan's arrival in WCW in 1994 changed the dynamics of the organization, and Sting's place in the pecking order shifted. Although he was still supremely popular, he was somewhat overshadowed by Hogan. The NWO came to prominence in 1996, and, at one point, it appeared that Sting had defected to the rogue operation.

But he hadn't. Instead, there was an imposter Sting working on behalf of the NWO, but the angle saw Sting declare himself a "free agent," and distancing himself from his old character. He reinvented himself to be a dark and ominous figure, often carrying a baseball bat and staring down at the ring from the rafters. The shift in attitude and appearance didn't mark his full-fledged turn to heel, but Sting's motives were sometimes unclear. Prior to Starrcade '97, he missed fourteen straight pay-per-views, but returned at that show for a much-hyped match against Hogan for the WCW Title, and using his patented Scorpion Deathlock, he won the belt. Sting feuded with the members of the NWO, and then joined an offshoot of the group known as the Wolfpack in 1998. After defeating Flair in July 1999, he became WCW President, and then turned heel for the first time two months later. Fortunately for the fans, it didn't stick. In April 2000, Sting was lumped into the "Millionaire's Club" because of his veteran status, then participated in a violent feud with Vampiro.

Following the sale of WCW in 2001, there were scores of rumors that he was joining the WWF, but it never materialized. He toured Europe and Australia with the WWA in 2002 and 2003, holding the world title of the promotion, and then joining TNA in June 2003 on a temporary basis. When he reappeared in 2006, it was more permanent. Sting won the NWA Title before the year was out, and added four TNA World Championships in the years that followed, defeating the likes of Jeff Jarrett, Kurt Angle, and Jeff Hardy. In 2011, he underwent a drastic metamorphosis into a Joker-esqe personality, complete with cackling and a heavy dose of unpredictability. The change added a unique edge to TNA that was unexpected from the longtime star. The gimmick displayed his versatility as a performer, and his matches were as entertaining as ever. But it ran its course, and Sting settled on a role, sans makeup, as the commissioner of all on-camera programming for *Impact*.

In the years that followed, Sting participated in the major Aces & Eights feud that dominated TNA, and engaged in a number of other feuds. Among them was against Magnus, who beat him on January 23, 2014, in a match that ended his tenure in TNA. Later that year he signed with the WWE for the first time in his long career, a move many of his fans hoped to see. He targeted Triple H at the Survivor Series, initiating a feud that culminated at WrestleMania 31 on March 30, 2015. At that event, he was defeated. He challenged Seth Rollins for the WWE World Title on September 20, 2015, but didn't get the win. Sting suffered a real world neck injury during the bout, and announced his retirement from the sport in 2016. He was inducted into both the WWE and TNA Halls of Fame, and honored for his great commitment to pro wrestling.

Born:	June 1, 1977
Height:	6'0"
Weight:	240
Real Name:	James Allen Cox
High School:	Franklin High School (TN)
Trained by:	Shane Morton
Career Span:	1997–Present

Titles Won:	16
Days as World Champion:	8
Age at first World Title Win:	34
Best Opponents:	Kurt Angle, Robert Roode, Sting
Movies:	1

Storm, James

An engaging personality in the business, "Cowboy" James Storm of Williamson County, Tennessee, was an amateur wrestler and transitioned to the local professional affiliates before getting a job with WCW in 2000. Two years later, he entered TNA and formed a long-running partnership with Chris Harris. As "America's Most Wanted," the duo dominated competition and won the NWA World Tag Team Title six times. In 2006, Storm briefly went out on his own before teaming with Robert Roode as "Beer Money," and, again, was very successful. The pair won the TNA belts four times, and in 2010, they joined Fortune. On October 18, 2011, two days after Roode came up short against TNA champion Kurt Angle, Storm pinned the titleholder and won his first world singles title. In what was supposed to be a match between friends, Roode blasted Storm with a beer bottle on October 26 to capture the belt, effectively destroying their bond. Storm remained a major player in TNA in the years that followed, but never returned to the top spot in the company. He departed the promotion in mid-2015, but returned in January 2016, reteaming with Bobby Roode to capture the World Tag Title, their fifth.

Born:	April 3, 1969
Height:	6'0"
Weight:	228
Real Name:	Lance Evers
College:	Wilfrid Laurier University
Finisher:	Canadian Maple Leaf
Groups:	Triple Threat (1997–98), Team Canada (2000–01), The Alliance (2001), The Canadians (2002), The Un-Americans (2002)
Tag Teams:	Sudden Impact w/ Chris Jericho, The Thrillseekers w/ Chris Jericho, The Impact Players w/ Justin Credible
Career Span:	1990–Present
Website:	www.stormwrestling.com

Storm, Lance

PPV Record:	19-22
WWE *Raw* TV Record:	27-39, 4 NC
WWE *Smackdown* TV Record:	10-17
Titles Won:	27
Best Opponents:	Booker T, Rob Van Dam, Jerry Lynn

Lance Storm was a smooth wrestler who let his outstanding ability speak for itself in the ring. After ending a pursuit to play volleyball in college, he went to Calgary to train under the Hart Brothers, and made his pro debut on October 2, 1990 against his future tag team partner, Chris Jericho. Astutely technical, Storm developed his skills in Asia and Europe, and then became better known to American fans while in SMW and ECW in the 1990s. He went to WCW in 2000 and was given a push as part of Team Canada, winning the US championship three times. Further success in the WWE followed, as Storm captured the World Tag Team Title on four occasions and the Intercontinental belt once before going into semi-retirement in 2004 because of injuries. He was a trainer at WWE's Ohio Valley until opening his own wrestling school. He offers insightful commentary on his official website.

Born:	December 18, 1975
Height:	5'4"
Weight:	120
Real Name:	Patricia Anne Stratigias
Trained by:	Ron Hutchison, Fit Finlay
College:	York University
Finisher:	Bulldog Headlock
Career Span:	2000–2011
Website:	www.trishstratus.com

Titles Won:	8
Days as World Champion:	828
Age at first World Title Win:	25
Best Opponents:	Jazz, Victoria, Lita
Halls of Fame:	1

Stratus, Trish

A native of the Toronto area, Stratus is a seven-time WWE Women's World Champion and is much more than just a blonde bombshell. She's an athletic wonder, a yoga enthusiast, and exceptionally charitable, devoting her time and energy to numerous causes. The oldest of three sisters, she broke into the business after working as a fitness model, featured initially in *MuscleMag International*, and trained at Ron Hutchinson's Toronto gym. Upon signing a WWF contract in November 1999, and furthering her training, she became the psuedo-manager behind Test and Albert. Stratus demonstrated her dedication for the sport by working long hours, learning the ways of the ring, and yearning to improve . . . and improve she did. Within a short time, she was one of the most talented divas on the promotion's roster, and her popularity skyrocketed. Fans could see that Stratus had the attitude and drive to be successful, not only as a wrestler in the ring, but within the madcap and drama-filled wrestling soap opera.

Stratus had on-screen romances with Chris Jericho, Carlito, and Jeff Hardy. However, her ring wars with Jazz, Lita, Victoria, and others were much more memorable. At the 2001 Survivor Series, she won a six-way match to capture her first WWF Women's Title. Many grueling battles for the belt occurred in the years that followed, and in 2002, she was honored as WWE's Babe of the Year. She was also recognized as the Diva of the Decade. Trish retired from the ring in 2006, and made sporadic appearances on *Raw* or *Smackdown*, particularly when the WWE visited Toronto. In 2011, she became a trainer for the revived *Tough Enough* series and returned to the ring at WrestleMania XXVII in a six-man tag team match, with her team being victorious. Stratus has spent time as an actress, performing in the 2011 film *Bail Enforcers*, and running a yoga studio. In just a little more than a decade on the mat, she's placed her name among the greatest women wrestlers in history, and secured her future place in the hall of fame.

Born:	June 2, 1978
Height:	5'10"
Weight:	215
Real Name:	Allen Neil Jones
Parents:	Troy and Betty Jones
Identities:	Mr. Olympia (masked)
Finisher:	Styles Clash
Groups:	Fortune (2010–11)
Career Span:	1998–Present

Styles, A.J.

Titles Won:	30
Days as World Champion:	407
Age at first World Title Win:	25
Best Opponents:	Christopher Daniels, Samoa Joe, Kurt Angle

A proven innovator in the ring, A.J. Styles is known around the world as one of the greatest active grapplers in the business. Owning technical knowledge, a repertoire of flashy high-flying maneuvers, and confidence behind the microphone, he is the prototype of the modern superstar akin to this generation's Shawn Michaels or Bret Hart. Styles doesn't stand 6'5" nor weigh 250 pounds, but he doesn't need that size to be successful. He utilizes the entire ring to his advantage, showing quickness and intelligence, and a developed psychology, all of which have earned him great respect. There's a reason why he's been pushed by TNA, New Japan, and now the WWE, and that's because he's one-of-a-kind. All his matches are must-see wrestling.

At Johnson-Gainesville High School, Styles was a standout football player and wrestler, winning two Class AA wrestling championships at 160 pounds. He earned a scholarship to Anderson College in South Carolina, but was lured into professional wrestling, training under Rick Michaels at a school run by the NCW co-founder. He began his successful career in 1998 around Georgia and started collecting championship belts, including the NCW TV and NWA Wildside Heavyweight crown. Following brief runs in WCW and the WWA overseas in Australia, Styles passed up an opportunity to join the WWE developmental league and eventually ended up in the budding TNA. He became the initial TNA X-Division champion on June 19, 2002 with a victory over Jerry Lynn in the finals of a four-man double-elimination match. The X-Division, which spotlighted many styles of wrestling with an emphasis on high-flying and death-defying maneuvers, was seemingly created with athletes like Styles in mind.

Styles' feud with Jerry Lynn created lots of buzz and gave TNA some of its earliest headlines. While in the midst of their war, the two teamed up to win the vacant NWA Tag Team Title in July 2002. There was no absence of excitement in X-Division bouts and they were often the highlight of TNA programs. Styles won a three-way match on June 11, 2003 for the NWA World Heavyweight Title, and at the age of twenty-five, he was the third youngest man to hold the coveted championship after Chris Candido and Tommy Rich. He'd captured the NWA belt two additional times, and on September 20, 2009, he finally won the TNA

World Title in a five-way match, and then turned heel in early 2010 with Ric Flair as his manager. Styles was heavily influenced by Flair, wearing suits to the ring, and began using the figure-four leglock as his finisher. He joined the group Fortune, and feuded with Immortal in 2011. During the summer, he resumed his longtime feud with Christopher Daniels, and they displayed more of their great ring chemistry.

In 2013, Styles won TNA's Bound for Glory series and propelled himself into a bout with World champion Bully Ray, which he won on October 20, 2013. However, a contract dispute with officials caused him to be stripped of the belt. But Styles continued to claim the belt and when he made his on-camera return, dropped his title to Magnus. He decided to leave TNA for good and turned up in the independents in 2014. He also ventured to New Japan, where he won the IWGP World Heavyweight crown on two occasions in 2014 and 2015. Styles joined the Bullet Club and was involved in a number of high profile bouts. In January 2016, he entered the WWE, and has since feuded with Chris Jericho and Roman Reigns.

Photo Courtesy of Mike Mastrandrea

Born:	March 24, 1982
Height:	6'5"
Weight:	260
Real Name:	Jacob Hager
High School:	Perry High School (OK)
College:	University of Oklahoma
Trained by:	Steve Keirn
Finisher:	Ankle-lock submission hold
Career Span:	2006–Present

Titles Won:	4
Days as World Champion:	186
Age at first World Title Win:	26
Best Opponents:	Christian, Chris Jericho, Rey Mysterio Jr.

Swagger, Jack

Oklahoma has produced innumerable wrestling champions, and Jack Swagger of Perry earned honors as both an amateur and a pro. A two-time high school champion, he continued his success at the University of Oklahoma, where he went on to become an All-American. Through Jim Ross, he signed with the WWE and landed on the ECW roster in 2008. Swagger played up his amateur background, billing himself as the "All-American American," and was hated for his cockiness. He went over Matt Hardy for the ECW World Title on January 12, 2009, and reigned for four months. At WrestleMania XXVI on March 28, 2010, he won the Money in the Bank match, and used that to take advantage of a hobbled Chris Jericho two nights later to win the World Title. He lost the belt on June 20, 2010, in a four-way bout. In 2011, he played a role in the Jerry Lawler-Michael Cole feud and joined a heel clique headed by Vickie Guerrero. Later, he took Zeb Colter as his manager and was a member of the "Real Americans" group.

Tara

Photo Courtesy of Dr. Mike Lano—Wrealano@aol.com

Born:	February 10, 1971
Height:	5'8"
Weight:	130
Real Name:	Lisa Marie Varon
College:	UCLA
Other Titles:	NPC Inland Empire Middleweight Title (1995) (bodybuilding), 1st Place in the 1997 ESPN2 Fitness America Competition (1997) and numerous other fitness awards and achievements
Finisher:	Moonsault, Widow's Peak, Black Widow
Groups:	Revolution (2001-02)
Career Span:	2000-Present

Titles Won:	7
Days as World Champion:	362
Age at first World Title Win:	31
Best Opponents:	Trish Stratus, Awesome Kong, ODB

Tara is one of the most talented women wrestlers in the world today. For years prior to becoming a pro grappler, her outstanding athleticism was on display in cheerleading and in various fitness competitions. She received some advice from Joanie Laurer and Torrie Wilson, and initially trained at UPW's Ultimate University in California before her 2000 debut. She later developed further at Ohio Valley before joining the WWE as "Victoria" in 2002. On November 17, 2002, she beat Trish Stratus to capture her first WWE Women's World Title. She'd win the belt a second time, and then capture the TNA Knockouts championship a total of four times in 2009-2010. She became known for carrying her pet tarantula to the ring and placing it on downed opponents. In July 2011, she teamed with Miss Tessmacher to capture the TNA Knockouts Tag Team Title.

Taylor, Terry

Born:	August 12, 1955
Height:	6'1"
Weight:	225
Real Name:	Paul W. Taylor
Parents:	Paul and Jacqueline Taylor
College:	Guilford College
Trained by:	Eddie Graham
Identities:	The Red Rooster, Terrence Taylor, Dr. Feelgood (Masked)
Nickname:	The Taylor Made Man
Groups:	The York Foundation (1991)
Tag Team:	The Fantastic Ones w/ Bobby Fulton
Career Span:	1979–2006

Titles Won:	28
Best Opponents:	Ric Flair, Ted DiBiase, Curt Hennig

Named Rookie of the Year by the National Wrestling Alliance in 1980, the popular Terry Taylor was seen by many fans as a potential successor to Ric Flair as World Heavyweight Champion. Among his early ring honors were the NWA World Junior Title and the Southern championship. By 1985, he was on the big stage, challenging Flair at the Superdome in New Orleans before 11,000 fans, and for more than thirty minutes, he looked every bit like the next NWA king. Unfortunately, it never materialized. Despite that fact, in his twenty-seven years on the mat, he appeared around the globe, and had plenty of success, including powerful backstage roles that influenced many careers. Taylor was also an important figure in training grapplers, working at the WCW Power Plant and operating his own wrestling school in Georgia. Originally from Vero Beach, Taylor enjoyed a stint with TNA as a director of talent relations before jumping back to the WWE to work for its NXT developmental organization.

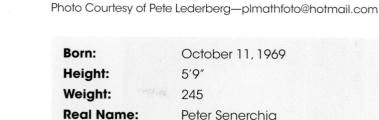

Born:	October 11, 1969
Height:	5'9"
Weight:	245
Real Name:	Peter Senerchia
Family:	Cousin of Chris and Joe Chetti
High School:	Franklin K. Lane High School (NY)
Identities:	Kid Krush
Finisher:	Tazmission, Katahajimi
Groups:	The Alliance (2001)
Tag Team:	The Tazmaniacs w/ Joe Chetti
Career Span:	1987–2006

Titles Won:	15
Best Opponents:	Sabu, Bam Bam Bigelow, Kurt Angle
Days as World Champion:	261
Age at first World Title Win:	29

Taz

A powerfully built grappler with legitimate skills, including knowledge of judo, Taz has been much more than a television commentator to the wrestling world. From Red Hook, Brooklyn, he was tutored in the fundamentals by Johnny Rodz and bounced around the independents before landing in Philadelphia for a budding promotion known as Eastern Championship Wrestling, where he was known in 1993 as Tazmaniac. Legendary Jimmy Snuka passed a symbolic "torch" to him the following year, and had a nine-month reign as ECW TV Champion between June 1997 and March 1998. On January 10, 1999, he beat Shane Douglas to capture the ECW World Heavyweight Title at the Guilty as Charged pay-per-view. Taz was a fighting champion for nine months, and lost the belt to Mike Awesome in a three-way match also involving Masato Tanaka on September 19.

The "Human Suplex Machine" signed with the WWF in early 2000, and on April 13, he returned to ECW to take the World Title off Mike Awesome, who had signed a contract with rival WCW, and did so with a submission victory. Taz appeared on WWF TV with the ECW belt and had a champion vs. champion match against Triple H on April 18 in Philadelphia. He lost the strap a short time later to Tommy Dreamer. Taz served as a commentator on *Smackdown* with Michael Cole from 2002 to 2006, and proceeded to perform the same role on the ECW program. In 2009, he left the WWE and joined TNA, debuting as commentator on August 20, and working alongside Mike Tenay on its weekly show on Spike. He remained in that position until 2015. Taz has also been an influential of Hardcore wrestling school and was a coach on the first season of *Tough Enough.*

Born:	February 2, 1950
Height:	6'1"
Weight:	235
Real Name:	Genichiro Shimada
Finisher:	Northern Lights Bomb
Promoted:	Wrestle Association R (WAR) (Japan)
Career Span:	1976–2015

Titles Won:	24
Days as World Champion:	713
Age at first World Title Win:	38
Best Opponents:	Jumbo Tsuruta, Keiji Mutoh, Stan Hansen
Tournament Wins:	4
Halls of Fame:	1

Tenryu, Genichiro

In the last thirty-five years, there have been few wrestlers more successful than Japanese legend Genichiro Tenryu. Transitioning from the Sumo ranks, he was trained in Amarillo by the Funk Brothers, and returned to All-Japan to work for Giant Baba. In February 1984, he captured the vacant United National Championship from Ricky Steamboat in Tokyo. That title would later be unified into the coveted AJPW Triple Crown, which he'd win from Jumbo Tsuruta on June 5, 1989 before 15,000 fans. Ten years later, on December 10, 1999, he defeated Keiji Mutoh at the Osaka Prefectural Gym and won the IWGP Title. With the victory, he became the second man in history to have held both the AJPW Triple Crown and the IWGP Title. Tenryu lost the IWGP belt to Kensuke Sasaki on January 4, 2000 at the Tokyo Dome. Tenryu regained the AJPW Triple Crown on October 28, 2000 in Tokyo, winning an eight-man tournament.

Born:	June 22, 1963
Height:	6'7"
Weight:	425
Real Name:	John Anthony Tenta
Parents:	John and Irene Tenta
High School:	North Surrey Secondary School (Surrey, B.C.)
Sumo Name:	Kototenta, Kototenzan
Identities:	Avalanche, The Shark, Golga
Groups:	Dungeon of Doom (1995–96), The Oddities (1998–99)
Tag Team:	The Natural Disasters w/ Typhoon
Career Span:	1987–2004
Died:	June 7, 2006, Sanford, FL 42 years old

Tenta, John

Titles Won:	5
Best Opponents:	Randy Savage, Sting, Hulk Hogan

The affable John Tenta was from North Surrey, British Columbia, where he took up amateur wrestling at fifteen years of age, winning many championships. After some college at LSU, he was courted to Japan to compete as a Sumo, and his size and athletic prowess garnered him an undefeated record in twenty-one matches. He retired prematurely in 1986, and entered pro wrestling for Giant Baba, spending two years working for All-Japan. Tenta turned up in the WWF as "Earthquake," a heel grappler managed by Jimmy Hart. He was most remembered injuring Hulk Hogan in 1990 and for his shocking splash on Jake Roberts' snake, Damien. He adopted a slew of gimmicks through the end of the decade, including a run as a member of the Oddities. In 2000, he ran a wrestling school in Florida, and two years later, he teamed with Genichiro Tenryu and had a good run in the annual Real World Tag League Tournament.

Born:	November 27, 1957
Height:	5'8"
Weight:	200
Real Name:	Satoru Sayama
Trained by:	Karl Gotch, Antonio Inoki
Identities:	Sammy Lee, Tigre Enmascarado, The Tiger, Super Tiger, Tiger King
Nickname:	El Tigre Enmascarado
Finisher:	Tiger Spin, Moonsault, Tiger Suplex
Career Span:	1976–Present

Titles Won:	7
Best Opponents:	Dynamite Kid, Kuniaki Kobayashi, Black Tiger
Halls of Fame:	1

Tiger Mask

For many years, the prototypical wrestler was mammoth in size and intimidating in all aspects. Most non-heavyweight stars were ignored by the mainstream until Tiger Mask helped lead a revolution in the early 1980s, transforming wrestling in the US, Mexico, and Japan into a culture that admired lighter, more nimble wrestlers. The colorful persona, created after a popular cartoon character in Japan, debuted in 1981, and Tiger Mask influenced a generation of performers with his quick-moving and inventive style. In his vibrant matches against the Dynamite Kid, an amazing amount of athleticism was demonstrated, and their bouts are still talked about with great esteem today. Three versions of Tiger Mask have followed in his footsteps, and the name symbolizes a high benchmark of wrestling skill that few can equal.

Photo Courtesy of Pete Lederberg—plmathfoto@hotmail.com

Born:	October 25, 1965
Height:	5'11"
Weight:	220–230
Real Name:	Charles Scaggs
Identities:	Black Wazuma
Finisher:	Twist Legdrop, Sommersault Splash
Groups:	The JOB Squad (1998-99)
Career Span:	1985-Present

Titles Won:	16
Best Opponents:	Sabu, Shane Douglas, Chris Benoit

Too Cold Scorpio

A product of Denver, Colorado, Too Cold Scorpio is a polished high-flyer and internationally known for his outstanding grappling abilities. In late 1993, he teamed with Marcus Alexander Bagwell to capture the WCW World Tag Team Title from the Nasty Boys, but lost the belts in a rematch at Halloween Havoc. Scorpio was a mainstay in Extreme Championship Wrestling during its heyday, winning the promotion's TV championship four times, defeating the likes of Jason and Eddie Guerrero. His four reigns were the most by any wrestler. Overseas in Japan, Scorpio also found a lot of success. He spent several years with the WWF between 1996 and 1999 as "Flash Funk," dazzling fans with his quickness and wide-ranging moveset. In August 2010, he participated in TNA's Hardcore Justice pay-per-view that featured wrestlers from the old ECW promotion In his victory over C.W. Anderson, his aerial attack was as enjoyable as it had been fifteen years earlier.

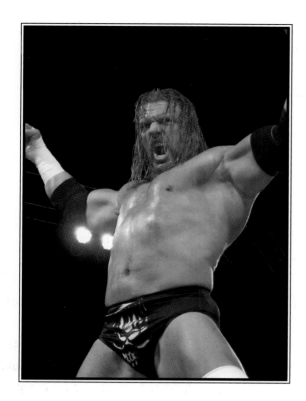

Triple H

Born:	July 27, 1969
Height:	6'5"
Weight:	260
Real Name:	Paul Michael Levesque
Parents:	Paul and Patricia Levesque
Wife:	Stephanie McMahon
High School:	Nashua High School (NH)
Identities:	Terra Rising, Jean-Paul Levesque
Nicknames:	Cerebral Assassin
Finisher:	The Pedigree
Groups:	D-Generation X (1997–2000), Evolution (2003)
Career Span:	1992–Present

Titles Won:	24
Days as World Champion:	1,155
Age at first World Title Win:	30
Best Opponents:	The Undertaker, Shawn Michaels, Steve Austin,
Halls of Fame:	2
TV Appearances:	Over 20
Movies:	4

A native of Nashua, New Hampshire, Triple H is a foremost pro wrestling superstar and one of WWE's legendary stars. He is known for his intense, knock-down drag-out ring combat, and has amassed fourteen World Title victories during his nearly two decades in the business. Nicknamed "The Game," he has drawn comparisons to Ric Flair throughout his career, but with the frame of a bodybuilder. In fact, he was more interested in training with weights than participating in organized sports and, after high school, he worked as a manager at a local Gold's Gym. He received some timely advice from bodybuilder and ex-wrestler Ted Arcidi, and decided to follow through with a path to becoming a pro grappler. Having always been a wrestling fan, Triple H attended Killer Kowalski's Malden school and made his debut in 1992. Within two years, he broke free from the independents for a job in WCW, where he fashioned himself as a British aristocrat.

There was little future in WCW, he quickly ascertained, and ventured to the WWF. It was there that he took the name, "Hunter Hearst Helmsley," the full designation of the moniker, "Triple H," and received his first significant push. In October 1996, he won the Intercontinental belt and came up victorious in the 1997 King of the Ring tournament. That same year, he teamed with Shawn Michaels, Chyna, and Rick Rude to form the first incarnation of D-Generation X, a rebellious group that would become immensely popular.

He won his first WWF Title on August 23, 1999, and viciously battled Vince McMahon. A storyline was enacted that saw Triple H marry Vince's daughter Stephanie, which became reality in October 2003. He collected championship wins from The Big Show and The Rock, and then feuded with Steve Austin before losing to The Undertaker at WrestleMania X-Seven. After befriending Austin and winning both the Intercontinental and tag team titles, he suffered a left quadriceps muscle tear during *Raw* on May 21, 2001.

The serious injury cost him the remainder of the year. He made his triumphant return on January 7, 2002 and proceeded to win both the Royal Rumble and the WWF Undisputed World Title at WrestleMania X-8 from Chris Jericho. During the summer, he entered a surprisingly violent feud with his old DX buddy Shawn Michaels. Eric Bischoff, on September 2, 2002, awarded Triple H the initial World Heavyweight Title, which, at the time, was exclusive to *Raw*. He was champion for more than nine months and formed Evolution with Ric Flair, Batista, and Randy Orton—although he'd eventually feud with all three. He traded the championship with both Michaels and Goldberg before finally losing the title to Chris Benoit at WrestleMania XX. A few months later, on September 12, 2004, Triple H won his fourth World Title from Randy Orton. The belt was declared vacant in December, but he rebounded to win it back on January 9, 2005. Batista went over at WrestleMania 21 and Triple H soon took a hiatus from the ring.

Notable feuds with Flair, John Cena, and the McMahons followed, and Triple H even reformed DX with Michaels in 2006. He was sidelined by another severe injury, this time a torn right quad, in January 2007, and missed a huge chunk of the year. On October 7, 2007, he beat Orton for his sixth WWE Title at No Mercy in what would be the first of three matches that night. He successfully retained against Umaga in the second contest, but then lost a Last Man Standing bout to Orton, meaning that he'd won and lost the championship in the same night. He beat Orton in a Fatal-Four way match on April 27, 2008 and kept the title until November when he was dethroned by Edge in Boston. On February 15, 2009, he captured his eighth WWE Title in an Elimination Chamber match at No Way Out. Of all his matches and feuds, Orton would be his most heated opponent, and the latter turned the dial up when he RKO'd Stephanie on *Raw*.

Orton beat him for the WWE belt on April 26, 2009, ending his run. From there he went on to reunite with Michaels against the members of Legacy and won the Tag Team Title from Big Show and Chris Jericho. He beat Sheamus at WrestleMania XXVI and, a year later, he again challenged The Undertaker's undefeated WrestleMania streak—but ended up with another loss. In July 2011, he assumed the role of on-camera "Chief Operating Officer" from Vince McMahon, but stepped back into the ring on April 2, 2012, to face The Undertaker once more, this time in a Hell in a Cell match. Triple H lost and Undertaker continued his WrestleMania winning streak. Beginning in 2013, he was part of the heel group "The Authority" and, in an attempt to halt Daniel Bryan's momentum, battled the latter at WrestleMania XXX. However, Bryan won and, later that night, beat Randy Orton and Batista in a three-way bout for the World Title. In January 2016, Triple H won the Royal Rumble, and captured the vacant WWE championship. He was defeated for the belt by Roman Reigns at WrestleMania 32.

Born:	June 16, 1959
Height:	6'3"
Weight:	280
Real Name:	James Brian Hellwig
Wife:	Dana Viale
Trained by:	Bill Anderson, Red Bastien
Identities:	Justice, Blade Runner Rock, Dingo Warrior, The Warrior
Finisher:	Splash, Gorilla Press
Career Span:	1985–2008
Died:	April 8, 2014, Scottsdale, AZ 54 years old

Titles Won:	7
Days as World Champion:	293
Age at first World Title Win:	30
Best Opponents:	Rick Rude, Randy Savage, Hulk Hogan

Ultimate Warrior, The

A high-energy, muscle-bound superstar, the Ultimate Warrior was enormously popular at the height of his WWF run. Exploding with unparalleled enthusiasm on the way to the ring, he mixed an unorthodox style with brute force and became a ring idol for many grappling fans. Originally from Indiana, he was a bodybuilder prior to joining a unique squad in 1985 known as "Power Team USA." Led by Rick Bassman and trained by Red Bastien, this quartet also featured Steve Borden, who'd gain future fame as Sting. After the group disbanded, Warrior and Sting ventured to the Mid-South Territory and the UWF as a tag team. Following a stint as a member of the Blade Runners, Warrior went to Dallas, where he appeared as the Dingo Warrior. That gimmick morphed into the "Ultimate Warrior" in 1987 for the World Wrestling Federation. Accompanied by a booming guitar rift, he sprinted to the ring, usually demolished his opponents in quick time, and vanished to the cheers of the crowd.

The Warrior engaged in an early feud with Hercules before entering contention for the Intercontinental Title. On August 29, 1988 at SummerSlam in New York, he toppled the Honky Tonk Man in twenty-eight seconds to capture the championship. In 1989, he traded the title back and forth with Rick Rude, and his popularity began to rival that of the promotion's number one face, Hulk Hogan. While no one expected the WWF's top two fan favorites to feud with each other, that is exactly what ended up happening. The two confronted each other at the 1990 Royal Rumble that concluded in a double clothesline, leveling both. Their war intensified in the weeks that followed, building toward their eventual match at WrestleMania VI at Toronto's Skydome. Hogan's WWF Title was on the line against the Warrior's Intercontinental Title, and after twenty-two minutes, Hogan missed a legdrop, and the Warrior landed a splash for the pin. It seemed at the time as if a symbolic torch had been passed and a new era of Warrior dominance had begun.

Surviving another feud with Rude, Warrior remained champion through the end of the year, and lost the belt to Sgt. Slaughter at the Royal Rumble on January 19, 1991 after being hit with a scepter by Randy Savage. Warrior feuded with Savage and the Undertaker in 1991, and after SummerSlam, he disappeared from the sport only to return eight months later. He chased Savage for the WWF Title and beat him by countout at SummerSlam 1992, but didn't win the title. Once again, he vanished from the business and a succession of appearance rumors followed. He reemerged in 1996, going over Triple H at WrestleMania in a short match. The Warrior remained active through the first part of the summer, only to part ways from the organization in an abrupt fashion in July 1996. Two years later, he tried to launch a revolution in WCW with his OWN group, but the stay in the promotion was brief. In 2008, he wrestled his final match in Spain, winning over Orlando Jordan.

Warrior was inducted into the WWE Hall of Fame on April 5, 2014. Over the next two days, he appeared at WrestleMania and *Raw*, and fans honored his exceptional career with earsplitting ovations. On April 8, he passed away suddenly in Scottsdale, Arizona. Warrior was fifty-four years of age.

Photo Courtesy of Dr. Mike Lano—Wrealano@aol.com

Born:	March 24, 1965
Height:	6'9"
Weight:	320
Real Name:	Mark William Calaway
Parents:	Frank and Betty Calaway
Trained by:	Ox Baker, Don Jardine
Finisher:	Heart Punch, Chokeslam
Tag Team:	The Brothers of Destruction w/ Kane
Career Span:	1987–Present

Titles Won:	17
Days as World Champion:	469
Age at first World Title Win:	24
Best Opponents:	Shawn Michaels, Triple H., Mick Foley
Halls of Fame:	1

Undertaker, The

The Undertaker went undefeated through 21 matches at WrestleMania, establishing one of the most exciting records in wrestling history. Sprung on the grappling world in 1990, his dark persona fit well into the colorful character-driven atmosphere of the WWF. Since that time, he's risen above the symbolism of any particular gimmick and has become a living, breathing icon for the promotion. Exceptionally agile for a large wrestler, he left fans in awe with his tight-rope walking, and his tombstone piledriver still appears to be one of the most powerful moves in the industry. Beginning his career in Texas, the Undertaker used several different names, winning the USWA Unified World Title as the "Master of Pain" on April 1, 1989. Before the end of the year, he was working for WCW as "Mean" Mark Callous.

Callous developed the chilling heart punch as his finisher and briefly teamed with Dan Spivey as a member of the Skyscrapers. He demonstrated his singles ability as a challenger to Lex Luger's US championship, but ended up in the WWF by the end of the year, initially imported by Brother Love. Paul Bearer assumed managerial rights to the Undertaker, and an early feud occurred against the popular Ultimate Warrior—even locking the latter in an "airtight" casket at one point as a display of his willingness to injure his opponents by whatever means. He was fast becoming immensely hated, and on November 27, 1991, he shocked the world by defeating Hulk Hogan for the WWF World Title. His reign lasted only six days, but affirmed his status as an impact player. Over the next few years, he began to develop a core base of fans and feuded with heels Kamala, Giant Gonzales, Yokozuna, and King Kong Bundy. Initially without much fanfare, his WrestleMania win streak built year after year until it was too exceptional to ignore.

On March 23, 1997 he pinned Sid Vicious for his second WWF Title and successfully turned back the challenges of Mankind, Steve Austin, and Vader in the months that followed. Upon losing the title to Bret Hart, Undertaker entered a feud with Shawn Michaels, and on October 5, they wrestled a classic "Hell in a Cell" match in St. Louis. Michaels was victorious after the Undertaker's purported brother Kane attacked him. The "siblings" fought a number of high-profile matches, including an "Inferno" bout in April 1998 with the ring surrounded by flames. On June 28, 1998, Undertaker fought Mankind in his second "Hell in a Cell" match, a bout that was seared into the minds of fans by the latter's wild bumps. On May 23, 1999, he beat Austin for the WWF belt and the next month, on June 27, pinned The Rock. The next night, however, Austin regained the belt.

In 2000, the Undertaker rose from the dead, after recovering from an injury, and made a spectacular return to the ring. Instead of his usual dead man gimmick, he was wearing a leather jacket and rode a motorcycle to the ring. The "American Bad Ass" emerged and his popularity flared to new heights. Back in action against Kane, Chris Benoit, and Kurt Angle, the Undertaker was stronger than ever, and by early 2001, he reconciled with his "brother" and formed a successful tag team. Following the onset of the WCW invasion a short time later, the Undertaker battled Dallas Page in an angle that involved the 'Taker's wife, Sara. On May 19, 2002, he beat Hulk Hogan for his fourth WWE World Title, only to lose it the next month to The Rock in a triple threat match in Detroit. On November 16, 2003, he was defeated by Vince McMahon in a "Buried Alive" match after Kane interfered, putting the Undertaker out of the business for a short time.

Of course, The Undertaker returned in time for WrestleMania XX. Using his "dead man" gimmick again with Bearer back at his side, he toppled Kane, continuing his winning streak. Heavy ring wars against JBL, Booker T, Randy Orton, and CM Punk followed. He beat Batista for the World Title at WrestleMania XXIV and had successive WrestleMania matches against Shawn Michaels in 2009-2010, winning both in dramatic fashion, with the second victory ending Michaels' wrestling career. In February 2011, he returned to the WWE, setting up a his WrestleMania XXVII match against Triple H, who he'd beaten ten years earlier on the same stage. The result was the same, and The Undertaker earned his nineteenth WrestleMania victory. He was carried from the ring after the hard-fought win and remained out of action for many months.

Triple H was his opponent at WrestleMania XXVIII as well and, once again, the 'Taker was victorious, extending his record to 20–0. A year later, he went over CM Punk, and his streak continued. However, he ran into the unstoppable Brock Lesnar at WrestleMania XXX on April 6, 2014, and the latter became the first man to beat the Undertaker at the grand event. In 25:47, Lesnar beat him and ended his streak at 21–1. Over the next two years, the Undertaker continued to appear at WrestleMania, and defeated Bray Wyatt and Shane McMahon.

Vader

Born:	May 14, 1955
Height:	6'4"
Weight:	425
Real Name:	Leon Allen White
College:	University of Colorado
NFL Draft:	Los Angeles Rams (1978) (3rd Round)
Pro Sports:	National Football League—Los Angeles Rams (1980–85)
Trained by:	Brad Rheingans
Identities:	Baby Bull, Bull Power, Big Van Vader, Super Vader
Nickname:	Mastodon
Finisher:	Vaderbomb, Moonsault
Career Span:	1985–2015

Titles Won:	19
Days as World Champion:	2,252 (including overlapping reigns)
Age at first World Title Win:	31
Best Opponents:	Antonio Inoki, Ric Flair, Shawn Michaels
Halls of Fame:	1

An amazingly agile and powerful big man, Vader won World championships in Europe, Mexico, Japan, and the United States. Following a pro football career that was hampered by injury, he developed his wrestling abilities, and with his unique look, rose up the ladder quickly. In Austria, he ended Otto Wanz's nearly nine-year stint as the CWA champion on March 22, 1987. That December, he shocked Japanese fans with a quick win over the legendary Antonio Inoki, and would go on to win the IWGP Title on three occasions. Vader toppled Sting for the first of three WCW World Titles on July 12, 1992, and in 1994, he won the UWFI World Title. Five years later, on March 6, 1999, he pinned Akira Taue for the vacant AJPW Triple Crown, adding another monumental achievement to his record. His feuds with Hulk Hogan, Sting, Shawn Michaels, Ric Flair, and The Undertaker were immensely heated, and Vader lived up to his monster heel billing. His son Jesse is an up-and-coming pro wrestler.

Born:	December 18, 1970
Height:	6'0"
Weight:	230
Real Name:	Robert Alexander Szatkowski
Identities:	Robbie V
Groups:	The Alliance (2001)
Tag Team:	Aerial Assault w/ Bob Bradley
Career Span:	1990–Present

Van Dam, Rob

Titles Won:	27
Days as World Champion:	156
Age at first World Title Win:	35
Best Opponents:	Sabu, Jerry Lynn, John Cena
TV Appearances:	Over 10
Movies:	4

Combining a natural athleticism with a kickboxing and martial arts background, Rob Van Dam has been a spectacular performer for over two decades. His ability to propel himself through the air to deliver his lethal Five-Star Frog Splash or the Van-Terminator is uncanny, and few peers can compare in terms of high-flying. Known as "RVD" and the "Whole F'n Show," Van Dam's popularity has been well-earned, and not many wrestlers hold pinfall victories over The Rock, Steve Austin, Sting, Kurt Angle, Ric Flair, and John Cena. Originally from Battle Creek, Michigan, he was trained by the master of the hardcore style, The Sheik, and wrestled in WCW and many independents before making a big name for himself in ECW. For 700 days, Van Dam held the ECW World TV Title from April 1998 to March 2000, elevating the championship to one of the most prestigious in the world. Along with Sabu, he won the ECW World Tag Team Title twice.

During the summer of 2001, Van Dam was part of an ECW invasion angle of the WWF along with Paul Heyman and others. He eventually unified both the European and Hardcore Titles with the Intercontinental Championship in 2002. He was also a top challenger to the heavyweight crown and, on June 11, 2006, he went over John Cena for the WWE belt. Two nights later, he was awarded the ECW World Title, making him the first wrestler to hold both belts simultaneously. On March 8, 2010, he arrived in TNA and, within weeks, won the promotion's World Title from A.J. Styles. In August, he was injured in an attack by Fortune and Abyss, forcing officials to vacate the TNA Title. He captured the X-Division championship before departing TNA in 2013, and ultimately rejoined the WWE. Since 2015, he's been appearing on the indie circuit and accepting film roles.

Photo Courtesy of Pete Lederberg—plmathfoto@hotmail.com

Born:	September 1, 1961
Height:	6'8"
Weight:	275
Real Name:	Sidney Raymond Eudy
Identities:	Lord Humongous, Vicious Warrior, Sid Justice
Nicknames:	Psycho, The Original Psycho, Y2S
Career Span:	1987–Present

Titles Won:	13
Days as World Champion:	382
Age at first World Title Win:	32
Best Opponents:	Shawn Michaels, Chris Benoit, Bret Hart

Vicious, Sid

The towering Sid Vicious was a major impact player in wrestling from his early days as one of the Four Horsemen to being a top challenger to the NWA, WCW, and WWF World Titles. Trained by Tojo Yamamoto, he earned a name for himself as a member of the Skyscrapers with Dan Spivey in 1989, but suffered an injury before winning any gold. He joined the Four Horsemen in 1990 and was a serious threat to Sting's NWA Title. His crushing powerbombs of Brian Pillman during War Games was one of the defining moments of the 1990s. In November 1996, he beat Shawn Michaels for the WWF World Heavyweight Title and won it again in early 1997. A few years later, in January 2000, he became the eighth man to win both the WWF and NWA/WCW Titles with a victory over Kevin Nash for the WCW World belt. At Sin in January 2001, he suffered a horrific leg injury during a match. Over the next few years, he made sporadic appearances on the indie scene, mostly as a special referee.

Born:	July 22, 1958
Height:	6'6"
Weight:	230
Real Name:	David Alan Adkisson
Parents:	Jack and Doris Adkisson
Family:	Brother of Chris, Kerry, Kevin, and Mike Von Erich
Wife:	Patricia Adkisson
College:	North Texas State University
Finisher:	Clawhold
Career Span:	1977–84
Died:	February 10, 1984, Tokyo, Japan 25 years old

Titles Won:	20
Best Opponents:	Harley Race, Ric Flair, Jack Brisco
Halls of Fame:	1

Von Erich, David

The tallest of five brothers, David Von Erich was a basketball standout at Lake Dallas High School and was twice All-State. Under the guidance of his father, Fritz Von Erich, he turned pro, like his brother Kevin before him, and joined the wars of the Sportatorium. Considered to be more similar in appearance to his father than his siblings, David displayed immense talent, and his career began to skyrocket. During a tour of Florida in 1981, he proved his versatility by turning heel. He took James J. Dillon as his manager, and beat Jack Brisco for the Southern championship. Von Erich won the cherished NWA Missouri Heavyweight crown from Ric Flair, and on February 3, 1984, he wrestled the United National Title away from Michael Hayes. He went to Japan for a scheduled three-week tour, and shortly after arrival, was found dead in his hotel of acute intestinal inflammation. His death stunned the wrestling community.

Photo Courtesy of Pete Lederberg—plmathfoto@hotmail.com

Born:	February 3, 1960
Height:	6'3"
Weight:	260
Real Name:	Kerry Gene Adkisson
Parents:	Jack and Doris Adkisson
Family:	Brother of Chris, David, Kevin, and Mike Von Erich
High School:	Lake Dallas High School (TX)
Nicknames:	The Modern-Day Warrior, Texas Tornado
Tag Team:	The Cosmic Cowboys w/ Kevin Von Erich
Career Span:	1978–93
Died:	February 18, 1993, Denton, TX 33 years old

Von Erich, Kerry

Titles Won:	42
Days as World Champion:	242
Age at first World Title Win:	24
Best Opponents:	Ric Flair, Curt Hennig, Jerry Lawler
Halls of Fame:	1

Another one of Jack Adkisson's popular and talented sons, Kerry Von Erich was a spectacular athlete, excelling in football at Lake Dallas as a running back and a linebacker, becoming All-State. He went to the University of Houston, where he was a noted discus thrower, and also turned pro in 1978. As part of the Von Erich clan, he participated in many exciting matches in Dallas at the Sportatorium. Following the shocking death of his brother, David, he beat Ric Flair for the NWA World Heavyweight Title on May 6, 1984 at Texas Stadium before 40,000 cheering fans, dedicating the win to his fallen sibling. Flair regained the belt later in the month in Japan. In 1990, he defeated Mr. Perfect for the WWF Intercontinental Title, using a clawhold and tornado punch to secure the victory. In addition, he was a four-time WCWA World and American Champion, and in 1983, he held the Missouri State Title.

On June 4, 1986, along US 373 in Argyle, Texas, he was in a near-fatal motorcycle accident. He suffered a very serious right ankle injury as well as a dislocated hip and lacerations to his right knee. His right foot was amputated and, unbeknownst to the wrestling world, he wore a prosthetic foot during his in-ring performances. When he headlined the AWA pay-per-view, SuperClash III, on December 13, 1988 in Chicago, there was an attempt by the WWF to have the Illinois Athletic Commission prevent Von Erich from wrestling due to his physical condition, but his match against Jerry Lawler went on as planned. He worked for the GWF, a local Dallas promotion, after leaving the WWF in the summer of 1992. Following his death, the GWF held a benefit show for his daughters on April 2, 1993. Among those who participated in the event were Kevin Von Erich, Chris Adams, and Michael Hayes. His daughter, Lacey, entered the profession and gained success while a member of the Beautiful People in TNA from 2009-2010.

Photo Courtesy of Dr. Mike Lano—Wrealano@aol.com

Von Erich, Kevin

Born:	May 15, 1957
Height:	6'2"
Weight:	235
Real Name:	Kevin Ross Adkisson
Parents:	Jack and Doris Adkisson
Family:	Older brother of Chris, David, Kerry, and Mike Von Erich
Trained by:	Jack Adkisson
Finisher:	Clawhold
Tag Team:	The Cosmic Cowboys w/ Kerry Von Erich
Career Span:	1976-95

Titles Won:	33
Days as World Champion:	313
Age at first World Title Win:	29
Best Opponents:	Ric Flair, Bruiser Brody, Chris Adams
Halls of Fame:	1

The oldest wrestling son of Fritz Von Erich, Kevin Von Erich was a standout fullback at Lake Dallas High School and as a tight end at North Texas State. He followed his father into the wrestling business, and, along with his brothers, was a hero at the Sportatorium in Dallas. Between 1978 and 1983, he held the American Title five times and also captured the all-important Missouri State crown in St. Louis. In 1986, he beat Black Bart for the WCWA World Title. With his siblings, he held an incredible number of tag team championships in Dallas. In honor of his late brother, David, he challenged Ric Flair for the NWA Title at the 2nd Annual Parade of Champions on May 5, 1985, but the match ended in a double countout. Following his retirement in 1995, he made a number of appearances, and was on hand to accept the honor as his family was inducted into the WWE Hall of Fame in 2009.

Born:	July 13, 1972
Height:	6′2″
Weight:	205
Real Name:	Sean Michael Waltman
Trained by:	Eddie Sharkey
Identities:	The Lightning Kid, The 1-2-3 Kid, Syxx, X-Pac, Syxx-Pac, Pac
Finisher:	Buzz Killer
Groups:	New World Order (1996–97, 2000) D-Generation X (1998–99, 1999–2000)
Career Span:	1990–Present

Titles Won:	25
Best Opponents:	Bret Hart, Eddie Guerrero, Shane McMahon

Waltman, Sean

A gifted mat wrestler with high-flying abilities, Sean Waltman grew up in Tampa and became a well-known grappling sensation while still a teenager. Trained by the Malenkos, he made a splash in the GWF in Dallas and was viewed as an underdog because of his lanky form. He maintained that status in the WWF and won some unexpected victories on *Raw*. Waltman captured the WWF World Tag Team Title four times with partners Marty Jannetty, Sparky Plugg, and twice with Kane. In WCW, he was a member of the NWO and held the World Cruiserweight Title; with the GWF and WWE Light Heavyweight Titles and the TNA X-Division Championship among his other achievements. In addition to his work as a member of the NWO, he was a part of another dominant faction: D-Generation X. He was engaged at one time to Joanie Laurer, and the two made a brief appearance during an episode of the *Anna Nicole Smith Show*.

Born:	June 4, 1973
Height:	5'7"
Weight:	185
Real Name:	John Michael Watson
High School:	Sayville High School (NY)
Trained by:	Sonny Blaze
Finisher:	Whippersnapper
Career Span:	1994–Present

Titles Won:	17
Days as World Champion:	42
Age at first World Title Win:	22
Best Opponents:	Cactus Jack, The Sandman, Steve Austin

Whipwreck, Mikey

In a world of behemoths, the 5'7" Mikey Whipwreck seemed to be an implausible heavyweight champion. In fact, he was commonly acknowledged as the underdog when he wrestled for ECW, where he began in 1994. Fans couldn't help but be awestruck by his well-rounded ring skills and ability to take hardcore bumps from much larger grapplers. Whipwreck proved indestructible, winning the ECW World TV Title twice, the World Tag championship three times, and, on October 28, 1995, he beat The Sandman for the World Heavyweight crown. The Sayville, New York athlete also held various indie belts and mentored the likes of Amazing Red and Jay Lethal.

Born:	May 14, 1960
Height:	6'1"
Weight:	265
Real Name:	Steven Franklin Williams
Parents:	Gerald and Dorthy Williams
High School:	Lakewood High School (CO)
College:	University of Oklahoma
College Ach.:	Big Eight Wrestling Champion (1980–82) (HWT), All-American Football Player (1982), All-American Wrestler (1978–81)
Pro Sports:	United States Football League—New Jersey Generals (1982) United States Football League—Denver Gold (1982)
Finisher:	Oklahoma Stampede
Groups:	The Varsity Club (1988–89, 1999)
Career Span:	1982–2009
Died:	December 30, 2009, Lakewood, CO 49 years old

Titles Won:	22
Days as World Champion:	435
Age at first World Title Win:	27
Best Opponents:	Kenta Kobashi, Mitsuharu Misawa, Bubba Rogers
MMA Record:	0-1

Williams, Steve

Williams was a powerhouse wrestler, known as "Dr. Death," and entered the business with outstanding amateur credentials. Under the tutelage of Bill Watts, he quickly made a splash in the Mid-South region, and on July 11, 1987, he beat Bubba Rogers for the UWF World Title in Oklahoma City. As a member of the impressive Varsity Club, he teamed with Mike Rotundo to beat the Road Warriors for the World Tag Team Title in April 1989, but they were stripped of the belts in May. In Japan, Williams established a strong legacy, forming a superlative tag team with Terry Gordy, and winning the All-Japan Tag Title five times between 1990 and 1993. The duo also won the NWA and WCW Tag Team Championship in 1992. On July 28, 1994 in Tokyo, Williams captured the coveted AJPW Japanese Triple Crown from Mitsuharu Misawa. Back in the US, Williams was a competitor in the WWF's Brawl for All tournament in 1998. He remained active into 2009 and passed away that December.

Windham, Barry

Born:	July 4, 1960
Height:	6'5"
Weight:	250
Real Name:	Barry Clinton Windham
Parents:	Robert and Julia Windham
College:	West Texas State University
Identities:	Blackjack Mulligan Jr., Dirty Yellow Dog, The Widowmaker, The Stalker
Finisher:	Bulldog Headlock, Superplex, Clawhold
Groups:	The Four Horsemen (1988–89, 1990–91), The Xtreme Horsemen (2001)
Tag Teams:	The Young Lions w/ Mike Rotundo, The US Express w/ Mike Rotundo, The New Blackjacks w/ Bradshaw, The West Texas Rednecks w/ Kendall Windham
Career Span:	1980–2008

Titles Won:	37
Days as World Champion:	147
Age at first World Title Win:	32
Best Opponents:	Ric Flair, Lex Luger, Steve Austin
Halls of Fame:	1

The pride of Sweetwater, Texas, Barry Windham has been one of the most successful wrestlers of the last thirty years. Trained by his father, Blackjack Mulligan, he initially began as a referee and developed into a fundamentally sound and entertaining grappler. During the 1980s, he chased Ric Flair for the NWA championship, and finally won the strap from The Great Muta on February 21, 1993. Between 1988 and 1998, he was a three-time World Tag Team Champion with Lex Luger, Dustin Rhodes, and Tully Blanchard. Windham also held the WCW World Tag Team Title on three occasions with Rhodes, Curt Hennig, and his brother Kendall. In 1988, he beat Nikita Koloff in a tournament final for the vacant US Heavyweight Title. He also won the WCW World TV Title from Steve Austin in 1992. Earlier in his career, he formed a highly successful tag team with his brother-in-law, Mike Rotunda. They won the US Tag Title in Florida twice before jumping to the WWF, where they won the World Tag Team Title on two occasions in 1985.

Born:	October 2, 1966
Height:	6'4"
Weight:	590
Real Name:	Agatupu Rodney Anoai
Trained by:	Afa
Identities:	Great Kokina, Kokina Maximus, Samoan Kokina
Finisher:	Splash
Career Span:	1984–2000
Died:	October 23, 2000, Liverpool, England 34 years old

Titles Won:	5
Days as World Champion:	280
Age at first World Title Win:	26
Best Opponents:	Bret Hart, Vader, Shawn Michaels
Halls of Fame:	1

Yokozuna

Nephew of the legendary Wild Samoans, Yokozuna was one of the most talented big men in wrestling history. From the Island of American Samoa, he weighed more than 500 pounds and made a huge impact on the World Wrestling Federation shortly after his debut in 1992. He used his bulk to win the 1993 Royal Rumble and earned a World Title shot at WrestleMania on April 4, 1993 in Las Vegas. WrestleMania, however, would see both success and failure as he initially won the heavyweight title from Bret Hart, at the time becoming the youngest WWF champion in history at age twenty-six. Minutes later, he was pinned by Hulk Hogan after an impromptu challenge was accepted and he lost the belt. Yokozuka beat Hogan to regain the belt on June 13, 1993 with some help from a ringside photographer, but dropped the title to Hart at WrestleMania X on March 20, 1994. In April 1995, he teamed with Owen Hart to win the WWF World Tag Team Championship. He died during a tour of England in 2000.

Born:	November 30, 1958
Height:	6'2"
Weight:	230
Real Name:	Thomas Erwin Zenk
High School:	Robbinsdale High School (MN)
College:	University of Minnesota
Trained by:	Eddie Sharkey, Brad Rheingans
Nickname:	Z-Man
Finisher:	Top Rope Dropkick
Career Span:	1984–95

Titles Won:	6
Best Opponents:	Arn Anderson, Bobby Eaton, Steve Austin

Zenk, Tom

The popular Tom Zenk of Minnesota made a name for himself while in the Pacific Northwest working for Don Owen, and formed a standout tag team with Rick Martel known as the Can-Am Connection in the WWF. The "Z-Man," as he was known, was a finalist in the vacant AWA World Title battle royal in 1989, and turned up in WCW a short time later, partnered with Brian Pillman. The high-flying duo won a tournament for the US Tag Team belts over the Freebirds on February 12, 1990. Later in the year, Zenk defeated Arn Anderson for the World Television Championship in Atlanta, winning the strap on December 4, 1990. He lost the belt in a return bout with Anderson on January 7, 1991. He was also a member of a World Six-Man Tag championship squad along with Big Josh and Dustin Rhodes.

Ziggler, Dolph

Born:	July 27, 1980
Height:	6'0"
Weight:	225
Real Name:	Nicholas Theodore Nemeth
High School:	St. Edward High School (OH)
College:	Kent State University
Trained by:	Lance Storm, Steve Keirn
Identities:	Nicky
Finisher:	Sleeperhold
Career Span:	2004–Present

Titles Won:	6
Days as World Champion:	0
Age at first World Title Win:	30
Best Opponents:	Edge, Rey Mysterio Jr., Kofi Kingston

Ohio's own Dolph Ziggler was a talented amateur grappler, capturing three MAC championships while at Kent State, and entered the WWE developmental system in 2004. Two years later, he was buried among the five-man unit known as the Spirit Squad and, in conjunction with the other members of the group, held the World Tag Team Title. Full of potential, Ziggler reemerged as a singles grappler in 2008, and formed a scripted relationship with Vickie Guerrero. He beat Kofi Kingston for the Intercontinental Title in 2010, and then defeated him again for the United States Championship in June 2011. Also, for a very brief moment in February 2011, he held the World Heavyweight Title, crowned by Guerrero, but was quickly dethroned by Edge. In 2013, he cashed in his Money in the Bank contract to regain the World Title, defeating Alberto Del Rio, but lost it back to the latter two months later. Ziggler's ultra-confidence, athleticism, and crafty in-ring skills make him one of the WWE's top rising stars.

Statistical Notes

+ Abbreviations: DCO is Double Countout, DDQ is Double Disqualification, and NC is No Contest.
+ Win/loss records include wins and losses incurred in tag team matches, handicap bouts, and any matches determined by disqualification or countout.
+ Loss count includes eliminations from battle royals or the Royal Rumble.
+ The ending year in "Career Span" is the final year they actively participated in a wrestling match—not counting any work done behind the scenes.
+ The title reign days of current champions have a cutoff of December 31, 2011.
+ The IWGP Heavyweight and AJPW Unified Triple Crown are included in "Days as World Champion" tabulations.
+ Professional wrestling is a sport in which match finishes are predetermined. Thus, win/loss records are not indicative of a wrestler's genuine success based on their legitimate abilities—but how much, or how little they were pushed by promoters.

Acknowledgments

As strange as it might sound, professional wrestling history is a complex labyrinth that has mystified researchers for decades. The aura of secrecy that has shrouded the business keeps those who partake in unraveling the sport's heritage quite busy; and it seems that as each year passes, more and more is finally revealed. I can only imagine where wrestling research will be in ten years, particularly as more historical databases appear online.

Of course, for me, a project of this magnitude could never have been accomplished without the help of many people. First and foremost, I would like to thank Amy Miller and everyone in the Interlibrary Loan department of the Broward County (FL) Library System, who provided me with a wonderful opportunity to research newspapers from all over the world—and trust me, I took advantage of the service, with over 500 requests over a period of several years. Days of research at the Jack Pfefer Collection housed at the University of Notre Dame was also pivotal, and curator George Rugg was helpful beyond belief.

The outstanding dedication and contributions of my fellow researchers was also crucial. Much gratitude goes out to historians J. Michael Kenyon, Don Luce, and Steve Yohe, who all have an unlimited knowledge on the subject, and promptly responded to my queries, regardless of the topic. These guys can write volumes on pro wrestling and have contributed to countless projects documenting its history. Yohe's penetrating biography of Ed "Strangler" Lewis is required reading for anyone interested in the sport's history.

I also have to thank historians and researchers Mark Hewitt, Fred Hornby, Steve Johnson, Greg Oliver, Dan Anderson, Koji Miyamoto, Tom Burke, Kit Bauman, George Lentz, Chuck Thornton, Haruo Yamaguchi, Daniel Chernau, Jim Zordani, Matt Farmer, Jim Mandl, Rich Tate, Dick Bourne, Hisaharu Tanabe, Glenn Helwig, Becky Taylor, Michael Norris, Karl Stern, Yasutoshi Ishikawa, Wayne Sine, Ronald Grosspietsch, Gerhard Schafer, and last but not least, the late Jim Melby, who was universally admired for his kindness and knowledge. He influenced me a great deal.

A special thanks to historians Libnan Ayoub and Scott Teal for not only being available to answer my questions, but for providing photos for this project from their vast collections. Libnan is the son of wrestling legend Wadi Ayoub, and is the author of *100 Years of Australian Professional Wrestling*. He is currently working on a documentary that will spotlight WCW in Australia between 1964 and 1978, and has a new website, www.worldwrestlinghistory.com.

Since 1968, Scott Teal has been documenting wrestling history and has over 100 publications to his credit. His company, Crowbar Press, has published fifteen autobiographies, and Scott has co-written nine of them, as well and has edited the others. Among them are highly recommended books by Lou Thesz, Nikita Koloff, and Ole Anderson. You can order his extraordinary works at his website, www.crowbarpress.com.

I must also thank John Pantozzi, Bob Bryla, and everyone affiliated with the Professional Wrestling Hall of Fame in Amsterdam, New York. Check out their website at www.pwhf.org, and make plans to visit this wonderful institution soon.

Dave Meltzer's ground-breaking *Wrestling Observer* newsletter was also a valuable resource as well as Graham Cawthon's website, www.thehistoryofwwe.com, which is a must see for any wrestling fan. Hours can also be spent at www.wrestlingclassics.com, a site that offers tons of history and has one of the best wrestling message boards on the Internet.

The professionalism of expert photographers Dr. Mike Lano, Peter Lederberg Bill Stahl, Dan Westbrook, Mike Mastrandrea, and George Tahinos made my job of obtaining pictures for this project easier than I could have ever imagined. I can't thank them enough for their unwavering assistance throughout this process. I recommend them to anyone in need of wrestling photography.

Dr. Mike Lano, wrestling's dentist journalist/historian, had his first newsstand magazine article with photos published in 1966. From that moment on, he's shot and covered nearly all the North American territories in their prime, plus Mexico, Japan, and Australia. His images have been featured in many magazines, including freelancing for the WWE, books, documentaries, and TV programs. He currently hosts a nationally syndicated radio show. You can contact Dr. Lano at Wrealano@aol.com.

Beginning in 1976, Pete Lederberg began collecting wrestling photos, and may possibly have the largest organized collection of photographs, negatives, and slides in the world. An accomplished photographer in his own right, he started shooting pictures for Paul Heyman and Eddie Gilbert in Continental in 1988, and continues to shoot at wrestling events around the country to this day. Check out his listings at his website, http://home.bellsouth.net/p/PWP-flwrestlingpix.

Bill Stahl picked up his first 35mm camera almost thirty years ago, and never could have imagined it would turn into a lifelong passion. Having refined his skills over the years by shooting sports and concerts, he is now ready to expand to portrait, fashion, and family photography. Check out his fantastic photos and contact him through his website, www.billstahlphotography.com.

Dan Westbrook has spent nearly thirty years photographing and writing about pro wrestling. Working out of the Los Angeles area, he served as the chief foreign correspondent for a number of Japanese newspapers and magazines beginning in 1972, and is currently putting together the highly anticipated book, *An Illustrated Archive of Southern California Wrestling in the 1960s*, which will cover both the WWA territory and the JWA in Japan.

Mike Mastrandrea is the SLAM! Wrestling staff photographer. The Toronto-based lensman has been shooting wrestling for over fifteen years. His work has been seen in publications across North America, Europe and Asia. http://slam.canoe.ca/Slam/Wrestling/Gallery/mastrandrea.html.

George Tahinos has been a wrestling photographer since 1993 and has worked for magazines in the United States, United Kingdom, Japan, Mexico, and Australia. He's photographed for many promotions, including ECW, TNA, ROH, WCW, 3PW, CZW, Shimmer, DGUSA, and other organizations throughout the NY-NJ-PA area.

The Wrestling Revue magazine archive is a spectacular resource, and with an online catalog of 6,000 images, www.wrestleprints.com, is definitely a place to spend time browsing. Brian Bukantis was of great help.

George Schire, an accomplished wrestling historian and author of the fantastic book, *Minnesota's Golden Age of Wrestling*, came through with a few needed photos at the last minute. I'd also like to recommend Jeff Leen's comprehensive biography of women's wrestling legend Mildred Burke entitled, *The Queen of the Ring*.

John Rauer, who also helped with some last minute pictures, is the producer of a Historic World Champions card collection. This enjoyable and informative series is a must-have, and can be seen at www. wrestlingsbest.com/collectibles/wrestuffcards017.html.

Additionally, there are many people involved in the business, family members of wrestlers and promoters, and other individuals who I consulted through the years. I'd like to thank: Dorothy Mondt Baldwin, Penny Banner, Richard Baumann, John Kim Bell, Mike Bothner, Richard Brown, Jane Byrnes and both the Byrnes and Riley families, Roger Carrier, Frank Cody, D'Angelo Dinero, Dr. Bruce Dunn, John Edgecumbe, Tom Ellis, Tina Farmer at the Boone County Library (AR), Viva Foy, Dory Funk Jr., Bob Geigel, Paul George, Holly Gilzenberg, Leilani Kai, Michael S. Karbo, John Ketonen, Dave Levin, Richard Longson, Ken Lucas, Eve Manoogian, Petros Manousakis, John McFarlin, Richard Muchnick, Sid Munn, Tommy Needham, Mark Nulty, Russell Owen, Geoff Pesek, Kevin Pesek, John Rohde, Bob Sand, Billy E. Sandow, Sandy Sparley, Dick Steinborn, Lou Thesz, Bob Thye, Diane Tourville, Bill and Nick Tragos, Maurice and Paul Vachon, Carol Walker, and Mikey Whipwreck.

On a personal note, I want to thank my editor, Jason Katzman, as well as Mark Weinstein and everyone at Skyhorse Publishing. Their guidance and recommendations turned fifteen years of research into a book I always hoped would be possible. The late Jim Cypher was a terrific literary agent and always offered sound advice. He is greatly missed.

Finally, a very special thanks goes out to my wife, Jodi, who believed in this project even before I did. I'd also like to thank Timothy and Barbara Hornbaker, Melissa Hornbaker, Virginia Hall, Frances Miller, and John and Christine Hopkins.

For more information on the history of professional wrestling, questions, or comments, go to www. legacyofwrestling.com.